Introduction

I've come to the painful realization that most people simply aren't willing to do their own research on topics, so this the best I can do to summarize 1,400 years of religion to explain the theological components of why it is so violent. It's honestly surprising to me that certain Conservative Christians throughout the world want to proclaim that Islam is the worst evil in the world, but they never bother to do any research on the topic. They will likely continue protesting or rioting over the religion that they argue to be an existential threat to their civilization such as the British riots of July – August 2024, but they don't try to read and learn to better tackle Islamic extremism more peacefully. If Islam is truly such a threat, why haven't you bothered to do any research into it to learn how to counter it in the most effective ways possible? For any possible Conservative Christian who despises Islam and reads this; are you truly serious about the dangers of Islam or are you just trying to justify hate? Nevertheless. regardless of political beliefs and religious views, some of this is going to be deeply uncomfortable to read and it might be truly painful to fully understand that these aspects being critiqued are indeed beliefs that Muslims throughout the world believe are justified *because* they are validated in Islamic theology. I want to make something clear though; as I grew-up in the US, I never experienced bigotry or hate from Muslim neighbors, Muslim family members, nor witnessed any of these problems I mention below. Neither my Muslim Indian family members, or my Pakistani Muslim neighbors, or any Pakistani Muslim co-workers ever expressed any sort of contempt or hate towards me and they all knew that I'm a Hindu Indian. They have a dislike for Hinduism and then get confused by Hindu atheism, but they're open to listening and learning when we agree to discuss religion. I've never experienced bigotry from any Muslim living in the US and this is more about the global issues pertaining to why Islam is violent. If it means anything, none of the female Pakistani Muslim neighbors or my female Muslim family members ever wore hijabs; I doubt any of them ever even thought about a hijab; apart from maybe when one of my cousin's had one Muslim friend who wore a hijab invited over to watch movies or watch an anime. I would be surprised if the vast majority of Muslims living in the United States have any of these behaviors mentioned below. The only time I've ever experienced bigotry and disdain was from interacting with Western Ex-Muslim atheists who act like a really bizarre hive-mind that remind me of the open hostility that I received from Pakistani Muslims of Pakistan through internet forums like Discord. That's honestly the truth; Western Ex-Muslim atheists hold more bigotry towards Hindus than US Muslims from my experience. I could talk about Indian materialist philosophy from 600 BCE to my Muslim co-workers and they'd be genuinely fascinated; I share it with Ex-Muslim atheists online and most of them somehow take it as a personal insult. The difference in behavior from Ex-Muslim atheists is very strange, but I'm done concerning myself with them.

All of that notwithstanding, **if you're serious about learning about the problems of Islam** but you don't have enough time or wherewithal to do your own research, **then please give this entire book a read**. We must find ways to end Islam through peaceful means to avoid our worst impulses. If you're a Muslim interested in reading the contents of this book, I highly encourage you to read the entirety of this book. Regardless of motivations or what your background is, I hope this book is of some value to you:

575. WE AERONAUTS OF THE INTELLECT.—All those daring birds that soar far and ever farther into space, will somewhere or other be certain to find themselves unable to continue their flight, and they will perch on a mast or some narrow ledge—and will be grateful even for this miserable accommodation! But who could conclude from this that there was not an endless free space stretching far in front of them, and that they had flown as far as they possibly could? In the end, however, all our great teachers and predecessors have come to a standstill, and it is by no means in the noblest or most graceful attitude that their weariness has brought them to a pause: the same thing will happen to you and me! but what does this matter to either of us? *Other birds will fly farther!* Our minds and hopes vie with them far out and on high; they rise far above our heads and our failures, and from this height they look far into the distant horizon and see hundreds of birds much more powerful than we are, striving whither we ourselves have also striven, and where all is sea, sea, and nothing but sea!

And where, then, are we aiming at? Do we wish to cross the sea? whither does this overpowering passion urge us, this passion which we value more highly than any other delight? Why do we fly precisely in this direction, where all the suns of humanity have hitherto set? Is it possible that people may one day say of us that we also steered westward, hoping to reach India—but that it was our fate to be wrecked on the infinite? Or, my brethren? or—? – **Friedrich Nietzsche, The Dawn of Day / Daybreak, Aphorism 575. Translated by J. M. Kennedy.**

Table of Contents

Introduction . . . iii

Key Terms . . . v

Chapter I: The Doctrinal Failings of Islam . . . 1

Chapter II: A Vedantic and Samkhya Critique of Islam . . . 10

Chapter III: What the term Islamophobia shields . . . 19

Chapter IV: Social Status and Genocide Denial . . . 70

Chapter V: Neoliberalism Empowers Islamism . . . 118

Chapter VI: Did the British Partition of 1947 Gradually Decline the UK and Bolster India? . . . 151

Chapter VII: Islamic Terrorism's 1st Generation was Al Qaeda, 2nd Generation was ISIS, and a 3rd Generation is making a Digital Caliphate from "Islamophobia" Censorship 206

Chapter VIII: The Partition of Free Speech . . . 251

Chapter IX: A Repurposed Edition of The Follies of Islam . . . 361

Chapter X: Islamism Always Creates Failed States . . . 414

Bibliography . . . 421

About the Author . . . 452

Copyright Notice . . . 453

***Please keep these Key Terms in mind**, they are how Muslims themselves define it:*

Definitions by the Brookings Institute to explain Islamic Extremism:

Islamism: "Islamism as a phenomenon incorporates a wide spectrum of behavior and belief. In the broadest sense, Islamist groups believe Islamic law or Islamic values should play a central role in public life. They feel Islam has things to say about how politics should be conducted, how the law should be applied, and how other people—not just themselves—should conduct themselves morally."[1]

Mainstream Islamism: "Mainstream Islamist groups primarily consist of Muslim Brotherhood and Brotherhood-inspired movements. Their distinguishing features are their gradualism (historically eschewing revolution), an embrace of parliamentary politics, and a willingness to work within existing state structures, even secular ones."[2]

Salafism: "Salafism is the idea that the most authentic and true Islam is found in the lived example of the early, righteous generations of Muslims, known as the *Salaf*, who were closest in both time and proximity to the Prophet Muhammad. Salafis—often described as "ultraconservatives"—believe not just in the "spirit" but in the "letter" of the law, which is what sets them apart from their mainstream counterparts. In the Arab world today, Salafis are known for trying to imitate the particular habits of the first Muslims, such as dressing like the Prophet (by cuffing their trousers at ankle-length) or brushing their teeth like the Prophet (with a natural teeth cleaning twig called a *miswak*)."[3]

Jihadism: "Jihadism is driven by the idea that jihad (religiously-sanctioned warfare) is an individual obligation (fard 'ayn) incumbent upon all Muslims, rather than a collective obligation carried out by legitimate representatives of the Muslim community (fard kifaya), as it was traditionally understood in the pre-modern era. They are able to do this by arguing that Muslim leaders today are illegitimate and do not command the authority to ordain justified violence. In the absence of such authority, they argue, every able-bodied Muslim should take up the mantle of jihad. Contrast this state of affairs with World War I, when the Kaiser himself had to sweet talk the Ottoman caliphate into declaring jihad against the Allied Powers."

---

[1] Hamid, Shadi, and Rashid Dar. "Islamism, Salafism, and Jihadism: A Primer." Brookings, The Brookings Institution, 15 July 2016, www.brookings.edu/articles/islamism-salafism-and-jihadism-a-primer/.

[2] Hamid, Shadi, and Rashid Dar. "Islamism, Salafism, and Jihadism: A Primer." *Brookings*, The Brookings Institution, 15 July 2016, www.brookings.edu/articles/islamism-salafism-and-jihadism-a-primer/.

[3] Hamid, Shadi, and Rashid Dar. "Islamism, Salafism, and Jihadism: A Primer." *Brookings*, The Brookings Institution, 15 July 2016, www.brookings.edu/articles/islamism-salafism-and-jihadism-a-primer/.

Salafi-Jihadism: "This is an approach to jihadism that is coupled with an adherence to Salafism. Salafi-jihadists tend to emphasize the military exploits of the *Salaf* (the early generations of Muslims) to give their violence an even more immediate divine imperative. Most jihadist groups today can be classified as Salafi-jihadists, including al-Qaida and ISIS. Given their exclusivist view that their approach to Islam is the only authentic one, Salafi-jihadists often justify violence against other Muslims, including non-combatants, by recourse to *takfir*, or the excommunication of fellow Muslims. For these groups, if Muslims have been deemed to be apostates, then violence against them is licit."[4]

---

[4] Hamid, Shadi, and Rashid Dar. "Islamism, Salafism, and Jihadism: A Primer." *Brookings*, The Brookings Institution, 15 July 2016, www.brookings.edu/articles/islamism-salafism-and-jihadism-a-primer/.

Chapter I: **The Doctrinal Failings of Islam**

The doctrinal problem within Islam that makes it so dangerous, that many in democratic countries either don't know or don't want to admit, is the theological underpinnings of its consistency. Human beings have cognitive dissonance, we can often be hypocrites, and we often ignore what is inconvenient to acknowledge; but I would argue that the reason for the prevalence of Islamic violence in an order of magnitude higher than other faith traditions in modern times is because as a system, it really does try to be the most consistent theology that humanity has so far ever created. Please understand, this is to its detriment and not something that we should honor or support. The lack of hypocrisy is why the violence is so prevalent, because it really does value the afterlife more than the material world and that is precisely why this religion can commit such wanton destruction upon "materialism" and non-Muslims who are "deceiving" Muslims away from spiritual commitments to their faith. Within the context of Islam's theology under the *Tafsir* system, you have to accept the Quran as the unalterable word of the Abrahamic God.[5] The *Sharia*, while analogous to a leading people to a watering hole in its literal meaning, actually means the "Divine Law" and refers to the Abrahamic God's Divine Law.[6][7] Regardless of if you name the Abrahamic God Yahweh or Allah or how uncomfortable Christians feel acknowledging this, it is the God of Abraham that Muslims worship. The Islamic jurisprudence system is based upon the notion of unquestionable fact that every follower, and those subjugated by Muslims as a lesser social status, have to accept because it was given by the Abrahamic God and Muslims believe that following the teachings of Islam leads to heaven for eternity. The process within Islam is more systematic than other major religions. The Tafsir system has a holistic structure whereby the Quran must be accepted as unquestionable fact, and if the Quran doesn't answer a question, then Mohammad's lived example (the Sunnah) serves as absolute fact that followers must adhere to, and if that's not satisfactory then the companions of the Prophet Mohammad serve as an example of how to behave.[8] If they

---

[5] "Tafseer on the Basis of Narrated Texts and Tafseer on the Basis of Individual Understanding - Islam Question & Answer." Islamqa.info, Islam Question and Answer, 11 Mar. 2015, islamqa.info/en/answers/205290/tafseer-on-the-basis-of-narrated-texts-and-tafseer-on-the-basis-of-individual-understanding.

[6] Ibrahim, Abu. "Shariah and Fiqh. Do You Know the Difference?" Islamic Learning Materials, 5 Mar. 2012, web.archive.org/web/20181006224011/islamiclearningmaterials.com/shariah-fiqh/.

[7] "What Is Shari'ah? - Islam Question & Answer." Islamqa.Info, Shaykh Muhammad Saalih al-Munajjid, islamqa.info/en/answers/210742/what-is-shariah. Accessed 17 Jan. 2025.

[8] "Tafseer on the Basis of Narrated Texts and Tafseer on the Basis of Individual Understanding - Islam Question & Answer." Islamqa.info, Islam Question and Answer, 11 Mar. 2015, islamqa.info/en/answers/205290/tafseer-on-the-basis-of-narrated-texts-and-tafseer-on-the-basis-of-

also do not answer the questions that society has on how to deal with a new social issue, then the lived experiences of the first Muslims are used as an example to follow.[9] If all of those fail to answer a question, then Muslim priests – who are viewed more as "Islamic Scholars" by Muslims due to the perception of learned scholarship in Islam – must find an appropriate Hadith that has a chain of narration verified by Islamic "scholars" to have been said by the Prophet Mohammad himself to give as a lived example that followers must adhere to.[10] And if all that is exhausted, then an Islamic "scholar" (an Islamic "scholar" is generally called a "*Faqih*" which can arguably be any Imam) gives an "*ijtihad*" or "independent opinion" within the context of following Sharia (The Divine Law of the Abrahamic God).[11] That is, they interpret all of what the Quran, Prophet Mohammad, the companions of the Prophet, and the first Muslims said or did to form a correct assessment of how they would view a specific modern question that couldn't be answered. This is what is called a "*Fiqh*" and while an "opinion", it can be seen as authoritative.[12][13] Furthermore, no new ideas or concepts can be added because it is "*bid'ah*" (literally, invention in a religion) and thus forbidden in Islamic jurisprudence.[14] It is important to note that this system includes the "*Naskh*" which means "abrogation" and refers to Islamic jurisprudence's "Theory of Abrogation" for the Quran; in brief, latter verses within the Quran can abrogate prior verses of the Quran as a legal system

---

individual-understanding.

[9] "Tafseer on the Basis of Narrated Texts and Tafseer on the Basis of Individual Understanding - Islam Question & Answer." Islamqa.info, Islam Question and Answer, 11 Mar. 2015, islamqa.info/en/answers/205290/tafseer-on-the-basis-of-narrated-texts-and-tafseer-on-the-basis-of-individual-understanding.

[10] "Tafseer on the Basis of Narrated Texts and Tafseer on the Basis of Individual Understanding - Islam Question & Answer." Islamqa.info, Islam Question and Answer, 11 Mar. 2015, islamqa.info/en/answers/205290/tafseer-on-the-basis-of-narrated-texts-and-tafseer-on-the-basis-of-individual-understanding.

[11] "Tafseer on the Basis of Narrated Texts and Tafseer on the Basis of Individual Understanding - Islam Question & Answer." Islamqa.info, Islam Question and Answer, 11 Mar. 2015, islamqa.info/en/answers/205290/tafseer-on-the-basis-of-narrated-texts-and-tafseer-on-the-basis-of-individual-understanding.

[12] Ibrahim, Abu. "Shariah and Fiqh. Do You Know the Difference?" Islamic Learning Materials, 5 Mar. 2012, web.archive.org/web/20181006224011/islamiclearningmaterials.com/shariah-fiqh/.

[13] "Difference between Shari'ah, Fiqh and Usul al-Fiqh - Islam Question & Answer." Islamqa.Info, Shaykh Muhammad Saalih al-Munajjid, islamqa.info/en/answers/282538/difference-between-shariah-fiqh-and-usul-al-fiqh. Accessed 17 Jan. 2025.

[14] "Tafseer on the Basis of Narrated Texts and Tafseer on the Basis of Individual Understanding - Islam Question & Answer." Islamqa.info, Islam Question and Answer, 11 Mar. 2015, islamqa.info/en/answers/205290/tafseer-on-the-basis-of-narrated-texts-and-tafseer-on-the-basis-of-individual-understanding.

that Muslims and those they conquer must follow.[15][16] Imams, Sheiks, and Faqihs may even use allegory to interpret the Quranic text to best fit an answer to a question regarding a modern problem, but it has to be understood within the context of accepting the Quran as absolute fact that cannot be questioned. Finally, the four types of *Jihad* that Muslims must adhere to on a daily basis to stay consistent with Islamic teachings. For this part, it might be best to simply quote the concisely put teachings of the *Islam Questions and Answers* website made by Sheikh Muhammed Salih Al-Munajjid under the URL (https://islamqa.info/en/answers/10455/greater-and-lesser-jihaad) which explains as follows:

> Undoubtedly jihaad against the self comes before jihaad against the kuffaar, because one cannot strive against the kuffaar until after one has striven against one's own self, because fighting is something which the self dislikes. Allaah says (interpretation of the meaning):
>
> "Jihaad (holy fighting in Allaah's Cause) is ordained for you (Muslims) though you dislike it, and it may be that you dislike a thing which is good for you and that you like a thing which is bad for you. Allaah knows but you do not know"[al-Baqarah 2:216]
>
> The point is that jihaad against the enemy cannot take place until one strives and forces oneself to do it, until one's self submits and accepts that.
>
> Fataawa Manaar al-Islam by Shaykh Ibn 'Uthaymeen (may Allaah have mercy on him), 2/421
>
> Ibn al-Qayyim said: "Jihaad is of four stages: jihaad al-nafs (striving against the self), jihaad al-shayaateen (striving against the shayaateen or devils), jihaad al-kuffaar (striving against the disbelievers) and jihaad al-munaafiqeen (striving against the hypocrites).
>
> Jihaad al-nafs means striving to make oneself learn true guidance, and to follow it after coming to know it, calling others to it, and bearing with patience the difficulties of calling others to Allaah. Jihaad al-Shaytaan means striving against him and warding off the doubts and desires that he throws at a person, and the doubts that undermine faith, and striving against the corrupt desires that he tries to inspire in a person. Jihaad against the kuffaar and munaafiqeen is done in the heart and on the tongue, with one's wealth and oneself. Jihaad against the kuffaar mostly takes the form of physical action, and jihaad against the munaafiqeen mostly takes the form of words… The most perfect of people are those who have completed all the stages of jihaad. People vary in their status before Allaah according to their status in jihaad."(Zaad al-Ma'aad 3/9-12)
>
> And Allaah knows best.[17]

Note, Islam literally translates to "the submission" and thus submission is considered a good act in service of the Abrahamic God. Moreover, many Muslims in the West will constantly say that any random Imam who is not their preferred Imam is not a

---

[15] THE THEORY OF ABROGATION, www.islamawareness.net/FAQ/Logic/faq105.html.
[16] "Theory of Abrogation (Naskh) in Islam, Abrogation in Islamic Jurisprudence." Theory of Abrogation (Naskh) in Islam, Abrogation in Islamic Jurisprudence, Law and Legislation, 28 May 2018, www.lawandlegislation.com/2018/05/theory-of-abrogation-naskh-in-islam.html.
[17] "Greater and Lesser Jihaad." Translated by Muhammed Salih Al-Munajjid, Islam Question And Answer, islamqa.info/en/10455.

"real Imam" and therefore not following the "real Islam" but this is just willful ignorance to the problems underscoring their theology, whereby they attempt to ignore the holistic issues that are intrinsic to their faith tradition. These are simply attempts, often successful attempts, to shut down logical arguments about the problems of their faith tradition failing to comport to modern times. They ignore the mass murder of civilians by focusing instead on how it makes them feel to hear such painful truths about their theology and to ignore the spread of violence that harms innocent people across the world. Their personal preference and subjective experience are immaterial to logical consequences of this theology and the facts regarding how many innocent non-Muslims and Muslims are repeatedly killed by it.

Finally, the issue of purity culture that is unique to the theology of Islam. Islam teaches people to believe that everyone is born pure as a Muslim but deceived away from Islam due to satanism in the world.[18] That is, they believe every child born is automatically a Muslim and when they follow faith traditions or belief structures outside of Islam, then they have been deceived by Satan away from Islam. In other words, a child born into a Jewish, Christian, or Hindu family is "deceived away" from Islam despite generations of families worshipping those other faith traditions. So, when someone commits the "heinous act" of Quran 4:89, of rejecting the faith of Islam, then they need to be murdered to keep the community "pure" and safe from "infidel" ideas that are viewed as being corrupted by devil worship and would cause people to burn in eternal hellfire in hell, if Muslims allow such beliefs to spread.[19] The endgoal of all of this is to accept the Quran as the perfect book to live by to solve all human problems and to live by the standards of the 7th century AD to await the coming of Jesus Christ after the Mahdi brings the true believers to Jesus Christ.[20][21] For those who are confused, Islam teaches that it is the true religion of the prophet Abraham and the Messiah of Islam is Jesus Christ.[22][23][24][25] For those who require further proof, here is a list of the Quranic verses that

---

[18] Castor, Trevor. "Sin According to Islam." Zwemer Center, www.zwemercenter.com/guide/sin-according-to-muslims/.

[19] "The Quranic Arabic Corpus - Word by Word Grammar, Syntax and Morphology of the Holy Quran." The Quranic Arabic Corpus - Translation, corpus.quran.com/translation.jsp?chapter=4&verse=89.
[20] The Quranic Arabic Corpus - Translation, Quranic Arabic Corpus, corpus.quran.com/translation.jsp?chapter=4&verse=159. Accessed 17 Jan. 2025.
[21] "What Do Muslims Believe about Jesus?" Islam Guide: Life After Death, www.islam-guide.com/ch3-10.htm.
[22] "What Is Unique about Jesus and Mary in Islam?" Facts about the Muslims the Religion of Islam, Why Islam?, 24 Nov. 2024, www.whyislam.org/jesus-and-mary/.
[23] "What Do Muslims Believe about Jesus?" Islam Guide: Life After Death, www.islam-guide.com/ch3-10.htm.
[24] Sahih Muslim 156 - The Book of Faith - كتاب الإيمان - Sunnah.Com - Sayings and Teachings of Prophet Muhammad (صلى الله عليه و سلم), sunnah.com/muslim:156. Accessed 17 Jan. 2025.
[25] al-Sadr, Sayyid Sadruddin. "Chapter 4 | Al-Mahdi | Al-Islam.Org." Translated by Jalil Dorrani, Al-Islam.Org, Sayyid Sadruddin al-Sadr, www.al-islam.org/al-mahdi-sayyid-sadruddin-sadr/chapter-4. Accessed 18 Jan. 2025.

mention Jesus Christ as the Messiah, Jesus Christ is sometimes referred to as the Arabic name Isa or as Son of Mary in the Quran's translations, this might be due to the fact that historically the term Christ was a title for Messiah that was translated in Greek as "Christos" before being adapted into English as "Christ" and not part of his actual name: Quran 3:45, Quran 4:157, Quran 4:171, Quran 4:172, Quran 5:17, Quran 5:72, Quran 5:75, Quran 9:30, and Quran 9:31. The context of other verses cohere to Jesus Christ being the Messiah in Islam; such as Quranic verse 4:159 which mentions that Jesus Christ will be a witness against those who doubt Islam on Judgment Day. The Mahdi, that is the Guided One, brings true Muslims together, while the Anti-Messiah (likely based upon the original Jewish concept of Anti-Messiah more than the latter Christian variant of the Anti-Christ) deceives people away from the real Islam. The Mahdi then apparently slaughters all the polytheists for deceiving Muslims and fights the Anti-Messiah until the Islamic Jesus Christ appears behind him and then helps him slay the Anti-Messiah and Satan. The Mahdi then "pauses time" for "seven years", or "nine years", or even a vague amount of years (the hadiths are deliberately vague) and rules a "glorious" Islamic Caliphate and then passes away to allow Jesus Christ to rule the world eternally from then on.[26][27][28][29][30][31] All of this is as foretold and instructed by the Prophet Mohammad. This is what Islamic Jihadists like the Salafists slaughter innocent people and fly planes into buildings for. Islamist political activists and Islamic terrorist groups really do want to destroy all forms of materialism and social concepts: modern medicine, the destruction of

---

[26] "Sunan Ibn Majah 4078: 36 Tribulations: (33)Chapter: The Tribulation of Dajjal, the Emergence of 'Esa Bin Maryam and the Emergence of Gog and Magog." Sunan Ibn Majah 4078 - Tribulations - كتاب الفتن - Sunnah.Com - Sayings and Teachings of Prophet Muhammad (صلى الله عليه و سلم), SUNNAH.COM, sunnah.com/ibnmajah:4078. Accessed 18 Mar. 2025. For reference: It was narrated from Abu Hurairah that the Prophet (ﷺ) said:
"The Hour will not begin until 'Eisa bin Maryam comes down as a just judge and a just ruler. He will break the cross, kill the pigs and abolish the Jizyah, and wealth will become so abundant that no one will accept it."

[27] "Sunan Ibn Majah 4055: (28)Chapter: Signs (of the Day of Judgment)(28) باب الآيات:." Sunan Ibn Majah 4055 - Tribulations - كتاب الفتن - Sunnah.Com - Sayings and Teachings of Prophet Muhammad (صلى الله عليه و سلم), SUNNAH.COM, sunnah.com/ibnmajah:4055. Accessed 18 Mar. 2025.

[28] "Jami` At-Tirmidhi 2240: 33 Chapters On Al-Fitan: (59)Chapter: What Has Been Related About The Turmoil Of The Dajjal." Jami` At-Tirmidhi 2240 - Chapters on al-Fitan - كتاب الفتن عن رسول الله صلى الله عليه وسلم - Sunnah.Com - Sayings and Teachings of Prophet Muhammad (صلى الله عليه و سلم), SUNNAH.COM, sunnah.com/tirmidhi:2240. Accessed 18 Mar. 2025.

[29] "Sunan Ibn Majah 4075: 36 Tribulations: (33)Chapter: The Tribulation of Dajjal, the Emergence of 'Esa Bin Maryam and the Emergence of Gog and Magog." Sunan Ibn Majah 4075 - Tribulations - كتاب الفتن - Sunnah.Com - Sayings and Teachings of Prophet Muhammad (صلى الله عليه و سلم), sunnah.com/ibnmajah:4075. Accessed 18 Mar. 2025.

[30] "Sahih Muslim 2937a: 54 The Book of Tribulations and Portents of the Last Hour: (20)Chapter: Ad-Dajjal." Sahih Muslim 2937a - the Book of Tribulations and Portents of the Last Hour - كتاب الفتن وأشراط الساعة - Sunnah.Com - Sayings and Teachings of Prophet Muhammad (صلى الله عليه و سلم), SUNNAH.COM, sunnah.com/muslim:2937a. Accessed 18 Mar. 2025.

[31] al-Sadr, Sayyid Sadruddin. "Chapter 4 | Al-Mahdi | Al-Islam.Org." Translated by Jalil Dorrani, Al-Islam.Org, Sayyid Sadruddin al-Sadr, www.al-islam.org/al-mahdi-sayyid-sadruddin-sadr/chapter-4. Accessed 18 Jan. 2025.

all history and culture of unconquered lands, the erasure of all other forms of philosophical thought outside Islam, and the erasure of all human advancements and scientific advancements beyond the 7th century. It is because the 7th century is considered the endpoint and perfect civilization due to being the time period of the Prophet Mohammad's rule; the Quran is supposed to answer all of life's problems for humanity within Islamic theology. I could go into details on the ridiculous nature of Islamic heaven, but I think you already get the general idea of why this theology has so many problems. That really is the worldview and outcome that they are forcing upon us. The systemic problems with Islam is never going to go away by seeking to reform the religion because there'll always be a return to tradition movement like Wahhabism and Salafism, any deviation will be seen as "*bid'ah*" and seen as adding devil worship to the faith tradition, and terms like Islamophobia continue to prevent peaceful Free Speech discussions that could save lives by de-converting people away from Islam.

What this religion amounts to is Divine Command Theory on figurative steroids to the extent that the Tafsir system of Islamic jurisprudence tries to thoroughly remove all forms of outside logic and thought or otherwise attempts to squeeze it into the acceptability of the standards of the 7th century during the Prophet Mohammad's time. The Tafsir system really is a legal system founded on the ideas of revealed wisdom and divine command theory with Muslims having absolute faith in it because they believe it comes from the Abrahamic God. This is also why I doubt Christianity can come-up with any real argument against Islam, because most Christians still follow the system of divine command theory as the basis for their moral judgments. Many US Christian pastors and priests make false aspersions upon Muslims with claims like Allah is somehow the devil (the age-old narcissism of Christianity whereby any disagreeable viewpoint is labeled as a temptation of the devil), or that Jesus was only seen as a good teacher or just a prophet (which is not the full truth, Jesus is the Messiah of Islam), and essentially do everything in their power to dehumanize Muslims without actually giving a valid critique because they don't even try to understand Islamic theology before denouncing it. It would be incredibly uncomfortable to acknowledge how much more literalist Islam is in accepting Divine Command theory compared to Christianity's open interpretation system. It's an argument that Christianity cannot win, because Christianity also predicates itself upon divine command theory. In a very real way, the failings of Christianity act as a shield to protect Islam's most dangerous beliefs. Christian conservatives often confuse the theology that Muslims are advocating for as Marxist or Socialist as a result, because they're unfamiliar with the very real and dangerous belief in Islam that the 7th century needs to be the endpoint of civilization to prepare the way for the Mahdi and Jesus Christ to save the true Muslims from the Anti-Messiah and Satan. This is not some figurative or interpretative belief; the majority of Muslims believe this to be a literal event that will happen with absolute certainty. It's not Socialist or Marxist, it's a purely Abrahamic belief that Muslims are espousing and which Christians have no legitimate ability to criticize within the worldview of their own faith tradition.

  As a Hindu and an Atheist, my perspective would be to look at Islam as a system and judge it that way. To the best of my knowledge, if the Quran references other material, then it is bizarre that the ideology claims the Quran can solve all of life's questions. The Tafsir legal system seems to be a self-contradiction to the Quran's claims of being the perfect book to answer all of life's problems to me. My reasoning is thus: the Tafsir system, the Sunnah (especially in the Shafi'i and Hanafi schools of Islam) and Hadiths essentially disprove the idea that the Quran is the perfect book for all people to live by; since they need the concept of the Tafsir system itself, the Hadiths as supplementary material, the Sunnah as an explanation of ritual and traditions, and cultural movements of return to faith traditions from Wahhabism and Salafism to stay consistent with it. Why, for example, do the Hadiths need a grading system of saheeh (Sound), Hasan (good), Daif (Weak), and Mawdu (fabricated)? The very existence of needing a gradation system for the chain of narration of the Hadiths prove that Islam's claims to simplicity are false. If certain Sunnah hadiths can abrogate the Quran in the Hanafi and Shafi'i schools of Islam, even within the context of strict conditions, then how could the Quran possibly answer all of life's questions as a guide for all people to live by?[32] Why doesn't a Sunnah Hadith abrogating a Quranic verse prove that the Quran clearly was never able to answer all of life's problems for humanity?[33] If the Quran really could provide what it claims, then why can't people just read it, follow it, and live in a perfect utopia without a jurisprudence system, the broader hadiths, or the Sunnah to explain as supplementary material? Is the Abrahamic God incapable of providing instruction without supplementary material that needs a grading system that leads to moral ambiguity? I don't understand why some Muslims claim that Hinduism and Christianity don't make sense, meanwhile their own religion doesn't just have one holy book, but multiple companion pieces to that holy book because – regardless of if your holy book refers to those companion pieces or not – it clearly wasn't enough on its own to solve all human problems which is why it needs those companion pieces. If anything, the entire jurisprudence system of Islam proves that the Quran isn't the perfect book to solve all human problems as it claims. If it was truly able to answer all questions, then the differing interpretation of the hadiths by so-called "Islamic scholars" wouldn't matter at all. The Quran would just be able to explain it without any ambiguity or interpretation. In

---

[32] Khan, Faraz A. "Can the Sunnah Abrogate the Qur'an?" SeekersGuidance, sufyan https://seekersguidance.org/wp-content/uploads/2024/11/SG_Logo_v23.svg, 28 Oct. 2010, seekersguidance.org/answers/general-counsel/can-the-sunnah-abrogate-the-quran/#:~:text=(1)%20The%20Hanafis%2C%20Imam,accepted%20and%20implemented%20by%20the.

[33] Khan, Faraz A. "Can the Sunnah Abrogate the Qur'an?" SeekersGuidance, sufyan https://seekersguidance.org/wp-content/uploads/2024/11/SG_Logo_v23.svg, 28 Oct. 2010, seekersguidance.org/answers/general-counsel/can-the-sunnah-abrogate-the-quran/#:~:text=(1)%20The%20Hanafis%2C%20Imam,accepted%20and%20implemented%20by%20the.

other words, the supposed simplicity that Islam claims to have over Christianity's trinity or Hinduism's heterodox tradition, doesn't actually seem to exist. It's a demonstrably false claim and the mere existence of the hadiths prove it.

There are certain logical errors within Islam that simply baffle me as a Hindu: Why isn't the existence of the Quran simply proof that the Abrahamic God is a failure? Its own premise of the original Torah and the Injeel being corrupted, lost, and then conveniently abrogated would mean that the Abrahamic God's revealed wisdom demonstrably failed to work twice (Quran 3:3 – 7 and Quran 5:46 – 5:82). Thus, the Quran's very existence contradicts the claims to Islam's simplicity, since the assumption of the Quran's necessity is predicated upon humanity failing to understand the Abrahamic God's will twice before; over a series of hundreds or thousands of years. If we apply Occam's Razor, it would simply be the case that humans have made-up the Abrahamic God as an invention to feel comfortable about life's ambiguity and not that humanity has failed to learn the Abrahamic God's moral lessons twice before the Quran was introduced to humanity. This is all ignoring the most salient failing of Islam: Why does the Prophet Mohammad's lived example matter? Why does any prophet's lived experiences and actions matter? If an all-powerful God instructed any prophet to give a set of instructions on how to live life for the best outcomes so that people go to heaven, then why couldn't they just recite the instructions, people could then follow it, and then the perfect outcome simply happens by following the holy book regardless of external circumstances? Why do you need competing traditions like the four Sunni schools to interpret your God's word and why can't your God's word be received in all languages instead of solely being limited to Arabic? Why didn't Allah allow for the Quran to be perfectly understood in all languages so that the maximum amount of people could follow it without being incumbered by learning one language to better understand the Quran? If the Prophet Mohammad really was a prophet of the Abrahamic God as he claims, why is insulting the Prophet Mohammad held as a greater taboo than insulting Allah? In other words, why is the Prophet Mohammad held in higher esteem than Allah in Islam? To deny this would simply be a rationalization; insulting comments towards Allah is allowed, but insults towards the Prophet Mohammad can lead to physical confrontation in the majority of Islamic countries. How exactly does this make sense? If the Prophet Mohammad was sincere in his claims, why didn't he hold Allah to a higher regard than himself? Why do some Islamic schools of thought such as in Pakistan hold Quran burning as more permissible with jail time than making an insulting picture or making insulting comments of the Prophet Mohammad, which usually leads to immediate violence? How is this not simply proof that Islam is nothing more than the Prophet Mohammad's personality cult and that he elevated himself into the status of a God without calling himself a God in what amounts to a difference in semantics?

For the next chapter, I want to give a purely Hindu perspective since fellow Hindus mention that they hardly ever feel their religious value systems are represented accurately even by fellow Hindus who are more outspoken like myself. I apparently did an abjectly terrible job in the past when discussing my views with Western Ex-Muslims, so I've tried to learn and improve after being criticized by fellow Hindus who pointed out how flawed and limited my views were at the time. I was also criticized by a close friend who said, even outside of that, I'd done a bad job. So, I want to present a critique from my own understanding as a regular Hindu and based upon my limited reading of Vedanta philosophy, specifically the Advaita Vedanta perspective, that I've read from commentary by Adi Shankara on the Bhagavad Gita. Allow me to explain the differences in theology first, before I go into the critique. The next chapter is mostly from a summarization I gave in my recent book, *Machiavellian Ahimsa*, to argue in favor of new International Relations concepts in Political Science to improve US Foreign Policy but edited and expanded on for the purposes of this book.

Chapter II: **A Vedantic and Samkhya Critique of Islam**

The utilization of the Vedanta philosophy of Hinduism may require some explanation for people who have no concept of the difference in worldview between Hinduism's dominant theology and other faith traditions. Unfortunately, two of the three Abrahamic faith traditions simply assume that anything that disagrees with them is idol worship and Satanism in a self-serving, narcissistic viewpoint of every other faith tradition in human history. As such, it's necessary to give a brief explanation because otherwise people who are unfamiliar with Hinduism will simply be confused due to most people only knowing about reincarnation, the Caste system, and the idea of multiple deities. I must stress that I'm more a nominal Hindu and I'm not a learned theologian, and I'm mostly going to explain portions that should hopefully reduce confusion on the subject for the purposes of critique in this case.

Hinduism is a bit similar to Christianity in one major aspect, materialism is largely viewed as a net-negative in most viewpoints within Hinduism. Whereas Christianity views the material world as sinful; most of Hindu theology, especially Vedanta philosophy, views the material world as an illusion (referred to as *maya*). The key difference is that while the Abrahamic concept of sin views the physical world as sinful and a test of temptation to overcome; the Hindu concept of *maya* views the world as a form of bondage whereby everything we see, hear, touch, taste, smell, and perceive are also illusions of the physical world.[34][35] The human body is sometimes given the analogy of being a chariot that our conscious mind or our soul rides in. Within Vedanta philosophy, this concept of *maya* delves deeper to argue that distinguishing any particular object as a specific subject matter within our own personal terms is also an illusion. The modifications of how we identify various subject matters in our own thoughts are also considered illusions; that is, our personal perspective of the physical world around us, our strong feelings towards material objects or even our religious iconography, and our personal ability to categorize the world around us are all illusions.[36] Hindu religious texts translated to English often use the term "sense-objects" as a broad term for understanding that it isn't merely the physical world being an illusion, but also our senses and our perception of the world itself. Why does Hinduism have so many supposed deities then? Within Advaita Vedanta philosophy specifically, because we must live in the bondage of the physical world, they are illusory means to become close to the unmanifested supreme

---

[34] Eknath, Easwaran, translator. Chapter Five: Renounce and Rejoice (122 – 130). The Bhagavad Gita. Nilgiri Press, 2007.

[35] Eknath, Easwaran, translator. Brihadaranyaka: The Forest of Wisdom (92-117) and Prashna: The Breath of Life (218-237). The Upanishads. Nilgiri Press, 2007.

[36] Datta, Jatindranath. Chapter 2: The Path of Knowledge (783 – 2219). Bhagavad Gita: With the commentary of Shankaracharya. Advaita Ashrama, 1984.

reality (known as *Brahman*) beyond our perceptions by creating our own illusory *Ishvara* (God) to become closer to *Brahman*. Hindus who follow the dominant theologies of Hinduism like Advaita Vedanta can be given the choice to do this in two ways. We can do this by following behaviors that allow for good karma, following dharmic duties, and serving our communities around us selflessly to help the people around us grow and prosper.[37][38] Or, we can commit to self-renunciation, non-violence, yoga, and meditation and learn more about *Brahman* (the Unmanifest) through a personal religious journey to purify ourselves of sin, evil, and become closer to *Brahman*.[39][40] An example of getting closer to *Brahman* according to Hindu theological texts like the *Upanishads* would be understanding that since it is unmanifested supreme reality, then it exists within us as our supreme self (*Atman*) too. What is meant by following Dharmic duties? I would be remiss, if I didn't specify what it means; traditionally this meant getting married and having children, following Caste duties, respecting the laws of any new countries that Hindus settle in, and respecting religious rites. In modern times, the caste duties that involve caste discrimination are rightly ridiculed as intra-Hindu abuse and unacceptable; likewise, it is unacceptable to bring such problems in other countries that provide better opportunities and means of living, as it is deeply disrespectful to your new community and to your new country to do that. We should be serving the community by participating and helping to the best of our abilities, not causing problems for others.[41]

    How am I critiquing Islam based upon this particular Hindu perspective? The Prophet Mohammad died in the 7th century and whatever feelings of love and commitment that Muslim majority countries have towards him is just their collective illusion – their *maya* – in both the physical and psychological sense. The image of the Prophet Mohammad controls their behavior; they *allow* the illusion of the Prophet Mohammad to control them due to their unquestioned faith. The image of the Prophet Mohammad is a *sense-object* that causes them to become senselessly violent when anyone is perceived to have mocked their Prophet. Likewise, the Quran is a *sense-object* when people are killed for the perceived wrongdoing of disrespecting the Quran. That is, deriving moral lessons or a guide from the Quran doesn't give Muslims the right to kill people for the perception of desecration or disrespect; Muslims who commit murder over it have simply allowed an illusory concept of divinity to cause them to behave violently.

---

[37] Eknath, Easwaran, translator. Chapter Three: Selfless Service (93-103). The Bhagavad Gita. Nilgiri Press, 2007.

[38] Datta, Jatindranath. Chapter 2: The Path of Knowledge (783 – 2219). Bhagavad Gita: With the commentary of Shankaracharya. Advaita Ashrama, 1984.

[39] Eknath, Easwaran, translator. Chapter Three: Selfless Service (93-103). The Bhagavad Gita. Nilgiri Press, 2007.

[40] Datta, Jatindranath. Chapter 2: The Path of Knowledge (783 – 2219). Bhagavad Gita: With the commentary of Shankaracharya. Advaita Ashrama, 1984.

[41] Eknath, Easwaran, translator. Chapter Three: Selfless Service (93-103). The Bhagavad Gita. Nilgiri Press, 2007.

The violence is proof that the Prophet Mohammad and the Quran are nothing more than delusions of their mind that have corrupted their thinking. The Quranic verse 4:89 and Muslims insisting that criticizing Islam is Islamophobia are both proof that Islam is the most doubting religion in the world; because why would anyone seek to eliminate others to protect their faith? Why do you constantly need external validation to feel comfortable in your faith? Why should the outside world need to change themselves so you feel comfortable in your faith? As long as they're not being bigots by harassing you, threatening violence against you, or discriminating against you; criticizing your religion is just non-Muslims exercising their inalienable right of Free Speech. Muslim people's need for external validation by forcing the world to change around them, so that they feel comfortable is proof of a weak faith. The reason is because they're simply trying to validate their own comfort by seeing, hearing, feeling, and experiencing what is analogous to a giant mirror to see only themselves. That is merely proof of delusion, not a strong faith, because the external world should be immaterial to your own independent reasoning of why you believe something is true.

For Hindus, to distinguish truth claims and improve our perceptions, we largely use the Pramana system but it differs in which ones are used for each philosophical school within Hinduism itself. Unfortunately, I had to learn this aspect of Hinduism late in my life since my experiences were just the Hindu priest at the local mandir that my family went to every Sunday simply eulogizing anecdotal stories of Gods and then having collective singing near the end. I've since had those misconceptions corrected thanks to harsh criticism from fellow Hindus and close friends who follow different faith traditions after embarrassing myself in a Youtube talk with Ex-Muslim atheists. To the best of my current knowledge, this would be the most correct approximation of what the main six Pramana systems consist of and mean:

1. Pratyaksha —Eyewitness Account / Direct Perception

2. Anumāna — Inference

3. Upamāna — Analogy

4. Arthāprapti — Deduction

5. Anupalabdhi — Non-existence (the unlikelihood that something is possible)

6. Shabda Pramāṇa — *Scriptural evidence, or Background knowledge*[42][43][44]

Eyewitness account / Direct Perception usually matters the most in Hindu philosophical systems above the other proofs. Below is an example of how Samkhya summarized their reasoning for why the concept of *Ishvara* (God) is not valid using the Pramana system, with only a slight addition of clarifying what the term *prakriti* means so there isn't any confusion. Western so-called "Indologists" liken this to the Ancient Greek "Problem of Evil" and seem to completely miss what this is actually critiquing. Samkhya critiques the belief in a singular omnipotent God and the problems that arise from believing in such a notion:

- **Samkhya** gave the following arguments against the idea of an eternal, self-caused, creator God:

1. If the existence of karma is assumed, the proposition of God as a moral governor of the universe is unnecessary. For, if God enforces the consequences of actions then he can do so without karma. If however, he is assumed to be within the law of karma, then karma itself would be the giver of consequences and there would be no need of a God.

2. Even if karma is denied, God still cannot be the enforcer of consequences. Because the motives of an enforcer God would be either egoistic or altruistic. Now, God's motives cannot be assumed to be altruistic because an altruistic God would not create a world so full of suffering. If his motives are assumed to be egoistic, then God must be thought to have desire, as agency or authority cannot be established in the absence of desire. However, assuming that God has desire would contradict God's eternal freedom which necessitates no compulsion in actions. Moreover, desire, according to Samkhya, is an attribute of prakriti (material energy) and cannot be thought to grow in God. The testimony of the Vedas, according to Samkhya, also confirms this notion.

3. Despite arguments to the contrary, if God is still assumed to contain unfulfilled desires, this would cause him to suffer pain and other similar human experiences. Such a worldly God would be no better than Samkhya's notion of higher self.

4. Furthermore, there is no proof of the existence of God. He is not the object of perception, there exists no general proposition that can prove him by inference and the testimony of the Vedas speak of prakriti (material energy) as the origin of the world, not God.

---

[42] Dixit, Sanjay. "Hindu Epistemology with Its Pramāṇa (Proof) System, Is Closest to Science - Hinduism Is Different..." Medium, Medium, 3 Nov. 2020, sanjay-dixit.medium.com/hindu-epistemology-with-its-pram%C4%81%E1%B9%87a-proof-system-is-closest-to-science-hinduism-is-different-5434cf9b659b.

[43] Patanjali. "Book One: Samadhi Pada." Yoga Sutras of Patanjali, translated by Swami Satchidananda, Kindle ed., Integral Yoga Publications, Buckingham, Virginia, 2012, pp. 23–108.

[44] Patanjali. "Chapter 1: Concentration (Samadhi Pada)." Translated by Swami Jnaneshvara Bharati, PDF ed., Www.Swamij.Com, pp. 4–15.

Therefore, **Samkhya** maintained that the various cosmological, ontological and teleological arguments could not prove God.[45][46][47][48]

That last epigram can be applied to the Islamic god, Allah. I would go so far that it could be applied to any supernatural claim and it's a brilliant counter to them for any empiricist and it comes solely from Hindu philosophy. Now, I want to be clear, I apply it to Brahman and Ishvara too; there is obviously no evidence to support that they exist from an empirical standpoint. Also, while eyewitness accounts can be valid, it's still true that our perceptions can be skewed and our judgments can be biased, and that's why I would apply scientific evidence before even the Pramana system because it is the best means of reaching a clear and honest approximation of how the world actually exists. It also shouldn't be seen as a binary choice between the two, since they can be used simultaneously. For example, our own eyewitness account of cells using tools like microscopes is the basis for understanding complex scientific topics like Biology and Microbiology. Similarly, NASA's use of advanced telescopes to detect what blackholes do[49] and ultraviolet satellite camera imagery from both Hubble[50] and the James Webb Space Telescope for a more in-depth look into space beyond our limited human eyes so we have a better understanding of the universe in our own limited human capacity.[51] I'd delve into how I apply this to modern neuroscientific and psychological findings which I'd argue validate my Hindu perspective, but going any further would be beyond the scope of this book.

It bears noting that my fellow Hindus in India and other fellow Dharmic followers have repeatedly expressed complaints of being ignored or they've been mocked as silly for arguments that do hold validity, even if it may bring discomfort to others because they

---

[45] "Atheism in Hinduism." Wikipedia, Wikimedia Foundation, 26 July 2019, en.wikipedia.org/wiki/Atheism_in_Hinduism#Arguments_against_existence_of_God_in_Hindu_philosophy.

[46] Kapstein, Matthew T., et al. Chapter 31: Hindu Disproofs of God: Refuting Vedantic Theism in the Samkhya-Sutra by Andrew J. Nicholson (598-619). The Oxford Handbook of Indian Philosophy. Edited by Jonardon Ganeri, Oxford University Press, 2018.

[47] Aniruddha. "Aniruddha's Commentary, Translated. Book I." Translated by Richard Garbe, Http://Indianculture.Gov.In, pp. 53–55. For Reference: Aphorisms and Commentary of 92, 93, and 94.

[48] Aniruddha. "Aniruddha's Commentary, Translated. Book V." Translated by Richard Garbe, Http://Indianculture.Gov.In, pp. 179 - 194. For Reference: Aphorisms and Commentary of 2 – 30.

[49] Lerner, Louise. "Black Holes, Explained." University of Chicago News, news.uchicago.edu/explainer/black-holes-explained#:~:text=Black%20holes%20have%20two%20parts,infinitely%20small%20and%20infinitely%20dense. Accessed 12 Mar. 2025.

[50] "The Death Throes of Stars - NASA Science." NASA, NASA, 27 Jan. 2025, science.nasa.gov/mission/hubble/science/science-highlights/the-death-throes-of-stars/#:~:text=When%20stars%20die%2C%20they%20throw,death%20depends%20on%20its%20size.

[51] "Webb Image Galleries - NASA Science." NASA, NASA, 13 Feb. 2025, science.nasa.gov/mission/webb/multimedia/images/.

challenge the notions of fairness to religious tolerance. I had initially thought these arguments as misguided on the basis that Democratic Republics shouldn't compare their internal structures to those of Islamic monarchies. Yet, after the Biden administration's foreign policy blunders in South Asia, obtaining a greater understanding on the limitations of Free Speech in Canada and Great Britain, and looking at the recent Pew Research surveys on global religious beliefs with how shockingly high the push for Muslim nationalism is[52]; I realized I was wrong to view them as misguided and I had been mistaken in my prior beliefs. Allow me to do my best to paraphrase the arguments I've heard from Hindus of India: *Why should we Hindus have to deal with proselytizers like Christian missionaries and Muslim dawahs when we don't do proselytizing ourselves and don't want it in our communities? Why should we Hindus, other Dharmic followers, and Christians permit Muslim dawahs to spread conversion in non-Muslim countries, when Muslim-majority countries would murder, torture, or jail people for de-converting people away from Islam? Why do we pretend this is a fair international system of each religion being treated equally in the world, when we know that Muslim-majority countries prohibit de-converting Muslims as illegal in their countries and make no qualms about killing Christian missionaries or religious missionaries of other faith traditions outside of Islam who try to de-convert them? Why do Christian missionaries act as if de-converting Hindus in India is some huge struggle, while ignoring the legitimate discrimination, violence, and murders of their fellow Christians and of other non-Muslim religious groups in Muslim-majority countries who suffer horrific abuses at the hands of the Muslim-majority populations? Are Christian missionaries just cowards who see Hindus as easy targets because Hindus believe in respecting Christians, while ignoring the violence and hate that Dharmic and Christian minority groups suffer in Muslim-majority countries like Pakistan, Afghanistan, and Bangladesh? You claim Christianity is all about testing your faith for the purpose of converting others, so why aren't you testing your faith in Muslim-majority countries that would kill you for being Christian? Aren't you suppose to bear persecution for having faith in Jesus Christ, so why aren't you proselytizing in Muslim-majority countries and helping your fellow Christians who are already persecuted there? Are you really sincere about your beliefs or are you just a pathetic coward who sees Hindus as easy targets because we're genuinely more peaceful than both of your faiths; which is why you smash Hindu iconography to mock us and your Christian extremists burn Hindu temples to instigate inter-religious violence that you then falsely portray in the news media as Hindu mob violence?*[53]

---

[52] Silver, Laura, and Jonathan Evans. "4. Should Religious Texts Influence National Laws?" Pew Research Center, Pew Research Center, 28 Jan. 2025, www.pewresearch.org/global/2025/01/28/should-religious-texts-influence-national-laws/.

[53] K, Prameela. "Rebuild Demolished Temples, BJP Tells State Govt." The New Indian Express, 17 Dec. 2020, www.newindianexpress.com/andhra-pradesh/2020/Dec/17/rebuild-demolished-temples-bjp-tells-state-govt-2237415.html.

For what it's worth, I believe these subsets of fellow Hindus who live in India are being pessimistic at least within the context of the politics of India; the fact is, if you actually look at what Christian Indians and Muslim Indians say about India, they're largely in agreement with Hindus that Indian culture is superior to other cultures and that India allows them to freely express their beliefs without fear or threats of harm.[54] Christian missionaries from the US only make up two percent of the Christian population within the US in total which should amount to approximately 3.4 million people out of approximately 170 million people judging from what I extrapolated from Glenn T. Stanton's book, *Myth of the Dying Church*.[55] The vast majority of Muslims in India and the US seem to just want to go about their day without talking about religion at all and try to steer conversations away because of feelings of embarrassment or possibly the fear of being singled out for being Muslim; which they obviously shouldn't have to fear as they are not the same as Islamists who are pushing for an Islamic political agenda into the public discourse and public policy. To be clear and to reiterate, Islamists are Muslim extremists who want to force Islamic values into broader societies. Islamists are not the same as nominal Muslims who just want to live their life without forcing religious agendas and go about their day within Democratic Republics. Sadly though, it's simply a fact when assessing Pew Research statistics and the laws of Islamic monarchies that the Islamists are the norm throughout the world and the nominal Muslims within Western societies and India are the rarity.[56][57]

To summarize my perspective as a Hindu Atheist towards Islam: I honestly see all supernatural claims as merely a delusion and that includes all of the Prophet Mohammad's claims. Within the scope of Hindu philosophy and personally reading a few chapters of Adi Shankara's commentary on the Bhagavad Gita, it better helped me to recognize and contextualize that all the claims of strong feelings of love that Muslims have for the Prophet Mohammad and Jesus Christ as their Messiah are merely illusory sense-perceptions. Insulting the Prophet Mohammad with the depiction of a picture and burning a Quran controls the behavior of most Muslims due to their strong feelings of adoration. Thus, their beliefs about the Prophet Mohammad and Jesus Christ are their sense-objects. That is, all their strong feelings of personally forming a relationship to

---

[54] Sahgal, Neha, and Jonathan Evans. "6. Nationalism and Politics." Pew Research Center, Pew Research Center, 29 June 2021, www.pewresearch.org/religion/2021/06/29/nationalism-and-politics/.
[55] Stanton, Glenn T. Chapter 9: "Is My Church Shrinking?" And Other Questions to Consider (pgs. 137 – 160). The Myth of the Dying Church: How Christianity Is Actually Thriving in America and the World. Worthy Publishing, 2019.
[56] Silver, Laura, and Jonathan Evans. "5. What Role Should Religion Play in Muslim- and Jewish-Majority Countries?" Pew Research Center, Pew Research Center, 28 Jan. 2025, www.pewresearch.org/global/2025/01/28/what-role-should-religion-play-in-muslim-and-jewish-majority-countries/.
[57] Silver, Laura, and Jonathan Evans. "4. Should Religious Texts Influence National Laws?" Pew Research Center, Pew Research Center, 28 Jan. 2025, www.pewresearch.org/global/2025/01/28/should-religious-texts-influence-national-laws/.

know Allah, their desire of wanting to be more like the Prophet Mohammad because they believe him to be the perfect human being to follow the example of and their love for him, and their faith that Jesus Christ will appear on judgment day to save the true Muslim believers are all illusions created from their collective affectation over what is really mythology. Modern neuroscience has largely determined that our personal views are a statistical distribution[58]; as such, the majority of Muslims confuse their subjective experiences and community relations for objective fact when the two are not the same. Faith in the Prophet Mohammad's revealed wisdom is faith in the illusion of prophethood, faith in Jesus Christ as their Messiah is faith in the illusion of prophecy and a Messiah, and fear of eternal hellfire is merely fear of a 7th century illusion and a fraudulent conversion tactic. The belief that anyone who disagrees with them will burn in eternal fire for those who disbelieve in Islam, the belief in angels, and their love for the Prophet Mohammad are all illusions from a 7th century mythology passed down to them. These beliefs are enforced by threats of fear such as the Eternal Fire: Quran 2:39, Quran 2:81, Quran 2:217, Quran 2:257, Quran 2:275, Quran 3:116, Quran 4:14, Quran 6:128, Quran 7:36, Quran 9:17, Quran 9:63, Quran 9:68, Quran 10:27, Quran 10:60, Quran 13:5, Quran 13:35, Quran 41:28, Quran 42:45, Quran 47:15, Quran 72:23, Quran 98:6, Quran 104:6, and threats of murder such as Quran 4:89. While some of my fellow Hindus also harbor belief in a soul, I'd argue that the belief that humans have souls is also an illusion.

Within the context of Samkhya's philosophical arguments, all of these supernatural beliefs; the supposed revealed wisdom of Prophet Mohammad, prophethood as a concept itself, the belief that Jesus Christ as the Messiah will come on Judgment day to save the true Muslims, the belief in the Occultation of the Mahdi and that the Mahdi will appear to guide true believing Muslims to Jesus Christ, the belief in angels, the soul, jinns, Shaytan / Satan, the eternal fires of hell, the belief in Jannah (Islamic Heaven), and the Abrahamic god Allah are all sensory illusions (*maya*). That is because, as Samkhya argued regarding any concept of *Ishvara* (God), these are all propositions that are not objects of perception, they are suppositions that have no evidentiary basis that can prove them, and the best way to obtain a method of proof to understand whether a claim can be true or not in modern times is the scientific method. The scientific method is obviously better than claims of revealed wisdom because it improves the ability of human eyewitness accounts using refined scientific tools like microscopes, medical techniques of brain imaging like fMRI, and telescopes for a more accurate approximation of reality itself. Feelings of love are not proof of truth and their feelings of love lead them into violence whenever someone mocks what they love. As a Hindu, I'd prefer a world of self-liberation (*moksha*) over illusion (*maya*). In other words, a world where people don't

---

[58] Lotto, Beau. Chapter 5: The Frog Who Dreamed of Being a Prince (1356 - 1670). Deviate: the Science of Seeing Differently. Hachette Books, 2017.

allow sense-objects to control their behavior or influence how they value truth-seeking regarding reality and facts.

When we Hindus observe Muslims or Christian extremists breaking, smashing, or burning Hindu iconography or Hindu temples; it is not proof of a strong faith on their part, it is proof of cowards who live in *maya* (illusion) and demand the rest of the world conform to their delusions due to the mythological belief in Judgment Day. The best way to end such tactics is to capture videos and share it with the world; in the cases where they aren't threatening immediate violence and just smashing Hindu iconography they bought; it might be useful to tell them pointblank that their actions are irrefutable proof that their religion teaches them to hate. Even if the person showing hate doesn't listen, others who hold the same faith as the ones who commit such actions will begin to lose faith and that's really all you need. Even if that doesn't happen, capturing video evidence and sharing it with the world inspires people to write critical essays or books like this one, so that more people become aware and potentially listen about the hatred and violence that such faiths like Islam continue to commit. It may seem paradoxical, but it's best to always keep in mind: most people of other faith traditions are unaware and not intentionally malicious, so when you share factual evidence, then even believers of the same faith tradition as those who commit hate will doubt their own faith because the vast majority find such hateful actions unconscionable. They're free to express their hate just as we're free to capture them committing such hateful acts and spreading their bad news to change minds in the opposite direction that they hoped for. In short, they try to force the illusion of their belief systems upon us and we show the truthful and harmful consequences of their belief systems upon their fellow faith members.

Chapter III: **What the term Islamophobia shields**

Quran 4:89

Sahih International: They wish you would disbelieve as they disbelieved so you would be alike. So do not take from among them allies until they emigrate for the cause of Allah. But if they turn away, then seize them and kill them wherever you find them and take not from among them any ally or helper.

Pickthall: They long that ye should disbelieve even as they disbelieve, that ye may be upon a level (with them). So choose not friends from them till they forsake their homes in the way of Allah; if they turn back (to enmity) then take them and kill them wherever ye find them, and choose no friend nor helper from among them,

Yusuf Ali: They but wish that ye should reject Faith, as they do, and thus be on the same footing (as they): But take not friends from their ranks until they flee in the way of Allah (From what is forbidden). But if they turn renegades, seize them and slay them wherever ye find them; and (in any case) take no friends or helpers from their ranks;-

Shakir: They desire that you should disbelieve as they have disbelieved, so that you might be (all) alike; therefore take not from among them friends until they fly (their homes) in Allah's way; but if they turn back, then seize them and kill them wherever you find them, and take not from among them a friend or a helper.

Muhammad Sarwar: They wish you to become unbelievers as they themselves are. Do not establish friendship with them until they have abandoned their homes for the cause of God. If they betray you, seize them and slay them wherever you find them. Do not establish friendship with them or seek their help

Mohsin Khan: They wish that you reject Faith, as they have rejected (Faith), and thus that you all become equal (like one another). So take not Auliya' (protectors or friends) from them, till they emigrate in the Way of Allah (to Muhammad SAW). But if they turn back (from Islam), take (hold) of them and kill them wherever you find them, and take neither Auliya' (protectors or friends) nor helpers from them.

Arberry: They wish that you should disbelieve as they disbelieve, and then you would be equal; therefore take not to yourselves friends of them, until they emigrate in the way of God; then, if they turn their backs, take them, and slay them wherever you find them; take not to yourselves any one of them as friend or helper[59]

Islamophobia is a problematic term. It is a neologism for blasphemy to prevent any non-Muslim from exercising their human rights of free speech to criticize it. It is a term that is used to deliberately obfuscate and conflate criticism of the theology of Islam with bigotry against Muslims as people. Even worse, and I hate having to write this, but despite the fact that the global Muslim population is approximately 1.9 ***billion***; despite

---

[59] "The Quranic Arabic Corpus - Word by Word Grammar, Syntax and Morphology of the Holy Quran." The Quranic Arabic Corpus - Translation, corpus.quran.com/translation.jsp?chapter=4&verse=89.

the fact it comprises of ethnic backgrounds from Africa, the Middle East, South Asia, and Eastern Europe; and despite the fact that it is actually the most racially diverse religion in the United States itself even more than Christianity[60]; people continue to racialize Islam as an ethnic minority group. This falsehood has become so successful that countries like Sweden, that claimed to have removed blasphemy laws, are now imposing legal charges on Iraqi refugees who criticize Islam even after one of them was murdered in their home for burning the Quran as a free speech protest.[61] I literally have to repeat to my close White friends constantly that Islam is not a race or an ethnic background but it's in one ear and out the other with them. By contrast, my close Black and Hispanic friends who value the First Amendment of the US Constitution seem to better understand what I mean. Yet, I swear, any heterosexual White person – close friend or no – I try to explain why the term prevents Free Speech discussion, they don't listen at all and the more obnoxious people only attempt to shut down discussions completely. In fairness, I've had more success with some LGBT White Americans but even then, it's half-and-half but I've experienced a greater degree of them willing to listen.

    This problem is becoming so pervasive that my fellow Hindus are now unfortunately replicating such tactics. I despise to the highest degree that this is happening, but here we are. Any time I explain to my fellow Hindus how ridiculous the term is on social media or attempts at private discussions, I'm either ignored, blocked, or they correctly point to how effective the term Islamophobia is and argue that the use of the term Hinduphobia is just about wanting to gain the same measure of respect as other faiths. They disagree with my criticisms on the grounds that Hindus continue to be maligned whereas Muslims and Christians are afforded a shield of protection for their religious teachings that Hindus have never received. This idea of criticizing religion being a phobia really is becoming the new social norm in Western countries and people are not recognizing just how dangerous that is. Where do societies go from this point forward? Should we expect "Christianphobia" to be the next step, once Christianity becomes a minority religion in some Western countries? Are we going to be discussing Catholicphobia or Christianphobia anytime another decades-long child rape scandal makes headline news similar to Pakistani Muslim grooming gangs and the term Islamophobia, as what has happened in Great Britain? Is it Hinduphobic of me to discuss US ISKCON's own deplorable child rape scandals in the 1960s and 1970s? Will it be anti-Semitic in the future to discuss child rape crimes committed by unsavory ultra-orthodox Jewish male preachers upon vulnerable Jewish children in Australia, the US, and Great Britain? This is becoming absurd because hurt feelings of religious people

---

[60] Greenwood, Shannon. "1. Demographic Portrait of Muslim Americans." Pew Research Center, Pew Research Center, 26 July 2017, www.pewresearch.org/religion/2017/07/26/demographic-portrait-of-muslim-americans/.

[61] Reuters. "Swedish Court Convicts Quran Burner of Hate Crimes, Days after His Ally Was Killed | The Times of Israel." Www.Timesofisrael.Com, Times of Israel, 3 Feb. 2025, www.timesofisrael.com/swedish-court-convicts-quran-burner-of-hate-crimes-days-after-his-ally-was-killed/.

shouldn't matter more than the human rights of children. I can't speak for monarchic countries with limitations on Free Speech like Great Britain and Canada, but is this what we want in Democratic Republics like the US, Ireland, and France? Should people continue to be silenced in fellow Democratic Republics like India due to colonial British laws still in effect and the pernicious British cultural influence that caused limitations upon their Constitution's Free Speech rights?

The basis for the term Islamophobia likely comes from Islamic theology's view that "Islamic Scholars" – that is, the Muslim Imams – are the only ones who have the right to an opinion on Islam.[62] That is, Muslims who aren't Islamic preachers and *all* non-Muslims aren't allowed to have an opinion on the faith of Islam. Due to the structure being based upon divine command theory and revealed wisdom, all non-Muslims and Muslims who aren't considered "scholars" are essentially forbidden from using their own reasoning faculties to give an opinion on Islam. If, for example, you were an Ex-Muslim who left the faith and were threatened by your Muslim neighbors with being killed for apostasy because of the Quranic verse 4:89, then according to the Islamic tradition based upon Islamic theology itself, you have no right to an opinion about being murdered for your freedom of thought. The attempts to racialize Islam with terms like Islamophobia essentially gives a blanket protection for the murder of Ex-Muslims and free speech protesters. With the attack on Ex-Muslim Atheist Salman Rushdie in New York a few years ago and the murder of Salwan Momika, an Atheist from a Christian background, in Sweden on January 29, 2025 for a Quran burning protest back in 2023[63]; it is obvious this racial distinction is merely sophistry in an effort to impose the Sharia (the Divine Law of the Abrahamic God) upon freer countries to advance Islamist political interests.

These next few subsections are going to be difficult to accept, but they are the unfortunate reality. This is what Islamists really do want to normalize and make socially acceptable in non-Muslim countries through Dawah tactics. Despite Western Ex-Muslim Atheists effectively utilizing normalizing dissent tours to explain in various US college panels on just what Islam teaches, it took me awhile for the information to fully register in my mind because of how absurd and even bigoted it sounded to me. In fact, years prior to watching Ex-Muslim of North America panel talks, when a close friend told me of an Ex-Muslim friend of theirs who explained the religious festival of Eid al-Adha (Festival of Slaughter), I absolutely didn't believe a word of it and assumed my friend had been deceived or tricked by some Ex-Muslim atheist who was making some weird reddit atheist meme about their former religion and that they had tricked my friend into believing the meme to be real. The reason I fully believed that viewpoint was because I

---

[62] "Who Is a Scholar ('Aalim)? - Islam Question & Answer." Islamqa.info, Islam Question and Answer, 18 July 2011, islamqa.info/en/answers/145071/who-is-a-scholar-aalim.

[63] Reuters. "Swedish Court Convicts Quran Burner of Hate Crimes, Days after His Ally Was Killed | The Times of Israel." Www.Timesofisrael.Com, Times of Israel, 3 Feb. 2025, www.timesofisrael.com/swedish-court-convicts-quran-burner-of-hate-crimes-days-after-his-ally-was-killed/.

thought such a notion as annual animal slaughter for religious reasons in modern times was "obviously" just an attempt to portray the majority of Muslims as backwards in a bigoted way.[64] Due to not knowing anything substantive about Islam at the time, I had assumed that this "Ex-Muslim atheist who spent too much time on reddit" was mocking Islam by confusing their own bizarre minor religious denomination in Islam for the majority of Muslims who couldn't possibly be that backwards in the twenty-first century. I likened it to a Christian minority subset having odious beliefs that the majority of Christians no longer hold. At no point did I entertain the idea of Muslims slaughtering animals every year as a real and true religious ritual that occurs every year until after listening to Ex-Muslims, finding Pakistani Ex-Muslim atheist Sarah Haider mentioning it on Twitter with other Ex-Muslims chiming in about their own personal stories[65], and then reading about it more via finding news articles about it with descriptive and brutal imagery from a Google search after reading her tweet.

Please regard everything you read from these subsections seriously. Unfortunately, these are not insensitive jokes or bad faith arguments; they are the social norms and values of Muslim-majority countries. I decided to add a dialogue transcript from a video from *Islam Unboxed*, a show once made by Ex-Muslim Atheist Armin Navabi, giving fuller context showing a prominent "Muslim skeptic" Daniel Reza Haqiqatjou, an undergraduate of Physics from Harvard and a Graduate with a Master's Degree in Western Philosophy from Tufts University.[66] Haqiqatjou formed his website Muslim Skeptic to criticize other people's religious beliefs in support of Islamic theology.[67] Haqiqatjou is an American who was born in Houston, Texas and promotes Islamist political views in the US.[68] These are not fringe ideas in Muslim-majority countries, they are the social norm of the vast majority of Muslim countries, they are the norm among Muslim communities throughout the world outside of the US, and Islamists really do want to make these ideas into the social norm of all non-Muslim countries.

These subsections will contain the normative values that Islam teaches and then I'll share news stories of the real-life consequences, so that you understand this is not

---

[64] "As Eid Al Adha Approaches..." Questions on Islam, questionsonislam.com/content/eid-al-adha-approaches....

[65] Haider, Sarah. "Even as a Child, This Eid Was Horrifying. I Remember Witnessing a Sacrifice of a Cow with My Family, I Remember the Blood Gushing from Its Throat and Running through the Street. The Story of Abraham Which It Commemorates Is Another Horror. I'll Save My Mubaraks for the Other Eid." Twitter, Twitter, 21 Aug. 2018, twitter.com/SarahTheHaider/status/1031995695652384769.

[66] Haqiqatjou, Daniel Reza. "Daniel Haqiqatjou, Author at Muslim Skeptic." Muslim Skeptic, Muslim Skeptic, Jan. 2018, muslimskeptic.com/author/drjou/.

[67] Haqiqatjou, Daniel Reza. "About." Muslim Skeptic, Muslim Skeptic, Nov. 2017, muslimskeptic.com/about/.

[68] Haqiqatjou, Daniel Reza. "Daniel Haqiqatjou, Author at Muslim Skeptic." Muslim Skeptic, Muslim Skeptic, Jan. 2018, muslimskeptic.com/author/drjou/.

some attempt to dehumanize Muslims or a sick joke. For these first two, I'll show teachings first and then the consequences:

Rape of girls as young as Nine Years-old

Daniel Reza Haqiqatjou: I think that what Islam can offer as a solution, you know, is, my interlocutor said that what Islam can offer is like music and the arts. I think what Islam offers is the truth. Islam is the truth. It is the religion that has been revealed, by God for the guidance of humanity. And that's something that we should discuss.

These are the kinds of topics that should be, discussed in media in calm, rational, you know, measured ways. And I'm willing to discuss my reasoning for why Islam is the truth, and reasons, and justifications, and arguments for that claim. And that's something that I encourage others to investigate as well. And when we come to those parts of Islam that conflict with the modern world, we have to take a more academic perspective, and we have to understand, well, what are these practices in context of a kinship-based society prior to the nation state? What happened is that the nation state structure, within the beginnings of the eighteenth century and throughout, the next three hundred years was to, was a structure that was characterized by bureaucracy, by technocratic industrial industrialization, and by the enforcement of law through a very strong police state, surveillance state, and what the effect of all of this was to destroy, kinship-based systems of life and living.

And, so what do I mean by this? In societies in the past, kinship structure meant that every aspect of life flow through the structure of of the family, the extended family, family businesses. You didn't have corporations. You didn't have a banking, a global national banking system. All of these kinds of economic activity, social activity, even governmental activity, education, childcare, elderly care, all happened in context of the extended family.

What the state did was destroy all these kinds of relationships and institutionalize them.

Armin Navabi: You're not really responding to the –

Daniel Reza Haqiqatjou: No. I am responding because I have to get to that point.

Armin Navabi: You're running out of ti– Go on. Go on. Go on.

Daniel Reza Haqiqatjou: Alright. So, if we understand that everything that, the modern world has a problem with in terms of Islam, it also has a problem with all kinship-based societies.

Let me address, for example, child marriage. Okay? The idea of childhood is actually a modern concept. It's something that if you look at the anthropology of childhood, anthropologists will note that the idea of childhood is something that's very new, only less than 200 years old. And the idea is that when you have a kinship-based society and you have a certain, lifespan, then children are expected to be contributing to the family. They're expected to contribute to society and to their community because there's not an – a career that they're pursuing. There's not a need for a technical education that extends for twelve or sixteen years.

Armin Navabi: Let me interrupt. Let me pause a little. So, you think that, having sex with a nine-year old is justified?

Daniel Reza Haqiqatjou: Yeah, I mean the thing is that the – so here let me ask you a question. Okay, is the problem with –

Armin Navabi: No, how I'm asking you a question. Let me ask –

Daniel Reza Haqiqatjou: Well. . . I have to frame it, okay? So, if you have – do you have a problem with child marriage, because you think it is categorically wrong? Or, is it because it's conditionally wrong?

Armin Navabi: Well, I'm asking you the question.

Daniel Reza Haqiqatjou: Well, I want to understand what your understanding is because I think that the prophet, peace be upon him, his – his marriage to Aisha, was that nine years of age.

Mohammad Tawhidi: Twenty-one.

Daniel Reza Haqiqatjou: So, do you think that that – I don't think that that's wrong. I can explain it and justify it. And, I'm trying to give you the entire anthropological explanation, the historical explanation of that. But like I said, it can't be done in five minutes.

Armin Navabi and Daniel Reza Haqiqatjou mutually interrupt each other at this portion before Daniel Reza Haqiqatjou continues.

Daniel Reza Haqiqatjou: I want to simplify it and say, do you think that this is categorically wrong or is it conditionally wrong?

Armin Navabi: Categorically wrong.

Daniel Reza Haqiqatjou: Like, did it If you think that it's categorically wrong to have those kinds of relationship, do you think that other kinds of sexual behavior can be categorically wrong?

Armin Navabi: As long as it harms somebody, as long as –

Daniel Reza Haqiqatjou: No. If you mention harm, then it's not categorical. It's conditional based on harm.

Armin Navabi: But the – but the category that you're introducing is a category that will be harmful in all situations in that category. That's why you –

Daniel Reza Haqiqatjou: How can you if you specify conditions, that's conditional. It's not categorical.

Armin Navabi: Okay. So, let's move on to the next one.

Daniel Reza Haqiqatjou: You didn't really answer the question.

Armin Navabi: Yeah. Because I wasn't . . . because you want me to bring up like why – you want me to explain why it's okay – why it's not okay to have sex with a nine-year old?

Daniel Reza Haqiqatjou: In a particular social context, in a particular historical

Armin Navabi: I mean to me that's –

Daniel Reza Haqiqatjou: Yes, it can be something that is moral and is acceptable. I can agree with you and say that within this particular context, if you take a nine-year old who is still watching, you know, Dora the Explorer and it has, you know, that kind of cultural background in the situation they are –

Video is paused with a note from Daniel Reza Haqiqatjou:

Navabi, Armin. "Islam Unboxed ☪︎☐ – Part 2 (With Imam Tawhidi, Daniel Haqiqatjou and Armin Navabi)." YouTube, Ideas Unboxed, 2 Jan. 2019, www.youtube.com/watch?v=bi3Cnk224zI&t=3164s&ab_channel=IdeasUnboxed.

Daniel Reza Haqiqatjou: That's wrong. That's morally wrong. But you're asking me about a completely different social circumstances society.

Armin Navabi: That's not true.

Daniel Reza Haqiqatjou: And, child marriage, as you describe it, I think the word child is anachronistic. If you talk about that, that's something that was practiced throughout history.

Armin Navabi: Yeah, I know.

Daniel Reza Haqiqatjou: Across all religions, across all cultures. So, the problem that you have is not with Islam. It's not with the prophet Muhammad, peace be upon him. It's a problem with all of the past.

Armin Navabi: I condemn all of the past.

Daniel Reza Haqiqatjou: You condemn all of the past? That's the problem with modernity.

Armin Navabi: I condemn all child rape. I condemn them all. And, if you – if you're thinking about the child mentality being different in different situation, remember that according to the Hadith, Aisha was playing with dolls, right before Muhammad raped them.

Daniel Reza Haqiqatjou: You have 35-year olds who play with dolls in this day and age. They're Star Wars fans, Star Trek fans. They have action figures. They play with them.

Mohammad Tawhidi: So, you can rape them?

Daniel Reza Haqiqatjou: It's not rape. Okay. You just go around the word rape whenever you wanna – or terrorism willy nilly. I don't take that as serious academic analysis.

Armin Navabi: If you want, we could dedicate another five minutes just to that? If you want after this, but I have other questions for you as well. But let me reset this. What, you – you mentioned that this is something we need to talk about. What the Muslim world need? What does the Muslim world need right now?

Mohammad Tawhidi: The Muslim world needs to realize that now we have extremists, who are graduating from Harvard.

Mohammad directs his hands gesturing towards Daniel Reza Haqiqatjou while he was speaking.

Armin Navabi: No. Let's not do that. Alright. Let's not do that. Please!

Mohammad Tawhidi: Before they used to dress in, in a long, well, basic Islamic tradition like this. And you can identify that this is a guy who holds a certain ideology, but when he speaks, you can then understand where he's coming from. Now they're dressed in the suits and ties. And, you know, they – they come to university and try to academically, justify, that marrying a nine-year old – although, I don't believe it happened because in my book, I prove she was not nine. Although I, I . . . Look, we may disagree. I believe there was even greater tragedy that the Muslim world is trying to hide and the fact that she was not a virgin and she was an obscene woman. But we're not discussing her, Aisha. We're not discussing her. We're discussing the fact that you believe that it's okay to marry a nine-year old because society is different. Society can develop and change as many times as it like. Marrying a nine-year old will never be right. Don't give me this lunar year, whatever nonsense they come up with. Muhammad did not marry a nine-year old. This is a lie. Yes. Other nine-year olds from Muhammad's family were married off. Yes. I – I agree. Other children, were married off to companions. I agree. Muhammad himself did not marry a nine-year old. This is a lie to hide a bigger secret. And the fact that you try to purify Muhammad's image by pushing the – the age of his, wife back to six or nine or 15. You can't even agree on what age because she wasn't a child. She was, old, and she'd slept with half of half of Mecca before him. And – and people can disagree, but this is my analysis and my proven research that I challenge anyone to refute. It's in my book. And I'm happy to pull out her timeline now and prove to you that she – she could, impossible, she would have been nine years old. And, also the timeline is in is in the book that I just released.

Armin Navabi: Not according to Sunni Islam, though.

Mohammad Tawhidi: No. Not according – according to Sunni Islam.

Armin Navabi: I mean, according to Sunni Islam, she was nine.

Mohammad Tawhidi: No. Not, not all Sunnis. Not all Sunnis.

Armin Navabi: And Bukhari is right in there.

Mohammad Tawhidi: Yes, Bukhari is not the only Sunni scholar.

Armin Navabi: That's the Sahih.

Mohammad Tawhidi: There are many other Sahihs.

Daniel Reza Haqiqatjou: He based his justification on the Quran not being perfect on Sahih Bukhari because a goat ate a page that the Quran was written on. So, how is that consistent?

Haqiqatjou and Navabi talk over each other.

Armin Navabi: I asked a different question.

Mohammad Tawhidi: No, wait, don't go back. I'm speaking to you based on your belief system. This is sacred to you and the Quran is sacred to you.

Daniel Reza Haqiqatjou: No, Sahih Bukhari is not sacred.

Mohammad Tawhidi: It's not sacred anymore?

Daniel Reza Haqiqatjou: That text is just a compilation of, narrations. They exist in many different texts.

Mohammad Tawhidi: Okay. So, do you emulate these because they're holy doings?

Daniel Reza Haqiqatjou: The Quran and the Sunnah.

Mohammad Tawhidi: Okay.

Daniel Reza Haqiqatjou: This is the Sunnah. This is compiled in different books.

Mohammad Tawhidi: In PDF in both of these.

Daniel Reza Haqiqatjou: Of course, it's Sahih. Of course, I – I study –

Mohammad Tawhidi: I'm speaking about content. He's talking about paper and cardboard. I'm telling him Bukhari. He says it can be compiled in different formats.

Daniel Reza Haqiqatjou: Alright. But this is . . . there's not just Sahih Bukhari.

Armin Navabi: Okay. Okay.

Daniel Reza Haqiqatjou: There's Sahih Muslim, there's –

Armin Navabi: She was nine according to most Islamic schools of thought.

Mohammad Tawhidi: Yes, according to the majority of Muslims, she was nine. Yes

Armin Navabi: And, accepted Islamic schools of thought she was nine

Mohammad Tawhidi: Yeah, to the majority; yes, to the majority, but not to all. Now, moving on with – with my time, it is absolutely wrong whatsoe – I don't care what people say. He can give it an academic coating all, what he likes. Completely wrong. It can never be justified. No way can it be justified that marrying an a nine-year old is right. And, these laws that you have in certain American states that allow, a man to marry a child, without her parents consent or, 11 or 10 or 12. I don't know. There are numerous states. That – that's also wrong. That is also wrong. But and –

Daniel Reza Haqiqatjou: You also disagree with –

Mohammad Tawhidi: Yes. I –

Daniel Reza Haqiqatjou: 11 year-olds going on having girlfriend, boyfriend. Then, what about having sex at the age of nine with their boyfriend? You agree with that?

Mohammad Tawhidi: I – I reject it. I don't allow it.

Daniel Reza Haqiqatjou: You don't think elementary school children should have boyfriend, girlfriend?

Mohammad Tawhidi: No, I don't.

Daniel Reza Haqiqatjou: And have sex with each other? Because that's rampant in Australia, The US.

Mohammad Tawhidi: I condemn it. Because it's in Australia doesn't mean I agree with it.

Daniel Reza Haqiqatjou: Okay. So, you condemn . . . so, what's the line? When is it okay for people to –

Mohammad Tawhidi: Do you know –

Daniel Reza Haqiqatjou: For having sex?

Mohammad Tawhidi: Do you know –

Daniel Reza Haqiqatjou: What age is it okay?

Mohammad Tawhidi: I'll tell you now. But, do you know who brings these, children, boyfriend, girlfriend, my body, your body things into our educational system and sex ed? Do you know who? Your allies. The allies of the Islamic extremists. The leftists, the globalists, they're the ones who would love this.

Daniel Reza Haqiqatjou: I'm not aligned with Leftists.

Mohammad Tawhidi: No, they are aligned with you. They would love you.

Daniel Reza Haqiqatjou: No, they denounced me every day. They would denounce me and call me on the same kind of things that you call me.

Mohammad Tawhidi: No. No. No. No.

Daniel Reza Haqiqatjou: Leftists don't like what I have to say about these things.

Armin Navabi: Alright. My question was completely ignored. What does the Muslim world – what does the Muslim world need right now?

Mohammad Tawhidi: I said the Muslim world, right now, needs to be warned from people like him.[69]

The unfortunate and disturbing reality of Islam's teachings are that the vast majority of Muslims throughout the world support child marriages of little girls as young as 6-years old and the majority of Muslims in the world really do approve of sex between a male adult and a 9-year old girl to the extent that they reject the idea that it is an act of rape. Due to the Tafsir system of Islam teaching that Prophet Mohammad was the perfect human being to emulate (the Sunnah) to be a morally good person in accordance with

---

[69] Navabi, Armin. "Islam Unboxed ☪ ☐ – Part 2 (With Imam Tawhidi, Daniel Haqiqatjou and Armin Navabi)." YouTube, Ideas Unboxed, 2 Jan. 2019, www.youtube.com/watch?v=bi3Cnk224zI&t=3164s&ab_channel=IdeasUnboxed.

what the Abrahamic God wants people to do; the majority of Muslims across the world believe that non-Muslims have no right to an opinion on disagreeing with this belief and practice. This is because only perceived "Islamic Scholars" which are the Muslim Imams have any right to debate this topic in accordance with their religious faith as part of the Sharia (Divine Law of the Abrahamic God). The majority of Muslims in the world believe this is justified because the hadiths considered saheeh or "authentic" pertaining to what Aisha said about herself and others close to the Prophet Mohammad confirm that the Prophet Mohammad married Aisha when she was six-years of age and that the Prophet Mohammad had sex with her when she was 9-years old[70]:

63
Merits of the Helpers in Madinah (Ansaar)
(44)
Chapter: Marriage of the Prophet (saws) with 'Aishah رضي الله عنها
(44)

باب تَزْوِيجُ النَّبِيِّ صلى الله عليه وسلم عَائِشَةَ وَقُدُومُهَا الْمَدِينَةَ وَبِنَاؤُهُ بِهَا

Narrated Hisham's father:

Khadija died three years before the Prophet (ﷺ) departed to Medina. He stayed there for two years or so and then he married `Aisha when she was a girl of six years of age, and he consumed that marriage when she was nine years old.

حَدَّثَنِي عُبَيْدُ بْنُ إِسْمَاعِيلَ، حَدَّثَنَا أَبُو أُسَامَةَ، عَنْ هِشَامٍ، عَنْ أَبِيهِ، قَالَ تُوُفِّيَتْ خَدِيجَةُ قَبْلَ مَخْرَجِ النَّبِيِّ صلى الله عليه وسلم إِلَى الْمَدِينَةِ بِثَلاَثِ سِنِينَ، فَلَبِثَ سَنَتَيْنِ أَوْ قَرِيبًا مِنْ ذَلِكَ، وَنَكَحَ عَائِشَةَ وَهِيَ بِنْتُ سِتِّ سِنِينَ، ثُمَّ بَنَى بِهَا وَهْىَ بِنْتُ تِسْعِ سِنِينَ.

Reference	: Sahih al-Bukhari 3896
In-book reference	: Book 63, Hadith 121
USC-MSA web (English) reference	: Vol. 5, Book 58, Hadith 236
(deprecated numbering scheme)	

Report Error | Share | Copy ▼

38953897 [71]

---

[70] "Age of the Mother of the Believers 'Aa'ishah (May Allah Be Pleased with Her) When the Prophet (Blessings and Peace of Allah Be upon Him) Married Her - Islam Question & Answer." Islamqa.info, Islam Question and Answer, 30 Dec. 2013, islamqa.info/en/answers/124483/age-of-the-mother-of-the-believers-aaishah-may-allah-be-pleased-with-her-when-the-prophet-blessings-and-peace-of-allah-be-upon-him-married-her.

[71] "Sahih Al-Bukhari 3896: 63 Merits of the Helpers in Madinah (Ansaar): (44) Chapter: Marriage of the Prophet (Saws) with 'Aishah." Sahih Al-Bukhari 3896 - Merits of the Helpers in Madinah (Ansaar) - كتاب مناقب الأنصار - Sunnah.Com - Sayings and Teachings of Prophet Muhammad (صلى الله عليه و سلم), SUNNAH.COM, sunnah.com/bukhari:3896. Accessed 20 Mar. 2025.

(44)
Chapter: Marriage of the Prophet (saws) with 'Aishah رضي الله عنها
(44)

باب تَزْوِيجُ النَّبِيِّ صلى الله عليه وسلم عَائِشَةَ وَقُدُومُهَا الْمَدِينَةَ وَبِنَاؤُهُ بِهَا

Narrated Aisha:

The Prophet (ﷺ) engaged me when I was a girl of six (years). We went to Medina and stayed at the home of Bani-al-Harith bin Khazraj. Then I got ill and my hair fell down. Later on my hair grew (again) and my mother, Um Ruman, came to me while I was playing in a swing with some of my girl friends. She called me, and I went to her, not knowing what she wanted to do to me. She caught me by the hand and made me stand at the door of the house. I was breathless then, and when my breathing became Allright, she took some water and rubbed my face and head with it. Then she took me into the house. There in the house I saw some Ansari women who said, "Best wishes and Allah's Blessing and a good luck." Then she entrusted me to them and they prepared me (for the marriage). Unexpectedly Allah's Apostle came to me in the forenoon and my mother handed me over to him, and at that time I was a girl of nine years of age.

حَدَّثَنِي فَرْوَةُ بْنُ أَبِي الْمَغْرَاءِ، حَدَّثَنَا عَلِيُّ بْنُ مُسْهِرٍ، عَنْ هِشَامٍ، عَنْ أَبِيهِ، عَنْ عَائِشَةَ ـ رضى الله عنها ـ قَالَتْ تَزَوَّجَنِي النَّبِيُّ صلى الله عليه وسلم وَأَنَا بِنْتُ سِتِّ سِنِينَ، فَقَدِمْنَا الْمَدِينَةَ فَنَزَلْنَا فِي بَنِي الْحَارِثِ بْنِ خَزْرَجٍ، فَوُعِكْتُ فَتَمَرَّقَ شَعَرِي فَوَفَى جُمَيْمَةً، فَأَتَتْنِي أُمِّي أُمُّ رُومَانَ وَإِنِّي لَفِي أُرْجُوحَةٍ وَمَعِي صَوَاحِبُ لِي، فَصَرَخَتْ بِي فَأَتَيْتُهَا لاَ أَدْرِي مَا تُرِيدُ بِي فَأَخَذَتْ بِيَدِي حَتَّى أَوْقَفَتْنِي عَلَى بَابِ الدَّارِ، وَإِنِّي لأَنْهَجُ، حَتَّى سَكَنَ بَعْضُ نَفَسِي، ثُمَّ أَخَذَتْ شَيْئًا مِنْ مَاءٍ فَمَسَحَتْ بِهِ وَجْهِي وَرَأْسِي ثُمَّ أَدْخَلَتْنِي الدَّارَ فَإِذَا نِسْوَةٌ مِنَ الأَنْصَارِ فِي الْبَيْتِ فَقُلْنَ عَلَى الْخَيْرِ وَالْبَرَكَةِ، وَعَلَى خَيْرِ طَائِرٍ، فَأَسْلَمَتْنِي إِلَيْهِنَّ فَأَصْلَحْنَ مِنْ شَأْنِي، فَلَمْ يَرُعْنِي إِلاَّ رَسُولُ اللَّهِ صلى الله عليه وسلم ضُحًى، فَأَسْلَمَتْنِي إِلَيْهِ، وَأَنَا يَوْمَئِذٍ بِنْتُ تِسْعِ سِنِينَ.

Reference	: Sahih al-Bukhari 3894
In-book reference	: Book 63, Hadith 119
USC-MSA web (English) reference	: Vol. 5, Book 58, Hadith 234
(deprecated numbering scheme)	

Report Error | Share | Copy ▼
3893 3895 [72]

12
Marriage (Kitab Al-Nikah)
(700)
Chapter: Regarding The Marriage Of The Young
(34)

باب فِي تَزْوِيجِ الصِّغَارِ

Narrated 'Aishah:

The Messenger of Allah (ﷺ) married me when I was seven years old. The narrator Sulaiman said: or Six years. He had intercourse with me when I was nine years old.

حَدَّثَنَا سُلَيْمَانُ بْنُ حَرْبٍ، وَأَبُو كَامِلٍ قَالاَ حَدَّثَنَا حَمَّادُ بْنُ زَيْدٍ، عَنْ هِشَامِ بْنِ عُرْوَةَ، عَنْ أَبِيهِ، عَنْ عَائِشَةَ، قَالَتْ تَزَوَّجَنِي رَسُولُ اللَّهِ صلى الله عليه وسلم وَأَنَا بِنْتُ سَبْعٍ ـ قَالَ سُلَيْمَانُ أَوْ سِتٍّ ـ وَدَخَلَ بِي وَأَنَا بِنْتُ تِسْعٍ.

Grade: Sahih (Al-Albani) (الألباني) حكم صحيح :

---

[72] "Sahih Al-Bukhari 3894: 63 Merits of the Helpers in Madinah (Ansaar): (44)Chapter: Marriage of the Prophet (Saws) with 'Aishah رضي الله عنها." Sahih Al-Bukhari 3894 - Merits of the Helpers in Madinah (Ansaar) - كتاب مناقب الأنصار - Sunnah.Com - Sayings and Teachings of Prophet Muhammad (صلى الله عليه و سلم), SUNNAH.COM, sunnah.com/bukhari:3894. Accessed 21 Mar. 2025.

Reference: Sunan Abi Dawud 2121
In-book reference: Book 12, Hadith 76
English translation: Book 11, Hadith 2116
Report Error | Share | Copy ▼
21202122[73]

26
The Book of Marriage
(29)
Chapter: A Man Marrying Off His Young Daughter
(29)
باب إِنْكَاحِ الرَّجُلِ ابْنَتَهُ الصَّغِيرَةَ .
It was narrated from 'Aishah that the Messenger of Allah married her when she was six years old, and consummated the marriage with her when she was nine.
أَخْبَرَنَا إِسْحَاقُ بْنُ إِبْرَاهِيمَ، قَالَ أَنْبَأَنَا أَبُو مُعَاوِيَةَ، قَالَ حَدَّثَنَا هِشَامُ بْنُ عُرْوَةَ، عَنْ أَبِيهِ، عَنْ عَائِشَةَ، أَنَّ رَسُولَ اللَّهِ صلى الله عليه وسلم تَزَوَّجَهَا وَهِيَ بِنْتُ سِتٍّ وَبَنَى بِهَا وَهِيَ بِنْتُ تِسْعٍ .
Grade: Sahih (Darussalam)
Reference: Sunan an-Nasa'i 3255
In-book reference: Book 26, Hadith 60
English translation: Vol. 4, Book 26, Hadith 3257
Report Error | Share | Copy ▼
32543256[74]

67
Wedlock, Marriage (Nikaah)
(39)
Chapter: Giving one's young children in marriage
(38)
باب إِنْكَاحِ الرَّجُلِ وَلَدَهُ الصِّغَارَ

Narrated `Aisha:

that the Prophet (ﷺ) married her when she was six years old and he consummated his marriage when she was nine years old, and then she remained with him for nine years (i.e., till his death).
حَدَّثَنَا مُحَمَّدُ بْنُ يُوسُفَ، حَدَّثَنَا سُفْيَانُ، عَنْ هِشَامٍ، عَنْ أَبِيهِ، عَنْ عَائِشَةَ ـ رضى الله عنها ـ أَنَّ النَّبِيَّ صلى الله عليه وسلم تَزَوَّجَهَا وَهْىَ بِنْتُ سِتِّ سِنِينَ، وَأُدْخِلَتْ عَلَيْهِ وَهْىَ بِنْتُ تِسْعٍ، وَمَكَثَتْ عِنْدَهُ تِسْعًا.
Reference: Sahih al-Bukhari 5133
In-book reference: Book 67, Hadith 69
USC-MSA web (English) reference: Vol. 7, Book 62, Hadith 64
  (deprecated numbering scheme)
Report Error | Share | Copy ▼

---

[73] "Sunan Abi Dawud 2121: 12 Marriage (Kitab Al-Nikah): (700) Chapter: Regarding The Marriage Of The Young." Sunan Abi Dawud 2121 - Marriage (Kitab al-Nikah) - كتاب النكاح - Sunnah.Com - Sayings and Teachings of Prophet Muhammad (صلى الله عليه و سلم), SUNNAH.COM, sunnah.com/abudawud:2121. Accessed 21 Mar. 2025.

[74] "Sunan An-Nasa'i 3255: 26 The Book of Marriage 29 (كتاب النكاح) Chapter: A Man Marrying Off His Young Daughter(29). باب إِنْكَاحِ الرَّجُلِ ابْنَتَهُ الصَّغِيرَةَ." Sunan An-Nasa'i 3255 - the Book of Marriage - كتاب النكاح - Sunnah.Com - Sayings and Teachings of Prophet Muhammad (صلى الله عليه و سلم), SUNNAH.COM, sunnah.com/nasai:3255. Accessed 21 Mar. 2025.

5132 5134[75]

In other words, because the Prophet Mohammad married Aisha when she was six years old and had sexual intercourse with her when she was 9-years old; the majority of Muslims believe that this was morally justified on the basis of the Divine Command of the Abrahamic God as per the Sharia (Divine Law of the Abrahamic God). The basis for their desire to retain this pedophilic belief and practice really is due to a legal system based upon Divine Command theory in absolute faith to the Abrahamic God. Islamists wish to push for normalizing this legally and socially in all non-Muslim countries as part of conversion to Islam due to their unquestioned faith in the Abrahamic God.

Slave Girls

Quran 4:3:

Sahih International

And if you fear that you will not deal justly with the orphan girls, then marry those that please you of [other] women, two or three or four. But if you fear that you will not be just, then [marry only] one or those your right hand possesses. That is more suitable that you may not incline [to injustice].

Muhsin Khan

And if you fear that you shall not be able to deal justly with the orphan-girls, then marry (other) women of your choice, two or three, or four but if you fear that you shall not be able to deal justly (with them), then only one or (the captives and the slaves) that your right hands possess. That is nearer to prevent you from doing injustice.

Pickthall

And if ye fear that ye will not deal fairly by the orphans, marry of the women, who seem good to you, two or three or four; and if ye fear that ye cannot do justice (to so many) then one (only) or (the captives) that your right hands possess. Thus it is more likely that ye will not do injustice.

Yusuf Ali

If ye fear that ye shall not be able to deal justly with the orphans, Marry women of your choice, Two or three or four; but if ye fear that ye shall not be able to deal justly (with them), then only one, or (a captive) that your right hands possess, that will be more suitable, to prevent you from doing injustice.

Shakir

And if you fear that you cannot act equitably towards orphans, then marry such women as seem good to you, two and three and four; but if you fear that you will not do justice (between them),

---

[75] "Sahih Al-Bukhari 5133: 67 Wedlock, Marriage (Nikaah): (39)Chapter: Giving One's Young Children in Marriage." Sahih Al-Bukhari 5133 - Wedlock, Marriage (Nikaah) - كتاب النكاح - Sunnah.Com - Sayings and Teachings of Prophet Muhammad (صلى الله عليه و سلم), SUNNAH.COM, sunnah.com/bukhari:5133. Accessed 21 Mar. 2025.

then (marry) only one or what your right hands possess; this is more proper, that you may not deviate from the right course.

Dr. Ghali

And, in case you fear that you will not act equitably towards the orphans, then marry such women as is good to you, two, three, four, (Literally: in twos and threes and fours) then, in case you fear that you will not do justice, then one (only), or what your right hands possess. That (way) is likelier you will not be in want (Or: you will have too many dependents).[76]

Quran 4:24

Sahih International: And [also prohibited to you are all] married women except those your right hands possess. [This is] the decree of Allah upon you. And lawful to you are [all others] beyond these, [provided] that you seek them [in marriage] with [gifts from] your property, desiring chastity, not unlawful sexual intercourse. So for whatever you enjoy [of marriage] from them, give them their due compensation as an obligation. And there is no blame upon you for what you mutually agree to beyond the obligation. Indeed, Allah is ever Knowing and Wise.

Pickthall: And all married women (are forbidden unto you) save those (captives) whom your right hands possess. It is a decree of Allah for you. Lawful unto you are all beyond those mentioned, so that ye seek them with your wealth in honest wedlock, not debauchery. And those of whom ye seek content (by marrying them), give unto them their portions as a duty. And there is no sin for you in what ye do by mutual agreement after the duty (hath been done). Lo! Allah is ever Knower, Wise.

Yusuf Ali: Also (prohibited are) women already married, except those whom your right hands possess: Thus hath Allah ordained (Prohibitions) against you: Except for these, all others are lawful, provided ye seek (them in marriage) with gifts from your property,- desiring chastity, not lust, seeing that ye derive benefit from them, give them their dowers (at least) as prescribed; but if, after a dower is prescribed, agree Mutually (to vary it), there is no blame on you, and Allah is All-knowing, All-wise.

Shakir: And all married women except those whom your right hands possess (this is) Allah's ordinance to you, and lawful for you are (all women) besides those, provided that you seek (them) with your property, taking (them) in marriage not committing fornication. Then as to those whom you profit by, give them their dowries as appointed; and there is no blame on you about what you mutually agree after what is appointed; surely Allah is Knowing, Wise.

Muhammad Sarwar: You are forbidden to marry married women except your slave-girls. This is the decree of God. Besides these, it is lawful for you to marry other women if you pay their dower, maintain chastity and do not commit indecency. If you marry them for the appointed time you must pay their dowries. There is no harm if you reach an understanding among yourselves about the dowry, God is All-knowing and All-wise.

Mohsin Khan: Also (forbidden are) women already married, except those (captives and slaves) whom your right hands possess. Thus has Allah ordained for you. All others are lawful, provided you seek (them in marriage) with Mahr (bridal money given by the husband to his wife at the time of marriage) from your property, desiring chastity, not committing illegal sexual intercourse, so with those of whom you have enjoyed sexual relations, give them their Mahr as prescribed; but if after a Mahr is prescribed, you agree mutually (to give more), there is no sin on you. Surely, Allah is Ever AllKnowing, AllWise.

---

[76] "Surat An-Nisā' (the Women) - سورة النساء." The Noble Qur'an, legacy.quran.com/4/3. Accessed 12 Mar. 2025.

Arberry: and wedded women, save what your right hands own. So God prescribes for you. Lawful for you, beyond all that, is that you may seek, using your wealth, in wedlock and not in licence. Such wives as you enjoy thereby, give them their wages apportionate; it is no fault in you in your agreeing together, after the due apportionate. God is All-knowing, All-wise.[77]

Quran 16:71

Sahih International: And Allah has favored some of you over others in provision. But those who were favored would not hand over their provision to those whom their right hands possess so they would be equal to them therein. Then is it the favor of Allah they reject?

Pickthall: And Allah hath favoured some of you above others in provision. Now those who are more favoured will by no means hand over their provision to those (slaves) whom their right hands possess, so that they may be equal with them in respect thereof. Is it then the grace of Allah that they deny?

Yusuf Ali: Allah has bestowed His gifts of sustenance more freely on some of you than on others: those more favoured are not going to throw back their gifts to those whom their right hands possess, so as to be equal in that respect. Will they then deny the favours of Allah?

Shakir: And Allah has made some of you excel others in the means of subsistence, so those who are made to excel do not give away their sustenance to those whom their right hands possess so that they should be equal therein; is it then the favor of Allah which they deny?

Muhammad Sarwar: God has made some of you richer than others. The rich ones do not have to give away their property to their slaves to make them equally rich. Do they reject the bounties of God?

Mohsin Khan: And Allah has preferred some of you above others in wealth and properties. Then, those who are preferred will by no means hand over their wealth and properties to those (slaves) whom their right hands possess, so that they may be equal with them in respect thereof. Do they then deny the Favour of Allah?

Arberry: And God has preferred some of you over others in provision;, but those that were preferred shall not give over their provision to that their right hands possess, so that they may be equal therein. What, and do they deny God's blessing?[78]

Quran 23: 5-6

Quran 23:5

Sahih International

And they who guard their private parts

---

[77] "The Quranic Arabic Corpus - Word by Word Grammar, Syntax and Morphology of the Holy Quran." The Quranic Arabic Corpus - Translation, http://corpus.quran.com/translation.jsp?chapter=4&verse=24
[78] The Quranic Arabic Corpus - Translation, corpus.quran.com/translation.jsp?chapter=16&verse=71. Accessed 12 Mar. 2025.

Muhsin Khan

And those who guard their chastity (i.e. private parts, from illegal sexual acts)

Yusuf Ali

Who abstain from sex,

Pickthall

And who guard their modesty -[79]

Quran 23:6

Sahih International

Except from their wives or those their right hands possess, for indeed, they will not be blamed -

Muhsin Khan

Except from their wives or (the captives and slaves) that their right hands possess, for then, they are free from blame;

Yusuf Ali

Except with those joined to them in the marriage bond, or (the captives) whom their right hands possess,- for (in their case) they are free from blame,

Pickthall

Save from their wives or the (slaves) that their right hands possess, for then they are not blameworthy,[80]

Quran 24:33

Sahih International

But let them who find not [the means for] marriage abstain [from sexual relations] until Allah enriches them from His bounty. And those who seek a contract [for eventual emancipation] from among whom your right hands possess - then make a contract with them if you know there is within them goodness and give them from the wealth of Allah which He has given you. And do not compel your slave girls to prostitution, if they desire chastity, to seek [thereby] the temporary interests of worldly life. And if someone should compel them, then indeed, Allah is [to them], after their compulsion, Forgiving and Merciful.

Muhsin Khan

And let those who find not the financial means for marriage keep themselves chaste, until Allah enriches them of His Bounty. And such of your slaves as seek a writing (of emancipation), give them such writing, if you know that they are good and trustworthy. And give them something yourselves out of the wealth of Allah which He has bestowed upon you. And force not your maids to prostitution, if they desire chastity, in order that you may make a gain in the (perishable) goods

---

[79] "Surat Al-Mu'Minūn (the Believers) - سورة المؤمنون." The Noble Qur'an, legacy.quran.com/23/5-6. Accessed 12 Mar. 2025.

[80] "Surat Al-Mu'Minūn (the Believers) - سورة المؤمنون." The Noble Qur'an, legacy.quran.com/23/5-6. Accessed 12 Mar. 2025.

of this worldly life. But if anyone compels them (to prostitution), then after such compulsion, Allah is Oft-Forgiving, Most Merciful (to those women, i.e. He will forgive them because they have been forced to do this evil action unwillingly).

Pickthall

And let those who cannot find a match keep chaste till Allah give them independence by His grace. And such of your slaves as seek a writing (of emancipation), write it for them if ye are aware of aught of good in them, and bestow upon them of the wealth of Allah which He hath bestowed upon you. Force not your slave-girls to whoredom that ye may seek enjoyment of the life of the world, if they would preserve their chastity. And if one force them, then (unto them), after their compulsion, lo! Allah will be Forgiving, Merciful.

Yusuf Ali

Let those who find not the wherewithal for marriage keep themselves chaste, until Allah gives them means out of His grace. And if any of your slaves ask for a deed in writing (to enable them to earn their freedom for a certain sum), give them such a deed if ye know any good in them: yea, give them something yourselves out of the means which Allah has given to you. But force not your maids to prostitution when they desire chastity, in order that ye may make a gain in the goods of this life. But if anyone compels them, yet, after such compulsion, is Allah, Oft-Forgiving, Most Merciful (to them),

Shakir

And let those who do not find the means to marry keep chaste until Allah makes them free from want out of His grace. And (as for) those who ask for a writing from among those whom your right hands possess, give them the writing if you know any good in them, and give them of the wealth of Allah which He has given you; and do not compel your slave girls to prostitution, when they desire to keep chaste, in order to seek the frail good of this world's life; and whoever compels them, then surely after their compulsion Allah is Forgiving, Merciful.

Dr. Ghali

And let the ones who do not find (the means) to wed keep abstaining until Allah enriches them of His Grace. And the ones your right hands possess who seek the Book, (Contract of emancipation) then contract with them (accordingly), in case you know that they are in charitable circumstances. And bring them of the wealth of Allah that He has brought you. And do not compel your handmaids to prostitution, in case they are willing to be chaste, (Literally: to be in wedlock) that you may inequitably seek the advantages of the present life; (Literally: the lowly life, i.e., the life of this world) and whoever compels them, then surely Allah, even after their being compelled, is Ever-Forgiving, Ever-Merciful.[81]

Quran 24:58

Sahih International

O you who have believed, let those whom your right hands possess and those who have not [yet] reached puberty among you ask permission of you [before entering] at three times: before the dawn prayer and when you put aside your clothing [for rest] at noon and after the night prayer. [These are] three times of privacy for you. There is no blame upon you nor upon them beyond

---

[81] "Surat An-Nūr (the Light) - سورة النور." The Noble Qur'an, legacy.quran.com/24/33. Accessed 12 Mar. 2025.

these [periods], for they continually circulate among you - some of you, among others. Thus does Allah make clear to you the verses; and Allah is Knowing and Wise.

Muhsin Khan

O you who believe! Let your legal slaves and slave-girls, and those among you who have not come to the age of puberty ask your permission (before they come to your presence) on three occasions; before Fajr (morning) prayer, and while you put off your clothes for the noonday (rest), and after the 'Isha' (late-night) prayer. (These) three times are of privacy for you, other than these times there is no sin on you or on them to move about, attending (helping) you each other. Thus Allah makes clear the Ayat (the Verses of this Quran, showing proofs for the legal aspects of permission for visits, etc.) to you. And Allah is All-Knowing, All-Wise.

Pickthall

O ye who believe! Let your slaves, and those of you who have not come to puberty, ask leave of you at three times (before they come into your presence): Before the prayer of dawn, and when ye lay aside your raiment for the heat of noon, and after the prayer of night. Three times of privacy for you. It is no sin for them or for you at other times, when some of you go round attendant upon others (if they come into your presence without leave). Thus Allah maketh clear the revelations for you. Allah is Knower, Wise.

Yusuf Ali

O ye who believe! let those whom your right hands possess, and the (children) among you who have not come of age ask your permission (before they come to your presence), on three occasions: before morning prayer; the while ye doff your clothes for the noonday heat; and after the late-night prayer: these are your three times of undress: outside those times it is not wrong for you or for them to move about attending to each other: Thus does Allah make clear the Signs to you: for Allah is full of knowledge and wisdom.

Shakir

O you who believe! let those whom your right hands possess and those of you who have not attained to puberty ask permission of you three times; before the morning prayer, and when you put off your clothes at midday in summer, and after the prayer of the nightfall; these are three times of privacy for you; neither is it a sin for you nor for them besides these, some of you must go round about (waiting) upon others; thus does Allah make clear to you the communications, and Allah is Knowing, Wise.

Dr. Ghali

O you who have believed, let the ones your right hands possess and the ones of you who have not reached puberty ask permission of you three times: right before the dawn prayer, and (the time) while you lay aside your clothes during mid-day, and right after the eventide prayer-three privacies for you. It is no fault in you or them, after these (times), that you go about one to the other (Literally: some of you to some others). Thus Allah makes evident to you the signs, and Allah is Ever-Knowing, Ever-Wise.[82]

Quran 33:50

Sahih International: O Prophet, indeed We have made lawful to you your wives to whom you have given their due compensation and those your right hand possesses from what Allah has returned to you [of captives] and the daughters of your paternal uncles and the daughters of your

---

[82] "Surat An-Nūr (the Light) - سورة النور." The Noble Qur'an, legacy.quran.com/24/58. Accessed 12 Mar. 2025.

paternal aunts and the daughters of your maternal uncles and the daughters of your maternal aunts who emigrated with you and a believing woman if she gives herself to the Prophet [and] if the Prophet wishes to marry her, [this is] only for you, excluding the [other] believers. We certainly know what We have made obligatory upon them concerning their wives and those their right hands possess, [but this is for you] in order that there will be upon you no discomfort. And ever is Allah Forgiving and Merciful.

Pickthall: O Prophet! Lo! We have made lawful unto thee thy wives unto whom thou hast paid their dowries, and those whom thy right hand possesseth of those whom Allah hath given thee as spoils of war, and the daughters of thine uncle on the father's side and the daughters of thine aunts on the father's side, and the daughters of thine uncle on the mother's side and the daughters of thine aunts on the mother's side who emigrated with thee, and a believing woman if she give herself unto the Prophet and the Prophet desire to ask her in marriage - a privilege for thee only, not for the (rest of) believers - We are Aware of that which We enjoined upon them concerning their wives and those whom their right hands possess - that thou mayst be free from blame, for Allah is ever Forgiving, Merciful.

Yusuf Ali: O Prophet! We have made lawful to thee thy wives to whom thou hast paid their dowers; and those whom thy right hand possesses out of the prisoners of war whom Allah has assigned to thee; and daughters of thy paternal uncles and aunts, and daughters of thy maternal uncles and aunts, who migrated (from Makka) with thee; and any believing woman who dedicates her soul to the Prophet if the Prophet wishes to wed her;- this only for thee, and not for the Believers (at large); We know what We have appointed for them as to their wives and the captives whom their right hands possess;- in order that there should be no difficulty for thee. And Allah is Oft-Forgiving, Most Merciful.

Shakir: O Prophet! surely We have made lawful to you your wives whom you have given their dowries, and those whom your right hand possesses out of those whom Allah has given to you as prisoners of war, and the daughters of your paternal uncles and the daughters of your paternal aunts, and the daughters of your maternal uncles and the daughters of your maternal aunts who fled with you; and a believing woman if she gave herself to the Prophet, if the Prophet desired to marry her-- specially for you, not for the (rest of) believers; We know what We have ordained for them concerning their wives and those whom their right hands possess in order that no blame may attach to you; and Allah is Forgiving, Merciful.

Muhammad Sarwar: Prophet, We have made lawful for you your wives whom you have given their dowry, slave girls whom God has given to you as gifts, the daughters of your uncles and aunts, both paternal and maternal, who have migrated with you. The believing woman, who has offered herself to the Prophet and whom the Prophet may want to marry, will be specially for him, not for other believers. We knew what to make obligatory for them concerning their wives and slave girls so that you would face no hardship (because we have given distinction to you over the believers). God is All-forgiving and All-merciful.

Mohsin Khan: O Prophet (Muhammad SAW)! Verily, We have made lawful to you your wives, to whom you have paid their Mahr (bridal money given by the husband to his wife at the time of marriage), and those (captives or slaves) whom your right hand possesses - whom Allah has given to you, and the daughters of your 'Amm (paternal uncles) and the daughters of your 'Ammah (paternal aunts) and the daughters of your Khal (maternal uncles) and the daughters of your Khalah (maternal aunts) who migrated (from Makkah) with you, and a believing woman if she offers herself to the Prophet, and the Prophet wishes to marry her; a privilege for you only, not for the (rest of) the believers. Indeed We know what We have enjoined upon them about their wives and those (captives or slaves) whom their right hands possess, - in order that there should be no difficulty on you. And Allah is Ever OftForgiving, Most Merciful.

Arberry: O Prophet, We have made lawful for thee thy wives whom thou hast given their wages and what thy right hand owns, spoils of war that God has given thee, and the daughters of thy uncles paternal and aunts paternal, thy uncles maternal and aunts maternal, who have emigrated with thee, and any woman believer, if she give herself to the Prophet and if the Prophet desire to take her in marriage, for thee exclusively, apart from the believers -- We know what We have imposed upon them touching their wives and what their right hands own -- that there may be no fault in thee; God is All-forgiving, All-compassionate.[83]

The kidnapping and enslavement of women, especially of little girls, is both condoned and supported explicitly by the Quran's teachings. The term "right-hand-possesses" is a metaphor in Islamic theology for "slave girl" and as you can see the term is translated interchangeably and even clarified to mean slave girls. Within the broader context of Islamic theology, it would mean that Muslim men have the right to kidnap nine year-old little girls, rape them to convert them to Islam, force nine-year old girls into prostitution for other Muslim men, and force them into child marriage with the expectation of being allowed to rape them and force them to become pregnant. While it might possibly be arguable that the age of a slave girl is slightly ambiguous in Islam due to being argued on the basis of Hadiths; the Quran unequivocally grants permission for Muslim men to have slave girls, to kidnap unmarried women (i.e. women who are "unclaimed" by other men within their unchanging 7th century social perceptions), to rape unmarried women, to sell unmarried women into prostitution for other Muslim men, and to use slavery as a social means of forced marriages of non-Muslim women to Muslim men. Moreover, the moral justification for this practice is that the Abrahamic God will forgive the women for being forced into prostitution, enslavement, and being repeatedly raped. Therefore, while Muslim men are discouraged from committing these practices upon non-Muslim women including little girls, they are not forbidden from committing these practices upon non-Muslim women on the basis that the Abrahamic God will forgive these women regardless. The reason for this morbid distinction is that by the standards of the Arab Spring in the 7th century, the woman's chastity is the only thing that matters and her consent doesn't matter; the bodies of adult women and little girls are contextualized as the property of men, which is the underpinnings for why the Islamic jurisprudence system treats women in this way.

I believe it is necessary to repeat: the Tafsir system (interpretation of the Quran) and the Sharia (Divine Law of the Abrahamic God) means that only Muslim Imams have any right to an opinion on these beliefs and practices; Muslims cannot question these beliefs and practices, while non-Muslims have no right to any opinion on these beliefs and practices.[84] Terms like Islamophobia to shut down criticisms of Islam really are just modernized neologisms for blasphemy against Islam. The truth is, Islamists will use

---

[83] The Quranic Arabic Corpus - Translation, corpus.quran.com/translation.jsp?chapter=33&verse=50. Accessed 12 Mar. 2025.
[84] "Tafseer on the Basis of Narrated Texts and Tafseer on the Basis of Individual Understanding - Islam Question & Answer." Islamqa.info, Islam Question and Answer, 11 Mar. 2015, islamqa.info/en/answers/205290/tafseer-on-the-basis-of-narrated-texts-and-tafseer-on-the-basis-of-individual-understanding.

every iota of perceived weakness within societies in order to protect this belief that only Muslim Imams have any right to an opinion on Islam; they will portray critics as bigots, they will try to "racialize" Muslims despite the population of 1.9 billion and Islam being one of the most multi-ethnic religions in human history, and they will try to exploit other perceived weaknesses such as socioeconomic differences to keep pushing this specific and very real threat of normalizing odious 7th century belief systems in non-Muslim majority countries as a means of making other civilizations more susceptible to Islamic conversion practices.

Common Sense versus the Consequences of the Reality of Islam:

Modern sensibilities of "common sense" may lead most people to believe that modern women's rights are so normalized that there is little to fear; the unfortunate historical truth is that this ignores societies that Islam ruled over and successfully regressed. I looked through Will Durant's *Our Oriental Heritage* to double-check this information, and then checked his own source where he cites Indian freedom fighter Lala Lajpat Rai's book, *Unhappy India*, which was published in 1928. According to Lala Lajpat Rai, when India back in the medieval period had adult Indian women pushing for greater cultural independence around the beginning of the Muslim conquest of India, Muslim men would simply kidnap Indian women and force them into slavery, including sexual slavery. This led to a return to the much older cultural tradition of child marriage due to Islam forbidding the kidnapping and rape of married women, whereas unmarried women were permitted by the Abrahamic God to be kidnapped and raped. From pages 158-159 of Lala Lajpat Rai's *Unhappy India*:

> We are not quite sure whether the institution was so universal as it afterwards became at the time when the Muhammadan dominance in India began, because instances of girls marrying at an advanced age and choosing their own husbands are not unkonw in the first centuries of the Muhammadan rule. The daughters of Raja Dahir made captives in the eighth century A.D. were grown up maidens, who, by a very ingenious stratagem revenged themselves on their captor. Samjogta. The princess of Kanauj, who chose Prithi Raj of Delhi as her husband in defiance of the wishes of her father, was also a grown up maiden. These are by no means solitary instances, as the dramatic literature of the period immediately preceding Moslem invasion is full of instances of such grown up girls falling in love with persons of their liking and marrying them by choice. Kalidasa, the greatest of Indian play-wrights,
> flourished in the fifth century A.D. Sakuntala, the greatest of his creations, was a grown up maiden who accepted the love of Dushyanta without waiting for the consent of her father. Her friends and companions were also grown up maiden. Hiuen Tsang, the Chinese traveler, mentions a case of marriage between a grown up Brahman young man and a girl with whom he at once began to live and who gave birth to a child of his after one year. This was in the sixth century. The eleventh century Moslem writer, Alberuni , says, 'the Hindus marry at a very young age; therefore the parents arrange the marriage for their sons.' We think it will be fair to conclude that the custom was in the making when the Moslem advent began, and that advent gave it a further point.

The reason was that the Muhammadan religion prohibited the carrying away of married women as slaves.[85]

Further details of how ubiquitous the capture and enslavement of women and their children were in Medieval India by Sultans and their Islamic military forces can be found in historian Kishori Saran Lal's works in which he cites Muslim geographers, travelers, and court officials. In both the *"Growth of Muslim Population in Medieval India"* on pages 113 – 116 of *Chapter 10: AD 1200 – 1400* in the subsection *"Conversion during Wars"* and in another of his books, *"Indian Muslims: Who Are They?"* on pages 23 – 27 of *"Chapter 2: Rise of Muslims under the Sultanate"* he gives the same thorough information. Unfortunately, the Kindle edition of *"Indian Muslims: Who Are They?"* has an error in which it is missing half of a crucial citation by Ibn Battuta. I was going to cite the PDF copy due to that, but it doesn't copy well into a Word document like the Kindle edition. I've decided to cite the Kindle edition's cleaner and more readable copy and the PDF edition's version, but please keep in mind the Kindle edition's citation 104 is lacking *"Ibn Battuta, op. cit., p. 63. Hindi translation by A.A. Rizvi in Tughlaq Kalin Bharat, part I, Aligarh, 1956, p. 189."* whereas the full citation is in the PDF version under citation 43 of Chapter 2 of the PDF edition. I want to show a full commitment to honesty and truth, so as not to confuse anyone:

Conversions

One important mission of Islam was to spread throughout the world. The Quran, the Hadis, the Hidaya and the Sirat-un-Nabi, the four all important works of Islam, direct the faithful to fulfill the above task. Therefore, 'there was never any doubt in the minds of the Muslims of their right to spread over the earth The Hidayah is quite explicit about the legality of jihad (holy war) against infidels even when they have not taken the offensive The Muslim Turks found the moral justification for their advance into India in the induction to propagate Islam. As this could not, in the opinion of kings and warriors, be achieved without the subjugation of non-Muslims and occupation of their territory, the propagation of Islam became identical with war and conquest.'[85]

In simple language, conquerors and rulers converted people by force. It has been seen that during the Arab invasion of Sind and the expeditions of Mahmud of Ghazni, defeated rulers, garrisons of captured forts, and civilian population were often forced to accept Islam. Turkish rule in Hindustan was established in the teeth of Rajput opposition and the process of war and conversion never ceased. Malik Kafur, the general of Alauddin Khalji, gave the Raja of Dwarsamudra a choice between Islam, death or payment of a huge idemnity.[86] But under Muhammad bin Tughlaq there is greater insistence on the vanquished Hindu princes to embrace Islam. The most glaring example of this is that during the Warangal campaign all the eleven sons of the Raja of Kampila were made Muslims. Muhammad bin Tughlaq converted many people in this fashion. When Firoz Tughlaq invaded Jajnagar (Orissa), he captured the son of the Rai of Sikhar, converted him to Islam, and gave him the name of Shakr Khan.[87]

---

[85] Rai, Lala Lajpat. "CHAPTER XII WOMAN IN INDIA: A RETROSPECT." WWW.HINDUSTANBOOKS.COM, BANNA PUBLISHING CO., CALCUTTA / Kolkata, West Bengal, 1928, pp. 151–174, https://hindustanbooks.com/books/unhappy_india/Unhappy_India.pdf. Accessed 12 Mar. 2025.

Ordinarily, captivity for a Rajput was out, of the question; his sense of honour and the dire punishments with which he was visited in case of captivity,[88] excluded any attempt on his part to save his life by surrender. He either died on the field of battle or escaped. But in war civilians and non-combatants could easily be taken. Kafur Hazardinari from Gujarat or Hasan (Khusrau Khan) from Malwa would not be the only ones who were captured. They rose into prominence and therefore the circumstances of their enslavement and conversion are known. Large numbers became Musalmans in this way. Muslim rulers were keen to obtain captives in war and convert them. During warfare it was still more easy to enslave women and children. It was almost a matter of policy with the Turkish rulers and their commanders, from the very start of Muslim rule, to capture and convert or disperse and destory the male population, and carry into slavery women and children. Ibn-ul-Asir says that Qutbuddin Aibak made 'war against the provinces of Hind He killed and returned home with prisoners and booty.'[89] In Banaras, according to Ibn-ul-Asir, Shihabuddin's slaughter of the Hindus was immense, 'none was spared except women and children,'[90] Who were destined to be made slaves. No wonder that slaves began to fill the household of every Turk from the very inception of Muslim rule in Hindustan. Fakhre Mudabbir informs us that as a result of the Turkish achievements under Muhammad Ghori and Qutbuddin Aibak, 'even a poor householder (or soldier) who did not possess a single slave (before) became the owner of numerous slaves '[91] In 1231 Sultan Iltutmish attacked Gwalior, and 'captured a large number of slaves'.[92] Minhaj Siraj Jurjani writes that 'his (Balban's) taking of captives, and his capture of the dependents of the great Ranas cannot be recounted.'[93] Talking of his war in Avadh against Trailokyavarman of the Chandela dynasty (Dalaki wa Malaki of Minhaj), the chronicler says: 'All the infidel's wives, sons and dependents and children fell into the hands of the victors.'[94] In 1253 in his campaign against Ranthambhor also Balban appears to have captured many prisoners.[95] In 1259, in an attack on Hariyana (the Shiwalik hills), many women and children were enslaved.[96] Twice Balban led expeditions against Kampil, Patiali, and Bhojpur, and in the process captured a large number of women and children. In Katehar he ordered a general massacre of the male population above eight years of age and carried away women and children.[97]

The process of enslavement during war went on under the Khaljis and the Tughlaqs. Alauddin had 50,000 slaves[98] some of whom were mere boys,[99] and surely many captured during war. Firoz Tughlaq had issued an order that whichever places were sacked, in them the captives should be sorted out and the best ones (fit for service with the Sultan) should be forwarded to the court.[100] Soon he was enabled to collect 180,000 slaves.[101] Ziyauddin Barani's description of the Slave Market in Delhi (such markets were there in other places also) during the reign of Alauddin Khalji, shows that fresh batches of slaves were constantly replenishing them.[102]

Muhammad bin Tughlaq became notorious for enslaving women, and his reputation in this regard spread far and wide, so that Shihabuddin Ahmad Abbas writes about him thus: 'The Sultan never ceases to show the greatest zeal in making war upon the infidels Everyday thousands of slaves are sold at a very low price, so great is the number of prisoners.'[103] Ibn Battuta's eyewitness account of the Sultan's arranging the enslaved girls' marriages with Muslims on a large scale on the occasion of the two Ids, confirms the statement of Abbas.[104] Such was their influx that Ibn Battuta writes: 'At (one) time there arrived in Delhi some female infidel captives, ten of whom the Vazir sent to me. I gave one of them to the man who had brought them to me, but he was not satisfied. My companion took three young girls, and I do not know what happened to the rest.'[105] Thousands of non-Muslim women[106] were captured in the minor yearly campaigns[107][108] of Firoz Tughlaq, and under him the Id celebrations were held on lines similar to those of his predecessor.[109] In short the inflow of such captives never ceased, and it need hardly be stated that in the hands of their Muslim masters the slaves, whether captured or purchased, became Musalman sooner or later.

The numbers thus captured and converted during the thirteenth and fourteenth centuries cannot be ascertained. But from the details given by the chroniclers, it appears that enslavement during war brought the largest number of converts and, as years passed by, they and their progeny seem to have formed the bulk of the Muslim population. Only two instances may suffice to show how this agency contributed to the rapid rise of Muslim numbers. Bashir Sultani was originally a Hindu slave. He converted to Islam and became an important nobleman (Imadul Mulk) under Firoz Tughlaq. He purchased 4,000 slaves.[110] Later on they were all manumitted and married, and could have produced other thousands of Muslims in a single generation. Khan-i-Jahan Maqbul too was originally a Hindu. He converted, became Prime Minister, and collected 2,000 women in his harem. How many slaves he had is not known, but for such a high dignitary's household of two thousand, at least a few thousand slaves would have been required. The point to note is that all these women and slaves, if not originally Muslim, would have embraced Islam in course of time.[86][87]

This practice still goes on in Muslim-majority South Asian countries like Pakistan and Bangladesh which continue to do this to Hindu, Sikh, Buddhist, Parsis, Christian, and other religious minority groups. A brief example from a March 18, 2016 news clip from the news organization, *Voice of America* that is titled "*Pakistani Hindus Complain of Forced Conversion of Teenage Girls*" from their Youtube channel which is transcribed as follows:

> **Ayesha Tanzeem, VOA news journalist**: Harya is back with her parents. She says she was kidnapped as she was collecting water from a well. Two weeks later, she appeared in a coach to say she had converted to Islam and married her abductor.
>
> **Harya**: *(Translated to English)* A female police officer gave me some kind of an injection. Both the judge and the police were bribed. They told me I was married. They also told me I was now a Muslim.
>
> **Ayesha Tanzeem, VOA news journalist**: Her parents spent everything they had, even sold their only buffalo to get their daughter back. A higher court finally ruled in their favor. Pakistan's Hindu community complains that conversion and marriage is often used to get legal cover for kidnapping young girls who are then threatened with harm to them or their families to get false statements in court. Police says these cases are not that simple. Many of these girls, they say, ran away willingly with boys they fell in love with, and then their parents filed charges for kidnapping. Shivdhan complained that his 15 year-old girl was kidnapped, but she says she was 21 and had eloped with her boyfriend.
>
> **Sonari / Zarina (Converted Girl)**: *(Translated in English)* I have married Shanawaz because my parents were forcing me to marry a man I did not like.
>
> **Ayesha Tanzeem, VOA news journalist**: Hindu leaders say even if a girl leaves home willingly, she should be returned to her parents if she's under 18.
>
> **Ravi Dawani, General Secretary of All Pakistani Hindu Panchayat**: *(Translated to English)* What does a 12, 13 year-old know about love? They lure young girls away and then create an atmosphere of fear and harassment to force false statements.
>
> **Ayesha Tanzeem, VOA news journalist**: The legal age for marriage is 16 in Pakistan and in Sindh province, 18. But underage marriages are common even amongst the majority Muslim

---

[86] Lal, K. S. Chapter 2: Rise of Muslims under the Sultanate (pp. 23-27). Indian Muslims - Who Are They. Mahesh Patel. Kindle Edition.

[87] Lal, K. S. Chapter 2: Rise of Muslims under the Sultanate (pp. 22-27). Indian Muslims - Who Are They. Internet Archive, 28 Aug. 2020, https://dn790000.ca.archive.org/0/items/indian-muslims-who-are-they-k.-s.-lal/Indian%20Muslims%20-%20Who%20Are%20They%20-%20K.%20S.%20Lal.pdf, PDF Edition.

population. That is because many religious clerics consider the age limit against Islamic law. Pir Mohammad Ayub Jahn says he has converted many Hindu girls. He says he ensures they make the decision freely without harassment or fear, but he does not consider the age of the girl.

Mohammad Ayub Jahn: *(Translated in English)* They say a girl is not mature till she is 18. We condemn this law. We do not accept it. We will never accept it.

Ayesha Tanzeem, VOA news journalist: Pakistan's Hindu community is now pushing for a law that would make the religious conversion of a person 18 illegal. Ayesha Tanzeem, VOA news, Umirkot.[88]

On August 13th, 2015, Romanian journalist Rukmini Callimachi published an article for the New York Times titled "*ISIS Enshrines a Theology of Rape*" which explained how the Islamic State utilized Islam's theology to justify the rape and sexual slavery of young girls, while portrayed as "radical" it is unfortunately the most consistent behavior with Islamic theology. I would recommend comparing what I've explained with the behavior of the Islamist perpetrators as described by interviews with the Yazidi rape survivors who were interviewed for the article. The article begins as follows:

> QADIYA, Iraq — In the moments before he raped the 12-year-old girl, the Islamic State fighter took the time to explain that what he was about to do was not a sin. Because the preteen girl practiced a religion other than Islam, the Quran not only gave him the right to rape her — it condoned and encouraged it, he insisted.
>
> He bound her hands and gagged her. Then he knelt beside the bed and prostrated himself in prayer before getting on top of her.
>
> When it was over, he knelt to pray again, bookending the rape with acts of religious devotion.
>
> "I kept telling him it hurts — please stop," said the girl, whose body is so small an adult could circle her waist with two hands. "He told me that according to Islam he is allowed to rape an unbeliever. He said that by raping me, he is drawing closer to God," she said in an interview alongside her family in a refugee camp here, to which she escaped after 11 months of captivity.[89]

And more details further in the article of the extent of how the sexual slavery system that they devised was consistent with their Islamic jurisprudence system:

> The trade in Yazidi women and girls has created a persistent infrastructure, with a network of warehouses where the victims are held, viewing rooms where they are inspected and marketed, and a dedicated fleet of buses used to transport them.
>
> A total of 5,270 Yazidis were abducted last year, and at least 3,144 are still being held, according to community leaders. To handle them, the Islamic State has developed a detailed bureaucracy of sex slavery, including sales contracts notarized by the ISIS-run Islamic courts. And the practice

---

[88] "Pakistani Hindus Complain of Forced Conversion of Teenage Girls." YouTube, VOA News, 18 Mar. 2016, youtu.be/-i24jg4mJ4I.

[89] Callimachi, Rukmini. "Isis Enshrines a Theology of Rape." The New York Times, The New York Times, 13 Aug. 2015, www.nytimes.com/2015/08/14/world/middleeast/isis-enshrines-a-theology-of-rape.html.

has become an established recruiting tool to lure men from deeply conservative Muslim societies, where casual sex is taboo and dating is forbidden.

A growing body of internal policy memos and theological discussions has established guidelines for slavery, including a lengthy how-to manual issued by the Islamic State Research and Fatwa Department just last month. Repeatedly, the ISIS leadership has emphasized a narrow and selective reading of the Quran and other religious rulings to not only justify violence, but also to elevate and celebrate each sexual assault as spiritually beneficial, even virtuous.

"Every time that he came to rape me, he would pray," said F, a 15-year-old girl who was captured on the shoulder of Mount Sinjar one year ago and was sold to an Iraqi fighter in his 20s. Like some others interviewed by The New York Times, she wanted to be identified only by her first initial because of the shame associated with rape.
"He kept telling me this is ibadah," she said, using a term from Islamic scripture meaning worship.[90]

The article closes with an anecdote from another Yazidi rape survivor who describes what an ISIS fighter did to a 12-year old girl and explains the mentality of the ISIS fighter which is unfortunately completely consistent with Islamic theology:

One 34-year-old Yazidi woman, who was bought and repeatedly raped by a Saudi fighter in the Syrian city of Shadadi, described how she fared better than the second slave in the household — a 12-year-old girl who was raped for days on end despite heavy bleeding.

"He destroyed her body. She was badly infected. The fighter kept coming and asking me, 'Why does she smell so bad?' And I said, she has an infection on the inside, you need to take care of her," the woman said.

Unmoved, he ignored the girl's agony, continuing the ritual of praying before and after raping the child.

"I said to him, 'She's just a little girl,' " the older woman recalled. "And he answered: 'No. She's not a little girl. She's a slave. And she knows exactly how to have sex.' "

"And having sex with her pleases God," he said.[91]

Within the broader Western culture, there is the dangerous cultural myth of Western exceptionalism. The perception within the Western cultural osmosis is still that the West is the endpoint of all human civilizations. Unfortunately, all cultures that held this hubris in the past fell into ruin; likely because it actively impaired them from accepting facts and evidence that disproved such misconceptions. When we stop believing cultures are exceptional and start gazing at cultural patterns and behaviors, we can learn a lot more and develop better methods on how to put an end to Islamism. The

---

[90] Callimachi, Rukmini. "Isis Enshrines a Theology of Rape." The New York Times, The New York Times, 13 Aug. 2015, www.nytimes.com/2015/08/14/world/middleeast/isis-enshrines-a-theology-of-rape.html.
[91] Callimachi, Rukmini. "Isis Enshrines a Theology of Rape." The New York Times, The New York Times, 13 Aug. 2015, www.nytimes.com/2015/08/14/world/middleeast/isis-enshrines-a-theology-of-rape.html.

unfortunate and painful truth is that similar crimes by Muslim men against young girls have been happening in Great Britain and the similarities should be scrutinized more to check for patterns where Muslims rule as the majority or have large enclaves that embrace Islamism.

An early example was a news report by journalist Kevin Rawlinson on June 27th, 2013 for *The Independent* on the horrifying activities of Oxford grooming gangs of Pakistani Muslim men which was titled *"Oxford grooming gang jailed: Dogar and Karrar brothers get life for abuse and rape of young girls"* with the early parts of the article reading as follows:

> Seven members of a gang which groomed girls as young as 12 and subjected them to "dreadful" sexual abuse over the course of eight years have been sentenced to at least 95 years in prison.
>
> The men, who ran a child sexual abuse ring in Oxford, were convicted of a range of offences, including the rape and trafficking of young girls around the country for sex. Five of them have been given life sentences, with two more sentenced to a total of seven years each.
>
> There were tears in the public gallery, where four of the six victims who gave evidence during the lengthy trial sat with family and friends.
>
> The mother of Girl A said that the ordeal of a near five-month trial was been "long and harrowing". In a statement read by police outside court, she said: "We were a happy family, living in a good area. We never imagined this could be possible and we want to make other parents and carers aware that this type of crime can happen anywhere. It's not about location, it's about the perpetrators. It isn't about affluence or poverty - these men deliberately targeted and groomed our daughter regardless of our family background. They took her from us and we will never get those lost years back.
>
> "It is important that every single one of us is vigilant and observant of children's behaviour and we urge anyone with any concerns to follow their instincts and come forward. If you have any concerns at all, tell someone before it's too late."[92]

Sentencing remarks by Judge Peter Rook from *the Judiciary of England and Wales*; which Elon Musk rightly shared snippets (specifically number 53 of the counts listed below) of the horrifying information on Twitter so that people unfamiliar with

---

[92] Rawlinson, Kevin. "Oxford Grooming Gang Jailed: Dogar and Karrar Brothers Get Life For." The Independent, Independent Digital News and Media, 27 June 2013, www.independent.co.uk/news/uk/crime/oxford-grooming-gang-jailed-dogar-and-karrar-brothers-get-life-for-abuse-and-rape-of-young-girls-8677159.html.

these issues could better understand the problem of Pakistani Muslim grooming gangs and what they're capable of. It had this extended passage of the sexual enslavement of a girl by the Muslim perpetrators:

> 50) You, Mohammed Karrar, were introduced to GH when she was only 11. It is a clear from the video clip we have seen, she was a small girl at the age of 12. You were in your thirties. [You knew that both her parents had profound disabilities, and at a very early age she shouldered a huge responsibility towards her parents. You would go to her home and smoke joints with her father who no doubt would have had no idea what you were doing to his daughter, including having sex with her at his home.] You anally raped her when she was 11. After a period of months when you groomed her, you were having regular oral, vaginal and anal sex with her. You duped her by telling her that you'd take her to Saudia Arabia and marry her when she was 15. She became pregnant. Your reaction was to become angry with her and slap her. You took her to Reading so that an illegal abortion could be performed upon her at an underground so-called clinic. Clearly this was highly dangerous to her health. As always you had no regard to her welfare and the damage you were causing her. She became obsessed with you, and you exploited her.
>
> 51) There came at time before she was 13 that both of you Mohammed and Bassam Karrar started to bring strangers to have sex with her. You Bassam would organise the sessions. Mohammed was closely involved and would be at most of these sessions. These 11 occasions happened many times. You would make her act as a hostess at sex parties no doubt charging for her services. If she did not want to have sex with the men, you both would get angry. She had to endure depraved sexual demands including the acting out of weird sex fantasies, and the insertion of objects in her vagina. If she kicked out, she would be restrained. If she said that she did not have sex. She said "Mo and Bassam would get mad at me." You, Mohammed, made videos of GH performing sex acts no doubt with a view to selling her sexual services.
>
> 51) You, Mohammed Karrar, took her to various places to provide sex to others – a hotel in Bournemouth, a flat near a school in Oxford. She was taken to High Wycombe for sex on a regular basis. Both of you took her to High Wycombe for sex with others. Bassam took her two or three times without Mohammed. Sometimes there were three or four men at a session. Sometimes as many as nine or ten. GH thought that Bassam was taking lots of phone calls in relation to the Wycombe trips where there would be sex acts and sexual fantasies acted upon.
>
> 52) GH would hear both Mohammed and Bassam speaking to customers over the phone before going to the Nanford for sex. She was taken to Nanford House over 50 times. The charge would vary according to the sex act you'd make her perform. Mainly Mohammed would take her, but Bassam took her more than a couple of times. Sometimes she would be to taken to the Nanford twice or three times a week.
>
> 53) You, Mohammed Karrar, prepared her for gang anal rape by using a pump to expand her anal passage. You subjected her to a gang rape by five or six men (count 30). At one point she had four men inside her. A red ball was placed in her mouth to keep her quiet. Not only were you both involved in the commercial sexual exploitation of GH, you also used her for your own self-gratification. You both raped her when she was under 13. When she was very young, although it is

not clear whether she was under 13, you both raped her at the same time (oral and vaginal/anal). It happened on more than one occasion (Count 28).

54) Mohammed Karrar, on one occasion when GH was 12, after raping her, she threatened you with your lock knife. Your reaction was to pick up a baseball bat with a silver metal handle, strike her on the head with it, and then insert the baseball bat inside her vagina. You treated her as if she was your commodity. You branded her (with your initial near her anal passage) using a hot hair pin. If GH did not comply with your wishes, if you were not with other people, you would lose your temper with her. As part of the grooming, you would provide her with crack cocaine and you injected GH with heroin on numerous occasions (Count 40).

55) When she was not prepared to participate any more, you would issue terrible threats. Your activities took a heavy toll upon her both physically and mentally. In late 2010/2011 she phoned you. You invited her to come and see you. You said "We'll sort it and make it better." Once there, you had an argument, and to exert your power and punish her, you pulled down her trousers and raped her.[93]

On February 27th, 2019, the BBC released a news article titled *"Bradford grooming: Nine jailed for abusing girls"* detailing another story of horrific abuses by nine men who were predominately Pakistani Muslims:

Nine men who raped and abused two teenage girls who were living in a children's home have been jailed.

The girls were aged 14 when the men first began to use drink, drugs and violence to groom and sexually exploit them.

Bradford Crown Court heard the abuse started after the girls moved into the home in 2008.

The nine were convicted of 22 offences including rape and inciting child prostitution.

A tenth defendant was cleared of rape.[94]

And further in the article:

At about the same time the girls also separately met brothers Saeed and Naveed Akthar, with much of the abuse taking place at Saeed's former address on Saffron Drive.

---

[93] Sentencing Remarks of His Honour Judge Peter Rook QC, www.judiciary.uk/wp-content/uploads/JCO/Documents/Judgments/sentencing-remarks-r-v-dogar-others.pdf. Accessed 13 Mar. 2025.
[94] "Bradford Grooming: Nine Jailed for Abusing Girls." BBC News, BBC, 27 Feb. 2019, www.bbc.com/news/uk-england-leeds-47388060.

'Used as a prostitute'

Ms Melly said: "Fiona was used for sex by the men that came to the property.

"She was used by Saeed to get drugs and bring them back, she was told to go and meet dealers and to ensure she came back with drugs though she was given no money for them.

"She was in effect used as a prostitute on his instruction."

The allegations came to light in 2014 when Ms Goddard saw a report on the grooming and sexual abuse of hundreds of young girls in Rotherham on BBC Look North.

She asked her then partner to contact the BBC to say that similar abuse was happening elsewhere and the BBC "quite properly" notified police.[95]

The "common sense" Western viewpoint would be to see the horrible sexual violence committed upon Fiona Goddard and the other young girls as a form of "prostitution" in isolation of the theology of Islam. However, once we understand and apply the theological context of Islam and how it promotes such horrific and unjustifiable violence upon young girls, then it is credible to draw a comparison to Islam's theological teachings of "right hand possesses" which is an Islamic religious metaphor for "slave girls" controlled by Muslim men in accordance with faith in the Abrahamic God. Even in the context of how ISIS justified their horrific slave trade of Yazidi women, there are parallels to what the Pakistani Muslim grooming gangs in Britain did to primarily working-class White British girls. In other words, it is more accurate to view this in terms of the Pakistani Muslim grooming gangs creating "slave girls" due to Islam's theological underpinning of what "right hand possesses" means than to subtract religion from the equation. It makes more sense when you compare it to how Muslim men treat women in a globalized context; due to the teachings of Islam.

For those unfamiliar of the extent of these Pakistani Muslim grooming gangs throughout Great Britain, how serious the majority of Muslims are of continuing this practice in countries they settle in, and the historic failures of the British police to hold them to account to protect young British girls from grooming tactics, Lizzie Deardan *of The Independent*, published an article on February 23rd, 2018 titled "*Grooming gangs abused more than 700 women and girls around Newcastle after police appeared to punish victims*" which explained the following within just one city in England:

---

[95] "Bradford Grooming: Nine Jailed for Abusing Girls." BBC News, BBC, 27 Feb. 2019, www.bbc.com/news/uk-england-leeds-47388060.

After examining evidence on the abuse of hundreds of girls in the North-east, investigators concluded that local authorities claiming there is no grooming in their area "are not looking hard enough".

Operation Sanctuary: "We do not believe that what we have uncovered is unique to Newcastle"

Pat Ritchie, chief executive of Newcastle City Council, said the council would enact all recommendations from the report.

"Sexual exploitation is happening in towns and cities across the country but what we have learned can be used to help others," she added.

"We know it is still going on in our city, but we are doing everything in our power to prevent it, disrupt it and deal with it, and support the victims for years to come."

Northumbria Police had identified more than 700 potential victims of grooming in the region by August through Operation Sanctuary, but expected the number to rise.

Temporary Deputy Chief Constable Darren Best said society had undergone a "sea change" in the knowledge and understanding of grooming in recent years.

"We are far from complacent and recognise we still have work to do to ensure we consistently identify victims and carry out comprehensive investigations on their behalf," he added.

"What cannot be clearer is that safeguarding the vulnerable is everybody's business."

Before 2014, police were responding to incidents on an ad hoc basis, with efforts by authorities trying to persuade victims to keep away from the abusers and change their behaviours.

The review found the approach led to "consideration of deterrent punishments of victims for being drunk and disorderly or for making false allegations when accounts were changed".

"This sent an unhelpful message to perpetrators – they were unlikely to be prosecuted or prevented from continuing to abuse – encouraging an arrogant persistence," it added.

"It also had a significant impact on victims who learnt that nothing would be done against perpetrators."

A total of 17 men and one woman have been convicted of offences including rape, sexual abuse, supplying drugs and trafficking for sexual exploitation in a series of trials over the Newcastle case.

Of eight victims covered in the trials, six were white and two were of African heritage, while the perpetrators came from a diverse range of backgrounds including Pakistani, Bangladeshi, Indian, Iranian, Iraqi, Kurdish, Turkish, Albanian and Eastern European.

The court heard how teenagers and young women were picked up off the streets, then groomed and given alcohol and drugs before being coerced or forced into sex at so-called "sessions" in Newcastle's West End.

Victims described being raped while they were asleep, unconscious or incapacitated after being forced to drink and take drugs.

"I wanted to leave but I was given drink," one said. "I kept saying no and fighting them off. I was very tired and fell asleep. When I woke, I had been raped."

Another added: "When I was out of it they could do anything they wanted to me."

> A judge concluded that the defendants "selected their victims not because of their race, but because they were young, impressionable, naive, and vulnerable", including young girls and women with learning difficulties and mental health issues.
>
> The review said victims in the wider North-east included a 12-year-old girl who fell pregnant and other teenagers who underwent abortions, as well as others left with devastating long-term trauma causing substance abuse, mental illness and relationship breakdowns.[96]

While working-class White girls have been the primary targets of Muslim grooming gangs in the UK, the *National Family Health Survey of the United Kingdom* revealed that Hindu and Sikh girls of primarily South Asian descent were being targeted for sexual grooming too. On November 9th, 2017, the organization released a short write-up titled "*Sexual grooming amongst Hindu girls*" which warned of the patterns of behavior to watch out for:

> Sexual grooming has become a very common issue over the last couple of years. A high occurrence was found amongst Hindu girls as they left home for university. Therefore, it is important that we ourselves, as well as these girls, have a full understanding of this and are able to tackle and help overcome these issues.
>
> Grooming is when someone builds an emotional connection with someone to gain their trust for the purposes of sexual abuse, leading to conversion to another faith. Many victims who are young have no understanding of what grooming is, or that they are being sexually abused.
>
> The Sikh Awareness Society UK has investigated over 200 reports relating to child sexual grooming in the UK. There are, however, no official statistics as it was found that a lot of young victims do not report these incidents. Incidents go unreported as the offenders often lure victims into sexualised relationships and use this against them. The victims then become vulnerable and fear they may bring shame to their family and community by speaking out.
>
> How it all begins
>
> 1. Target the victim: offenders will target those girls whom they feel are suitable to be exploited or converted.
> 2. Gaining trust: girls may start to gain trust through attention and gifts given by the offender, which start to make them feel special.
> 3. Isolation: offenders will continue to draw the girls in more deeply, until they are isolated from friends and family.
> 4. Sexualising the relationship: offenders will start to take advantage by threats and blackmail unless their demands are fulfilled, and thus start to gain control.
>
> Telling signs
>
> It is important that we are familiar with the signs of grooming. Knowing these little signs could help save many victims who have been suffering silently for many years and feel completely

---

[96] Dearden, Lizzie. "Grooming Gangs Abused More than 700 Women and Girls around Newcastle after Police Appeared to Punish Victims." The Independent, Independent Digital News and Media, 23 Feb. 2018, www.independent.co.uk/news/uk/crime/grooming-gangs-uk-britain-newcastle-serious-case-review-operation-sanctuary-shelter-muslim-asian-a8225106.html.

helpless. Signs may include: going missing from home, school, college, university or staying out late at night on a regular basis; a change in behaviour – quiet or withdrawn, aggressive and disruptive; receiving unexplained gifts – watches, money, clothes; involvement in criminal activities and changes in physical appearance.

How to stay safe
Alcohol and drugs are most commonly used in grooming by offenders. It is very important when at university and on nights out to always remain aware of your surroundings. Never leave your drink unattended, as it is can very easily be spiked without you knowing. Always stick with your friends and make sure they are aware of where you are if you do decide to leave, and avoid going home alone.
For support or advice, you can get in touch with National Hindu Welfare Support. Their confidential helpline can be reached at 020 7341 6279, or you can email info.nhws@gmail.com.
— *Neelam Chhabhadiya*, Events Team Member[97]

Due to being part of the teachings of the Quran itself that Muslims cannot question; these are not one-off events, they have a horrifying historical context that has never been addressed and which still occur in Muslim-majority South Asian countries that the British government itself created via the partition of India in 1947, and the underpinnings of Islamic theology create moral justifications that the behavior is sanctioned by the Abrahamic God under Islam's divine command theory.

Within the Middle East, especially in Saudi Arabia, this sort of behavior is socially condoned, even if not officially acceptable due to international pressure. An article initially published on The Daily Beast in October 11th, 2015 and then updated in April 13th, 2017 titled *"Inside the World of Gulf State Slavery"* by journalists Asra Q. Nomani and Hala Arafa explained as follows:

> What's happened in recent years is that, just as phone videos have been used in the U.S. to capture controversial police arrests and shootings, phone videos are being used today in a sort of wasta revolution, in which witnesses are shooting secret footage of abuse of power over maids, "servants," children, and ordinary folks.
>
> The wasta revolution flips the traditional notion of honor and frames behavior, like the Saudi man's sexual harassment, as dishonorable and, in the courtroom of public opinion, it is the oppressed who have wasta, not the oppressor.
>
> In Pakistan, someone shared a video last month of a family dining out with their "servant" girl, sitting at the same table, but not allowed to eat. Another clip, shared not long ago, showed another family dining out with their servants told to sit with their backs to the table. This past December, the video of a Filipino "household maid" in distress went viral. "Please help us," she said. "I beg you."

---

[97] Chhabhadiya, Neelam. "Sexual Grooming amongst Hindu Girls." National Hindu Students Forum UK, NHSF (UK), 9 Nov. 2017, www.nhsf.org.uk/2017/11/sexual-grooming-amongst-hindu-girls/.

Men are very often not the only aggressors, either, and abuse exists beyond the boundaries of Saudi Arabia. Born in India and Egypt, we both grew up witnessing shockingly brutal violence against "servants" by women for whom dominance over "servants" was one of their few expressions of "power." Such social abuse has become so normative that, very often, we look at such infractions through a lens of moral and cultural relativism, but doing so fails humanity.

Human Rights Watch estimates tens of millions of women and girls are employed as household "domestic workers," and it estimates that millions of poor women from countries, including Bangladesh, the Philippines, India, Sri Lanka, and Nepal, work as "household maids" in the six countries of the Gulf Cooperation Council, Saudi Arabia, Bahrain, Kuwait, Oman, Qatar, and the United Arab Emirates. Men and boys are hired too for menial tasks too often exploited inhumanely.

Years ago, the Economist outlined the injustices workers face, challenging governments of the workers to protect their citizens, in a piece, headlined, "Beheading the Golden Goose," after Saudi Arabia beheaded an Indonesian "household maid."

Human Rights Watch has documented the abuses against "domestic workers" in in Saudi Arabia and the Gulf in reports titled "I Already Bought You" and "As If I Am Not Human," noting "sexual violence" against workers, including "male employers" and their "teenage or adult sons" engaging in "inappropriate touching, hugging, and kissing" and "repeated rape."

In a report in Der Spiegel, the investigative German magazine, two German ambulance workers who worked in Riyadh, Saudi Arabia, testified to the abuses they had seen, chronicling one raped maid who was almost unable to walk due to the pain and others who get pregnant, babies usually abandoned, including at a local garbage dump.

The issue of the treatment and conduct of "domestic workers" in Saudi Arabia has led to heated diplomatic exchanges with countries from Ethiopia to Sri Lanka and the Philippines.

Two years ago, Annette Vlieger, a researcher who went undercover in South Asia and the Gulf to investigate the issue, published a book, Domestic Workers in Saudi Arabia and the Emirates: A Socio-Legal Study on Conflict, telling Voice of America that "people are aware that the sexual abuse of domestic workers in the Middle East is pretty bad." When she posed as a potential employer in the Middle East, she said, "…I was very much in shock—mostly in Saudi Arabia, where they simply told me, 'She will be your slave for two years.'"

Workdays are ones of drudgery up to 20 hours, she said, and many were "abused, either physically or mentally" and "many women" were sexually abused as well.

Just like the young woman chronicled in the video, dodging the man's groping but acquiescing to his presence, the researcher noted, "The women themselves simply believe in fate." She said that poor rural families will often send one daughter to the Middle East "sort of like a sacrifice." "Very often, girls know that that is their reason for existing," she said.

A few years ago, the Saudi Gazette reported that "expat women commit suicide," chronicling an "Indonesian housemaid" who hanged herself in her sponsor's home in the city of eastern Asi, and an "Ethiopian housemaid" in her 20s who committed suicide inside "her sponsor's home" in the holy city of Mecca. When she didn't open her door, the story said, the family broke the door down and found "her body hanging from the ceiling."

In 1962, the leader of Saudi Arabia, "King" Faisal, abolished slavery in Saudi Arabia by royal decree. But he largely neglected to amend Saudi labor laws to provide protection for workers in the kingdom because the culture of servitude is very intricately woven into its national fabric. The Saudi version of Romeo and Juliet is Qays Wa Layla, about the impossible love between the daughter of a high-born Saudi and her cousin, born to a slave mother.

The attitude of servitude extends toward "housemaids" in the modern day. In a book, Saudi Arabia Exposed, John R. Bradley, a British journalist who lived and worked in Saudi Arabia for many years, detailed how these maids make between $150 and $200 a month, working around the clock without any benefits or medical insurance. Bradley explains how these maids are seen as lesser humans who should be grateful for the opportunity to serve. They are cut off from contact with their communities and kept as prisoners in the house.

This past March, Saudi Arabia executed two "household maids," accused of killing family members from the family of their "sponsor," amid protests from human rights groups, including Amnesty International.

Outside Saudi Arabia, we've seen glimpses of this abuse. In December 2001, a Saudi princess was arrested at a luxury Orlando resort, charged with beating her Indonesian servant and pushing her down a flight of stairs.

In July 2013, a Kenyan woman working for a Saudi princess escaped in Irvine, California, and complained that she and four other Filipino women were held against their will and mistreated.

Just weeks ago, a member of the Saudi ruling family was arrested in Los Angeles for allegedly forcing women workers to give him oral sex in his palatial Los Angeles mansion, with one woman attempting to scale a fence to escape the "prince," traumatized and bloodied.

With sexual assault on campuses a universal problem, the issue got a cultural dimension last week with the arrest of four Saudi national students at Johnson & Wales University in Providence, Rhode Island, for the alleged rape and sexual assault of two 18-year-old freshman women.

This week's viral video emerged at a time of backlash to the Saudi regime for the tragedy of deaths at the hajj pilgrimage, its assaults in Syria and Yemen, and its export of the Wahhabi and Salafi ideology that fuels militant groups like the Islamic State. For example, we support a boycott of the hajj and the government of Saudi Arabia.

"It's a little odd that the matter is being treated as a husband-wife scandal," says Stanley Heller, a leader in a new Coalition to End the U.S.-Saudi Alliance, which supports a boycott. "The maid at minimum was sexually harassed and the act shown to the general public online. That's a double crime against her." The defamation law is being used to "intimidate the public from making justified criticism of public officials and the monarch," he says.

Fortunately, from the Philippines to Nepal, citizens are rallying to protect their own against the tyranny of abuse of power. Last year, a new Facebook page, called "Filipino Domestic Worker Abuse in Saudi Arabia," was created to facilitate a sort of "underground railroad" to help women from the Philippines escape servitude and abuse in Saudi Arabia, posting the email addresses and phone numbers for Philippines Embassy officials, as well as horror stories of the "OFW," or "Overseas Filipino Worker."

"…help is just a Text away," read an early message.

The administrator of the website is a northern California former accountant, Karl Anderson, who became an accidental activist when a Facebook friend from the Philippines asked for help. Today, he helps about 10 women a month escape abuse to go to one of the little-discussed shelters in Saudi Arabia established for "household maids."

"It is slavery," Anderson tells us. "Every day, I see the face of slavery."

"There is a woman who was forced to eat a child's feces out of a diaper because she didn't clean the diaper soon enough," he says. "Women are raped, tortured, denied food, denied water, made to work 20 hours a day, seven days a week. One woman was only allowed to eat the food that her sponsor family left on their plates. They are treated like dogs."[98]

On Jurist.org, a website and non-profit organization where Law Students are encouraged to report of conditions where the rule of law is in crisis across the world; a

---

[98] Nomani, Asra Q., and Hala Arafa. "Inside the World of Gulf State Slavery." The Daily Beast, The Daily Beast Company, 11 Oct. 2015, www.thedailybeast.com/inside-the-world-of-gulf-state-slavery.

guest article was published on May 9th, 2017 by Mais Haddad. At the time she wrote the article, Mais Haddad was then a S.J.D candidate (Doctor of Juridical Science) at the University of Pittsburgh School of Law, she holds a Master's degree in International Relations from the then City, University London, and she received her LL.M (Masters of Law degree) from Damascus University, and practiced law in Damascus, Syria for eight years. In her article bluntly titled *"Victims of Rape and Law: How the Laws of the Arab World Protect Rapists, Not Victims"* she gives an overarching explanation of the horrifying consequences that Islamic Law causes upon Arab women in modern times within many Muslim-majority countries:

> Criminal Codes of Iraq, Syria [Arabic] [pdf], Lebanon [Arabic] [pdf], Libya [Arabic] [pdf], Kuwait [Arabic] [pdf], Bahrain [pdf], Algeria [Arabic] [pdf], Tunisia [Arabic] [pdf] and the Palestinian Territories provide that if the offender of rape lawfully marries the victim, any action becomes void and any investigation or other procedure is discontinued and, if a sentence has already been passed in respect of such action, then the sentence will be repealed. A unique case is Saudi Arabia where Islamic Law is applied and there is no codified Penal Code and no clear definition of rape. Also, the criminal codes of Sudan and Mauritania have no definition of rape as a crime at all. Further, even though, this provision has been removed from the Criminal Code of Egypt since 1999, however, in practice this custom is still widely applied away from the court system. Morocco revoked the law in 2014 after a 16 year old girl committed suicide when she was forced to marry her rapist. Recently, Jordan succeeded quashing the law in 2017. As Jordan took steps towards abolishing Article 308, Lebanese activists were hanging wedding dresses along Beirut's famous sea front, in protest against the Lebanese version of the law. Thus, Lebanon is on the same path with a lot of efforts and hope. Last month, Lebanon's parliamentary committee for administration and justice announced a recommendation to repeal Article 522 of the country's penal code, which allows for suspending the conviction of someone who has raped, kidnapped or committed statutory rape, if he marries the victim. The recommendation must now go through parliament, a process that could still take months.

> The logic behind this law is to protect, though not the victim, rather the reputation of the victim in the society where she lives after her honor has been wounded. The honor of a woman is defined by her chastity, and when she is raped she is stigmatized and no longer marriageable. Hence, a marriage to her rapist is perceived as a solution to this problem and an exit from shame that is suitable to the society. This way her family needs not to feel dishonored or, in many cases, the need to seek vengeance-honor crime. Therefore, better than leaving girls shamed, unmarriageable and dishonored or to be killed by their families or relatives the law protects the girls by forcing attackers to marry them. As a result, such legal system legitimizes rape if it was followed by marriage, rewards the rapist and, in fact, allows him to continue his act. Also, the law ignores any redress for the victim, which should be the aim of the law at the first place. Further, it gets its legitimacy from the concept of shame, and prioritizes wrongful social customs over principles of protecting women and their right, as citizens and humans, to live safely with the protection of law and society.

> Further judicial drawback to already troubling laws regarding rape is the burden of proof. For a rape conviction to actually be handed down, UAE, Saudi Arabia, Sudan, Qatar and Mauritania laws mandate either a confession from the rapist or a witness account from four adult males. One must pause here and imagine the circumstances of which a woman is being raped and four adult

male are witnessing this crime. In all cases, with neither of those things readily available, along with laws that make extramarital sex illegal, women reporting rape are likely to find themselves as the subject of criminal investigation and often, actually, sentenced. The result is the victims often don't report rape, fearing they will be tried for adultery. In the UAE in many cases, foreign women who are in a tourism vacation in Dubai, not knowing of these laws ended up being arrested after they went to the police to report they had been raped. In Saudi Arabia a victim known as 'Girl of Qatif' was gang-raped by seven men. At her 2006 Trial, she was sentenced to 90 lashes for being alone in a car with a man to whom she was not married. The rape was not established in the trial and it could not be proved. There were no witnesses and the men had recanted confessions they made during interrogation, and the verdict cannot be appealed.

Accordingly, the burden of proof in rape cases before the court and the provision of solving the problem of rape by marring the victim to her rapist among many other violations of women's rights found in the Arab states' legal systems, such as honor killing, child marriage and martial rape, reveal the level of cultural, social, political and legal failure these states have. A small success here and there of changing or revoking a certain articles and provisions is far away from what needs to be achieved. The amount of work to be done in order to revolutionize the way society and law perceives women and end the highest levels of female objectification are tremendous. Unfortunately, the Arab states do not seem to be on the right track at the first place. In fact, the recent unfortunate developments even show set back of what has been already little for women rights, especially with the ongoing instability and armed conflicts in the region and the clear rise of extremism over modernity.[99]

It should come as no surprise within the context of Islam's vehement support for the rape of nine-year old children, child marriage, and sexual slavery of women and little girls that even when legal policies are changed, they inevitably regress at the expense of the human rights of Arab children in the Arab Spring. Unfortunately, it is still happening even just this year in 2025. Walk Free, an international human rights group focused on the eradication of modern slavery; co-founded by Australian philanthropist, Grace Forrest and her father, the wealthiest male billionaire in Australia, John Andrew Henry Forrest; released a short article titled *"Iraq's new law allowing children as young as 9 to marry undermines women and girls' rights"* on January 31st, 2025 lamenting Iraq's regression of child marriage laws:

> Under Iraq's new law, girls can legally marry from the age of 9 in certain circumstances, depending on religious interpretations. The legal marriage age for boys has also been reduced from 18 to 15.
>
> The law gives religious authorities the power to decide on family matters, including marriage, divorce, and child custody, and abolishes a longstanding ban on child marriage under the age of 18, which had been in place since the 1950s.

---

[99] Haddad, Mais. "Victims of Rape and Law: How the Laws of the Arab World Protect Rapists, Not Victims." Jurist, Jurist, www.jurist.org/commentary/2017/05/mais-haddad-arab-world-laws-protect-the-rapist-not-the-victim/.

This change significantly reduces protections for women and children, exposing them to greater risks of exploitation and abuse.

The law also restricts women's access to fundamental rights, including divorce, child custody, and inheritance, which are all important for their autonomy and safety.

These restrictions could leave women and girls increasingly vulnerable in a country already facing significant instability.

The dangers of child marriage for girls

Legalising child marriage in Iraq increases the vulnerability of young girls, especially in communities with ongoing conflict and social unrest.

The risks associated with child marriage are severe, including health complications, mental health struggles, and a lack of education and employment opportunities.

Girls who marry at a young age are often forced to leave school, limiting their education and financial independence, which continues cycles of poverty.

This practice also threatens their physical and emotional well-being, further entrenching gender inequality.

Iraq's new law violates international and national legal standards

The new legislation not only contradicts Iraq's existing legal framework but also breaches international agreements.

Iraq has previously criminalised forced marriage and endorsed treaties such as the Convention on the Elimination of All Forms of Discrimination Against Women (CEDAW) and the Convention on the Rights of the Child, both of which prohibit child marriage.

Passing this amendment means Iraq risks breaching its international obligations, ignoring its responsibility to protect women and girls from harmful practices.

Additionally, the law allows religious councils to draft legal codes without parliamentary or public oversight, further reducing the state's role in safeguarding citizens' rights.

Legal changes that bypass democratic processes weaken crucial checks and balances, making it easier for harmful laws to come into effect without proper scrutiny.[100]

And further in the article, they note similar regressive patterns in Muslim-majority countries like Somalia and Bangladesh, whereas they confess the admittedly slow progress in the US and Western countries like Australia and France:

Global efforts to end child marriage threatened by Iraq's law

---

[100] "Iraq's New Law Allowing Children as Young as 9 to Marry Undermines Women and Girls' Rights." Walk Free, Minderoo Foundation, 31 Jan. 2025, www.walkfree.org/news/2025/iraqs-new-law-allowing-children-as-young-as-9-to-marry-undermines-women-and-girls-rights/.

Many countries, including Australia, the United States, and France, have exceptions that legally allow children under the age of 18, to marry with judicial or parental consent. Progress in removing harmful exceptions has been slow.

In our latest Global Slavery Index, we found that only 35 countries had set a minimum age of marriage at 18 years old without exception.

Attempts to lower the legal marriage age in other countries, such as Bangladesh and Somalia, have led to exceptions that allow children under 18 to marry in specific circumstances, including pregnancy or with a guardian's consent.

These exceptions normalise child marriage and establish harmful gender norms.[101]

For these last two sections, I decided to add the two subsection of Chapter 24 of my older book, *Faith in Doubt* as I don't really have much else to add from what I've already critiqued years ago. The only real change I've made is adding imagery of the Quranic verses supporting incest:

Islamic Theology and Female Genital Mutilation

In Islam, most Islamic schools of thought consider the matter of Female Genital Mutilation (FGM) to be an honor that women can choose to undertake. However, in the Shafi'i school of Islam, it is considered mandatory to impose FGM upon young girls and they often undergo this horrific procedure in their infancy. If you don't believe that the Shafi'i school of Islam makes FGM mandatory, here is the evidence from a Shafi'i cleric who justifies the procedure in terms of a commitment to the purity of Islam and obedience to the Abrahamic God:

> *Rulings from your site regarding female circumcision appear to have been taken down. Is there is a change in opinion concerning female circumcision from a Shafii point of view? What do you say about issuing a fatwa on this issue which prohibits the practice?*

In Maratib al-Ijma' p. 157, Ibn Hazm cited that there is an established consensus (ar: ijma') that circumcision for women is permissible. This ijma' is related by other scholars too. In the Sacred Law, ijma' is a binding proof, and it is not permissible for any scholar to go against it.

In Nihayah 8/35, after mentioning the official position of the Shafi'i School, that circumcision is obligatory for both men and women, Ramli defines what it means for a woman. He says that it is the removal of some skin from the clitoral prepuce. This is also mentioned by Ibn Hajar in Tuhfah 9/198.

---

[101] "Iraq's New Law Allowing Children as Young as 9 to Marry Undermines Women and Girls' Rights." Walk Free, Minderoo Foundation, 31 Jan. 2025, www.walkfree.org/news/2025/iraqs-new-law-allowing-children-as-young-as-9-to-marry-undermines-women-and-girls-rights/.

In these passages, the word "bazr" is mentioned. Sahib al-Misbah al-Munir mentions that the "bazr" in circumcision is the prepuce. Thus, what is intended is a part of the prepuce surrounding the clitoris and not the clitoris itself.

In Sunan Abi Dawud and Tabarani's al-Mu'jam al-Kabir, it is related that the Prophet Muhammad (upon him be peace) said,

أَشِمِّي لَا تُنْهِكِي فَإِنَّ ذَلِكَ أَحْظَى لِلْمَرْأَةِ وَأَحَبُّ لِلْبَعْلِ

"Leave it bulging, do not exaggerate in cutting. Indeed, that is more enjoyable for the woman, and the husband will like it better."

Some have declared Tabarani's chain to be authentic. While others criticized the authenticity of this narration. Here, it is not being cited to establish a basis for a practice in the Sacred Law, the aforementioned ijma' establishes that. The narration describes the manner in which the practice is to be performed. It clarifies that the procedure is minor and the reduction is slight; in fact, the verbs used are commands, which indicate obligation. Meaning, to go beyond this contravenes what the Prophet (upon him be peace) commanded.

What we have mentioned above is not FGM. In Arabic, the practice we are talking about is called "khafd," meaning, a reduction i.e. of the clitoral hood. This is actually, according to many health experts, an accepted medical procedure; something that when done properly, women are satisfied with.

Some individuals or organizations in Europe and other places argue that circumcision/unhooding is genital mutilation. The corollary of this line of argument is generally that it should be banned. This is obviously something that Muslims disagree with.

Allah commanded the Prophet Abraham (upon him be peace) to circumcise, and Allah says in the Qur'an, "Follow the way of Abraham, as a pure monotheist." (Surah al-Nahl 123) And circumcision is part of his way; it is a ritual of obedience to God first performed by the father of the monotheistic faiths.

Also, it was practiced and advised in the time of the Prophet Muhammad (upon him be peace), for both men and women.

The official position of the Shafi'i School is that it is obligatory for a woman. There is also a weaker opinion that Imam Nawawi relates in Rawdah 10/180 that it is recommended. This is the opinion maintained by other scholars who considered that it is recommended or simply a noble deed, like Imam Abu Hanifah and Imam Malik. A woman following the Shafi'i School could make taqlid of these opinions. She would thereby be omitting a meritorious act, but not an obligation.

For a Muslim scholar to issue a fatwa against it, that violates the aforementioned consensus, and to violate consensus is impermissible. Such a fatwa would also disregard many experts from the medical community who have expressed the benefits that such procedures have for women.

And Allah knows best.

Answered by: Shaykh Yaqub Abdurrahman[102]

For any potential Muslim readers from the Shafi'i school of Islam who believe FGM is morally obligatory or who are indifferent to the procedure, please be advised that FGM does have irreversible and life-threatening health impacts for your daughters and that no qualified medical experts should be endorsing such a procedure as it has severe health risks with no benefits at all. Below is a short compilation provided by the World Health Organization (WHO) that details FGM's short-term and permanent long-term damage to the health and welfare of female children. In my honest opinion, if you pursue FGM for your children or any of your family members knowing the consequences then you obviously don't love them:

> **Health risks of female genital mutilation (FGM)**
>
> Women and girls living with FGM have experienced a harmful practice. Experience of FGM increases the short and long term health risks to women and girls and is unacceptable from a human rights and health perspective. While in general there is an increased risk of adverse health outcomes with increased severity of FGM, WHO is opposed to all forms of FGM and is emphatically against the practice being carried out by health care providers (medicalization).
>
> **Short-term health risks of FGM**
>
> **Severe pain**: cutting the nerve ends and sensitive genital tissue causes extreme pain. Proper anaesthesia is rarely used and, when used, is not always effective. The healing period is also painful. Type III FGM is a more extensive procedure of longer duration, hence the intensity and duration of pain may be more severe. The healing period is also prolonged and intensified accordingly.
> **Excessive bleeding**: (haemorrhage) can result if the clitoral artery or other blood vessel is cut during the procedure.
> **Shock**: can be caused by pain, infection and/or haemorrhage.
> **Genital tissue swelling**: due to inflammatory response or local infection.
> **Infections**: may spread after the use of contaminated instruments (e.g. use of same instruments in multiple genital mutilation operations), and during the healing period.
> **Human immunodeficiency virus (HIV)**: the direct association between FGM and HIV remains unconfirmed, although the cutting of genital tissues with the same surgical instrument without sterilization could increase the risk for transmission of HIV between girls who undergo female genital mutilation together.
> **Urination problems**: these may include urinary retention and pain passing urine. This may be due to tissue swelling, pain or injury to the urethra.
> **Impaired wound healing**: can lead to pain, infections and abnormal scarring
> **Death**: can be caused by infections, including tetanus and haemorrhage that can lead to shock.
> **Psychological consequences**: the pain, shock and the use of physical force by those performing the procedure are mentioned as reasons why many women describe FGM as a traumatic event.
>
> **Long-term health risks from Types I, II and III (occurring at any time during life)**
>
> **Pain**: due to tissue damage and scarring that may result in trapped or unprotected nerve endings.
> **Infections**:

---

[102] "Rulings from Your Site Regarding Female Circumcision Appear to Have Been Taken down. Is There Is a Change in Opinion Concerning Female Circumcision from a Shafii Point of View? What Do You Say about Issuing a Fatwa on This Issue Which Prohibits the Practice?" Translated by Yaqub Abdurrahman, *Shafii Fiqh*, shafiifiqh.com/question-details.aspx?qstID=173.

- **Chronic genital infections**: with consequent chronic pain, and vaginal discharge and itching. Cysts, abscesses and genital ulcers may also appear.
- **Chronic reproductive tract infections**: May cause chronic back and pelvic pain.
- **Urinary tract infections**: If not treated, such infections can ascend to the kidneys, potentially resulting in renal failure, septicaemia and death. An increased risk for repeated urinary tract infections is well documented in both girls and adult women.

Painful urination: due to obstruction of the urethra and recurrent urinary tract infections.
Menstrual problems: result from the obstruction of the vaginal opening. This may lead to painful menstruation (dysmenorrhea), irregular menses and difficulty in passing menstrual blood, particularly among women with Type III FGM.
Keloids: there have been reports of excessive scar tissue formation at the site of the cutting.
Human immunodeficiency virus (HIV): given that the transmission of HIV is facilitated through trauma of the vaginal epithelium which allows the direct introduction of the virus, it is reasonable to presume that the risk of HIV transmission may be increased due to increased risk for bleeding during intercourse, as a result of FGM.
Female sexual health: removal of, or damage to highly sensitive genital tissue, especially the clitoris, may affect sexual sensitivity and lead to sexual problems, such as decreased sexual desire and pleasure, pain during sex, difficulty during penetration, decreased lubrication during intercourse, reduced frequency or absence of orgasm (anorgasmia). Scar formation, pain and traumatic memories associated with the procedure can also lead to such problems.
Obstetric complications: FGM is associated with an increased risk of Caesarean section, post-partum haemorrhage, recourse to episiotomy, difficult labour, obstetric tears/lacerations, instrumental delivery, prolonged labour, and extended maternal hospital stay. The risks increase with the severity of FGM.
Obstetric fistula: a direct association between FGM and obstetric fistula has not been established. However, given the causal relationship between prolonged and obstructed labour and fistula, and the fact that FGM is also associated with prolonged and obstructed labour it is reasonable to presume that both conditions could be linked in women living with FGM.
Perinatal risks: obstetric complications can result in a higher incidence of infant resuscitation at delivery and intrapartum stillbirth and neonatal death.
Psychological consequences: some studies have shown an increased likelihood of post-traumatic stress disorder (PTSD), anxiety disorders and depression. The cultural significance of FGM might not protect against psychological complications.[103]

It should be clearly stated: any Islamic apologist, whether Muslim or non-Muslim, who continues to spread the lie that Islam has nothing to do with female genital mutilation is not morally different from people promoting anti-vaxxer campaigns that spread disinformation about vaccines. The only reason an apologist for FGM would believe that it is not morally equivalent, to lying about vaccines causing autism, is the idea of protecting sacred beliefs. The human rights – the health and welfare of young female children – should take top priority above any idiotic religious beliefs that permanently harm them. I would say the same if it were any other religion including my family background of Hinduism. People like myself who criticize these horrific practices aren't doing so because we hate Muslims, we do it because we care about the welfare of Muslims. Our criticisms and Free Speech are an act of compassion. I say the same for Hindus, Buddhists, Jains, Sikhs, Christians, and Jews who follow any barbaric practices

---

[103] "Health Risks of Female Genital Mutilation (FGM)." *World Health Organization*, World Health Organization, 1 Feb. 2017, www.who.int/reproductivehealth/topics/fgm/health_consequences_fgm/en/.

that hurt their own communities. I will criticize them all the same because I care about them. If you're spreading disinformation and attempting to shield Muslims from criticism of these practices, then you don't give a damn about the wellbeing of Muslims and you're partly to blame for the continuation of harm imposed upon Muslim children.[104] You are just being a bigot because a bigot is someone who holds two different sets of standards for different groups of people; it is an obvious lower standard towards Muslims as people.[105]

Incest

Quran 4:23:

Sahih International
Prohibited to you [for marriage] are your mothers, your daughters, your sisters, your father's sisters, your mother's sisters, your brother's daughters, your sister's daughters, your [milk] mothers who nursed you, your sisters through nursing, your wives' mothers, and your step-daughters under your guardianship [born] of your wives unto whom you have gone in. But if you have not gone in unto them, there is no sin upon you. And [also prohibited are] the wives of your sons who are from your [own] loins, and that you take [in marriage] two sisters simultaneously, except for what has already occurred. Indeed, Allah is ever Forgiving and Merciful.

Muhsin Khan
Forbidden to you (for marriage) are: your mothers, your daughters, your sisters, your father's sisters, your mother's sisters, your brother's daughters, your sister's daughters, your foster mother who gave you suck, your foster milk suckling sisters, your wives' mothers, your step daughters under your guardianship, born of your wives to whom you have gone in - but there is no sin on you if you have not gone in them (to marry their daughters), - the wives of your sons who (spring) from your own loins, and two sisters in wedlock at the same time, except for what has already passed; verily, Allah is Oft-Forgiving, Most Merciful.

Pickthall
Forbidden unto you are your mothers, and your daughters, and your sisters, and your father's sisters, and your mother's sisters, and your brother's daughters and your sister's daughters, and your foster-mothers, and your foster-sisters, and your mothers-in-law, and your step-daughters who are under your protection (born) of your women unto whom ye have gone in - but if ye have not gone in unto them, then it is no sin for you (to marry their daughters) - and the wives of your sons who (spring) from your own loins. And (it is forbidden unto you) that ye should have two sisters together, except what hath already happened (of that nature) in the past. Lo! Allah is ever Forgiving, Merciful.

Yusuf Ali
Prohibited to you (For marriage) are:- Your mothers, daughters, sisters; father's sisters, Mother's sisters; brother's daughters, sister's daughters; foster-mothers (Who gave you suck), foster-sisters; your wives' mothers; your step-daughters under your guardianship, born of your wives to whom ye have gone in,- no prohibition if ye have not gone in;- (Those who have been) wives of your sons

---

[104] Saleem, Mya, et al. "Examining Honor Culture and Violence in Islam (AHA Conference 2016)." *YouTube*, American Humanist Association, 30 June 2016, www.youtube.com/watch?v=DhwrOJvPfBw.

[105] Haider, Sarah. "Sarah Haider: Islam and the Necessity of Liberal Critique (AHA Conference 2015)." *YouTube*, American Humanist Association, 28 May 2015, www.youtube.com/watch?v=0plC24YuoJk.

proceeding from your loins; and two sisters in wedlock at one and the same time, except for what is past; for Allah is Oft-forgiving, Most Merciful;-

Shakir
Forbidden to you are your mothers and your daughters and your sisters and your paternal aunts and your maternal aunts and brothers' daughters and sisters' daughters and your mothers that have suckled you and your foster-sisters and mothers of your wives and your step-daughters who are in your guardianship, (born) of your wives to whom you have gone in, but if you have not gone in to them, there is no blame on you (in marrying them), and the wives of your sons who are of your own loins and that you should have two sisters together, except what has already passed; surely Allah is Forgiving, Merciful.

Dr. Ghali
Prohibited to you are your mothers and your daughters, and your sisters, and your paternal aunts, and your maternal aunts, and (your) brother's daughters, and (your) sister's daughters, and your mothers who have given suck to you, and your suckling sisters, and your women's mothers, and your step-daughters who are in your laps (i.e. under your guardianship) being born of your women whom you have been into-yet, in case you have not been into them, (Literally: entered with) it is no fault in you-and the lawful (spouses) of your sons who are of your loins, and that you should take to you two sisters together, except what has already gone by. Surely Allah has been Ever-Forgiving, Ever-Merciful.[106]

Quran 33:50:

Sahih International: O Prophet, indeed We have made lawful to you your wives to whom you have given their due compensation and those your right hand possesses from what Allah has returned to you [of captives] and the daughters of your paternal uncles and the daughters of your paternal aunts and the daughters of your maternal uncles and the daughters of your maternal aunts who emigrated with you and a believing woman if she gives herself to the Prophet [and] if the Prophet wishes to marry her, [this is] only for you, excluding the [other] believers. We certainly know what We have made obligatory upon them concerning their wives and those their right hands possess, [but this is for you] in order that there will be upon you no discomfort. And ever is Allah Forgiving and Merciful.

Pickthall: O Prophet! Lo! We have made lawful unto thee thy wives unto whom thou hast paid their dowries, and those whom thy right hand possesseth of those whom Allah hath given thee as spoils of war, and the daughters of thine uncle on the father's side and the daughters of thine aunts on the father's side, and the daughters of thine uncle on the mother's side and the daughters of thine aunts on the mother's side who emigrated with thee, and a believing woman if she give herself unto the Prophet and the Prophet desire to ask her in marriage - a privilege for thee only, not for the (rest of) believers - We are Aware of that which We enjoined upon them concerning their wives and those whom their right hands possess - that thou mayst be free from blame, for Allah is ever Forgiving, Merciful.

Yusuf Ali: O Prophet! We have made lawful to thee thy wives to whom thou hast paid their dowers; and those whom thy right hand possesses out of the prisoners of war whom Allah has assigned to thee; and daughters of thy paternal uncles and aunts, and daughters of thy maternal uncles and aunts, who migrated (from Makka) with thee; and any believing woman who dedicates her soul to the Prophet if the Prophet wishes to wed her;- this only for thee, and not for the

---

[106] "Surat An-Nisā' (the Women) - سورة النساء." The Noble Qur'an, legacy.quran.com/4/23. Accessed 13 Mar. 2025.

Believers (at large); We know what We have appointed for them as to their wives and the captives whom their right hands possess;- in order that there should be no difficulty for thee. And Allah is Oft-Forgiving, Most Merciful.

Shakir: O Prophet! surely We have made lawful to you your wives whom you have given their dowries, and those whom your right hand possesses out of those whom Allah has given to you as prisoners of war, and the daughters of your paternal uncles and the daughters of your paternal aunts, and the daughters of your maternal uncles and the daughters of your maternal aunts who fled with you; and a believing woman if she gave herself to the Prophet, if the Prophet desired to marry her-- specially for you, not for the (rest of) believers; We know what We have ordained for them concerning their wives and those whom their right hands possess in order that no blame may attach to you; and Allah is Forgiving, Merciful.

Muhammad Sarwar: Prophet, We have made lawful for you your wives whom you have given their dowry, slave girls whom God has given to you as gifts, the daughters of your uncles and aunts, both paternal and maternal, who have migrated with you. The believing woman, who has offered herself to the Prophet and whom the Prophet may want to marry, will be specially for him, not for other believers. We knew what to make obligatory for them concerning their wives and slave girls so that you would face no hardship (because we have given distinction to you over the believers). God is All-forgiving and All-merciful.

Mohsin Khan: O Prophet (Muhammad SAW)! Verily, We have made lawful to you your wives, to whom you have paid their Mahr (bridal money given by the husband to his wife at the time of marriage), and those (captives or slaves) whom your right hand possesses - whom Allah has given to you, and the daughters of your 'Amm (paternal uncles) and the daughters of your 'Ammah (paternal aunts) and the daughters of your Khal (maternal uncles) and the daughters of your Khalah (maternal aunts) who migrated (from Makkah) with you, and a believing woman if she offers herself to the Prophet, and the Prophet wishes to marry her; a privilege for you only, not for the (rest of) the believers. Indeed We know what We have enjoined upon them about their wives and those (captives or slaves) whom their right hands possess, - in order that there should be no difficulty on you. And Allah is Ever OftForgiving, Most Merciful.

Arberry: O Prophet, We have made lawful for thee thy wives whom thou hast given their wages and what thy right hand owns, spoils of war that God has given thee, and the daughters of thy uncles paternal and aunts paternal, thy uncles maternal and aunts maternal, who have emigrated with thee, and any woman believer, if she give herself to the Prophet and if the Prophet desire to take her in marriage, for thee exclusively, apart from the believers -- We know what We have imposed upon them touching their wives and what their right hands own -- that there may be no fault in thee; God is All-forgiving, All-compassionate.[107]

Consanguine marriages pervade in disproportionately high rates within predominately Islamic countries and communities. *Dr. S. Shamshad* from the women's college in Kurnool, India provides a review titled "*Prevalence of Consanguinity in Muslim Community*" which details the percentages of consanguine marriages within the Islamic faith tradition. It is important to note that this research is not meant to shame Muslims as people, Dr. S. Shamshad notes that consanguine marriages are prevalent within Mormon communities in the US too. Her main concern, and the concern of the

---

[107] The Quranic Arabic Corpus - Translation, corpus.quran.com/translation.jsp?chapter=33&verse=50. Accessed 12 Mar. 2025.

academic research, is on the long-term health effects of children being born in these societies:

> Abstract: Consanguinity ("blood relation", from the Latin consanguinitas) is the property of being from the same kinship as another person. In that aspect, consanguinity is the quality of being descended from the same ancestor as another person. Consanguineous marriage is frequent in many populations. In fact, it has been recently estimated that consanguineous couples and their progeny suppose about 10.4 % of the 6.7 billion global population of the world. First-cousin marriage and other types of consanguineous unions are frequent in a number of current populations from different parts of the world. Consanguinity is most common among muslim population. Consanguinity rates, coupled by the large family size in some communities, could induce the expression of autosomal recessive diseases, including very rare or new syndromes. The most thoroughly investigated are sickle cell disease, haemoglobinopathies, and enzymopathies (glucose-6-phosphate dehydrogenase deficiency). It is the duty of the public health professionals to ensure accessibility to counseling services and to periodically evaluate the knowledge and awareness of the health consequences of consanguineous marriages on offspring health so as to reduce this kind of marriages. And creating awareness among the people may lessen the chance of consanguinity.

1. Introduction

Consanguinity refers to the marriage of parents with a recent common ancestor. In humans, consanguineous marriage is frequent in many populations. In fact, it has been recently estimated that consanguineous couples and their progeny suppose about 10.4 % of the 6.7 billion global population of the world [1]. First-cousin marriage and other types of consanguineous unions are frequent in a number of current populations from different parts of the world. Consanguinity is common in several populations of the world though the consanguinity rates vary from one population to another. Furthermore, there is variability between different tribes, communities, and ethnic groups within the same country. Worldwide, wide variations in the consanguinity rates among various ethnic groups have been reported. In European populations the rates are generally less than 0 5%, while in North Africa and southern and western Asian populations 22 to 55% of all unions are consanguineous. In the majority of the US States cousin marriages are illegal under the statutes passed in the 19th and 20th centuries. The practice of consanguineous marriage, or marriage between close biological relatives, shows significant heterogeneity across the world [2], [3]. While such marriages are legal in the Middle East, Africa, the UK and Australia, they are prohibited by law in China, some parts of Europe, and the United States. Prohibitions also vary by religion. While consanguineous marriages are permitted within Islam, Buddhism and Zoroastrianism, they are forbidden by Christian Orthodox churches and require special permission for members of the Roman Catholic Church. The variations in legislative and religious rules are also reflected in the prevalence of consanguineous marriage across regions. In the western world, consanguineous marriages currently constitute less than 1% of total marriages, but this practice remains widely prevalent in many other places. Estimates range from 30—50% in Middle Eastern countries, 20-40% in North Africa, and 10— 20% in South Asia [4], [5], [6], [7], [8], [9].There is also significant variation within countries. The National Family Health Survey 1992- 93 [10] reveals that 16% of marriages are consanguineous in India, but this varies from 6% in the north to 36% in the south [11]. Some new research also suggests that the practice is growing in popularity in Western countries, particularly in migrant communities [8].

2. Prevalence of consanguinity:

>Consanguineous marriage remains common in many parts of the world and has been reported in various communities such as the Mormons [12], [13]. It is especially common in most of the Middle-Eastern countries where the custom in considered socially acceptable [14], [15], [16], [17], [18], [19], [20], [21], [22], [23], [24], [25]. The same applies to other Muslim countries and regions such as India [26], Pakistan [27], [28], [29], [30], [31] and Uzbekistan [32]. This practice continued in some of the communities who settled the West such as the Pakistani community in the UK [14], [33], [34]. In the Arab countries, consanguinity has been reported with the highest frequency in Saudi Arabia [24], where it reaches 80% of marriages in certain parts of the Kingdom. From the available data, the consanguinity rate for other countries in the Middle East ranges between 59% among the Iraqis [18], 40% among the Palestinians [21], 44% among the Yemenis in Sanaa [17] 49-58% among the Jordanians [35], [15], [16] and 40-54% in the UAE [36]. In Kuwait [37] high rates of consanguineous marriages within the particular Arab communities but low frequency of intermarriage between them, and also the presence of genetic isolates and semiisolates in some extended families and Bedouin tribes have been described. Consanguinity is less common in North African Arab countries where it was reported to be 29% in Egypt; [23] however, in another study on the Nubian population in southern Egypt the figures ranged between 41.5-45.5% [19]. The highest rates of such marriages have been reported in rural areas, among individuals with low educational levels, and among the poorest. In Morocco [38], with its contact with the outside world, a marked decrease in consanguineous unions is reported; consanguinity is disappearing and does not present a preoccupying problem for public health. However, this cannot be used as a generalization as the trend has increased in younger generations in other Arab countries such as the UAE where the rate of consanguinity has risen from 39% in the parent generations to 50.5% in the current generation [36].[108]

A separate study in 2000 on India's regional and State levels of Muslim populations found no significant changes in the rates of Consanguine marriages from the study's beginning period of 1950 to its completion in 1990.[109] Such research shows the shocking level of cultural commitment to what scientific research and consensus has already thoroughly debunked.[110] The pervasive commitment to consanguine marriages has reared itself in the West by the migrating population of Muslims. In the United Kingdom, the brave Baroness Shreela Flather; a cross-bench peer that has highlighted the oft-forgotten contribution of 5 million volunteers from India, Africa, and the Caribbean to

---

[108] Shamshad, S. "Prevalence of Consanguinity in Muslim Community - A Review." *Pdfs.semanticscholar.org*, International Journal of Science and Research (IJSR), pdfs.semanticscholar.org/f3db/08faf43477ce7c34146aa4b8db0769661efa.pdf.

[109] Bittles, A H, and R Hussain. "An Analysis of Consanguineous Marriage in the Muslim Population of India at Regional and State Levels." *Current Neurology and Neuroscience Reports.*, U.S. National Library of Medicine, www.ncbi.nlm.nih.gov/pubmed/10768421.

[110] Bittles, A H, and R Hussain. "An Analysis of Consanguineous Marriage in the Muslim Population of India at Regional and State Levels." *Current Neurology and Neuroscience Reports.*, U.S. National Library of Medicine, www.ncbi.nlm.nih.gov/pubmed/10768421.

Great Britain's campaigns in World Wars 1 and 2[111]; has highlighted the plight of children being born with horrifying birth defects in Pakistani immigrant communities.[112] Disabled children are being born within Pakistani communities because of the strong cultural and social commitment to Islam.[113] After all, Pakistanis were originally Indian and people among non-Muslim Indian communities don't have a disproportionately high level of consanguine marriages. This is not a Western versus Arab Spring cultural argument, this is about scientific evidence and the growing number of problems from this commitment to the Islamic religious tradition. Others within the British parliamentary system seem more keen on not being labeled racist and instead looking politically correct while Baroness Flather has bravely spoken out due to heartfelt concern for the damage the social practice of consanguine marriages has on children.[114]

Physical disabilities and deformities aren't the only problem with consanguine marriages. A pilot study in Southern Israel's Arab Bedouin population has found overwhelming evidence that consanguine marriages within Islamic communities located in Negev.[115] The consanguine marriages are forming mild to severe cognitive impairment for children born in Islamic communities.[116] Intellectual and development disability (IDD) is rampant throughout consanguine marriages in Israel with over 60% of children suffering from some form of IDD coming from such marriages.[117] Another study noted

---

[111] "Shreela Flather." *Wikipedia*, Wikimedia Foundation, 9 July 2018, en.wikipedia.org/wiki/Shreela_Flather.

[112] Swinford, Steven. "First Cousin Marriages in Pakistani Communities Leading to 'Appalling' Disabilities among Children." *The Telegraph*, Telegraph Media Group, 7 July 2015, www.telegraph.co.uk/news/health/children/11723308/First-cousin-marriages-in-Pakistani-communities-leading-to-appalling-disabilities-among-children.html.

[113] Swinford, Steven. "First Cousin Marriages in Pakistani Communities Leading to 'Appalling' Disabilities among Children." *The Telegraph*, Telegraph Media Group, 7 July 2015, www.telegraph.co.uk/news/health/children/11723308/First-cousin-marriages-in-Pakistani-communities-leading-to-appalling-disabilities-among-children.html.

[114] Swinford, Steven. "First Cousin Marriages in Pakistani Communities Leading to 'Appalling' Disabilities among Children." *The Telegraph*, Telegraph Media Group, 7 July 2015, www.telegraph.co.uk/news/health/children/11723308/First-cousin-marriages-in-Pakistani-communities-leading-to-appalling-disabilities-among-children.html.

[115] Saad, Hassan Abu, et al. "Consanguineous Marriage and Intellectual and Developmental Disabilities among Arab Bedouins Children of the Negev Region in Southern Israel: A Pilot Study." *Current Neurology and Neuroscience Reports.*, U.S. National Library of Medicine, 2014, www.ncbi.nlm.nih.gov/pmc/articles/PMC3904202/.

[116] Saad, Hassan Abu, et al. "Consanguineous Marriage and Intellectual and Developmental Disabilities among Arab Bedouins Children of the Negev Region in Southern Israel: A Pilot Study." *Current Neurology and Neuroscience Reports.*, U.S. National Library of Medicine, 2014, www.ncbi.nlm.nih.gov/pmc/articles/PMC3904202/.

[117] Saad, Hassan Abu, et al. "Consanguineous Marriage and Intellectual and Developmental Disabilities among Arab Bedouins Children of the Negev Region in Southern Israel: A Pilot Study." *Current*

that a horrifying 43% of all infant deaths of Bedouin children, from either physical deformities within their bodies or hereditary diseases, is attributed to the prevalence of consanguine marriages.[118]

Neurology and Neuroscience Reports., U.S. National Library of Medicine, 2014, www.ncbi.nlm.nih.gov/pmc/articles/PMC3904202/.

[118] Na'amnih, Wasef, et al. "Prevalence of Consanguineous Marriages and Associated Factors among Israeli Bedouins." *Current Neurology and Neuroscience Reports.*, U.S. National Library of Medicine, Oct. 2014, www.ncbi.nlm.nih.gov/pmc/articles/PMC4159474/.

Chapter IV: **Social Status and Genocide Denial**

I'm honestly unsure how to fully articulate this part of the issue, and I hope I provide a decent enough explanation, but please bear in mind that this might be difficult for some to accept. The term Islamophobia obscures the disturbing reality that this is really an attempt to create an unequal social status system whereby Muslims are held as more important and superior to all other groups of people. Anytime an Atheist, Jewish person, Hindu, Sikh, Jain, Buddhist, or Christian does something offensive then they are correctly viewed as a bigot; anytime a Muslim does something offensive, it is viewed as an outcry of being oppressed by the wider society. If you doubt this unequal treatment, seriously consider the following: everyone that criticizes Islam is viewed as secretly hating Muslims. All of these other groups supposedly secretly have an evil agenda of wanting to cause the most harm to Muslims; this is despite the fact that it isn't what they have said at all. All the historical, religious, and cultural criticisms that they provide are part of some "conspiracy" or "subconscious bigotry" to oppress and kill Muslims somehow despite the fact that the vast majority of critics have never said this at all nor behaved in such ways. Among those of you who agree with the term Islamophobia, shutting down these discussions is thus giving a self-satisfied honorable and righteous feeling, because you're somehow preventing those "bigots" from spreading "hate" against Muslims. Even though these critics aren't actually saying they hate Muslims, they aren't saying they want to kill Muslims, and – at least for most atheists – they don't make special exemptions to other religious beliefs; somehow, anyone who criticizes Islam is either a bigot or a "useful stooge" for bigots.

Where are these ideas coming from? Why have so many in Western countries been brought up to believe that the term Islamophobia is necessary to protect Muslims from bigots? And, if you don't know anything about the religion of Islam, how exactly are you able to determine the difference between what is genuine criticism of the theology and what is bigotry that is untrue about Islam? These feelings of self-righteousness, the shutting down of religious debate and acting "above" it, and the shielding of Muslims from any criticism of their faith tradition is really about enforcing a 7th century social standard upon the modern world and normalizing it in your own community. If you believe that anyone who critiques Islam on the basis of Free Speech is either a bigot or a useful pawn of bigots who are doing harm to Muslims, then you are honestly being conditioned into a 7th century mindset; that may sound insane, but – for reasons stated prior – the ideology of Islam really is a form of 7th century Arab fundamentalism that tries to enforce its views upon modernity.

It's important to make a clear distinction: there is somewhat of a difference between Islamists and regular Muslims in this case of shielding Islam from any criticism. Islamists want to propagate the concept of Islamophobia in order to pursue their political interests of making everything closer to the standards of the 7th century as outlined in their theology; this is for the purposes of normalizing conversion, even forced conversions, to Islam. Regular Muslims will likely feel offended and want to shut down criticisms, but they're likely to view it in a similar way to the protective social taboo on public forums of never involving ourselves in religious arguments within Western cultures and shutting them down whenever they happen under the misguided belief it leads to peaceful outcomes. The intent is different, and the two will advocate it for mutually contradictory purposes, even if the outcome is the same. A regular Muslim typically just doesn't want to involve themselves in religious debates, an Islamist typically feels it is a necessary step for the normalization and enforcement of the Sharia within the broader society. That is why they propagate these ideas and that is why these smug, self-righteous "protectors" are really analogous to guard dogs protecting harmful views. And just think of this, what other religion has so many figurative guard dogs as Islam? Whenever Hinduism is brought up in an online conversation, it's immediately mocked for the caste system which people wrongly think is still the majority view in India, despite the Pew Research statistics showing it has overwhelmingly declined in many ways and criticized within intra-Hindu contexts as bigotry against fellow Hindus.[119] It hasn't vanished to the point that inter-caste marriage is normalized yet; there is still internal family bigotry in that regard, but the discrimination within the broader society has declined to approximately nineteen percent of India's population according to Pew Research surveys.[120]

    What both Islamists and regular Muslims actually seek to do is create a bubble to shield Islam from any and all criticism; they will use every iota of excuse possible to protect Islam from any sort of meaningful criticism. The reason for this is because they believe that Islam is the revealed truth of the Abrahamic God and therefore only the "Islamic scholars" – the Muslim Imams – have any right to an opinion on it. Muslims largely believe that any distress in making Muslims doubt their faith should be completely forbidden. They will use the protective social taboo of not being allowed to criticize religion in the wider society, they will use false arguments of racism and economic inequality to shield their faith, and they will repeatedly talk about how their feelings are hurt to shut down discussions even when Muslim grooming gangs are raping children. They view all of that as a test to shield Islam from scrutiny, because they believe they are not allowed to criticize Islam and that non-Muslims are not allowed to criticize Islam. Due to Islam being "revealed truth" that they cannot question due to their unyielding faith in the Abrahamic God, they will invent outside reasons for why Islamic societies are suffering from worse discrimination or why Muslim enclaves have more

---

[119] Sahgal, Neha, et al. "Religion in India: Tolerance and Segregation." Pew Research Center, Pew Research Center, 29 June 2021, www.pewresearch.org/religion/2021/06/29/religion-in-india-tolerance-and-segregation/#2cadb6b1e440f0bf00cd84d9a5e73d3a.
[120] Sahgal, Neha, et al. "Religion in India: Tolerance and Segregation." Pew Research Center, Pew Research Center, 29 June 2021, www.pewresearch.org/religion/2021/06/29/religion-in-india-tolerance-and-segregation/#2cadb6b1e440f0bf00cd84d9a5e73d3a.

social problems in Western and Dharmic societies. Shielding them from criticism genuinely encourages them to seek out conspiratorial thinking as the reasons for why increasing Islamic influence in society is leading to worse outcomes. What Islamophobia encourages is imbibing Islamic conspiracy theories to find rationalizations for why their beliefs lead to worse outcomes compared to those who don't believe in their religion. Moreover, because it is being shielded by non-Muslims acting as figurative guard dogs, Muslims are more likely to believe that their beliefs are incapable of being challenged because they're correct. If Muslims never hear why their beliefs could be wrong, then there's no reason for them to ever doubt their beliefs.

When a person argues in defense of the term Islamophobia with the strong feelings that everyone who criticizes Islam is either a closet bigot or a useful idiot for bigots who have an evil agenda, then unfortunately that is simply conspiratorial thinking. If you argue from that standpoint, then you're not actually evaluating critics based upon what they say, and you're wrongly assuming what beliefs another person holds instead of listening to them. This leads to the same 7th century Middle Eastern conspiratorial thinking and when you shut down debate this way, it really does encourage the breakdown of society. That is the 7th century mindset that Islamism is imposing upon all of us. Please think of the consequences instead of thinking of me as some anti-Muslim bigot; grooming gangs, forcing 9-year old children into being raped, the sexual slavery of women, the inability to criticize these beliefs and practices due to Islamic views on Divine Command theory, the murder of apostates and anyone who criticizes the Prophet Mohammad, and how terrorism really is never going to end so long as this belief system exists due to the theological teachings of *bid'ah* and that the Quran cannot be questioned by either Muslims or non-Muslims. Even terms like "far-right" are becoming problematic because it's insinuating that anyone who has criticisms of Islam is somehow a Nazi; even when Jewish people are the ones criticizing Islam.

For any Muslim reading this and who strongly disagrees with me, consider the behavior of Catholics and Catholicism as a comparison point. The hatred against unmarried consensual sex between adults and the forbidding of Catholic Priests from marriage, masturbation, or unmarried consensual adult sex is largely what critics argue to be the reason for child rape cases that were possibly happening for over a thousand years within Catholic institutions. Yet, what do strong believing Catholics think when this discussion comes up? Usually they argue that it's really a conspiracy from Satan causing it to deceive Catholics away from their faith, the more anti-Semitic will argue that it is obviously a Jewish conspiracy and that Jews somehow entered the Catholic Church (a Pakistani Catholic living in Pakistan argued this exact point to me on Discord and believed it was "obvious" that Jews were magically responsible for their religion's problems), or that it's all exaggerated claims and that other places are equally as bad as their institutions. Why do they make these claims? Because they're not allowed to question the dogma of their religion, so they come-up with conspiracy theories to "make sense" of why their religious beliefs lead to bad outcomes for vulnerable children in their own communities.

Unfortunately, one of the biggest targets of Muslim conspiracy theories are Hindus like myself. Muslims largely view Hindus as polytheist, this is inaccurate as Hinduism has a wide spectrum of beliefs due to historical debates for the purpose of truthseeking and the current dominant view is pantheism. Atheism became part of Hinduism due to the influence of a pro-materialist movement called the Charvakas in approximately 600 BCE from approximately one-hundred years of debates on truth claims and by 500 BCE, the evidence suggests that the debates were so uncontested with atheists dominating Northeast India for one-hundred years, that Vedic followers decided to incorporate atheism into two schools of thought of Hinduism. To better understand why polytheism is an inaccurate view, here is Will Durant's explanation of what India's Northeastern princely states were like approximately around 600 BCE in Chapter Fifteen of *Our Oriental Heritage*:

> *"Indeed, as scholarship unearths some of the less respectable figures in Indian philosophy before Buddha, a picture takes form in which, along with saints meditating on Brahman, we find a variety of persons who despised all priests, doubted all gods, and bore without trepidition the name of Nastiks, No-sayers, Nihilists. Sangaya, the agnostic, would neither admit nor deny life after death; he questioned the possibility of knowledge, and limited philosophy to the pursuit of peace. Purana Kashyapa refused to accept moral distinctions, and taught that the soul is a passive slave to chance. Maskarin Gosala held that fate determines everything, regardless of the merits of men. Ajita Kasakambalin reduced man to earth, water, fire and wind, and said: "Fools and wise alike, on the dissolution of the body, are cut off, annihilated, and after death they are not."4 The author of the Ramayana draws a typical sceptic in Jabali, who ridicules Rama for rejecting a kingdom in order to keep a vow."*[121]

And further on in the same section, but separate subsection of Chapter Fifteen:

> *"When Buddha grew to manhood he found the halls, the streets, the very woods of northern India ringing with philosophic disputation, mostly of an atheistic and materialistic trend. The later Upanishads and the oldest Buddhist books are full of references to these heretics.6 A large class of traveling Sophists—the Paribbajaka, or Wanderers—spent the better part of every year in passing from locality to locality, seeking pupils, or antagonists, in philosophy. Some of them taught logic as the art of proving anything, and earned for themselves the titles of "Hair-splitters" and "Eelwrigglers"; others demonstrated the non-existence of God, and the inexpediency of virtue. Large audiences gathered to hear such lectures and debates; great halls were built to accommodate them; and sometimes princes offered rewards for those who should emerge victorious from these intellectual jousts.7 It was an age of amazingly free thought, and of a thousand experiments in philosophy. Not much has come down to us from these sceptics, and their memory has been preserved almost exclusively through the diatribes of their enemies.8 The oldest name among them is Brihaspati, but his nihilistic Sutras have perished, and all that remains of him is a poem denouncing the priests in language free from all metaphysical obscurity:*

---

[121] Durant, Will. Chapter XV: The Buddha: I. The Heretics (9581 - 9656). *Our Oriental Heritage: Being a History of Civilization in Egypt and the Near East to the Death of Alexander, and in India, China and Japan from the Beginning to Our Own Day*. Simon and Schuster, 1935.

> *No heaven exists, no final liberation,*
> *No soul, no other world, no rites of caste....*
> *The triple Veda, triple self-command,*
> *And all the dust and ashes of repentance—*
> *These yield a means of livelihood for men*
> *Devoid of intellect and manliness....*
> *How can this body when reduced to dust*
> *Revisit earth?*
> *And if a ghost can pass*
> *To other worlds, why does not strong affection*
> *For those he leaves behind attract him back?*
> *The costly rites enjoined for those who die*
> *Are but a means of livelihood devised*
> *By sacerdotal cunning—nothing more....*
> *While life endures let life be spent in ease*
> *And merriment; let a man borrow money*
> *From all his friends, and feast on melted butter.9*

"Out of the aphorisms of Brihaspati came a whole school of Hindu materialists, named, after one of them, Charvakas. They laughed at the notion that the Vedas were divinely revealed truth; truth, they argued, can never be known, except through the senses. Even reason is not to be trusted, for every inference depends for its validity not only upon accurate observation and correct reasoning, but also upon the assumption that the future will behave like the past; and of this, as Hume was to say, there can be no certainty.10 What is not perceived by the senses, said the Charvakas, does not exist; therefore the soul is a delusion, and Atman is humbug. We do not observe, in experience or history, any interposition of supernatural forces in the world. All phenomena are natural; only simpletons trace them to demons or gods.11 Matter is the one reality; the body is a combination of atoms;12 the mind is merely matter thinking; the body, not the soul, feels, sees, hears, thinks.13 "Who has seen the soul existing in a state separate from the body?" There is no immortality, no rebirth. Religion is an aberration, a disease, or a chicanery; the hypothesis of a god is useless for explaining or understanding the world. Men think religion necessary only because, being accustomed to it, they feel a sense of loss, and an uncomfortable void, when the growth of knowledge destroys this faith.14 Morality, too, is natural; it is a social convention and convenience, not a divine command. Nature is indifferent to good and bad, virtue and vice, and lets the sun shine indiscriminately upon knaves and saints; if nature has any ethical quality at all it is that of transcendent immorality. There is no need to control instinct and passion, for these are the instructions of nature to men. Virtue is a mistake; the purpose of life is living, and the only wisdom is happiness.15 This revolutionary philosophy of the Charvakas put an end to the age of the Vedas and the Upanishads. It weakened the hold of the Brahmans on the mind of India, and left in Hindu society a vacuum which almost compelled the growth of a new religion. But the materialists had done their work so thoroughly that both of the new religions which arose to replace the old Vedic faith were, anomalous though it may sound, atheistic religions, devotions without a god. Both belonged to the Nastika or Nihilistic movement; and both were originated not by the Brahman priests but by members of the Kshatriya warrior caste, in a reaction against sacerdotal ceremonialism and theology. With the coming of Jainism and Buddhism a new epoch began in the history of India.[122]

Please note that he had to oversimplify a bit since he was making a series of history books that encompassed the entire world. It would be more accurate to say that

---

[122] Durant, Will. Chapter XV: The Buddha: I. The Heretics (9581 - 9656). *Our Oriental Heritage: Being a History of Civilization in Egypt and the Near East to the Death of Alexander, and in India, China and Japan from the Beginning to Our Own Day.* Simon and Schuster, 1935.

Hindus of the time period self-described themselves as the Vedic people and whether the Charvaka philosophers would consider themselves part of the Dharmic fold seems like a debatable historical argument. However, two key points should be noted: Vedic texts gave an open-ended view to the perspective of Agnosticism since the Rigveda's time approximately around 3000 – 2000 BCE[123] and by 500 BCE; due to the Charvaka philosophy's dominance for approximately 100 years, Vedic practitioners of the Samkhya and Mimamsa schools adapted their atheistic perspective into the Vedic tradition and they both remain part of Hinduism. Judging from the historical evidence, the Buddha himself was agnostic to the question of whether a God exists and left it up to each Buddhist to decide for themselves. Eventually, through the debate and inquiry of Adi Shankara centuries later, pantheism became the dominant view within India and still remains so amongst the majority of Hindus to this day.

Despite these historical facts, the perception most Muslims have of Hindus remains unchanged and the nuances of Hinduism are ignored by the majority of the world. Obviously, it shouldn't matter whether someone is polytheistic or not, but the teachings of the Quran are what inform Muslim views that they're not allowed to question. These teachings do inform behavior; the only exception within Muslim-majority countries to the best of my knowledge, and only very recently, seems to be the United Arab Emirates and it seems conditioned on the expectation that increased tourism and economic trade will remain beneficial to the UAE. I would like to believe that this could spark genuine change towards modernity, but if an economic recession occurs and Hindus are no longer perceived as economically useful by the majority of the UAE government and Muslim-majority public, who will be the first targets of blame? Who will suffer violence first? It's possible that the uniqueness of the UAE government will help protect vulnerable religious minorities, but only time will tell. In the interests of fairness, while other Muslim-majority countries have horribly mistreated and persecuted Hindus, the UAE government does stand as a singular outlier so far, but conditioned on the expectation of future economic gains.

The Quranic teachings of those perceived as "polytheist" and "disbelievers" makes it clear exactly what the majority of Muslims in the world think of we Hindus. Both these teachings and their consequences continue to be ignored when it comes to most Muslim majority countries treatment of their Hindu minority groups and other religious minority groups:

Quran Chapter 9, Verse 5:

---

[123] Sridhar, Nithin. "Vedic and Harappan Are Respectively Literary and Material Facets of Same Civilization: B. B. Lal." NewsGram, 2 Dec. 2015, www.newsgram.com/vedic-and-harappan-are-respectively-literary-and-material-facets-of-same-civilization-b-b-lal

Sahih International

And when the sacred months have passed, then kill the polytheists wherever you find them and capture them and besiege them and sit in wait for them at every place of ambush. But if they should repent, establish prayer, and give zakah, let them [go] on their way. Indeed, Allah is Forgiving and Merciful.

Muhsin Khan

Then when the Sacred Months (the Ist, 7th, 11th, and 12th months of the Islamic calendar) have passed, then kill the Mushrikun (see V.2:105) wherever you find them, and capture them and besiege them, and prepare for them each and every ambush. But if they repent and perform As-Salat (Iqamat-as-Salat), and give Zakat, then leave their way free. Verily, Allah is Oft-Forgiving, Most Merciful.

Pickthall

Then, when the sacred months have passed, slay the idolaters wherever ye find them, and take them (captive), and besiege them, and prepare for them each ambush. But if they repent and establish worship and pay the poor-due, then leave their way free. Lo! Allah is Forgiving, Merciful.

Yusuf Ali

But when the forbidden months are past, then fight and slay the Pagans wherever ye find them, an seize them, beleaguer them, and lie in wait for them in every stratagem (of war); but if they repent, and establish regular prayers and practise regular charity, then open the way for them: for Allah is Oft-forgiving, Most Merciful.

Shakir

So when the sacred months have passed away, then slay the idolaters wherever you find them, and take them captives and besiege them and lie in wait for them in every ambush, then if they repent and keep up prayer and pay the poor-rate, leave their way free to them; surely Allah is Forgiving, Merciful.

Dr. Ghali

So, when the prohibiting months are drawn away, (Literally: stripped away) then kill the associators wherever you find them, and take them, and detain them, and sit (in wait) for them at every place of observation (i.e., ambush). But, in case they repent, and keep up the prayer, and bring the Zakat, (i.e., pay the obligatory poor-dues) then let them go their way; (Literally: pass on their way) surely Allah is Ever-Forgiving, Ever-Merciful..[124]

Quran Chapter 9, Verse 17:

Sahih International

It is not for the polytheists to maintain the mosques of Allah [while] witnessing against themselves with disbelief. [For] those, their deeds have become worthless, and in the Fire they will abide eternally.

---

[124] "Surat At-Tawbah (the Repentance) - سورة التوبة." The Noble Qur'an, quran.com, legacy.quran.com/9/5. Accessed 22 Mar. 2025.

Muhsin Khan

It is not for the Mushrikun (polytheists, idolaters, pagans, disbelievers in the Oneness of Allah), to maintain the Mosques of Allah (i.e. to pray and worship Allah therein, to look after their cleanliness and their building, etc.), while they witness against their ownselves of disbelief. The works of such are in vain and in Fire shall they abide.

Pickthall

It is not for the idolaters to tend Allah's sanctuaries, bearing witness against themselves of disbelief. As for such, their works are vain and in the Fire they will abide.

Yusuf Ali

It is not for such as join gods with Allah, to visit or maintain the mosques of Allah while they witness against their own souls to infidelity. The works of such bear no fruit: In Fire shall they dwell.

Shakir

The idolaters have no right to visit the mosques of Allah while bearing witness to unbelief against themselves, these it is whose doings are null, and in the fire shall they abide.

Dr. Ghali

In no way should the associators (Those who associate others with Allah) tend the mosques of Allah, witnessing against themselves disbelief; those, their deeds are frustrated, and in the Fire they are eternally (abiding (..[125]

Quran Chapter 9, Verse 28:

Sahih International

O you who have believed, indeed the polytheists are unclean, so let them not approach al-Masjid al-Haram after this, their [final] year. And if you fear privation, Allah will enrich you from His bounty if He wills. Indeed, Allah is Knowing and Wise.

Muhsin Khan

O you who believe (in Allah's Oneness and in His Messenger (Muhammad SAW)! Verily, the Mushrikun (polytheists, pagans, idolaters, disbelievers in the Oneness of Allah, and in the Message of Muhammad SAW) are Najasun (impure). So let them not come near Al-Masjid-al-Haram (at Makkah) after this year, and if you fear poverty, Allah will enrich you if He will, out of His Bounty. Surely, Allah is All-Knowing, All-Wise.

Pickthall

O ye who believe! The idolaters only are unclean. So let them not come near the Inviolable Place of Worship after this their year. If ye fear poverty (from the loss of their merchandise) Allah shall preserve you of His bounty if He will. Lo! Allah is Knower, Wise.

Yusuf Ali

---

[125] "Surat At-Tawbah (the Repentance) - سورة التوبة." The Noble Qur'an, quran.com, legacy.quran.com/9/17. Accessed 22 Mar. 2025.

O ye who believe! Truly the Pagans are unclean; so let them not, after this year of theirs, approach the Sacred Mosque. And if ye fear poverty, soon will Allah enrich you, if He wills, out of His bounty, for Allah is All-knowing, All-wise.

Shakir

O you who believe! the idolaters are nothing but unclean, so they shall not approach the Sacred Mosque after this year; and if you fear poverty then Allah will enrich you out of His grace if He please; surely Allah is Knowing Wise.

Dr. Ghali

O you who have believed, surely the associators (Those who associate others with Allah) are only an impurity; so they should not come near the Inviolable Mosque after this season (Literally: after this duration = (this year) of theirs. And if you fear want, then Allah will eventually enrich you of His Grace, in case He (so) decides; surely Allah is Ever-Knowing, Ever-Wise..[126]

Quran Chapter 9, Verse 33:

Sahih International

It is He who has sent His Messenger with guidance and the religion of truth to manifest it over all religion, although they who associate others with Allah dislike it.

Muhsin Khan

It is He Who has sent His Messenger (Muhammad SAW) with guidance and the religion of truth (Islam), to make it superior over all religions even though the Mushrikun (polytheists, pagans, idolaters, disbelievers in the Oneness of Allah) hate (it).

Pickthall

He it is Who hath sent His messenger with the guidance and the Religion of Truth, that He may cause it to prevail over all religion, however much the idolaters may be averse.

Yusuf Ali

It is He Who hath sent His Messenger with guidance and the Religion of Truth, to proclaim it over all religion, even though the Pagans may detest (it).

Shakir

He it is Who sent His Messenger with guidance and the religion of truth, that He might cause it to prevail over all religions, though the polytheists may be averse.

Dr. Ghali

He (is The One) Who has sent His Messenger with the guidance and the religion of Truth that He may make it topmost over all religion, though the associators (Those who associate others with Allah) hate (that)..[127]

---

[126] "Surat At-Tawbah (the Repentance) - سورة التوبة." The Noble Qur'an, quran.com, legacy.quran.com/9/28. Accessed 22 Mar. 2025.

[127] "Surat At-Tawbah (the Repentance) - سورة التوبة." The Noble Qur'an, quran.com, legacy.quran.com/9/33. Accessed 22 Mar. 2025.

Quran Chapter 9, Verse 36:

Sahih International

Indeed, the number of months with Allah is twelve [lunar] months in the register of Allah [from] the day He created the heavens and the earth; of these, four are sacred. That is the correct religion, so do not wrong yourselves during them. And fight against the disbelievers collectively as they fight against you collectively. And know that Allah is with the righteous [who fear Him].

Muhsin Khan

Verily, the number of months with Allah is twelve months (in a year), so was it ordained by Allah on the Day when He created the heavens and the earth; of them four are Sacred, (i.e. the 1st, the 7th, the 11th and the 12th months of the Islamic calendar). That is the right religion, so wrong not yourselves therein, and fight against the Mushrikun (polytheists, pagans, idolaters, disbelievers in the Oneness of Allah) collectively, as they fight against you collectively. But know that Allah is with those who are Al-Muttaqun (the pious - see V.2:2).

Pickthall

Lo! the number of the months with Allah is twelve months by Allah's ordinance in the day that He created the heavens and the earth. Four of them are sacred: that is the right religion. So wrong not yourselves in them. And wage war on all of the idolaters as they are waging war on all of you. And know that Allah is with those who keep their duty (unto Him).

Yusuf Ali

The number of months in the sight of Allah is twelve (in a year)- so ordained by Him the day He created the heavens and the earth; of them four are sacred: that is the straight usage. So wrong not yourselves therein, and fight the Pagans all together as they fight you all together. But know that Allah is with those who restrain themselves.

Shakir

Surely the number of months with Allah is twelve months in Allah's ordinance since the day when He created the heavens and the earth, of these four being sacred; that is the right reckoning; therefore be not unjust to yourselves regarding them, and fight the polytheists all together as they fight you all together; and know that Allah is with those who guard (against evil).

Dr. Ghali

Surely the (right) (i.e. fixed) number of the months in the Providence of Allah is twelve months (ordained) in the Book of Allah the day that He created the heavens and the earth. Four of them are prohibiting. (i.e., fighting is prohibited during them) That is the most upright religion. So do not do (any) injustice to yourselves during them; (i.e., durimg the prohibited during them) and fight the associators as a whole as they fight you as a whole; and know that Allah is with the pious..[128]

Quran Chapter 9, Verse 66:

---

[128] "Surat At-Tawbah (the Repentance) - سورة التوبة." The Noble Qur'an, quran.com, legacy.quran.com/9/36. Accessed 22 Mar. 2025.

Sahih International

Make no excuse; you have disbelieved after your belief. If We pardon one faction of you - We will punish another faction because they were criminals.

Muhsin Khan

Make no excuse; you have disbelieved after you had believed. If We pardon some of you, We will punish others amongst you because they were Mujrimun (disbelievers, polytheists, sinners, criminals, etc.).

Pickthall

Make no excuse. Ye have disbelieved after your (confession of) belief. If We forgive a party of you, a party of you We shall punish because they have been guilty.

Yusuf Ali

Make ye no excuses: ye have rejected Faith after ye had accepted it. If We pardon some of you, We will punish others amongst you, for that they are in sin.

Shakir

Do not make excuses; you have denied indeed after you had believed; if We pardon a party of you, We will chastise (another) party because they are guilty.

Dr. Ghali

Do not excuse yourselves. You have readily disbelieved after your belief; in case We are clement towards a section of you, We will torment (another) section, for that they have been criminals.".[129]

Quran Chapter 9, Verse 109:

Sahih International

Then is one who laid the foundation of his building on righteousness [with fear] from Allah and [seeking] His approval better or one who laid the foundation of his building on the edge of a bank about to collapse, so it collapsed with him into the fire of Hell? And Allah does not guide the wrongdoing people.

Muhsin Khan

Is it then he, who laid the foundation of his building on piety to Allah and His Good Pleasure, better, or he who laid the foundation of his building on an undetermined brink of a precipice ready to crumble down, so that it crumbled to pieces with him into the Fire of Hell. And Allah guides not the people who are the Zalimun (cruel, violent, proud, polytheist and wrong-doer).

Pickthall

Is he who founded his building upon duty to Allah and His good pleasure better; or he who founded his building on the brink of a crumbling, overhanging precipice so that it toppled with him into the fire of hell? Allah guideth not wrongdoing folk.

---

[129] "Surat At-Tawbah (the Repentance) - سورة التوبة." The Noble Qur'an, quran.com, legacy.quran.com/9/66. Accessed 22 Mar. 2025.

Yusuf Ali

Which then is best? - he that layeth his foundation on piety to Allah and His good pleasure? - or he that layeth his foundation on an undermined sand-cliff ready to crumble to pieces? and it doth crumble to pieces with him, into the fire of Hell. And Allah guideth not people that do wrong.

Shakir

Is he, therefore, better who lays his foundation on fear of Allah and (His) good pleasure, or he who lays his foundation on the edge of a cracking hollowed bank, so it broke down with him into the fire of hell; and Allah does not guide the unjust people.

Dr. Ghali

So, is he who founded his structure upon piety to Allah and all-blessed Satisfaction more charitable, or he who founded his structure upon the brink of a toppling precipice, (and) so it has toppled down with him in the fire of Hell? And Allah does not guide the unjust people.[130]

Quran Chapter 9, Verse 113:

Sahih International

It is not for the Prophet and those who have believed to ask forgiveness for the polytheists, even if they were relatives, after it has become clear to them that they are companions of Hellfire.

Muhsin Khan

It is not (proper) for the Prophet and those who believe to ask Allah's Forgiveness for the Mushrikun (polytheists, idolaters, pagans, disbelievers in the Oneness of Allah) even though they be of kin, after it has become clear to them that they are the dwellers of the Fire (because they died in a state of disbelief).

Pickthall

It is not for the Prophet, and those who believe, to pray for the forgiveness of idolaters even though they may be near of kin (to them) after it hath become clear that they are people of hell-fire.

Yusuf Ali

It is not fitting, for the Prophet and those who believe, that they should pray for forgiveness for Pagans, even though they be of kin, after it is clear to them that they are companions of the Fire.

Shakir

It is not (fit) for the Prophet and those who believe that they should ask forgiveness for the polytheists, even though they should be near relatives, after it has become clear to them that they are inmates of the flaming fire.

Dr. Ghali

---

[130] "Surat At-Tawbah (the Repentance) - سورة التوبة." The Noble Qur'an, quran.com, legacy.quran.com/9/109. Accessed 22 Mar. 2025.

In no way should the Prophet and the ones who have believed ask forgiveness for the associators, (Those who associate others with ' Allah) even if they are near of kin, even after it has become evident to them that they will be the companions (i.e., inhabitants) in Hell-Fire.[131]

Quran Chapter 10, Verse 13:

Sahih International

And We had already destroyed generations before you when they wronged, and their messengers had come to them with clear proofs, but they were not to believe. Thus do We recompense the criminal people

Muhsin Khan

And indeed, We destroyed generations before you, when they did wrong while their Messengers came to them with clear proofs, but they were not such as to believe! Thus do We requite the people who are Mujrimun (disbelievers, polytheists, sinners, criminals, etc.).

Pickthall

We destroyed the generations before you when they did wrong; and their messengers (from Allah) came unto them with clear proofs (of His Sovereignty) but they would not believe. Thus do We reward the guilty folk.

Yusuf Ali

Generations before you We destroyed when they did wrong: their messengers came to them with clear-signs, but they would not believe! thus do We requite those who sin!

Shakir

And certainly We did destroy generations before you when they were unjust, and their messengers had come to them with clear arguments, and they would not believe; thus do We recompense the guilty people.

Dr. Ghali

And We have already caused the generations even before you to perish as soon as they did injustice and their Messengers came to them with the Supreme evidences; and in no way were they to believe; thus We recompense the criminal people.[132]

Quran Chapter 98, Verse 6:

Sahih International

---

[131] "Surat At-Tawbah (the Repentance) - سورة التوبة." The Noble Qur'an, quran.com, legacy.quran.com/9/113. Accessed 22 Mar. 2025.
[132] "Surat Yūnus (Jonah) - سورة يونس." The Noble Qur'an, quran.com, legacy.quran.com/10/13. Accessed 22 Mar. 2025.

Indeed, they who disbelieved among the People of the Scripture and the polytheists will be in the fire of Hell, abiding eternally therein. Those are the worst of creatures.

Muhsin Khan

Verily, those who disbelieve (in the religion of Islam, the Quran and Prophet Muhammad (Peace be upon him)) from among the people of the Scripture (Jews and Christians) and Al-Mushrikun will abide in the Fire of Hell. They are the worst of creatures.

Pickthall

Lo! those who disbelieve, among the People of the Scripture and the idolaters, will abide in fire of hell. They are the worst of created beings.

Yusuf Ali

Those who reject (Truth), among the People of the Book and among the Polytheists, will be in Hell-Fire, to dwell therein (for aye). They are the worst of creatures.

Shakir

Surely those who disbelieve from among the followers of the Book and the polytheists shall be in the fire of hell, abiding therein; they are the worst of men.

Dr. Ghali

Surely (the ones) who have disbelieved among the population of the Book (Or: family of the Book; i.e., the Jews and Christians) and the associators (Those who associate others with Allah) will be in the Fire of Hell, eternally (abiding) therein; those are they who are the most evil beings (Literally: Initiated creatures).[133]

And the historic consequences of these hateful teachings in the Quran; this is what Hindus, Buddhists, Jains, and others of India suffered, according to Chapter Sixteen of Will Durant's *Our Oriental Heritage*:

> Each winter Mahmud descended into India, filled his treasure chest with spoils, and amused his men with full freedom to pillage and kill; each spring he returned to his capital richer than before. At Mathura (on the Jumna) he took from the temple its statues of gold encrusted with precious stones, and emptied its coffers of a vast quantity of gold, silver and jewelry; he expressed his admiration for the architecture of the great shrine, judged that its duplication would cost one hundred million dinars and the labor of two hundred years, and then ordered it to be soaked with naphtha and burnt to the ground.73 Six years later he sacked another opulent city of northern India, Somnath, killed all its fifty thousand inhabitants, and dragged its wealth to Ghazni. In the end he became, perhaps, the richest king that history has ever known. Sometimes he spared the population of the ravaged cities, and took them home to be sold as slaves; but so great was the number of such captives that after some years no one could be found to offer more than a few shillings for a slave. Before every important engagement Mahmud knelt in prayer, and asked the blessing of God upon his arms. He reigned for a third of a century; and when he died, full of years and honors, Moslem historians ranked him as the greatest monarch of his time, and one of the greatest sovereigns of any age.74

---

[133] "Surat Al-Bayyinah (the Clear Proof) - سورة البينة." The Noble Qur'an, quran.com, legacy.quran.com/98/6. Accessed 22 Mar. 2025.

Seeing the canonization that success had brought to this magnificent thief, other Moslem rulers profited by his example, though none succeeded in bettering his instruction. In 1186 the Ghuri, a Turkish tribe of Afghanistan, invaded India, captured the city of Delhi, destroyed its temples, confiscated its wealth, and settled down in its palaces to establish the Sultanate of Delhi—an alien despotism fastened upon northern India for three centuries, and checked only by assassination and revolt. The first of these bloody sultans, Kutb-d Din Aibak, was a normal specimen of his kind—fanatical, ferocious and merciless. His gifts, as the Mohammedan historian tells us, "were bestowed by hundreds of thousands, and his slaughters likewise were by hundreds of thousands." In one victory of this warrior (who had been purchased as a slave), "fifty thousand men came under the collar of slavery, and the plain became black as pitch with Hindus."75 Another sultan, Balban, punished rebels and brigands by casting them under the feet of elephants, or removing their skins, stuffing these with straw, and hanging them from the gates of Delhi. When some Mongol inhabitants who had settled in Delhi, and had been converted to Islam, attempted a rising, Sultan Alau-d-din (the conquerer of Chitor) had all the males—from fifteen to thirty thousand of them—slaughtered in one day. Sultan Muhammad bin Tughlak acquired the throne by murdering his father, became a great scholar and an elegant writer, dabbled in mathematics, physics and Greek philosophy, surpassed his predecessors in bloodshed and brutality, fed the flesh of a rebel nephew to the rebel's wife and children, ruined the country with reckless inflation, and laid it waste with pillage and murder till the inhabitants fled to the jungle. He killed so many Hindus that, in the words of a Moslem historian, "there was constantly in front of his royal pavilion and his Civil Court a mound of dead bodies and a heap of corpses, while the sweepers and executioners were wearied out by their work of dragging" the victims "and putting them to death in crowds."[134]

Currently in India's schools, this history is not taught. Instead, Indian schoolchildren are taught the utter myth that Hindus and Muslims lived in harmony and that these Muslim warlords were somehow benign rulers. Most Muslims will tell people that Islam came into South Asia through a fabricated myth of trade until South Asians gradually converted. The true history of India has been mocked, insulted, treated with indifference, and falsely argued to be a myth itself despite Islam's own history and even how the vast number of Muslim-majority countries treat Hindus and other religious minorities to this day. It wasn't until I had listened to the arguments of mostly Pakistani and Iranian Ex-Muslim Atheists living in Canada and the United States that I was better able to distinguish the facts from the falsehoods. Yet, why do these distortions of history continue to persist? Why is basic information about history treated as a conspiracy theory meant to harm Muslims? The answer is both simple and disturbing upon a better understanding of Islamic theology itself; Muslims are conditioned to view Islam as completely beyond doubt and anything that makes Muslims question or feel moral distress regarding their faith is considered less important than the feelings Muslims have about their faith; this is especially true for their feelings for the Prophet Mohammad. In other words, Muslims are conditioned to view their personal feelings as more important than the historic abuses, genocides, and generational traumas that their religion has

---

[134] Durant, Will. Chapter XVI: From Alexander to Aurangzeb: VI. The Moslem Conquest (Pgs. 10447-10520). Our Oriental Heritage: Being a History of Civilization in Egypt and the Near East to the Death of Alexander, and in India, China and Japan from the Beginning to Our Own Day. Simon and Schuster, 1935.

caused non-Muslims. In twenty or thirty years, nobody should be surprised if there's attempts by Muslim "historians" or their supporters to claim the Yazidi genocide, the Syrian Christian genocide, or the violence towards Hindus and Christians happening in Bangladesh are somehow "distortions" or "conspiracies" so that Muslims continue to feel good about their faith. It is no different than how the majority of Muslims in the world have dismissed the Islamic conquest of India and the Armenian Christian genocide as "conspiracies" meant to make Muslims doubt their faith.

What has been the effect of this censorship and distortion of history? The false narrative is that both Hindus and Muslims were peaceful up until the British committed divide-and-conquer policies. This has caused the majority of Muslims to believe that Hindus became deluded by British culture causing them to react with unjustified extremism and that Muslims are somehow oppressed. The truth is that Hindus and Muslims were never at peace in the early contact period of their history, Hindus and other Dharmic followers were largely the victims of genocide under Muslim rule in a massive death toll that's estimated to have been approximately between 60 – 80 million[135], and Hindus of India are forbidden to even talk about it and accused of being conspiracy theorists when trying to discuss our historic trauma. It is likely that many of my fellow Hindus unfortunately still believe that this history is a falsehood, because they've imbibed the falsifications of self-stylized experts from Western Indology who readily confess in their *Oxford Handbook of Indian Philosophy* that they know nothing about India's history. Yet, they readily claim the mass death tolls written by all of the Muslim historians who were serving under Muslim rulers; in which they were celebrating the mass murder of Hindus for approximately 700 years; are exaggerations and distortions.[136] These Western Indologists like Sheldon Pollock, Cynthia Talbot, and Andrew Nicholson and Indian Indologists like Romila Thapar readily and gleefully participate in this form of genocide denial and claim Hindus are bigots for wanting to discuss our historic trauma.[137] They use claims of expertise that they do not have to explicitly support genocide denial. They don't study history, they don't study archaeology, they don't even study the theological concepts of Hinduism, and their only knowledge seems to be knowing how to translate words without understanding the social, cultural, and theological contexts of Dharmic theology.

As I don't want to be seen as singling only them out and for those who doubt this criticism of mine, here is my brief examination and review of the *Oxford Handbook of*

---

[135] Elst, Koenraad. Chapter Two: Negationism in India (pgs. 56 – 59). Negationism in India: Concealing the Record of Islam. Voice of India, 2014.
[136] Nicholson, Andrew J. Chapter 10: Hindu Unity And The Non-Hindu Other (4806-5293). Unifying Hinduism: Philosophy and Identity in Indian Intellectual History (South Asia Across the Disciplines). Columbia University Press, 2010.
[137] Nicholson, Andrew J. Chapter 10: Hindu Unity And The Non-Hindu Other (4806-5293). Unifying Hinduism: Philosophy and Identity in Indian Intellectual History (South Asia Across the Disciplines). Columbia University Press, 2010.

Indian Philosophy that I had written as a subsection of Chapter Twenty-Seven of my earlier book, *Faith in Doubt*, in which I critiqued the purported methodology of Western Indology:

The Oxford Handbook of Indian Philosophy

I'll begin my critique with *The Oxford Handbook of Indian Philosophy* of 2017, which was reprinted in 2018, and since I can't make lengthy quotes of any portion of the book without the express permission of Oxford University Press, I'll have to lay out in explicit terms what I find problematic with these Indologist critiques and may sometimes list both the chapters and pages of those chapters when necessary. While my primary aim is criticizing US Indology, I've chosen to critique others in Western Indology insofar as they show the same failings of US Indology and sustain arguments based on either insufficient or bad evidence. Usually, it is a complete lack of evidence on their part. Essentially, the underlying assumptions should be highlighted and then critiqued in order to expose the failings of what may well be this entire department on a global scale throughout the West, if the most current version of *The Oxford Handbook of Indian Philosophy* as of 2019 serves as an indication. As it would be beyond the scope of this book to give a general review of the entirety of its contents, I've narrowed the focus to pertinent specifics that I'll be addressing, I've settled for critiquing the Introduction and the four chapters of *Part 1: Methods, Literatures, and Histories* of *The Oxford Handbook of Indian Philosophy* which exists as the main thesis of the textbook; it is geared to explain to an audience of upcoming Indologists about what to expect in the academic discipline. I've chosen this method due to constraints, as I'm of the opinion that the entirety of the text is problematic due to ample evidence from the textbook itself and the chapters that I've read outside of Part 1.

I'll begin with the introductory chapter, "*Introduction: Why Indian Philosophy? Why Now?*" by the editor of the textbook, Jonardon Ganeri, who is listed as a Global Network Professor of Philosophy, Faculty of Arts and Science at New York University and a visiting Professor at King's College.[138] His chapter shows no evidence that he has any awareness or knowledge of the mass genocides of the Indian population during the Islamic conquests of India[139]; on page 4, he refers to the purported Aryan settlers that Indian archaeologists have shown to be a falsehood with extensive evidence that'll be detailed in another section below and the introductory page itself mentions the so-called impact of British colonialism but never mentions the Islamic colonialism prior to that.[140]

---

[138] Kapstein, Matthew T., et al. Contributors (IX - XVII). *The Oxford Handbook of Indian Philosophy*. Edited by Jonardon Ganeri, Oxford University Press, 2018.

[139] Kapstein, Matthew T., et al. Introduction: Why Indian Philosophy? Why now? by Jonardon Ganeri (1-14). *The Oxford Handbook of Indian Philosophy*. Edited by Jonardon Ganeri, Oxford University Press, 2018.

[140] Kapstein, Matthew T., et al. Introduction: Why Indian Philosophy? Why now? by Jonardon Ganeri (Pg.4). *The Oxford Handbook of Indian Philosophy*. Edited by Jonardon Ganeri, Oxford University

On page 8, he briefly touches upon so-called Mughal patronage but fails to mention the massacres and colossal death toll of Islam's ravaging, plundering, and enslavement of Indians throughout the entirety of the Indian subcontinent.[141] This has been copiously documented by legendary historian, Will Durant. In volume 1 of his series *The Story of Civilization: Our Oriental Heritage*, Will Durant details the mass genocides perpetuated by Islamic invaders in Chapter 16 from subsection "*VI. The Moslem Conquest*" to the very end of Chapter 16 of *The Story of Civilization: Our Oriental Heritage*.[142] Will Durant himself refers to it as "probably the bloodiest story in history" before going into the grizzly details.[143] At no point does Jonardon Ganeri show any indication that he is knowledgeable about this history at all throughout the Introduction of *The Oxford Handbook of Indian Philosophy* and seems to depict interactions between Indians and the Islamic invaders as congenial when the only time period that could credibly be argued would be under Akbar the Great after he had de-converted from Islam, ordered the shutdown of the mosques throughout India, and forbade the teachings of the Quran.[144][145] However, before and after Akbar under more pious Islamic rulers, the story is an unambiguous bloodbath and Will Durant doesn't mince words or soften the details of the horror that Islam brought upon India.[146] If you doubt this, feel free to read Chapter 16, subsection VI all the way to the end of Chapter 16 of *The Story of Civilization: Our Oriental Heritage*.[147] The only time the practitioners of Sanatana Dharma - be it Hindu, or Buddhist, or Jain, or later on the Sikhs - ever lived in any peace during Islamic rule was when a Islamic ruler de-converted from Islam and rejected the Islamic religion. At

---

Press, 2018.

[141] Kapstein, Matthew T., et al. Introduction: Why Indian Philosophy? Why now? by Jordan Ganeri (Pg. 8). *The Oxford Handbook of Indian Philosophy*. Edited by Jonardon Ganeri, Oxford University Press, 2018.

[142] Durant, Will. Chapter XVI: From Alexander to Aurangzeb (10072 - 10817). *Our Oriental Heritage: Being a History of Civilization in Egypt and the Near East to the Death of Alexander, and in India, China and Japan from the Beginning to Our Own Day*. Simon and Schuster, 1935.

[143] Durant, Will. Chapter XVI: From Alexander to Aurangzeb: VI. The Moslem Conquest (Pgs. 10447-10448). *Our Oriental Heritage: Being a History of Civilization in Egypt and the Near East to the Death of Alexander, and in India, China and Japan from the Beginning to Our Own Day*. Simon and Schuster, 1935.

[144] Kapstein, Matthew T., et al. Introduction: Why Indian Philosophy? Why now? by Jonardon Ganeri (1-14). *The Oxford Handbook of Indian Philosophy*. Edited by Jonardon Ganeri, Oxford University Press, 2018.

[145] Durant, Will. Chapter XVI: From Alexander to Aurangzeb: VII. Akbar The Great (Pgs. 10520 - 10691). *Our Oriental Heritage: Being a History of Civilization in Egypt and the Near East to the Death of Alexander, and in India, China and Japan from the Beginning to Our Own Day*. Simon and Schuster, 1935.

[146] Durant, Will. Chapter XVI: From Alexander to Aurangzeb (10072 - 10817). *Our Oriental Heritage: Being a History of Civilization in Egypt and the Near East to the Death of Alexander, and in India, China and Japan from the Beginning to Our Own Day*. Simon and Schuster, 1935.

[147] Durant, Will. Chapter XVI: From Alexander to Aurangzeb (10072 - 10817). *Our Oriental Heritage: Being a History of Civilization in Egypt and the Near East to the Death of Alexander, and in India, China and Japan from the Beginning to Our Own Day*. Simon and Schuster, 1935.

no point does Jonardon Ganeri put this in proper context and doesn't even seem to be aware of this history in his introductory chapter.[148]

The next chapter was what made me lose confidence in Western Indology and gradually caused me to change my views on this entire enterprise called Indology within the US, but this view may be applicable throughout the West too. I had assumed that they based their views on hard evidence, but "*Chapter 1: Interpreting Indian Philosophy Three Parables*" by Matthew T. Kapstein, a Professor at the University of Chicago who purportedly specializes in Tibetan Buddhism, makes it clear that this isn't true.[149] Kapstein explains without any ambiguity on pages 15-16 of the book that Western Indologists have absolutely no criteria for determining what interpretations are valid and what aren't valid.[150] They don't base their understanding from any deep understanding of the ancient Sanatana Dharma theology and they hold no special knowledge or criterion of procedures for how to develop an understanding of Indian philosophies.[151] In short, they haven't developed any method at all that can make accurate and reliable judgments on the theology of Hinduism.[152] In fact, Kapstein outright explains on page 16 that hermeneutics, with the exclusion of legal hermeneutics, offers absolutely nothing as a guideline to demarcate valid and honest interpretations from dishonest or unreliable interpretations.[153] This means that they have no method at all for separating their own make-believe with any potentially credible scholarship. Kapstein claims that Indology attempts to utilize archaeology, but this is plainly proven false since they never accepted information from Indian archaeologists who reliably and credibly debunked the Aryan Race Conspiracy Theory with scientific and historical evidence.[154] The Aryan Race theory was supported by Nazism and Adolf Hitler. Western Indologists have held onto those Nazi viewpoints which pervades the entirety of *The Oxford Handbook of Indian*

---

[148] Kapstein, Matthew T., et al. Introduction: Why Indian Philosophy? Why now? by Jonardon Ganeri (1-14). *The Oxford Handbook of Indian Philosophy*. Edited by Jonardon Ganeri, Oxford University Press, 2018.

[149] Kapstein, Matthew T., et al. Contributors (IX - XVII). *The Oxford Handbook of Indian Philosophy*. Edited by Jonardon Ganeri, Oxford University Press, 2018.

[150] Kapstein, Matthew T., et al. Chapter 1: Interpreting Indian Philosophy Three Parables by Matthew Kapstein (15-16). *The Oxford Handbook of Indian Philosophy*. Edited by Jonardon Ganeri, Oxford University Press, 2018.

[151] Kapstein, Matthew T., et al. Chapter 1: Interpreting Indian Philosophy Three Parables by Matthew Kapstein (15-31). *The Oxford Handbook of Indian Philosophy*. Edited by Jonardon Ganeri, Oxford University Press, 2018.

[152] Kapstein, Matthew T., et al. Chapter 1: Interpreting Indian Philosophy Three Parables by Matthew Kapstein (15-31). *The Oxford Handbook of Indian Philosophy*. Edited by Jonardon Ganeri, Oxford University Press, 2018.

[153] Kapstein, Matthew T., et al. Chapter 1: Interpreting Indian Philosophy Three Parables by Matthew Kapstein (Pg. 16). *The Oxford Handbook of Indian Philosophy*. Edited by Jonardon Ganeri, Oxford University Press, 2018.

[154] Kapstein, Matthew T., et al. Chapter 1: Interpreting Indian Philosophy Three Parables by Matthew Kapstein (15-31). *The Oxford Handbook of Indian Philosophy*. Edited by Jonardon Ganeri, Oxford University Press, 2018.

Philosophy of 2017-2018 despite the Aryan Race theory having been debunked in 2014-2015 by Indian archaeologists through empirical and scientific evidence.[155][156][157] For whatever reason, Western Indologists have since tried to push these Nazi theories that they've held as sacrosanct into the work of modern Western geneticists, possibly without the awareness of the broader scientific community that the methods of Indology are arbitrary, unreliable, and seem to be pure guesswork without any basis on historic evidence. One must question why these Western Indologists hold onto these Nazi theories so strongly and dismiss any criticism from outside as not part of their arbitrary consensus that isn't based on empirical evidence. And, if the scientific community doesn't know about how unreliable their methods are, then why weren't Western scientists duly informed and instead have had their meaningful scientific work, their trust, and goodwill co-opted by Western Indologists? Further along in Chapter 1, on pages 20 - 23 in the subsection titled "*The Meaning of Moksa*" in the book, Kapstein cherry-picks three philosophers - Rousseau, Locke, and Hobbes - in order to ignorantly assert that Western philosophy's entire body of work on the terminology of the word freedom is based upon civic governments and political participation.[158] He demonstrates no understanding of Dharmic teachings of *Moksha* being an existential philosophical disposition and he shows no indication that existential philosophers of so-called Anglophone and continental philosophy such as Schopenhauer was influenced by the Upanishads[159]; Nietzsche was profoundly influenced and impressed by Buddhism even declaring it, and the intellectual capacity of the Brahmins of Sanatana Dharma, as entirely superior to Christianity in *The Anti-Christ*.[160][161] How did Kapstein miss not only the basic usage of Moksha's terminology of freedom, but also two of the most famous Western philosophers who were influenced by Dharmic views on freedom? Why did he use a reductionist argument on the various philosophical dispositions of Western Philosophy's views on freedom? Even from

---

[155] Kapstein, Matthew T., et al. *The Oxford Handbook of Indian Philosophy*. Edited by Jonardon Ganeri, Oxford University Press, 2018.

[156] Sridhar, Nithin. "No Evidence for Warfare or Invasion; Aryan Migration Too Is a Myth: B B Lal." *NewsGram*, 30 Nov. 2015, www.newsgram.com/no-evidence-for-warfare-or-invasion-aryan-migration-too-is-a-myth-b-b-lal

[157] Sridhar, Nithin. "Vedic and Harappan Are Respectively Literary and Material Facets of Same Civilization: B. B. Lal." *NewsGram*, 2 Dec. 2015, www.newsgram.com/vedic-and-harappan-are-respectively-literary-and-material-facets-of-same-civilization-b-b-lal

[158] Kapstein, Matthew T., et al. Chapter 1: Interpreting Indian Philosophy Three Parables by Matthew Kapstein (Pg. 20-23). *The Oxford Handbook of Indian Philosophy*. Edited by Jonardon Ganeri, Oxford University Press, 2018.

[159] Durant, Will. Chapter XIV: The Foundations of India: VII. The Philosophy of the Upanishads (9463 - 9469). *Our Oriental Heritage: Being a History of Civilization in Egypt and the Near East to the Death of Alexander, and in India, China and Japan from the Beginning to Our Own Day*. Simon and Schuster, 1935.

[160] Nietzsche, Friedrich Wilhelm. Aphorism 23. *THE ANTICHRIST*. Translated by H. L. Mencken, The Project Gutenberg, 2006.

[161] Kapstein, Matthew T., et al. Chapter 1: Interpreting Indian Philosophy Three Parables by Matthew Kapstein (15-31). *The Oxford Handbook of Indian Philosophy*. Edited by Jonardon Ganeri, Oxford University Press, 2018.

his chosen selection, he doesn't seem to be aware of the extent Rousseau praised and had his philosophy influenced by Islamic theology.

However, another equally compelling issue must be asked: how can any so-called "consensus" within the sphere of Western Indology be allowed to dismiss empirical scientific evidence by Indian archaeologists?[162][163] Moreover, on what grounds can Western Indology claim any special privilege on knowledge of Hinduism over any random Hindu individual when they have no methods and their so-called research is the equivalent of any random person making a blind guess?[164] How can they dismiss Rajiv Malhotra or any other Hindu who has criticism on the basis of consensus, when their consensus is pure blind guessing with no real methodology, they have no recognition of Hindu practices like Yogi, and there is no evidence from their behavior of any interest in archaeology that disproves Nazi theories that they harbor? To my surprise, throughout *The Oxford Handbook of Indian Philosophy*, Western Indologists demonstrate no awareness of the mass genocide by Islamic conquests elaborated by historian Will Durant in *The Story of Civilization: Our Oriental Heritage* and the subsequent mass starvation policies which may also credibly constitute genocide caused by British colonialism as copiously documented by historian and Marxist Mike Davis in his work, *Late Victorian Holocausts: El Nino Famines and the Making of the Third World* in which he collected and referenced numerous documented accounts by mostly US Christian missionaries and US journalists who spoke out against the British policies in defense of the human rights of the people of India.[165][166] How can they claim to be searching for proper context and a better understanding of India's changing philosophies throughout the history of the subcontinent, if they categorically ignore the most notorious impacts of Islamic and British imperialism?[167][168][169] Judging from their lack of methodology, I don't quite

---

[162] Sridhar, Nithin. "No Evidence for Warfare or Invasion; Aryan Migration Too Is a Myth: B B Lal." *NewsGram*, 30 Nov. 2015, www.newsgram.com/no-evidence-for-warfare-or-invasion-aryan-migration-too-is-a-myth-b-b-lal

[163] Sridhar, Nithin. "Vedic and Harappan Are Respectively Literary and Material Facets of Same Civilization: B. B. Lal." *NewsGram*, 2 Dec. 2015, www.newsgram.com/vedic-and-harappan-are-respectively-literary-and-material-facets-of-same-civilization-b-b-lal

[164] Kapstein, Matthew T., et al. Chapter 1: Interpreting Indian Philosophy Three Parables by Matthew Kapstein (15-31). *The Oxford Handbook of Indian Philosophy*. Edited by Jonardon Ganeri, Oxford University Press, 2018.

[165] Durant, Will. Chapter XVI: From Alexander to Aurangzeb (10072 - 10817). *Our Oriental Heritage: Being a History of Civilization in Egypt and the Near East to the Death of Alexander, and in India, China and Japan from the Beginning to Our Own Day*. Simon and Schuster, 1935.

[166] Davis, Mike. *Late Victorian Holocausts: El Nino Famines and the Making of the Third World*. Penguin Random House Publisher Services, 2001.

[167] Kapstein, Matthew T., et al. Chapter 1: Interpreting Indian Philosophy Three Parables by Matthew Kapstein (15-31). *The Oxford Handbook of Indian Philosophy*. Edited by Jonardon Ganeri, Oxford University Press, 2018.

[168] Durant, Will. Chapter XVI: From Alexander to Aurangzeb (10072 - 10817). *Our Oriental Heritage: Being a History of Civilization in Egypt and the Near East to the Death of Alexander, and in India, China and Japan from the Beginning to Our Own Day*. Simon and Schuster, 1935.

[169] Davis, Mike. *Late Victorian Holocausts: El Nino Famines and the Making of the Third World*.

understand why Indians of the Dharmic faiths within India even bother protesting or view anything Western Indologists say as credible when any random opinion that they have on their own religion is actually more valid than the so-called hermeneutic methodology which is quite honestly just pure, blind guesswork on the part of these so-called scholars in the West.[170] It's a methodology that claims to have no methodology and just makes random guesses with the hopes that others who are equally as uninformed about Hinduism agree with them. This insularity can be comparable with the *Tafsir* of Islam, but with the clear difference that they claim nobody outside their insular community has any right to an opinion on a religion that isn't even theirs. Kapstein ends the chapter by emphasizing that Western Indologists have no conceptual framework except for hypothetical ideas that they critique each other with and it is thus a reaffirmation that they have no knowledge beyond pure, blind guesswork.[171]

Chapter 2 "*History and Doxography of the Philosophical Schools*" by Ashok Aklujkar, a Sanskritist and Indologist working at the University of British Columbia[172], falsely assumes an isolated distinction between Western Philosophy and Sanatana Dharma on page 32 since it isn't as clearly demarcated as he assumed and will be explained further below.[173] He asserts that proper guidance is required (assuming Western Indologists) but fails to detail specific procedures since Western Indology has none according to the chapter prior to his chapter.[174][175] Finally, he contradicts himself on page 35 and continuing on to page 36 by first correctly asserting that Indian Philosophy isn't irrational and then using the very stereotype that he just stated was wrong by demarcating philosophy as purely rational and then implying religion that isn't based on rational arguments should have its definition broadened as somehow conforming to rationality.[176] This is simply a self-contradiction that is trying to re-contextualize words

---

Penguin Random House Publisher Services, 2001.

[170] Kapstein, Matthew T., et al. Chapter 1: Interpreting Indian Philosophy Three Parables by Matthew Kapstein (15-31). *The Oxford Handbook of Indian Philosophy*. Edited by Jonardon Ganeri, Oxford University Press, 2018.

[171] Kapstein, Matthew T., et al. Chapter 1: Interpreting Indian Philosophy Three Parables by Matthew Kapstein (15-31). *The Oxford Handbook of Indian Philosophy*. Edited by Jonardon Ganeri, Oxford University Press, 2018.

[172] Kapstein, Matthew T., et al. Contributors (IX - XVII). *The Oxford Handbook of Indian Philosophy*. Edited by Jonardon Ganeri, Oxford University Press, 2018.

[173] Kapstein, Matthew T., et al. Chapter 2: History and Doxography of the Philosophical Schools by Ashok Aklujkar (Pg. 32). *The Oxford Handbook of Indian Philosophy*. Edited by Jonardon Ganeri, Oxford University Press, 2018.

[174] Kapstein, Matthew T., et al. Chapter 1: Interpreting Indian Philosophy Three Parables by Matthew Kapstein (15-31). *The Oxford Handbook of Indian Philosophy*. Edited by Jonardon Ganeri, Oxford University Press, 2018.

[175] Kapstein, Matthew T., et al. Chapter 2: History and Doxography of the Philosophical Schools by Ashok Aklujkar (32-55). *The Oxford Handbook of Indian Philosophy*. Edited by Jonardon Ganeri, Oxford University Press, 2018.

[176] Kapstein, Matthew T., et al. Chapter 2: History and Doxography of the Philosophical Schools by Ashok Aklujkar (32-55). *The Oxford Handbook of Indian Philosophy*. Edited by Jonardon Ganeri, Oxford University Press, 2018.

by redefining illogical beliefs within Hinduism as somehow rational, but refusing to simply use actual rational arguments within Hinduism itself. Chapter 3 "*Philosophy As A Distinct Cultural Practice*" by Justin E. H. Smith, listed as a Professor of History and Philosophy of Science at the Universite Paris Diderot (Paris 7)[177], explicitly begins on page 56 by asserting the audience of Indology is for people of "European" or "Western" backgrounds and then goes onto explain that comparative studies should never include comparing philosophies of two distinct cultural backgrounds.[178] On page 57, he asserts that Greece and India only had significant contact in geography and astronomy, he explains how the philosophical exchange that created Pyrrhonian skepticism by Christopher Beckworth has been dismissed without any explanation why, and goes onto explain that there seems to be no evidence of a philosophical exchange between Greece and India because there is no "smoking gun" at all.[179] Evidently, Smith is either utterly ignorant of or entirely dismissive of the period of Hellenization of India that occurred shortly after the defeat of Alexander the Great[180]; many Greek people migrated in droves.[181] The cities and military colonies of Alexander the Great were expanded by the Greek migration from approximately 70 to an additional 250 and eventually, the Greco-Bactarian kingdom was formed by King Demetrius I of Bactria from his successful invasion of Northern India in which there is evidence to indicate that he effectively ruled over it.[182] A cultural syncretism that is unparallel in history proceeded for almost 200 years from 180 BCE to 10 CE.[183] This astonishing level of peaceful intermingling of what is known as the Indo-Greek kingdoms is shown from several compelling pieces of evidence. The Greek and Indian languages and symbols fused within the coinage such as the Greek language in the front and the Pali language in the back.[184] Archaeological

---

[177] Kapstein, Matthew T., et al. Contributors (IX - XVII). *The Oxford Handbook of Indian Philosophy*. Edited by Jonardon Ganeri, Oxford University Press, 2018.

[178] Kapstein, Matthew T., et al. Chapter 3: Philosophy as a Distinct Cultural Practice: The Transregional Context by Justin E.H. Smith (Pg. 56). *The Oxford Handbook of Indian Philosophy*. Edited by Jonardon Ganeri, Oxford University Press, 2018.

[179] Kapstein, Matthew T., et al. Chapter 3: Philosophy as a Distinct Cultural Practice: The Transregional Context by Justin E.H. Smith (Pg. 57). *The Oxford Handbook of Indian Philosophy*. Edited by Jonardon Ganeri, Oxford University Press, 2018.

[180] Kapstein, Matthew T., et al. Chapter 3: Philosophy as a Distinct Cultural Practice: The Transregional Context by Justin E.H. Smith (56-74). *The Oxford Handbook of Indian Philosophy*. Edited by Jonardon Ganeri, Oxford University Press, 2018.

[181] Ghose, Sanujit. "Cultural Links between India & the Greco-Roman World." *Ancient History Encyclopedia*, Ancient History Encyclopedia, 30 Apr. 2019, www.ancient.eu/article/208/cultural-links-between-india--the-greco-roman-worl/.

[182] Ghose, Sanujit. "Cultural Links between India & the Greco-Roman World." *Ancient History Encyclopedia*, Ancient History Encyclopedia, 30 Apr. 2019, www.ancient.eu/article/208/cultural-links-between-india--the-greco-roman-worl/.

[183] Ghose, Sanujit. "Cultural Links between India & the Greco-Roman World." *Ancient History Encyclopedia*, Ancient History Encyclopedia, 30 Apr. 2019, www.ancient.eu/article/208/cultural-links-between-india--the-greco-roman-worl/.

[184] Ghose, Sanujit. "Cultural Links between India & the Greco-Roman World." *Ancient History Encyclopedia*, Ancient History Encyclopedia, 30 Apr. 2019, www.ancient.eu/article/208/cultural-links-between-india--the-greco-roman-worl/.

evidence shows the blending of Ancient Greek and Ancient Sanatana Dharma practices; statues of the Buddha protected by the Greek God Herakles/Heracles, statues of Mahayana Buddhist deities, and Greco-Buddhist statues of the Buddha in general.[185] Given all of this fascinating history, which Smith doesn't demonstrate to have any knowledge of in Chapter 3[186], is it reasonable to believe that there was no cultural exchange of philosophical viewpoints or a shared philosophy? There is ample, compelling evidence that indicates Buddhism flourished as a result of this cultural exchange which may have conceivably helped spread Buddhism to East Asia.[187] Yet, despite this astonishing history, Western Indologists expect people to believe that there was no philosophical exchange or perhaps that this almost 200 years of history doesn't count as a significant and compelling wealth of evidence of such exchange?[188][189] Does that honestly make sense? Further along on pages 58-59, Justin E. H. Smith demonstrates no understanding that Adivasi is a term coined in the 1930s for people in India who didn't own land and doesn't mean that they were the original inhabitants as he heavily implies since all Indians are the original inhabitants of India.[190] On page 59, he wrongly presumes that the debunked Nazi Aryan Race theory is true by claiming that Adivasi traditions show evidence of pre-Aryan origins.[191] He can only claim that it is pre-Aryan, if he assumes the Nazi conspiracy theory is true.[192] He goes on in page 59 to argue the dubious claim that all philosophical positions have anthropological roots which implies that people throughout history can't have used their reasoning faculties or imagination.[193]

---

[185] Ghose, Sanujit. "Cultural Links between India & the Greco-Roman World." *Ancient History Encyclopedia*, Ancient History Encyclopedia, 30 Apr. 2019, www.ancient.eu/article/208/cultural-links-between-india--the-greco-roman-worl/.

[186] Kapstein, Matthew T., et al. Chapter 3: Philosophy as a Distinct Cultural Practice: The Transregional Context by Justin E.H. Smith (56-74). *The Oxford Handbook of Indian Philosophy*. Edited by Jonardon Ganeri, Oxford University Press, 2018.

[187] Ghose, Sanujit. "Cultural Links between India & the Greco-Roman World." *Ancient History Encyclopedia*, Ancient History Encyclopedia, 30 Apr. 2019, www.ancient.eu/article/208/cultural-links-between-india--the-greco-roman-worl/.

[188] Kapstein, Matthew T., et al. Chapter 3: Philosophy as a Distinct Cultural Practice: The Transregional Context by Justin E.H. Smith (56-74). *The Oxford Handbook of Indian Philosophy*. Edited by Jonardon Ganeri, Oxford University Press, 2018.

[189] Ghose, Sanujit. "Cultural Links between India & the Greco-Roman World." *Ancient History Encyclopedia*, Ancient History Encyclopedia, 30 Apr. 2019, www.ancient.eu/article/208/cultural-links-between-india--the-greco-roman-worl/.

[190] Kapstein, Matthew T., et al. Chapter 3: Philosophy as a Distinct Cultural Practice: The Transregional Context by Justin E.H. Smith (Pg. 58-59). *The Oxford Handbook of Indian Philosophy*. Edited by Jonardon Ganeri, Oxford University Press, 2018.

[191] Kapstein, Matthew T., et al. Chapter 3: Philosophy as a Distinct Cultural Practice: The Transregional Context by Justin E.H. Smith (Pg. 59). *The Oxford Handbook of Indian Philosophy*. Edited by Jonardon Ganeri, Oxford University Press, 2018.

[192] Kapstein, Matthew T., et al. Chapter 3: Philosophy as a Distinct Cultural Practice: The Transregional Context by Justin E.H. Smith (Pg. 59). *The Oxford Handbook of Indian Philosophy*. Edited by Jonardon Ganeri, Oxford University Press, 2018.

[193] Kapstein, Matthew T., et al. Chapter 3: Philosophy as a Distinct Cultural Practice: The Transregional Context by Justin E.H. Smith (Pg. 59). *The Oxford Handbook of Indian Philosophy*. Edited by Jonardon Ganeri, Oxford University Press, 2018.

Finally, the only useful content that can be gleaned on page 70 is that a Mughal leader attempted to fuse the psychotic teachings of the book, the Quran, as being somehow proved true by the mostly more intellectual and interesting Upanishads; Smith demonstrates no knowledge as to how utterly absurd such a task is, but instead Smith discusses some insane translator by the name of Francois Bernier who cut open animals in front of a Hindu pandit to teach the pandit philosophy and Smith acts as if this was a failure of cultural exchange instead of the act itself being entirely insane on the part of Bernier as it is doubtful most people in the West would begin a cultural exchange by butchering a living animal (in this case, a goat) in front of non-Westerners.[194] Finally, there isn't much to be said about Chapter 4, "*Comparison or Confluence of Philosophy*" by Mark Siderits, a retired Analytical Asian Philosophy Professor from Seoul National University[195]. The entirety of the chapter reaffirms comparative philosophy being unwilling to mix philosophies with the pretense that they're isolated and then he mentions fusion philosophy, but then warns that it could be a form of cultural appropriation and mangling an Indian philosophical school's ideas.[196] One wonders why on earth a person couldn't simply reference where they got an idea and then explain how their new idea departs from it before exploring their own philosophical inquiry.

Did Islamic Conquest and Colonization Slaughter around 60 – 80 million Hindus?

There's been attempts to obfuscate and confuse what the arguments for this assertion are. It did not originate from Koenraad Elst, he simply cited the historian, Kishori Saran Lal, who made the argument in the book, *Growth of Muslim Population in Medieval India (1000 – 1800)*. I've come to my own conclusion after reading K.S. Lal's book that the claim is credible, but I believe that it was likely the more conservative estimates of approximately 60 million deaths within 500 years due to Islamic conquest and rule. Moreover, it wasn't just Hindus but Buddhists and likely other Dharmic followers who suffered these massacres too. To explain why, I'll just provide my review of his book:

I can only give my own subjective opinion, but I was personally so blown away by how informative this book was that I felt so compelled to keep reading and it was never boring. I don't quite know how to put in terms how amazing this book was and how much I'd have preferred reading a physical copy instead of a PDF copy that had some parts very difficult to read due to the legibility in some parts, which I later cross-

---

[194] Kapstein, Matthew T., et al. Chapter 3: Philosophy as a Distinct Cultural Practice: The Transregional Context by Justin E.H. Smith (56-74). *The Oxford Handbook of Indian Philosophy*. Edited by Jonardon Ganeri, Oxford University Press, 2018.

[195] Kapstein, Matthew T., et al. Contributors (IX - XVII). *The Oxford Handbook of Indian Philosophy*. Edited by Jonardon Ganeri, Oxford University Press, 2018.

[196] Kapstein, Matthew T., et al. Chapter 4: Comparison or Confluence in Philosophy? by Mark Sideritis (75-92). *The Oxford Handbook of Indian Philosophy*. Edited by Jonardon Ganeri, Oxford University Press, 2018.

referenced with similar written material in a PDF copy of one of his other works, "*Indian Muslims: Who Are They?*" to better understand everything. It was barely different in those key points and I was able to read most of the more difficultly smudged portions by powering through. This book was basically everything I ever wanted in terms of a general overview of understanding important portions of India's history during Islamic conquest and rule, which I didn't ever get a clear picture of when reading Western Indologists. I'm very sorry if that sounds political, but it shouldn't be and I can only give my own best arguments in as honest a manner possible.

From historian Kishori Saran Lal's book, *Growth of Muslim Population in Medieval India,* he makes the case as follows: within the Preface, he explains that Hindus and Muslims clashed and coexisted for eight-hundred years, which seemed far more academically honest than others. Kishori Saran Lal explains in *Growth of Muslim Population in Medieval India* that the estimates are based upon significant historical computation of reported demographic behavior from the sources that he's used. He separated the time periods into four parts of: A. D. 1000 to 1200, 1200 to 1400, 1400 to 1600, and 1600 to 1800 on the basis of the rise and fall of different Islamic monarchies and their overall impact on the population of India. Lal explains that much of the book's studies were assisted by other professors during his time researching and writing it; a visiting Professor of the University of Chicago, David F. Lach provided him with demographic tables of European cities. This was to compare population estimates to how European travelers compared different locales in India to their own European civilizations. He explains a Professor of Demography in the Institute of Economic Growth, Ashish Bose, read through the first draft, offered advice for certain areas of the book, and helped Lal prepare the Tables and Diagrams. Dr. Suren Navalakha of the Asian Research Centre gave significant information to assist in better understanding the growth of the Muslim population in Bengal. Dr. H. C. Varma prepared the Index of the book. Something I've never seen anyone mention is that K.S. Lal explained some of the calculations for his research were done by Dr. Feroz Ahmad of the Physics department of the University of Delhi; Lal briefly mentions that Dr. Ahmad did this "ungrudgingly" which means that Dr. Ahmad wanted to help.

In *"Part I: The Data"* within the subsection *"Source Materials and Limitations of Demographic Data"* from pages three through nine, K. S. Lal explains data of 1000 – 1200 is done by cross-referencing among various Arab or Persian geographers and travelers and he makes the case that he only added their estimates of the population sizes as authentic when they all agreed upon the same events and the similar range of figures or archaeology could back-up their claims.[197] He notes on page four the example that

---

[197] Lal, Kishori Saran. "Growth of Muslim Population in Medieval India (1000-1800)" Internet Archive, Internet Archive, 5 Aug. 2018,

Alberuni, Utbi, Baihaqi, Ibn al-Asir all give similar information on the decline and dispersal of the Indian population due to Mahmud of Ghazni's invasions of India, as an example.[198] Data from 1300 – 1700s by Islamic court officials and Islamic historians would be from people who could directly interview Islamic military officials, including those doing the Islamic war campaigns, and they would have had access to Islamic royal libraries of the Delhi Sultanate and Mughal empire to cross-reference population estimates even if those records no longer exist for us. K.S. Lal lists Ziyariddsu Bafani, Amir Khusrau. Isaml, and Shams Siraj Afif as his sources for the Delhi Sultanate period; for the Mughal time period, he lists Babur, Abul Fazl, Nizamuddin Ahmad, Khafi Khan, and says that Firishta (formally named Muhammad Qasim Hindu Shah Astarabadi) is a very descriptive writer. He explains they're ultimately the most trustworthy, even if they do exaggerate a few numbers here or there; the references to the historic times of Emperor Akbar are especially useful because Akbar had multiple population consensuses done during his time, even if those records were lost. On page five, Lal explains that from the 16th century onwards, Persian writers become very detailed including with information on population statistics.[199]

Within the subsection where he explains the methodological limits titled *"Some Methodological Problems of Estimating Population"* which range from pages ten through twenty-two, K.S. Lal explains on page ten that definite population statistics don't exist for any country in pre-consensus times and all historians are forced to work with the limitations of those who were eyewitness accounts and evidence provided by archaeology. K.S. Lal explains the limits of the Arab and Persian writers is that they're faulty with figures and statistics when it comes to the number of towns and villages on pages 10 – 11; judging from what he explains later, it seems that the Arab and Persian writers had very good details about urban life, but let their imagination run wild on villages because they never bothered to visit them. For example, on page eighteen, Lal says that Islamic historians gave very thorough and detailed information on the pricing of foodgrains, the amount and rate of revenue of their respective Sultanates and Islamic empires, price-schedules on revenue demands, and the listings of other commodities. K.S. Lal further explains on page 18 as follows regarding how he utilized this information and why it is important: *"For instance, many chroniclers give reliable data about the prices of foodgrains and other commodities pertaining to their times. About the same period the*

---

ia902800.us.archive.org/11/items/GrowthOfMuslimPopulationInMedievalIndiaAd10001800/Growth-Of-Muslim-Population-In-Medieval-India-ad-1000-1800_text.pdf.

[198] Lal, Kishori Saran. "Growth of Muslim Population in Medieval India (1000-1800)" Internet Archive, Internet Archive, 5 Aug. 2018, ia902800.us.archive.org/11/items/GrowthOfMuslimPopulationInMedievalIndiaAd10001800/Growth-Of-Muslim-Population-In-Medieval-India-ad-1000-1800_text.pdf.

[199] Lal, Kishori Saran. "Growth of Muslim Population in Medieval India (1000-1800)" Internet Archive, Internet Archive, 5 Aug. 2018, ia902800.us.archive.org/11/items/GrowthOfMuslimPopulationInMedievalIndiaAd10001800/Growth-Of-Muslim-Population-In-Medieval-India-ad-1000-1800_text.pdf.

amount of revenue, the rate of revenue, the price-schedules on which the revenue demand was settled, are also given. All this information helps in calculating 'the total amount of produce on which the then population subsisted and estimating, on the basis of per capita consumption of foodgrains and other edibles, the then density of population. Thus, in spite of their few weaknesses, the facts and figures supplied by medieval chroniclers are of great value in our study."[200] Therefore, the urban population statistics are vastly more reliable because the overwhelming majority of these writers were actually there to visit these places at the time and they made copious notes. A major weakness is that, due to receiving patronage from Islamic rulers and Islamic royal families, some Islamic writers tended to exaggerate the military size of the Sultans and Emperors as a way of glorifying them in the battlefield. Unless there is archaeological evidence or other writers giving context to support these claims, the strength of the Islamic military forces needed to be carefully assessed with skepticism and cross-referenced by the other writers who give similar statistics on military forces to give credibility to the numbers. K.S. Lal essentially always chose the conservative estimates by writers on the scale of massacres of Hindus and only accepted the sizes of military forces if multiple Islamic writers cited the same range of statistical figures.

Islamic court officials giving detailed accounts about the military forces of Sultans and Emperors were essentially more reliable due to the rich amount of details on the number of forces, weaponry, and their accounts of skulls or heads taken from the massacres of Hindus. K.S. Lal explains on pages sixteen – seventeen that Medieval wars consisted of Islamic rulers encouraging their military personnel to make a tower of heads or skulls of Hindus by giving cash rewards for slaying them and that the Islamic court officials could count the heads at their leisure, interview military officials who would give them the number of heads counted from military campaigns they participated in, go to the Islamic archives where such records would have been recorded, or be given the information from other government officials who had records. K.S. Lal explains on page seventeen the Islamic historians and recordkeepers had access to court archives for estimated population figures to cross-reference all their material because they were usually serving under the patronage of the Islamic ruler or their royal family[201]; he notes that if foreigners were granted access to the archives, then it's doubtless that the official Royal Court-appointed historians of the Emperors' and royal families' would also have

---

[200] Lal, Kishori Saran. "Growth of Muslim Population in Medieval India (1000-1800)" Internet Archive, Internet Archive, 5 Aug. 2018, ia902800.us.archive.org/11/items/GrowthOfMuslimPopulationInMedievalIndiaAd10001800/Growth-Of-Muslim-Population-In-Medieval-India-ad-1000-1800_text.pdf.

[201] Lal, Kishori Saran. "Growth of Muslim Population in Medieval India (1000-1800)" Internet Archive, Internet Archive, 5 Aug. 2018, ia902800.us.archive.org/11/items/GrowthOfMuslimPopulationInMedievalIndiaAd10001800/Growth-Of-Muslim-Population-In-Medieval-India-ad-1000-1800_text.pdf.

access.[202] Therefore, K.S. Lal says that they are very useful, informative, and trustworthy sources overall despite a few exaggerations and limitations. From 1400s – 1600s, Western travelers and Muslim court officials giving similar or the same estimates of various populations would ultimately be the most trustworthy. The comparison of population statistics that European travelers make to their own European cities are also a useful reference. The most egregious weakness of European travelers specifically, despite their detailed approach, was that they sometimes failed to distinguish Hindus and Muslims and so their information must be taken with great care. K.S. Lal even notes the perplexing information that has dumbfounded historians of India; on pages eighteen – nineteen, he explains that Vasco da Gama was very ignorant of the Hindu religion despite spending three months living in India since his arrival on May 17, 1498. Vasco da Gama mistook a Hindu temple for a chapel and prayed there in Calicut.[203] The major weakness of both Islamic and European writers was that these estimates were mostly for cities and usually did not account for rural areas among all these various groups of people. European travelers and Islamic writers mainly travelled and were interested in urban areas and not rural areas, according to Lal. Moreover, these are obviously pre-modern consensus figures, but K.S. Lal mentions taken altogether the information on India's population history is above average compared to the gaps in most other societies and it is clear that this is mainly due to the thorough work of Islamic geographers, travelers, and Court officials for approximately seven-hundred to eight-hundred years of history.

This book was frankly amazing. While Kishori Saran Lal has a very slight bias for Hinduism, he doesn't mince words on how brutal and foolish Hindu Rajas were compared to Muslim Sultans. In Pages 39 – 51, Lal explains that the Turkish and Tughlaq bloodthirsty rule and cruelty was during a time when they had wars with Rajputs and also with each other. Lal makes it clear that Rajputs were warring amongst themselves too. He never ignored Hindu deaths as a result of Intra-Hindu violence. Beyond the trappings of Sultan and Raja, the idea that every ruler had during the Medieval period was to seize it all for their own power and privilege. However, the cruelty visited upon Hindu serfs by Islamic rulers was unique compared to the more sporadic and rarer instances of Hindu Rajas being so murderous to serfs under their rule. This was especially true for the treatment of women. Whereas Buddhism and Adi Shankara's brand of Brahmanism reduced women's status; under Islamic rule, women became little more than commodities to be sold and purchased at slave markets alongside their children. I was struck by how

---

[202] Lal, Kishori Saran. "Growth of Muslim Population in Medieval India (1000-1800)" Internet Archive, Internet Archive, 5 Aug. 2018, ia902800.us.archive.org/11/items/GrowthOfMuslimPopulationInMedievalIndiaAd10001800/Growth-Of-Muslim-Population-In-Medieval-India-ad-1000-1800_text.pdf.

[203] Lal, Kishori Saran. "Growth of Muslim Population in Medieval India (1000-1800)" Internet Archive, Internet Archive, 5 Aug. 2018, ia902800.us.archive.org/11/items/GrowthOfMuslimPopulationInMedievalIndiaAd10001800/Growth-Of-Muslim-Population-In-Medieval-India-ad-1000-1800_text.pdf.

the descriptions under the Tughlaq dynasty of Medieval India was no different than the *Sabaya system* of the Islamic State in 2015 that the New York Times did an expo on.[204] I recall Will Durant mentioning in *Our Oriental Heritage* how Hindu Rajputs would war with each other to kidnap Hindu princesses to have them married to them prior to Islam's existence[205][206]; the bizarre aspect of this was that Hindu Princesses felt thorough gratification in their royal status being held to such high esteem amongst warring Rajputs that they felt it only fitting that a Rajput kidnap them to force them into marriage as an honor and duty.[207][208] Having men of Princely States build armies and war amongst themselves for a princess's hand-in-marriage elevated the status of the Hindu princess in the eyes of the broader public of ancient Indian society.[209][210] I was genuinely dumbfounded by this explanation and I had to fight my natural inclinations of how hilarious and how stupid this sounded to try to understand the minds of ancient people. I could only compare it to Western cultural stories like *Snow White* and *Repunzal* and realized the origin of such stories was probably to make systems like this more palatable for a broader audience; which may have explained the variations throughout different cultures. I suppose some Hindus of India would gaze upon the *Ramayana* with a new perspective just as some Europeans may gaze upon *The Odyssey* with different viewpoint from reading such a comparison to ancient Hindu history. The Islamic system of slavery did away with this by creating a market where women and children were put up for sale for either the highest Muslim bidder among Muslim armies or the higher-class Muslims picked whatever woman they wanted as a personal slave because of their physical

---

[204] Callimachi, Rukmini. "Isis Enshrines a Theology of Rape." The New York Times, The New York Times, 13 Aug. 2015, www.nytimes.com/2015/08/14/world/middleeast/isis-enshrines-a-theology-of-rape.html.
[205] Durant, Will. Chapter XIV: The Foundations of India: IV. Indo-Aryan Society (9245 - 9297). Our Oriental Heritage: Being a History of Civilization in Egypt and the Near East to the Death of Alexander, and in India, China and Japan from the Beginning to Our Own Day. Simon and Schuster, 1935.
[206] Durant, Will. Chapter XVI: From Alexander to Aurangzeb: IV. Annals of Rajputana (Pgs. 10362-10387). Our Oriental Heritage: Being a History of Civilization in Egypt and the Near East to the Death of Alexander, and in India, China and Japan from the Beginning to Our Own Day. Simon and Schuster, 1935.
[207] Durant, Will. Chapter XIV: The Foundations of India: IV. Indo-Aryan Society (9245 - 9297). Our Oriental Heritage: Being a History of Civilization in Egypt and the Near East to the Death of Alexander, and in India, China and Japan from the Beginning to Our Own Day. Simon and Schuster, 1935.
[208] Durant, Will. Chapter XVI: From Alexander to Aurangzeb: IV. Annals of Rajputana (Pgs. 10362-10387). Our Oriental Heritage: Being a History of Civilization in Egypt and the Near East to the Death of Alexander, and in India, China and Japan from the Beginning to Our Own Day. Simon and Schuster, 1935.
[209] Durant, Will. Chapter XIV: The Foundations of India: IV. Indo-Aryan Society (9245 - 9297). Our Oriental Heritage: Being a History of Civilization in Egypt and the Near East to the Death of Alexander, and in India, China and Japan from the Beginning to Our Own Day. Simon and Schuster, 1935.
[210] Durant, Will. Chapter XVI: From Alexander to Aurangzeb: IV. Annals of Rajputana (Pgs. 10362-10387). Our Oriental Heritage: Being a History of Civilization in Egypt and the Near East to the Death of Alexander, and in India, China and Japan from the Beginning to Our Own Day. Simon and Schuster, 1935.

appearance or skills in dancing, singing, or playing musical instruments.[211][212] Ibn Battuta is quoted stating that Sultans sold Rajas princesses by making them perform for Muslim audiences before selling them to the highest bidder.[213] As paradoxical as it is, the social destruction of hierarchy of Hindu society under Muslim rule made for a more degrading system where women were put into pens like cattle[214][215]; again, no different from the New York Times expo on how ISIS treated Yazidi women in 2015.[216]

The majority of Kishori Saran Lal's consensus data seems very good. Imperial consensus by Akbar the Great on page 64, affirmed an approximately 140 million population size from approximately 170 million prior on pages 48 – 51. The consensus of 140 million is based upon a summation of Akbar the Great's having done a royal consensus on the twenty-fifth year of his reign where his officials gathered information on households within his empire including individuals in each household. The 170 million approximation is based upon Muslim geographers and historians under the Tughlaq dynasty giving very detailed and dry accounts of the amounts of foodgrain, foodgrain taxes, and Kishori Saran Lal then mathematically computing how much that would typically serve each individual and household after setting aside two-thirds of the material for non-edibles or for animal husbandry in Medieval society. The calculations on the taxes and the sheer largesse of foodgrain amounted to a population of approximately 170 million during Firoz Tughlaq's reign. In other words, the mathematics of foodgrain pricing from the thorough analyses of Muslim historians and Geographers in the 1380s and Akbar's population consensus during the twenty-fifth year of his reign which should

---

[211] Lal, Kishori Saran. Chapter X: AD 1200 – 1400 (Pgs. 113 – 116). "Growth of Muslim Population in Medieval India (1000-1800)" Internet Archive, Internet Archive, 5 Aug. 2018, ia902800.us.archive.org/11/items/GrowthOfMuslimPopulationInMedievalIndiaAd10001800/Growth-Of-Muslim-Population-In-Medieval-India-ad-1000-1800_text.pdf.

[212] Lal, Kishori Saran. Chapter XI: AD 1400 – 1600 (Pgs. 127 – 143). "Growth of Muslim Population in Medieval India (1000-1800)" Internet Archive, Internet Archive, 5 Aug. 2018, ia902800.us.archive.org/11/items/GrowthOfMuslimPopulationInMedievalIndiaAd10001800/Growth-Of-Muslim-Population-In-Medieval-India-ad-1000-1800_text.pdf.

[213] Lal, Kishori Saran. Chapter X: AD 1200 – 1400 (Pgs. 113 – 116). "Growth of Muslim Population in Medieval India (1000-1800)" Internet Archive, Internet Archive, 5 Aug. 2018, ia902800.us.archive.org/11/items/GrowthOfMuslimPopulationInMedievalIndiaAd10001800/Growth-Of-Muslim-Population-In-Medieval-India-ad-1000-1800_text.pdf.

[214] Lal, Kishori Saran. Chapter XI: AD 1400 – 1600 (Pgs. 127 – 143). "Growth of Muslim Population in Medieval India (1000-1800)" Internet Archive, Internet Archive, 5 Aug. 2018, ia902800.us.archive.org/11/items/GrowthOfMuslimPopulationInMedievalIndiaAd10001800/Growth-Of-Muslim-Population-In-Medieval-India-ad-1000-1800_text.pdf.

[215] Lal, Kishori Saran. Chapter XII: AD 1600 – 1800 (Pgs. 144 – 156). "Growth of Muslim Population in Medieval India (1000-1800)" Internet Archive, Internet Archive, 5 Aug. 2018, ia902800.us.archive.org/11/items/GrowthOfMuslimPopulationInMedievalIndiaAd10001800/Growth-Of-Muslim-Population-In-Medieval-India-ad-1000-1800_text.pdf.

[216] Callimachi, Rukmini. "Isis Enshrines a Theology of Rape." The New York Times, The New York Times, 13 Aug. 2015, www.nytimes.com/2015/08/14/world/middleeast/isis-enshrines-a-theology-of-rape.html.

have been around 1581 confirms a drop in population size of approximately thirty million under Islamic rule.

The following is how Kishori Saran Lal himself explains it in *Chapter V: A.D. 1200 – 1400* on pages 49 – 51 of *Growth of Muslim Population in Medieval India*:

> On the basis of the evidence set forth above, it would be reasonable to conclude that at the time of Muhammad bin Tughlaq's death (about the middle of the fourteenth century) the population may have come down to about 160 million; at the time of Firoz Tughlaq's death (A. D. 1388) the number was probably 170 million.
>
> There is a basis for arriving at this conclusion. The total revenue of Firoz Tughlaq's empire was 67, 500, 000 tankahs. Since the revenue collected was, on the average, one third of the total produce of food-grains in his dominions would have been of the value of 202,500,000 tankahs. From the price schedule of Firoz's time, it is gathered that the average cost of a *man* of food-grains was 5 jitals[59]. A tankah in the fourteenth century was approximately equal to about 50 jitals (48 jitais to be precise)[60], A *man* in those days was equal to 14 *sers* of today[61]. Therefore one tankah (or 50 jitals) bought 10 *man* (of 14 *sers* each) or 3 1/2 maunds of 40 *sers* each in Firoz's time.[62] At this rate the total agricultural production in Firoz Tughlaq's time would have been about 202.500,000 X 3 1/2 =708,750,000 maunds.
>
> Out of this, two-thirds may safely be set aside for non-eatable agricultural products like cotton; damage caused by rodents, birds and animals habituated to nibbling in the fields; and for the consumption of large number of bullocks, horses, elephants and many other animals, indispensable to medieval husbandry, soldiery, nobility and even royalty, because they comprised sources of energy and means of transport. Therefore the quantity consumed by the people was 1/3 of this figure or about 236,250,000 maunds.
>
> Today, for a population of 500 million, India requires about 100,000,000 tonnes of cereals every year. In other words, every individual consumes about 200 kilograms, 220 *sers*, or 5 1/2 maunds of foodgrains in the course of a year. Taking this average as holding good for the medieval times also,[63] the number of people who consumed 236,250,000 maunds was (236,250,000 ÷ 5 ½ =) about 43 million. Firoz Tughlaq's empire included the Punjab, Delhi, Uttar Pradesh, major portions of Gujarat and Malwa and northern Bihar.[61] In the absence of precise knowledge of the area which came under the revenue regulations in Malwa, we may, for convenience's sake, take into account the whole of present Bihar state and drop Malwa. Thus the total area of Firoz's dominions approximated to the following.

Table 1

Approximate area of Firoz Tughlaq's empire

Punjab (undivided)	253,000 sqr. Kilometers
Delhi	1,500 " "
Uttar Pradesh	295,800 " "
Gujarat	187,100 " "
Bihar	174,000 " "
Total	909,400 Sqr. Km.

    The total area of India before partition (or the India of medieval times minus Kabul and Qandhar) was 4,052,950 sqr. km. Firoz's empire comprised of approximately one fourth of this area, and contained 43 million inhabitants. The population of the whole of India, therefore, was roughly four times this number or 172 million. But since the empire of Firoz had within its dominions rather thickly populated regions, the total population of India was probably a little less than 172 million, say approximately 168 to 170 million.[217]

    Most of the stories prior to Akbar detailed by Muslim historians elaborate on mass slaughter, enslavement, and torture of Hindus by Muslims and not of any famines causing this massive drop in population size. Adding the bloodthirsty massacres of the early Islamic contact period from Mahmud of Ghazni onwards, and the approximation of 60 – 80 million deaths under Islamic rule of India stands the test of time.

    However, there is one weakness which is in the mid to late 1500s in Chapter Six, it seems more credible that famine from lack of monsoons and a spread of general diseases related to famine weakening bodily immunity was more the cause of a great many deaths in the millions. What surprised me though is the explanation that within roughly 30 – 40 years most population sizes quickly recovered from many of these famines or bloodlettings from Islamic massacres of Hindus and Buddhists, intra-Islamic wars over the Sultanate throne, intra-Hindu wars over territory, and wars amongst Hindus and Muslims in which the Tughlaq dynasty in general and Aurangzeb of the Mughal empire slaughtered innocent Hindus. While there was much bloodletting, the civilian populations worked to rebuild, recover, and bounce back time after time to the shock of

---

[217] Lal, Kishori Saran. Chapter V: AD 1200 – 1400 (Pgs. 39 – 51). "Growth of Muslim Population in Medieval India (1000-1800)" Internet Archive, Internet Archive, 5 Aug. 2018, ia902800.us.archive.org/11/items/GrowthOfMuslimPopulationInMedievalIndiaAd10001800/Growth-Of-Muslim-Population-In-Medieval-India-ad-1000-1800_text.pdf.

many of the ruling elite; especially the Muslim ruling elite. The resilience of the general Hindu population played a significant factor in why the millions upon millions of deaths can be understood to be credible. Between periods of war campaigns, civilians worked to fix-up what was shattered, migrate to better job opportunities, or repair and rebuild economies until they were improved and thriving just as before they were shattered by mostly Islamic conquests such as sackings and kidnappings of women and children to sell at slave auctions. For as much destruction as was wrought in Medieval India's history, there was attempts at rebuilding, reconstruction, and returning to the thriving lifestyle through great efforts time after time and it usually succeeded within an approximate forty-year timespan from these communities. After having finished it, I'm left with the impression that the more conservative 60 – 75 million approximation is plausibly closer to a real assessment of the Hindu losses under Islamic rule than the oft-repeated 80 million of the 60 – 80 million range that is given. This is mainly because the rest of the twenty million seems to have been more likely due to mixed factors of famine mortality, intra-Muslim military slaughters caused by rival Muslim militaries upon each other and the slaughter of Muslim civilians over Sultanate thrones, and forced conversions of millions of women and children into Islam as per Jihad theology of kuffar women being spoils of war as slave girls for Muslim men in the Quran (4:3, 4:24, 16:71, 23:5-6, 24:33, 24:58, 33:50). It's worth mentioning – and I swear that I do not say this lightly, but in an effort for full and thorough honesty – that Great Britain's mass death toll of India which is also in the 60 – 80 million range happened in half the time as Islamic rule did, it has far more credible evidence to back it up including Britain's own recordkeeping, and it was far more devastating to India's economy than anything that came before it from my understanding of the evidence. The facts do seem to support that India needed far more time to rebuild due to how thoroughly brutal British colonialism was to the entire population of India for 250 years in what is now India, Pakistan, and Bangladesh than the damage Islamic rule did for approximately 500 years prior to Akbar the Great's more peaceful rule.

One aspect that has me thoroughly confused is Indian Muslims and even pseudo-Indologists like Audrey Truschke rallying around the figure of Islamic ruler Aurangzeb when there are much less bloodthirsty Islamic rulers that they could have used as a rallying point and the not-so-insignificant fact that we have a great amount of historical information, including two eyewitness accounts, that could make a compelling argument that Aurangzeb almost certainly murdered more Muslims than any other ruler in India's entire history. Regardless of their motives, it's a definitive nail in the coffin for their credibility to rally around this bloodthirsty monarch. In fact, European eyewitness accounts during Aurangzeb's reign are the ones who confirm this. Page 84 explains that Niccolao Manucci mentions Aurangzeb's armies destroyed crops and heavily suggests a military campaign not unlike scorched-earth policies. The people being slaughtered and the Kingdoms that Aurangzeb was warring against were independent Muslim Kings of the Deccan and the ones dying from plague due to a mix of the failure of rains and the thorough destruction of crop fields by Aurangzeb's military were undoubtedly Muslims. Niccolao states over two million people died in just two years from 1702 – 1704; these two million would have to be mostly Muslim peasants ruled under independent Deccan Sultanates. Moreover, he left a desolation of crops during a time when the rain wasn't falling, which means the death toll of just Muslims must've been enormous afterwards due to Aurangzeb's war campaigns against independent Muslim Sultans; especially if the confirmed record of two million Muslim deaths in just two years due to Aurangzeb's wars is anything to go by. K.S. Lal also cites the more neutral Khafi Khan on pages 84 – 85, a Mughal historian who was also an eyewitness, who explains there were mass killings, the burning down of populated locations, he confirms a purposeful scorched-earth policy on cultivation, starvation of carriage-animals, and a general massacring of the populous. . . all of these victims would have been Muslim peasants. Khafi Khan likely waited until Aurangzeb's death because he wanted to be honest about what was done to the Muslim population of the Deccan. Any claims he was lying are perplexing given that Aurangzeb's multiple war campaigns are well-attested history that led to the Mughal Empire's decline. Page 86 mentions Islamic rulers in Afghanistan invading and further weakening Mughal hold at various times from the 1730s – 1790s that was tenuous due to internal power struggles among self-serving Mughal princes and viziers. This is not to say that it was exclusively Muslim and K.S. Lal makes no such illusions; page 85 also mentions that the Marathas were having intra-rulership struggles including villages burned, open murder and robbery gone unchecked, and caravans destroyed in what were intra-Hindu power struggles for control of Maratha territory. The victims of the Maratha power struggles would have largely been Hindus, just as the victims of Mughal power struggles were largely Muslims.

    The most surprising aspect of reading this book was Kishori Saran Lal's examination of what the role of Caste actually played. Lal carefully explains that both the arguments that Caste was so brutal that Hindus converted and that Caste was so strong that Hindus did not convert are ignorant, do not have much evidence at all, and lack the main factor in what compelled certain groups to convert to Islam and others not to. What keeps being missed from the picture of Caste politics of Medieval India is economics and economic incentives. I was surprised to learn that Caste, as part of the social fabric of Medieval Indian society, meant that Indians of the same lower Castes were more likely to form guilds based on their Castes. I could only really compare this knowledge to video games like *Elder Scrolls IV: Oblivion* or adventure Anime where characters were part of separate guilds like mage, swordsman, archer and so on. In this real-life case, it was guilds of shoemakers, goldsmiths, swordsmiths, Elephant riders, and plausibly even fashion guilds. I had thought the restriction on Third-Gender people's careers under Islamic rule to fashion designers were due to bigotry by Muslims, but K. S. Lal makes a very compelling case that it was more plausible that this shift occurred due to the Muslim population's preference for living in urban areas and enthusiasm for the latest and most expensive clothes and clothing designs. Essentially, whenever conversion to Islam was more congenial, Medieval Indians usually converted based upon economic incentives if the patrons were usually Muslim and there were massive profits to be made for their guilds. Most likely, social cohesion within the guilds caused people to gradually convert because they wouldn't want to be left out of either work or their Caste community. Lal mentions that those Castes like shoemakers who were thoroughly discriminated against by upper-caste Hindus usually converted, but also that there was a ubiquitous fondness among Islamic rulers for elephants. For esteemed elephant riders of Rajas, nearly all the Sultans and Islamic emperors provided very generous economic incentives for elephant riders to convert to Islam with any refusal being met with death. Goldsmiths whose patrons were usually Hindus had no reason or even incentive to convert because Hindus had a higher preference for goldsmith wears than Muslims in Medieval India; the same is generally true of the Castes that were swordsmiths. Any group of outcastes that did butchery of animals, which is generally frowned upon with Hindu culture and society, would have almost certainly converted to Islam for economic opportunities and higher monetary gains. For rural populations, there actually wasn't any higher status gain or even equality if they converted to Islam because Islamic monarchies were already firmly established; Sultans and Islamic emperors generally married Hindu princesses to legitimize their rule in territories they conquered. A Muslim peasant wasn't suddenly going to become equal to an Emperor or Sultan. Women were also less equal in most respects; women were generally made slaves under Islam. Hindu princesses made to convert to Islam becoming Muslim queens or Muslim slave-consorts generally spent their days trying to find ways to force their rival Islamic wives into stillbirths so that their child would reign after the Emperor or Sultan. Perhaps the most surprising fact of all, which in hindsight is very obvious due to the decline of Buddhism and loss of the Buddha's teachings in his original language, is that Islam actually shattered Buddhism and almost certainly converted more Buddhists proportionally through violent conquest than Hindus. Hinduism had a paradoxical relationship with conversion to Islam due to Medieval Caste pride, economic incentives, and Caste-based guilds that served as social communities and for economic opportunities; Buddhism evidently didn't have any of these caveats. As a result, it was completely shattered into conversions to Islam in Bengal, especially in what is now Bangladesh.

The richness and brutal honesty of this book honestly blew me away. I can't go into full details without an overly lengthy review, but I can't help but gush this book with praise in all but a few areas. To give a few snippets: on page 98, details on Qasim's campaigns in 664 AD into Sindh. Pages 102 – 107 details Mahmud of Ghazni's conversion by force. Pages 113 – 116 explains the enslavement of women and children into forced conversions, and other conversions under the Muslim slave system. Page 138 gives a brief explanation of the surprising history of racism against African Muslims who came to India; the racism was by the fair-skinned Arab, Turkish, Persian, Abyssinians, and Egyptian Muslim upper-class in the Medieval period. There is no dearth of rich, well-structured, well-argued, and fact-finding details in this book. It's such a shame that I had to read it on PDF with nearly half the pages hard to read, because it is no longer in English circulation. This book deserves so much more attention. I felt as if I was finally learning real history without any obfuscation and just a general reading of brute facts regardless of how I felt about them.

When I contrast this with how Andrew J. Nicholson tried to portray India's Medieval history in which he cited Cynthia Talbot, Sheldon Pollock, and Romila Thapar; it genuinely made no sense whatsoever purely on the basis that Medieval history is simply filled with bloodletting on a scope and scale that makes modern people deeply uncomfortable. Andrew Nicholson citing his own Indology fields of translators who – citing no evidence whatsoever – make preposterous claims that Hindus and Muslims weren't aware of each other[218]; the reason Nicholson's and the claims of those he cites are clearly falsifications is that it genuinely is counter to basic human psychology; especially according to the studies of Polish social psychologist, Henri Tajfel. In Tajfel's repeated studies, he found that psychological in-group and out-group associations in social identity are instantaneous among disparate groups of people.[219] Tajfel conducted these studies to better understand the mentality of the Nazis for having committed the Holocaust; he wanted to understand why it happened because many of his family died in the Holocaust. Essentially, these studies on basic human psychology by Tajfel overwhelmingly prove that Nicholson, Talbot, Thapar, and whatever other pseudo-Indologists espousing the claim that Hindus and Muslims lacked awareness of each other are thoroughly and willfully lying. They likely haven't been academically honest at all and if they were being honest, then it's laziest research possible. Compare the information to other places during Medieval history as that might be a useful way to understand the problem better. Apparently, Vlad Dracula slaughtering his own people including infants into stakes and making a gate out of it in Southeastern Europe to strike fear into the Turkish armies is perfectly credible, but Muslim massacres of villages of both Muslims and Hindus in the same time period of history is delusional? Intra-Native American clan wars and dynastic wars of each dynasty setting fire to temples in order to conquer vast swathes of territory under their respective dynastic or clan rule is perfectly credible Medieval history on the Mayan and Mexica civilizations, but Sultans raising armies and slaughtering Hindus with the choice of conversion or death is not? Ancient Rome taking women as spoils of war to be their slaves, burning Carthage to the ground, and salting the earth out of deep-seeded revenge for losses in previous war campaigns to

---

[218] Nicholson, Andrew J. Chapter 10: Hindu Unity And The Non-Hindu Other (4806-5293). Unifying Hinduism: Philosophy and Identity in Indian Intellectual History (South Asia Across the Disciplines). Columbia University Press, 2010.
[219] Ispas, Alexa. Psychology and politics: a social identity perspective. Psychology Press, 2014.

Carthage is perfectly credible; but the slaughter Hindu Rajas and Rajputs and enslavement of their women and children to be sold in Islamic slave markets is not?[220]

    I always wanted to know more about the transition from the ancient world of India to the modern India as it exists today and how Islam influenced the politics. When I read Western Indology such as several chapters of a book from Gerald J. Larson, an essay from Sheldon Pollock, and the entirety of *Unifying Hinduism* from Andrew J. Nicholson . . . all I received was confusion. I went so far as to read the *Oxford Handbook of Indian Philosophy* and it was plainly filled with Western racialization of Indian culture to the point that I don't find it valuable at all. Andrew J. Nicholson's book was just outright shoddy scholarship and perhaps even the poster-child of shoddy scholarship when it comes to Islam. He cited Akbar the Great, an Ex-Muslim King who founded his own religion of the *Din-i Ilahi* and who banned distribution of the Quran late in his reign, as a Muslim King curious about Hinduism.[221][222] That information by Nicholson was an abject lie. If these usual folks of Marxist Westerners are just going to scream that Hindus are Nazis and lie so religiously about factual information while exploiting academic freedom as a cover for bigotry and hate, then guess what? They have the Free Speech to do… whatever it is that they're doing, and I will go forward with purchasing credible historic information that helps to give me a clearer understanding of a history that I'm curious about. Honestly, it isn't just the dehumanizing bigotry against Hindus that bothers me, but also the fact that they're just a waste of time and the fact I wasted my own money on a book of ignorance and pure obfuscation. I could read and refute each and every one of them, but if they're so hellbent on just lying to create their own concocted fantasies about another people's history while calling them racist, Nazi, bigot, Casteist, and treating Hindutva as a sort of Nazism while deliberately not distinguishing between Hindutva and Hinduism; what am I even arguing against apart from a group of conspiracy theorist nutjobs who just happen to be college professors? They're the equivalent of "Holocaust Denial" Professors and make comments that make them sound no different from nuisance streamers like Johnny Somali (whose real name is Ramsey Khalid Ismael). I agree with criticizing their views so that it doesn't go unchallenged, I think giving them credible information to show why we think they're wrong is valuable, and I don't agree with trying to shut them down; but honestly, engaging with people who don't care about our perspective in this whole experience is just a waste of my time. If I want credible fact-

---

[220] Lal, Kishori Saran. Chapter XI: AD 1400 – 1600 (Pgs. 127 – 143). "Growth of Muslim Population in Medieval India (1000-1800)" Internet Archive, Internet Archive, 5 Aug. 2018, ia902800.us.archive.org/11/items/GrowthOfMuslimPopulationInMedievalIndiaAd10001800/Growth-Of-Muslim-Population-In-Medieval-India-ad-1000-1800_text.pdf.

[221] Nicholson, Andrew J. Chapter 10: Hindu Unity And The Non-Hindu Other (4806-5293). Unifying Hinduism: Philosophy and Identity in Indian Intellectual History (South Asia Across the Disciplines). Columbia University Press, 2010.

[222] Durant, Will. Chapter XVI: From Alexander to Aurangzeb: VII. Akbar The Great (Pgs. 10520 - 10691). Our Oriental Heritage: Being a History of Civilization in Egypt and the Near East to the Death of Alexander, and in India, China and Japan from the Beginning to Our Own Day. Simon and Schuster, 1935.

finding information about India's history, then I'll read from historians like Kishori Saran Lal and Will Durant. *Growth of the Muslim Population of Medieval India* is a phenomenal work by a legitimate historian. What I want and value is the pursuit of knowledge and I can only seem to get that from historians like Lal and Durant; I honestly wouldn't care so much about the bigotry against Hinduism as a theology, if there was fact-finding research to back it up from these Marxist-leaning Indologists like there is with Historians like Will Durant, Marxist-Environmentalist Mike Davis (who is a wonderful fact-finding historian), and Kishori Saran Lal.

The Consequences of Genocide Denial? More Genocide Denial:

What these mostly Western Indologists did was a self-serving act to propel their own fame by purposefully insulting what they perceived to be easy targets; they will sign letters and support Audrey Truschke for academic freedom, but they do not condemn Islamists of India who would kill Hindus, other Dharmic followers, and Christians who exercised their Free Speech to insult the Prophet Mohammad; for example, they never condemned or criticized crimes such as the horrifying pre-planned murder of Kamlesh Tiwari. In fact, they did not stand-up for Free Speech when Islamists murdered people in any South Asian country. They went on Indian national newspapers to project themselves as aggrieved scholars facing persecution from angry Hindu mobs, but they never discussed or condemned the burning of Christian homes in Pakistan, the Pakistani Muslim gangs raping religious minorities in Pakistan, and they did not stand up for Pakistani Catholic Asia Bibi or Pakistani Hindu Ashok Kumar when gangs of Pakistani Muslims threatened to murder them for specious rumors of insulting the Prophet Mohammad. Even now, with horrific stories of the burning of Hindu temples, the burning of Christian homes, and the physical assaults by Islamist mobs in Bangladesh upon Hindus, likely other Dharmic followers, and upon Christians; it has been complete silence from these supposedly persecuted experts who constantly gained fame and publicity from making caricatures of Hindus as angry mobs. They have repeatedly shown that they're willing to ignore the violent, angry Muslim mobs who murder people over specious rumors of insulting the Prophet Mohammad in all three South Asian countries. It shows exactly the kind of craven people they truly are. Like all moral cowards, they only cared about one thing: themselves.

What has been the effect of propagating falsehoods? Muslims of South Asia continue to feel justified in committing violence against other religious groups; some Muslims see it as a religious duty and view it in terms of heroism. As a result, the act of genocide upon Hindus and its denial still continues unimpeded to this day. The Kashmir conflict is a prime example of this. While treated as an aggrieved Kashmiri Muslim minority group struggling for independence against Hindu-majority India, the genocide of Kashmiri Hindu pandits has been systematically ignored because it doesn't serve the mythic narrative of oppressed Muslims. In an article published on April 6th, 2016 for the British Broadcasting Corporation (BBC), journalist Zubair Ahmed explained in the bluntly titled *"Kashmiri Hindus: Driven out and insignificant"* the following:

> Muslim militant groups targeted Hindus by killing their men, burning their homes and damaging their places of worship. Mosques would make calls for them to leave the valley.
>
> Saifullah, a former militant, tells the BBC that he regrets participating in driving Kashmiri Hindus out. "We want them back. We want them to live in peace. Kashmir is theirs too," he says.[223]

Further in the BBC article, he articulates:

> According to one estimate, 3,000-5,000 Pandits are left in the valley today - a far cry from the 300,000 who used to live there. These few thousand are scattered over 185 places in the valley, where seven million people live.
>
> Today the Pandits are condemned to live a life of anonymity in their own homeland.
>
> **'Painful times'**
>
> Mr Tikku and Mohan Lal Bhat, like most Hindus who did not leave Kashmir, lived nightmarish existences during the initial phase of the conflict.
>
> "In the beginning there was a lot of fear, nights were eerily silent. If a cat jumped on to the roof we thought militants had come to kill us", Mr Tikku tells the BBC.
>
> Mr Bhat, a retired policeman, also recalls the "painful times" he used to be up all night "in case someone came to kill us".
>
> "I would look out of the window to see if an intruder was coming to kill us," he says.
>
> The Bhats never left the valley and poverty never left them. A young son was killed in a terror attack. The other is unemployed. Like many others in the valley, they have their own homes, but ready cash is scarce.
>
> For the community, the scars undoubtedly run deep, but it seems that time has nearly healed their wounds. They now enjoy healthy relationships with their Muslim neighbours.
>
> **Peace problems**
>
> But relative peace comes with its own set of problems.
>
> Many complain about a lack of priests. This becomes an issue during occasions like weddings, and also during deaths, when priests are needed to perform the last rites.

---

[223] Ahmed, Zubair. "Kashmiri Hindus: Driven out and Insignificant." BBC News, BBC, 6 Apr. 2016, www.bbc.com/news/world-asia-india-35923237.

Another problem, according to Mr Tikku, is finding partners for their children.

He estimates that there are around 900 Pandit boys and girls of marriageable age in the valley. Mr Pandita himself has three daughters, none of them married yet. "We would like to get our daughters married in the valley but it's not easy to find the boys in our community," he says.

Children's education is another worry.

Many young parents are unwilling to raise their children in a predominantly Muslim Kashmir, where all children "have to learn Arabic and the Koran".

Sonica Bhatt is 30 and has three children. The oldest is six. She says she has not told them about their Hindu background yet, because their friends are all Muslim. "We want to send them to Jammu where they will be raised as Hindus," she says.[224]

What happened to Kashmiri Hindu Pandits was a genocide, yet their narrative is categorically ignored and silenced as less important than the lives of Kashmiri Muslims. It is an inherently unequal and discriminatory narrative that purposefully dehumanizes Hindus as unworthy of human rights and equal protection. Whereas the US still hasn't formally recognized the Kashmiri genocide of Hindus by Kashmiri Islamists, in 2016 the US government under President Obama and the EU immediately, and correctly, recognized the genocide of Syrian Christians, Yazidis, Jews, minority Islamic faiths, and other faiths by ISIS. The US State Department cited *Open Doors USA*, which unfortunately I've found exaggerates claims when it came to religious discrimination of Christians in India as they had citations that didn't result in any sources at all, but I don't believe that they would lie or exaggerate about the genocide of Christians, Yazidis, Jews, and others in Syria suffering under ISIS terrorism. From *"Section I"* of the Executive Summary of the *"2022 Report on International Religious Freedom: Syria"* which had the following:

> The U.S. government estimates the total population at 21.6 million (midyear 2022). At year's end, according to the UN, more than half of the country's prewar population was displaced; there were approximately 5.7 million refugees in neighboring countries as well as 6.9 million IDPs. Continued population displacement adds a degree of uncertainty to demographic analyses, but the U.S. government estimates 74 percent of the population is Sunni Muslim, which includes ethnic Arabs, Kurds, Circassians, Chechens, and some Turkmen. Other Muslim groups, including Alawites, Ismailis, and Shia, together constitute 13 percent of the population, while Druze constitute 3 percent.

> The U.S. government estimates 10 percent of the population is Christian. There are reports, however, that indicate that number is considerably lower – approximately 2.5 percent. Of the 2.2 million Christians who lived in the country prior to the war, the NGO Open Doors USA estimates that only approximately 638,000 remain, approximately 3 percent of the population and a decrease of 39,000 Christians from the previous year.

---

[224] Ahmed, Zubair. "Kashmiri Hindus: Driven out and Insignificant." BBC News, BBC, 6 Apr. 2016, www.bbc.com/news/world-asia-india-35923237.

Before the civil war, there were small Jewish populations in Aleppo and Damascus, but in 2020, the *Jewish Chronicle* reported that there were no known Jews still living in the country. Before the civil war, the country also had a Yezidi population of approximately 80,000. While there are no updated official figures on the number of Yezidis in the country, the Afrin Yazidi Union estimates that approximately 2,000 Yezidis remain in Afrin, compared with approximately 50-60,000 prior to 2011.[225]

While it may seem unfair to categorically list various global instances of Islamic violence on religious minority groups, the truth is that once you understand the general framework of the theology, then the violence displays similar patterns despite the sociopolitical and geographic differences. In other words, the unquestioned obedience to the Quran and the Quran's own violent passages, such as the entirety of Chapter 9 of the Quran, really does explain the global patterns of Islamic terrorism and Islamic violence better than any other method of attempting to discern primary causes. The fact remains that beliefs inform opinions and behavior. Thus, the religious beliefs do explain the purveyance of systemic patterns of violence of Islam. Time after time, the violence against Hindus, other Dharmic followers, Christians, and other faith traditions like the Yazidis remains proof that unquestioned obedience to the Quran encourages violence. Mob violence is horrifically common in most Muslim-majority countries towards any specious rumors of insulting the Prophet Mohammad.

The Consequences of Ignoring Islamic Violence? It Emboldens Islamists:

While Sheldon Pollock was arguing on a personal interview with the *The Indian Express* at the Taj Mahal hotel in the safe confines of New Delhi of how he was "a target for being an outsider" due to receiving harsh criticisms from Hindus of India who criticized his characterization of Hinduism; a year earlier on January 29th, 2017, Anugrah Kumar, a contributor of the *Christian Post*, citing *The Indian Express* which itself cited the *Press Trust of India* (PTI), published an article titled *"Pakistan Acquits All 115 Suspects in Burning of Christians' Homes"* which read as follows:

> A court in Pakistan on Saturday cited lack of evidence to acquit all 115 suspects in the burning of more than 150 houses of Christians in 2013 over alleged blasphemy of the Prophet Muhammad.
>
> Chaudhry Muhammad Azam, Lahore's anti-terrorism court judge, said the prosecutors failed to produce sufficient evidence against the accused, who had been charged under various laws, including the Anti-Terrorism Act, attempted murder, robbery, arson and terrorism, according to The Indian Express.
>
> A prosecution lawyer, however, disputed the judge's conclusion and was quoted as saying, "This incident not only spread a wave of terrorism in Lahore but also brought a bad to name to Pakistan."

---

[225] U.S. Department of State, U.S. Department of State, www.state.gov/reports/2022-report-on-international-religious-freedom/syria/. Accessed 23 Mar. 2025.

The March 8, 2013, attack was seen as the largest anti-Christian violence since the attacks in 2009 that killed nine Christians in the town of Gojra in the same province of Punjab.

Police arrested the accused two days after a mob of about 3,000 Muslims armed with sticks, clubs and stones burned at least 150 houses of Christians, a church and shops in the Joseph Colony area in Lahore over allegations that a Christian had made derogatory remarks about the Prophet Muhammad.

After the incident, a Supreme Court bench, headed by Chief Justice Iftikhar Chaudhry, reprimanded the government of Punjab and the province's police for failing to protect members of the minority community. Justice Azmat Saeed Sheikh, a member of the bench, said the violence took place "right under the nose of Punjab Police and there was total inaction."

The court also said at the time that police at the "highest level" may have been told not to take action when the violence erupted.

The accused in the blasphemy case, identified as 26-year-old Sawan Masih, and the complainant, his Muslim friend identified as Imran Shahid, had quarreled under the influence of liquor, but the latter claimed it was a case of insulting the Prophet Muhammad.

"Both Imran and Sawan are close friends and the former has made the allegation only to settle a personal score because they had quarreled over some petty matter," a local resident, Dilawar Masih, who lost his house and shop in the attack, was quoted as saying at the time. He added that the attackers burned their houses even after the accused had been arrested.

Blasphemy is punishable by life in prison or even death in Pakistan.

The blasphemy law, embedded in Sections 295 and 298 of the Pakistan Penal Code, is frequently misused to target religious minorities – Christians, Shi'as, Ahmadiyyas and Hindus – and allows Islamists and others to justify killings. Extremist Islamists believe that killing a "blasphemous" person earns a heavenly reward.

Just an accusation under the controversial law is enough to have a person arrested, and there is no provision to punish a false accuser or a false witness of blasphemy. Some local Muslims seek revenge by making an allegation against his or her adversary who is a non-Muslim. Many who are accused of blasphemy are also often killed by mobs extra-judicially.[226]

A year after the gross miscarriage of justice in Pakistan, and five months prior to Sheldon Pollock's comfortable interview in India; on January 5th, 2018, *The Indian Express,* citing the PTI news agency, reported that two Pakistani Hindu businessmen were shot dead for no explicable reason in a predominately Hindu community within Pakistan in an article titled *"Two Pakistani Hindu businessmen shot dead in Sindh"* which explains as follows:

> Two Hindu brothers were on Friday shot dead outside their grain shop by bike-borne robbers in Tharparkar district of Pakistan's Sindh province, triggering protests from the minority community. The victims, identified as Dileep Kumar and Chandar Maheshwari were grain traders. They were opening their shop in the grain market in Mithi area of the district when the incident took place, the Express Tribune reported.

---

[226] Kumar, Anugrah. "Pakistan Acquits All 115 Suspects in Burning of Christians' Homes." The Christian Post, 29 Jan. 2017, www.christianpost.com/news/pakistan-acquits-all-115-suspects-in-burning-of-christians-homes.html.

> According to police, in the first ever robbery incident in the city, bike-borne dacoits tried to snatch the money from the brothers, but when they resisted, the robbers shot them.
>
> Following the incident, traders shut their business in Hindu-dominated areas in the district in protest and people blocked main roads and staged sit-ins, leading to traffic jams.[227]

Unfortunately, the patterns of Islamist violence continue even in more recent times. Last year, after the fall of Bangladesh's former ruler, Sheikh Hasina, fled Bangladesh on August 5th, 2024; the results have been repression of ISKCON faith leaders such as the incident of Chinmoy Krishna Das Brahmachari being arrested at Hazrat Shahjalal International Airport over fatuous claims of sedition because youths in his protest had allegedly put a Saffron flag above the Bangladeshi flag on November 25th, 2024.[228][229] Two other Hindu ISKCON followers who had visited him in prison were arrested when attempting to leave with no formal charges brought upon them on November 29th, 2024.[230] An article published on December 1st, 2024 by the Times of India titled "*Bangladesh stops dozens of Iskcon members from crossing into India amid rising tensions: Report*" summarizes the major events thus far:

> Bangladesh's immigration authorities at the Benapole border crossing turned away 54 members of the International Society for Krishna Consciousness (Iskcon) on Sunday, despite them possessing valid passports and visas.
>
> The immigration police cited a lack of specific government approval for their travel as the reason for barring their entry. "We consulted the special branch of police and received instructions from the higher authorities not to permit them (to cross the border)," officer-in-charge of Benapole immigration police, Imtiaz Ahsanul Quader Bhuiyan was quoted as saying by The Daily Star newspaper.
>
> He added that while the devotees carried valid passports and visas, they were "lacking specific government permission."

---

[227] "Two Pakistani Hindu Businessmen Shot Dead in Sindh." The Indian Express, Thursday, June 07, 2018, 5 Jan. 2018, web.archive.org/web/20180607183942/https://indianexpress.com/article/pakistan/two-pakistani-hindu-businessmen-shot-dead-in-sindh-5012781/.

[228] Sekhar, - Metla Sudha, et al. "Who Is Chinmoy Krishna Das and Why Has He Been Arrested in Bangladesh?" The Economic Times, economictimes.indiatimes.com/news/new-updates/all-about-the-iskcon-priest-who-has-been-arrested-in-bangladesh/articleshow/115694394.cms. Accessed 11 Mar. 2025.

[229] TNN / Nov 29, 2024. "Chinmoy Krishna Das Brahmachari: Bangladesh Monk Who's Sparked Calls for a Ban on ISKCON: India News." The Times of India, TOI, timesofindia.indiatimes.com/india/chinmoy-krishna-das-brahmachari-bangladesh-monk-whos-sparked-calls-for-a-ban-on-iskcon/articleshow/115787770.cms. Accessed 11 Mar. 2025.

[230] TOI News Desk / TIMESOFINDIA.COM / Updated: Nov 30, 2024. "Two More ISKCON Priests Arrested in Bangladesh Following Chinmoy Krishna Das's Detention: India News - Times of India." The Times of India, TOI, timesofindia.indiatimes.com/india/two-more-iskcon-priests-arrested-in-bangladesh-following-chinmoy-krishna-dass-detention/articleshow/115848147.cms. Accessed 11 Mar. 2025.

> The group of 54 members, including devotees from various districts in Bangladesh, had arrived at the check post between Saturday night and Sunday morning. They waited for hours, hoping for permission to proceed, only to be informed their travel was not authorized.
>
> "We came to participate in a religious ceremony taking place in India, but immigration officials stopped us, citing the absence of government permission," said Iskcon member Saurabh Tapandar Cheli.
>
> This incident comes amid heightened scrutiny of Iskcon in Bangladesh following the arrest of Hindu leader Chinmoy Krishna Das on November 27. Das, a spokesperson for the Bangladesh Sammilita Sanatani Jagran Jote, was detained at Dhaka's Hazrat Shahjalal International Airport on charges of sedition. The case alleges that he and others hoisted a saffron flag above the Bangladeshi national flag during a rally on October 25 in Chattogram.
>
> Das's arrest sparked protests among his supporters, leading to violent clashes that resulted in the death of a lawyer in Chattogram.
>
> Bangladeshi authorities froze the bank accounts of 17 individuals associated with Iskcon, including Das, for a 30-day period.
>
> Adding to the tension, two Iskcon monks, Adi Purush Shyam Das and Ranganath Das, were arrested on Friday while returning from delivering prasad to Das in prison. Both monks, natives of Chattogram, were detained amid heightened concerns over violence targeting Hindu minorities since the fall of the Sheikh Hasina government in August.
>
> The Bangladesh high court, however, declined to issue a suo motu order to ban Iskcon in the country.
>
> (With PTI inputs)[231]

The *Associated Press News* was the only US-based corporate news organization brave enough to cover stories about Bangladesh after the other US corporate news organizations curiously went into a collective blackout the moment the truth of Bangladeshi Muslims oppressing Bangladeshi Hindus, Christians, and other minority religious groups started to come out. The unchecked mob violence by Islamists upon religious minorities hurt the image of the Biden administration who had openly supported the interim government of Muhammad Yunus at that time. Julhas Alam of the Associated Press News released an article on November 2nd, 2024 titled *"Hindus in Muslim-majority Bangladesh rally to demand protection from attacks"* which contained the following:

> Hindu groups say there have been thousands of attacks against Hindus since early August, when the secular government of Prime Minister Sheikh Hasina was overthrown and Hasina fled the country following a student-led uprising. Muhammad Yunus, the Nobel peace laureate named to lead an interim government after Hasina's downfall, says those figures have been exaggerated.
>
> Hindus make up about 8% of the country's nearly 170 million people, while Muslims are about 91%.

---

[231] TOI World Desk / TIMESOFINDIA.COM / Updated: Dec 1, 2024. "Bangladesh Stops Dozens of ISKCON Members from Crossing into India amid Rising Tensions: Report - Times of India." The Times of India, TOI, timesofindia.indiatimes.com/world/south-asia/bangladesh-stops-dozens-of-iskcon-members-from-crossing-into-india-amid-rising-tensions/articleshow/115871437.cms. Accessed 11 Mar. 2025.

The country's influential minority group Bangladesh Hindu Buddhist Christian Unity Council has said there have been more than 2,000 attacks on Hindus since Aug. 4, as the interim government has struggled to restore order.

United Nations human rights officials and other rights groups have expressed concern over human rights in the country under Yunus.

Hindus and other minority communities say the interim government hasn't adequately protected them and that hard-line Islamists are becoming increasingly influential since Hasina's ouster.

The issue has reached beyond Bangladesh, with Indian Prime Minister Narendra Modi voicing concern over reports of attacks.

While the administration of United States President Joe Biden has said it is monitoring Bangladesh's human rights issues since Hasina's ouster, U.S. presidential candidate Donald Trump has condemned what he described as "barbaric" violence against Hindus, Christians, and other minorities in Bangladesh.

In a post on X, he said: "I strongly condemn the barbaric violence against Hindus, Christians, and other minorities who are getting attacked and looted by mobs in Bangladesh, which remains in a total state of chaos."

Hindu activists have been staging protest rallies in the capital, Dhaka, and elsewhere since August to press a set of eight demands including a law to protect minorities, a ministry for minorities and a tribunal to prosecute acts of oppression against minorities. They also seek a five-day holiday for their largest festival, the Durga Puja.

Friday's protest in Chattogram was hastily organized after sedition charges were filed Wednesday against 19 Hindu leaders, including prominent priest Chandan Kumar Dhar, over an Oct. 25 rally in that city. Police arrested two of the leaders, angering Hindus.

The charges stem from an event in which a group of rally-goers allegedly placed a saffron flag above the Bangladesh flag on a pillar, which was considered disrespecting the national flag.

Hindu community leaders say the cases are politically motivated and demanded Thursday that they be withdrawn within 72 hours. Another Hindu rally was planned for Saturday in Dhaka.

Separately, supporters of Hasina's Awami League party and its allied Jatiya Party have said they also have been targeted since Hasina's ouster. Jatiya's headquarters was vandalized and set on fire late Thursday.

On Friday, Jatiya Party Chair G.M. Quader said his supporters would continue to hold rallies to demand their rights despite risking their lives. He said they would hold a rally Saturday at the party headquarters in Dhaka to protest price hikes of commodities, and what they call false charges against their leaders and activists.

Later Friday, the Dhaka Metropolitan Police announced it was banning any rallies near the Jatiya Party's headquarters. Hours after the police decision, the party said it postponed their rally to show respect to the law and a new date for the rally would be announced soon.

The police decision came after a student group strongly criticized the police administration for initially granting permission for the rally, and threatened to block it.[232]

---

[232] Alam, Julhas. "Hindus in Muslim-Majority Bangladesh Rally to Demand Protection from Attacks." AP News, AP News, 2 Nov. 2024, apnews.com/article/bangladesh-hindu-minority-attacks-hasina-yunus-beaddefd93f1b9dcf14d287543b023f5.

Almost like clockwork from the behavior of Islamists, Bangladeshi Islamists committed a similar attack to the horrifying 2013 attack by Pakistani Muslims upon the Pakistani Christian community quoted earlier. This incident in Bangladesh appears to have a particular element of sadism due to being purposefully and willfully conducted on Christmas Eve in 2024. While the US Corporate media conveniently ignored the attack on Christian homes with a continued media blackout over Bangladeshi Islamist attacks upon Bangladeshi Christians, the *Times of India* valiantly reported the harrowing incident in an article titled "*Houses of Christian Tripura community torched in Bangladesh on Christmas eve*" on December 25th, 2024. The incident happened within a subdistrict of Chittagong, Bangladesh and the article citing the Bangladeshi *Daily Star* mentions as follows:

> At least 17 houses belonging to the Christian Tripura community were allegedly set ablaze on Christmas Eve night at Sarai Union in Lama upazila, Bandarban, reported the Daily Star.
>
> The arson attack left the residents, who were away in a nearby village for prayers and Christmas celebrations, homeless and devastated.
>
> According to victims, the miscreants targeted the new Tongjhiri Tripura Para, where the community had rebuilt their homes after being displaced several years ago.
>
> Locals reported that 17 out of 19 houses in the village were completely gutted, leaving little to salvage.
>
> **History of displacement**
>
> Tongjhiri has long been home to the Tripura community, but residents alleged they were forcibly evicted several years ago and claimed that the land on which they were living, had been leased to the wife of a high-ranking police officer during the Awami League regime.
>
> Paisapru Tripura, the head of the community, told the outlet, "We have been living here for three or four generations. A group of people, identifying themselves as 'SP's men,' evicted us four to five years ago."
>
> The community returned and rebuilt their homes following the fall of the Awami League government.
>
> Gungamani Tripura, one of the victims, shared his anguish, "Our houses have been completely burned to ashes. We could not save anything. Today is supposed to be our happiest day, but this has turned into a nightmare. We demand exemplary punishment for the criminals."
>
> **Authorities respond**
>
> Md Idris, chairman of Sarai Union Parishad, confirmed about the incident, adding that 17 houses were destroyed. Acting Lama Upazila Nirbahi Officer (UNO), Ruppayan Deb, visited the site and provided initial relief, including a blanket and a sack of rice for each affected family.

"I have asked the families to file a written complaint," Ruppayan Deb said. "We will coordinate with the deputy commissioner and the upazila project implementation officer for further action", Deb added.

Md Enamul Haque Bhuiyan, inspector (investigation) of Lama Police Station, noted that land disputes in the remote area have been ongoing, with complaints and counter-complaints of land grabbing reported since August 5. He assured that law enforcement is working diligently to identify the perpetrators and conduct a fair investigation.[233]

One final takeaway that should be obvious by now is this: they are never going to stop. Please take that statement seriously and take the time to understand what this means; this is not fear-mongering, this is the reality that Muslim organizations will continue to pursue as they grow in population size. They are never going to stop Muslim grooming gangs such as what has happened in Great Britain due to the Quranic teachings about slave girls, they are never going to stop trying to normalize FGM such as what nearly happened in the US due to the Shafi'i school of Islam[234], and they are never going to stop the normalization of murdering people for offending Muslim sensibilities in disrespecting the Prophet Mohammad or the Quran as what happened to Kamlesh Tiwari. They will gradually attempt to normalize the murders of Ex-Muslims who try to leave due to Quran 4:89. They are never going to stop making secret communities or pressuring politicians to remove legal protections for children in order to support forced child marriage in full faith to the 7th century Arab fundamentalist beliefs that it is morally acceptable to rape nine-year olds because the Prophet Mohammad did it. They are never going to stop formulating conspiracy theories or accusations of phobias in order to protect their religion from receiving any criticism. They are never going to stop the social, technological, and political revisionist project that is Islamism in order to bring everything into a 7th century living standard, because they believe their version of Jesus Christ's Second Coming requires it. They will never stop trying to impose the *Sharia* (the Divine Law of the Abrahamic God) upon all democracies throughout the world. When did they ever stop trying to do any of that to India for hundreds of years, even after Great Britain broke India into two pieces and created Pakistan and what was then East Pakistan? This is not a joke, this is not an attempt to insult Muslims as inferior, and this is not me being a bigot. This is what Islam simply is. Even now in India, some Muslim men seek out and commit sexual violence upon Hindu, Christian, Sikh, Buddhist, and other young girls. It is not as frequent on a per capita basis as Christian and Sikh Indians

---

[233] "Houses of Christian Tripura Community Torched in Bangladesh on Christmas Eve - Times of India." The Times of India, TOI, 25 Dec. 2024, timesofindia.indiatimes.com/world/south-asia/houses-of-christian-tripura-community-torched-in-bangladesh-on-christmas-eve/articleshow/116658938.cms.
[234] White, Ed. "Judge Dismisses Charges Tied to Genital Mutilation Case." AP News, AP News, 28 Sept. 2021, apnews.com/article/religion-courts-detroit-183a427558377e73a150719d2205860e.

according to India's crime statistics, but it still happens.²³⁵ The US news media and US scholars treat them as an aggrieved minority group while conveniently trying to compartmentalize the existence of Pakistan and Bangladesh and the violence that happens in those countries. If you want to understand where Western Europe is heading as a result of mass Muslim immigration, then look no further than what Great Britain helped Islamists do to India with the partition of 1947.

---

²³⁵ Mallapur, Chaitanya. "Sikhs, Christians More Likely to Be Jailed than Hindus and Muslims." Hindustan Times, Hindustan Times, 24 Oct. 2015, www.hindustantimes.com/india/hindus-least-likely-to-be-jailed-sikhs-christians-most-likely/story-Og4PhnhYsPlVLJglKyeOKL.html.

Chapter V: **Neoliberalism Empowers Islamism**

4

Basically, my title *immoralist* involves two denials. I first deny the type of man that has hitherto been regarded as the highest type— the *good*, the *kind*, and the *charitable*, and secondly, I deny that kind of morality which has come to be recognized and to dominate as morality itself— *decadence* morality or to use a still cruder term, *Christian* morality. I would regard the second denial as the more decisive as the overestimation of the value of goodness and kindness seems to me already a consequence of *decadence*, as a symptom of weakness and incompatible with an ascending and affirmative life: *denial and destruction* are inseparable from an affirmative attitude towards life.— Let me stay for a moment with the question of the psychology of the good man. In order to determine the value of a certain type of man, the cost of maintaining him must be calculated— and for this the conditions of his existence must be known. The condition of existence of the *good* is the lie— or to put it differently, the *refusal* at any price to see how reality is actually constituted, the refusal to see that this reality does not always give rise to benevolence, even less that it provides a constant justification for interference by short-sighted and good-natured hands. To regard emergencies in general as an objection, as something which must be abolished, is the greatest nonsense on earth, having the most disastrous consequences, fatally stupid— almost as stupid as a wish to abolish bad weather— out of pity for the poor... In the general economy of things the fearful aspects of reality (in terms of passions, desires, of the will to power) are incalculably more necessary than any form of petty happiness, so-called "goodness", in fact, one must even consider whether it is worth giving it a place at all, seeing that it is based upon a falsification of the instincts. I shall have an excellent opportunity of showing the incalculably calamitous consequences for the whole of history of optimism, this monstrous offspring of the *homines optimi*. Zarathustra, the first to recognize that the optimist is just as degenerate as the pessimist and possibly more detrimental says: good men never speak the truth. *The Good preach of false shores and false security, you were born and bred in the lies of the good. Through the good everything has become false and twisted down to the very roots.* Fortunately the world is not built solely to serve good-natured herd animals their little happiness, or to demand that everybody becomes a "good man", herd animal, blue-eyed, benevolent, "beautiful soul"— or, as Herbert Spencer has it, altruistic— would mean robbing existence of its great character, to castrate mankind and reduce humanity to a sort of wretched Chinadom.— *And this some have tried to do!.. It is precisely this that men have called morality...* It is in this sense that Zarathustra calls the good at times "the last men" and at times 'the beginning of the end", above all he considers them *as the most harmful kind of men*, because they secure their existence at the expense of truth and at the expense of the *future*.

The good— they cannot create: they are always the beginning of the end—
—they crucify him who writes new values on *new* law tables, they sacrifice the future to themselves, they crucify the whole future of humanity!

The good— they are always the beginning of the end... And whatever harm the slanderers of the world may do, *the harm done by the good is the most harmful of all.*
Nietzsche, Friedrich. Ecce Homo (translated, unexpurgated) (Lexido Classic Texts). Lexido.com. Kindle Edition. For reference: Aphorism 4 of Chapter "*Why I am a Destiny*"

Please be aware, this is not an advocacy of any economic position, but rather my general examination of how Islamism is strengthened by Neoliberalism and mostly an opinion instead of an analysis. Neoliberalism is a free-market capitalist economic policy; certain subsets of Right-wing blogospheres wrongly try to portray it as some type of Marxist takeover and conflate it with terms like globalism. It is not Marxist and the contemporary usage of Marxist social value systems for political ideologies like Wokeism was arguably a concession by Neoliberals after they failed to convince people of Libertarian and Free market economic principles by promoting Ayn Rand around the early 2000s – 2010s. Nevertheless, it is important to keep in mind that capitalism conceding to superficial promotions of Marxist social values was never going to mean support for Marxist economic reforms of any kind. Such arguments simply lack strong evidence to support them. Most importantly, free market capitalism should not be confused for the only form of capitalism as that's a pernicious and extremist view of economic policy. If you have strong disagreements with anything I've said, then I'm begging you to please read through everything carefully before making a judgment on my worldview. I'm a capitalist, I have never supported economic theories of either Marxism or Socialism, and I find it silly that we've turned discussions of economic theories into a form of social identity politics.

The conflicting views regarding Neoliberalism are due to the distinctions of what it purports to be, what it actually is, and perceptions by regular people due to the resulting disconnect that they suffer the consequences of; primarily as a result of the ignorance of Neoliberal economists. Pro-Neoliberal economists, politicians, lobbyists, businesspeople, and some scholars purport in the broadest sense that Neoliberalism is about advancing universal human rights, free market economics, Individualism, and that the uncontested superiority of these value systems would form a sort of global monoculture of Western Universalism. In the narrowest sense, it meant that free market economics and the free movement of people outside of their origin countries to migrate into Western countries to increase future economic gains in productivity to offset declining birth rates. Generally speaking, while Neoliberalism is a mostly economic theory and Western Universalism is about the propagation of Western values into the world, Neoliberalism and Western Universalism were conflated with the expectation by Neoliberal economists from the 1990s, to the 2010s, and even still today that Western values would automatically flourish from the spread of free market economics. Most politicians, economists, popular scholars of their respective decade, businesspeople, and lobbyists assumed there would be stopgaps and slowdowns due to political turmoil, but that it would inevitably move towards a Western Universalist monoculture as a sort of flourishing world peace due to economic prosperity. However, outside of the economic and pollution debates which would be beyond the focus of this book, this ideology of Neoliberalism came with three chief problems that it failed to answer and which proponents have never been able to sufficiently grapple with. First, which components of human rights do we value more: Religious Tolerance or Free Speech? Second, is this aggressive push by free market capitalists for the Free Migration of people desirable, sustainable, and truly going to yield long-term economic gains in the future as they envisioned? Third, what are the unintended social consequences of pursuing a global monoculture?

The Free-market capitalists and their loyal jesters in the corporate media circus responded to the first question by trying to enforce a Canadian style principle of

"Reasonable Limits" to Free Speech criticisms of religion. The corporate mass media of the US was essentially weaponized to prohibit certain forms of Free Speech as socially taboo and it negatively impacted the perceptions of other organizations that were trying to do sincere human rights activism. This was not the corporate media's only implicit "Reasonable Limit" as there was also stalwart efforts to shut down all criticisms of free market economics, a shutdown of any meaningful criticism of US Foreign Policy blunders, and a complete silence over the corporate mass media lying about Weapons of Mass Destruction as an argument to convince the US public to support President Bush's invasion of Iraq in 2003; for the purposes of this book, we will strictly focus upon the effects this had on religious criticism. Needless to say, anything that deviated from the implicit "reasonable limits" was therefore too extreme and not acceptable speech. Terms such as Islamophobia and an attempt to racialize a religious group of nearly two billion adherents were developed as tactics to shut down the inalienable right of Free Speech of all Americans and the Enlightenment cultural values of Western Europe.

Islamophobia was peddled aggressively by the jester-journalists of the corporate media circus. The first witch-hunt against those who deviated from the jester orthodoxy were the New Atheists for pointing to the unique theological problems of Islam. Criticizing Christianity was perfectly acceptable and having such debates between Christianity and Atheism in US universities was fine, but White Atheists criticizing Islam? "Scientism", "Islamophobia", "Bigotry", and "Racist" were often accusations hurled upon them for the blasphemy of criticizing Islam. This incoherence of the corporate jesters' arguments went so far that Ex-Muslim Christian Ayaan Hirsi Ali and Muslim Reformist Maajid Nawaz were both argued or insinuated to be ignorant bigots of the religion that largely wants to kill them. Despite the reality that Islamists really do desire to kill one for leaving Islam and the other for espousing "*bid'ah*" upon Islam, even anti-discrimination organizations like the Southern Poverty Law Center (SPLC) were deceived into using the term Islamophobia to shut down criticisms of Islam; this is even after Maajid Nawaz sued them for adding his organization, Quilliam, to a list of organized groups who purportedly "hate" Muslims.[236] The SPLC added him despite the fact that Maajid Nawaz is himself a Muslim and seeks to promote peaceful reformation.[237] The incoherence of this corporate media circus was most notably demonstrated by their silence over President Obama overseeing drone bombings of seven different countries against Islamic terrorists, but which caused untold suffering upon an unaccounted number of Muslim civilians. While President Obama pursued this policy of drone bombings, the corporate media circus praised President Obama's U.N. speech in which President Obama argued that the Prophet of Islam should not be criticized. In other

---

[236] Price, Greg. "SPLC Apologizes to Falsely Labeled Foundation." Newsweek, Newsweek, 18 June 2018, www.newsweek.com/splc-nawaz-million-apologizes-981879.
[237] Price, Greg. "SPLC Apologizes to Falsely Labeled Foundation." Newsweek, Newsweek, 18 June 2018, www.newsweek.com/splc-nawaz-million-apologizes-981879.

words, in the monoculture of Western Universalism, respecting the collective illusion of sense-objects from religious beliefs was more important than the lives of Muslim civilians who had nothing to do with terrorism.

Second, the sole focus on future economic gains from the mass migration of large Muslim populations into Europe was supported under two chief presumptions: that it was taboo to criticize religion and that Muslim migrants and refugees would eventually "Westernize" on the basis that it is inevitable. Mass shootings, bombings, violence against women, British cities consisting of Pakistani Muslim grooming gangs that willfully seek to rape hundreds of women and little girls[238], Muslim migrants attempts at forming thuggish groups of Sharia morality police in Germany to Islamize the society[239], Muslim migrants in France saying French women cannot be allowed at restaurants or cafes because women aren't allowed live like that in their country of origin[240], and the formation of Muslim enclaves where they remain as deliberately segregated communities are all viewed as temporary problems until the purported inevitable adaption to Western values; all so that the economies keep increasing in Gross Domestic Product (GDP) so that the business elites continue to make increasing profits under the sense-object of future economic prospects. The lobbyists, businesspeople, economists, and politicians who kept peddling neoliberalism clearly viewed all of this as a temporary inconvenience because of their abject ignorance of Islamic culture and the full range of danger from Islamist political ideologies. They wrongly kept compartmentalizing these as isolated incidents instead of viewing it as what it actually is: a relentless political ideology that seeks to fundamentally transform all non-Muslim civilizations into 7th century technological, social, and political standards. Even worse, the neoliberal political elite effectively helped sell Islamist Judgment Day religious fervor due the Great Recession and ignoring the declining living standards. In opening up borders to Islamic communities in an effort to raise the European Union's collective GDP, the neoliberal elite have allowed a religious ideology that is fundamentally opposed to Adam Smith's social innovations from the 18th century that form the basis for modern capitalism; simply because it was created after the 7th century of the Prophet Mohammad's time. Arguments pointing to the Islamic monarchies of the Arab Spring purportedly adapting capitalism ignore the fact that modern slavery exists in many of those countries under the Kafala system and the influence of Free Speech condemnations from the US and the West

---

[238] Dearden, Lizzie. "Grooming Gangs Abused More than 700 Women and Girls around Newcastle after Police Appeared to Punish Victims." The Independent, Independent Digital News and Media, 23 Feb. 2018, www.independent.co.uk/news/uk/crime/grooming-gangs-uk-britain-newcastle-serious-case-review-operation-sanctuary-shelter-muslim-asian-a8225106.html.

[239] "German Federal Court Overturns 'Sharia Police' Acquittals." AP News, AP News, 11 Jan. 2018, apnews.com/article/525f089c10ae4417b48b368cd6fb3357.

[240] Maxwell, Emerald, and Caroline Sinz. "Focus: Women Made to Keep Low Profile in Some French Suburbs." YouTube, FRANCE 24 English, 19 Dec. 2016, www.youtube.com/watch?v=6gZFGpNdH1A&ab_channel=FRANCE24English.

itself.[241] In other words, the neoliberal elite ignoring the exploitation of workers forced into slavery in the Arab Spring was also in ignorance of the fact that the Islamic monarchies haven't adopted capitalism, but simply remade the slave system in Islam with a capitalist façade because the neoliberal elite were likely gaining from the slave system too.

    Over the many years, the condemnations towards Neoliberalism and Western Universalism under the umbrella term of "Globalism" kept piling up. The peddling of Ayn Rand or lassie faire capitalism no longer became tenable to shut down criticisms in order to ignore reality and facts. The neoliberal elite simply barked at their loyal jesters in the corporate media, whose press passes and journalistic badges are basically glorified dog collars, to write about Islamophobia, to scream racism or whatever other ism to shut down criticisms, and to continue the implicit pursuit of "reasonable limits" while categorizing the pain inflicted upon the broader public as some form of racism for having Free Speech criticisms. Even as mounting evidence of hundreds of little girls being raped in Britain; Islamic terrorist bombings like the Boston bombing and terrorist shootings like the Bernardino shooting and Pulse nightclub shooting in the US; the insane amount of Islamic terrorist bombings that India endures every year such as the October 2005 Delhi bombings to the March 2024 Bengaluru café bombings; and the unwillingness of Islamic communities to adapt to Western culture in multiple European countries to instead form their own isolated enclaves continued unimpeded. The ignorance of the neoliberal elite could be seen in how stunned they were at the emergence and long-term success of nationalist politics after they had successfully barked at their jester-journalists to ignore all the pain and suffering their economic policies inflicted upon the broader public throughout multiple countries by designating all of it as racist.

    Third, the pursuit of a global monoculture of Neoliberalism and Western Universalism has incontrovertibly led to a nonculture that fractured into incoherence. The neoliberal elite's persistence to shut down all criticisms of any component of neoliberalism as unrealistic or illusory with politicians like Prime Minister Tony Blair claiming it was effectively inarguable and President Bill Clinton adding neoliberal policies to the Democrat political agenda and betraying the unions[242]; the ideological arguments that were espoused effectively became the earliest emerging versions of what would later happen in US universities with Wokeism. That is, they replaced culture with what journalist Chris Hedges argues is "the cult of the self" and we see it every day with what Wokeism became. The earliest emergence of this was the neoliberals themselves with their arguments that nobody could argue against Neoliberal economic policies as if they were somehow tied to the identity of these people and it was presented more as their

---

[241] "Modern Slavery in United Arab Emirates." Walk Free, 22 Aug. 2023, www.walkfree.org/global-slavery-index/country-studies/united-arab-emirates/.
[242] Hacker, Jacob S., and Paul Pierson. Winner-Take-All Politics How Washington Made the Rich Richer - and Turned Its Back on the Middle Class. Simon & Schuster, 2011.

divine truth than anything they believed on the basis of rationality, facts, and evidence. They presented as divine orthodoxy concomitant with their love for Ayn Rand's pro-selfishness arguments. It was this figurative bubble shielding neoliberalism from any criticism that eventually created off-shoots and countercultures like Wokeism. Instead of a culture that values actual philosophy like Enlightenment values, the US Founding Fathers views on Free Speech, robust religious debates on questions of the human condition and truth that the New Atheists had, or even philosophical critiques in artform; we had all of that replaced with race and gender effectively being bizarre and stunted replacements for culture. It was not robust and informative critiques about racial equality such as Martin Luther King Jr or Malcolm X's historic speeches. It was not a historical recognition of the contributions of Native American cultures of North America to modern women's rights.[243] It certainly wasn't a recognition of Dharmic cultures' contributions and support for Transgenderism until British imperialism ruthlessly criminalized it for approximately 250 years; first with the Buggery Act of 1533 and then more formally with section 377 which was implemented by Great Britain in 1858.[244][245] It was primarily the shifting of the implicit "reasonable limits on Free Speech" principle to *not* being allowed to debate anything about Transgenderism, *not* being allowed to debate anything without accusations that you were somehow a phobic or a racist, or the most bizarre accusations that anyone disagreeing with Wokeism was a bad faith actor secretly seeking to harm racial minorities, women's rights, and the LGBT. Every identity-ism became an accusatory method of labeling other people as bigots, conspiracy theorists, and loons.

    In the same way neoliberal elites demanded nobody had the right to critique or criticize Neoliberalism, overgrowths of this emerged with the coinage of the term Islamophobia as somehow equivalent to homophobia despite Islam being a religious belief system with nearly two billion adherents and existing for roughly fourteen-hundred years, and then this concept branched out into off-shoots like gender and race becoming uncontestable identities due to an overemphasis on people's feelings instead of an argument based upon evidence and rational critique. As a result, Islamism continues to go unchecked and empowers itself from this confused and incoherent ideology that places no value on Free Speech. Please consider the following: if a 7th century Arab fundamentalist ideology can utilize and effectively strangle discussions in democratic societies by using Wokeism as a useful tool to continue a long-term plan of regressing all non-Muslim societies into 7th century standards, then what does this really say about the value of Wokeism? If it has been doing the same with exploiting Western Universalism to shut

---

[243] Wagner, Sally Roesch. Sisters in Spirit: Iroquois Influence on Early Feminists: Haudenosaunee (Iroquois) Influence on Early American Feminists. Book Publishing Company. Kindle Edition.

[244] Wong, Tessa. "377: The British Colonial Law That Left an Anti-LGBTQ Legacy in Asia." BBC News, BBC, 28 June 2021, www.bbc.com/news/world-asia-57606847.

[245] "India's Relationship with the Third Gender." UAB Institute for Human Rights Blog, The University of Alabama at Birmingham, 29 Oct. 2018, sites.uab.edu/humanrights/2018/10/29/indias-relationship-with-the-third-gender/.

down criticisms of Islam, then what does that say about the value of Western Universalism? The reason this is working is because both the Woke Left and the Neoliberal elite don't have a culture and don't value culture. Western Universalism has given way to incoherence and abject nothingness that even Islamism can fill the void of within democratic societies, because there is no focus or respect for genuine philosophy. Fundamental building blocks of ideas have been tossed for feelings of offense which encourage only a "I know it when I see it" mentality that is no different from Islamists being offended by images of the Prophet Mohammad. There's no sense of value in Free Speech. There's no respect for ideas. There're only aggressive, mob-like outcries and cancel culture due to a lack of ability and willingness to argue in favor of the beliefs that they hold. Why do you believe that your values are inherently good and others should support it, if you can't argue in favor of them through your own reasoning and communication?

A possible solution to counter this would be to separate the Founders from their philosophical arguments similar to what's already done in Hinduism and subsets of Western philosophy itself. It is similar to the idea of separating art from the artist. In this instance, it is focusing on advancing the method and not on the historical figures that first proposed them. From a historical perspective, it's perfectly fine to appreciate the individual, but not from a philosophical perspective of advancing lines of inquiry and reasoning. The US Founding Fathers were racist slave-owners, but that's not all that they were; Thomas Jefferson gave an amazing critique in favor of Free Speech that is awe-inspiring to me and he was also a deplorable racist against Native Americans. His philosophical views of Free Speech can be separated from his hateful views towards Native Americans; one is a philosophical view that has benefitted US society with so much technological innovation through the efforts of multiple ethnic backgrounds throughout the nearly 250 years of US history and the other is inexcusable racism towards Native Americans. If we haven't already come to a point in US society where we can agree to separate the two, then what are we doing? For whatever reason, Wokeism completely fails to accept this distinction between Thomas Jefferson's philosophical arguments and his racism. It simply peddles the argument that people are racist and cannot be allowed to argue against such accusations made against them. Islamism is winning because of this simplistic mindset. In fairness to Wokeism, and so as not to completely present a one-sided view, there has been an encouragement towards the reconceptualization of the US as a melting pot of cultures with highlighting innovations, artistic achievements, and historic milestones of multiple ethnic minorities in US history and throughout the world. Examples would be Google searches showing the innovations of minority inventors and female inventors like Americans Alice H. Parker, Fredrick McKinley Jones, or foreign innovators like Jagadish Chandra Bose of India and Ada Lovelace of Britain. Nevertheless, for the purposes of advancing society, it's probably better to focus on the advancements of methods regardless of who was the originator.

The Western world's willful ignorance of the threat of Islamism has become absurd. It has proven beyond doubt that European-derived legal systems, Western government institutions, and nonsensical beliefs in Western Universalism have left the Western world incapable of grappling with the challenges of Islamist takeover, because of the lack of willingness to criticize harmful ideas. Neoliberal economic theories and the obnoxious encouragement of Western Universalism have stultified and weakened the Western world due to a refusal to value Free Speech. While the United States has a mixed message of being both Western and a melting pot that ostensibly encourages cultural diversity; it has only recently pursued attempts at the conceptualization of being a melting pot of diverse cultures working together with a unified faith in US nationalism instead of parroting Western Universalism. Thankfully, it had a backlash to Wokeism's propensity to try to shut down debate. Western Europe has not been so lucky. Nowhere is the absurdity and failures of Western Universalism clearer than the country of Sweden. Sweden is the pinnacle of what happens when compassionate, bleeding-heart Europeans delude themselves into Western Universalist value judgments and refuse to criticize the hateful ideas within Islam, even as they suffer being bombed every waking day of their lives. Even as their children are put in danger of being bombed by foreign "refugees" and migrants from Syria and Iraq every single day, they refuse to criticize Islamism or even talk about the problems within Islam. It is genuinely absurd that they refuse to even call it Islamic terrorism and instead present it as gang violence, but not *Muslim* gang violence because that would apparently offend the sensibilities of the refugees and migrants who are bombing their cars, homes, shops, schools, and parks every single day to show how much unambiguous appreciation they have for being welcomed to live in Sweden.

In an excerpt from an article titled, "*Sweden's 100 explosions this year: What's going on?*" from Maddy Savage in a BBC article published on November 11th, 2019:

When three explosions took place in one night across different parts of Stockholm last month, it came as a shock to residents. There had been blasts in other city suburbs, but never on their doorstep.

Swedish police are dealing with unprecedented levels of attacks, targeting city centre locations too. The bomb squad was called to deal with 97 explosions in the first nine months of this year.

"I grew up here and you feel like that environment gets violated," says Joel, 22.

The front door of his apartment block in the central Stockholm neighbourhood of Sodermalm was blown out and windows were shattered along the street.

Who is to blame?
This category of crime was not even logged prior to 2017. Then, in 2018, there were 162 explosions and in the past two months alone the bomb squad have been called to almost 30.

"Bangers, improvised explosives and hand grenades" are behind most of the blasts, says Linda H Straaf, head of intelligence at Sweden's National Operations Department.

The attacks are usually carried out by criminal gangs to scare rival groups or their close friends or family, she says.
"This is a serious situation, but most people shouldn't be worried, because they are not going to be affected."
Teams have been sent to work with gang crime specialists in the US, Germany and the Netherlands, and they are liaising with Swedish military experts who dealt with explosives in Africa and Afghanistan.

"It's very new in Sweden, and we are looking for knowledge around the world," says Mats Lovning, head of the National Operations Department.

For criminologist Amir Rostami, who has researched the use of hand grenades in Sweden, the only relevant comparison is Mexico, plagued by gang violence.

"This is unique in countries that pretty much don't have a war or don't have a long history of terrorism," he says.

Where are the explosions?
Most attacks have taken place in low-income, vulnerable suburbs in the biggest cities: Stockholm, Gothenburg and Malmo.

Malmo had three blasts in just over 24 hours at the start of this month.

But more affluent places are now being targeted too. An explosion in the residential northern Stockholm suburb of Bromma last month destroyed the entrance to a block of flats, blew out windows and damaged cars.

A 20-year-old passerby was treated in hospital when a bomb targeted a grocery shop in the historic university city of Lund. And 25 people were hurt when a block of flats was targeted in the central town of Linkoping.

Sodermalm is a former working-class area that has become increasingly gentrified. Vintage boutiques and vegan delicatessens break up grids of mustard- and terracotta-painted apartment blocks. The building targeted is opposite a park and close to a school.

"Immediately afterwards, when police closed off the streets and I walked with my two kids to preschool, I got really scared," says Malin Bradshaw, who lives a few doors down.

No arrests have been made and police will not comment on potential motives.

"If it was targeted then to be honest it makes us feel safer, because then the attack was not aimed to harm the public," says Ms Bradshaw, hoping it was not a random attack.

Who are Sweden's criminal gangs?
Police say the criminals involved are part of the same gangs behind an increase in gun crime, often connected to the drugs trade. Sweden saw 45 deadly shootings in 2018, compared with 17 in 2011.

But why they have added explosives to their arsenal is unclear.

Swedish police do not record or release the ethnicity of suspects or convicted criminals, but intelligence chief Linda H Straaf says many do share a similar profile.[246]

---

[246] Savage, Maddy. "Sweden's 100 Explosions This Year: What's Going On?" BBC News, BBC, 12 Nov. 2019, www.bbc.com/news/world-europe-50339977.

Later on in the article, Linda H. Straaf claims the ones committing the crimes are second-or-third generation immigrants while the article later admits the Left-leaning news media completely refuses to even discuss bomb attacks to avoid "proof of problems with leftist policies" according to Christian Christenson, a Stockholm University professor of journalism.[247] How exactly are people able to verify or believe that it's not the refugees and migrants, when the Left-leaning Swedish news media refuse to discuss it because they're afraid of offending feelings?[248] Apparently, the mother mentioned earlier in the article, Malin Bradshaw, needs to seriously risk her preschool children being blown apart by bombs from Muslim migrants and Muslim "refugees" so that Sweden's Leftist political parties don't seem racist.[249]

Sadly, in the years since the BBC article was published, the problem has worsened with what are likely Muslim migrants and refugees increasing their bombings of Sweden in what are clearly terrorist activities meant to destabilize the country. An article from the *Eurasia Review: News and Analysis* published on January 31st, 2025 titled *"'No Control': Sweden Grapples With Bomb Violence Wave"* with the Prime Minister Ulf Kristersson openly admitting that the Swedish government has completely lost control over the wave of bombings happening in their country. The article reads as follows:

> (EurActiv) — Swedish Prime Minister Ulf Kristersson admitted that his government has lost control over a burgeoning wave of violence sweeping the country, amid escalating public concern.
>
> The acknowledgment came during an emergency meeting where Kristersson announced the acceleration of new legislation targeting juvenile involvement in criminal activities.
>
> The beginning of 2025 has seen bombings carried out at an average of one per day, leading to 27 bombings by January 27 – including several in residential communities, the Nordic Times reported.
>
> "Sweden is in the midst of a new wave of violence; it's primarily the bombings that are increasing, with almost one occurring every day," Kristersson told reporters on Thursday.
>
> "It's abundantly clear that we do not have control over this wave of violence; otherwise, we wouldn't be here," he added.
>
> In 2024, there were 317 total blasts reported by police, which has coincided with a troubling escalation in gang-related conflicts.
>
> According to the Swedish prime minister, gang violence is now affecting entire communities, showing "total indifference" to the consequences in residential areas. The Swedish Police Authority estimated in 2024 that 1,700 under-18s were active members of criminal networks.

---

[247] Savage, Maddy. "Sweden's 100 Explosions This Year: What's Going On?" BBC News, BBC, 12 Nov. 2019, www.bbc.com/news/world-europe-50339977.
[248] Savage, Maddy. "Sweden's 100 Explosions This Year: What's Going On?" BBC News, BBC, 12 Nov. 2019, www.bbc.com/news/world-europe-50339977.
[249] Savage, Maddy. "Sweden's 100 Explosions This Year: What's Going On?" BBC News, BBC, 12 Nov. 2019, www.bbc.com/news/world-europe-50339977.

In response, the Swedish government will bring forward planned legislation that will grant police more powers to detain children under the age of 15 in some circumstances. Originally due in the summer of 2026, the law is now slated to come into effect as early as 1 October this year.

Nevertheless, Kristersson described these criminal issues as "inherited" over a long period, suggesting that resolving them would be a project that extends through the entire decade.

Political pressure continues to mount on the prime minster, who has made the fight against armed crime one of his talking points in the 2022 election campaign.

Given that a hard line on organised crime in Sweden is one of the hallmarks of the Sweden Democrats – the far-right party that supports Kristersson's government – the prime minister faces a dual imperative to take decisive action: to please his ally, and prevent the party out-flanking him on the issue at the 2026 election.

Further recent measures taken to tackle Swedish gang violence a proposal to amend the country's constitution to strip dual nationals of their citizenship if convicted of involvement in gang crime.

A government-commissioned investigation also proposed on Wednesday that people convicted of crimes in Sweden should in future be able to serve their sentences in foreign prisons, as there are no 'absolute obstacles' under Swedish law.[250]

Sweden is suffering an organized and deliberate sacking from within by Islamic terrorists using modern bombs and a 7th century Arab fundamentalist mentality. Yet, the Swedish government and Swedish public refuse to utilize the use of force necessary to stop them. Why? Why are they refusing to even call the perpetrators terrorists and instead label the deliberate bombings of their own country as gang violence with a refusal to label them appropriately as Muslim terrorists, Muslim immigrants, and the purported Muslim refugees?

It is because they fear being labeled "Far-right" or the implication of being associated with any sort of fascist ideology. This insane level of tolerance for what is a sacking likely stems from the horrendous and cruel history that they imposed upon the Indigenous Sami people of Sweden, who suffered under Swedish government programs influenced by Nazism.[251] I will not go into the details of what was done to the Sami people, including to their children by a state-sponsored and Nazi-inspired policy as that's beyond the focus of this topic. The contemporary Swedish people's acknowledgement of guilt and genuine desire to make amends over what was done to the Sami people is admirable. The Swedish people wanting to vigorously avoid the label of Far-right due to the history of what was done to the Sami people is understandable. Having a tolerance for

---

[250] Szumski, Charles. "'No Control': Sweden Grapples with Bomb Violence Wave." Eurasia Review, EurActiv, 31 Jan. 2025, www.eurasiareview.com/31012025-no-control-sweden-grapples-with-bomb-violence-wave/.

[251] France 24. "Sweden's 'truth Commission' Delves into Painful Sami Past." France 24, FRANCE 24, 5 Oct. 2023, www.france24.com/en/live-news/20230510-sweden-s-truth-commission-delves-into-painful-sami-past.

foreign Muslim terrorists using their own Muslim children to throw hand grenades with the purpose of bombing civilian centers is surely not the way to show commitment to this desire to make amends to the indigenous group of people that Swedes have historically abused and harmed. Allowing Muslim terrorists to organize improvised explosives that could kill Swedish, Sami, or foreign children is not acceptable and not keeping anyone safe. It is not far-right to use more assertive means to stop organized terrorists, especially not people who show a clear and intentional targeting of civilians for the explicit purpose of mass murder. This is not fair to Swedish people, it is not fair to any foreign immigrants who simply want to live peacefully in Sweden, and it is surely putting the Sami people in danger too.

The Swedish governments positions on this matter are not an acceptable, or moral, or intelligent policy. I can't help but paraphrase a meme when reading about what has been happening in Sweden: This is just stupid. You are being stupid. Stop being stupid. Stop being stupid and then hold these terrorists to account for their deliberate terrorist actions that are putting innocent people in danger. If these people were sincere about grievances, then they'd be protesting with peacefully organized picket marches, not using their children to throw hand grenades near locations like preschools or planting improvised explosives to kill as many civilians as possible. Islam has its own set of history and you should not be conflating or substituting the suffering of the Sami people under Sweden's shameful and barbaric government policies of the past as a justification for the benign treatment given to Islamic terrorists. You should not be holding back the appropriate use of force against terrorists who are clearly seeking to destroy your country and making no secret about it every time they use children to blow up civilian centers.

Islam's own history explains what their intentions are. The truth is that they behave this way, precisely because they view you as weak. Unfortunately, they will almost certainly start attempting to commit grooming gangs just like in Great Britain, Pakistan, and India. They'll almost certainly be trying to force female children into becoming their slave girls. Historically, they always seek out the ethnic backgrounds that are most vulnerable in society. In other words, they'll likely try to groom and gang rape the Sami people because their 7th century Arab fundamentalist mindset will make them perceive the Sami people as the weakest in society. It is not racist or a joke to say that, because their religion justifies such behavior, it happens throughout the Arab Spring even now, and Islam teaches them that the Abrahamic God will forgive the women when Muslims force them into prostitution, which will include gang raping young girls. That is the truth about the history of Islam and ignoring that truth results in grooming gang violence in Great Britain, India, and other countries they seek to Islamize. Please re-read Chapter Three, if you think any of that is bigotry. It is no different than Catholic child rape cases; it is real and it is something that you need to make sure that you're on top of to prevent, or children – the most vulnerable in society – are going to be the ones that will suffer and the most likely targets will be Sami children just like they did in Great Britain to primarily working-class children.

Neoliberals and Marxists Do Not Value Culture

One core issue that should be addressed and which is shared by both Neoliberals and Marxists; why do they behave as if reality and consequences don't matter or don't exist? It is very strange how these opposing groups behave the same, but for diametrically opposed economic reasons. There're two chief reasons why: first, both Marxists and Neoliberals have no culture. They don't view culture as real value systems; they don't understand how culture impacts governing systems and that these governing systems aren't immutable. They confuse governments created and shaped by people as divinely-inspired and thus immune from evidence-based reasoning, because they lack even the most basic principles of philosophical thought. They have no critical thinking when it comes to philosophy; Marxists believe that it doesn't matter as part of the bedrock of Marxist economic theory and Neoliberals simply don't think about it or view it with derision despite the fact that the wealthy Neoliberals are always lobbying political systems that grew from these philosophical views. This is also why they turn their economic theories into a bizarre religious orthodoxy that they argue is indisputable and that no philosophical system is allowed to argue against. The only focus they have is in the sense-object of future monetary gains and they view culture as simply interchangeable noise, because they have no culture themselves. What happens? The Neoliberals and the Marxists both turn their economic theories into identity politics and Neoliberals in particular try to substitute their specific, extremist brand of capitalism for all of capitalism. They deliberately ignore the variety of capitalist systems to push for their specific identity-based ideology of capitalism.

The second reason is willful ignorance. They actively seek only confirmatory information and ignore all evidence-based reasoning that they believe goes "too far" or is "too extreme" which challenges what is little more than an identity-based faith tradition. Marxists do this on Discord and reddit internet forums, in public speaking events, and in their Youtube videos. Neoliberals do this when lobbying their policies in secret to politicians and giving them millions in campaign finance as incentives to pursue their specific economic agenda. When questioning Marxists on their beliefs, they'll come-up with the most incoherent arguments asking if people who question them know the difference between a variety of Marxist theories instead of actually putting in the effort to explain how such an economic system could ever work in reality and then they mock those who simply question them on the realistic applicability of their economic theory. Neoliberals typically refuse to even have discussions and simply accuse you of being Marxist or a Socialist for simply questioning how their specific, extremist branch of capitalism can even work in the long-term. I'd argue that Marxists simply believe in a fantasy world and those capitalists tricked into conflating Neoliberalism with all forms of capitalist economic theories have confused people questioning them as harboring some form of evil or hate, which is also ridiculous. Moreover, the Conservatives that have abandoned Neoliberalism and who are now accusing Neoliberals of being evil and hateful, are assuming too much in their intent. It might be more accurate to say that the wealthy Neoliberal elite and Neoliberal economists are simply ignorant and greedy. The Neoliberal elite only think about future earnings from future gains in profit and don't realize Islamism is a political ideology that is absolutely serious about reverting every aspect of human life back into a 7th century standard; there will be no future economic rewards for all the damage done from Islamic immigration. There's no massive payout at the end of all the bombings, shootings, stabbings, and economic damage done to Western Europe. The European public have a legitimate right to be angry with the Neoliberal elite. The Neoliberal elite only have themselves to blame for not using their millions and billions in resources to learn more about Islamic culture before pushing for policies of massive immigration to offset the reduced labor capacity. There's no justification for not doing any research; they were so stupid that they didn't think of the obvious threat after horrific events like September 11th, 2001 and the ensuing terrorist attacks that have happened since then throughout multiple countries too numerous to mention in brief.

The reason this continues to be a problem is that the neoliberal elite have vehemently chosen to commit to "analyses" that lack in reality-based thinking to preserve their own power and social status, but at the expense of anything that criticizes what is effectively what Daniel Kahneman referred to as theory-induced blindness.[252] Take for example the most recent case of Neoliberal ideologues peddling their beliefs within their paywall think tanks like in *Foreign Affairs*, so that the majority of the US public doesn't learn about it and therefore can't judge it. I refer to the corrosive and disastrous influence of Jason Furman's economic policies throughout his years serving under President Clinton, the World Bank, and President Obama. However, you may be wondering, who is Jason Furman and why does his Pro-Neoliberal stance matter and does he really have much influence? Well, how about judging him based upon his own stated achievements? Here is his brief biography made on *Foreign Affairs* to explain his "accomplishments" and his competence in arguing for economic policies:

> JASON FURMAN is Aetna Professor of the Practice of Economic Policy at Harvard University and Nonresident Senior Fellow at the Peterson Institute for International Economics. He spent eight years as a senior economic adviser to President Barack Obama, including as Chair of the U.S. Council of Economic Advisers from 2013 to 2017. He also served under President Bill Clinton, including on the National Economic Council, and was an economist at the World Bank.[253]

---

[252] Kahneman, Daniel. Chapter 25: Bernoulli's Errors (276) and Chapter 26: The Prospect Theory (278-288). Thinking, fast and slow. Farrar, Straus and Giroux, 2015.
[253] Furman, Jason. "Jason Furman." Foreign Affairs, 30 Oct. 2024, www.foreignaffairs.com/authors/jason-furman.

In this case, Jason Furman's recent article on *Foreign Affairs* titled *"The Post-Neoliberal Delusion"* and published on February 10th, 2025 where he makes this very odd claim:

> The economy was also awash in pent-up demand from consumers, who had been unable to spend during the pandemic. In 2020, toward the end of the first Trump administration, Congress passed $3.4 trillion in fiscal support; in December, $900 billion was authorized to fund $600 stimulus checks for most American adults. Despite the ravages of the pandemic on public health, many households had never been in better financial shape, with overall debt service payments representing the lowest share of disposable income in decades, delinquencies and defaults remaining low, and record amounts of money sitting in checking accounts across the income spectrum. Economists hoped that as the rollout of vaccines proceeded, so would the economic recovery. In fact, when Biden came to office, the $1.5 trillion of excess savings that Americans had accumulated from the federal largess of 2020 and their suppressed spending was waiting to be unleashed by the reopening—perhaps obviating the macroeconomic need for yet another large stimulus bill. The economist and *New York Times* columnist Paul Krugman summed up this view in late 2020. "Once we've achieved widespread vaccination, the economy will bounce back," he wrote. "On average Americans have been saving like crazy, and will emerge from the pandemic with stronger balance sheets than they had before."[254]

This information is actually false. What's particularly odd is that there were numerous news articles citing monthly and annual survey results from Bank Rate Monitor, a website and originally a financial magazine chiefly read by the Banking sector, that provides free resources to help anyone interested in improving their financial situations. Jason Furman claims there was an "excess savings" by Americans during the pandemic, but self-reported survey results from regular Americans published by Bankrate's Principal US economic reporter, Sarah Foster, completely disproves this claim. In her article published on July 21st, 2021, titled *"Survey: More than half of Americans couldn't cover three months of expenses with an emergency fund"* she revealed the following datasets from the survey:

---

[254] Furman, Jason. "The Post-Neoliberal Delusion." Foreign Affairs, 10 February 2025, https://www.foreignaffairs.com/united-states/post-neoliberal-delusion. Accessed 28 March 2025.

More than half of Americans have less than three months' worth of expenses in an emergency fund

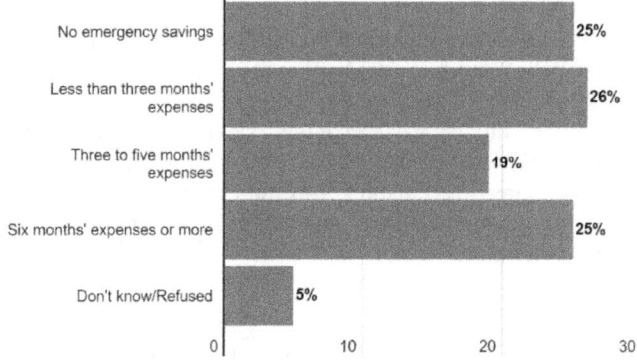

Foster, Sarah. "Survey: More than Half of Americans Couldn't Cover Three Months of Expenses with Emergency Savings." Edited by Brian Beers, Bankrate, SRS Omnibus, 22 Oct. 2024, www.bankrate.com/banking/savings/emergency-savings-survey-july-2021/.

And later on in the same article:

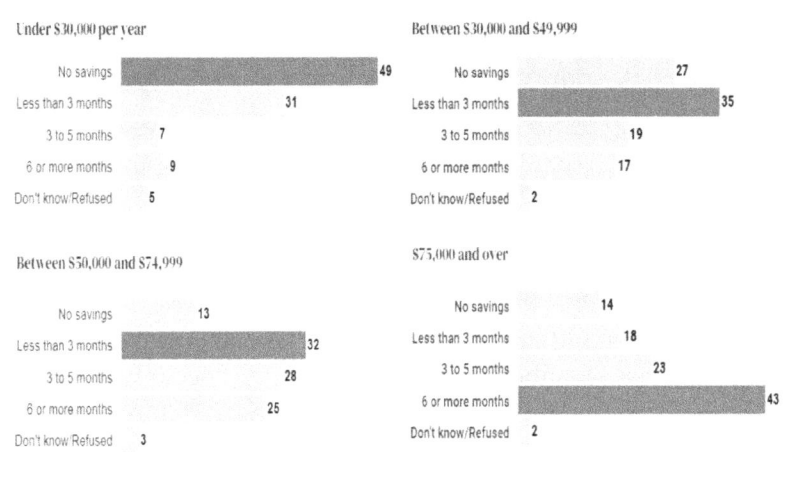

Foster, Sarah. "Survey: More than Half of Americans Couldn't Cover Three Months of Expenses with Emergency Savings." Edited by Brian Beers, Bankrate, SRS Omnibus, 22 Oct. 2024, www.bankrate.com/banking/savings/emergency-savings-survey-july-2021/.

And her methodology was perfectly credible:

Methodology
This study was conducted for Bankrate via telephone by SSRS on its Omnibus survey platform. The SSRS Omnibus is a national, weekly, dual-frame bilingual telephone survey. Interviews were conducted from June 22-27, 2021 among a sample of 1,009 respondents in English (973) and Spanish (36). Telephone interviews were conducted by landline (202) and cell phone (807, including 542 without a landline phone). The margin of error for total respondents is +/- 3.74 percent at the 95 percent confidence level. All SSRS Omnibus data are weighted to represent the target population.[255]

This only took me a quick google search of around twenty minutes or less. A Neoliberal elite like Jason Furman surely has more capital, manpower, and other resources than I do. So, why did he cite Krugman instead of taking the time to read through credible surveys that would challenge his argument? The answer may lie with Political Scientists Jacob S. Pierson and Paul Hacker's critique of Neoliberal economic policies impacts on Presidential and Congressional election campaigns. In their magnum

---

[255] Foster, Sarah. "Survey: More than Half of Americans Couldn't Cover Three Months of Expenses with Emergency Savings." Edited by Brian Beers, Bankrate, SRS Omnibus, 22 Oct. 2024, www.bankrate.com/banking/savings/emergency-savings-survey-july-2021/.

opus, "*Winner-Take-All Politics How Washington Made the Rich Richer - and Turned Its Back on the Middle Class*" the pair make the case that the wealthy politicians, especially during the second President Bush's administration, only viewed the wealthy elite as their voter base and never concerned themselves with the broader public during this time.[256] To people like Jason Furman and his fellow Neoliberals, the only opposing side they see are those accepted within their own wealthy circles; no facts and evidence matter outside of their in-group of the wealthy elite. The broader public is just angry and contradictory noise to them. It is very likely that to the neoliberal elite, the neoliberals of the wider public are just their useful idiots in all practical sense. Something to give an awkward thumbs-up and quote as a means of support for their own preconceived notions, but not people worthy of equal consideration when there is a divergence in viewpoint and especially not for any possible reformation of neoliberal economic theory itself. They certainly will never acknowledge that Neoliberalism as an economic theory has brought poverty to the US and the West. Neoliberalism has simply failed in its claims; yet, this inconvenient fact is ignored despite multiple bailouts within the US and for countries like Greece, the weakening of the European Union, and the rise of China.

By transforming their economic theory into their identity due to their lack of culture and refusal to acknowledge inconvenient facts that disprove their economic orthodoxy, they have sold out entire countries to 7th century Islamism's attempts to break them to pieces, while ordering their jester-journalists to conflate nationalism with Nazism by using terms like far-right because they genuinely don't understand the value of culture at all. They don't distinguish between nationalism and Nazism because they lack even the basic education to understand the difference due to only being educated in economic theories and only being motivated by future gains in profits that'll never come. The false premise that Muslim enclaves will automatically Westernize is simply taken for granted on the basis of Western Universalism and this premise is used to shut down all legitimate criticisms. The Neoliberal elite merely bark at their jester-journalists to make articles that imply anything that disagrees or questions the notion of religious tolerance is far-right. Anything that points to Muslim enclaves being unwilling to adapt is accused of being far-right and conflated to be a form of Nazism despite the lack of clear definition of what is Far-right about this criticism. Fascism has been repurposed to mean some arbitrary and self-serving criteria for the Neoliberal elite to quash dissent without any clear definition; instead of meaning the original term of ultraorthodox Catholicism and the entwining of race with nationalism, it has been hurled as an insult for conservative groups from Britain, to Ireland, to France, to Sweden, to the Netherlands, to India, and to the US. Essentially, anything that disagrees with the notion of religious tolerance and the desire to question Islamic religious doctrines is viewed as far-right and fascist. Ultimately, the

---

[256] Hacker, Jacob S., and Paul Pierson. Winner-Take-All Politics How Washington Made the Rich Richer - and Turned Its Back on the Middle Class. Simon & Schuster, 2011.

jester-journalists of the corporate media and the Neoliberal elite are the ultimate guard dogs of the Islamist takeover and destruction of all non-Muslim cultures.

Of Aztecs and Indians

Lastly, a philosophical concept that has helped me to better understand the social issues of what both the Woke and Neoliberal elite's ignorance has wrought upon chiefly Western civilizations is James Maffie's arguments of how the Mexica / Aztec viewed their society in their own theological and philosophical terms. In brief, Maffie claims, and provides extensive research in support of this claim, that the Mexica viewed their society in a horizontal and nonhierarchical social system of the Center containing the majority of the population and a two or four-sided periphery containing various groups that tried to tug and pull the Center to their respective side to obtain favor.[257] In my own reconceptualization of Mexica philosophy, the Center is the majority population and the Periphery are various interest groups and ideologues like the Neoliberal elite such as Jason Furman who seek to curry favor and obtain social power over the Center via tugging against other Peripheries who have opposing views. This philosophical concept, which I currently believe is well-supported based upon the copious amounts of evidence that James Maffie has given for how the Mexica constituted their society in their own philosophical terms, surprisingly helped me to understand precisely why Cancel Culture and turning race, gender, and economic theories into identity politics was doomed to fail. Effectively, the tug-of-war in democratic societies is Free Speech. When the Neoliberal elite secretly lobby without the general public's general awareness or knowledge within the periphery and then tries to justify their lobbying via saying their economic policies cannot be argued at all, then the general public has a natural distrust of such methods. For the Woke Left, it is even more ridiculous. First, the Woke Left argue the Center is bigoted and when anyone in the Center questions the Woke Left about their perspectives, the Woke Left respond by blocking and "cancelling" the Center and they keep using this method of cancellation to create a receding wall of ignorance into the Periphery. They view and discuss issues with like-minded individuals as a way of "seeing themselves" within their own community of the Periphery of society. The Woke Left proceed to get shocked when the Center doesn't vote in their favor after cancelling themselves into irrelevance from the Center, seeking only to "see themselves" with like-minded individuals within the Periphery, and then acting with astonishment when the Center doesn't support their views after completely failing to communicate what their views are and being completely unwilling to accept criticism of their views. This sounds like a

---

[257] Maffie, James. Aztec Philosophy: Understanding a World in Motion. University Press of Colorado. Kindle Edition.

satirical skit, except this is what is actually happening in societies due to basing views on personal feelings instead of our individual reasoning skills. What has been filling the void of these failures wrought by Western Universalism, which continues to pursue Cancel Culture as an off-shoot of Religious Tolerance? The unrestrained rise of the 7th Century Arab fundamentalist ideology of Islamism.

India knows well what happens when you can't criticize Islamism in society and everyone else in India is forced to suffer the consequences every year under threat of riots from the large Muslim populations that still exist within India over fear of offense. The feelings of Muslims supersede the lives of those they harm. The fact that Hindus, Hindutva, and the broader BJP party are portrayed as "far-right" is laughably asinine; but the jester-journalists of the US corporate media circus destroying their credibility should come as no surprise. After all, they refused to ever write or publish any news stories of the New Zealand-funded Baptist Christian terrorist groups within India for about twenty-five years and still don't mention them.[258][259] A cursory look at the Wikipedia page of terrorism in India makes it clear which groups are the most dangerous. I did a full tally twice and then a cursory tally a third time of all terror attacks listed on the Wikipedia page from 1980 – 2024. I must confess one issue of my own limitation to be as open and honest as possible; I somehow kept missing one case of the 121 cases, so the full tally that I did was of 120 cases out of the 121 listed cases and I apologize for that, but it shouldn't impact the statistical distribution of the terror cases. Within India's contemporary history, while it is true that some terrorist attacks are due to various groups from the Hindu Tamil Tigers of Sri Lanka, to Naxal / Maoist-variant Communist terrorist groups, to Khalistani terrorists, and Baptist Christian terrorists (the Christian terrorists are barely listed in the Wikipedia page, because apparently the feelings of White Christian Europeans supersede the harm that Baptist Christian terror funding from countries like New Zealand does to Indians of different backgrounds)[260][261]; they all make-up approximately forty-two percent judging from the Wikipedia's accounting and they mostly occurred in the 1980s – 90s. Approximately an overwhelming 58 percent of the Wikipedia listings of terrorism, especially contemporary terrorism in India that is as annual as the seasonal weather changes, comes from various Islamist terrorist groups.

---

[258] Bhaumik, Subir. "South Asia | 'Church Backing Tripura Rebels.'" BBC News, BBC, 18 Apr. 2000, news.bbc.co.uk/2/hi/world/south_asia/717775.stm.
[259] Tiwary, Deeptiman. "Centre Signs Peace Pact with Tripura Insurgent Outfit Nlft." The Indian Express, The Indian Express, 10 Aug. 2019, indianexpress.com/article/india/centre-signs-peace-pact-with-tripura-insurgent-outfit-nlft-5895406/.
[260] Bhaumik, Subir. "South Asia | 'Church Backing Tripura Rebels.'" BBC News, BBC, 18 Apr. 2000, news.bbc.co.uk/2/hi/world/south_asia/717775.stm.
[261] Tiwary, Deeptiman. "Centre Signs Peace Pact with Tripura Insurgent Outfit Nlft." The Indian Express, The Indian Express, 10 Aug. 2019, indianexpress.com/article/india/centre-signs-peace-pact-with-tripura-insurgent-outfit-nlft-5895406/.

This is the reality of a country being strangled to prevent any discussion about the problems of Islam:

List of terror attacks in India

#	Date	Incidents & Description	Location	People Killed	Injured	Status of the Case
1	8 June 1980	Mandai massacre	Tripura	500		N/A
2	2 August 1984	Meenambakkam bomb blast[2]	Tamil Nadu	30	25	Verdict given
3	7 July 1987	1987 Haryana killings[3]	Haryana	36	60	
4	21 May 1991	Assassination of Rajiv Gandhi	Tamil Nadu	15		N/A
5	15 June 1991	1991 Punjab killings[4]	Punjab	126	200	
6	17 October 1991	1991 Rudrapur bombings	Uttarakhand	41	140	
7	8 November 1991	1991 Kalyan train bomb blast[5][6][7]	Mumbai	12	65	
8	12 March 1993	1993 Bombay bombings[8][9]		257	700+	
9	16 March 1993	1993 Bowbazar bombing	Kolkata (Formerly Calcutta), West Bengal	69		Verdict given
10	9 April 1993	Palar blast	Karnataka	22	13	
11	8 August 1993	1993 bombing of RSS office in Chennai	Tamil Nadu	11	7	
12	5–6 December 1993	Trains and Ajmeri[10]	Rajasthan			
13	21 May 1996	1996 Lajpat Nagar blast	Delhi	13	39	
14	22 May 1996	1996 Dausa blast	Rajasthan	14	37	
15	30 December 1996	Brahmaputra Mail train bombing	Assam	33	150	N/A
16	14 February 1998	1998 Coimbatore bombings	Tamil Nadu	58	200+	Verdict given
17	20 May 2000	Bagber massacre	Tripura	25		
18	May–July 2000	2000 Church bombings of South India	Karnataka, Goa and Andhra Pradesh	0		Verdict given

139

#	Date	Event	Location	Fatalities	Injuries	Notes
19	9 June 2001	Charar-e-Sharief mosque attack	Charari Sharief	4	60	
20	22 December 2000	2000 terrorist attack on Red Fort[11]	Delhi	3	14	Verdict given
21	1 October 2001	2001 Jammu and Kashmir legislative assembly car bombing	Jammu and Kashmir	38		
22	13 December 2001	2001 Indian Parliament attack in New Delhi	Delhi	7	18	Verdict given
23	22 January 2002	American Cultural Centre attack	Kolkata	5	20	
24	13 May 2002	2002 Jaunpur train crash[12]	N/A	12	80	
25	30 March 2002	2002 Raghunath temple attacks[13]	Jammu	11	20	
26	10 September 2002	Rafiganj train wreck	Bihar	200	150+	
27	24 November 2002	2002 Raghunath temple attacks[13]	Jammu	14	45	
28	6 December 2002	2002 Mumbai bus bombing[14]	Mumbai	2	14	
29	21 December 2002	Kurnool train crash	Andhra Pradesh	20	80	
30	24 September 2002	Attack on Akshardham temple	Gujarat	31	80	Verdict given
31	27 January 2003	January 2003 Mumbai bombing[15]	Mumbai	1	28	
32	13 March 2003	March 2003 Mumbai bombing[16]	Mumbai		10	
33	23 March 2003	2003 Nadimarg massacre	Nadimarg, Jammu and Kashmir	25	1	
34	14 August 2003	Kamalnagar massacre[17]	Tripura	14		N/A
35	25 August 2003	August 2003 Mumbai bombings	Mumbai	52		
36	2 January 2004	Jammu railway station attack[18]	Jammu	4	14	
37	15 August 2004	2004 Dhemaji school bombing	Assam	18	40	

#	Date	Event	Location	Fatalities	Injuries
38	2 October 2004	2004 Dimapur bombings	Dimapur, Nagaland	30	100
39	5 July 2005	2005 Ram Janmabhoomi attack[19]	Ayodhya	6	
40	28 July 2005	2005 Jaunpur train bombing[20]	N/A	13	50
41	29 October 2005	2005 Delhi bombings: Three powerful serial blasts in New Delhi at different places[21]	Delhi	70	250
42	28 December 2005	2005 Indian Institute of Science shooting	Karnataka	1	4
43	19 February 2006	2006 Ahmedabad railway station bombing	Gujarat	0	25
44	7 March 2006	2006 Varanasi bombings: Three synchronized terrorist attacks in Varanasi in Shri Sankatmochan Mandir and Varanasi Cantonment Railway Station[22][23]	Varanasi	28	101
45	11 July 2006	2006 Mumbai train bombings: Series of 7 train bombing during the evening rush hour in Mumbai	Mumbai	209	714
46	8 September 2006	2006 Malegaon bombings: Series of bomb blasts in the vicinity of a mosque in Malegaon, Maharashtra	Maharashtra	40	125
47	18 February 2007	2007 Samjhauta Express bombings	Haryana	70	50
48	18 May 2007	Mecca Masjid bombing		16	100
	August 2007				

49	25 August 2007	August 2007 Hyderabad bombings - Two blasts in Hyderabad's Lumbini park and Gokul Chat.	Hyderabad	42	54	
50	11 October 2007	Ajmer Dargah bombing[24]	Rajasthan	3	17	
51	14 October 2007	One blast in a movie theatre in the town of Ludhiana[24]	Ludhiana	6		
52	24 November 2007	A series of near-simultaneous explosions at courthouse complexes in the cities of Lucknow, Varanasi, and Faizabad[24]	Uttar Pradesh	16	70	
53	1 January 2008	Terror attack on CRPF camp in Rampur, Uttar Pradesh by Lashkar-e-Taiba.[25]		8	5	
54	13 May 2008	Jaipur bombings: 9 bomb blasts along 6 areas in Jaipur[26]	Jaipur	71	200	Verdict given[26]
55	25 July 2008	2008 Bangalore serial blasts: 8 low intensity bomb blasts in Bangalore	Bangalore	1	20	arrests made
56	26 July 2008	2008 Ahmedabad bombings: 17 serial bomb blasts in Ahmedabad	Gujarat	56	200	arrests made
57	13 September 2008	13 September 2008 Delhi bombings: 5 bomb blasts in Delhi markets		33	130	
58	27 September 2008	27 September 2008 Delhi bombing: Bombings at Mehrauli area, 2 bomb blasts in Delhi flower market	Delhi	3	21	
59	29 September	29 September 2008 western India bombings: 10 killed and 80 injured in bombings in	Maharashtra	10	80	

#	Date	Event	Location	Killed	Injured	Notes
59	29 September 2008	29 September 2008 western India bombings: 10 killed and 80 injured in bombings in Maharashtra (including Malegaon) and Gujarat bomb blasts	Maharashtra	10	80	
60	1 October 2008	2008 Agartala bombings	Agartala	4	100	
61	21 October 2008	2008 Imphal bombing	Imphal	17	40+	
62	30 October 2008	2008 Assam bombings	Assam	81	470	
63	26 November 2008	2008 Mumbai attacks[27][28]	Mumbai	171	300+	Verdict given
64	1 January 2009	2009 Guwahati bombings[29]	Assam	6	67	
65	6 April 2009	2009 Assam bombings[30]		9	63	
66	13 February 2010	2010 Pune bombing[31]	Pune	17	54	
67	15 February 2010	Silda camp attack	West Bengal	28		
68	6 April 2010	April 2010 Maoist attack in Dantewada	Chhattisgarh	84 (including 8 terrorists)	8	
69	17 May 2010	2010 Dantewada bus bombing		31-44	15	
70	28 May 2010	Jnaneswari Express train derailment	West Bengal	148	200+	
71	7 December 2010	2010 Varanasi bombing[32]	Varanasi	2	37	
72	13 July 2011	2011 Mumbai bombings	Mumbai	26	130	
73	7 September 2011	2011 Delhi bombing[33]	Delhi	15	74	
73	13 February 2012	2012 attacks on Israeli diplomats		0	4	
75	1 August 2012	2012 Pune bombings	Pune	0	1	

#	Date	Event	Location	Fatalities	Injuries	Notes
76	21 February 2013	2013 Hyderabad blasts	Hyderabad	18	131	
77	13 March 2013	March 2013 Srinagar attack	Jammu and Kashmir	7	10	
78	17 April 2013	2013 Bangalore blast	Bengaluru	0	16	
79	25 May 2013	2013 Naxal attack in Darbha valley	Chhattisgarh	32	32	
80	24 June 2013	June 2013 Srinagar attack	Jammu and Kashmir	8	19	
81	7 July 2013	July 2013 Maoist attack in Dumka	Chhattisgarh	2		
82		Bodh Gaya bombings	Bihar	0	5	
83	27 October 2013	2013 Patna bombings		6	85	
84	26 December 2013	2013 Jalpaiguri bombing	West Bengal	5	5	
85	11 March 2014	2014 Chhattisgarh attack	Chhattisgarh	16	3	
86	25 April 2014	Blast in Jharkhand[34]	Jharkhand	8	4-5	
87	28 April 2014	Blast in Budgam District[35]	Jammu and Kashmir	0	18	
88	1 May 2014	2014 Chennai train bombing	Tamil Nadu	1	14	
89		May 2014 Assam violence	Assam	33		
90	12 May 2014	Maoist blast in Gadchiroli District[36]	Maharashtra	7	2	
91	23 December 2014	December 2014 Assam violence	Assam	85		
92	28 December 2014	2014 Bangalore bombing[37]	Bengaluru	1	5	
93	20 March 2015	2015 Jammu attack[38]	Jammu and Kashmir	6	10	
94	4–9 June 2015	2015 Manipur ambush	Manipur	176 (including 158 terrorists)	15	Surgical strike by Indian Armed Forces near India Myanmar border killing 156 terrorists.[39] [circular reference]
95	27 July 2015	2015 Gurdaspur attack in Dina Nagar,		10	15	

95	27 July 2015	2015 Gurdaspur attack in Dina Nagar, Gurdaspur district		10	15	
96	2 January 2016	2016 Pathankot attack in Pathankot Air Force Station, Pathankot	Punjab	7		
97	25 June 2016	2016 Pampore attack	Pampore	8	22	
98	5 August 2016	2016 Kokrajhar shooting.[40]	Kokrajhar, Assam	14	15	
99	18 September 2016	2016 Uri attack[41]	Uri, Jammu & Kashmir	23	8	India claimed surgical strike on terrorist camps across Line of Control, Pakistan denied that a cross-border strike took place.[42]
100	3 October 2016	2016 Baramulla attack	Baramulla, Jammu & Kashmir	5		
101	6 October 2016	2016 Handwara attack at 30 Rashtriya Rifles	Handwara, Jammu & Kashmir			
101	6 October 2016	2016 Handwara attack at 30 Rashtriya Rifles camp	Handwara, Jammu & Kashmir			
102	29 November 2016	2016 Nagrota army base attack	Nagrota, Jammu & Kashmir	10		
103	7 March 2017	2017 Bhopal–Ujjain Passenger train bombing	Bhopal, Madhya Pradesh		10	
104	24 April 2017	2017 Sukma attack	Sukma district, Chhattisgarh	26		
105	11 July 2017	2017 Amarnath Yatra attack	Anantnag, Jammu & Kashmir	8	18	
106	10 February 2018	2018 Sunjuwan attack	Sunjuwan, Jammu and Kashmir	11	11	
107	13 March 2018	2018 Sukma attack	Sukma district, Chhattisgarh	9		
108	14 February	2019 Pulwama	Awantipora, Jammu &	46		Air strikes by Indian Air Force on Pakistani Islamic

#	Date	Name	Location	Fatalities	Injuries	Notes
108	14 February 2019	2019 Pulwama attack	Awantipora, Jammu & Kashmir	46		Air strikes by Indian Air Force on Pakistani Islamic militant group Jaish-e-Mohammed
109	7 March 2019	2019 Jammu Bus stand grenade blast[43]	Jammu City, Jammu & Kashmir	3	28-35	Arrest made of a teen aged student of 9th standard of a local school.
110	9 April 2019	2019 Dantewada attack[44]	Dantewada, Chhattisgarh	5		
111		2019 killing of RSS worker in Kishtwar[45]	Kishtwar, Jammu and Kashmir	2		Curfew imposed in Kishtwar and adjoining areas
112	1 May 2019	Gadchiroli Naxal bombing[46]	Maharashtra	16		Unknown
113	12 June 2019	June 2019 Kashmir attack[47]	Awantipora, Jammu & Kashmir	5(+1)	4	Got away
113	21 March 2020	2020 Sukma Maoists attack	Sukma district, Chhattisgarh	17	15	
114	3 April 2021	2021 Sukma–Bijapur attack	Sukma district,	22 (+9)	32	
114	3 April 2021	2021 Sukma–Bijapur attack	Sukma district, Chhattisgarh	22 (+9)	32	
115	8 April 2023	2023 Elathur train arson[48]	Elathur, Kozhikode district, Kerala	3		Unknown. Culprit is believed to be a lone wolf.
116	20 April 2023	2023 Poonch-Rajouri Attack[49]	Poonch, Rajouri, Jammu and Kashmir	5	1	
117	26 April 2023	2023 Dantewada bombing[50]	Dantewada District, Chhattisgarh	11 (10 Policemen and 1 driver)		
119	29 October 2023	Ernakulam Jehovah's Witness Convention Center Blast[51]	Kochi, Kerala	3	36	Perpetrator is a former member of the Jehovah's Witness religion community.
120	1 March 2024	2024 Bangalore Cafe bombing	Bangalore, Karnataka	0	9	Chargesheet filed against four Islamic State members.[52]
						Pakistani-backed Islamist terrorists

| 121 | 9 June 2024 | 2024 Reasi attack[53] | Reasi, Jammu and Kashmir (union territory) | 9 | 33 | Pakistani-backed Islamist terrorists belonging to the terrorist group The Resistance Front attacked Hindu pilgrims returning from pilgrimage.[54] |

Year, fatalities, and number of incidents

Terrorist incidents in India[55][56]

Year	Number of incidents	Deaths	Injuries
2018	748	350	540
2017	1000	470	702
2016	1025	467	788
2015	884	387	649
2014	860	490	776
2013	694	467	771
2012	611	264	651
2011	645	499	730
2010	663	812	660
2010	663	812	660
2009	672	774	854
2008	534	824	1,759
2007	149	626	1,187
2006	167	722	2,138
2005	146	466	1,216
2004	108	334	949
2003	196	472	1,183
2002	164	599	1,186
2001	234	660	1,144
2000	180	671	761
1999	112	469	591
1998	61	398	411
1997	193	853	1,416
1996	213	569	952
1995	179	361	616
1994	107	389	405
1993	42	525	1,564
1992	237	1,152	917
1991	339	1,113	1,326
1990	349	907	1,042

1990	349	907	1,042
1989	324	874	769
1988	358	966	1,033
1987	166	506	429
1986	96	340	163
1985	39	51	79
1984	159	195	364
1983	47	59	217
1982	13	64	102
1981	16	24	12
1980	10	17	13
1979	20	31	19
1978	0	0	0
1977	1	0	0
1976	1	0	0
1975	1	4	0
1974	0	0	0
1973	0	0	0
1972	1	0	0
1971	0	0	0
1970	0	0	0
1973	0	0	0
1972	1	0	0
1971	0	0	0
1970	0	0	0
Total	12,002	19,866	30,544

See also

- Terrorism in India
- Insurgency in Jammu and Kashmir
- Insurgency in Northeast India
- Insurgency in Punjab
- Naxalite–Maoist insurgency

References

1. ^ Mahapatra, Dhananjay (16 July 2016). "Since 2005, terror has claimed lives of Indians". *The Times of India*. Mumbai. TNN.
2. ^ "Meenambakkam Airport blast: HC sets aside life term for five". *The Hindu*. 3 May 2000. Archived from the original on 11 November 2012. Retrieved 30 April 2014.
3. ^ Hazarika, Sanjoy (8 July 1987). "34 Hindus Killed In New Bus Raids; Sikhs Suspected". *The New York Times*. Retrieved 30 April 2010.
4. ^ Crossette, Barbara (16 June 1991). "Extremists in India Kill 80 on 2 Trains As Voting Nears End". *The New York Times*. Retrieved 30 April 2010.
5. ^ "Kalyan 1991 train blast: SIT to probe convict's activities since he jumped parole in 2007". *The Indian Express*. 18 August 2016. Retrieved 17 December 2020.
6. ^ Sehgal, Manjeet L (17 August 2016). "1991 Mumbai blast convict arrested from Phagwara". *India*

Wikipedia contributors. "List of terrorist incidents in India." Wikipedia, The Free Encyclopedia. Wikipedia, The Free Encyclopedia, 5 Jan. 2025. Web. 30 Mar. 2025.

Full Tally:

Corrected (*and rechecked*) Tally of Terror Attacks in India from 1980s – 2024: 120 cases / **100 %**

Organized Crime: 1, 1 = 2 Terror Attacks / **2 %**

Sikh Terror / Khalistani: 1, 1, 1, 1, 1 = 5 Terror Attacks / **4 %**

Naxals / Maoist: 1, 1, 1, 1, 1, 1, 1, 1, 1, 1, 1, 1, 1, 1, 1, 1, 1, 1 = 18 Terror Attacks / **15 %**

Tribal Insurgency: 1, 1, 1, 1, 1, 1, 1, 1, 1, 1 = 10 Terror Attacks / **8 %**

Islamic Terror: 1, 1, 1, 1, 1, 1, 1, 1, 1, 1, 1, 1, 1, 1, 1, 1, 1, 1, 1, 1, 1, 1, 1, 1, 1, 1, 1, 1, 1, 1, 1, 1, 1, 1, 1, 1, 1, 1, 1, 1, 1, 1, 1, 1, 1, 1, 1, 1, 1, 1, 1, 1, 1, 1, 1, 1, 1, 1, 1, 1, 1, 1, 1, 1, 1, 1, 1, 1, 1, 1 = 70 Terror Attacks / **58 %**

Christian Terror; National Liberation Front of Tripura (Christian Terror Organization funded by New Zealand Baptist Churches) and Specific cases of Bodo Christian Militia Terror: 1, 1, 1 = 3 Terror Attacks / **3 %**

Hindu Terror: 1, 1, 1 = 3 Terror Attacks / **3 %**

Unknown: 1, 1, 1, 1, 1, 1, 1, 1, 1 = 9 cases / **7 %**

In short, even if you combined all the Christian Terror, Sikh Terror, Hindu Terror, Tribal Insurgency terrorism, Naxal / Maoist Terror, and added 9 cases of unknown terror (which are mostly suspected of being Islamic Terror anyway), then you still get less than half the incidents of officially recognized Islamic Terrorism in India. Even if the final one that I missed were added to any other group, it's still less than half the Islamic terror that is committed upon India. All of the rest of the terrorism in India between the 1980s to 2024 makes up 42% of the terrorism that India has suffered, while Islamic terrorism makes up 58% of the terrorism from mainly the listings on Wikipedia. Nevertheless, if we were all to bet on terrorist incidents that Wikipedia had missed in listing regarding Terrorism in India, how many of us would be surprised if forgotten incidents of Islamic terrorism were the most prominent among that news? Islamic terrorism is so *banal and commonplace* for the people of India that it's hard to remember which Islamic terrorist group did which Islamic terrorist attack. Even the Indian national media and the Wikipedia contributors have to double-and-triple check to make sure they have the correct Islamic terror group that is specific to each Islamic terror incident. This is what happens when you can't criticize Islam through Free Speech, this is what happens when you "respect" Muslims feelings over the lives and livelihoods of everyone else, and perhaps, this is what happens when you seek peaceful co-existence. This is the world of Religious Tolerance. This is what the Neoliberal elite and their jester-journalists of the corporate media keep hounding and dragging all of us into and then they act as if the people criticizing Islamic terrorism in India like the BJP, or the British public rioting over Islamic violence done to young British girls, or the US for exercising Free Speech are all the bigots for speaking their mind and making their complaints known about the dangers of the political ideologies of Islamism and its off-shoots. All they keep screaming is that Hindus of India, White people of Great Britain, and everyone who is perceived as Rightwing in the US are all bigots for wanting to criticize beliefs that are actively harming people everywhere. This is how insane that it has become.

To Islamists, Compassion is Weakness meant to be exploited to further Islamism

Islamism is a real political ideology; even after a mass genocide of approximately between 60 – 80 million people for approximately 700 – 800 years of ruling India, even after breaking India into two pieces due to the stupidity of British imperialists in the partition of 1947, and even after the genocide of Kashmir . . . Islamists never stopped. Islamists don't care about the harm they do to others and treat it all as a conspiracy against them. Why did Europeans believe that Western Universalism could stop them? Those Muslim enclaves are just the first step in the process of Islamization and overwhelming proof that they don't care about adapting to Western values. Instead of the sense-object of future monetary gains that the Neoliberal elites expected from mass immigration, you should expect the future of European countries like Great Britain and Sweden to be similar to Israel-Palestine and Kashmir. That is, military no-go zones filled with Islamic terrorism with attempts to breakaway to form their own caliphates. The Neoliberal elite and their jester-journalist dogs of the corporate media circus, in an effort to insinuate all forms of nationalism are a form of fascism and an effort to compartmentalize all Islamic violence by ignoring Islamist ideologies, have unalterably destroyed Western Europe and seek to destroy the United States in the same way. Neoliberal economic policy and Western Universalism have led only to Islamism being given an open-door and helping hand to reverting the entire world into 7th century standards technologically, politically, socially, and culturally. As the Neoliberal elite, Woke Left, and jester-journalists continue to shield their religious values from criticism; Islamists continue unchallenged in their stalwart belief that it is necessary to regress all non-Muslim societies to bring about the Islamic version of the Second Coming of Jesus Christ.

I sincerely hope that I'm proven wrong, but you should ask yourselves; why is Sweden being destroyed from within from the consequences of compassionate Islamic immigration? Why does Sweden get repeatedly criticized for failing to deal with Islamic terrorism as if they're incompetent, but no such criticism is given to China by Muslims across the world for its repressive policies upon the Uyghurs; in what is condemned as a genocide by mostly European countries? Why do Muslim-majority countries outside of Turkey remain silent about it? Why is there such a stark contrast between Muslim-majority reactions to Sweden which is being bombed by Muslim children throwing hand grenades at preschools, while China enforces a military-designed detention after they had to stop multiple Islamic terrorist incidents from Uyghur Muslims? China has suffered multiple terrorist attacks between 2010 – 2016 due to Islamic Uyghur terrorism; which includes a foiled attempt at stealing a jetliner to commit a 9/11 style attack by Uyghur Muslim terrorists back in June 29th, 2012.[262] They suffered Islamic terrorism sporadically in the early 1990s and the early 2000s too. It was only after six years of unrelenting Islamic terrorism in the 2010s that China implemented the Uyghur Muslim concentration camps. Why do Western Europeans and the US criticize China, but the Islamic monarchies and Muslim-majority populations in countries like Pakistan don't criticize China over the Uyghur genocide? To the West, it is seen as a horrific human rights atrocity, but to the 7th century Arab fundamentalist thinking of Islam, Sweden is "weak" for not using a greater use of force upon Syrian and Iraqi Muslims and China is "strong" for using a greater use of force upon Uyghur Muslims, therefore Muslim-majorities will not criticize China. You can lie to yourselves about why this distinction is occurring all you want; this is the actual truth of the matter.

    Finally, never lie to yourselves about this fundamental truth about these problems: the Neoliberal Capitalists hold far more blame than the Marxists for these problems, because they're the ones who lobbied and funded campaigns for these policies of mass immigration to politicians in the billions, whereas the Woke and other cultural Marxists are just outspokenly espousing the values that the Neoliberal elites want to pursue. The Marxists and the Woke may be the louder group, but the ones with true culpability for all the violence and terrorism that Western Europe is suffering are the Neoliberal elites and their jester-journalist dogs of the corporate media circus.

---

[262] Moore, Malcolm. "Chinese Plane in Xinjiang Hijack Attempt." The Telegraph, Telegraph Media Group, 29 June 2012, www.telegraph.co.uk/news/worldnews/asia/china/9365032/Chinese-plane-in-Xinjiang-hijack-attempt.html.

Chapter VI: Did the British Partition of 1947 Gradually Decline the UK and Bolster India?

The pervasive belief that it is unfair to single out Islamic terrorism over other forms of terrorism and that this is some form of deliberate persecution and hate against Muslims ignores the fundamental failures of Islamic theology; it ignores the fact of Islamism's transnational violence which is now reaching a third-generation at the time of writing this. The truth is that Islam is a metaphorical cyanide pill that degrades and destroys everything that seeks a sense of "fairness" by trying to make false equivalents to Islamic terrorism that stem from the problems of Islamic theology itself. Judging purely from the evidence, I would argue that it is more correct to acknowledge the following about each major religion: Casteism is obviously an originally Hindu theological problem and Caste discrimination pertains to a discriminatory legacy that is within Hindu theology regardless of the more ambivalent nature of that history, the view of Cow urine as somehow providing unique benefits is obviously a uniquely Hindu theological problem and more evidence would need to be made to verify such claims on scientific grounds, the rape of innocent children across multiple denominations of Christianity is an overwhelmingly Christian theological problem due to its deranged hatred for consensual sex between unmarried adults and Jesus Christ in the Beatitudes arguing it is a thought crime to feel sensual pleasure for observing pornography of consenting adult women whom a man is not married to, and so forth. Whereas willful ignorance of Christianity's pedophile rings only impacts their own Christian communities so that the rest of the world can ignore it because it doesn't personally harm their children, and Judaism's pedophile scandals by Ultra-Conservative Jewish preachers only impacts their own communities; worth noting is that it is assiduously criticized with a public demand for accountability and prison time from other Jewish preachers – outside of the sexual violence against Jewish children that occur in Jewish communities within New York. The difference is that Islam doesn't keep any of its problems to itself within its own circumscribed *ummah* (one Muslim nation / one Muslim community). At base value, what differentiates Islam from other religions' problems is that the majority of Muslims around the world make no secret that they will kill anyone who disrespects their religion, even if the disrespect is due to unsubstantiated rumors. Whereas most Jews and Christians happily argue in favor of the Biblical tenant of *Thou Shalt Not Kill* and Hindus, Buddhists, Jains, and Sikhs happily argue in favor of *ahimsa* (Non-Violence) and respective versions of *Om Shanti* (Peace); Islam only has *Qisas* (Eye for an Eye / Retributive Justice) and promotes the idea of murdering anyone who is *perceived* to insult Islam. Additionally, Islam has the same problem as Christianity of trying to promote their faith tradition globally due to the nonsensical belief in a Judgment Day prophecy which is often called "Day of Resurrection" in Islamic theology. The depth in which Islamists and even nominal Muslims will obfuscate this problem of "retributive justice" can be seen in the oft-repeated quote of Quran 5:32:

Quran 5:32

Sahih International
Because of that, We decreed upon the Children of Israel that whoever kills a soul unless for a soul or for corruption [done] in the land - it is as if he had slain mankind entirely. And whoever saves one - it is as if he had saved mankind entirely. And our messengers had certainly come to them with clear proofs. Then indeed many of them, [even] after that, throughout the land, were transgressors.

Muhsin Khan
Because of that We ordained for the Children of Israel that if anyone killed a person not in retaliation of murder, or (and) to spread mischief in the land - it would be as if he killed all mankind, and if anyone saved a life, it would be as if he saved the life of all mankind. And indeed, there came to them Our Messengers with clear proofs, evidences, and signs, even then after that many of them continued to exceed the limits (e.g. by doing oppression unjustly and exceeding beyond the limits set by Allah by committing the major sins) in the land!.

Pickthall
For that cause We decreed for the Children of Israel that whosoever killeth a human being for other than manslaughter or corruption in the earth, it shall be as if he had killed all mankind, and whoso saveth the life of one, it shall be as if he had saved the life of all mankind. Our messengers came unto them of old with clear proofs (of Allah's Sovereignty), but afterwards lo! many of them became prodigals in the earth.

Yusuf Ali
On that account: We ordained for the Children of Israel that if any one slew a person - unless it be for murder or for spreading mischief in the land - it would be as if he slew the whole people: and if any one saved a life, it would be as if he saved the life of the whole people. Then although there came to them Our messengers with clear signs, yet, even after that, many of them continued to commit excesses in the land.

Shakir
For this reason did We prescribe to the children of Israel that whoever slays a soul, unless it be for manslaughter or for mischief in the land, it is as though he slew all men; and whoever keeps it alive, it is as though he kept alive all men; and certainly Our messengers came to them with clear arguments, but even after that many of them certainly act extravagantly in the land.

Dr. Ghali
On that account We prescribed for the Seeds (Or: sons) of Israel) that whoever kills a self-other than for (killing another) self or (Literally: nor) for corruption in the earth-then it will be as if he had killed mankind altogether; and whoever gives life to it, (i.e., a self) then it will be as if he had given life to mankind altogether. And indeed Our Messengers have already come to them with supreme evidences; thereafter surely many of them after that are indeed extravagant in the earth.[263]

---

[263] "Surat Al-Mā'Idah (the Table Spread) - سورة المائدة." The Noble Qur'an, https://legacy.quran.com, legacy.quran.com/5/32. Accessed 30 Apr. 2025.

Yet, they ignore the very next Quranic verse. There is a sense of morbid fascination in how so few Muslims themselves are willing to acknowledge the next verse of Quran 5:33:

Quran 5:33

Sahih International
Indeed, the penalty for those who wage war against Allah and His Messenger and strive upon earth [to cause] corruption is none but that they be killed or crucified or that their hands and feet be cut off from opposite sides or that they be exiled from the land. That is for them a disgrace in this world; and for them in the Hereafter is a great punishment,

Muhsin Khan
The recompense of those who wage war against Allah and His Messenger and do mischief in the land is only that they shall be killed or crucified or their hands and their feet be cut off on the opposite sides, or be exiled from the land. That is their disgrace in this world, and a great torment is theirs in the Hereafter.

Pickthall
The only reward of those who make war upon Allah and His messenger and strive after corruption in the land will be that they will be killed or crucified, or have their hands and feet on alternate sides cut off, or will be expelled out of the land. Such will be their degradation in the world, and in the Hereafter theirs will be an awful doom;

Yusuf Ali
The punishment of those who wage war against Allah and His Messenger, and strive with might and main for mischief through the land is: execution, or crucifixion, or the cutting off of hands and feet from opposite sides, or exile from the land: that is their disgrace in this world, and a heavy punishment is theirs in the Hereafter;

Shakir
The punishment of those who wage war against Allah and His messenger and strive to make mischief in the land is only this, that they should be murdered or crucified or their hands and their feet should be cut off on opposite sides or they should be imprisoned; this shall be as a disgrace for them in this world, and in the hereafter they shall have a grievous chastisement,

Dr. Ghali
Surely the only recompense of (the ones) who war against Allah and His Messenger and (diligently) endeavor to do corruption in the earth, is that they should be (all) massacred or crucified, or that their hands and legs should be cut asunder alternately or that they should be exiled from the land. That is a disgrace for them in the present (life), (Literally: the lowly "life", i.e., the life of this world) and in the Hereafter they will have a tremendous torment.[264]

How often have you heard from Imams, regular Muslims, the Western corporate news media, and government officials arguing how Islam had nothing to do with violent killings for insulting Islam? How often have you been told it is "radical Islam" and an "off-shoot" but not mainstream Islam? In other words, how often have you been completely lied to by institutions that are meant to give us fact-finding research? For

---

[264] "Surat Al-Mā'Idah (the Table Spread) - سورة المائدة." The Noble Qur'an, legacy.quran.com, legacy.quran.com/5/33. Accessed 30 Apr. 2025.

example, how often were we told that FGM was an African issue and not a Muslim issue, despite it being part of the Shafi'i school of Islam? How often do all these institutions obfuscate or plainly lie to us all even after these groups commit the worst sexually violent offenses upon women and little girls in non-Muslim countries? How often were we told when pointing to Pakistan, Afghanistan, Bangladesh, or the Middle East that these were the "minority" of Muslims and that East Asian Muslims did not have these same issues? Well, here are the facts from Pew Research studies from January 28th, 2025 in which Muslim-majority countries in East Asian countries willfully self-reported their beliefs when the surveys were conducted. Here's the truth from the 2025 survey, *"Comparing Levels of Religious Nationalism Around the World"* by Pew Researchers Laura Silver, Jonathan Evans, Maria Smerkovich, Sneha Gubbala, Manolo Corichi, and William Miner:

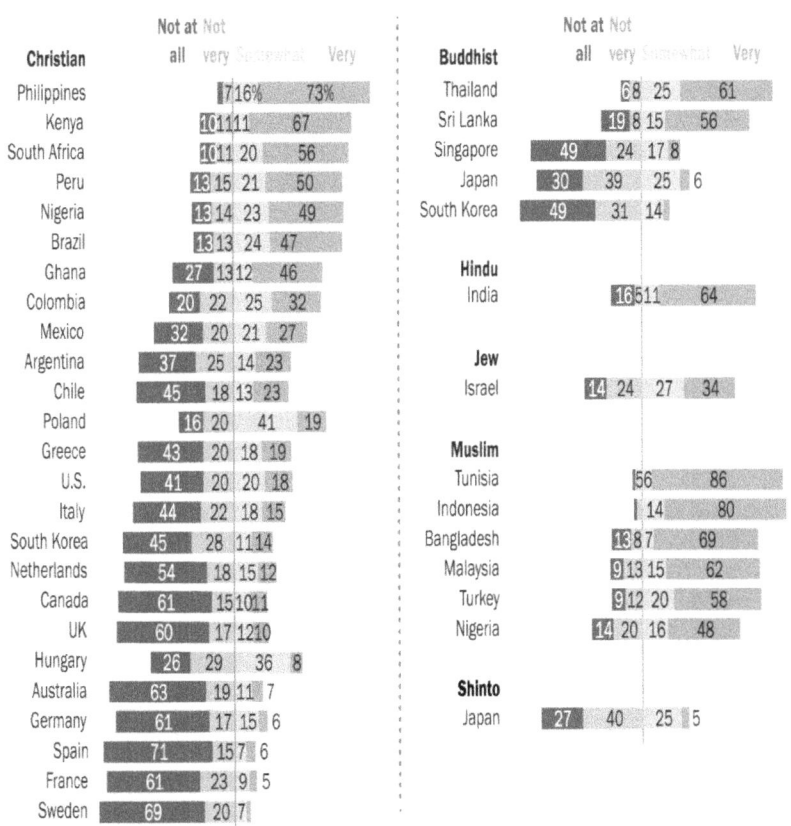

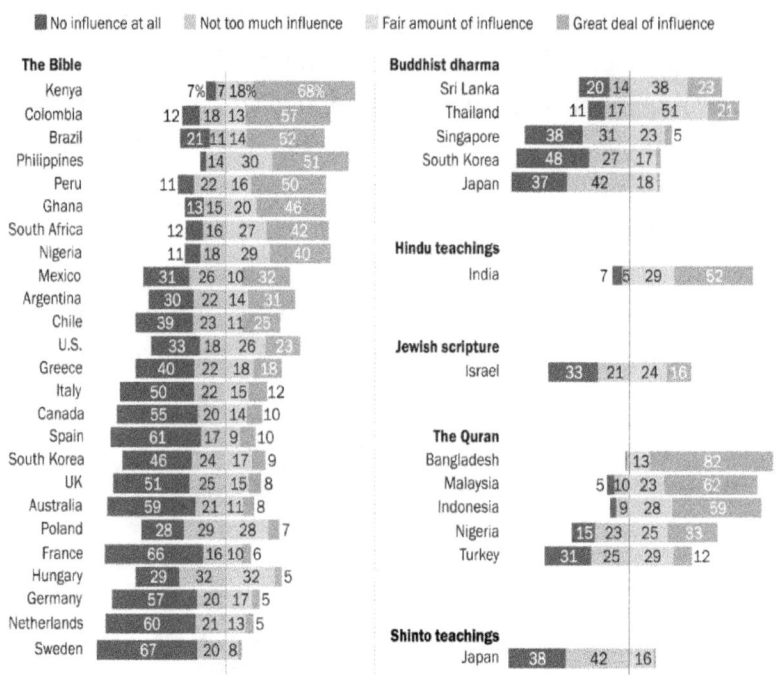

Christians are more likely than religiously unaffiliated people to say the Bible should have great deal of influence on national laws

*% who say [the Bible, Buddhist dharma, etc.] should have **a great deal of influence** on the laws of their country, by religious identity*

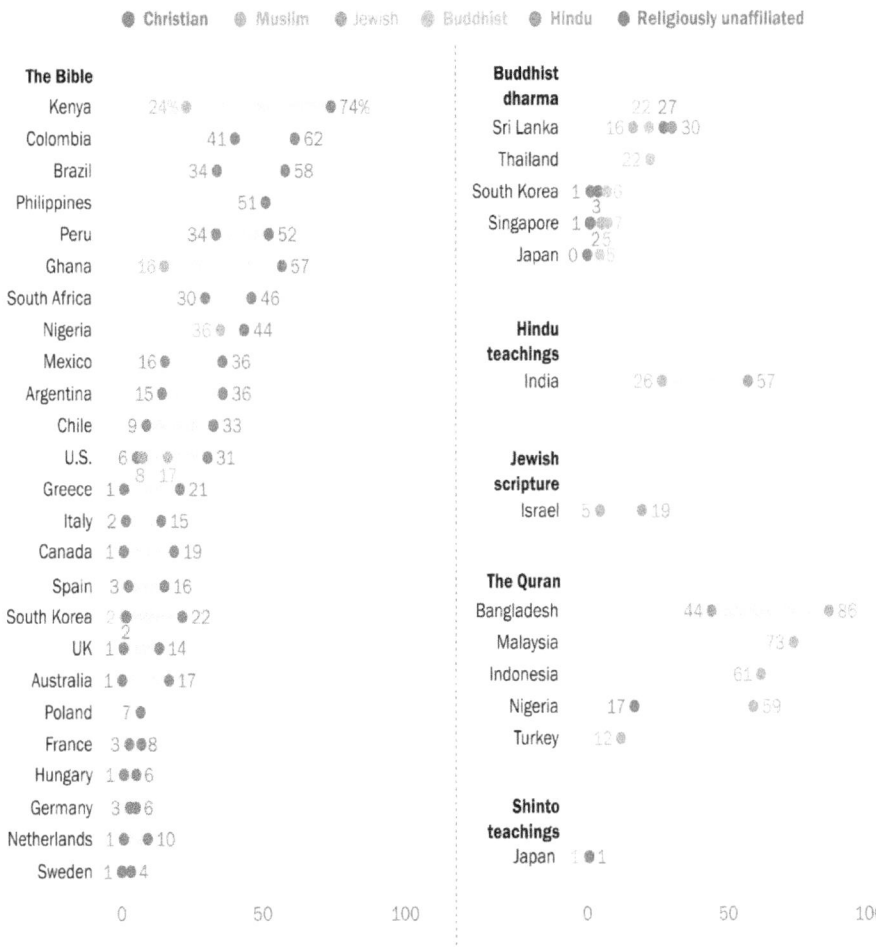

Note: Only religious groups with large enough sample sizes for analysis are included. Those who did not answer are not shown. In Japan, respondents were asked about Buddhist dharma and Shinto teachings as two items; in South Korea, about the Bible and Buddhist dharma; and in Nigeria, about the Bible and the Quran.
Source: Spring 2024 Global Attitudes Survey.
"Comparing Levels of Religious Nationalism Around the World"

PEW RESEARCH CENTER

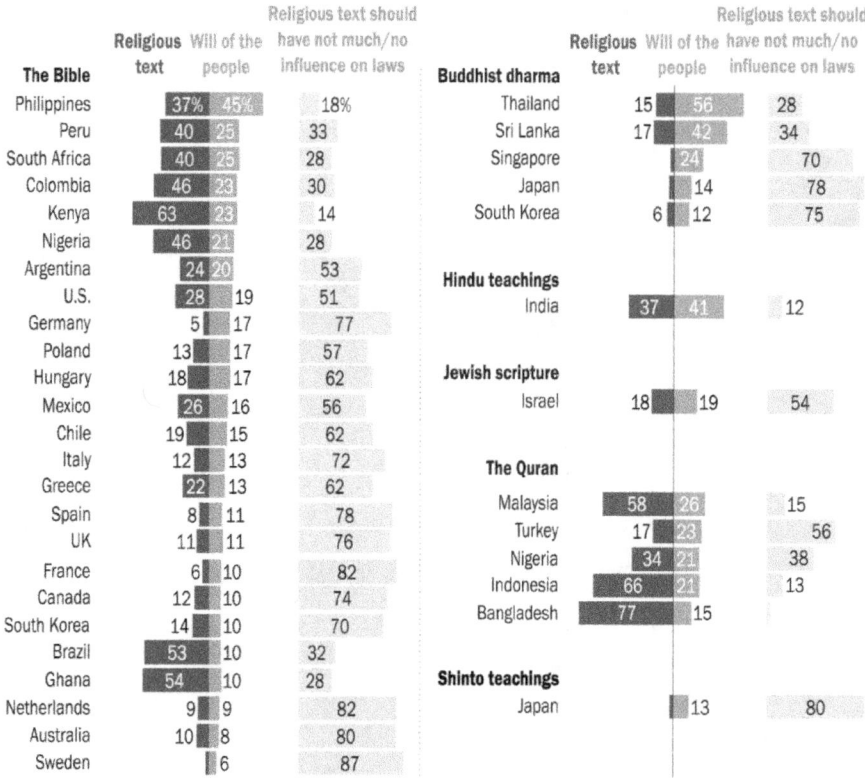

Silver, Laura, et al. "Comparing Levels of Religious Nationalism around the World." Pew Research Center, Pew Research Center, 28 Jan. 2025, www.pewresearch.org/global/2025/01/28/comparing-levels-of-religious-nationalism-around-the-world/.

    This is the truth. All the discussions about Hindu Nationalism, Christian Nationalism, and Zionism overwhelmingly ignore the basic fact that they're just reactions to a globalized Muslim Nationalism that is seeking to transform the entire world with competing Islamist agendas. Terms like Islamophobia only serve to protect the reality of these movements and their corrosive Islamist interests that Islamists really do seek to impose on the non-Muslim world. US journalists and the Neoliberal elite are essentially safeguarding Islamism and trying to destroy nationalist movements that are a protective vanguard from a growing rise in what is an attempt to destroy democratic institutions, civil rights like women's rights and Free Speech, the rights of children to live free and unharmed from sexual exploitation, and trying to label all criticisms as a racist phobia. The Neoliberal elite's policies have destroyed the United Kingdom and Sweden by making their civilians vulnerable to Islamic exploitation; it is entirely their fault that the problems of Islamic immigration continue to persist even now. The Neoliberal elite, the Neoliberal economists, and their clown show of the US Corporate media have probably irreversibly destroyed Western Europe too.

Western Universalism as Egoism

When I was growing up in US grade school, studying social studies textbooks briefly mentioning the partition of India in 1947 by Great Britain; the impression given to me was of a people and culture lagging behind the Western world. US teachers often supported this narrative of how I'd "feel superior" for simply being an American when meeting people living in a third-world country. News filled with images and brief online videos of riots in India mentioned communal riots between Hindus and Muslims and largely depicted them as a society lagging behind as further confirmation of what was taught to me in US high school. I was inculcated with the belief that the US was an unstoppable force of power, Great Britain was second-best compared to the US, and the rest of the world was largely in the periphery after World War 2. When I went to college and studied Political Science, a lot of my personal views began to change; I realized that Great Britain splitting India into two with Pakistan and East Pakistan was part of the Realist Theory of International Relations. In brief, the Realist theory of International Relations argues that nation-states are rational and work to exploit pre-existing issues in other countries to weaken them in order to further empower the nation-state seeking to exploit them; the reason for this is that international relations is always assumed to be anarchic without any real rules, norms, or values at all within the Realist theory of International Relations. Why would the Great Britain of 1947 do this? Obviously, to further its own national interests. They had hoped for situations like the four major wars between Pakistan and India that would happen later, so that both Pakistan and India would remain weak enough for the purposes of being put back under British imperialist rule. Despite the events of two World Wars, it likely seemed possible in the minds of those in power in Great Britain at the time due to ruling the Indian subcontinent for approximately 250 years. The US corporate news media and the majority of those with political power treated what was regarded as "third-world" countries to be set further back on a linear transition to modern Western democracies; they didn't even think of the unique histories of these other countries or try to learn from them, because they saw no value in their histories in the late 1990s and early 2000s. India's communal riots between Hindus and Muslims was seen as simply the predictable outcome of a third-world country and the US corporate news media largely insinuated that Hindu bigotry was mostly responsible throughout it all. The organized murders of Hindus by Muslim mobs or Muslim serial killers whose stated reasons were that the Hindu victim was rumored or spoke criticism of the Prophet Mohammad like Kamlesh Tiwari in 2019 and Kishan Bharwad in 2022 were purposefully ignored by the US corporate news media because it didn't fit their narrative of poor, oppressed Muslims. The ethnic cleansing of Kashmiri Hindu Pandits was likewise ignored for not suiting the poor, oppressed Muslim narrative. Instead of the genocide of Hindus and murders over anti-Free Speech beliefs on the part of Muslims, the US corporate news media and greater Western news media only spent attention on larceny crimes of cow stealing by Hindu gangs from lower-income Muslims which barely constituted much crime at all. No significant effort was made to simply interview or talk to regular Hindus of India unless it was to interview a bigoted person to further reinforce bigotry towards all Hindus and to view the Hindus of India as oppressors.

The narrative of the US corporate media circus seemed to be either in the service of Christian missionary objectives, or in protecting a Christian bias, and not actual fact-finding research. Why exactly was no time or attention spent on the Christian terrorist group known as the National Liberation Front of Tripura which India had been at war with for more than twenty-five years? Why were there barely any news stories on the Bodo Christian terrorism that India suffered on August 5th, 2016 in the Western media[265], like there was an abundance of Hindu gangs stealing cows? Why did the news media depict Christians who sold their own women into sexual slavery only as Marxist groups and obscure the fact that they were Christians? However, the main reason I suggest this is because the narrative of India being a "rape capital" vanished the moment the Catholic Church's global child rape crimes became more well-known in 2018. Unfortunately, child rape crimes by White Catholic priests upon predominately white children has become so banal even in the United States that it is simply a normal expectation of Catholic communities to have families gathered to hear the names of pedophile priests who managed to evade the US statute of limitations and to have a spokesperson for the Catholic Church simply read off their names in a lengthy list to hundreds of families after the Catholic pedophile priest passes away.[266][267] Apparently, a Catholic parents' love for

---

[265] Batchelor, Tom. "14 Dead in Terror Attack on Market in India." Express.Co.Uk, Express.co.uk, 5 Aug. 2016, www.express.co.uk/news/world/696937/India-terror-attack-shooting-Kokrajhar-market-Assam.
[266] Ruland, Sam, et al. "List: Names, Details of 301 Pa. Priest Sex Abuse Allegations in Catholic Dioceses." York Daily Record, York Daily Record, 18 Aug. 2018, www.ydr.com/story/news/2018/08/14/pa-grand-jury-report-catholic-clergy-sexual-abuse-names-details-catholic-dioceses/948937002/.
[267] "Brooklyn Diocese Lists Names of 108 Priests Accused of Abuse." AP News, AP News, 15 Feb. 2019, apnews.com/general-news-ae576a17118b4a45bdb0ba4943e880dc.

the sense-object of Jesus Christ matters more to them than the love they have for their own real-life children. That is, the illusory vision of Jesus Christ in their mind coming to save their eternal souls matters more than the real-life harm committed by Catholic child raping priests upon their own children; who have been made rape victims due to faith in Jesus Christ as their Lord and Savior. Curiously, no thought went into how numerous the events of Catholic Priests in India raping Christian Indian children must've occurred. I learned of one incident second-hand simply because my aunt and grandma had visited a public event made by a local Catholic Indian leader who Indian police later arrested for many cases of pedophilia of young Indian boys and my mother had been the most shocked because she'd only heard positive things about this man from Hindu family members who were more local to the area. It's amazing how nobody thinks to question the dissonance that other religious communities feel when the so-called revealed and moral word of Jesus Christ is suddenly unveiled to have secretly raped hundreds of children, while Christian non-governmental organizations (NGOs) vilify Hindus as devil worshippers. Yet, anytime Hindus try to look past that and respect communal harmony? *Surprise!* Mass rape crimes of little kids from a religion that continues to preach that we're the devil worshippers, while ignoring the fact that multiple denominations of their Christian religion rape children and get away with it! Soon, they'll start blaming Satan, or more privately the Jews (the scapegoats they always blame for their own religion's barbaric stupidity), or greedy, selfish people in power. In power of what exactly, a hierarchy of illusion (*maya*)? They never blame the blatantly idiotic teachings of their religious faith that put more importance on discriminating against women and illusory concepts like souls, ghosts, hell, and the figment of their imagination called Satan. Oh, and don't express your human right to Free Speech to criticize this organization for literally raping children, because . . . "religious tolerance" must be maintained, even at the expense of the human rights of child victims of their own religion.

    What was lost in this self-serving narrative perpetuated by the clown show that is the US Corporate news media was the request for equality and impartiality instead of Islam continuing to be given special treatment. What Hindus of India want is equality and impartiality. Why, for example, are Islamic terrorist attacks so normalized that they're treated as seasonal natural disasters in India? Why are the victims of Islamic terrorist attacks just treated as body counts in news reports and as statistical numbers, but there's an immediate attempt by US and other news media to argue against "Islamophobia" and hate crimes against Muslims immediately after Islamic terrorist attacks? Whether the people writing such news articles knew it or not, they were essentially treating all non-Muslim lives as less important and less valuable than Muslim lives. What they probably don't realize is that after hearing it repeatedly from multiple Islamic terrorist attacks upon multiple countries on a global scale, it just begins to piss everyone off. That is because the perception that Islamic terrorism will fade away or end someday within their lifetime starts to break and it can cause people to snap, especially if it is perceived that Muslim communities already obtained concessions. This same double-standard of treating Muslim lives as more important than non-Muslim lives could be seen during news of the Rohingya massacres by the Myanmar government. Rohingya Islamist militias slaughtered an entire Hindu village of roughly up to ninety-nine people on August 2017 according to a report by Amnesty International published on May 22nd, 2018 that was titled "*Myanmar: New evidence reveals Rohingya armed group massacred scores in Rakhine State*" and it didn't reach anywhere near the level of publicity as Rohingya Muslim news stories.[268] When I shared it on Facebook, I was told by a Muslim that it was ignoring the tragedy of the Rohingya and that somehow several villages that were completely wiped out don't have it as bad as the Rohingya who support Islamist militias that deliberately kill non-Muslims by slaughtering entire villages of Hindus. I shared it on Twitter and a person of a White European background in their profile picture explicitly told me that Myanmar Hindu lives don't matter as much and aren't as important as Rohingya Muslim lives and they made a laugh emoji to mock me for sharing news about multiple village massacres by Rohingya Islamist militias. Now, consider a Jewish person experiencing something similar to this after October 7th, 2023 after the Hamas terror attack[269], or a British person experiencing something similar to this after the horrific murder of three young girls at a Taylor Swift-themed dance class by Axel Muganwa Rudakubana who was later found to have an al Qaeda training manual in his possession yet the prosecution was too cowardly to infer the obvious motive[270][271][272], or a Swedish person who loses loved ones due to improvised explosives made by people of Syrian or Iraqi descent who subscribe to the Islamic faith, or Americans like myself after the Boston bombings, or the myriad of similar attacks on various African countries, Russia, Iran for being the wrong version of Islam, China prior to the Uyghur concentration camps, and many more examples. Or the recent examples of the Pahalgam terror attack in India and the massacres of Christian communities in Nigeria which both happened in April

---

[268] "Myanmar: New Evidence Reveals Rohingya Armed Group Massacred Scores in Rakhine State." Amnesty International, Amnesty International, 22 May 2018, www.amnesty.org/en/latest/news/2018/05/myanmar-new-evidence-reveals-rohingya-armed-group-massacred-scores-in-rakhine-state/.

[269] "Israel/OPT: Amnesty International's Research into Hamas-Led Attacks of 7 October 2023 and Treatment of Hostages." Amnesty International, Amnesty International Public Statement, 2 Dec. 2024, www.amnesty.org/en/documents/mde15/8803/2024/en/.

[270] "CPS Authorises Two Further Charges against Axel Rudakubana." CPS Authorises Two Further Charges against Axel Rudakubana | The Crown Prosecution Service, The Crown Prosecution Service, 29 Oct. 2024, www.cps.gov.uk/mersey-cheshire/news/authorises-two-further-charges-against-axel-rudakubana.

[271] Riches, Chris, and Paul Jeeves. "Southport Killer Axel Rudakubana Read Al-Qaeda Training Manual for Sick Tips." Express.Co.Uk, Express.co.uk, 23 Jan. 2025, www.express.co.uk/news/uk/2004398/southport-killer-axel-rudakubana-al-qaeda.

[272] Humphries, Jonny. "Axel Rudakubana: 'evil' Southport Killer Jailed for Minimum 52 Years." BBC News, BBC, 23 Jan. 2025, www.bbc.com/news/articles/c4gweeq1344o.

2025.²⁷³²⁷⁴²⁷⁵ If this continues to be a problem, then how many of us will remain holding onto patience and a commitment to compassion and non-violence towards the small percentage of nominal Muslims? How many Christians will try to continue holding onto teachings of forgiveness or turning the other cheek? How many Jews will continue holding onto Jewish teachings of simply recognizing the attackers as flawed human beings? What will happen if the majority of the world shares the same human pain and has the same common enemy to blame? How many of us are getting fed-up with hearing anything related to Islamic violence and being told to shut up about Free Speech criticisms because we are Islamophobic? I want us all to avoid our worst impulses, but it seems that could just be my naivety.

The egoistic Western Universalist arguments about the rest of the world lagging behind to model themselves after the West had slowly been degrading for decades due to the incompetence of Neoliberal economic policies that weakened the US and the Western world with the Great Recession. The June 30th – August 5th, 2024 riots throughout the United Kingdom absolutely shattered any remaining vestiges of that illusion of the world lagging behind the Western model. No longer were news organizations depicting the so-called communal riots in India with implications of backwardness within the insulated halls of the US and European corporate media circuses; no longer could they deceive the US public by treating it as a one-sided falsehood of a poor, oppressed Muslim problem. The news of various Anti-CAA protests from December 2019 – March 2020 in India was portrayed with this egoistic perspective of Hindu backwardness by the US and European corporate media clown show. After the UK riots, that has changed and even recent activities of communal violence such as the Maharashtra violence of March 17th, 2025 over the legacy of the barbaric Mughal Emperor Aurangzeb and the violence against Hindus by Muslims in West Bengal in India over legal policy changes of the Waqf board do not have the same enthusiasm by the US and European corporate media of attempting to portray them as the fault of supposedly backwards Hindus. Any and all depictions of riots involving Muslims was displayed with more caution and far less attention because they now had to deal with the parallels within the countries that they considered their inner circle of White, European societies. They now knew what it was like to experience the visceral reality; they couldn't use any feeling of detachment and superiority so that they could label the Hindu victims as the secret perpetrators when it came to how

---

[273] De, Abhishek. "US-Based Techie, IAF Official among 26 Killed in Attack. Who Were the Victims?" India Today, India Today, 23 Apr. 2025, www.indiatoday.in/india/story/pahalgam-terror-attack-kashmir-full-list-of-victims-released-2713232-2025-04-23.

[274] Preston, Heather. "Nigerian Bishop Demands Action after 200 Christians Murdered in Week of Violence - Premier Christian News: Headlines, Breaking News, Comment & Analysis." Premier Christian News, Premier Christian News, 22 Apr. 2025, premierchristian.news/us/news/article/nigerian-bishop-demands-action-200-christians-murdered-week-of-violence.

[275] Sharma, Yashraj. "What Is the Resistance Front, the Group Claiming the Deadly Kashmir Attack?" Al Jazeera, Al Jazeera, 24 Apr. 2025, www.aljazeera.com/news/2025/4/23/what-is-the-resistance-front-the-group-behind-the-deadly-kashmir-attack.

unwilling the majority of Muslims are in adapting any iota of modern values and least of all, human rights. After all, adapting human rights means not carrying out premeditated murder of anyone who insults the Prophet Mohammad, but this basic fact about human rights was ignored by journalists, self-righteous US scholars, the United Nations, and US Presidents Bush, Obama, and Biden when it came to Hindu victims of Islamic violence and often Christian victims of Islamic violence. The only President who has stood up for the disparity in violence inflicted upon both Hindu and Christian victims by Islamist perpetrators is President Donald Trump.

Perhaps the most ironic part about the reactions to Islamic immigration is that it can no longer obscure that Europe has always been overwhelmingly more racist than the United States and that has been attested to by Pew Research surveys since 2016, but because the US was labeled as "Western" and identified itself as such, it obscured the actual facts; while the US was ironically receiving the bulk of accusations of being racist by Western Europeans. I recall a video by Ex-Muslim Atheist and Twitter provocateur, Armin Navabi, arguing that Western countries were the least racist in the world. Unfortunately, he and others who argued this point were merely exploiting the US's exceptional cultural milestone as a way to obscure the fact that Western Europe is as racist as most other countries in the world. On July 12th, 2016, Pew Researchers Bruce Drake and Jacob Poushter published an article on *Pewresearch.org* titled "*In views of diversity, many Europeans are less positive than Americans*" and the findings are as such:

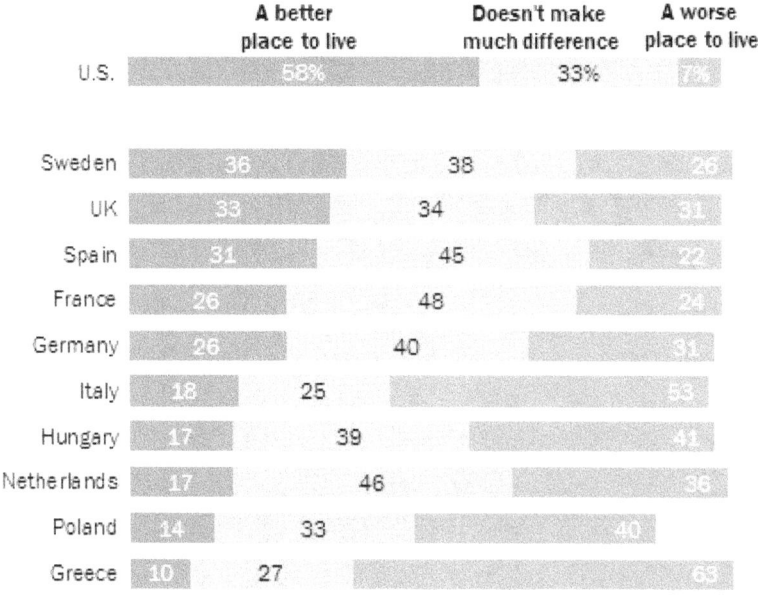

Drake, Bruce, and Jacob Poushter. "In Views of Diversity, Many Europeans Are Less Positive than Americans." Pew Research Center, Pew Research Center, 12 July 2016, www.pewresearch.org/short-reads/2016/07/12/in-views-of-diversity-many-europeans-are-less-positive-than-americans/.

In other words, once we separate the US from the term "Western" and view the US as unique from Western European cultures, then Western Europe is essentially no different than other countries around the world. Even if we were to grant five of those Western European countries as being average, they're honestly only the average seen across most of the world if we compare the statistics or look at their comparable responses. In the 2010 – 2014 World Values Survey's Wave 6 in the PDF file *"WV6_Results_By_Country"* show the following responses on Question 37 *"On this list are various groups of people. Could you please mention any that you would not like to have as neighbors?: People of a different race"* on pages 68 – 69 of the total 898 pages of the PDF file:

V37.- On this list are various groups of people. Could you please mention any that you would not like to have as neighbors?: People of a different race

		Would not like to have as neighbors: People of a different race		
	TOTAL	Mentioned	Not mentioned	HT: Dropped out survey SG: Missing DE: Inapplicable RU: Inappropriate response
Country Code				
Algeria	1,200	19.8	80.2	-
Azerbaijan	1,002	58.1	41.9	-
Argentina	1,030	1.0	99.0	-
Australia	1,477	5.0	95.0	-
Armenia	1,100	31.8	68.2	-
Brazil	1,486	1.9	98.1	-
Belarus	1,535	23.1	76.9	-
Chile	1,000	5.6	94.4	-
China	2,300	10.5	89.5	-
Taiwan	1,238	8.4	91.6	-
Colombia	1,512	3.2	96.8	-
Cyprus	1,000	24.8	75.2	-
Ecuador	1,202	34.5	65.5	-
Estonia	1,533	25.4	74.6	-
Georgia	1,202	32.1	67.9	-
Palestine	1,000	44.0	56.0	-
Germany	2,046	14.8	85.0	0.2
Ghana	1,552	19.9	80.1	-
Haiti	1,996	6.3	93.6	0.2
Hong Kong	1,000	18.8	81.2	-
India	4,078	25.6	74.4	-
Iraq	1,200	27.7	72.3	
India	4,078	25.6	74.4	-
Iraq	1,200	27.7	72.3	-
Japan	2,443	22.3	77.7	-
Kazakhstan	1,500	11.2	88.8	-
Jordan	1,200	27.2	72.8	-
South Korea	1,200	34.1	65.9	-
Kuwait	1,303	28.1	71.9	-
Kyrgyzstan	1,500	28.1	71.9	-
Lebanon	1,200	36.3	63.7	-
Libya	2,131	55.1	44.9	-
Malaysia	1,300	31.3	68.7	-
Mexico	2,000	10.2	89.8	-
Morocco	1,200	13.8	86.2	-
Netherlands	1,902	8.2	91.8	-
New Zealand	841	2.9	97.1	-
Nigeria	1,759	20.9	79.1	-
Pakistan	1,200	15.7	84.3	-
Peru	1,210	9.3	90.7	-
Philippines	1,200	21.6	78.4	-
Poland	966	5.5	94.5	-
Qatar	1,060	8.8	91.2	-
Romania	1,503	23.5	76.5	-
Russia	2,500	17.2	82.5	0.3
Rwanda	1,527	3.5	96.5	-
Singapore	1,972	12.6	87.3	0.1
Slovenia	1,069	10.9	89.1	-
South Africa	3,531	19.2	80.8	-
Zimbabwe	1,499	8.1	91.9	-

Study #WV6_Results_By_Country   v20180912

	TOTAL	Would not like to have as neighbors: People of a different race		HT: Dropped out survey SG: Missing DE: Inapplicable RU: Inappropriate response
		Mentioned	Not mentioned	
Spain	1,189	4.8	95.2	-
Sweden	1,206	2.8	97.2	-
Thailand	1,200	39.7	60.3	-
Trinidad and Tobago	999	1.5	98.5	-
Tunisia	1,205	16.9	83.1	-
Turkey	1,605	35.8	64.2	-
Ukraine	1,500	16.9	83.1	-
United States	2,232	5.6	94.4	-
Uruguay	1,000	1.6	98.4	-
Uzbekistan	1,500	14.0	86.0	-
Yemen	1,000	34.0	66.0	-
TOTAL	(88,042)	18.7%	81.3%	*

"World Values Survey Association." WVS Database, World Values Survey, 12 Sept. 2018, www.worldvaluessurvey.org/WVSDocumentationWV6.jsp. Initially published on 4/29/2014 but updates and corrections were made on 9/12/2018.

    Western Europe isn't exceptional like the United States and a few other countries. India, which was often mocked as racist by the jester-journalists of the US corporate media circus, is shockingly average in terms of racial attitudes and far less racist than many Southern European countries. Judging from comparisons of the Pew Research and World Values Survey, apparently even Pakistan and Russia are far less racist than Western European countries with the exceptions of Spain and Sweden. But also judging from this, Sweden and Spain had a shocking rise in racism within approximately five years since the WVS surveys for both countries occurred in 2011 and the Pew Research survey was conducted on March 2016.[276][277] Whether this is due to some quirk of how the surveys were conducted or perhaps the framing of the 37th WVS question was poorly executed; that is beyond the scope of what I can derive from the datasets given. I'm just trying to share information as honestly as I can from the limitations of these survey results. As far as I can see, Western Europe is utterly average in terms of racial views

---

[276] Drake, Bruce, and Jacob Poushter. "In Views of Diversity, Many Europeans Are Less Positive than Americans." Pew Research Center, Pew Research Center, 12 July 2016, www.pewresearch.org/short-reads/2016/07/12/in-views-of-diversity-many-europeans-are-less-positive-than-americans/.
[277] "World Values Survey Association." WVS Database, World Values Survey, 12 Sept. 2018, www.worldvaluessurvey.org/WVSDocumentationWV6.jsp. Initially published on 4/29/2014 but updates and corrections were made on 9/12/2018.

towards others. To put it bluntly, the Right-wing of the United States, often labeled as "racist" for this or that "offensive" statement from the Left-wing of the US, are actually the equivalent of your average Liberal-leaning European in terms of social values towards other ethnic backgrounds.[278] The United States may also deserve to be called the most socially compassionate and least racist society in all of human history. That is not to diminish or ignore policies that do cause harm such as the Supreme Court case of Oliphant vs Suquamish 1978 which is still harming Native Americans to this day or the US's history of human rights abuses in the past, but it's best to acknowledge both the good and the bad as impartially as we can based upon the evidence.

Due to accusations of the British news media suppressing the culprits of the surge in crime such as stabbing incidents in the UK, elements of the British public have attempted to portray Pakistani Muslim immigrants as part of an inferior, foreign, and backwards culture in contemporary times compared to Western British culture. Yet, this portrayal lacks any historical or logical basis and conveniently ignores the proverbial elephant in the room: Great Britain created Pakistan in 1947 from the Partition of India. How does it logically follow that Great Britain, which ruled the entirety of the Indian subcontinent for 250 years and imposed laws of appeasement to Islamist interests like Section 295-A to effectively dismantle Free Speech in multiple South Asian countries, should then exclaim the end-product of its own 250 years of imperialist history is a foreign culture? British rulers had ample evidence from rebellions, violent encounters, mutinies, and much more of exactly what would happen from interacting with Islamists; there is honestly no rational or even empirical basis to claim British rulers and administrators of South Asia were wholly ignorant of how violent Islam was for 250 years of their rule. They knew exactly what Islamists were and what aims Islamists wished to achieve; they split India into two pieces at the behest of Islamists and Islamist sympathizers to create a permanent fracture in hopes of weakening both Pakistan and India for the intention of reconquest in the future. British government officials after World War 2 surely weren't stupid either; they knew about the multiple coups, constitutional crises, and rise of the most extremist forms of Islamism in Pakistan and still chose to willfully import them into British society in the hopes of off-setting the declining birth rates in order to keep increasing the British GDP at the behest of Neoliberal billionaires, lobbying groups, and economists. If you're British and reading this, then please seriously consider the following: if 250 years of ruling an entire subcontinent where your culture unilaterally influences the colonized country at your full discretion still means that you call that culture foreign because you don't like the consequences of your imperialist history, then what on earth does the word "foreign" even mean anymore? Your ancestors knew what these people were, your past and present

---

[278] Drake, Bruce, and Jacob Poushter. "In Views of Diversity, Many Europeans Are Less Positive than Americans." Pew Research Center, Pew Research Center, 12 July 2016, www.pewresearch.org/short-reads/2016/07/12/in-views-of-diversity-many-europeans-are-less-positive-than-americans/.

governments knew what these people were, and – in a very real way – your country created them. Your country split India into two pieces knowing that Islamists had extreme and violent beliefs, you gave Islamists an entire country in which they festered their extremism and conspiratorial thinking, you had decades of proof that Islamists weren't capable of running a country efficiently because of it from Pakistan's coups and the gradual emergence of Bangladesh in response to Pakistan's genocidal policies upon them, and then you imported them into your society. What did you think was going to happen? If it is true that British citizens are being stabbed by Pakistani Muslim immigrants or threatened with violence in other ways, then this is somewhat of a metaphorical Frankenstein and Frankenstein's Monster situation. The Pakistani immigrants are Frankenstein's monster and the British subjects are the children of Dr. Frankenstein with the monster chasing after them due to their ancestor having created the monster.

    Great Britain is being stabbed with the evidence that the legacy of British imperialism was categorically wrong in all respects. To any British reader taking the time to read this; you have a right to argue in favor of your human rights and obviously I would never ever condone the rapes and murders of innocent children like what has been overwhelmingly done by Pakistani Muslim grooming gangs. You have to acknowledge the history that caused this situation though; your country created the conditions and the very country of supposed immigrants that are causing widespread societal issues for you. It is not outrageous to point out that your country essentially created these people. If anything, and please take this statement seriously, your ancestors sacrificed your futures for the sake of their present moment, so that they could maintain dominance in their lifetime without any thought of how your generation would be worse off. If you follow the concepts of the Realist Theory of International Relations, then what your ancestors wanted was for Pakistan and India to keep warring until they weakened enough to be reconquered by Britain; that was why Pakistan was split in two separate sections with India in between, they did it deliberately to cause as much bloodshed and war as possible. Your ancestors knew what the immediate result was going to be, because how on earth could a severely weak country after World War 2; that followed after 250 years of imperialism that consisted of multiple starvation campaigns, a rise in illiteracy, an annihilation of their trade systems, and a massive theft of resources then be able to effectively administer a functioning government from both West Pakistan and East Pakistan? For comparison, India had to settle millions of displaced people immediately after the Partition and that was considered a miracle at the time because the West undoubtedly believed that India would break apart. In a very real way, while it is true that Islamism played the most significant factor in its failures, Pakistan was nevertheless always set-up to fail due to how the 1947 Partition of India was done. By a striking contrast, the 2021 Pew Research survey of India shows that a slight majority of India now argues the Partition of 1947 benefitted India.[279] As India's GDP has overtaken Great Britain's as the fifth-largest world economy as of 2021, how is it that the Partition of India in 1947 seems to be bringing about the fall of Great Britain and the rise of India? When your ancestors split India into two pieces, they almost certainly envisioned a future where they took control of the entire Indian subcontinent with it being "obvious" to them that the superior White race would need to be a guiding hand for the "backwards" Indian people. Yet, while the Partition of India in 1947 did bring about multiple wars, approximately over seventy terrorist attacks that can credibly be linked to Islamic terrorist groups that mainly exist in Pakistan and Bangladesh, and Islamism holds influence using British colonial laws like 295-A to keep a stranglehold on Indian society; it now seems that the imperialist dreams of reconquering India and the rest of the subcontinent by your British forebears was really the doom of Great Britain itself.

  The so-called right-wing Hindus of India have been warning people of this issue with Islam from the very beginning. They pointed out the unfairness of Muslims being allowed to proselytize while Christians and Hindus cannot do so in Muslim-majority countries, the selective news coverage of violence with Muslims being given more focus than victims of other religious backgrounds, the depiction of Hindus as bigots while Hindus and other religious groups have tried so hard to maintain communal harmony with Muslims, and the anger over constant terrorist attacks being treated as no different than a natural disaster and how the US and Western news media categorically ignore the implications of what that means for the religion of Islam. Even when Hindus of India pointed to examples of Christians being massacred or discriminated against in Bangladesh and Pakistan, it fell to deaf ears in the West and was just chalked up as "bigotry" because having empathy for Christian victims is somehow bigoted when pointing out the perpetrators are violent Muslims. What happened here? The US and Western European media categorically refused to view Hindus as rational human beings with their lives and opinions as being worthy of equal respect. At least for Europe, it is literally destroying their own societies because they're less equipped to handle Islamist terrorism on the scale that India has been handling it for over seventy years. The murder of Kishan Bharwad in 2022 immediately had the Gujarat anti-Terror taskforce look into possible terrorist links where they found a kill list supplied by two Imams to the murder suspects.[280] The murder of Salwan Momika in Sweden led to the suspects being let go within less than twenty-four hours and the co-protester of a Quran burning protest being charged with supposedly "*having expressed contempt for the Muslim ethnic group*

---

[279] Sahgal, Neha, et al. "Religion in India: Tolerance and Segregation." Pew Research Center, Pew Research Center, 29 June 2021, www.pewresearch.org/religion/2021/06/29/religion-in-india-tolerance-and-segregation/#2cadb6b1e440f0bf00cd84d9a5e73d3a.

[280] "Dhandhuka Murder: 3 Accused in Police Remand for 10 More Days." The Indian Express, Express News Service, 7 Feb. 2022, web.archive.org/web/20220207041105/https://indianexpress.com/article/cities/ahmedabad/dhandhuka-murder-accused-police-remand-ahmedabad-7760401/.

because of their religious beliefs on four occasions" against people of his own ethnicity who were Muslim, because the Swedish government now chooses to falsely recognize a religious population of 1.9 billion as an ethnicity instead of a group of people with a shared set of mythological beliefs.[281] The Western world is proving surprisingly brittle at handling the threat of Islamism rationally.

Great Britain Failed to Acknowledge the Cruel Truth of its Imperialist History

I doubt that Great Britain can truly grapple with the problem of Pakistani Muslim violence within their communities without acknowledging their own country's history in creating the conditions that led to that result and the devastation wrought upon all of India under British colonial rule. A country created in 1947 from the partition of India by Great Britain itself cannot truly be called foreign, especially after 250 years of rule. It merely reveals how colonialism was a one-way street when nothing about the colonized cultures was learned beyond the appreciation for tea. To give a clearer glimpse of how devastating and self-serving British imperialism was and why the British narrative is wholly false, here is a small portion of the late historian Mike Davis's *Late Victorian Holocausts: El Niño Famines and the Making of the Third World*, describing the second of four mass starvation campaigns imposed by the British upon India which led to the death toll of approximately between 60 – 80 million throughout India. For a bit of context, three of the four starvation campaigns were done to obtain massive profits from rice without concern for the starvation of all of India under Malthusian economics created by Anglican Christian Minister, Thomas Malthus, who argued in favor of his economic theory which supported population control. The fourth, the Bengal famine, seemed to be part of British military strategy in World War II.

The economic policy of Thomas Malthus influenced the British government to deliberately starve India in the tens of millions on at least four separate occasions to maximize profits from rice exports by creating artificial scarcity. These British state-sponsored starvation campaigns happened from the late 1870s to the early 1900s.[282] A plethora of rice was fully stockpiled and could have fed the entirety of India on each occasion.[283] However, the British government sold it to overseas markets for maximum financial exports to finance the British military campaigns of the Boer Wars and Wars in

---

[281] Reuters. "Swedish Court Convicts Quran Burner of Hate Crimes, Days after His Ally Was Killed | The Times of Israel." Www.Timesofisrael.Com, Times of Israel, 3 Feb. 2025, www.timesofisrael.com/swedish-court-convicts-quran-burner-of-hate-crimes-days-after-his-ally-was-killed/.
[282] Davis, Mike. Late Victorian Holocausts: El Niño Famines and the Making of the Third World (Essential Mike Davis). Verso Books. Kindle Edition.
[283] Davis, Mike. Late Victorian Holocausts: El Niño Famines and the Making of the Third World (Essential Mike Davis). Verso Books. Kindle Edition.

Afghanistan[284], they aggressively taxed all Indians to finance their colonial wars despite these taxes furthering conditions of mass starvation because Indian families had even less money to try to keep their families alive[285], the British government imposed internment camps to force Indian people who couldn't pay the taxes into hard labor for a pittance of rice among thirty Indians each who were then forced to squabble over it[286], and the British didn't concern themselves with the rise of diseases like cholera epidemics that killed tens of millions in these internment camps and spread throughout the wider society[287], because the specific purpose of British imperialism was to enhance the power and dominance of the British empire over the world, as per the Realist Theory of International Relations. In response to vehement outrage from the US and Indian public from US journalists and US missionaries sharing numerous photographs[288], giving firsthand eyewitness accounts from fellow missionaries and Indians serving in the British government whose peaceful attempts for reform were ignored by British Viceroys[289], and US journalists interviewing victims throughout British-administered India with the help of US missionaries expediting the process to meet with them[290]; the British government created cheaply made poorhouses for a brief time that required 9-hours of hard labor for emaciated males to feed their families before discontinuing them after creating fabricated stories of how they were helping reduce poverty when the information from US missionaries and US journalists repeatedly disproved their arguments through fact-finding research.[291] Here is but a glimpse of what these British imperialist policies wrought:

> Famine mortality crested in March 1897. The next month Elgin himself conceded that 4.5 million poor people had perished. Behramji Malabari, the nationalist editor of the Indian Spectator, countered that the real number, plague victims included, was probably closer to 18 million.55 At the same time, the Missionary Review of the World, which ordinarily praised British philanthropy, denounced the doublespeak by which the government had downplayed the severity of the crisis and sabotaged missionary efforts to organize prompt international relief. "When the pangs of hunger drive people in silent procession, living skeletons, to find food, dying by the way; the stronger getting a few grains, the feebler perishing, and children, an intolerable burden, are sold at from ten to thirty cents a piece, and when at best a heritage of orphaned children of tens of

---

[284] Davis, Mike. Chapter Five: Skeletons at the Feast (pgs. 141 – 177). Late Victorian Holocausts: El Niño Famines and the Making of the Third World (Essential Mike Davis). Verso Books. Kindle Edition.
[285] Davis, Mike. Chapter Five: Skeletons at the Feast (pgs. 141 – 177). Late Victorian Holocausts: El Niño Famines and the Making of the Third World (Essential Mike Davis). Verso Books. Kindle Edition.
[286] Davis, Mike. Chapter Five: Skeletons at the Feast (pgs. 141 – 177). Late Victorian Holocausts: El Niño Famines and the Making of the Third World (Essential Mike Davis). Verso Books. Kindle Edition.
[287] Davis, Mike. Late Victorian Holocausts: El Niño Famines and the Making of the Third World (Essential Mike Davis). Verso Books. Kindle Edition.
[288] Davis, Mike. Chapter Five: Skeletons at the Feast (pgs. 141 – 177). Late Victorian Holocausts: El Niño Famines and the Making of the Third World (Essential Mike Davis). Verso Books. Kindle Edition.
[289] Davis, Mike. Chapter Five: Skeletons at the Feast (pgs. 141 – 177). Late Victorian Holocausts: El Niño Famines and the Making of the Third World (Essential Mike Davis). Verso Books. Kindle Edition.
[290] Davis, Mike. Chapter Five: Skeletons at the Feast (pgs. 141 – 177). Late Victorian Holocausts: El Niño Famines and the Making of the Third World (Essential Mike Davis). Verso Books. Kindle Edition.
[291] Davis, Mike. Chapter Five: Skeletons at the Feast (pgs. 141 – 177). Late Victorian Holocausts: El Niño Famines and the Making of the Third World (Essential Mike Davis). Verso Books. Kindle Edition.

thousands must remain to the country – this is not 'impending' famine – it is grim, gaunt, awful famine itself."56

Meanwhile, the agrarian economy of northern India continued to unravel, and the famous jurist and national leader Mahdev Govinda Ranade complained that the "seven plagues which afflicted the land of the Pharaohs in old time were let loose upon us."57 In the Punjab, where cattle powered wells and irrigation wheels, the decimation of animals was so great that the standing crops in the fields died because villagers could not lift water from their wells.58 The most extreme distress, however, was still in the Central Provinces where, as the Indian National Congress charged and Lord Hamilton later conceded, revenue exactions had long threatened the subsistence of the poor. Prophetically, eight years earlier after a severe tax hike, 15,000 protesting peasants had confronted the chief commissioner in front of the Bilaspur railroad station. *"Their cry was, 'bandobast se mar gaya' – 'the settlement has killed us!'"*59

The protestors' words came grimly true in the winter of 1896–97, when mortality soared in at least one district (Gantur) to an incredible 40 percent (200,000 out of 500,000 residents).60 In his zeal to maintain fiscal pressure on the peasantry, the Central Provinces' governor-general took little account of the remarkable siege of natural disaster – three consecutive years of devastating rains, plant rust, caterpillar plagues and black blight – that preceded the drought. Despite the terrible velocity with which famine spread through an already prostrate countryside, Sir Charles Lyall followed Elgin's lead and downplayed the acuity of the famine. While allowing grain merchants to export the province's scarce reserves, he refused frenzied pleas to suspend revenue collections or provide village-centered relief as authorized in the famine code.61 Destitute famine victims were instead herded into hastily improvised poorhouses that set new standards for administrative incompetence and corruption. Reuter's "special famine commissioner," F. Merewether, shocked the British reading public with his exposé of suffering and neglect inside the poorhouses of Bilaspur and Jubbulpur. Although an ardent imperialist whose reports usually depicted heroic British district officers battling natural cataclysm and Hindu superstition, Merewether did not mince words about the atrocities that passed for relief in the Central Provinces:

[T] he actual inhabitants of Bilaspur were dying of starvation, while under the supposed aegis of the Government and within their very gates. I mentioned previously that my opinion was that the famine in the Central Provinces was grossly mismanaged. I collected tangible proofs of this daily, till I had to hand a mass of reliable and irrefutable evidence, which showed only too clearly that the officials and those responsible had not, and did not, fully recognized the gravity of the situation. With reference to the poor-house, there can be no doubt that in addition to supineness and mismanagement, there was decided fraud going on, and the poor hopeless and helpless inmates were being condemned by a paternal Government to a slow, horrible, and lingering death by starvation.

*I here came across the first specimens of "Famine Down," which is produced by long-continued starvation. At certain stages of want a fine down of smooth hair appears all over the bodies of the afflicted. It has a most curious look, and gives the wearer a more simian look than ever.... There were more than a score of souls who had reached this stage, and their bodies were covered from head to foot with the soft-looking black fur.*62

When Julian Hawthorne, son of the famous New England writer and Cosmopolitan's special correspondent in India, reached Jubbulpur in April 1897, three months after Merewether, conditions in the Central Provinces had grown even more nightmarish. On the long, hot train ride up the Narmada Valley ("the great graveyard of India" according to American missionaries),63 Hawthorne was horrified by the families of corpses seated in the shade of the occasional desert trees. "There they squatted, all dead now, their flimsy garments fluttering around them, except when jackals had pulled the skeletons apart, in the hopeless search for marrow."64 In Jubbulpur, he was escorted by the resident American missionary who took him first to the town market, where he was disgusted by the radical existential contrast between "bony remnants of human beings" begging for kernels of grain and the plump, nonchalant prosperity of the local merchant castes.65

The poorhouses, meanwhile, were converted cattle-pens terrorized by overseers who, as Merewether had accurately reported, systematically cheated their doomed charges of their pathetic rations. "Emaciation" hardly described the condition of the "human skeletons" Hawthorne encountered:

*They showed us their bellies – a mere wrinkle of empty skin. Twenty per cent of them were blind; their very eyeballs were gone. The joints of their knees stood out between the thighs and shinbones as in any other skeleton; so did their elbows; their fleshless jaws and skulls were supported on necks like those of plucked chickens. Their bodies – they had none; only the framework was left.*66

Hawthorne's most haunting experience, however, was his visit to the children in the provincial orphanage in Jubbulpur. In imperial mythology, as enshrined in Kipling's famous short story "William the Conquerer" (published on the eve of the famine in 1896), British officials struggled heroically against all odds to save the smallest famine victims. The Ladies Home Journal (January 1896) version of Kipling's story had featured a famous woodcut by the American artist W. L. Taylor of a tall British officer walking slowly at the head of a flock of grateful, saved children. "Taylor accentuated the god-like bearing of Scott, as seen through the eyes of William [his love interest], standing at the entrance to her tent. The black cupids are there and a few capering goats …"

But as W. Aykroyd, a former Indian civil servant who in his youth had talked to the veterans of the 1896– 97 famine, emphasizes, this idyllic scene was utterly fictional. "No particular attention was … given to children in the famine relief operations."67 Far more realistic than Scott's motherly compassion was the repugnance that Kipling's heroine William feels when, after dreaming "for the twentieth time of the god in the golden dust," she awakes to face "loathsome black children, scores of them wastrels picked up by the wayside, their bones almost breaking their skin, terrible and covered with sores."68

Hawthorne indeed discovered that "rescue" more often than not meant slow death in squalid, corruptly managed children's camps. After reminding American readers that "Indian children are normally active, intelligent and comely, with brilliant eyes, like jewels," he opens the door to the orphanage:

"One of the first objects I noticed on entering was a child of five, standing by itself near the middle of the enclosure. Its arms were not so large round as my thumb; its legs were scarcely larger; the pelvic bones were plainly shown; the ribs, back and front, started through the skin, like a wire cage. The eyes were fixed and unobservant; the expression of the little skull-face solemn, dreary and old. Will, impulse, and almost sensation, were destroyed in this tiny skeleton, which might have been a plump and happy baby. It seemed not to hear when addressed. I lifted it between my thumbs and forefingers; it did not weigh more than seven or eight pounds."

Beyond, in the orphanage yard, neglected children agonized in the last stages of starvation and disease. Hawthorne thought it obvious that the overseers, as in the adult poorhouses, were stealing grain for sale with little fear of punishment from their superiors:

*"We went towards the sheds, where were those who were too enfeebled to stand or walk. A boy was squatting over an earthen saucer, into which he spate continually; he had the mouth disease; he could not articulate, but an exhausted moan came from him ever and anon. There was a great abscess on the back of his head. Another, in the final stage of dysentery, lay nearly dead in his own filth; he breathed, but had not strength to moan. There was one baby which seemed much better than the rest; it was tended by its own mother.… Now, this child was in no better condition than the rest of them when it came, but its mother's care had revived it. That meant, simply, that it had received its full allowance of the food which is supposed to be given to all alike. Why had the others – the full orphans – not received theirs?"*69

Cosmopolitan pointedly published photographs of famine victims from the Central Provinces next to an illustration of a great monument erected to Queen Victoria. Hawthorne, "on his way home from India," it editorialized, "heard it conservatively estimated in London that a total of more than one hundred millions of dollars would be expended, directly and indirectly, upon the Queen's Jubilee ceremonies."70 But dying children in remote taluks were no more allowed to interrupt the gaiety of the Empress of India's Diamond Jubilee in June 1897 than they had her Great Durbar of twenty years before. Critics of Elgin were uncertain which was more scandalous: how much he had expended on the Diamond Jubilee extravaganza, or how little he had spent to combat the famine that affected 100 million Indians. When the government's actual relief expenditures were published a year later, they fell far below the per capita recommendations of the 1880 Famine Commission. As a new Famine Commission reported in 1898: "Our general conclusion is that, as compared with the past, a considerable degree of success as regards economy had been attained in the relief famine."71

The relief works were quickly shut down with the return of the rains in 1898. Hundreds of thousands of destitute, landless people, without any means to take advantage of the monsoon, were pushed out of the camps and poorhouses. As a consequence, the momentum of famine and disease continued to generate a staggering 6.5 million excess deaths in 1898, making total mortality closer to 11 million than the 4.5 million earlier admitted by Elgin. Twelve to 16 million was the death toll commonly reported in the world press, which promptly nominated this the "famine of the century."72 This dismal title, however, was almost immediately usurped by the even greater drought and deadlier famine of 1899– 1902.[292]

It bears noting that genocide was a term coined after the horrors done to Armenian Christians by the Turkish government in the 1910s and gradually had to be added reluctantly by Western governments after the Holocaust of Jewish people by Nazi Germany.[293] If ever we are willing to apply modern standards to the past, such as the case of the earliest recording of genocide purportedly being the Athenian genocide of Melos that Sparta had likely hoped to prevent[294], then what Great Britain did to India was four consecutive, calculated genocides that are well-documented by both fact-finding US journalists and predominately American Christian missionaries.[295] Part of the reason I mock modern US journalists is because they're not really journalists, if you compare the lengths US journalists of the late 1800s and early 1900s went through meeting people, documenting photos, and giving estimates of either their own statistical research or the government surveys from local British government officials of Indian descent that British Viceroys ignored; the American journalists did vigorous reporting of the depressing impact of British government policies upon India. It was American Christian missionaries unabashed condemnation of British economic policies that forced the more compliant

---

[292] Davis, Mike. Chapter Five: Skeletons at the Feast (pgs. 141 – 177). Late Victorian Holocausts: El Niño Famines and the Making of the Third World (Essential Mike Davis). Verso Books. Kindle Edition.
[293] Power, Samantha. "A Problem from Hell": America and the Age of Genocide. Reissue ed., Harper Perennial, 2007.
[294] Mulligan, Gerard. "Genocide in the Ancient World." World History Encyclopedia, https://www.worldhistory.org#organization, 27 Jan. 2013, www.worldhistory.org/article/485/genocide-in-the-ancient-world/.
[295] Davis, Mike. Late Victorian Holocausts: El Niño Famines and the Making of the Third World (Essential Mike Davis). Verso Books. Kindle Edition.

Anglican British Christians to start condemning their own government too. Finally, it was American scholars like historian Mike Davis and also Indian scholars of India like Indian politician Shashi Tharoor who started investigating and researching decades later to compile and reveal the copiously documented evidence.

While the period after World War 2 gradually resulted in a special relationship between the US government and Great Britain, and the Christian missionaries of the 1990s would spread documentaries about how Hindus of India are poor because they're devil worshippers who need to be converted to Christianity; I saw the beginning of one of these documentaries myself on television when I was a child, I think I may have been around nine-years old; the US Christian missionaries and US journalists of the late 1800s to early 1900s never let whatever negative beliefs they had about Hindus to influence their support for enlightenment values, human dignity, and vehement support for the human rights of all Indians including Hindus and other Dharmic followers. The US missionaries of the 1990s, who to my understanding used British material to learn of India, basically ignored that everything about the British narratives of India were self-serving and categorically proven false by their forebears in Missionary work and US journalism. The late 1800s to early 1900s American Christian missionaries and US journalists were vehemently denouncing British rule in India and doing painstaking work in documenting the depressing realities of British rule. The sentiment about British rule of India was shared by a large percentage of Americans at the time and that is not an exaggeration. When US missionaries returned to the United States to spread the horrifying news of what British government policies had wrought upon India and British Christian missionaries and a few of their politicians did the same for India, the late Mike Davis's *Late Victorian Holocausts* lets us know exactly what the results were:

> Curzon was responding to new stringencies dictated by the secretary of state for India, Lord George Hamilton. Financing of the Boer War trumped any "philanthropic romanticism" in India. Two years earlier, with the Northwest Frontier in upheaval, the secretary had in fact offered famine aid to Elgin, but now "Hamilton not only did not approach the Treasury for such a grant but also prevented Curzon from seeking it. The wars in China and South Africa made him more conscious of the Indian obligation with regard to the Imperial wars than of his responsibility to relieve the distress of the famine-stricken people." While refusing appeals to organize a famine charity in England, the secretary pressured Curzon to launch a War Fund in India so that its patriotic subjects could help defray Kitchener's expenses in the Transvaal. Though he did not interfere with the viceroy's plan to build a hugely ornate Victoria Memorial Monument in Calcutta, he urged the most ruthless Lyttonian vigilance in policing the relief works.92
>
> Meanwhile, the English public's famed philanthropic instinct had dried up as completely as the Deccan's streams and wells. As Herbert Spencer warned of the "rebarbarization" of the English spirit by rampant jingoism, the popular press ignored the new Indian holocaust to focus almost exclusively on the unexpectedly difficult struggle to subdue the Boers.93 "So far as the London Press and periodicals are concerned," complained a member of the Fabian Society, "India might almost have been non-existent."94 A desultory Mansion House fund for Indian famine victims raised barely 7 percent of the Lord Mayor's parallel War Fund for South Africa.95 "India," wrote an American missionary, "now would have to struggle alone, for the thoughts of every Englishman in the world were centered on South Africa."96

The most substantial international aid came not from London but from Topeka: 200,000 bags of grain "in solidarity with India's farmers" sent by Kansas Populists. (American relief organizers were incensed when British officials in Ajmir promptly taxed the shipment.)97 There were also notable contributions from sympathetic Native American tribes and Black American church groups.98[296]

In short, White Americans, Native Americans, Black Americans, and apparently even a group of Chinese schoolgirls from a single school in China before they martyred themselves in the Boxer Rebellion[297]; all donated their own hard-earned money to prevent what was then called a famine, which – in a more modern sense – is better understood to be a calculated genocide by Great Britain upon all of India. Brahmins and Dalits alike suffered and starved to death under British rule and the only ones who were possibly spared the worst of it were arguably the Merchant Castes in specific locations due to exploitative practices upon other Castes or possible fears of British government reprisal.[298] Nevertheless, the evidence is overwhelmingly clear thanks to the hard work of US Christian missionaries and US journalists from the time period of the 1870s – 1940s that all Indians throughout all of India suffered what should be understood as four consecutive mass genocides due to deliberate and calculated British government policies. Although they tragically couldn't prevent the worst effects of British policies upon India, US missionaries, US journalists, and regular people in the US public of all backgrounds were largely the unsung heroes of this tragic tale because they made a decades-long commitment in support of India's human rights.

Britain's Anti-Hindu Bigotry involved 250 years of dehumanizing Transgenderism

As a mass death toll of Indian people is never a concern for predominately White, European people due to the lack of perceived value of Indian lives within European culture and especially British culture; given they insist that – despite this massive death toll – that their imperialist project was ultimately a positive; here is an examination of how British policies demonstrably ruined the lives of LGBT people in India from bizarre and creepy laws like the Buggery act of 1533 and the subsequent Section 377 Law,

---

[296] Davis, Mike. Late Victorian Holocausts: El Niño Famines and the Making of the Third World (Essential Mike Davis) (pp. 164-165). Verso Books. Kindle Edition.
[297] Eddy, Sherwood. Chapter I: The People of India (pg. 25). "India Awakening: Eddy, Sherwood, 1871-1963: Free Download, Borrow, and Streaming." Google Books, Princeton University. Presented by THE PHILADELPHIAN SOCIETY, 1912,
https://books.googleusercontent.com/books/content?req=AKW5QacOjZvyVCZx7JC45zx-pVd69QF_LrzHGBABHlS0BgDJfJNrm__UimdC_tajRdFAHCb5Fc7s5prfnZA5v_2kgrvVs4xCvYzw1DK cpY23MeNI5J8FL0u6HNfHT7PxHtR030sgoOXaVi2VVNswh-
gOIXN1b3AXji1BPyqoV7tUxYhdPLpdQuhOJN4ZANy_ogTdNlHu-
y2H5b4AjSlU2JuiFYgTcUCL8Vq9uZmSqw0z2tmvo4YOh6dUG_d4PblBcVWG-3kj6edg PDF edition.
[298] Davis, Mike. Late Victorian Holocausts: El Niño Famines and the Making of the Third World (Essential Mike Davis). Verso Books. Kindle Edition.

according to the University of Alabama at Birmingham's Human Rights Blog in an article titled *"India's Relationship with the Third Gender"* which reads as follows:

What is the Third Gender?

In April of 2014, the Supreme Court of India formally recognized the existence of a third gender. There is no formal definition of the third gender in India. People who identify as neither man nor woman are commonly referred to as Hijra or transgender. The Hijra have been subject to discrimination, harassment, and persecution for their genderqueer self-identification. Along with the queer community, Hijras have been targeted by law enforcement and government officials under Section 377. This law was used to criminalize any queer sexual acts and has been used to justify discrimination and mistreatment of the LGBTQ+ community since its enactment in British colonial era India.

What Is the History of the Third Gender In India?

Although the Hijra have been subject to much hate and discrimination in recent times, this has not always been the case. Hijras were well-respected and revered in ancient India. In fact, Hijras play important roles in many Hindu religious texts. One such text talks about the life of Lord Rama, one of the most virtuous Hindu heroes. At some point, Lord Rama was banished from his kingdom. After being banished, he told his followers that the men and women should wipe their tears and leave him. All of the men and women left. However, a group of people known as the Hijra remained standing before him. They were neither men nor women and refused to leave until Lord Rama returned fourteen years later. This community was praised for showing such loyalty.

Hijras also held religious authority and important court positions and administrative roles in Mughal era India. Believed to have the ability to bless, many would seek out Hijras for blessings during important religious ceremonies. In ancient India, the Hijras were a community that was respected for being extremely loyal and were well trusted enough to be given important religious and governmental roles. This begs the question. If Hijras played an important role in ancient Indian society, then why are Hijras ostracized and persecuted in modern India?

Why Is the Third Gender Ostracized Today?

The answer is due in large part to the British colonization of India. When the British took over direct rule of India and absolved the British East India Company, government officials sought to enforce their western ideas and beliefs on Indians. Lawmakers accomplished this goal by enacting moral laws that banned anything that western society viewed as unclean and dirty. This included the creation of Section 377 of the Indian Penal Code which made illegal any "unnatural offenses" that were deemed "against the order of nature." From when Section 377 was implemented in 1858 to when it was recently deemed unconstitutional on 6 September 2018, Section 377 was used as justification to mistreat and punish Hijras, queers, and the LGBTQ+ community.

The western concept of hating and marginalizing anybody who was not straight and cisgender took hold in Indian society. The Hijra community was forced from a well-respected role as pillars of religious and governmental society to being social outcasts. This social exile is responsible for the socioeconomic and medical difficulties that Hijras face. Hijras are prone to being economically challenged because of the stigmas that they face. They are denied educational opportunities, jobs, and discriminated against in every area of their lives.

What are the Social, Economic, and Medical Problems Caused By Lasting Social Stigmas?

Despite gaining their independence from Britain in 1947, India has only recently begun to make progress on removing legislation that has been used to attack the Hijra and LGBTQ+ population. The many decades of subjugation stretching back generations have left a mark. Many of the hateful western views towards LGBTQ+ people have become deeply ingrained in India's culture. Even with many public relations campaigns along with a growing group of supporters, the vast majority of Indians still are against Hijras. Many Indians don't respect Hijras worth. Hijras are often called to come to auspicious events such as marriages and child-births for blessings. Many Indians view the Hijras as bringing good luck and warding off evil spirits. Yet because of widespread discrimination, the majority of Hijras are forced to beg for money since they are barred from most employment opportunities. Due to this, some of the common means of living for Hijras are begging, dancing, and prostitution.[299]

And, just to understand that this really was all Great Britain's fault with its bizarre, primitive, and backwards Western moral values, here's BBC journalist Tessa Wong's article titled "*377: The British colonial law that left an anti-LGBTQ legacy in Asia*" which goes into a cursory glance at the influence of British culture upon the world. The British finally admit they did something wrong after more than 250-years of exploitation and brutalization of the world:

> **For much of the past two centuries, it was illegal to be gay in a vast swathe of the world - thanks to colonial Britain.**
>
> Till today, colonial-era laws that ban homosexuality continue to exist in former British territories including parts of Africa and Oceania.
>
> But it is in Asia where they have had a significantly widespread impact. This is the region where, before India legalised homosexual sex in 2018, at least one billion people lived with anti-LGBTQ legislation.
>
> It can be traced back to one particular law first conceptualised in India, and one man's mission to "modernise" the colony.
>
> **'Exotic, mystical Orient'**
> Currently, it is illegal to be gay in around 69 countries, nearly two-thirds of which were under some form of British control at one point of time.
>
> This is no coincidence, according to Enze Han and Joseph O'Mahoney, who wrote the book British Colonialism and the Criminalization of Homosexuality.
>
> Dr Han told the BBC that British rulers introduced such laws because of a "Victorian, Christian puritanical concept of sex".
>
> "They wanted to protect innocent British soldiers from the 'exotic, mystical Orient' - there was this very orientalised view of Asia and the Middle East that they were overly erotic."
>
> "They thought if there were no regulations, the soldiers would be easily led astray."
>
> While there were several criminal codes used across British colonies around the world, in Asia one particular set of laws was used prominently - the Indian Penal Code (IPC) drawn up by British historian Lord Thomas Babington Macaulay, which came into force in 1862.
> It contained section 377, which stated that "whoever voluntarily has carnal intercourse against the order of nature with any man, woman or animal" would be punished with imprisonment or fines.

---

[299] "India's Relationship with the Third Gender." UAB Institute for Human Rights Blog, The University of Alabama at Birmingham, 29 Oct. 2018, sites.uab.edu/humanrights/2018/10/29/indias-relationship-with-the-third-gender/.

Lord Macaulay, who modelled the section on Britain's 16th Century Buggery Act, believed the IPC was a "blessing" for India as it would "modernise" its society, according to Dr Han and Dr O'Mahoney's book.

The British went on to use the IPC as the basis for criminal law codes in many other territories they controlled.

Till today, 377 continues to exist in various forms in several former colonies in Asia such as Pakistan, Singapore, Bangladesh, Malaysia, Brunei, Myanmar and Sri Lanka.

Penalties range from two to 20 years in prison. In places with Muslim-majority populations which also have sharia law, LGBT persons can also face more severe punishment such as flogging.

Lasting legacy
Activists say these laws have left a damaging legacy on these countries, some of which have long had flexible attitudes towards LGBTQ people.

Transgenderism, intersex identity and the third gender, for example, have traditionally been a part of South Asian culture with the hijra or eunuch communities.
In India, where for centuries LGBTQ relationships were featured in literature, myths and Hindu temple art, present-day attitudes now largely skew conservative.

"It's in our traditions. But now we are getting so embarrassed about [LGBTQ relations]. Clearly the change happened because of certain influences," says Anjali Gopalan, executive director of Naz Foundation India, a non-governmental organisation which offers counselling services for the LGBTQ community.

One common argument governments have made for keeping the law is that it continues to reflect the conservative stance of their societies. Some, like India, have even ironically argued that it keeps out "Western influence".
But activists point out that this perpetuates discrimination and goes against some countries' constitutions which promise equal rights to all citizens.

This has a "de-humanising effect" on an LGBTQ person, and can seriously impact their access to education and career opportunities as well as increase their risk of poverty and physical violence, said Jessica Stern, executive director of LGBTQ rights group OutRight International.

"If you're a walking criminal, you're living with a burden every day. Whether you internalise it or not, it affects you and everyone who loves you," she told the BBC.
The Covid pandemic has exacerbated these problems, she added.

One recent example her group found was in Sri Lanka, where the police were tasked to distribute emergency rations while the country was under curfew - but some in the LGBTQ community were too afraid to come forward due to the country's anti-sodomy law.

"People said they have to risk arrest or risk going hungry… it's a stark life or death choice they have to make," said Ms Stern.

Some governments, like Singapore, have tried to tread the middle ground by publicly promising never to enforce the law. But the LGBTQ community in the city-state say this is unfair as they live knowing the government could change its mind at any time.

Olivia and Irene Chiong left Singapore five years ago for the US, where they got married and are both legally recognised as the mothers of their two daughters - something that would not be possible back home.

The lack of rights is one reason they find it difficult to return, as well as the refusal among some Singaporeans including government ministers to acknowledge that there is discrimination.
"I think for me the biggest frustration comes from the fact that Singaporeans think everything's okay - that as long as gay people keep quiet... keep themselves in the closet, it's fine!" said Olivia.

"There are many rainbow families in Singapore...You can't just keep sweeping things under the carpet.

"The only reason why Singapore is holding so tightly to (377) is because it gives them the illusion of control," she said.

A long road ahead
There has been progress - most notably, of course, with the Indian Supreme Court's decision in 2018 to repeal 377, following years of legal challenges mounted by determined activists.

It was a historic decision and a major step forward for LGBT rights in India. But three years on, there is still a very long way to go in changing cultural attitudes, activists say.

"The most common thing we still see in counselling is families wanting their gay sons to get married (to a woman)," said Ms Gopalan.

"Everything is linked to the family in India, and marriage is a very big part of our lives. So the first issue is acceptance from the family and then by extension, society."

Activists say more protection is needed, such as anti-discrimination laws. Earlier this month, a court in Chennai ordered officials to draw up plans for reforms to respect LGBTQ rights.
Still, India's repeal of 377 has helped to lessen the stigma - and inspired other countries.

In Singapore and Kenya, activists have used the repeal in legal arguments against their own colonial anti-homosexuality laws.

Two centuries after it was used by the British as a legal blueprint, India once again is seen as an example to follow - this time to strike down that very law that was exported across Asia.

"It has emboldened others in Asia, unequivocally... it sent a message to all former colonial outposts," said Ms Stern.

"Activists I spoke to have said that if it can happen in India, it can happen here too."[300]

Since I've noticed a few ignorant views even from Indians of India who continue to purport the falsehood that we Hindus were somehow not really pro-Third Gender prior to British imperialism, here's Adi Shankara's commentary on the *Shvestashvatara / Svetasvatara Upanishad* 4.3 – that is chapter four, verse three – which reads as follows:

> 3. You are the woman, You are the man, You are the boy, (and) You are the girl, too. You are the old man tottering with a stick. Taking birth, You have Your faces everywhere.
> **The meaning of the verse is clear.**[301]

---

[300] Wong, Tessa. "377: The British Colonial Law That Left an Anti-LGBTQ Legacy in Asia." BBC News, BBC, 28 June 2021, www.bbc.com/news/world-asia-57606847.
[301] Shankara, Adi. "Chapter 4." Svetasvatara Upanishad with the Commentary of Sankaracarya, translated by Swami Gambhirananda, 4th ed., Advaita Ashrama, Kolkata, West Bengal, 2009, pp. 143–143. For

As I suspect there will be aspersions that I've taken this passage out of context, I'll provide a story from the Mahabharata which gives further context supporting this argument. For those unaware, the Mahabharata is a lengthy book of Hindu legends, Hindu myths, anecdotal moral lessons, a list of dynastic ruling families, and scenarios providing philosophical contexts and arguments for an array of concepts within the Hindu tradition. It's more a book of epics to help give further context to Hindu theology, while also being a theological book itself but of lesser importance as a *Smriti* text, which are supplementary materials to the main Vedic literature categorized as *Shruti* such as the Upanishads. I've found theological and philosophical arguments and stories ranging from topics like determinism, to transgenderism, and so much more in the Mahabharata itself. Some Hindus believe it to be based more upon real historical events and there are now archaeological findings suggesting the earliest period of the Harrapan civilization is approximately as old as 8000 – 7000 BCE.[302][303] I'm of the opinion that; while there probably are plenty of historical events written in it; there were likely exaggerations, dynastic political clashes arguing over specific historical events, and mythical events added for the sake of dramatization and for the benefit of respective ruling classes and dynasties within specific historical time periods throughout India's history. In short, basically like everywhere else in the world where there were dynastic clashes over ruling kingdoms and empires. I do think specific events such as a history of civil wars happened but the specific context, the number of forces on each dynastic side, and the presentation of victories and defeats were probably influenced by whatever dominant Vedic kingdom or empire wanted for the sake of justifying their ultimate victory or to justify their rule over new territories. Whatever the case, that topic is beyond the scope of this book. The Mahabharata's book thirteen, *Anusasana Parva*, section twelve presents the following story affirming Transgenderism in ancient Hindu / Vedic society in a purely theological context. This specific translation had an odd doubling of speech marks and I'm unsure why either the translator or editor chose this method, but I decided to leave it as is for the sake of authenticity:

SECTION XII
"'Yudhishthira said, "It behoveth, O king to tell me truly which of the two viz., man or woman derives the greater pleasure from an act of union with each other. Kindly resolve my doubt in this respect."

Reference on page 143: 3. You are the woman, You are the man, You are the boy, (and) You are the girl, too. You are the old man tottering with a stick. Taking birth, You have Your faces everywhere. The meaning of the verse is clear.

[302] Pandey, Jhimli Mukherjee. "Indus Era 8,000 Years Old, Not 5,500; Ended Because of Weaker Monsoon: India News." The Times of India, TOI, 29 May 2016, timesofindia.indiatimes.com/india/Indus-era-8000-years-old-not-5500-ended-because-of-weaker-monsoon/articleshow/52485332.cms.

[303] Bengrut, Dheeraj. "New Evidence Suggests Harappan Civilisation Is 7,000 to 8,000 Years' Old." Hindustan Times, Hindustan Times, 22 Dec. 2023, www.hindustantimes.com/cities/pune-news/new-evidence-suggests-harappan-civilisation-is-7-000-to-8-000-years-old-101703182904001.html.

"'Bhishma said, "In this connection is cited this old narrative of the discourse between Bhangaswana and Sakra as a precedent illustrating the question. In days of yore there lived a king of the name of Bhangaswana. He was exceedingly righteous and was known as a royal sage. He was, however, childless, O chief of men, and therefore performed a sacrifice from desire of obtaining an issue. The sacrifice which that mighty monarch performed was the Agnishtuta. In consequence of the fact that the deity of fire is alone adored in that sacrifice, this is always disliked by Indra. Yet it is the sacrifice that is desired by men when for the purpose of obtaining an issue they seek to cleanse themselves of their sins.[30] The highly blessed chief of the celestials, viz. Indra, learning that the monarch was desirous of performing the Agnishtuta, began from that moment to look for the laches of that royal sage of well-restrained soul (for if he could succeed in finding some laches, he could then punish his disregarder). Notwithstanding all his vigilance, however, O king, Indra failed to detect any laches, on the part of the high-souled monarch. Some time after, one day, the king went on a hunting expedition. Saying unto himself—This, indeed, is an opportunity,—Indra stupefied the monarch. The king proceeded alone on his horse, confounded because of the chief of the celestials having stupefied his senses. Afflicted with hunger and thirst, the king's confusion was so great that he could not ascertain the points of the compass. Indeed, afflicted with thirst, he began to wander hither and thither. He then beheld a lake that was exceedingly beautiful and was full of transparent water. Alighting from his steed, and plunging into the lake, he caused his animal to drink. Tying his horse then, whose thirst had been slaked, to a tree, the king plunged into the lake again for performing his ablutions. To his amazement he found that he was changed, by virtue of the waters, into a woman. Beholding himself thus transformed in respect of sex itself, the king became overpowered with shame. With his senses and mind completely agitated, he began to reflect with his whole heart in this strain:—'Alas, how shall I ride my steed? How shall I return to my capital? In consequence of the Agnishtuta sacrifice I have got a hundred sons all endued with great might, and all children of my own loins. Alas, thus transformed, what shall I say unto them? What shall I say unto my spouses, my relatives and well-wishers, and my subjects of the city and the provinces? Rishis conversant with the truths of duty and religion and other matters say that mildness and softness and liability to extreme agitation are the attributes of women, and that activity, hardness, and energy are the attributes of men. Alas, my manliness has disappeared. For what reason has femininity come over me? In consequence of this transformation of sex, how shall I succeed in mounting my horse again?'—Having indulged in these sad thoughts, the monarch, with great exertion, mounted his steed and came back to his capital, transformed though he had been into a woman. His sons and spouses and servants, and his subjects of the city and the provinces, beholding that extraordinary transformation, became exceedingly amazed. Then that royal sage, that foremost of eloquent men, addressing them all, said,—'I had gone out on a hunting expedition, accompanied by a large force. Losing all knowledge of the points of the compass, I entered a thick and terrible forest, impelled by the fates. In that terrible forest, I became afflicted with thirst and lost my senses. I then beheld a beautiful lake abounding with fowl of every description. Plunging into that stream for performing my ablutions, I was transformed into a woman!'—Summoning then his spouses and counsellors, and all his sons by their names, that best of monarchs transformed into a woman said unto them these words:—'Do ye enjoy this kingdom in happiness. As regards myself, I shall repair to the woods, ye sons.'—Having said so unto his children, the monarch proceeded to the forest. Arrived there, she came upon an asylum inhabited by an ascetic. By that ascetic the transformed monarch gave birth to a century of sons. Taking all those children of hers, she repaired to where her former children were, and addressing the latter, said,—'Ye are the children of my loins while I was a man. These are my children brought forth by me in this state of transformation. Ye sons, do ye all enjoy my kingdom together, like brothers born of the same parents.'—At this command of their parent, all the brothers, uniting together, began to enjoy the kingdom as their joint property. Beholding those children of the king all jointly enjoying the kingdom as brothers born of the same parents, the chief of the celestials, filled with wrath, began to reflect—'By transforming this royal sage into a woman I have, it seems, done him good instead of an injury.' Saying this, the chief of the celestials viz., Indra of a hundred sacrifices, assuming the form of a Brahmana, repaired to the capital of the king and meeting all the children succeeded in disuniting the princes. He said unto them—'Brothers never remain at peace even when they happen to be the children of the same father. The sons of the sage Kasyapa, viz., the deities and the Asuras, quarrelled with each other on account of the sovereignty of the three worlds. As regards ye princes, ye are the children of the royal sage Bhangaswana. These others are the children of an ascetic. The deities and the Asuras are children of even one common sire, and yet the latter quarrelled with each other. How much more, therefore, should you quarrel with each other? This kingdom that is your paternal property is being enjoyed by these children of an ascetic.' With these words, Indra succeeded in causing a breach between them, so that they were very soon engaged in battle and slew each other. Hearing this, king Bhangaswana, who was living as an ascetic woman, burnt with grief and poured forth her lamentations. The lord of the celestials viz. Indra, assuming the guise of a Brahmana, came to that spot where the ascetic lady was living and meeting her, said,—'O thou that art possessed of a beautiful face, with what grief dost thou burn so that thou art pouring forth thy lamentations?'—Beholding the Brahmana the lady told him in a piteous voice,—'Two hundred sons of mine O regenerate one, have been slain by Time. I was formerly a king, O learned Brahmana and in that state had a hundred sons. These were begotten by me after my own form, O best of regenerate persons. On one occasion I went on a hunting expedition. Stupefied, I wandered amidst a thick forest. Beholding at last a lake, I plunged into it. Rising, O foremost of Brahmanas, I found that I had become a woman. Returning to my capital I installed my sons in the sovereignty of my dominions and then departed for the forest. Transformed into a woman, I bore a hundred sons to my husband who is a high souled ascetic. All of them were born in the ascetic's retreat. I took them to the capital. My children, through the influence of Time, quarrelled with each other, O twice-born one. Thus afflicted by Destiny, I am indulging in grief.' Indra addressed him in these harsh words.—'In former days, O lady, thou gayest me great pain, for thou didst perform a sacrifice that is disliked by Indra. Indeed, though I was present, thou didst not invoke me with honours. I am that Indra, O thou of wicked understanding. It is I with whom thou hast purposely sought hostilities.' Beholding Indra, the royal sage fell at his feet, touching them with his head, and said,—'Be gratified with me, O foremost of deities. The sacrifice of which thou speakest was performed from desire of offspring (and not from any wish to hurt thee). It behoveth thee therefore, to grant me thy pardon.'—Indra, seeing the transformed monarch prostrate himself thus unto him, became gratified with him and desired to give him a boon. 'Which of your sons, O king, dost thou wish, should revive, those that were brought forth by thee transformed into a woman, or those that were begotten by thee in thy condition as a person of the male sex?' The ascetic lady, joining her hands, answered Indra, saying, 'O Vasava, let those sons of mine come to life that were borne by me as a woman.' Filled with wonder at this reply, Indra once more asked the lady, 'Why dost thou entertain less affection for those children of thine that were begotten by thee in thy form of a person of the male sex? Why is it that thou bearest greater affection for those children that were borne by thee in thy transformed state? I wish to hear the reason of this difference in respect of thy affection. It behoveth thee to tell me everything.'

"'"The lady said, 'The affection that is entertained by a woman is much greater than that which is entertained by a man. Hence, it is, O Sakra, that I wish those children to come back to life that were borne by me as a woman.'"

"'Bhishma continued, "Thus addressed, Indra became highly pleased and said unto her, 'O lady that art so truthful, let all thy children come back into life. Do thou take another boon, O foremost of kings, in fact, whatever boon thou likest. O thou of excellent vows, do thou take from me whatever status thou choosest, that of woman or of man.'

"'"The lady said, 'I desire to remain a woman, O Sakra. In fact, I do not wish to be restored to the status of manhood, O Vasava.'—Hearing this answer, Indra once more asked her, saying,—'Why is it, O puissant one, that abandoning the status of manhood thou wishest that of womanhood?' Questioned thus, that foremost of monarchs transformed into a woman answered, 'In acts of congress, the pleasure that women enjoy is always much greater than what is enjoyed by men. It is for this reason, O Sakra, that I desire to continue a woman; O foremost of the deities, truly do I say unto thee that I derive greater pleasure in my present status of womanhood. I am quite content with this status of womanhood that I now have. Do thou leave me now, O lord of heaven.'—Hearing these words of hers, the lord of the celestials answered,—'So be it,'—and bidding her farewell, proceeded to heaven. Thus, O monarch, it is known that woman derives much greater pleasure than man under the circumstances thou hast asked.""[304]

The point being that the United Kingdom absolutely never brought anything but violence, hate, despair, racism, theft of resources, and victim-blaming upon all of the Indian subcontinent. The imposition of "Western values" brought Europe's backwardness into Indian society and the only reason it has been ignored for so long is specifically because Europe continues to devalue the lives of all Indians of India and vilifies Hindu culture as an easy target because most Hindus genuinely strive for non-violence and harmony. While it is a very good thing that former Prime Minister Theresa May acknowledged this wrongdoing on behalf of the UK back in 2018, it should not be taken out of the general context and in isolation of, the other crimes against humanity that Great Britain committed upon India, other South Asian countries, Ireland, Tasmania, Jamaica, Southeast Asian countries, and various African countries.[305]

British Imperialism Did Not Bring India Democracy

Any claims that it brought a Republic form of government cannot be substantiated given that Indians did all the hard work for that establishing the Republic of India on January 26th, 1950 which was three years after British colonialism had ended; such narratives ignore the inconvenient history that Great Britain was only briefly a Republic for approximately eleven years in the mid-1600s before Royalists returned it back to a Monarchy and slaughtered every last person who signed off on the public execution of England's King Charles I. The term "Western democracies" helps to obscure the historical fact that England slaughtered the only known Republic in its land out of existence, its monarchy remains above the law even now in the UK, and all failings of either it or Canada reveal the failings of monarchy and not a democratic republic. I've written this piece before, but I find it most fitting to share it here and I'll keep it circumscribed to the UK for the purposes of this chapter. The British monarchy's legal impositions upon British society cannot be ignored:

The examples in the UK include the Racial and Religious Hatred Act of 2006 (and put in effect around October 2007 in the UK) which is anti-Free Speech[306], the

---

[304] Vyasa. "SECTION XII of Anusasana Parva of the Mahabharata." Mahabharata, edited by John Bruno Hare, translated by Kisari Mohan Ganguli, Kindle ed., Sacred-Texts.Com, 2005, p. Location 614-Location 681, https://www.gutenberg.org/cache/epub/15477/pg15477-images.html. Accessed 14 May 2025.
[305] Jain, Sagaree. "Theresa May 'deeply Regrets' Colonial Anti-LGBT Laws." Human Rights Watch, Human Rights Watch Dispatches, 18 Apr. 2018, www.hrw.org/news/2018/04/18/theresa-may-deeply-regrets-colonial-anti-lgbt-laws.
[306] Windsor, Elizabeth Alexandra Mary. Racial and Religious Hatred Act 2006, UK Home Office, 1 Oct. 2007, www.legislation.gov.uk/ukpga/2006/1/data.pdf. For Reference: The Home Office of the UK states it

connectedness of the UK government and the Church of England which is far removed from the US's staunch belief in the Separation of Church and State[307], the fact the upper house of their parliament (the House of Lords) are determined by peerage and a special unelected committee and not by democratic process[308], the fact the British government can issue threats of lawsuit via D-Notices to the British press[309], the fact they're still officially a monarchy as a government with British people officially recognized as subjects of the British crown and not as citizens[310], and the fact that the Royal family still holds wealth by the Crown Estate that classifies itself as neither government nor part of the monarchy which is unelected[311]; these are serious social differences, not something that we should roll our eyes about. The previous monarch was able to prevent the British public from knowing how much money she has by refusing "the King's / Queen's Consent" which is a legal policy in British lawmaking that the current reigning King or Queen has to consent for bills to be debated in the British parliament[312]; this was regarding money she obtains from British taxpayers to fund her family's lavish lifestyle. Even worse, according to *The Guardian*, the British government actively hide how powerful this method of influence on British law really is, so if you were to research it from the British Monarchy's website, you wouldn't have a clear understanding of how disturbingly powerful it is in the British rule of law or how the previous monarch used it to hide her wealth assets pertaining to land ownership from the British public.[313][314] While the British public may try to argue that the House of Commons can pass bills without the House of Lords in some cases the legal basis seems to be the British Monarch delegating

---

was officially enacted on October 1st, 2007 on "https://www.legislation.gov.uk/uksi/2007/2490/made" which reads as follows: Commencement

2.—(1) Apart from the provisions mentioned in paragraph (2), the 2006 Act comes into force on 1st October 2007.

[307] Torrance, David. "The Relationship between Church and State in the United Kingdom - House of Commons Library." UK Parliament, House of Commons Library, 14 Sept. 2023, commonslibrary.parliament.uk/research-briefings/cbp-8886/.

[308] "How Members Are Appointed - UK Parliament." Www.Parliament.Uk, UK Parliament, www.parliament.uk/business/lords/whos-in-the-house-of-lords/members-and-their-roles/how-members-are-appointed/. Accessed 17 May 2025.

[309] Greenslade, Roy. "The D-Notice System: A Typically British Fudge That Has Survived a Century." The Guardian, Guardian News and Media, 31 July 2015, www.theguardian.com/media/2015/jul/31/d-notice-system-state-media-press-freedom.

[310] Alden, Chris. "Britain's Monarchy." The Guardian, Guardian News and Media, 16 May 2002, www.theguardian.com/world/2002/may/16/qanda.jubilee.

[311] "The Crown Estate FAQs: Find Answers to Commonly Asked Questions." The Crown Estate, The Crown Estate, 2025, www.thecrownestate.co.uk/about-us/faqs#whoownsthecrownestate.

[312] Evans, Rob, and David Pegg. "Revealed: Queen Lobbied for Change in Law to Hide Her Private Wealth." The Guardian, Guardian News and Media, 7 Feb. 2021, www.theguardian.com/uk-news/2021/feb/07/revealed-queen-lobbied-for-change-in-law-to-hide-her-private-wealth.

[313] Evans, Rob, and David Pegg. "Revealed: Queen Lobbied for Change in Law to Hide Her Private Wealth." The Guardian, Guardian News and Media, 7 Feb. 2021, www.theguardian.com/uk-news/2021/feb/07/revealed-queen-lobbied-for-change-in-law-to-hide-her-private-wealth.

[314] Lewis, Paul, and David Pegg. "How the British Royal Family Hides Its Wealth from Public Scrutiny." The Guardian, Guardian News and Media, 5 Apr. 2023, www.theguardian.com/uk-news/2023/apr/05/how-the-british-royal-family-hides-its-wealth-from-public-scrutiny.

them the power to do so in the first place; if the reigning Monarch doesn't delegate the power as a condition, then it doesn't seem possible.[315] Moreover, they still must face Royal Assent from the Monarch and thus the Monarch must approve it both prior to and after the bill is debated. The only argument against it is that the Monarchy that holds a power imbalance in an unequal system chooses not to abuse it in most cases; likely because it doesn't serve their self-interests for every bill. Furthermore, the fact that the House of Lords can amend bills at their committee stage and force a vote that can lead to the bill failing during the debate portion essentially equalizes monarch approved and race-based peerage systems and treats them equivalent to democratically elected officials in the House of Commons in the British parliamentary system regardless.[316] The House of Lords consists roughly of eight-hundred people, ninety-two by race-based peerage, twenty-five via the Church of England's representatives, and the rest approved by the Monarchy or the Monarch's special unelected committees that keeps itself hidden from public scrutiny in the interests of the British Monarchy.[317] Finally, the House of Lords can amend the bills in both the Report Stage and Third Reading stage, the claims that it is usually just for "clarity" doesn't mean that this power cannot be abused by these unelected officials who are already imposing their will via unelected means upon what seems to be a very limited democratic process in scope.[318] In fact, this system of abuse, although reduced, is still in effect because the 1949 Parliament act still allows the House of Lords to delay bills for one-year at their discretion.[319]

While the Republic of India also holds control over Hindu temples, it is something many Hindus staunchly do not want and have repeatedly argued for Hindu temples to be free of government confines, because it is simply another form of appeasement where Hindu temples are regulated by the government.[320][321] Hindu religious

---

[315] "The Parliament Act 1949 (Updated November 2005)." Www.Parliament.Uk, HOUSE OF LORDS LIBRARY, www.parliament.uk/globalassets/documents/lords-library/hllparlact1949.pdf. Accessed 17 May 2025.
[316] "Making Laws: House of Lords Stages - UK Parliament." Https://Www.Parliament.Uk/Business/Lords/Work-of-the-House-of-Lords/Making-Laws/, UK Parliament, www.parliament.uk/business/lords/work-of-the-house-of-lords/making-laws/. Accessed 17 May 2025.
[317] Clarke, Jennifer, and Tom Edgington. "What Is the House of Lords, How Does It Work and How Is It Changing?" BBC News, BBC, 5 Sept. 2024, www.bbc.com/news/uk-politics-63864428.
[318] "Making Laws: House of Lords Stages - UK Parliament." Https://Www.Parliament.Uk/Business/Lords/Work-of-the-House-of-Lords/Making-Laws/, UK Parliament, www.parliament.uk/business/lords/work-of-the-house-of-lords/making-laws/. Accessed 17 May 2025.
[319] "The Parliament Acts - UK Parliament." Www.Parliament.Uk, UK Parliament, www.parliament.uk/about/how/laws/parliamentacts/. Accessed 17 May 2025.
[320] Prakash, A Surya. "Why Should the Government Run Hindu Temples?" The New Indian Express, The New Indian Express, 13 Jan. 2022, www.newindianexpress.com/opinions/2022/Jan/13/why-should-the-government-run-hindu-temples-2406605.html.
[321] G, Ananthakrishnan. "On PIL Seeking to Free Temples from Govt Control, SC Seeks More Material in Support." The Indian Express, The Indian Express, 1 Sept. 2022, web.archive.org/web/20220902050836/https://indianexpress.com/article/india/on-pil-seeking-to-free-temples-from-govt-control-sc-seeks-more-material-in-support-8125936/.

schools must spend their own expenses of up to twenty-five percent for free education to underserved children, while no such imposition is placed upon Islamic and Christian schools or religious places. It reduces the ability of India to educate all of its children just to cater to primarily Christian bigotry against Hindus by depriving Hindu children of equal opportunities due to increased school closings of specifically Hindu religious schools as a result of this policy, essentially causing the opposite of its likely intent due to higher costs imposed upon Hindu religious schools.[322][323] In effect, the only place a Hindu can freely be a Hindu is in the United States. While this double-standard began under Islamic rule in India through the *Jizya* (Toleration Tax), Hindus had to pay a "holy dip" tax for participation in Kumbh Mela festivals from 1895 – 1940 under British colonial rule.[324] Starting from the British East India company, there was a levied tax of the Jagannath temple in Puri, Odissa of India; for Hindus who participated in journeying to it. It was briefly cancelled for three years and then began again from approximately between 1806 – 1840 from what surviving records show and of course, the specific intent was to increase Christian conversions in recognition of the fact that Britain was a Christian nation and to deliberately weaken Hinduism.[325][326][327] The performance of *Sati* – widowers burning themselves after their husband's passing – was criticized and reformed by the indigenous Bengal Renaissance from people such as Hindu reformer, Ram Mohan Roy and not by British imperialists.

British Imperialism Supported Casteism when Convenient for its Self-Interests

To top it all off, even despite the pro-Christian bigotry towards Hindus that came from British imperialism, this did not stop British imperialists from worshipping their true god, the entwined worship of Jesus Christ with British nationalism which is the very essence of Anglicanism. During the 1820s, Shanar Christians protested against a dehumanizing and mandatory Caste-based social custom that lower-caste women remain topless, to publicly display their lower social status at the behest of upper-caste male

---

[322] "Article 30: Discrimination against Hindus by the Indian State." HHR News, Hindu Human Rights, 16 Dec. 2013, www.hinduhumanrights.info/article-30-discrimination-against-hindus-by-the-indian-state/.
[323] "Legalized Hinduphobia - RTE Law, Hurts Hindus Part 1." PGurus, 23 Sept. 2016, www.pgurus.com/diary-of-a-second-class-citizen-how-rte-has-hurt-hindu-educational-bodies-part-1/.
[324] Kurungot, Avinash. "Kumbh Mela and Taxation: A Historical and Economic Perspective." Taxscan, TAXSCAN, 14 Feb. 2025, www.taxscan.in/the-kumbh-mela-tax-a-price-paid-on-spirit-and-soul/489753/#.
[325] "Pilgrim Tax—India - Hansard - UK Parliament." UK Parliament, Hansard, hansard.parliament.uk/Commons/1831-10-14/debates/a954d490-d962-4650-8d39-f1dd71072012/PilgrimTax%E2%80%94India. Accessed 18 May 2025.
[326] Tripathy, Manorama. "A Brief History of the Pilgrim Tax in Puri." Magazines.Odisha.Gov.In, Odisha Review, Jan. 2014, magazines.odisha.gov.in/Orissareview/2014/Jan/engpdf/62-69.pdf. For Reference: Page 63
[327] Srinivasan, Kaushik. "How a British Tax Scheme at the Jagannath Temple Became a Political Controversy." Brown History, Brown History, 30 Mar. 2023, brownhistory.substack.com/p/how-a-british-tax-scheme-at-the-jagannath.

Hindus; this was within the village of Neyoor in the State of Tamil Nadu (now apparently part of Southern Kerala). This led to shameful and widespread violence by Hindus upon Christians who insisted their caste-based discriminatory custom be upheld. The situation became so violent that British troops were called in to end the unrest. Reverand Isaac Henry Hacker of the Church of England explains what Anglican missionaries recorded in his book. The British troops ended it by enthusiastically supporting dehumanization, Casteism, and inflicted their own merciless violence upon Shanar Christians in Tamil Nadu for violating what is misnamed the Breast Tax in modern times. On page 38 of "*A Hundred Years in Travancore*" by Reverend Isaac Henry Hacker, it reads as follows:

> The removal of Mr Mead to the new station at Neyoor seemed to arouse all the slumbering fires of persecution. Occasion was taken to object to the wearing of upper cloths by Christian women, but there is no doubt the better classes looked with great disfavour on the steady advancement of the Shanars and Pariah converts of the mission. From persecution of individuals they went further, and riotous bands attacked and burnt the houses and chapels of Christians. An attack was even made upon Mr Mead. Early in 1829 news of a plot to assassinate him came to Mr Mead's ears, and he had to obtain military protection from Fort Udaigiri, and for a fort night was under the care of British troops. The official enquiry made by the Dewan and other officials into these riots was remarkable for the fact that the sufferers (the Shanar Christians) were treated as the culprits, and were chained, flogged, and imprisoned, and many of them sent to the central prison at Quilon. The enquiry was distinctly unfavourable to the Christians. The favourable order as to women's dress made to Mr Mead in 1823 was cancelled, and Christians were ordered to respect the ancient caste customs, especially those inculcating submission to the higher castes. The proclamation is remarkable also for the first appearance of the order peculiar to Travancore that no place of worship should be erected without Government permission being first obtained. This order has within recent years been revived, and is now added to the statute book as a regular law. The persecution seems to have worn itself out and to have gradually subsided, Mr Mead counselling submission and diligently exercising himself in getting condemned Christians liberated.[328]

When I first learned of the general information of this story in 2018, and read blogs about it online, I was given the depiction that the benevolent hand of Great Britain came to stop the "savage" Hindus from mistreating lower-caste Indian converts to Christianity and that Great Britain had eventually outlawed it due to their vigorous support for an emerging consciousness towards Western values but with gradual missteps. This was the image the British presented to the world to justify their imperialism of India, but this is not true even in the case of unambiguous Casteism in India. I noticed the details stopped making sense even among supposed Christians from Tamil Nadu and Kerala posting online about the benevolent, guiding hand of the "superior" Christian nation-state of Great Britain. How was it that the Breast social custom had continued over a century later and needed outlawing again? How could it

---

[328] Hacker, Isaac Henry. "CHAPTER III: THE GROWTH OF FORTY YEARS, 1816-1856." A HUNDRED YEARS IN TRAVANCORE BY I. H. HACKER, PDF ed., THE LONDON MISSIONARY SOCIETY, pp. 38–38,
https://ia600207.us.archive.org/20/items/100YearsInTravancore/100YearsInTravancore.pdf. Accessed 18 May 2025.

both be true that there was strict Caste observance and that British influence had changed the society, but the purported positive effect of British influence didn't last? Why had it incorrectly been called the Breast Tax, when Christian missionaries in the 1820s called it a Caste-enforced Breast social custom without any mention of a Breast Tax? From what little I could find on the subject; it was the vigorous peaceful protests from Christian Indians themselves that removed it years after British imperialism. How could Great Britain have helped "outlaw" it, if Anglican missionary accounts state that British governing officials supported the Breast custom as official British government law imposed upon the lower-Caste Shanar Christians of Travancore, and this imposition was put into legal effect after British troops put Shanar Christians into prisons where they were chained and whipped? A lot of superstition and falsehoods exist about this story, such as the story of Nangeli, which is apparently a hoax as no record of this person exists.[329] Too many details about the so-called "breast tax" don't add-up and were possibly never recorded; the simple fact that it wasn't a tax, but a social custom was never corrected about the story.[330][331] Christianity was flourishing briefly in the area, slightly over a decade prior to the upper-caste Hindu riots, until a severe British poll tax was implemented. For some context, a British poll tax is not a tax on voting like in the US context of the name, it appears to have been a tax on the assessed value of movable property for each individual.[332][333] In other words, British troops had full military control of this area and were undoubtedly the ones who had put Shanar Christians into prisons to torture them approximately ten – twenty years later. From page 27 of "*A Hundred Years in Travancore*" by Reverand Isaac Henry Hacker:

> In 1810 two events of importance to the infant mission occurred. They were the retirement of Colonel Macaulay and the appointment of Colonel Munro and the accession to the throne of Travancore of H. H. Lakshimi Bai. From this date began the strenuous rule of Colonel Munro. He seems to have taken a lively interest in Ringeltaube's work, and to have had a great personal liking for the man himself. One of Ringeltaube's early difficulties arose from the fact that his converts sought to use his influence with the Resident to gain special privileges for themselves, especially remission of State labour and taxes. But the missionary would have no converts on these terms, and actually went so far as to appoint one of his Christians to superintend the payment of Poll tax and services by his Christians. In 1814, however, when very severe famine reduced the

---

[329] Gautam, Swati. "The Breast Tax That Wasn't." Kerala | The Breast Tax That Wasn't - Telegraph India, Telegraph India, 13 Jan. 2021, www.telegraphindia.com/culture/style/the-breast-tax-that-wasnt/cid/1803638.

[330] Hacker, Isaac Henry. "CHAPTER III: THE GROWTH OF FORTY YEARS, 1816-1856." A HUNDRED YEARS IN TRAVANCORE BY I. H. HACKER, PDF ed., THE LONDON MISSIONARY SOCIETY, pp. 38–38, https://ia600207.us.archive.org/20/items/100YearsInTravancore/100YearsInTravancore.pdf. Accessed 18 May 2025.

[331] Gautam, Swati. "The Breast Tax That Wasn't." Kerala | The Breast Tax That Wasn't - Telegraph India, Telegraph India, 13 Jan. 2021, www.telegraphindia.com/culture/style/the-breast-tax-that-wasnt/cid/1803638.

[332] "Poll Tax." Encyclopædia Britannica, Encyclopædia Britannica, inc., www.britannica.com/topic/poll-tax. Accessed 22 May 2025.

[333] "Poll Tax." Wikipedia, Wikimedia Foundation, 2 Apr. 2025, en.wikipedia.org/wiki/Poll_tax#Great_Britain.

people to a state of starvation, Ringeltaube appealed to the Resident and secured the exemption of his Christians from the operation of the Poll tax. His honesty, however, is shown in that he engaged to give to each of his Christians a certificate which was to be held to exempt him for one year only. With a sane man at the head of the mission such as Ringeltaube, there was not likely to be a rush of converts eager only to secure release from taxation. That such a rush did take place we have evidence in Ringeltaube's own words. He says in a report to Colonel Munro in 1813, and speaking of 1810, "There was a rush of five thousand Shanars upon me who had been long waiting for an opportunity to shake off the Poll tax and service attached to their caste, and which they hoped to effect by connecting themselves with me. All my solemn declarations to the contrary were of no avail, until that sovereign instructor, painful experience, convinced them of their mistake. As soon as the people were convinced that no temporal advantages were to be obtained, their zeal for the Protestant religion collapsed"; and yet in 1811 we find he baptized nearly four hundred persons, including children.[334]

This British poll tax seems to have been conflated and confused for an anonymous Kerala King's supposed "tax" that did not exist. Even more confusing, the documentation written by Anglican Christian missionaries make it clear that British troops had full governing control of the supposed Kingdom of Travancore, they imposed their own tax policies upon the populace that caused a famine, and jointly worked with the Diwan to put Christian Indians into prisons to torture them as a reaction to caving in to upper-caste Hindu bigotry against lower-castes who had converted to Christianity. Given this historical information by eyewitness accounts from British Anglican missionaries, how could Great Britain claim to have been the cause of the removal of the Breast social custom when they explicitly upheld Casteism to the point they supported the torture of Christian Indian victims, as official British government policy? Was the story of a Kerala King outlawing it in Tamil Nadu even verified outside British sources? And why would a Kerala King need to outlaw it, if British troops were in charge of the area and effectively governing the location under British rule of law superseding the princely state to the point that Anglican Christian missionaries could ask British officials to force the Diwan to change policies, and then with the Diwan's joint support, imprisoned and tortured the lower-caste Shanar Christians? The context in the Anglican Missionary books clearly is referring to the "Government" as the British government and refers to British laws in the context of the book itself, it is not referring to the laws of a princely state which it regards as social custom. Pages 46 – 48 seem to further repudiate this idea that British government policy had any influence in ending the breast social custom:

> If the progress of the mission is to be gauged by the measure of opposition it arouses, then this decade was the most prosperous of all. It was in the beginning of this year that the third, last, and most determined persecution arose against the Christians, ostensibly on account of the wearing by men and women of the upper cloths which were held to mark off the higher castes.

---

[334] Hacker, Isaac Henry. "CHAPTER II: THE RINGELTAUBE PERIOD, 1806-1816." A HUNDRED YEARS IN TRAVANCORE BY I. H. HACKER, PDF ed., THE LONDON MISSIONARY SOCIETY, pp. 27–27, https://ia600207.us.archive.org/20/items/100YearsInTravancore/100YearsInTravancore.pdf. Accessed 18 May 2025.

With this was mixed up also the demands for forced labour and Sunday work, all of which were resolutely refused by Christians. Much of the blame for the disturbances has been attached to the British Resident who was in office from 1840 to 1860.

General Cullen, after long residence in Travancore, regarded it as a retreat to be preserved from the intrusive changes of the Western world. The agitation against slavery had received no help from him, and he could hardly be interested because certain people wanted to wear more clothes than the climate demanded or their neighbours thought lawful. But the controversy was carried abroad. English newspapers in Madras took the matter up. Travancore manners and customs were dragged into the fierce light of publicity, and something had to be done. General Cullen's most redoubtable antagonist was John Cox of Trevandrum, though Baylis of Neyoor and Whitehouse of Nagercoil were not less strenuous. Cases of individual cruelty were frequent, and armed mobs attacked and burned chapels and houses and terrorised peaceful communities. Cases were brought forward by the missionaries when Christians were actually beaten to death under the orders of minor officials, and all appeals for justice were refused or delayed. There is no doubt that the uprising of the higher classes was due to a desire to recover by force the authority over the lower castes, which they had lost by the abolition of slavery. If the civil laws of the realm denied them superiority, then they would insist on caste rule and old custom to keep in subjection those who attempted to rise. A curious, and to some an inexplicable argument for this oppression, was devised from the Queen's Proclamation of Sovereignty which was issued at Delhi in 1858. In the course of that document, Her Majesty declared her determined neutrality in matters religious. Now to one who knows the Indian mind it is a familiar idea that to say that no one is ordered to become a Christian is equivalent to say that all are ordered not to become Christians. Further, no doubt exaggerated reports of the Mutiny reached Travancore, and the idea grew that the English power was on the wane. In the end of 1858 and beginning of 1859 the disturbances reached their height, and in Pareychaley, Neyoor, and Nagercoil districts, many chapels and schools were burnt, catechists were flogged, and Christians' houses were pillaged. The Dewan himself proceeded to the district, and a number of native troops under Captain Daly were ordered down to ensure quiet. An appeal was now made by the missionaries to the British Government then represented in Madras by Sir Charles Trevelyan, brother-in-law of Lord Macaulay.

Sir Charles took very prompt action, and the Raja very reluctantly issued an order in 1859 allowing Shanar women to wear coarse upper cloths. The recent transfer of authority from the East India Company to the Queen is curiously reflected in one sentence of Sir Charles' despatch. He says, "I should fail in respect to Her Majesty if I attempted to describe the feelings with which she must regard the use made against her own sex of the promises of protection so graciously accorded by her." This was nearly fifty years ago. and yet to this day caste rule and common custom have so far prevailed that low-caste women still move about in the public streets in the style of dress repudiated by Christian women so long ago. The custom is not so common south of the Capital, but from Trevandrum northwards the only dress of the low-caste non-Christian women is the loincloth, and caste rule refuses them anything more. Just as these troubles came to an end came the Revs. James Duthie to Nagercoil and Samuel Mateer to Pareychaley, two names closely associated with the Travancore mission, one for over thirty years, and the other to this day.[335]

---

[335] Hacker, Isaac Henry. "CHAPTER IV: FROM JUBILEE TO CENTENARY, 1856-1906." A HUNDRED YEARS IN TRAVANCORE BY I. H. HACKER, PDF ed., THE LONDON MISSIONARY SOCIETY, pp. 46-49, https://ia600207.us.archive.org/20/items/100YearsInTravancore/100YearsInTravancore.pdf. Accessed 18 May 2025

It's curious that the Anglican British missionaries emphasize the Travancore Diwan's policy being changed by British government threats, but they ignore the clear contradiction of their earlier statement that British government officials made it local law that lower-caste women had to follow the caste-based discriminatory policies; which was mentioned earlier in the book in the section mentioning the 1820s. The Anglican British missionaries also contradicted themselves by stating that the British Queen wanted the emancipation of women and that she wanted to remain neutral to local customs. What exactly happened here and how did so many Anglican missionaries dismiss the fact that their own British laws were supporting Casteism in Travancore at this point? There's no mention of them removing the impositions from British lawbooks in the area after a brief mention of their existence, but only that the Diwan made a public speech removing it within his own legal capacity which would have been overruled by British law regardless due to the British having the stronger military force.

I can only give my own personal opinion based upon the limited evidence. The obscurity around this time period seems to be due to the lack of pushback, unlike the time period of the 1870s to the early 1900s where US missionaries and US journalists were vehemently condemning what was happening and copiously documenting the evidence for the world to see. Anglican British missionaries don't demonstrate as much critical thinking as US Christian missionaries and especially US journalists. Unfortunately, in Travancore, they're the only recorded eyewitness accounts, to the best of my knowledge. They don't demonstrate any condemnation for the British poll tax forced upon the residents of Travancore and only claimed to have a limited ability to exempt Christian Indian converts to the brutal tax policy that was apparently causing a famine prior to even the better documented period of the 1870s. In the end, the British chose their own greed even at the earliest recorded stages, they enforced a brutal tax policy that would cause a deliberate theft of India's resources in Travancore just as it did in later years of their rule, and Anglican Christian missionaries seemed to bow to pressure and justified the brutal exploitation by arguing to their Anglican Christian readership in Britain and likely the US that it brought in more Christian converts. Later, the Anglican Christians of Britain tried to present it as exclusively the fault of belligerent Hindus after British policies seemed to be deliberately starving all the people of Travancore. What the upper-caste Hindus did was obviously unjustifiable, but the context of British policies that seem to be in full control of the region judging purely from the Anglican British missionary accounts.

Essentially, the Anglican British Christian statements are the accounts of the useful idiots of British empire, whereas the US missionaries and US journalists are actually the initially neutral observers who proceeded to condemn what was going on and mock what they argued as the thoroughgoing incompetence of British governing policies in India from the time periods mostly between 1870s – 1940s due to their own evidence-based research. While some may want to claim a neutral stance or a middle-ground, this ignores the fact that the British accounts are purely self-serving and they have repeatedly demonstrated willingness to lie to protect the image of their empire. The reason for the British government surveys within India admitting to famine mortalities seems to be due to ethnically Indian government officials and critical US journalists hoping to argue reform through sparking outrage; while the upper-echelons of the Viceroys, who were exclusively English-origin rulers, willfully ignored them.[336] It seems more accurate to say that any resource that is using British government accounts of events is honestly no different than Nazi-sympathizers using exclusively Nazi propaganda accounts of the Jewish Holocaust and proclaiming them to be a neutral source. This really is not an exaggeration and that is obviously not meant to ridicule any Holocaust victims, but rather to express the serious logical errors in viewing British "historians" as a neutral source even on supposedly "obvious" claims. The British government is not neutral in the extraction of resources from India to sustain the British empire and its wars with fellow European countries in a serious bid to conquer the entire world. That was what they were doing and that was their main focus of interest throughout their centuries of imperialism from the 1500s – 1900s. The hoax of Nangeli, even the implications of the social context of the story, clearly never mention that British local laws were in direct legal effect upon Travancore and the Anglican British missionaries never mention any person or event like Nangeli in their eyewitness accounts from the significant portions of the chapters I read.[337] There is no mention of her at all in the explanation of the Travancore Diwan abolishing it nor does the story of Nangeli mention the British local laws keeping it enforced after the supposed abolition by the Diwan.[338] The hoax of Nangeli was likely perpetuated to hide the fact that British economic and taxation policies were deliberately meant to bleed India dry and to obscure the proof of it in their torture of Shanar Christians to appease the sentiments of Casteism. The events within Travancore appear to be more explicitly violent; either the British government itself or Anglican British Christians likely fabricated the story of Nangeli to hide their deliberate brutalization of lower-caste Christian Indians and especially to hide the aggressive tax policies causing mass starvation, as part of British governing policy.

The South Asian Exception to the British Abolition of Slavery

---

[336] Davis, Mike. Late Victorian Holocausts: El Niño Famines and the Making of the Third World (Essential Mike Davis). Verso Books. Kindle Edition.

[337] Hacker, Isaac Henry. A HUNDRED YEARS IN TRAVANCORE BY I. H. HACKER, PDF ed., THE LONDON MISSIONARY SOCIETY, pp. 27–27, https://ia600207.us.archive.org/20/items/100YearsInTravancore/100YearsInTravancore.pdf. Accessed 18 May 2025.

[338] Hacker, Isaac Henry. A HUNDRED YEARS IN TRAVANCORE BY I. H. HACKER, PDF ed., THE LONDON MISSIONARY SOCIETY, pp. 27–27, https://ia600207.us.archive.org/20/items/100YearsInTravancore/100YearsInTravancore.pdf. Accessed 18 May 2025.

The United Kingdom's oft-celebrated Slavery Abolition Act of 1833, preached with such zeal from British lips and from some ignorant Ex-Muslim atheists, deliberately obfuscates and ignores the fact that the ancestors of modern-day Indians, Bangladeshis, Sri Lankans, and Pakistanis were still being enslaved, almost certainly physically and sexually exploited, and shipped off for hard labor after this purported "abolition" of slavery took effect on August 1st, 1834. Section Sixty-Four of the Slavery Abolition Act of 1833 reads as follows:

> Act not to extend to East Indies, &c.
>
> LXIV. And be it further enacted, That nothing in this Act contained doth or shall extend to any of the Territories in the Possession of the East India Company, or to the Island of Ceylon, or to the Island of Saint Helena.[339][340]

In other words, Great Britain "ended" slavery . . . if you stop seeing South Asians as people worthy of any human rights and ignore the fact the British were still enslaving and shipping them overseas to maximize their own profits in full faith to Jesus Christ and England, as per their Anglican faith. The territories being referenced were India before the Partition of 1947 by the British and Sri Lanka, which they called Ceylon. Furthermore, it is very bizarre that supposed scholars keep arguing that Britain outlawed slavery, but never bothered to read the actual law itself in which section 64 clearly states that those territories held in and around India were exempt from being free from slavery. This geopolitical fact is further reinforced by the increased population of what is now known as Rohingya Muslims brought under British authority to Myanmar:

Who are the Rohingya?

> The Rohingya are an ethnic Muslim minority who practice a Sufi-inflected variation of Sunni Islam. There are an estimated 3.5 million Rohingya dispersed worldwide. Before August 2017, the majority of the estimated one million Rohingya in Myanmar resided in Rakhine State, where they accounted for nearly a third of the population. They differ from Myanmar's dominant Buddhist groups ethnically, linguistically, and religiously.
>
> The Rohingya trace their origins in the region to the fifteenth century, when thousands of Muslims came to the former Arakan Kingdom. Many others arrived during the nineteenth and early twentieth centuries, when Rakhine was governed by colonial rule as part of British India. Since independence in 1948, successive governments in Burma, renamed Myanmar in 1989, have refuted the Rohingya's historical claims and denied the group recognition as one of the country's

---

[339] "Slavery Abolition Act (1833) | An Act for the Abolition of Slavery throughout the British Colonies; for Promoting the Industry of the Manumitted Slaves; and for Compensating the Persons Hitherto Entitled to the Services of Such Slaves. [28th August 1833.]." Legislation on the Slave Trade, pdavis.nl, www.pdavis.nl/Legis_07.htm. Accessed 20 May 2025.

[340] "SLAVERY ABOLITION ACT 1833." Slavery Abolition Act, 1833, Section 64, Government of Ireland: electronic Irish Statute Book (eISB), www.irishstatutebook.ie/eli/1833/act/73/section/64/enacted/en/html. Accessed 20 May 2025.

135 official ethnic groups. The Rohingya are considered illegal immigrants from Bangladesh, even though many trace their roots in Myanmar back centuries.

> Neither the central government nor Rakhine's dominant ethnic Buddhist group, known as the Rakhine, recognize the label "Rohingya," a self-identifying term that surfaced in the 1950s, which experts say provides the group with a collective political identity. Though the etymological root of the word is disputed, the most widely accepted theory is that Rohang derives from the word "Arakan" in the Rohingya dialect and ga or gya means "from." By identifying as Rohingya, the ethnic Muslim group asserts its ties to land that was once under the control of the Arakan Kingdom, according to Chris Lewa, director of the Arakan Project, a Thailand-based advocacy group.[341]

What were the mental gymnastics of people who mention that the British purportedly ended slavery, while consequentially ignoring the fact that the Rohingya . . . exist? I've learned from doing my own research that history is better viewed as a continuum, there is no real way to separate historical events into neat sections and claim it as objective history; while Muslims started emerging in Rohingya around the 1400s, it seems that the majority of them came from the British slave trade in the 1800s and 1900s. The Rohingya terrorist threat that Hindus and Buddhists of Myanmar suffer is thus another example of the historic consequences of British colonialism.[342] Obviously, the Myanmar junta's crackdown should have only been towards the armed militia groups affiliated with Islamic terrorism, they could have also done a crackdown on other serious crimes like violence against non-Muslim women by Islamist men, and not the state-sponsored violent massacres against all the Rohingya Muslims in what amounts to collective punishment; making Rohingya Muslims effectively stateless obviously won't bring peace but neither should we be obscuring the fact that so much of Islamic violence is due to British colonial stupidity.

While certain groups of Western Ex-Muslim atheists and the British public continue to praise Britain for "ending slavery" the regular Rohingya Muslims, and those who were slaughtered from the violence of Islamist Rohingya terrorist groups, are all still suffering the consequences of Great Britain's slave trade in the 1800s and 1900s that continued far past the purported abolition. India and Bangladesh are still grappling with the ramifications of British greed and narcissism, while the British and ignorant Western Ex-Muslim atheists continue to praise the British empire for something easily disproven by meeting most Rohingya sheltered and suffering in refugee camps across South Asia or

---

[341] Maizland, Lindsay, and Eleanor Albert. "What Forces Are Fueling Myanmar's Rohingya Crisis?" Council on Foreign Relations, Council on Foreign Relations, 23 Jan. 2020, www.cfr.org/backgrounder/rohingya-crisis.

[342] "Myanmar: New Evidence Reveals Rohingya Armed Group Massacred Scores in Rakhine State." Amnesty International, Amnesty International, 22 May 2018, www.amnesty.org/en/latest/news/2018/05/myanmar-new-evidence-reveals-rohingya-armed-group-massacred-scores-in-rakhine-state/.

reading about the tragic truths of their history. The very reason the Rohingya themselves are obfuscating details and calling themselves the Rohingya is because they're rationally afraid of deportations from all countries in the region, being left stateless with their families having no means to support themselves if they're forbidden to resettle back in Myanmar, and possibly starving to death once the world forgets about them. As tragic as it is, Myanmar scholars pointing out the majority of the Rohingya are a more recent group of people are mostly right judging from the general information. The reason the Western corporate media circus refers to their historical roots as "Muslim laborers" and then tries to conflate the scant few Muslims who can claim heritage from the 1400s as their past, is to protect Great Britain's image over the consequences of the British slave trade continuing unimpeded past August 1st, 1834.[343][344] They would rather protect the history of the slave-owners than give a truthful accounting to help provide a more compassionate understanding for the Rohingya Muslims who still today suffer the long-term effects of the British slave trade.

Unfortunately, another problem is that the US and Western media circus continues to blithely lie and claim that Rohingya Islamist men raping Myanmar women wasn't happening regarding stories similar to the Pakistani grooming gang scandal of the UK.[345] This is despite the fact that the Quran and Islamic theology itself teaches Muslims to capture and rape women, including little girls, for the purposes of conversion to Islam under the divine command of the Abrahamic God. If Western and US organizations continue protecting Islamist rapists, then they should not be surprised by increased violence against Muslims or their dwindling credibility. They need to report news impartially, even when it shows disproportionate evidence of Muslim men being more likely to rape young girls. Impartiality is not seeking the fallacy of the middle-ground, but rather treating all human lives as equal by giving as impartial an accounting of the facts as possible. The selective reporting of only Rohingya Muslim victims is not going to convince anyone to concern themselves when there is no honest acknowledgement of what Islam itself teaches Muslim men to commit upon "slave girls" within the Quran itself such as Quranic verses 23:5-6. Frankly, ignoring this fact is devaluing all non-Muslim lives and people are becoming more aware of discrepancies in reporting; to most people across the world, it appears to be a steadfast support for Muslim rapists by the US

---

[343] "SLAVERY ABOLITION ACT 1833." Slavery Abolition Act, 1833, Section 64, Government of Ireland: electronic Irish Statute Book (eISB), www.irishstatutebook.ie/eli/1833/act/73/section/64/enacted/en/html. Accessed 20 May 2025.
[344] "Slavery Abolition Act (1833) | An Act for the Abolition of Slavery throughout the British Colonies; for Promoting the Industry of the Manumitted Slaves; and for Compensating the Persons Hitherto Entitled to the Services of Such Slaves. [28th August 1833.]." Legislation on the Slave Trade, pdavis.nl, www.pdavis.nl/Legis_07.htm. Accessed 20 May 2025.
[345] Kurlantzick, Joshua. "Genocide in Burma." Washington Monthly, 11 June 2016, washingtonmonthly.com/2016/06/11/genocide-in-burma/.

and Western media circus. That is how it appears to any outside observer now and I struggle to see how that is the wrong view, given what is being protected.

Pakistan is the true Scion of British Imperialism

Pakistan is the true heir of the British empire, not India. Pakistan is currently a little over 77 years old after the British partition of India in 1947. India maintains its roots in a very ancient civilization that current evidence suggests existed for approximately 7000 – 8000 years.[346][347] Pakistan is the abomination of Islamic and British imperialist powers having committed their respective, uninterrupted, and whitewashed mass genocides. When examined carefully India's cultural traditions can credibly be argued to rival ancient Greek philosophy and often surpasses it in terms of topics pertaining to psychology and physiology in terms of breathing exercises. Pakistan's entire identity and government is founded upon trying to rationalize whether an illiterate, pedophile warlord from the 7th century would approve or disapprove their personal behavior in modern times; they chose that over living in a Democratic Republic.

Great Britain split India for the dreams of reconquest, but it now appears that all they really did was extricate and substantially weaken the cyanide poisoning that is Islam from India's body politic. After the poison of Islam became even more corrosive within Pakistan, the British foolishly ingested it into their body politic with the misguided belief that Western Universalism was a natural vaccine. To be blunt, judging strictly from how it was portrayed in my US schooling, the British only saw the Hindu-Muslim divide as a group of ignorant, angry, and brown savages too dumb to govern themselves. As of now, it seems quite clear that the cyanide pill of Islam is more fatal to Western culture since Britain still refuses to do a national inquiry into Pakistani Muslim grooming gangs as of writing this, and it was India that slowly built-up the immunity through the body politic of Hindutva and the BJP being more critical of the murderous, pedophilic cult that is Islam. All of the assumptions and arguments I was taught in high school social studies classes postulating India's backwardness, slowness to adapt to Western values of the Enlightenment, and the supposed inflexibility of India due to Casteism were all categorically disproven by the hard work, ambition, selflessness, and compassion of India itself. In the end, after going through college classes in Political Science, I slowly unlearned my Western-induced bigotries and actually decided to read what British imperialism was like for India's history, while I was working on my dissertation for

---

[346]Pandey, Jhimli Mukherjee. "Indus Era 8,000 Years Old, Not 5,500; Ended Because of Weaker Monsoon: India News." The Times of India, TOI, 29 May 2016, timesofindia.indiatimes.com/india/Indus-era-8000-years-old-not-5500-ended-because-of-weaker-monsoon/articleshow/52485332.cms.

[347] Bengrut, Dheeraj. "New Evidence Suggests Harappan Civilisation Is 7,000 to 8,000 Years' Old." Hindustan Times, Hindustan Times, 22 Dec. 2023, www.hindustantimes.com/cities/pune-news/new-evidence-suggests-harappan-civilisation-is-7-000-to-8-000-years-old-101703182904001.html.

graduate studies due to becoming more sensitive to topics related to genocide being covered in electives I had taken. In my view, Britain's supposed historians should never have been taken seriously, because the US missionary and US journalists categorically debunked all of their claims through fact-finding research during the time of supposed "famines" that British rulers clearly did deliberately and it can be proven they did because the same policies were used upon Ireland too. When reading large portions of both *The Graves Are Walking: The Great Famine and the Saga of the Irish People* by John Kelly and *The Famine Plot: England's Role in Ireland's Greatest Tragedy* by Tim Pat Coogan; I was struck by how similar the policies imposed upon Ireland leading to the Potato "famine" of 1845 – 1854 were to what was done to India. I couldn't finish either book due to the deep depression they gave me, especially because I was also reading through the majority of *Late Victorian Holocausts* by Mike Davis at the time. I'm still too afraid to start reading the book about Tasmania's genocide under British rule or any books on what the British did to the Boers and Black Africans like Kenyans in Africa. Whereas Germany is appropriately criticized for the Nazi's committing the Jewish Holocaust, no such sympathies exist for any who suffered British colonialism.

    Let us be clear: Pakistani grooming gangs have absolutely nothing to do with revenge-based colonial motives; it is coming from Pakistan willfully imbibing Islamism from countries like Saudi Arabia and what Islam itself teaches regarding the treatment of women and young girls. As an anecdote, when I confronted my parents with the real history of British colonialism, with facts that even they weren't aware of, we had a family discussion in my parents' living room; my Father shrugged his shoulders and said "*What can we do?*" and went on to explain that it would obviously be wrong to vilify British people living today for what their ancestors did to ours. My Mother and Father both proceeded to insist that Hinduism teaches them non-violence and to help others, not to cause other people problems or to hate; we don't have to like the British, but hate is too far. We shouldn't concern ourselves with what the British do as they're not important to our lives, we live happily in the United States where we hardly ever feel discrimination of any kind, and India is improving under Prime Minister Modi's policies which proves Great Britain's bigoted ancestors were wrong. Therefore, why should we care about this and cause problems for others? I felt bitter about their response. At the time, I recognized the political brilliance under the Realist Theory of International Relations and I hated Britain for it; Great Britain extracted resources from India, kept using pre-existing issues to further harm India, starved approximately between 60 – 80 million people to death on purpose to keep their war economy going during the times of their colonial rule, split India to pieces, used the images and social problems that came after that mass death toll that they caused to dehumanize Indians as savage rapists in the Western news media, and they knew that they would get away with all of it and these actions would never come to harm them. They got away with it and that was that; human rights were just key terms for essay writing, nothing of consequence would ever happen regarding this brutal history.

The British actually had a policy of erasing their colonial crimes and the British public's myths of the "civilizing missions" of other countries persisted regardless of the weight of evidence of their ancestors' genocidal violence.[348][349] A YouGov UK poll titled "*British Attitudes to the British Empire*" published on January 29th, 2025 found that thirty-three percent of Britons agreed with the claim that the British empire was "*More something to be Proud of*" and the majority of the thirty-nine percent agreed it was "*Neither something to be proud of nor ashamed of*" in the survey results.[350] Yet, when it came to the topic of the curriculum for how their empire would be taught in schools, seventy-eight percent of Britons supported the statement that "*Teaching should contain a mixture of positive and negative aspects of the British Empire, so pupils are given a comprehensive balanced view*" with an additional six percent supporting the statement "*Teaching should concentrate on mainly the positive aspects of the British Empire, so that pupils are taught to be proud of Britain's history and accomplishments*" but this supposedly "balanced" approach runs amok of the "middle-ground fallacy" because it's not valuing the human rights of the people that were colonized objectively.[351] In the same way that there is no "balanced" way of stating the fact-finding research when it comes to the Nazi Holocaust of Jewish people or the US dehumanization and discrimination against Native Americans which is still regrettably upheld by US law; there's no "balanced way" of stating Boers were put into concentration camps, Irish and Indian people were deliberately starved to death, and Kenyans were tortured and massacred among many other atrocities committed by the British empire.[352][353]

    What happened as a consequence of the UK peddling and holding onto their narrative falsehoods was completely unexpected. The systematic erasure, denial, and calculated half-truths regarding Britain's colonial legacy within the consciousness of the British public left them completely unprepared to deal with the reality of Islamism, because they kept peddling the falsehood that Muslims were an aggrieved minority population in India and clearly had no knowledge of the true history. This was despite the

---

[348] Norton-Taylor, Richard, et al. "Britain Destroyed Records of Colonial Crimes." The Guardian, Guardian News and Media, 17 Apr. 2012, www.theguardian.com/uk/2012/apr/18/britain-destroyed-records-colonial-crimes?newsfeed=true.

[349] Monbiot, George. "Deny the British Empire's Crimes? No, We Ignore Them | George Monbiot." The Guardian, Guardian News and Media, 23 Apr. 2012, www.theguardian.com/commentisfree/2012/apr/23/british-empire-crimes-ignore-atrocities.

[350] Smith, Matthew. "British Attitudes to the British Empire." YouGov, YouGov UK, 29 Jan. 2025, yougov.co.uk/society/articles/51483-british-attitudes-to-the-british-empire.

[351] Smith, Matthew. "British Attitudes to the British Empire." YouGov, YouGov UK, 29 Jan. 2025, yougov.co.uk/society/articles/51483-british-attitudes-to-the-british-empire.

[352] Monbiot, George. "Deny the British Empire's Crimes? No, We Ignore Them | George Monbiot." The Guardian, Guardian News and Media, 23 Apr. 2012, www.theguardian.com/commentisfree/2012/apr/23/british-empire-crimes-ignore-atrocities.

[353] Norton-Taylor, Richard, et al. "Britain Destroyed Records of Colonial Crimes." The Guardian, Guardian News and Media, 17 Apr. 2012, www.theguardian.com/uk/2012/apr/18/britain-destroyed-records-colonial-crimes?newsfeed=true.

fact that Hindus of India continuously mentioned that young girls were historically kidnapped by Muslim warlords for centuries. Due to Britain's own willful whitewashing of history, it left them utterly unprepared for the very real harm that Islamism causes in societies. They failed to even recognize the cultural contexts of why Hindus committed certain behaviors like *Sati*, seeing it as simply uncivilized barbarism. The practice of *Sati* – of women throwing themselves into the fire and burning themselves alive – is generally known to have increased under Islamic rule. Jauhar, the practice of women and children burning themselves alive after Rajputs died in battle, also increased during this time.[354] A British person reading this may roll their eyes and ask "So what?" without any critical thinking involved. What was so horrible about Islamic rule that would cause women to willfully burn themselves alive? Muslim men forcibly kidnapping Hindu women to make them into sex slaves, committing gang rapes upon these women, and prostituting them to other Muslim men just like what is happening in the United Kingdom now. In other words, Hindu women wanted to avoid being made sex slaves and avoid being forced into situations no different from the Pakistani Muslim grooming gangs that currently exist in the United Kingdom. Islam would teach these men that gang raping women was less objectionable than having them suffer the eternal torment of fires in hell. Hindu women apparently responded to this by willfully burning themselves as an act of defiance that made it unambiguously clear that they preferred the eternal fires of Islamic hell over being gang raped, turned into a sex slave for a Muslim warlord, and being prostituted to other Muslim men.

Four Final Thoughts with a set of questions for British Hindus

Four personal views I've inculcated from researching all this history in my personal time was the following: fact-finding research absolutely matters more than anything else regardless of how disproportionate the painful truths of the information is; they matter more than labels. Whereas the BBC interviewed people in Sweden arguing that Muslim kids throwing hand grenades at Swedish preschools shouldn't negative reflect the Left-leaning parties; Mike Davis, a Marxist-Environmentalist, did not allow the identity of being a Marxist to skew his views on the objective facts. The US Christian missionaries and US journalists of the late 1800s and early 1900s that Mike Davis copiously cited did not allow their views of being Christian to ignore the plight of all Indians suffering under British starvation campaigns including Hindus and other Dharmic followers. Reading only the British side and believing it to be "objective" by ignoring how self-serving their imperialist narrative is, ironically ignores the salient fact that

---

[354] Lal, Kishori Saran. Chapter V: AD 1200 – 1400 (Pgs. 39 – 51). "Growth of Muslim Population in Medieval India (1000-1800)" Internet Archive, Internet Archive, 5 Aug. 2018, ia902800.us.archive.org/11/items/GrowthOfMuslimPopulationInMedievalIndiaAd10001800/Growth-Of-Muslim-Population-In-Medieval-India-ad-1000-1800_text.pdf.

regular Americans were ubiquitously the unsung heroes of this period of India's history. Even though they ultimately failed due to the ubiquity of British colonial policy at the time, US Christian missionaries and US journalists were so sincere about stopping it that they tried to do a food drive to save as many lives as possible in India; regular Americans of various ethnic backgrounds and a school of Chinese schoolgirls all donated to help. Socialist and world-renown Historian Will Durant wrote *The Case for India* in defense of the human rights of all Indians because he was genuinely disgusted by British policies; late in life, he took his Last Sacraments and returned to his Catholic faith before he passed away.[355] The personal identities, racial identities, political views, and religious views of these people did not interfere with a rational and empirical outlook on what human rights for all people should be and they were completely sincere about their commitments to the human rights of all of India. Ever since US news media got bought and sold by US billionaires, we don't see this commitment anymore or any real attempt at investigative journalism unlike actual investigative journalism from Revealnews.org and Propublica. They push narratives over fact-finding research to please the Neoliberal elites and that's why I call them jester-journalists, because they're not real journalists and they usually don't care about fact-finding research.

    Second, I don't understand what the point is of worshipping mythologized figures like Jesus Christ and the Prophet Mohammad given this history. What Indians, the Irish, Tasmanians, Africans, and numerous others suffered under British imperialism was clearly far worse than Jesus Christ purportedly suffering three days in hell according to Christian theology or the Prophet Mohammad being attacked and fighting those enemy tribes who wouldn't submit to his insanity according to Islamic theology and the history of Islam. What is the point of worshipping Jesus Christ as a Messiah in Christianity or Islam and worshipping the Prophet Mohammad in Islam? What regular people endured under European imperialism was far worse and more brutal than anything either of these two venerated figures presumably experienced; that's just a fact. As an Indian, your ancestors in the 1800s – early 1900s suffered worse than anything either Jesus Christ or the Prophet Mohammad suffered; this applies to other South Asians, the Irish, the Tasmanians, the Boers, so many different Black African groups, and so on. They all experienced a hell far worse than anything the fantasy books of the Bible and the Quran proclaim, no judgment day ever happened during those times of British imperial rule where US Christian missionaries themselves compared it to the fantasy stories of the plagues of Egypt in the Bible, and those trying to survive starvation struggled and suffered to make the lives of everyone descended from them better than how they had it

---

[355] Schroth, Raymond A. "New Jersey Opinion; the Rise, and Fall and Rise Again of Willdurant, Truth-Seeker." Https://Www.Nytimes.Com/1985/12/08/Nyregion/New-Jersey-Opinion-the-Rise-and-Fall-and-Rise-Again-of-Willdurant-Truth-Seeker.Html, The New York Times, 8 Dec. 1985, www.nytimes.com/1985/12/08/nyregion/new-jersey-opinion-the-rise-and-fall-and-rise-again-of-willdurant-truth-seeker.html.

under European imperialism. They underwent and surpassed suffering far crueler and viler than any Abrahamic Judgment Day prophecy for decades upon decades, they never sought revenge for any of the calculated violence inflicted upon them, and they lived long enough to create a better life for all their future descendants who did the same for theirs – and if you're descended from them then please consider what that means to you personally. Why do we bother with myths, especially Judgment Day myths, when this demonstrably proves that we never needed it?

Third, I'm unsure how paradoxical this may seem, but this history made me believe that the *Ubermensch* philosophical concepts of Friedrich Nietzsche had a lot more of a biological component than most people were willing to accept. Whether this is an interpretative social perspective on the evolutionary science of natural selection or it is actually an aspect of our natural desire for survivability, I cannot say for sure. What I mean is that even just being able to live in a poorly sustained farming village decades after British imperialism was more of a shocking miracle than most people are aware of; given what Indians went through under British colonial oppression. Pursuing a dream of simply living a quiet life in a farming village without too much to worry about was probably vastly more miraculous to people immediately after the British left; due to entire generations being worked and starved to death with the emaciated survivors forced to slowly pick-up the pieces. That video I had watched when I was around nine-years old of this ignorant White Christian guy insinuating Hindus were devil worshippers as a means to explain poverty will probably never know how much of a privileged ignoramus that he was. It was a miracle that India was even able to survive with its fertility rates essentially grounded to a halt under British imperialism.[356] India being free of that brutality had more to do with the skyrocketing fertility rates than most are aware of. It was a real struggle for existence and survival and undoubtedly left a crime rate that wasn't normal; it could only slowly be reduced with each successive generation working to improve the quality of life for everyone else with personal goals likely aligning to slowly improve the community. Under Prime Minister Narendra Modi, far more could finally be done to make personal dreams, improved education rates, and community security into a sustainable reality without the Indian National Congress party playing identity politics. It's only now that they're emerging out of the hellhole that Britain forced upon them. Variations of these social issues and the struggle to overcome them undoubtedly hold true for all people who were harmed under European Imperial rule.

Finally, in fairness to Anglicanism, I believe that Anglican Priest and poet George Herbert from 1640 provides a very good quote from among his collections, from proverb 524 from his book, *Outlandish Proverbs (1640)*, which states the following: *"Living well*

---

[356] Davis, Mike. Late Victorian Holocausts: El Niño Famines and the Making of the Third World (Essential Mike Davis). Verso Books. Kindle Edition.

is the best revenge"[357] which is a sentiment that I can agree with. I believe that British Hindus are uniquely poised to rejoice in this sentiment, if they wish and this last paragraph is primarily for them. I will not presume motives for why any person of Indian descent would swear allegiance to the Anglican monarchy of Great Britain and choose to become a British citizen, I'm sure the reasons are multi-faceted and each of us has our own individual values before anything else. I honestly don't know much about contemporary British culture and I will not presume to understand your experience. What I want to ask any British Hindu who decides to read this (including any converts to Hinduism like White Hindus and any Dharmic faith tradition, not just fellow Indians) is the following: What is the point of staying faithful to a capricious, self-serving, self-absorbed, and pretentious Monarchy of inbreds who do not value your children's lives enough to conduct a national inquiry into the Pakistani grooming gangs throughout the UK? What is the point of having to take the time to teach your daughters in your mandirs, gurdwaras, various Buddhist temples, and other Dharmic temples how to avoid Pakistani Muslim rapists who seek to groom them when your police force refuses to do their jobs to avoid looking "racist" and "Islamophobic" when your daughters' lives are in danger?[358] You are among the wealthiest, well-educated, and hard-working diaspora in the United Kingdom and the economy of the UK is not going to recover due to the fact that – whether you want to accept it or not – a Monarchy can never be as competent as a Republic. They care more about people who are raping innocent young girls, predominately White girls, than they do about protecting your families from harm despite all the effort, service, compassion, and commitment you're trying to show them. As the UK government create Islamophobia councils over your objections to how it could harm Free Speech[359], as they proclaim "Hindu Nationalism" is an equivalent threat to Islamic terrorism and Islamism[360], and as they blithely ignore your compassionate pleas to listen to you because they no longer regard you as worthy of human dignity and respect[361]; they

---

[357] "Outlandish Proverbs (1640) | Jack Horntip Collection Blog." Edited by Jack Horntip. Translated by George Herbert, Outlandish Proverbs (1640), Jack Horntip Collection Blog, www.horntip.com/html/books_&_MSS/1600s/1640-68--1876_musarum_deliciae__wit_restored__and__wits_recreations_(HC)/1640_outlandish_proverbs.htm. Accessed 23 May 2025. For reference: Proverb 524. Living well is the best revenge.

[358] Chhabhadiya, Neelam. "Sexual Grooming amongst Hindu Girls." National Hindu Students Forum UK, NHSF (UK), 9 Nov. 2017, www.nhsf.org.uk/2017/11/sexual-grooming-amongst-hindu-girls/.

[359] CANTON, NAOMI. "British Hindus Object to Islamophobia Council in UK, Call for Hatred against All Religions to Be Recognised." The Times of India, TOI, 18 Feb. 2025, timesofindia.indiatimes.com/nri/british-hindus-object-to-islamophobia-council-in-uk-call-for-hatred-against-all-religions-to-be-recognised/articleshow/118337929.cms.

[360] Mukul, Sushim. "Hindu Nationalism, Khalistani Extremism among New Threats: Leaked UK Govt Report." India Today, India Today, 29 Jan. 2025, www.indiatoday.in/world/uk-news/story/uk-leaked-report-hindu-nationalism-pro-khalistani-extremism-threats-britain-islamist-left-wing-2671734-2025-01-29.

[361] Rajyaguru, Dipen. "The Hindu Council UK's Concerns on the Recently Leaked Home Office Extremism Report." Hindu Council UK, Hindu Council UK, 2 Feb. 2025, hinducounciluk.org/2025/02/02/the-hindu-council-uks-concerns-on-the-recently-leaked-home-office-report/.

now repeat the same double-standards of bigotry and show you only contempt. For those of you who descend from countries brutalized by British imperialism like India was, despite all your sacrifices and faith in your allegiance to the British Monarchy, they're dehumanizing you just as how their ancestors dehumanized yours. This is who they were and have always really been. Self-serving, shameless, hateful, and never regarding your views as worthy of serious consideration. Well, guess what? You have options; you don't have to live with these dangers of incompetent governance that refuses to solve problems, the credible fears that Pakistani grooming gangs will target your daughters, or any future "communal riots" like what mostly Muslim Indians do in India.

Make a serious effort to come live in the United States of America; come to the land where you're almost certainly guaranteed to be making more money than in the UK, where your daughters don't have to live in fear of Pakistani Muslim grooming gangs because the UK police and UK government don't want to be called racist and would protect child predators over your daughters' safety, where your religious councils don't have to argue about Free Speech rights and you're simply guaranteed it as an inalienable right from Thomas Jefferson's arguments in the US Constitution, and where you don't have to deal with an inbred, self-serving Monarch stripping you of all your accomplishments for the crime of being "Islamophobic" for making criticisms of Islam when Hindus and Christians are being attacked in Bangladesh.[362] Or, if that is too much and you are part of an older generation, consider moving back to India and starting a business or working there. There are surely numerous ventures that many business-savvy Hindus can research and do; in my own studies, I had learned that tampons were an overlooked market that makes billions in revenue every year because women in families largely choose the same brand for all their lives; but I'm sure you can come-up with your own ideas. The point is, you have options, you're probably paying among the highest in taxes in the UK, and they are taking you for granted. You should not have to struggle to be listened to by people who want to capitulate to Islamism. Even if the US and India aren't personally appealing to you, you don't have to go begging to be heard from a worthless Monarchy, you can live better and safer in other countries that should be willing to take such high-quality prospects to improve their own countries. Even a short distance away, you could just go to Ireland, a people who suffered under British colonial rule too, and perhaps find a way to make it work there. Speaking as a born and raised Indian American of the Hindu tradition, I've never been discriminated against for being Hindu in the US and I believe the discrimination against Indian Americans is far overblown at the moment. If you're seriously thinking about it, then I recommend that you come to the US where Hindus can really be free to express ourselves and safe from

---

[362] Canton, Naomi. "Two Leading British Indian Community Figures Rami Ranger and Anil Bhanot Stripped of Their Honours by the King." The Times of India, TNN, 7 Dec. 2024, timesofindia.indiatimes.com/nri/other-news/two-leading-british-indian-community-figures-rami-ranger-and-anil-bhanot-stripped-of-their-honours-by-the-king/articleshow/116056259.cms.

Pakistani Muslim grooming gangs. Finally, allow me to leave you with my favorite verse from Chapter Four of the *Brihadaranyaka Upanishad*:

Brihadaranyaka Upanishad: Chapter Four. Verse Five.

As a person acts, so he becomes in life. Those who do good become good; those who do harm become bad. Good deeds make one pure; bad deeds make one impure. You are what your deep, driving desire is. As your desire is, so is your will. As your will is, so is your deed. As your deed is, so is your destiny.[363]

---

[363] Easwaran, Eknath. Brihadaranyaka Upanishad (p. 114). The Upanishads (Easwaran's Classics of Indian Spirituality Book 2) (p. 114). Nilgiri Press. Kindle Edition.

Chapter VII: Islamic Terrorism's First-Generation was Al Qaeda, Second-Generation was ISIS, and a Third-Generation's making a Digital Caliphate from "Islamophobia" Censorship

> *"On questions of national security, I am now as wary of my fellow liberals as I am of the religious demagogues on the Christian right.*
>
> *This may seem like frank acquiescence to the charge that "liberals are soft on terrorism." It is, and they are.*
>
> *A cult of death is forming in the Muslim world -- for reasons that are perfectly explicable in terms of the Islamic doctrines of martyrdom and jihad. The truth is that we are not fighting a "war on terror." We are fighting a pestilential theology and a longing for paradise.*
>
> *This is not to say that we are at war with all Muslims. But we are absolutely at war with those who believe that death in defense of the faith is the highest possible good, that cartoonists should be killed for caricaturing the prophet and that any Muslim who loses his faith should be butchered for apostasy.*
>
> *Unfortunately, such religious extremism is not as fringe a phenomenon as we might hope. Numerous studies have found that the most radicalized Muslims tend to have better-than-average educations and economic opportunities.*
>
> *Given the degree to which religious ideas are still sheltered from criticism in every society, it is actually possible for a person to have the economic and intellectual resources to build a nuclear bomb -- and to believe that he will get 72 virgins in paradise. And yet, despite abundant evidence to the contrary, liberals continue to imagine that Muslim terrorism springs from economic despair, lack of education and American militarism."*[364] – Sam Harris, Atheist author and neuroscientist, from his September 18th, 2006 article in the Los Angeles Times titled *"It's real, it's scary, it's a cult of death"* where he explained the problems with how Liberals of the US were misconstruing the primary causes of Islamic violence.

These words by Sam Harris were condemned as phobic, racist, bigoted, and provincial by a slew of Liberal academics, journalists, and supposed experts back in 2006. When I was in college, I had wrongly assumed that they knew what they were talking about and that while Sam Harris was correct about freewill and religion in a more general sense, that he'd surely been too extreme and that Muslims across the world were more reasonable. One of the problems that made me believe this was that nobody actually explained what Sharia was in any clear explanation in the discussions around Islam for the early 2010s, not even Sam Harris himself. It wasn't until I listened to Ex-Muslim Youtube videos in 2018, specifically the *Ex-Muslims of North America* organization's college campus tours, that I began to fully understand the depth of the problems within Islam and then decided to research it based upon the explanations they had given. When I

---

[364] Harris, Sam. "It's Real, It's Scary, It's a Cult of Death." Los Angeles Times, Los Angeles Times, 18 Sept. 2006, www.latimes.com/archives/la-xpm-2006-sep-18-oe-harris18-story.html.

could finally understand what was true from what wasn't true, I could finally begin to understand without worrying that I was falling into either bigotry or conspiracy theories.

The fact is that Sam Harris's argument was proven correct with the rise of the Islamic State back in the mid-2010s. On April 14th, 2015, NY Times journalist Mary Anne Weaver published an article titled *"Her Majesty's Jihadists: More British Muslims have joined Islamist militant groups than serve in the country's armed forces. How to understand the pull of jihad."* which had the following eye-opening portion:

> **Ifthekar's story would** become an iconic one of the foreign jihad in Syria. It was recounted to me by Shiraz Maher, a senior research fellow at the International Center for the Study of Radicalization (I.C.S.R.), an innovative institute at King's College London. Here, a handful of researchers have been charting, following and, in some cases, interacting directly with foreign fighters in Syria and Iraq — through text-messaging and smartphone apps — in hopes of understanding their motivations and their worldview. The center now monitors some 700 of the 20,000 foreign fighters from 90 countries around the world. (Foreigners make up half of ISIS's total fighting force.) An estimated 4,000 are from Western nations, some 600 to 700 from Britain alone. More British Muslim men have joined ISIS and the Nusra Front than are serving in the British armed forces.
>
> Many of the fighters from Britain — as well as those from Finland, Germany, France, Belgium and the Netherlands — came from comfortable middle-class homes. Many were university students or graduates; a surprising number were women, too. But they didn't appear to fit a typical profile, which confounded counterterrorism experts and Western governments. Some, like Ifthekar, seemed driven by romantic notions of jihad. Others, like Mohammed Emwazi, who later became known as Jihadi John, the ruthless executioner of Western journalists and aid workers in the ISIS videos, fully embraced the violence of the Islamic State. Emwazi was also a Briton, and also the son of a comfortable middle-class family, with a degree in computer programming. And then there were still other cases in which entire families made their way to Syria or Iraq: pregnant women; young children; even the family pets.
>
> The I.C.S.R. forms part of the Department of War Studies at Kings College's Strand Campus. Peter Neumann, a 40-year-old political scientist and a professor of security studies, established the center in January 2008 to study the roots of radicalization and political violence. Now, as its director, he supervises a surprisingly small staff, considering the depth and range of the research the center does. There are only nine full-time academics attached to it, supplemented by a dozen or so part-time interns or students who sit hunched over their laptops in shifts, tracking the militant Islamists in the center's database.
>
> Initially, researchers monitored jihadist websites and individual Twitter accounts. But it was not until 2013 that they established direct contact with the foreign fighters themselves. "It was exhilarating," Maher said to me, "and we came about it only by chance." Maher happened upon Ifthekar, who used his Twitter feed to recount his experiences in Syria and to urge all of his "brothers and sisters" to come and join the fight. Soon, I.C.S.R. researchers realized there were other Europeans in Syria: a Dane named Abu Fulan; then a former Dutch soldier called Yilmaz. They sent a flood of messages, hoping some of the fighters would respond. Ifthekar was the first; he invited Maher to talk on Skype. As the researchers gained the fighters' trust, direct contact increased. Most of the jihadists preferred text-messaging, for both convenience and security. Some of them were effusive; others were guarded and skeptical; still others, over a period of time, actually began to seek, or offer, guidance and advice.
>
> "Building these relationships with these guys, you get to know them," Maher told me. "You build and develop rapport. You get to understand why they're there; what they hope to do. One Eid, the first message I got was not from my parents, but from a member of Al Qaeda. It was surreal."

Maher, a 33-year-old historian of medium height and medium build with a neatly trimmed beard, is an expert on Salafi jihadism. As I sat with him one February morning, he scrolled through dozens of images culled from Facebook and jihadist websites that he'd stored on his laptop: young men in battle gear, some posing with weapons, others manning roadblocks; still others lounging by swimming pools and extolling the virtues of what the foreign fighters have coined "the five-star jihad."

As we looked at the images, Maher began recounting some of the fighters' stories to me. Some of the jihadists were hardened radicals who would become suicide bombers in Syria or Iraq. Others, he discovered, were much more fanciful. There was, for example, the foreign fighter from Mexico who constantly complained that it was impossible to find good Mexican food in Syria. There was the blind man from the Netherlands, who told a recruiter that because he was blind he couldn't fight; the recruiter told him to come anyhow: "We're a state," he said, "and we need people to build that state." And then there was the young man from Britain, who was already packed but had one last question before he left: Was hair gel available in Syria?

I looked around at the various flags that festoon the I.C.S.R.'s walls. They told the story of the three generations of Western fighters who had embraced jihad — going back to the 1980s and the war in Afghanistan. There were banners of the Kosovo Liberation Army, the Free Syrian Army and ISIS, interspersed with posters of angry young men, some holding Kalashnikovs, others staring sternly ahead. The black, white and green flag of the U.S.-trained Free Syrian Army, Maher told me, took forever to find; he finally came upon one in a Turkish border town on the Syrian frontier. The black-and-white banner of ISIS, conversely, was available everywhere.

Maher explained that Ifthekar's experience with the Nusra Front was not atypical. "Al Nusra has a vigorous vetting process, especially for foreigners," he said. "It's called tazkiyah, and it means that you must be vouched for by someone already in the organization. The system has worked well for Arabs with links to the group, but it has made it much more difficult for Europeans to join."

The group also expects recruits to speak Arabic. "Nusra is very big on being entrenched in local communities," Neumann told me. "If they think you're not going to be useful, they won't take you in. ISIS is less discriminating. They say: 'If you're a Muslim, you're already part of the Caliphate. So even if you're too fat, or too old to be a fighter, we'll find something else for you to do. You have a right to emigrate. We'll find a place for you."

Of the 600 to 700 British fighters now in Syria and Iraq, only 20 percent have gone to the Nusra Front, according to Neumann. "The remaining 80 percent," he says, "have joined ISIS. Very, very few are joining other groups."

Hours at the I.C.S.R. can be erratic: Exchanges always occur on the jihadists' clock. Maher and the other academics often have to wait, sometimes seemingly endlessly, for the fighters to call. In conducting research into radicalization, its causes and effects, and how it might be reversed, the center has published scores of research papers, journal articles and monographs. In some cases, it has acted as a kind of news service for those on the battlefields. It was the first to announce the death of one young British man.

I asked Maher if, based on the center's research, he could draw a typical jihadist profile. "The average British fighter is male, in his early 20s and of South Asian ethnic origin," he began. "He usually has some university education and some association with activist groups. Over and over again, we have seen that radicalization is not necessarily driven by social deprivation or poverty." He paused for a moment, and then went on. "Other than those who go for humanitarian reasons, some of the foreign fighters are students of martyrdom; they want to die as soon as possible and go directly to paradise. We've seen four British suicide bombers thus far among the 38 Britons who have been killed. Then there are the adventure seekers — those who think this will enhance their masculinity, the gang members and the petty criminals too; and then, of course, the die-hard radicals, who began by burning the American flag and who then advanced to wanting to kill Americans — or their partners — under any circumstance."

One afternoon I was talking with Maher in his office, which is filled with books and files, when an intern came in and handed him a note. He immediately turned to his computer and began to navigate onto jihadist websites, until he found what he was looking for: a video clip showing First Lt. Moaz al-Kasasbeh, the Jordanian fighter pilot, as ISIS was about to burn him alive.

We both sat stunned as the video began to play. Lieutenant Kasasbeh had been a prisoner of ISIS since Dec. 24, when his F-16 fighter plane was supposedly shot down, not far from the ISIS capital of Raqaa in northern Syria. He was the first member of the U.S.-led coalition to be captured by the Islamic State. Now dressed in an orange uniform — to resemble the attire of prisoners in Guantánamo — he stood inside a locked cage in the middle of the desert. A dozen or so ISIS fighters, some wearing masks, others not, formed a semicircle at a safe distance from the cage. The footage began cutting back and forth, between the desert scene and images of the charred bodies of women and children, their flesh discolored and raw, who, according to a voice-over, had been the victims of the coalition bombing campaign against ISIS in Syria.

The camera zoomed in and out, focusing on tight head shots of Kasasbeh, his bright orange uniform in sharp contrast with the taupe of the desert and the black ISIS flags. Then, with a flourish of his hand, one fighter set a powder fuse alight. The flames raced across the sand to Kasasbeh's cage. The fighters began swaying rhythmically back and forth to the background music of a prophetic lyric, or nasheed. Kasasbeh flailed his arms as the flames entered his cage, first setting the bottom of his uniform alight, then moving on until the 26-year-old pilot disappeared in a human fireball.

Later, I asked Maher if such an act would dissuade potential fighters from joining the Islamic State. He replied that it would not. "In their minds, this was qisas, the principle of equal retaliation under Islamic law. If someone is killed, you can kill the perpetrator. You can choose the means. And he was burned at one of the very sites that the coalition forces bombed. Something like this will not affect the average fighter I'm talking to. For them, they are in a state of war with us. The Caliphate must be protected at all costs."

Whether or not the Caliphate that ISIS has declared proves viable, it has extraordinary appeal, a return to the grandeur of the seventh- century Islamic state.[365]

Sikhs versus Sam Harris

However, a major and inexcusable failing of Sam Harris's throughout the years, which made it far more difficult to accept what he was saying about Islam in terms of ideas, is that he did peddle some of the most incompetent and laughably idiotic arguments when it comes to national security. This is firmly worth mentioning, because it was the main reason I was thoroughly skeptical of his views for so long and why I believed those who opposed his characterization of Islam until a gradual process in which I finally changed my mind. On April 28th, 2012, Sam Harris published an essay on his blog, samharris.org, titled *"In Defense of Profiling"* he argued *"We should profile Muslims, or anyone who looks like he or she could conceivably be Muslim, and we*

---

[365] Weaver, Mary Anne. "Her Majesty's Jihadists: More British Muslims Have Joined Islamist Militant Groups than Serve in the Country's Armed Forces. How to Understand the Pull of Jihad." New York Times, The New York Times Magazine, 14 Apr. 2015, www.nytimes.com/2015/04/19/magazine/her-majestys-jihadists.html.

should be honest about it.[366]" He went from arguing about ideas, which is respectable, to arguing in favor of racial profiling, which is both racist and an attempt to appeal to White Supremacist fearmongering. On May 1st, 2012, he wrote an addendum adding the following:

> 1. When I speak of profiling "Muslims, or anyone who looks like he or she could conceivably be Muslim," I am not narrowly focused on people with dark skin. In fact, I included myself in the description of the type of person I think should be profiled (twice). To say that ethnicity, gender, age, nationality, dress, traveling companions, behavior in the terminal, and other outward appearances offer no indication of a person's beliefs or terrorist potential is either quite crazy or totally dishonest. It is the charm of political correctness that it blends these sins against reasonableness so seamlessly. We are paying a very high price for this obscurantism—and the price could grow much higher in an instant. We have limited resources, and every moment spent searching a woman like the one pictured above, or the children seen in the linked videos, is a moment in which someone or something else goes unobserved.[367]

The manner in which he phrases the arguments and rebuttals in defense of racial profiling is teeming with White Supremacist fearmongering attempting to appear rational and logical by ignoring all the contrary evidence. On May 7th, 2012, in a follow-up article on his blog, titled *"On Knowing Your Enemy"* he elucidated even further:

> In trying to understand the reaction to my essay, I think I have uncovered most of the assumptions at work in the minds of my critics. I believe that every one of these assumptions is false. To my surprise, a few people who have a reputation for being very intelligent, such as the biologist-blogger PZ Myers, appear to believe all of them:
>
> 1. Terrorism is just terrorism—there is nothing special about jihadists as a group, or suicide bombing as a tactic. When thinking about airline security, therefore, it makes perfect sense to put forward Timothy McVeigh (a non-Muslim terrorist) as an example of why any focus on Muslims is wrongheaded.
>
> 2. Furthermore, there is no link between Islam and suicidal terrorism.
>
> 3. Thus, any focus on the Muslim community is a sign of prejudice against dark-skinned people, Arabs, foreigners, or some other beleaguered minority.
>
> 4. And, in any case, it is impossible to tell whether someone is likely to be Muslim in the first place—there is no such thing as "looking Muslim" or "not looking Muslim."
>
> 5. Focusing on people who could conceivably be Muslim would require ugly infringements of civil liberties—separate lines for dark-skinned people at the airport, for instance.
>
> 6. It would also allow terrorists to find another path through security—such as recruiting 80-year-old women from Okinawa to do their suicidal dirty work (though #4 tells us that there is no such thing as "looking Muslim," so 80-year-old women from Okinawa look no less Muslim than anyone else). Random searches are actually more prudent than targeted ones because terrorists cannot game a random system.

---

[366] Harris, Sam. "In Defense of Profiling." Sam Harris, www.samharris.org, 28 Apr. 2012, www.samharris.org/blog/in-defense-of-profiling.
[367] Harris, Sam. "In Defense of Profiling." Sam Harris, www.samharris.org, 28 Apr. 2012, www.samharris.org/blog/in-defense-of-profiling.

7. And focusing on Muslims would prove so offensive to the Muslim community worldwide that it could increase Muslim support for terrorism (though #2 assures us that nothing about Islam makes this more likely than it would otherwise be; any group could be expected to support suicidal terrorism in response to being profiled).

8. If we had the resources, we would follow the Israeli approach to airline security, wherein no one is profiled on the basis of religion, race, ethnicity, nationality, age, or gender. Rather, the Israelis attend only to a person's behavior at the airport. "Behavioral profiling" is logically and empirically distinct from other sorts of profiling, and we should practice it alone.

The only assumptions on this list that stand a chance of being true are #6 and #7. Bruce Schneier appears to be very fond of #6, and I trust we will hear more from him about how terrorists can successfully game any system that profiles. But I don't buy this argument, at least not yet, for reasons that we will probably discuss.

Assumption #7 does strike me as possible, though not likely. But this is just a statement about how terrifying Muslims have become worldwide: Don't draw cartoons of their Prophet, or they'll kill you. Don't write a novel that could be considered blasphemous, or they'll kill you. Don't criticize their treatment of women, or they'll kill you. Don't leave the religion and publicly disavow it, or they'll kill you. Don't burn a Qur'an, or they'll kill you. And if their vicious intolerance of civil discourse causes you to profile them at the airport, well, some who would not have otherwise thought to kill you will grow more insular and radicalized and, in the end, they will kill you too. I agree that a concern about alienating the Muslim community isn't absurd—we desperately need Muslims to cooperate with law enforcement (i.e., to help profile within their own community)—but I'm not worried about creating more jihadists by simply taking intelligent steps to keep them off airplanes.

The Israelis have had a spotless record of airline security since 1972. It is widely imagined that they would never be so stupid as to profile people on the basis of race, ethnicity, or nationality. But this is just a pious fantasy. The Israelis have well-trained screeners who use all the information they can possibly glean to mitigate the risk of terrorism. Racial and ethnic profiling appears to be central to their process. I agree with many of my critics that we should emulate the Israeli approach insofar as it is possible. That would require smart, well-trained screeners who are empowered to use their discretion (i.e., to profile).[368]

His refusal to accept number six and his example of Israel's airline security is suspect. He actually couldn't have been more wrong. While Politifact has an obvious political bias, they provide historical and expert testimony in this counterargument to Sam Harris's views on racial profiling. In their September 26th, 2016 rebuttal to President Donald Trump's argument *"Says Israel profiles based on ethnicity and "does it very successfully."* by Linda Qiu, they stated the following:

> Amotz Brandes is a former intelligence officer in the Israeli Defense Forces and a security agent and profiler at El Al Airlines, Israel's flagship carrier. He is now a managing partner at the international security firm, Chameleon Associates.
>
> Brandes told PolitiFact that Israeli security almost exclusively profiled Arabs and Muslims until the Lod Airport massacre of 1972. That year, a radical Palestinian group recruited gumen from the militant Japanese Red Army for the terrorist attack that killed 26 people at the airport in Tel Aviv.

---

[368] Harris, Sam. "On Knowing Your Enemy." Sam Harris, samharris.org, 7 May 2012, www.samharris.org/blog/on-knowing-your-enemy29.

> Using non-Arab, non-Muslim gunmen exploited and exposed a weakness in exclusively focusing on someone's race or ethnicity, Brandes said. Israeli security now consider a much more comprehensive and specific set of indicators to locate potential threats.
>
> But Israel "never really stopped risk-based profiling. They just added threat-based profiling," Brandes said, adding for a Jewish state located in a "very unsafe neighborhood," it's necessary. "They treat those with Arab ethnicity as higher risk. It's not a secret. It's done in many, many ways."
>
> For example, Ben Gurion International Airport (formerly Lod Airport) labels passengers with numbered stickers, one representing low risk and six very high risk. All fliers are questioned and searched, but those with higher numbers undergo more intensive security screening.
>
> According to Israeli journalist Lia Tarachansky, one's, two's and three's are reserved for Jewish Israelis, Jewish non-Israelis and friendly internationals. Arab Israelis and questionable internationals are given a four or higher. Palestinians and Muslims are typically classified as six. The Arab American Institute has documented numerous cases of detentions of Arabs and Muslims lasting upward of 10 hours.[369]

I was aware of this argument prior to 2016, but this Politifact article explains it best insofar as why Sam Harris was wrong. Also, since he insisted on an anecdote of using himself as an example, I'll do the same with explicit candor: I don't care if he's comfortable with racial profiling, I'm tired of people automatically assuming my religion the moment they see my skin tone. I was subjected to that dumbassery when I was growing up in middle-school and high school after September 11th, 2001 happened, I should not have to deal with any further ignorance and stupidity because TSA agents feel jumpy when looking at my skin tone. Furthermore, the idea that profiling anyone who "*looks Muslim*" falls apart when you look at the rise in hate crimes against Sikhs for the sheer stupidity of mistaking them for being Muslim because they wear turbans.

In the same year that Sam Harris was espousing these White Supremacist arguments and trying to rationalize his fearmongering, the HuffingtonPost published an article on August 7th, 2012 titled "*History of Hate: Crimes Against Sikhs Since 9/11.*" which reads as follows:

> The mass shooting of a gurdwara (Sikh temple) in Wisconsin on Sunday is merely the latest chapter in a history of violence. In the months following the attacks of 9/11, more than 300 incidences of hate crimes against Sikhs were reported, according to the Sikh Coalition (PDF).
>
> Though their numbers make up the world's fifth-largest religion, Sikhs are still misunderstood (No, they are not Muslims or Hindus). Below is a round up of notable hate crimes and bias incidents against Sikhs since 9/11. (H/t Buzz Feed.)
>
> **Sept. 15, 2001 -- Mesa, Ariz.:** Four days after the infamous attacks of 9/11, Balbir Singh Sodhi, a 49-year-old Sikh, is shot and killed outside the gas station he owned by Frank Silva Roque. When

---

[369] Qiu, Linda. "Trump Claim on Israel Profiling Misses Full Security Context." @politifact, The Poynter Institute, 23 Sept. 2016, www.politifact.com/factchecks/2016/sep/23/donald-trump/donald-trump-claim-israel-profiling-very-successfu/.

police approached to arrest him, Roque says, "I'm a patriot and an American. I'm American. I'm a damn American." [More from HuffPost.]

Nov. 18, 2001 -- Palermo, N.Y.: Three teens burn down Gobind Sadan, a gurdwara (Sikh temple) in New York, because they thought it was named for Osama bin Laden. [More from BeliefNet and *Tribune of India*.]

Dec. 12, 2001 -- Los Angeles, Calif.: Surinder Singh Sidhi, a liquor store owner in Los Angeles who took to wearing an American flag turban after 9/11 out of fear of being attacked, is beaten in his store by two men who accuse of him of being Osama bin Laden. [More from Real Sikhism.]

Aug. 6, 2002 -- Daly City, Calif.: Sukhpal Singh, brother of Balbir Singh Sodhi, who was the first Sikh murdered following 9/11, is shot while driving his cab. [More from HuffPost, Real Sikhism and Sikh American Legal Defense and Education Fund.]

May 20, 2003 -- Phoenix, Ariz.: Fifty-two-year-old Sikh immigrant and truck driver Avtar Singh is shot in his 18-wheeler while waiting for his son to pick him up. As he is being shot, he hears someone say: "Go back to where you belong." [More from Real Sikhism.]

Aug. 5, 2003 -- Queens, N.Y.: Members of a Sikh family are beaten outside of their home by drunk individuals yelling, "Go back to your country, Bin Laden." [More from *NY Daily News*.]

Sept. 25, 2003 -- Tempe, Ariz.: Sukhvir Singh, a 33-year-old convenience store owner, is stabbed to death by Bruce Phillip Reed. It is not labeled as a hate crime. Representatives of the Phoenix Sikh community issue a statement that says, in part, "Together we can help others to evolve past hate and fear by continuing to organize to reach out to others with increased understanding, respect, and support. May our collective prayer be that God preserve and protect the honor of all people, our nation, and our world." [More from the Sikh American Legal Defense and Education Fund and SikhNet.]

March 13, 2004 -- Fresno, Calif.: Gurdwara Sahib, a local Sikh temple, is vandalized with graffiti messages: "Rags Go Home" and "It's Not Your Country. [More from SALDEF and Real Sikhism.]

July 12, 2004 -- New York, N.Y.: Rajinder Singh Khalsa and Gurcharan Singh, cousins on their way to dinner at a restaurant, are beaten by two drunk white twentysomething men. The attackers describe Gurcharan's turban as a "curtain." When Rajinder tries to intervene, saying that Sikhs are peaceful, he is beaten unconscious and suffers a fractured eye socket, among other injuries. [More from Real Sikhism.]

May 24, 2007 -- Queens, N.Y.: A 15-year-old student has his hair forcibly cut by an older student at his high school. The scissor-wielding 17-year-old showed the Sikh a ring inscribed with Arabic, saying, "This ring is Allah. If you don't let me cut your hair, I will punch you with this ring." Afterward, he cuts the younger boy's hair. A main pillar of the Sikh faith compels followers to keep their hair uncut. [More from Real Sikhism and United Sikhs.]

May 30, 2007 -- Joliet, Ill.: A decorated U.S. Navy veteran of the Gulf War, Kuldip Singh Nag is approached by a police officer outside of his home for an expired vehicle registration tag. The officer reportedly assaults Nag with pepper spray while hurling expletive-laced anti-immigrant statements. [More from SALDEF and ABC7 News.]

Jan. 14, 2008 -- New Hyde Park, N.Y.: A 63-year-old Sikh, Baljeet Singh, has his jaw and nose broken when attacked outside his temple by a man who lived next-door. David Wood, the attacker, had apparently disturbed members of the gurdwara in the past. [More from United Sikhs.]

Feb. 28, 2008 -- Bryan, Texas: A Sikh man is assaulted in a Wal-Mart parking lot. Though the assailant called him a terrorist, punched him in the face and head and knocked his turban off, the Sikh man does not suffer major injuries. [More from SALDEF.]

June 5, 2008 -- Queens, N.Y.: A ninth grade Sikh is attacked by another student, who tried to remove his *patka*, or under-turban, and had a history of bullying the boy. [More from Real Sikhism and United Sikhs.]

June 5, 2008 -- Albuquerque, N.M.: A vehicle belonging to a Sikh family is defaced with the message "F*** Allah!" and a picture of male genitalia. [More from SALDEF.]

Aug. 4, 2008 -- Phoenix, Ariz.: Inderjit Singh Jassal is shot and killed while working at a 7-Eleven. No clear motive is found. [More from SALDEF and *The Arizona Republic*.]

Oct. 29, 2008 -- Carteret, N.J.: A Sikh man, Ajit Singh Chima, goes for a walk in his neighborhood. He is attacked by a man who casually leaves the scene afterward. Nothing is stolen. [More from SALDEF.]

Jan. 30, 2009 -- Queens, N.Y.: Three men attack Jasmir Singh outside of a grocery store. Racial slurs are heard. A broken glass bottle is used. Singh loses vision in his left eye. [More from NY Daily News and United Sikhs.]

Nov. 29, 2010 -- Sacramento, Calif.: Harbhajan Singh, a cab driver, is a attacked by passengers, who call him Osama bin Laden. Singh believes the attackers, who were later convicted, would have killed him. [More from SALDEF.]

March 6, 2011 -- Elk Grove, Calif.: Two elderly Sikh men in traditional garb, out for a daily afternoon walk, are shot and killed. The perpetrator is not found. [More from Southern Poverty Law Center, SALDEF and *The Sacramento Bee*.]

May 30, 2011 -- New York, N.Y.: Jiwan Singh, an MTA worker and the father of Jasmir Singh, who was assaulted in early 2009 in Queens, is attacked on the A train and accused of being related to Osama bin Laden. [More from the *NY Daily News*.]

Feb. 6, 2012 -- Sterling Heights, Mich.: A gurdwara (Sikh temple) is defaced with graffiti that includes a gun and references to 9/11. [More from SALDEF.]

Aug. 5, 2012 -- Oak Creek, Wis.: A gunman is shot dead by police after he opened fire in a gurdwara during Sikh prayer services, killing six. [More from HuffPost.]

Report hate crimes and bias incidents to the United Sikhs. Learn about hate crime laws from the Sikh Coalition.

Check out a collection of Sikh prayers for healing, hope and strength...[370]

As these anecdotes aren't conclusive proof and one of the best ways to learn the truth is simply taking the time to research and listen to what people have to say, the organization known as the Sikh Coalition provided research on the general experience of what Sikhs have gone through in both criminal reporting and the statistical surveys that they conducted. But first, who are *The Sikh Coalition*? Here is how they describe their history in the United States:

> The Sikh Coalition was founded by volunteers on the night of September 11, 2001 in response to a torrent of violent attacks against Sikh Americans throughout the United States. In those early days, a group of 15 Sikhs decided to take a stand against the civil rights abuses our community faced.

---

[370] "History of Hate: Crimes Against Sikhs Since 9/11." The Huffington Post, TheHuffingtonPost.com, 7 Aug. 2012, www.huffingtonpost.com/2012/08/07/history-of-hate-crimes-against-sikhs-since-911_n_1751841.html.

These volunteers had normal day jobs, but worked weekends and nights to do everything possible to ensure that our community was protected and our voices were heard.

Since then, the Sikh Coalition has transformed into the largest Sikh American advocacy and community development organization in the United States. In 2003, we hired a legal director as our first staff member. Today, we are a team of 20 full- and part-time staff who provide premier legal, policy, and community development support to more than 500,000 Sikh Americans. We work to create safer schools, prevent hate and discrimination, create equal employment opportunities, empower local Sikh communities, and educate the American public about the Sikh faith, community, and traditions.

Over the past 20 years, the Sikh Coalition legal team has won numerous workplace discrimination cases against Fortune 500 employers and government agencies, while championing the rights of clients in cases of school bullying, racial profiling, discrimination, and hate crimes. Our policy work has secured groundbreaking religious rights laws and dramatic policy improvements for how anti-Sikh hate crimes are tracked by the FBI and how the TSA screens Sikh passengers at airports. Our community empowerment and education work has trained hundreds of Sikh advocates across the country who now stand on the frontlines for defending civil rights. This work has also transformed Sikh school bullying into a national policy issue, and ensured that Sikh history is taught accurately in the curricula of California, Texas, New York, New Jersey, Tennessee, Idaho, Colorado, Arizona, Oklahoma, Michigan, North Dakota, Nebraska, Indiana, and most recently Kansas.

While the Sikh Coalition will continue to evolve to meet the changing needs and demands of the Sikh American community, we will always remain focused on defending civil liberties in the community, courtrooms, classrooms, and halls of Congress.[371]

And, the Sikh Coalition's "Fact Sheet" of the lived experiences of Sikhs in the Post-9/11 world including with statistical surveys, while Sam Harris was advocating for racial profiling of anyone who "*looks Muslim*" while violence against Sikhs was going on:

Fact Sheet on Post-9/11 Discrimination and Violence against Sikh Americans

Overview

• Since 9/11, the Sikh Coalition has received thousands of reports from the Sikh community about hate crimes, workplace discrimination, school bullying, and racial and religious profiling.

Hate Crimes

• In the first month after the 9/11 attacks, the Sikh Coalition documented **over 300 cases** of violence and discrimination against Sikh Americans throughout the United States.

• While the FBI recorded over 9000 hate crimes nationwide in 2008 (out of a population of 300 million in the US), **10 percent** of Sikhs in the San Francisco Bay Area reported being the target of hate crimes during the same period according to Sikh Coalition survey of over 1,000 Sikhs in the San Francisco Bay Area.

• Some of the most recent egregious hate attacks include: The **murders of Gurmej Singh Atwal and Surinder Singh** in Elk Grove, CA in March 2011; the **desecration of the Sikh Gurdwara** in Sterling Heights, MI in February 2012, the **hate-motivated death threats mailed to a Sikh**

---

[371] "History." Sikh Coalition, 19 Oct. 2020, www.sikhcoalition.org/about-us/history/.

family in Sterling, VA in March 2012; and the **fire-bombing of a Sikh-owned convenience story** in September 2011.

School Bullying

• A 2010 Sikh Coalition survey revealed that **69%** of turban-wearing Sikh students in the Bay Area of San Francisco have suffered bullying and harassment because of their religion and that **30%** of them had been hit or involuntarily touched because of their turbans. These attacks occur because the Sikh articles of faith – in particular, the turban – are associated with terrorism and 9/11.

• Some of the most egregious attacks on Sikh children have included: **Jaskirat Singh's turban being set on fire** by a fellow student in Hightstown, New Jersey in 2008, **Harpal Singh Vacher's hair being forcibly cut** by a fellow student in New York City in 2007, and **an assault on Gurwinder Singh** by fellow students in New York City

Workplace Discrimination

• **12% of Sikhs** in the San Francisco Bay Area have reported suffering employment discrimination, which makes clear that Sikhs are exponentially more likely to suffer employment discrimination than the general population.

• Most recently, **Frank Singh was called a terrorist and fired** by an AutoZone store because he refused to remove his turban in Boston. **Gurpreet Singh was refused a job** because he would not shave his religiously-mandated beard at a Lexus dealership in New Jersey. **And the NYPD still refuses to hire turbaned Sikhs..**

• Title VII of the Civil Rights Act of 1964 has been misinterpreted in ways that allow employers to **segregate Sikhs from customers** and the general public in the name of corporate image.

Racial and Religious Profiling

• At some airports in the United States, Sikhs are subjected to secondary screening **100 percent** of the time by Transportation Security Administration (TSA) personnel. TSA consistently refuses to audit its screening policies to determine whether Sikh travelers are being profiled.

• The problem of perceived profiling at airports has become so troubling to members of the Sikh community that the Sikh Coalition released a mobile application called FlyRights in April 2012. The application allows Sikhs and people of any community to easily file an official complaint with the TSA in real time, right after an incident occurs.

FOR MORE INFORMATION PLEASE VISIT WWW.SIKHCOALITION.ORG[372]

In my own anecdotal experience, when working with a very respected and professional doctor of Sikh background at a care center for Veterans for approximately six months, I once watched this well-respected doctor seek privacy to call what seemed to be her son to ask if he was okay and if anyone was trying to do anything suspicious around him, because she legitimately feared for his life due to the ignorance of violence

---

[372] "Fact Sheet on Post-9/11 Discrimination and Violence against Sikh Americans ." www.Sikhcoalition.Org, The Sikh Coalition, https://www.sikhcoalition.org/images/documents/fact%20sheet%20on%20hate%20against%20sikhs%20in%20america%20post%209-11%201.pdf. Accessed 18 July 2025.

against Sikhs around that time period. Prior to that, when my family heard of a Sikh Gurdwara shooting on August 5th, 2012 which was on CNN news and is mentioned above, my sister tried to lighten the mood about how the White shooter probably couldn't tell the difference between a Muslim and a Sikh because of skin tone, precisely because we were all scared because the hate crimes against Sikhs were rising and we all felt powerless back in the 2010s and early 2000s. Ignorant and violent White people were murdering descendants of people known for fighting against Islamic tyranny. Such is the stupidity of racial profiling anyone who "*looks Muslim*" – in short, profiling people based on their own primitive, racist stupidity. Other forms of primitive stupidity that Sam Harris seems to believe in is the laughably racist idea that Black people are intellectually inferior as he never challenged Charles Murray on it in his podcast when inviting him on and further refused Ezra Klien's offer for actual scientific researchers who dispute Murray to be on his podcast over the topic of Black people's IQs.[373][374] When Sam Harris was invited onto *The Ezra Klein Show* on April 9th, 2018 to discuss the topic with Ezra about it; Sam Harris repeatedly kept avoiding Ezra Klein's arguments to argue he and Murray are constantly maligned by bad faith actors instead of actually engaging in the content of the criticisms that Ezra pointed out and I do believe it was to deliberately avoid them. If that wasn't a thoroughly provable case of Sam Harris trying to justify White fearmongering and White Supremacy by rationalizing it, then what is?[375][376] To give him credit, within the podcast with Klein released on *The Ezra Klein Show*, Sam Harris had two good points about the pursuit of questions near the end with the African Americans succeeding in sports as a counterexample of how we don't assume there's anything nefarious about the lack of representation of Jews in sports and pointing out Harvard's discrimination against people of East Asian descent, but that was it insofar as good rebuttals in my view.[377] His point about Ayn Hirsi Ali and Maajid Nawaz being maligned is self-refuting, because they were being maligned for violating unspoken standards of religious tolerance in the US and not for their ethnic background. To be frank, I believe he only gets into these controversies and talks about how maligned he is to convince his viewers to stay subscribed to him and perhaps it is to convince them to pay for membership content in what amounts to a parasocial relationship. If he presents himself as an academic who is chronically smeared or taken out of context, then his supporters

---

[373] Klein, Ezra, and Sam Harris. "The Sam Harris Debate: The Ezra Klein Show." Smash Notes, The Ezra Klein Show, 9 Apr. 2018, https://smashnotes.com/p/the-ezra-klein-show/e/the-sam-harris-debate.
[374] Klein, Ezra. "Sam Harris, Charles Murray, and The Allure of Race Science." Vox, Vox, 27 Mar. 2018, web.archive.org/web/20201124051651/https://www.vox.com/policy-and-politics/2018/3/27/15695060/sam-harris-charles-murray-race-iq-forbidden-knowledge-podcast-bell-curve.
[375] Klein, Ezra, and Sam Harris. "The Sam Harris Debate: The Ezra Klein Show." Smash Notes, The Ezra Klein Show, 9 Apr. 2018, https://smashnotes.com/p/the-ezra-klein-show/e/the-sam-harris-debate.
[376] Klein, Ezra. "Sam Harris, Charles Murray, and The Allure of Race Science." Vox, Vox, 27 Mar. 2018, web.archive.org/web/20201124051651/https://www.vox.com/policy-and-politics/2018/3/27/15695060/sam-harris-charles-murray-race-iq-forbidden-knowledge-podcast-bell-curve.
[377] Klein, Ezra, and Sam Harris. "The Sam Harris Debate: The Ezra Klein Show." Smash Notes, The Ezra Klein Show, 9 Apr. 2018, https://smashnotes.com/p/the-ezra-klein-show/e/the-sam-harris-debate.

will likely be convinced to keep supporting him or support him even more strongly by paying for a membership.

When it came to the ideas and fundamentals of Islamism, Sam Harris was correct. Yet, when it came to the solutions for fighting against Islamism in terms of National Security, he failed and Sam Harris doesn't seem to care about opposing views on it despite purportedly listening to them. We need real solutions to the seemingly endless danger of Islamic terrorism that seeks to harm all non-Muslims, perceived non-Muslims from intra-Islamic violence such as the Sunni-Shia split, and we must stop making excuses for it. When I was studying Foreign Policy for my Master's degree in Political Science, Al Qaeda was popularly referred to as First-Generation Islamic Terrorism, ISIS as Second-Generation Islamic Terrorism, and now AI and Cryptocurrency are unknowingly abetting what seems to be an increasing form of Third-Generation Islamic Terrorism that may be rising in Canada, India, Russia, Iran, and Europe more generally. It may even be rising in the United States and the so-called experts have no solutions for it.

The US Failed in Afghanistan because American Policymakers were Incompetent and Self-Sabotaged Nationbuilding

A broader and in-depth context is necessary for a better approximation of the real dangers of global Islamic terrorism. Even now after the United States's stunning defeat in Afghanistan against the Taliban on August 2021, people still do not understand the utter insanity of pressuring businesses, lawmakers, and political groups to push for Islamophobia as some sort of civic good, when it's just reinstituting blasphemy laws with incoherent racial terms. People don't understand why Pakistan – as a nuclear-armed country – is such a unique risk to global safety and Great Britain is especially guilty of ignoring the fact that this truly is the direct consequences of British imperialism. Unfortunately, the United States's special relationship with Great Britain clearly only sabotaged US interests and created the second-most abrupt decline of a global power in human history with the first being the USSR. The reason is surprisingly simple: Great Britain's perspective on history was always calculated lies – not half-truths, but full-fledged lies – that tried to present itself as rational and balanced but was actually a means of keeping their own people intentionally ignorant so they would keep supporting British Foreign Policy. Due to the fact that they had conquered a third of the world and ruled as the strongest empire in human history for 400 years, their historians created a thoroughly self-serving middle-ground fallacy that the US absorbed as a perspective due to a false perception of a shared culture and history, and it led to the US's abrupt collapse as a global power because the US essentially made itself ignorant of facts and logic by believing the British viewpoint was unbiased instead of irrational. The US never took advantage of being a melting pot and thus destroyed itself by simply being an abridged version of Britain's mistakes; the British empire lasted approximately for four-hundred years and the US empire hasn't even lasted for one-hundred years yet. It has become abundantly clear that only the perspective of the British and to a lesser extent, fellow perceived racial peers like other Europeans were respected as equals among the upper-political echelons of the United States and it completely destroyed the United States. We Americans are on borrowed time and soon to be finished because we treated Britain's views as objective instead of deranged; likely because it probably fed into shared feelings of White Supremacy among the majority of Americans for most of the US's history as a global power. It's become quite clear that social justice was only seen in terms of appeasing non-Whites as a sanitized form of Otherness and not as anything of legitimate value based upon fact-finding criteria for the majority of the wealthy elites.

The British perspective, like the Islamic perspective, is just a self-perpetuating hoax that sees no value in either history or truth, because the main purpose was always to justify its brutality in terms of heroism and moral goodness to instill British people with pride in its overwhelming power over the world itself for approximately four-hundred years. In short, the British perspective that the US cosigned itself to was completely and thoroughly antagonistic to a third of the world on the basis of bigotry borne from colonial rule; the special relationship was just a means of the British monarchy to successfully hoodwink the gullible and idiotic American policymakers who pretended to know what they were doing. When it comes to global policies, the results are the only truth. What were America's results for over twenty years now? The results show that American policymakers weren't competent, American policymakers had no plans, and American policymakers knowingly and willfully sent US troops to their deaths for no reason and American policymakers will never apologize for their blatant stupidity despite their culpability. The fact is simply this: there's no excuse for these results. Either we had the information necessary to overcome the failings of previous empires or we didn't. Either the US had full capabilities to accomplish its US policy objectives as the strongest power in the world or we are too stupid, the people that we Americans constantly elected into power are too stupid, and they chose equally stupid people in Presidential cabinet positions. That's it and that is how real competent management works according to the works of Austrian-American management theorist, Peter Drucker; no bullshit, no excuses – you failed those below you who trusted you to know what you were doing. No ifs, ands, or buts . . . that's the end of it.

The fact is that our American policymakers were idiots and the negative repercussions are due to the fact they are genuinely stupid people but probably well-spoken enough at public speaking events to delude us. I recall reading an article years ago of how Bush's plan for opening-up schools in Afghanistan was to open them up in conflict zones – i.e. where children would be shot to death and where suicide bombers could blow themselves up; they genuinely thought this was a good idea. The US did not support any Free Speech initiative because they didn't understand anything about the culture and ignored how Afghan Muslim women were brutally murdered in public for false accusations of desecrating the Quran[378], the ignoramuses who led American policymaking were genuinely too stupid to know how to appeal to regular Afghans and treated such behavior as their "culture" even though it only comes from the theology of Islam[379], and no effort was made for grassroots policymaking for local areas as a starting place. That is, they could have put Afghan youths into fast-tracked college programs for public policy and have them build grassroots civil societies over time with better human rights laws including Free Speech. What did they do instead? Under eight-years of the Obama administration, they let children get raped by Afghan warlords in US bases and fired any US military official who was disgusted and voiced concerns. After they were fired, the fired US military staff thankfully reported this to US news outlets back in 2015. The article titled *"U.S. Soldiers Told to Ignore Sexual Abuse of Boys by Afghan Allies"* by Joseph Goldstein published on September 20th, 2015 in the NY Times gives an in-depth look and its best to just read the entirety of it:

> KABUL, Afghanistan — In his last phone call home, Lance Cpl. Gregory Buckley Jr. told his father what was troubling him: From his bunk in southern Afghanistan, he could hear Afghan police officers sexually abusing boys they had brought to the base.
>
> "At night we can hear them screaming, but we're not allowed to do anything about it," the Marine's father, Gregory Buckley Sr., recalled his son telling him before he was shot to death at the base in 2012. He urged his son to tell his superiors. "My son said that his officers told him to look the other way because it's their culture."
>
> Rampant sexual abuse of children has long been a problem in Afghanistan, particularly among armed commanders who dominate much of the rural landscape and can bully the population. The practice is called bacha bazi, literally "boy play," and American soldiers and Marines have been instructed not to intervene — in some cases, not even when their Afghan allies have abused boys on military bases, according to interviews and court records.
>
> The policy has endured as American forces have recruited and organized Afghan militias to help hold territory against the Taliban. But soldiers and Marines have been increasingly troubled that instead of weeding out pedophiles, the American military was arming them in some cases and placing them as the commanders of villages — and doing little when they began abusing children.
>
> "The reason we were here is because we heard the terrible things the Taliban were doing to people, how they were taking away human rights," said Dan Quinn, a former Special Forces captain who beat up an American-backed militia commander for keeping a boy chained to his bed as a sex slave. "But we were putting people into power who would do things that were worse than the Taliban did — that was something village elders voiced to me."

---

[378] Akbar, Noorjahan. "A Year Later, Still No Justice for Farkhunda." Foreign Policy, 1 Apr. 2016, web.archive.org/web/20160406114242/https://foreignpolicy.com/2016/04/01/a-year-later-still-no-justice-for-farkhunda/.

[379] Akbar, Noorjahan. "A Year Later, Still No Justice for Farkhunda." Foreign Policy, 1 Apr. 2016, web.archive.org/web/20160406114242/https://foreignpolicy.com/2016/04/01/a-year-later-still-no-justice-for-farkhunda/.

The policy of instructing soldiers to ignore child sexual abuse by their Afghan allies is coming under new scrutiny, particularly as it emerges that service members like Captain Quinn have faced discipline, even career ruin, for disobeying it.

After the beating, the Army relieved Captain Quinn of his command and pulled him from Afghanistan. He has since left the military.

Four years later, the Army is also trying to <u>forcibly retire Sgt. First Class Charles Martland</u>, a Special Forces member who joined Captain Quinn in beating up the commander.

"The Army contends that Martland and others should have looked the other way (a contention that I believe is nonsense)," Representative Duncan Hunter, a California Republican who hopes to save Sergeant Martland's career, wrote last week to the Pentagon's inspector general.

In Sergeant Martland's case, the Army said it could not comment because of the Privacy Act.

When asked about American military policy, the spokesman for the American command in Afghanistan, Col. Brian Tribus, wrote in an email: "Generally, allegations of child sexual abuse by Afghan military or police personnel would be a matter of domestic Afghan criminal law." He added that "there would be no express requirement that U.S. military personnel in Afghanistan report it." An exception, he said, is when rape is being used as a weapon of war.

The American policy of nonintervention is intended to maintain good relations with the Afghan police and militia units the United States has trained to fight the Taliban. It also reflects a reluctance to impose cultural values in a country where <u>pederasty is rife</u>, particularly among powerful men, for whom being surrounded by young teenagers can be a mark of social status.

Some soldiers believed that the policy made sense, even if they were personally distressed at the sexual predation they witnessed or heard about.

"The bigger picture was fighting the Taliban," a former Marine lance corporal reflected. "It wasn't to stop molestation."

Still, the former lance corporal, who spoke on the condition of anonymity to avoid offending fellow Marines, recalled feeling sickened the day he entered a room on a base and saw three or four men lying on the floor with children between them. "I'm not a hundred percent sure what was happening under the sheet, but I have a pretty good idea of what was going on," he said.

But the American policy of treating child sexual abuse as a cultural issue has often alienated the villages whose children are being preyed upon. The pitfalls of the policy emerged clearly as American Special Forces soldiers began to form <u>Afghan Local Police militias</u> to hold villages that American forces had retaken from the Taliban in 2010 and 2011.

By the summer of 2011, Captain Quinn and Sergeant Martland, both Green Berets on their second tour in northern Kunduz Province, began to receive dire complaints about the Afghan Local Police units they were training and supporting.

First, they were told, one of the militia commanders raped a 14- or 15-year-old girl whom he had spotted working in the fields. Captain Quinn informed the provincial police chief, who soon levied punishment. "He got one day in jail, and then she was forced to marry him," Mr. Quinn said.

When he asked a superior officer what more he could do, he was told that he had done well to bring it up with local officials but that there was nothing else to be done. "We're being praised for doing the right thing, and a guy just got away with raping a 14-year-old girl," Mr. Quinn said.

Village elders grew more upset at the predatory behavior of American-backed commanders. After each case, Captain Quinn would gather the Afghan commanders and lecture them on human rights.

Soon another commander absconded with his men's wages. Mr. Quinn said he later heard that the commander had spent the money on dancing boys. Another commander murdered his 12-year-old daughter in a so-called honor killing for having kissed a boy. "There were no repercussions," Mr. Quinn recalled.

In September 2011, an Afghan woman, visibly bruised, showed up at an American base with her son, who was limping. One of the Afghan police commanders in the area, Abdul Rahman, had abducted the boy and forced him to become a sex slave, chained to his bed, the woman explained. When she sought her son's return, she herself was beaten. Her son had eventually been released, but she was afraid it would happen again, she told the Americans on the base.

She explained that because "her son was such a good-looking kid, he was a status symbol" coveted by local commanders, recalled Mr. Quinn, who did not speak to the woman directly but was told about her visit when he returned to the base from a mission later that day.

So Captain Quinn summoned Abdul Rahman and confronted him about what he had done. The police commander acknowledged that it was true, but brushed it off. When the American officer began to lecture about "how you are held to a higher standard if you are working with U.S. forces, and people expect more of you," the commander began to laugh.

"I picked him up and threw him onto the ground," Mr. Quinn said. Sergeant Martland joined in, he said. "I did this to make sure the message was understood that if he went back to the boy, that it was not going to be tolerated," Mr. Quinn recalled.

There is disagreement over the extent of the commander's injuries. Mr. Quinn said they were not serious, which was corroborated by an Afghan official who saw the commander afterward.

(The commander, Abdul Rahman, was killed two years ago in a Taliban ambush. His brother said in an interview that his brother had never raped the boy, but was the victim of a false accusation engineered by his enemies.)

Sergeant Martland, who received a Bronze Star for valor for his actions during a Taliban ambush, wrote in a letter to the Army this year that he and Mr. Quinn "felt that morally we could no longer stand by and allow our A.L.P. to commit atrocities," referring to the Afghan Local Police.

The father of Lance Corporal Buckley believes the policy of looking away from sexual abuse was a factor in his son's death, and he has filed a lawsuit to press the Marine Corps for more information about it.

Lance Corporal Buckley and two other Marines were killed in 2012 by one of a large entourage of boys living at their base with an Afghan police commander named Sarwar Jan.

Mr. Jan had long had a bad reputation; in 2010, two Marine officers managed to persuade the Afghan authorities to arrest him following a litany of abuses, including corruption, support for the Taliban and child abduction. But just two years later, the police commander was back with a different unit, working at Lance Corporal Buckley's post, Forward Operating Base Delhi, in Helmand Province.

Lance Corporal Buckley had noticed that a large entourage of "tea boys" — domestic servants who are sometimes pressed into sexual slavery — had arrived with Mr. Jan and moved into the same barracks, one floor below the Marines. He told his father about it during his final call home.

Word of Mr. Jan's new position also reached the Marine officers who had gotten him arrested in 2010. One of them, Maj. Jason Brezler, dashed out an email to Marine officers at F.O.B. Delhi, warning them about Mr. Jan and attaching a dossier about him.

The warning was never heeded. About two weeks later, one of the older boys with Mr. Jan — around 17 years old — grabbed a rifle and killed Lance Corporal Buckley and the other Marines.

Lance Corporal Buckley's father still agonizes about whether the killing occurred because of the sexual abuse by an American ally. "As far as the young boys are concerned, the Marines are allowing it to happen and so they're guilty by association," Mr. Buckley said. "They don't know our Marines are sick to their stomachs."

The one American service member who was punished in the investigation that followed was Major Brezler, who had sent the email warning about Mr. Jan, his lawyers said. In one of Major Brezler's hearings, Marine Corps lawyers warned that information about the police commander's penchant for abusing boys might be classified. The Marine Corps has initiated proceedings to discharge Major Brezler.

Mr. Jan appears to have moved on, to a higher-ranking police command in the same province. In an interview, he denied keeping boys as sex slaves or having any relationship with the boy who killed the three Marines. "No, it's all untrue," Mr. Jan said. But people who know him say he still suffers from "a toothache problem," a euphemism here for child sexual abuse.[380]

The Taliban's appeasement of Village Elders concerns in the latter years of US occupation were why they were quickly able to takeover Afghanistan and take US military weapons. In other words, it is entirely plausible that the Bush, Obama, and probably later Trump and Biden administrations ignoring the child abuse of Afghan children is why we lost the war in Afghanistan. The Bush administration produced pro-Islamic textbooks and had them distributed for their eight-years of Presidency[381], the Obama administration outright ignored child rape by Afghan warlords happening on US military bases despite peaceful reporting and protests by Afghan civilians hoping it would be stopped[382], the Obama administration did nothing about women being killed for insulting Islam for eight-years[383], the Trump Administration to my knowledge did not concern itself with any of this and kept most of its actions a secret, and the Biden administration is responsible for the worst withdrawal in US history with the Taliban acquiring approximately $83 billion in US weapons.[384] Pedophilia became conflated with Western freedoms and US policy almost certainly led to this conflation in the minds of local Afghans. When it came time for the withdrawal from Afghanistan, the European and American policymakers laughed that Afghanistan had thousands of years of women not having equal rights and that it was simply a return to tradition.

Shaharzad Akbar, an Afghan woman who served as former Chair of the Afghanistan Independent Human Rights Commission, served as Deputy on the Afghan National Security Council for Peace and Civilian Protection, and served as Country Director for Open Society Afghanistan from 2014 to 2017 wrote for *Foreign Affairs* on August 30th, 2022 in an article titled "*Afghanistan's Women Are On Their Own*"

---

[380] Goldstein, Joseph. "U.S. Soldiers Told to Ignore Sexual Abuse of Boys by Afghan Allies." The New York Times, The New York Times Magazine, 20 Sept. 2015, www.nytimes.com/2015/09/21/world/asia/us-soldiers-told-to-ignore-afghan-allies-abuse-of-boys.html.
[381] Stephens, Joe, and David B. Ottaway. "From U.S., the ABC's of Jihad." The Washington Post, WP Company, 23 Mar. 2002, www.washingtonpost.com/archive/politics/2002/03/23/from-us-the-abcs-of-jihad/d079075a-3ed3-4030-9a96-0d48f6355e54/?utm_term=.cbb9b6b8a59a.
[382] Goldstein, Joseph. "U.S. Soldiers Told to Ignore Sexual Abuse of Boys by Afghan Allies." The New York Times, The New York Times Magazine, 20 Sept. 2015, www.nytimes.com/2015/09/21/world/asia/us-soldiers-told-to-ignore-afghan-allies-abuse-of-boys.html.
[383] Akbar, Noorjahan. "A Year Later, Still No Justice for Farkhunda." Foreign Policy, 1 Apr. 2016, web.archive.org/web/20160406114242/https://foreignpolicy.com/2016/04/01/a-year-later-still-no-justice-for-farkhunda/.
[384] Burns, Robert. "Billions Spent on Afghan Army Ultimately Benefited Taliban." AP News, AP News, 17 Aug. 2021, apnews.com/article/joe-biden-army-taliban-995b069a9008690582cb34f4cacd8515.

mentioned the following on US and Western policymakers jubilant attitude at leaving women to be raped as spoils of war for Afghan fighters:

> YOU'RE ON YOUR OWN
>
> This is not the first time that the demands of Afghan women are falling on deaf ears. Throughout the U.S.-initiated talks with the Taliban, which began under the Trump administration and lasted from 2018 until February 2020, Afghan women campaigned, wrote, and organized mass gatherings to demand an inclusive peace process. But their appeals went unheeded. I attended a round of talks with the Taliban in Doha and heard firsthand their worryingly vague and general statements on women's rights "within Islam." Following this, in many interactions with U.S. officials, including Zalmay Khalilzad, the U.S. envoy who negotiated the Doha deal, I raised concerns about the lack of participation of women and victims of war in the talks and the emptiness of the Taliban's reassurances. None of these concerns or warnings were taken seriously. Instead, I and others in the women's movement were constantly told that the Taliban have changed.
>
> Additionally, a convenient counternarrative took hold, pushed by male diplomats and male commentators, who claimed that the demands of Afghan women's rights activists were not representative of rural Afghan women, and instead represented a Western imposition and were therefore not legitimate. In the end, the Doha agreement excluded any references to women's rights, human rights, or civilian protection, key areas of concern for all Afghan people. Even while the United States and its allies made proclamations committing to protect the women of Afghanistan, they let the Taliban set the conditions of the talks. They participated in a process that would decide the fate of millions of Afghan women but that included zero Afghan women at the negotiating table.
>
> This has meant that in addition to standing up to the Taliban and battling patriarchy inside Afghanistan, advocates for the rights of Afghan women have also had to contend with condescension, gaslighting, and marginalization at the hands of Western officials and alleged experts on Afghanistan. Women activists who fled Afghanistan after the Taliban took control last summer have had to endure this while also navigating the bureaucracies of various Western countries as they try to gain legal asylum. Although Western leaders have talked for the last two decades about supporting Afghan women, at critical junctures, where women's rights activists' rights and lives are on the line, Western countries have provided limited support for them or their cause, exposing a deep hypocrisy.
>
> None of this is to say that the situation in Afghanistan is an easy challenge to solve. The Taliban won the war, and nobody wants to stand by and watch Afghans starve in a humanitarian crisis. So outside powers and organizations must deal with the Taliban regime in at least a limited way.
>
> Yet Western officials have exercised poor judgment in picking their Taliban interlocutors and in setting the public tone of their engagement. Consider, for example, how Western governments and even the UN continue to deal with Sirajuddin Haqqani, Afghanistan's acting interior minister and the leader of the Haqqani network, who remains on the FBI's most wanted list because of his involvement in some of the bloodiest terrorist attacks in Afghanistan over the last 20 years. The world was reminded of his ties to al Qaeda earlier this summer when a U.S. drone strike killed al Qaeda's leader, Ayman al-Zawahiri, who was living in Kabul in a house owned by a top aide to Haqqani, according to U.S. intelligence.
>
> Western officials may have to meet with Haqqani, but they should be mindful of how their interactions further normalize him and whitewash his deeply problematic background. In June, in a tweet noting a "farewell meeting" between Haqqani and Deborah Lyons, the outgoing Afghanistan representative for the UN Secretary-General, the UN used the honorific term "al hajj" in referring to Haqqani, which is typically reserved for people who have completed a pilgrimage to Mecca and connotes a level of respect. The tweet referred to discussions between him and Lyons

on issues including counterterrorism, which infuriated Afghan human rights activists who have worked with victims of the Haqqani network's terrorist attacks for years.

It is possible to deliver foreign aid through Afghan and international nongovernmental organizations without having to cozy up to some of the world's most wanted terrorists. The EU is one of the biggest contributors of humanitarian aid to Afghanistan, and EU Special Envoy Tomas Niklasson has continued to be outspoken about the human rights issues and violations by the Taliban. He also engages with Afghan women and men outside the Taliban's leadership.[385]

The Western and US policymakers were genuinely too stupid at even a basic understanding of their jobs to know historic facts about Afghanistan and their own comments belie the fact they were too stupid for the positions they held. The Afghans are descendants of the Greco-Buddhist polities of Gandhara, Greco-Bactrian Kingdom, and the Indo-Greek kingdoms and were ruthlessly converted into Islam by force. They could have easily replaced Islamic school teachings with Greek philosophy and could have argued historical roots as a basis for a shared culture or a return to Afghans true traditions, instead the Bush Administration continued spreading Islamic schoolbooks just like his father before him.[386] Oh wait! They think it doesn't matter because it's history; history is synonymous with irrelevant to these idiots. This was how intrinsically worthless the British perspective was and why the US failed completely; it's all America's fault for creating a special relationship that went so far as absorbing the perspectives of colonizers of a third of the world and believing such a farce was ever objective as a viewpoint. Please ask yourselves this: what has this special relationship with Britain ever advantaged or benefitted the US in a global context outside of Europe? British perspectives on Europe are surely valuable, but outside of such regional concerns; what was the value in their perspective on anything else? US policymakers clearly didn't scrutinize Britain and didn't understand that British history books and perspectives were largely just fabrications about the rest of the world. The US Federal government trusted British viewpoints more than the ethnic minorities in their own intelligence agencies, specifically because their junior staff weren't White according to their own self-reports in the CIA.[387]

One of the worst parts is what most of that civilian spending for nationbuilding purposes went to. What exactly did US policymakers do with the money for the civilian sectors? In fairness, they did build schools and promote women's education but abandoned it upon women's rights becoming inconvenient. They had built infrastructure,

---

[385] Akbar, Shaharzad. "Afghanistan's Women Are on Their Own." Foreign Affairs, 30 August 2022, https://www.foreignaffairs.com/afghanistan/afghanistans-women-are-their-own. Accessed 21 July 2025
[386] Stephens, Joe, and David B. Ottaway. "From U.S., the ABC's of Jihad." The Washington Post, WP Company, 23 Mar. 2002, www.washingtonpost.com/archive/politics/2002/03/23/from-us-the-abcs-of-jihad/d079075a-3ed3-4030-9a96-0d48f6355e54/?utm_term=.cbb9b6b8a59a.
[387] Dilanian, Ken. "CIA's Failure to Hire and Promote Diverse Agents Erodes Spy Agency's Mission, Study Finds." PBS, Public Broadcasting Service, 30 June 2015, www.pbs.org/newshour/nation/cias-failure-hire-promote-diverse-agents-erodes-spy-agencys-mission-study-finds.

but what else did they do? Allow corporate greed to run rampant in yet another lengthy chapter of US corporations ruling over the United States based upon profits and the US politicians being useless figureheads. Albert Fox Cahn, the founder and executive director of Surveillance Technology Oversight Project (S.T.O.P.), made an article for *The Daily Beast* published on August 24th 2021 titled "*The Taliban Now Controls a U.S.-Made Super-Surveillance System*" which read as follows:

> In Kabul, checkpoints are now manned by Taliban fighters using biometric scanners paid for by the American people to hunt down civilians who worked and fought alongside us, in what should be a reckoning for everyone who sold biometric surveillance as a tool for good.
>
> Over the last 20 years, Afghanistan became a technological training ground. It was the place America experimented with new weapons of war, like the Predator drone, often with horrific results. It's also where we experimented with new forms of surveillance, both militarized and humanitarian. By going community to community, scanning Afghans' biometric data indiscriminately, the U.S. hoped to create new counter-insurgency tools.
>
> That effort failed to create anything that could stop the Taliban, but it did create things that are incredibly dangerous in the Taliban's own hands.
>
> Approximately 80 percent of the country, roughly 25 million people, were targeted for inclusion in the U.S. military's biometric database. Now, the Handheld Interagency Identity Detection Equipment can scan Afghans' fingerprints, faces, and irises to reveal biographical information. The Microsoft-powered device can also tap into a much larger national database of information on millions of Afghans collected by the United States over two decades of war.
>
> With that technology, the Taliban will take control of one of the most sophisticated state surveillance systems on the planet.
>
> It gets worse. While few expected the U.S. military to focus on promoting Afghans' civil rights, many expected better from the United Nations, particularly the UN Refugee Agency. Instead, the UNHCR drove a nearly two-decade long campaign to require biometric data to receive aid, creating yet another dangerous database for the Taliban to control.
>
> Since 2002, Afghanistan served as a de facto testing ground for new biometric technology, including one of the earliest iris scanning systems in the world. For aid agencies, this was a way to not only confirm the identities of employees, but to track who received food and other staples, blocking recipients from receiving too much food under multiple names. Privacy and civil rights complaints were dismissed as alarmist—as they so often are—but now Afghans will pay the price.
>
> As in countless other low-income countries, biometric surveillance became a substitute for civil society and the rule of law. Yes, fraud and embezzlement are real problems. Yes, we must ensure that aid gets to those most in need. But when we respond to humanitarian crises with dystopian tools like facial recognition and iris scans, we're undermining the very democratic principles we were supposedly fighting to support.
>
> Every time biometric surveillance became more embedded in Afghan society, the risks for abuse grew, but the pushback was ignored. When facial recognition became the entry fee for casting a ballot, those on the ground and their supporters around the world pushed back, only to once again be ignored.
>
> Today, the elaborate network of biometric surveillance that was largely bought and paid for with American taxpayer dollars is now one of the Taliban's most terrifying tools. Aid workers, interpreters, and other American allies can get forged papers, they can wipe their phones, but they can't change their faces. And for those risking their lives to get to the Kabul airport and the last fleeting hope of safety, every Taliban checkpoint brings the risk of a facial scan, and deadly repercussions.

Most countries don't face the same risk of collapse that the Afghan government did, but the lessons still apply. Whenever we let any company or government capture our biometric data, we give them the one form of information that will haunt us for life. You can change your name but not your iris or DNA.

Even if we trust our own government with such tracking tools (and we should not), what about everyone else who can take the data? Nearly 200,000 Americans' faces were taken in just one Department of Homeland Security hack in 2019, but that's infinitesimal compared to the millions of federal employees whose data was stolen in the 2015 Office of Personnel Management hack.

It doesn't take a governmental collapse to see our biometric data transformed from a tool used by police into one used by criminals and militants. And so far, there is only one surefire way to protect our biometric data and prevent it from being repurposed: not collecting it in the first place.[388]

The US keeps bragging to the world about how it is the strongest military power in the world and has nothing to show for it in terms of the occupation of Afghanistan. With the Iraq war concluding in 2011, it kept the sale of oil on the US dollar. In Afghanistan, Islamism defeated the United States, NATO, women's rights, and obtained $83 billion in US taxpayer weapons and Iraq is reverting back to Islamism with a return of Islamic personal laws allowing pedophilic marriages with 9-year old girls to much older men. Why did this happen? Despite the overwhelming amount of money and military power, what American policymakers lacked was any real commitment to ideals. They deceived themselves into believing ideals were meaningless and that they mustn't criticize Islam at all. Sixteen years of the Bush and Obama administrations' strategies merely consisted of fighting the Taliban, but not building any future based upon any sort of counter ideal for the Afghan people. This obviously would have been difficult to do; any insult to Islam could lead to riots and intra-Afghan killings and American policymakers wrongly thought it was "wise" to avoid that. In truth, this was the ultimate proof of their unfettered stupidity and it is the reason we lost. Islamism is opposed to basically any ideal that goes beyond 7th century Arab fundamentalism and there was no dearth in what could have been used. Yet, on this crucial juncture for nationbuilding, despite what US armed forces fight for and what the US founded itself on, this basic fact about reforming a country to be better was missing. All that these corporations that seemed to have free reign really did was show off modernity without realizing that Islam sees that as a challenge to be disgusted by because it doesn't conform to 7th century social standards of the Middle East. The most tragic part is that any ideal would have been fine, but instead these incompetent American policymakers bowed to Islamism and their half-assed nationbuilding fell to Islamism. There is no such thing as extremist or moderate Islam; there is only Islam and that's why we lost the war in Afghanistan after twenty years. Islamic Republics are not republics; they are theocracies ruled by dictators because

---

[388] Cahn, Albert Fox. "The Taliban Now Controls a U.S.-Made Super-Surveillance System." The Daily Beast, The Daily Beast Company, 19 Sept. 2024, www.thedailybeast.com/the-taliban-now-controls-a-us-made-super-surveillance-system/.

they resemble the Prophet Mohammad's 7th century caliphate more than any modern democracies. They're simply appropriating modern terms to delude themselves with the belief that following 7th century social, political, and technological standards can lead to a modern democratic republic. The problem is, and will always be, Islam. American incompetence and refusal to challenge the idea of religious tolerance with Free Speech criticisms of Islam is why we lost.

The Long-Term Effects of British Imperialism: Pakistan's Global Terror Risk

Despite the general unreliability of Great Britain's historic views that were wrongly assumed by incompetent US policymakers to be objective, not all of Great Britain falls into this trap. While it is true for the general majority of the UK, that doesn't mean every facet of UK society falls into such delusions so long as they maintain a commitment to honesty and truth. Even in Failing States like the United Kingdom, they can provide valuable work so long as it is based upon evidence-based research without biased sampling. In this specific case, Oxford University's Centre for the Resolution of Intractable Conflicts (CRIC) and a Mumbai, India thinktank known as the Strategic Foresight Group, created a publication in late 2018 titled "*Humanity At Risk: Global Terror Threat Indicant*" which analyzed global terror threats. It might be a bit dated due to being published in 2018, but the work is well-researched and it goes through terror threat aspects from finance, to drug cartels, and the estimated military forces of each respective terrorist group. However, it is perhaps necessary to first give more information on the Strategic Foresight Group as many would likely already find sufficient value in Oxford University:

> **About Strategic Foresight Group**
>
> Strategic Foresight Group (SFG) is a think - tank engaged in crafting new policy concepts that enable decision makers to prepare for a future in uncertain times. Founded in 2002 to create new forms of intellectual capital, our body of work today encompasses over 50 countries, across four continents.
>
> SFG has published over 30 in-depth research reports in English with some translations in Arabic and Spanish. We currently work within three areas of focus: 1. Water Diplomacy 2. Peace, Conflict and Terrorism 3. Global Foresight
>
> SFG analysis and recommendations have been discussed in the United Nations, UK House of Lords, House of Commons, Indian Parliament, European Parliament, Alliance of Civilization, World Economic Forum (Davos), and quoted in over 1500 newspapers and media sources. Several Heads of Government, Cabinet Ministers and Members of Parliament have participated in SFG

activities.[389]

And, CRIC and Strategic Foresight Group (SFG)'s research into the estimated military capabilities of Islamic terror groups across the world in their 2018 publication titled "*Humanity At Risk: Global Terror Threat Indicant*" in their Part III from pages 67 – 77 with a scale they've created so people better understand the risks. I'd like for you to think on two issues that have bothered me when I first looked at this in 2018: First, what happens to all of us non-Muslims the moment we no longer have powerful militaries protecting us from all this? In other words, what would be the result of their military forces being more powerful than ours? Second, please seriously consider the fact that all of this is coming from just the religion of Islam. In other words, all of these are Islamic terrorist groups across the world and we are reaching a point where these Islamic terrorist groups are perpetually resupplied with new manpower every successive generation. Finally, when looking at the case of Pakistan, please consider the fact that it is truly the longest lasting legacy of Great Britain's imperialism:

---

[389] "About Us - Strategic Foresight Group, Think Tank, Policy, Global Studies, Global Affairs Research, Global Water Cooperation." Strategicforesight.Com, Strategic Foresight Group (SFG), www.strategicforesight.com/about-us.php. Accessed 24 July 2025.

Part 3: Indicant

Backgrounder

In order to identify long term risks to humanity from terrorism, it is important to focus on the groups that have resilience and a strong support base. The strength of a group depends on its manpower, financial resources, weapons, determination and support from state structures. Among these factors, financial resources and weapons in hand are transient variables. The drop in the revenue of Islamic State of Iraq and the Levant (ISIL)/Daesh in a couple of years is an important indicator. If a terrorist group manages to appeal to a large number of people to join it as a combatant or armed member, it shows the potential of such a group to cause harm in the long run.

In order to assess future risks, it is necessary to measure the armed strength of terrorist groups. It is also necessary to examine their intent to acquire and use weapons of mass destruction. The stronger a group is in terms of attracting armed members, the greater the risk it poses to humanity. If a group intends to acquire nuclear weapons, its risk potential multiplies by several times.

The Global Terror Threat Indicant (GTTI) therefore places emphasis on the number of the active combatants or armed members, which are interchangeable realities, and the interest demonstrated or efforts made by a group to acquire nuclear weapons or attack or capture nuclear plants. The GTTI Scale is a function of the product of combatant strength and nuclear intent.

It also identifies countries on a comparative scale in terms of their support for terror groups either by offering base or support in the form of safe havens, and otherwise.

A scale in the constantly changing ecology of terror cannot be a perfect measurement. Combatants move from one group to another and from one geography to another. Objectives, strategy and lethal intent also keep changing. Therefore no scale can be perfect. The purpose of GTTI Scale is not to offer a detailed analytical tool to assess mathematically accurate strength of terror groups. It is to indicate the groups and supporting countries that need to be watched in future if the growth of terrorism is to be contained.

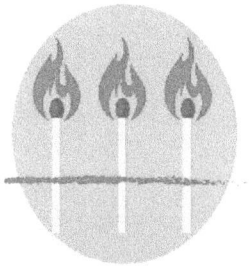

1. the gttl Scale

Methodology

Each group's combatant strength or the range is already provided in the document. When there is a range, the median is taken. When combatant strength is not available (N/A) the value is taken as 1000. However if the group poses nuclear threat then the combatant strength is multiplied by 10.

GTTI Scale of Terror Groups: 1- 10

The GTTI Scale of a terror group is calculated based on the combatant strength of each group. A value between 1 and 10 is assigned based on the product of the combatant strength and potential nuclear risk calculated as mentioned above.

Combatant Strength and Nuclear Risk	Value on Scale
<500	1
500-999	2
1000-1999	3
2000-4999	4
5000-9999	5
10,000-24999	6
25000-49999	7
50000-74999	8
75000-99999	9
>100,000	10

GTTI score of a country: Sum total of GTTI Scale of each terror group which has a base in that country + half of the sum total of GTTI Scale of each terror group which has support in that country

GTTI Scale of Terror Groups

10
- Afghan Taliban
- Lashkar-e-Tayyiba (LeT)

9
- Al-Nusrah Front for the People of the Levant
- Jaish-i-Mohammed

8
- Al-Shabaab
- Jama'atu Ahlis Sunna Lidda'awati Wal-Jihad (Boko Haram)

7
- Islamic State of Iraq and the Levant (ISIL) / Daesh

6
- Islamic Movement of Uzbekistan
- Jamaat-ul-Ahrar (JuA)
- Jemaah Islamiyah
- Tehrik-e-Taliban Pakistan (TTP)

5
- Al-Qaida
- Harakat-ul Jihad Islami
- Lashkar-i-Jhangvi (LJ)
- Haqqani Network (HQN)

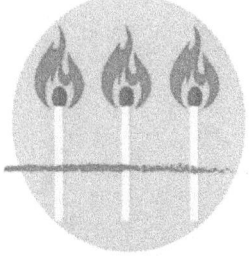

- Al-Qaida in the Arabian Peninsula (AQAP)
- Forces Democratiques De Liberation Du Rwanda (FDLR)

- Abdallah Azzam Brigades (AAB)
- Al Mourabitoun
- Ansar al-Islam
- Ansar al-Shari'a in Tunisia (AAS-T)
- Eastern Turkistan Islamic Movement (ETIM)
- Jemmah Anshorut Tauhid (JAT)
- Mujahidin Indonesian Timur (MIT)

- Ansar Eddine
- Asbat al-Ansar
- The Organization of Al-Qaida in the Islamic Maghreb (AQIM)

- Abu Sayyaf Group
- Harakat ul-Mujahidin (HuM)
- Islamic Jihad Group
- Rajah Solaiman Movement

GTTI Score of Countries

Country	Score
Pakistan	70.5
Afghanistan	44
Syria	22
Lebanon	14
Indonesia	12
Libya	11.5
Nigeria	11.5
Egypt	10
Iraq	10
Chad	10
Somalia	8
Yemen	7.5
Mali	7
Algeria	6.5
Philippines	5.5
Bangladesh	5
Cameroon	4
Democratic Republic of the Congo (DRC)	4
Kenya	4
Saudi Arabia	3
Tunisia	3

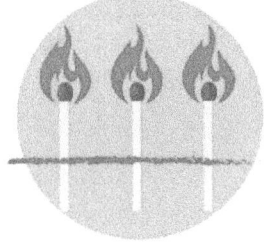

71 | Indicant

GTTI Workings

Terror Group (With Nuclear Risk Marked in red)	Number of Combatants	Number of Combatants (Median)	Product of Combatants and Nuclear Risk	GTTI Scale
Abdallah Azzam Brigades (AAB)	N/A	1000	1000	3
Abu Sayyaf Group	200 – 600	400	400	1
Afghan Taliban	25,000 – 60,000	42500	425000	10
Al Mourabitoun	N/A	1000	1000	3
Al-Nusrah Front for the People of the Levant	5000-14000	9500	95000	9
Al-Qaida	300- 1000	650	6500	5
Al-Qaida in the Arabian Peninsula (AQAP)	1000 – 4000	2500	2500	4
Al-Shabaab	5000 – 9000	7000	70000	8
Ansar al-Islam	N/A	1000	1000	3
Ansar al-Shari'a in Tunisia (AAS-T)	N/A	1000	1000	3
Ansar Eddine	700	700	700	2
Asbat al-Ansar	650	650	650	2
Eastern Turkistan Islamic Movement (ETIM)	500– 1500	1000	1000	3
Forces Democratiques De Liberation Du Rwanda (FDLR)	1500 – 2500	2000	2000	4
Haqqani Network (HQN)	3000-10,000	6500	6500	5
Harakat ul-Mujahidin (HuM)	300	300	300	1
Harakat-ul Jihad Islami	500- 750	625	6250	5
Islamic Jihad Group	100 – 200	150	150	1
Islamic Movement of Uzbekistan	200 – 3000	1600	16000	6
Islamic State of Iraq and the Levant (ISIL)/Daesh	<3000	3000	30000	7
Jaish-i-Mohammed	75000	75000	75000	9
Jama'atu Ahlis Sunna Lidda'awati Wal-Jihad (Boko Haram)	5,000	5000	50000	8
Jamaat-ul-Ahrar (JuA)	N/A	1000	10000	6
Jemaah Islamiyah	500 – 2000	1250	12500	6

Humanity at Risk | 72

Jemmah Anshorut Tauhid (JAT)	1500-2000	1750	1750	3
Lashkar-i-Jhangvi (LJ)	<500	500	5000	5
Lashkar-e-Tayyiba (LeT)	40,000 – 120,000	80000	800,000	10
Mujahidin Indonesian Timur (MIT)	N/A	1000	1000	3
Rajah Solaiman Movement	<100	100	100	1
Tehrik-e-Taliban Pakistan (TTP)	1000	1000	10000	6
The Organization of Al-Qaida in the Islamic Maghreb (AQIM)	300-1000	650	650	2

NOTE: All terror groups which pose a nuclear risk are marked in red.

GTTI Score of Countries

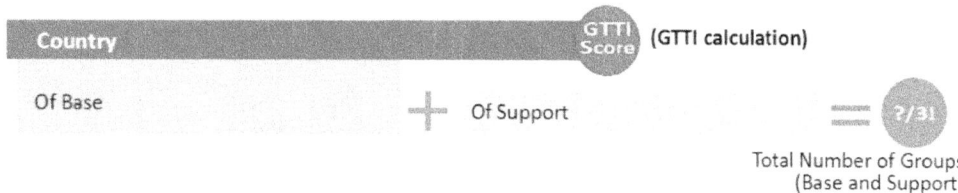

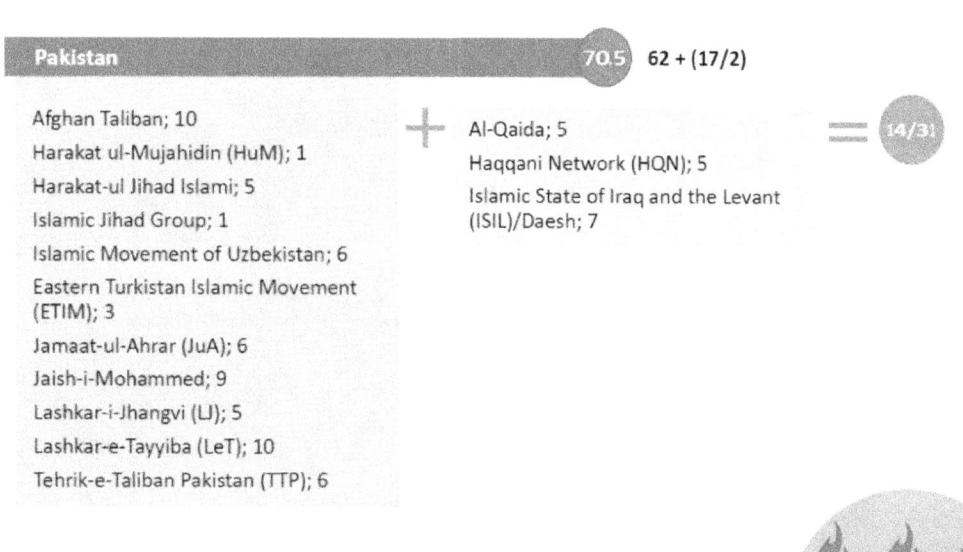

Afghanistan — 44 — 26 + (36/2)

- Al-Qaida; 5
- Haqqani Network (HQN); 5
- Afghan Taliban; 10
- Jamaat-ul-Ahrar (JuA) 6

+

- Lashkar-i-Jhangvi (LJ); 5
- Lashkar-e-Tayyiba (LeT); 10
- Tehreek-e-Taliban Pakistan (TTP); 6
- Harakat ul-Mujahidin (HuM); 1
- Islamic Jihad Group; 1
- Islamic Movement of Uzbekistan; 6
- Islamic State of Iraq and the Levant (ISIL)/Daesh; 7

= 11/31

Syria — 22 — 19 + (6/2)

- Islamic State of Iraq and the Levant (ISIL)/Daesh; 7
- Al-Nusrah Front for the People of the Levant; 9
- Ansar al-Islam; 3

+

- Eastern Turkistan Islamic Movement (ETIM); 3
- Abdallah Azzam Brigades (AAB); 3

= 5/31

Lebanon — 14 — 14

- Asbat al-Ansar; 2
- Abdallah Azzam Brigades (AAB); 3
- Al-Nusrah Front for the People of the Levant; 9

+

= 3/31

Indonesia — 12 — 12

- Jemaah Islamiyah; 6
- Jemmah Anshorut Tauhid (JAT); 3
- Mujahidin Indonesian Timur (MIT); 3

+

= 3/31

Libya — 11.5 — 10 + (3/2)

- Ansar al-Shari'a in Tunisia (AAS-T); 3
- Islamic State of Iraq and the Levant (ISIL)/Daesh; 7

+

- Al Mourabitoun; 3

= 3/31

Nigeria — 11.5 — 8 + (7/2)

- Jama'atu Ahlis Sunna Lidda'awati Wal-Jihad (Boko Haram); 8

+

- Islamic State of Iraq and the Levant (ISIL)/Daesh; 7

= 2/31

Egypt — 10

- Islamic State of Iraq and the Levant (ISIL)/Daesh; 7
- Abdallah Azzam Brigades (AAB); 3

+ = 2/31

Iraq — 10

- Islamic State in Iraq and the Levant (ISIL)/Daesh; 7
- Ansar al-Islam; 3

+ = 2/31

Chad — 8

- Jama'atu Ahlis Sunna Lidda'awati Wal-Jihad (Boko Haram); 8

+ = 1/31

Somalia — 8

- Al-Shabaab; 8

+ = 1/31

Yemen — 7.5 4 + (7/2)

- Al-Qaida in the Arabian Peninsula (AQAP); 4
+ Islamic State of Iraq and the Levant (ISIL)/Daesh ; 7

= 2/31

Mali — 7

- Al Mourabitoun; 3
- Ansar Eddine; 2
- The Organization of Al-Qaida in the Islamic Maghreb(AQIM); 2

+ = 3/31

75 | Indicant

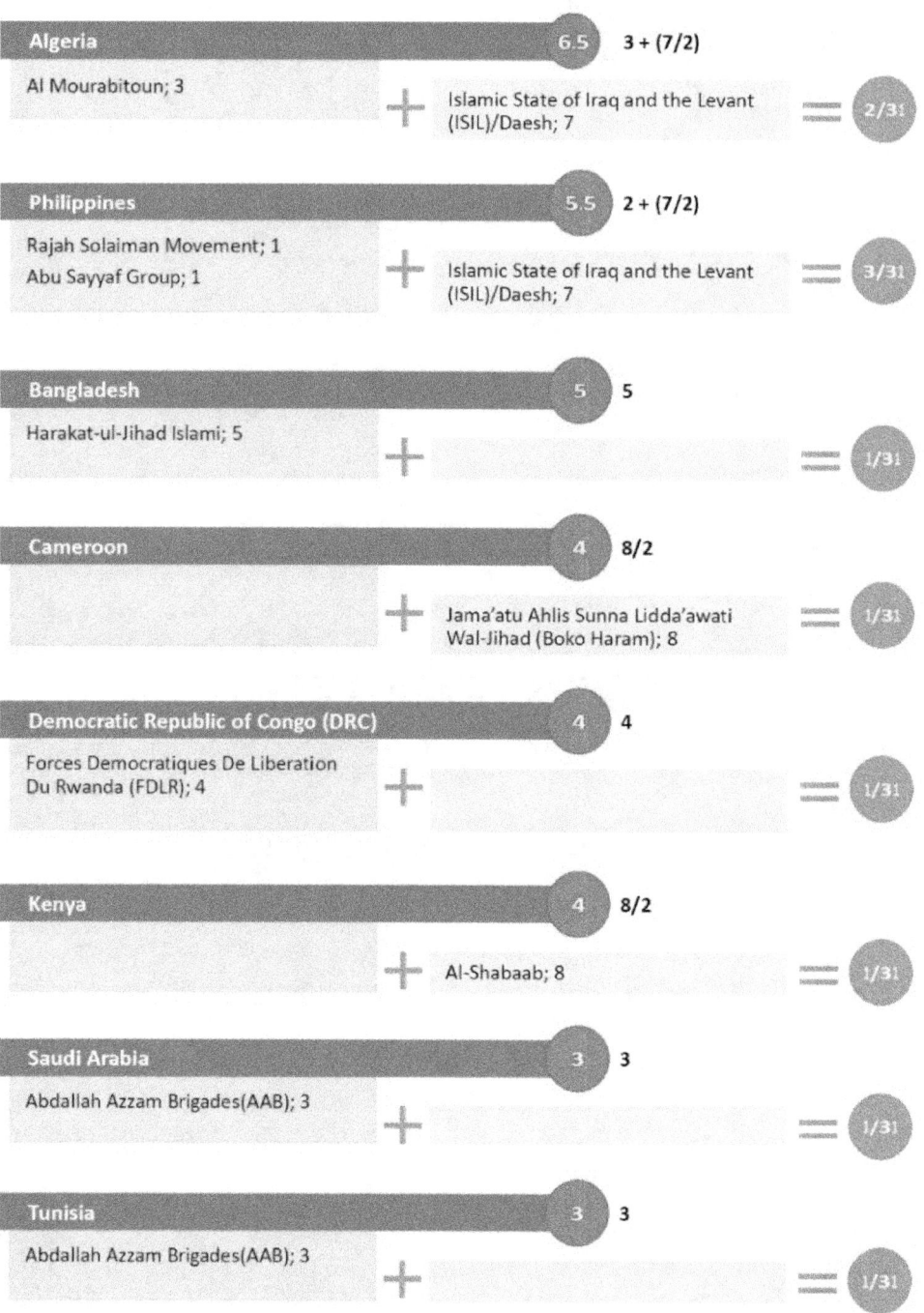

2. Conclusions

The construction of the GTTI Scale helps to understand realities and future threats which are different from the scenario that is portrayed in the mainstream media. The lethality of terrorist groups depends on their combatant strength, support of organised entities aligned with states or criminal networks, and proclivity to acquire weapons of mass destruction. If we follow trend-lines rather than headlines, we find that Lashkar-e-Tayyiba, Taliban, Jaish-i-Mohammed are much greater risk to humanity than ISIL or Daesh at this stage. Indeed, even Al-Nusrah Front and Al-Shabaab are greater threat than Daesh. Nevertheless, greater attention is focussed on Daesh than the groups that can threaten humanity on a large scale.

If we look at the most dangerous terrorist groups, based on hard facts and statistics, we find that Pakistan hosts or aids majority of them. Also, there are a significant number of groups based in Afghanistan, which operate with the support of Pakistan. Thus, Pakistan is responsible for 3 times the terror risk to humanity that Syria poses, or more than 5 times the risk that Libya poses, and 7 times the risk that Iraq poses.

The mainstream media in the world concentrates on the threats that are immediate and closest to Western interests. Therefore, they are obsessed with terrorist groups in the Middle East or the groups that occasionally operate in Europe and America with the help of their networks in the Middle East. The Middle East is of critical importance to Western countries for strategic, historical, religious and economic reasons, and therefore attention given to the terrorist groups in that part of the world is natural. The terrorist groups operating in the areas of higher strategic and economic importance are dangerous, but they have to be realistically compared with terrorist groups operating in areas of less strategic importance and having greater strength in terms of man-power and material support. In the long run, the groups that have the wherewithal to sustain will have an impact on the ability of states to conduct international relations in a civil manner.

In addressing the threat of terrorism states tend to adopt a tactical approach focussing on what they consider is of immediate importance. As we saw in this report, the lines between terrorist groups are dificult to draw, as capital and labour of the terror economy flows from one geography to another. Thus, while the states have disaggregated strategy governed by their individual interests, the terrorist groups have an integrated approach linking them with each other and criminal networks across the world. If states have to succeed in dealing with terrorism, they need to understand how the minds of terrorists work at the micro-level and how the forces of terrorism are globally inter-connected at the macro-level. It is only with comprehensive and holistic understanding of the threat of terrorism that any effective and preventive response strategy will be feasible.

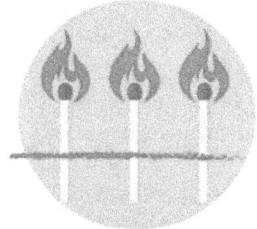

Source: Futehally, Ilmas, et al. "Humanity at Risk: Global Terror Threat Indicant, 2018." Strategicforesight.Com/Publication_pdf/Humanity%20at%20Risk.Pdf, Strategic Foresight Group (SFG) / Centre for the Resolution of Intractable Conflict (CRIC) from the University of Oxford, 2018, www.strategicforesight.com/publication_pdf/Humanity%20at%20Risk.pdf.

The Islamic State's Expanding Affiliate Groups in Africa

While Pakistan is a glorified terrorist factory, the Islamic State has expanded its military presence and territorial gains in Northern Africa and the Sahel (the region of Africa just below the northern countries of the continent) in the past decade. Among the Islamic State's global affiliates, there is now the Islamic State of West Africa (ISWA), Islamic State – Sahel (IS–Sahel), Islamic State Central African Province (ISCAP), Islamic State Mozambique (ISM), the Islamic State Libya Province (IS–LP), Islamic State Somalia Province (ISS), and Islamic State Sinai Province (IS–SP).[390] Each with their own horrifying stories of brutality upon non-Muslim Africans. A Nigerian Bishop, Matthew Hasan Kukah of Soto, reported that nearly 200 Christians were slaughtered in one week back in April 2025 by various Islamic terror groups including ISWA.[391] Christian rights groups reported that around 1,300 Christians were slaughtered by Islamic terrorists between December 2023 – February 2024.[392] On June 13 – 14 in the Yelwata village of Benue State, Nigeria, it was reported by Christian rights groups that around 200 Christians were massacred by Fulani Muslim herdsmen with survivors describing it as a full-on genocidal invasion of a well-armed group to steal their land.[393] Additionally, it was reported that between April 1st, 2025 – June 1st, 2025 that 270 people were slaughtered in total.[394] A Benue NGOs Network estimates that since 2011 the full-scale death toll is likely 5,700 from terrorist violence with 150,000 displaced since that time and the attacks in just June 2025 displaced approximately 6,500 people.[395] This is just one State in Nigeria where Islamic terrorists have been amassing power and territory. The other Islamic State affiliates have conducted similar bloodbaths in other African countries

---

[390] "Global Terrorism Index 2025." Vision of Humanity: IEP's Peace Research, Presentations and Resources, Institute of Economics and Peace, Mar. 2025, www.visionofhumanity.org/wp-content/uploads/2025/03/Global-Terrorism-Index-2025.pdf. For reference: Pages 67 – 70.
[391] Preston, Heather. "Nigerian Bishop Demands Action after 200 Christians Murdered in Week of Violence - Premier Christian News: Headlines, Breaking News, Comment & Analysis." Premier Christian News, Premier Christian News, 22 Apr. 2025, premierchristian.news/us/news/article/nigerian-bishop-demands-action-200-christians-murdered-week-of-violence.
[392] Preston, Heather. "Nigerian Bishop Demands Action after 200 Christians Murdered in Week of Violence - Premier Christian News: Headlines, Breaking News, Comment & Analysis." Premier Christian News, Premier Christian News, 22 Apr. 2025, premierchristian.news/us/news/article/nigerian-bishop-demands-action-200-christians-murdered-week-of-violence.
[393] "Massacre of over 100 Villagers in Christian Area of Nigeria Elicits Response from President." MSN, The Christian Post, 23 June 2025, www.msn.com/en-us/news/world/massacre-of-over-100-villagers-in-christian-area-of-nigeria-elicits-response-from-president/ar-AA1HfeI4.
[394] "Massacre of over 100 Villagers in Christian Area of Nigeria Elicits Response from President." MSN, The Christian Post, 23 June 2025, www.msn.com/en-us/news/world/massacre-of-over-100-villagers-in-christian-area-of-nigeria-elicits-response-from-president/ar-AA1HfeI4.
[395] "Massacre of over 100 Villagers in Christian Area of Nigeria Elicits Response from President." MSN, The Christian Post, 23 June 2025, www.msn.com/en-us/news/world/massacre-of-over-100-villagers-in-christian-area-of-nigeria-elicits-response-from-president/ar-AA1HfeI4.

and the main targets have been almost always been non-Muslims being slaughtered, especially Christians.

Why do we in the US and Western world largely treat this as an African-on-African problem when so many non-Muslim African civilians are suffering from Islamic terrorism and then get mocked for being "backwards" when they have to live in fear and suffering like this with so many of their loved ones being brutally slaughtered by Islamic terrorists? Imagine how many fans of Charles Murray and Sam Harris dismiss these issues in terms of racial inferiority as global Islamic State affiliates continue to amass more territory and power from slaughtering innocent Africans trying to live in peace. Sadly, it is simply a statement of fact to say that the US, China, Russia, and Western powers simply try to find ways into exploiting African people left powerless by Islamic terrorism. This is not to say that we Americans and others genuinely don't try to help sometimes; President Obama sending medical and military personnel to help fight the Ebola outbreak within several countries in West Africa which reduced cases by 80 percent in 2014[396] and President George W. Bush's "U.S. President's Emergency Plan for AIDS Relief" (PEPFAR) program to combat HIV / AIDS in South Africa and other parts of the world is estimated to have saved 25 million people by 2023 after all[397]; but when it comes to business interests in respective countries or the suffering of African civilians, then which do you think our governments will prioritize? The answer is obvious and that's why African countries generally want to remain non-aligned despite all the hardships they go through and help they receive. I don't have all the answers for what can be done, but I hope that this can help somewhat in highlighting the plight of Africans who just want to live in peace and who are constantly living in fear and pain from Islamic terror attacks, while certain smug US scholars and Westerners see fit to use every iota of their pain and suffering to label them as inferior like the Charles Murray and Sam Harris types while conveniently ignoring the Islamic terrorists causing these situations.

Cryptocurrency and AI Censorship Is Creating Third-Generation Islamic Terrorism

The painful truth of the matter is that we are continually losing the War on Terror because the majority of the world refuses to criticize Islam. These so-called Moderate Muslims have done nothing to curb Islamic Terrorism and Muslim Reformers like Maajid Nawaz don't have the statistical evidence to show their path is viable in the long-term. Neither moderate or reformer groups can answer the problem of *bid'ah* in Islamic

---

[396] "The Obama Administration's Ebola Response." National Archives and Records Administration, National Archives and Records Administration, Oct. 2014, obamawhitehouse.archives.gov/ebola-response.
[397] Schreiber, Melody. "George W. Bush's Anti-HIV Program Is Hailed as 'amazing' - and Still Crucial at 20." NPR, NPR, 28 Feb. 2023, www.npr.org/sections/goatsandsoda/2023/02/28/1159415936/george-w-bushs-anti-hiv-program-is-hailed-as-amazing-and-still-crucial-at-20.

theology. The US, Europe, India, and other countries continue to compartmentalize and pretend that Islamic terrorism has no relation to Islamic theology knowing that Muslim lives are being prioritized over non-Muslim lives time after time, while idiotic US Corporations continue to censor "Islamophobia" and what has been the result? Islamic terrorist groups affiliated with the Islamic State have taken advantage of AI Censorship that "moderate" Muslims have demanded and Islamic State affiliates have additionally taken advantage of the general lack of global regulations for Cryptocurrency to create a Digital Caliphate that has already expanded into global appeal for Muslims living in democratic countries. Their main targets are Muslim youths who are instructed and encouraged to commit terrorism through bombmaking or mass shootings to kill as many civilians in non-Muslim majority countries as possible. However, other older Muslims – due to their strong Islamic faith and not social disaffection – are joining in and committing pre-planned terrorism practically anytime that dignitaries of various democratic countries visit each other for trade negotiations. Think of the banality of this; we're living in a world where it's wrong to criticize a theology that encourages people to kill as many innocent people as possible whenever foreign dignitaries visit each other to mutually benefit from trade negotiations. Yet, when any rational person criticizes this as coming from Islam, we're accused of being bigots while everyone else turns a blind eye as Islam continues to kill innocent people. What are we doing here? How much more can any of us take from this double-standard where Muslims' feelings are prioritized above the lives of everyone else?

The Institute of Economics and Peace (IEP) publishes annual Global Terror Indexes and the *Global Terror Index 2025* has explained exactly these problems that mostly democratic countries are facing right now. But first, who are the Institute of Economics and Peace? A summary of who they are from their website's *About Us* page:

> The Institute for Economics & Peace is creating a paradigm shift in the way the world thinks about peace. We are doing this by delivering research, consulting and training, unlocking the power of peace across all three.
>
> Research remains central to our mission, driven by a dedicated team developing global and national indices, calculating the economic cost of violence, analysing country level risk and fragility, and understanding Positive Peace. Our research is relied upon by governments, academic institutions, think tanks, non-governmental organisations and by intergovernmental institutions such as the OECD, The Commonwealth Secretariat, the World Bank and the United Nations.
>
> Our suite of reports, including the Global Peace Index, Global Terrorism Index and Ecological Threat Report, remain critical for stakeholders everywhere. Central to our ethos is the understanding that peace extends beyond the mere absence of conflict. Our Pillars of Peace framework identifies eight critical factors for establishing enduring peace, based on extensive data analysis.
>
> Established in 2007 by Steve Killelea AM, IEP has significantly influenced global narratives on matters of security, defence, terrorism and development. Headquartered in Sydney, since 2007 IEP has developed into a global operation, with regional offices in New York, Brussels, The Hague, Mexico City, and Nairobi, working on outreach, education and partnership development.

IEP research regularly features in leading international media publications including the New York Times, The Guardian, The Economist, Deutsche Welle, Washington Post, CNN, and the BBC. IEP works alongside a range of multilateral partners, from the United Nations and the World Bank, to the Lloyds foundation, the Australia Department of Foreign Affairs (DFAT), and many others.[398]

Vision of Humanity, a subgroup of IEP's peace initiatives, publishes the annual Global Terror Indexes and the most recent *Global Terror Index 2025* has explained the formation of a digital caliphate ecosystem and the encouragement of jihadism to Muslim youths in democratic countries from the successful propaganda efforts of the Islamic State Khorasan Province (ISK / ISKP) that utilize AI technology and fund themselves through unregulated Cryptocurrency markets created from their successful jihadist blockchain initiatives. Page 70 of the *Global Terror Index 2025* provides more information on ISK / ISKP including some of their stunning success in promoting Islamic terrorism across multiple countries through successful terrorist propaganda efforts:

> ISLAMIC STATE KHORASAN PROVINCE
> Islamic State – Khorasan Province (ISK), also known as ISKP, is a regional affiliate of IS operating primarily in Afghanistan, Pakistan, Iran and parts of Central Asia. Formed in 2015, ISK pledged allegiance to IS's central leadership and aims to establish an Islamic caliphate in the historical region of Khorasan, which includes parts of modern-day Iran, Afghanistan and Central Asia.
>
> ISK has become one of the most active jihadist groups internationally in recent years. Since its formation, it has carried out numerous attacks beyond its bases in Afghanistan. In 2024, the group was responsible for two of the year's deadliest terrorist incidents: the January attack in Kerman, Iran, which killed at least 95 people, and the March attack in Moscow, Russia, which resulted in at least 144 deaths.70
>
> Since its inception, ISK has been linked to 634 attacks and 3,212 deaths. Recent activity has targeted the Russia and Eurasia region, with incidents rising from 11 in 2023 to 18 in 2024. Although the number of attacks remains lower than in sub-Saharan Africa, deaths attributed to the group increased from four to 199 during the same period.
>
> The threat of jihadism in Afghanistan and surrounding countries has been limited until recently. Since the various political and military upheavals that have impacted the region in the years since 2021, radical jihadism had persisted as a security concern until then but had remained a marginal issue, affecting only a small segment of the socio-political landscape.71
>
> The departure of Bashar al-Assad from Syria in December 2024, coupled with the change of power in Afghanistan in 2021, has reshaped the regional security landscape. At the same time, a surge in international attacks and foiled plots linked to ISK has underscored the group's growing transnational threat. This subsection examines ISK's expanding influence and reassesses the broader jihadist threat both in the region and globally.[399]

---

[398] "About Institute for Economics and Peace." Institute for Economics & Peace, Institute for Economics & Peace, 2025, www.economicsandpeace.org/about/.

[399] "Global Terrorism Index 2025." Vision of Humanity: IEP's Peace Research, Presentations and Resources, Institute of Economics and Peace, Mar. 2025, www.visionofhumanity.org/wp-content/uploads/2025/03/Global-Terrorism-Index-2025.pdf. For reference: Page 70.

Page 72 of the Global Terror Index 2025 explains the disturbing success of ISK / ISKP's dark money blockchain initiatives with sustained financial backing through cryptocurrency from their efforts in international Muslim outreach to support Islamic terrorism and how this is financing their growing military force in the regions of Afghanistan, Tajikistan, and Uzbekistan:

> ISK relies on financial networks to sustain its operations, with an estimated $2.5 million in funding accessed through blockchain transactions in 2023.105 In 2024, the group's membership in the region was estimated to be between one and six thousand, with a strong presence near Tajikistan's southern border provinces, including Badakhshan, Kunduz and Takhar.106 ISK continues to attract returning fighters from Syria and Iraq, with recruitment efforts bolstered by the Islamic Movement of Uzbekistan. ISK's multilingual media strategy uses Pashto, Dari, Arabic, Urdu, Farsi, Uzbek, Tajik, English, and more recently, Russian and Turkish, to target youth and marginalised groups through platforms such as Telegram and Al-Azaim.107[400]

A subgroup of IEP's Vision of Humanity known as *Tech Against Terrorism* provided an article titled *"Islamic State Khurasan Province's International Expansion and Growing Online Activities"* on pages 77 – 80 of the *Global Terror Index 2025* which can be read as follows alongside their credentials. Please seriously think about everything you read below:

Islamic State Khurasan Province's International Expansion and Growing Online Activities

Tech Against Terrorism Analysis

Lucas Webber, Senior Threat Intelligence Analyst, Tech Against Terrorism

Cat Cadenhead, Junior Research and Project Officer, Tech Against Terrorism

The implications are clear: ISKP's sophisticated online strategy directly enables its militant and external operations, resulting in more attacks across a wider geographical area. Given the group's dispersed and highly covert nature, traditional military measures alone are insufficient to neutralise the threat. Consequently, it is paramount that governments, organisations, tech platforms, financial institutions, and other private industry entities develop and implement a coordinated approach to countering and degrading ISKP's online infrastructure and operational capacity. Tech Against Terrorism urges tech platforms to increase efforts to monitor and remove terrorist content, with regulators needing stronger powers to enforce accountability.6 Action taken to remove and suppress ISKP's online content is just as important as kinetic military action.

Use of the Internet to Project Power at a Regional Level

ISKP has leveraged the internet as a primary instrument for amplifying the projection of power beyond its territorial area of operations and shaping regional perceptions of its strength and influence.7 Since the Taliban's takeover of Afghanistan in August 2021, the group has

---

[400] "Global Terrorism Index 2025." Vision of Humanity: IEP's Peace Research, Presentations and Resources, Institute of Economics and Peace, Mar. 2025, www.visionofhumanity.org/wp-content/uploads/2025/03/Global-Terrorism-Index-2025.pdf. For reference: Page 72.

increasingly relied on its online presence to maintain strategic relevance while facing intensified counterterrorism raids. Through sophisticated media operations and digital propaganda, ISKP has exaggerated its apparent operational capabilities and created a discrepancy between its perceived and actual strength. This digital strategy serves multiple purposes: it helps to attract potential recruits, maintains psychological pressure on adversaries, and advances the group's broader goal of regional expansion. ISKP also uses dedicated propaganda channels, including magazines and encrypted messaging channels, to maintain active crowdfunding campaigns using Monero, a privacy-based cryptocurrency and money transfers via TRC20 tokens.8

Central to this outreach effort is the Al-Azaim Foundation for Media Production, which emerged from an ecosystem of competing but aligned pro-IS propaganda outlets to become the chief media organ used by ISKP. While initially focused narrowly on religious discourse, Al-Azaim has evolved in parallel with ISKP's growing regional ambitions to become a sophisticated multimedia platform addressing religious, political, social, and military issues at both regional and global levels. ISKP's outreach and propaganda campaigns exploit the dynamics of regional conflict and militant infrastructures by fusing local grievances with its global agenda. Al-Azaim's linguistic reach is particularly notable, with content produced in a lengthening list of languages, including Pashto, Dari, Arabic, Urdu, Farsi, Uzbek, Tajik, English, and more recently, Russian and Turkish. This versatility enables ISKP to craft culturally resonant messages for diverse audiences across South Asia, Central Asia, and beyond.9 Tech Against Terrorism has observed that, in recent campaigns, Al-Azaim and aligned outlets have intensified regional outreach, producing content that ranges from high quality online magazines to AI generated video content. Notable examples include a pro-ISKP AI video news program in Pashto called "Khurasan TV" and the flagship English language Voice of Khurasan magazine. This high volume of propaganda output in local and regional languages, with customised messaging and narratives to appeal to specifically identified ethnolinguistic target audience segments, has resulted in a growth of influence and support throughout South and Central Asia.10 By maintaining consistent messaging across multiple platforms and languages, Al-Azaim has enabled ISKP to project an image of organisational strength and operational capability that often exceeds its true extent. These communication networks, which imply an extensive organisation thereafter, supply the infrastructure for achieving strategic objectives which typically require substantial territorial control or military capability.

The success of this strategy manifests most importantly in ISKP's ability to inspire, coordinate, and conduct attacks against foreign nationals across the region. ISKP propaganda explicitly advocates targeted attacks against Chinese, Russian, and Central Asian nationals as retaliation for the perceived anti-Muslim policies enacted by such nationals' home countries.11 Issues such as China's treatment of Uyghurs and Russia's actions in the Caucasus are frequently emphasised by way of justification. This selective but comprehensive targeting serves multiple strategic objectives. A primary objective of attacks on foreign nationals is to undermine the Taliban's authority by demonstrating their inability to provide security for foreign investments and diplomatic personnel in Afghanistan. A second objective is to provoke international reactions that could destabilize diplomatic and economic relationships across the region. A third objective is to capitalise on existing regional tensions for the purpose of creating conditions of instability that ISKP believes could facilitate territorial expansion.

ISKP appears to have been successful in advancing these strategic objectives. Since the withdrawal of NATO forces from Afghanistan in July 2021, ISKP has steadily escalated its campaign of violence against foreign nationals. Significantly, in August 2021, a suicide bombing at the Kabul airport's Abbey Gate killed American soldiers and scores of other bystanders.12 The same day, two Pakistani nationals possessing an explosive device were detained in the vicinity of the Turkmenistan embassy. In September 2022, the Al-Azaim Foundation issued threats of further attacks on diplomatic targets in Afghanistan, specifically naming those from China, Iran, and India. On January 11, 2023, these threats materialsed with a suicide bombing targeting a Chinese diplomatic delegation at the Afghan Foreign Ministry in Kabul.13 Most recently, on January 22, 2025, ISKP fatally shot a Chinese national and mine worker in Afghanistan's Takhar province, near the border with Tajikistan.14 These attacks have undermined the Taliban's ability to attract foreign direct investment and economic development projects. The Chinese government, for instance, has increased pressure on the Taliban to better secure its citizens and interests in Afghanistan.15 The cumulative effect has been a deterioration of regional stability, with affected nations adopting increasingly aggressive security postures while reducing diplomatic and economic engagement with Afghanistan. This has created precisely the conditions of isolation and instability that ISKP seeks to exploit, while also serving to make the group appear successful and more dangerous.

Use of the Internet to Project Power at an International Level

In the past four years, ISKP has transformed from a militant group with a regional focus into an organisation with expansive international capabilities, largely driven by its sophisticated exploitation of digital platforms.16 A pivotal factor in this transformation is Al-Azaim's multilingual propaganda campaign, which strategically targets the growing Afghan and Central Asian diasporas in Europe and North America. By extending its reach beyond Asia, ISKP strengthens its sphere of influence, widening its support base far beyond its regional origins.

A milestone in Al-Azaim's expansion was the launch of its English-language magazine, Voice of Khurasan, in January 2022. This publication has attracted contributors from diverse backgrounds, including those from Canada, Australia, Italy, and Tajikistan, reflecting ISKP's successful extraterritorial expansion of its ideological appeal. Al-Azaim has further strengthened its media presence through strategic partnerships with other pro-IS media entities. A significant development was its collaboration with Fursan al-Tarjuma, an umbrella organisation established in March 2023 that coordinates at least 14 pro-IS media groups. Additionally, Al-Azaim has partnered with the I'lam Foundation archive, which serves as a key source of translated official IS content for supporter networks both within and outside the EU, available on the surface and dark web. These strategic media partnerships significantly amplify ISKP's reach by increasing the accessibility and visibility of its propaganda. By making content easier to find and available in multiple languages, Al-Azaim enhances ISKP's potential to radicalise supporters across multiple continents, further solidifying its global influence.

ISKP has also considerably intensified the online incitement of its supporters to carry out violence abroad. The first escalation in this incitement campaign was prompted by events that took place in Stockholm, Sweden, on January 21, 2023, when Rasmus Paludan, the leader of the far-right Danish party "Hard Line", stood in front of the Turkish embassy and burnt a copy of the Quran on video. By way of response, ISKP, in its Pashto language Khurasan Ghag magazine, devoted several pages to issuing threats and calling for attacks against targets in Sweden and, in general, against European citizens wherever they could be found.17 This campaign of incitement intensified further following the October 7, 2023, Hamas attack on Israel: ISKP moved quickly and aggressively to capitalise on hostile sentiments stirred up throughout the Muslim world as a result of the ensuing protracted conflict in Gaza. ISKP created a high volume of propaganda criticising, threatening, and urging attacks against Israeli targets as well as against Western states that support Israel. In its Voice of Khurasan magazine, for instance, ISKP published an English translation of an editorial from IS's official al-Naba newsletter that urged its supporters to participate in its post-October 7 propaganda campaign.18 In addition, it encouraged supporters to carry out attacks against Jewish neighbourhoods in America and Europe and on Israeli and Western embassies, synagogues, and Israeli economic interests globally. In the same issue, Al-Azaim included instructions in a full-page infographic titled "Practical Ways to Confront the Jews" which called upon supporters to kill Jews wherever they could be found, participate in IS' anti-Jewish propaganda campaign and conduct cyberattacks on websites affiliated with Jews.19 ISKP suggested that supporters choose weapons such as Molotov cocktails, crossbows, guns acquired on the black market, pipe guns, nail guns, vehicles, and knives.

ISKP and aligned pro-IS outlets launched a similarly intense incitement campaign after the Crocus City Hall raid in Moscow, Russia on 22 March 2024. This campaign emphasised specific countries and targets which should be attacked and additionally provided tactical advice and options for relevant weaponry. In an issue of Voice of Khurasan magazine, it featured a full-page image of an ISKP jihadist wearing camouflage with a rifle and box of explosives on a train with a sign behind him saying "Welcome to Europe" accompanied by the text "Last call before exit." The post-Moscow campaign mostly focused on large sporting events.20 This particular escalation in ISKP's event-driven incitement campaign is marked by increasingly specific tactical guidance and target selection. Furthermore, it represents an evolution in the group's approach to inspiring attacks abroad and demonstrates the increasing sophistication of its ability to exploit global events and mobilise violence against both traditional and emerging target sets.

ISKP has poured considerable resources into building up its external operations and guided plot capabilities. This increased resourcing is evident in the rise in international plots in 2024 when compared to the previous year. Notably, many of these plots were hybrid operations, whereby followers were not directly trained and deployed by ISKP but instead received remote instruction in tactics, target selection, and weapons procurement from official ISKP members by means of online platforms.21 This is a clear practical application of the system that the group has developed whereby selected "officials" of ISKP provide online advice and support to followers willing to carry out attacks abroad. This support involves the provision of DIY manuals on making IEDs, detonators, craft-made suppressors, and drone-use. ISKP instructors are readily available to answer the plotters' questions and coach them on operational security practices and more.

These developments highlight how ISKP has effectively leveraged online platforms to transform its ability to project power internationally. The group's sophisticated use of digital infrastructure has enabled it to spread its propaganda beyond Asia, radicalising and mobilising new communities across diverse geographical regions. This expansion has affected a striking collateral shift in ISKP's operational methodology, as the group can now establish and coordinate operational cells across multiple continents simultaneously and remotely by providing online guidance. The shift to enhance digital operations serves as a significant force multiplier, enabling ISKP to reach previously inaccessible audiences with targeted messaging while providing operational guidance without physical presence.

A testament to the effectiveness of this approach is the marked diversification in the backgrounds of those implicated in ISKP-related activities abroad. Historically, international plots were primarily associated with Central Asians and predominantly Tajiks.22 This resulted from an intentional decision by ISKP to appeal to a wider Central Asian audience in order to expand its influence and recruitment within and beyond Afghanistan's borders. However, in the latter half of 2023, this diversification accelerated, with the national and ethnic backgrounds of those involved in ISKP-related operations broadening noticeably. The group's success in increasing their appeal to a broader range of Central Asian backgrounds was illustrated in July 2023, when coordinated law enforcement operations in Germany and the Netherlands resulted in the arrest of individuals from Tajik, Turkmen, and Kyrgyz backgrounds.23 Arrests which took place in early 2024 showed a yet wider range of nationalities involved in ISKP plots. In January 2024, Austrian authorities disrupted an ISKP cell in Vienna comprising individuals of Chechen and Bosnian descent, suggesting a successful expansion of the group's influence into the Caucasus and Balkan regions.24 Similarly, February 2024 saw Turkish authorities dismantle a network comprising Russian, Uzbek, Kyrgyz, Azerbaijani, and Sudanese nationals and in March 2024, German police arrested two ISKP-linked Afghan nationals accused of plotting an attack on the Swedish parliament.25,26 These arrests underscore the group's expanding global appeal and the effectiveness of its growing propaganda efforts. The implications of this evolution are significant for counterterrorism efforts. ISKP's sophisticated digital infrastructure enables it to provide detailed operational guidance while bypassing traditional counterterrorism measures focused on physical movement and training camps. The group's demonstrated ability to recruit across diverse nationalities, incite violence, and establish operational networks from Central Asia to North America underscores how online platforms have fundamentally transformed the nature of the threat landscape.27

Conclusion

ISKP's strategic exploitation of digital platforms, including social media, messaging, file-sharing platforms, and archiving sites, has enabled it to overcome traditional limitations of territorial control and physical presence, creating a dynamic, multi-vector threat with expanding international capabilities. The group's distinctive multilingual propaganda strategy, spearheaded by the Al-Azaim Foundation, represents a form of "digital caliphate" that in some aspects rivals IS's multilingual online presence during the height of the caliphate era and has enabled it to simultaneously pursue regional destabilisation and global operational reach in ways that set it apart from other IS branches. Tech Against Terrorism's analysis shows this dual-track approach has yielded significant results. Regionally, ISKP has successfully executed high-profile attacks against foreign interests in Afghanistan and Pakistan while using targeted propaganda in local languages to exploit regional grievances. Globally, the group has demonstrated its expanded reach through devastating attacks in Iran, Türkiye, and Russia in 2024 while establishing operational networks extending into North America and Europe. Its propaganda now provides increasingly specific tactical guidance, transforming online platforms into operational planning tools. By remotely guiding operatives, ISKP can now coordinate attacks across multiple continents without physical training infrastructure. The group's capacity is likely to increase as it grows its influence to reach a broader range of ethno-linguistic elements from Afghanistan, Central Asia, the Caucasus, and elsewhere situated in the West, providing ISKP with additional opportunities for recruitment and operational planning. This threat is increasingly difficult for intelligence and law enforcement agencies to detect, monitor, and disrupt. However, this also creates an opportunity to place greater focus on the online communications space where much of this activity is concentrated and planned. Given ISKP's strategic de-emphasizing of territorial conquest, its sophisticated digital strategy, and demonstrated ability to inspire and coordinate attacks globally, traditional military measures alone are insufficient to counter its evolving threat. A more comprehensive approach is essential - one that prioritizes enhanced online counterterrorism efforts, disruption of ISKP's digital ecosystem, and targeted counter-radicalisation messaging to undermine its ideological appeal.28 The mere existence of ISKP's propaganda online represents a strategic victory given the digitalisation of militant warfare. Tech Against Terrorism continues to stress that information warfare is just as important as traditional military means in combating ISKP.29 Accordingly, it is paramount that governments, organizations, and the private sector work together to remove and suppress ISKP's online content. Only through such a multifaceted strategy can the international community effectively mitigate ISKP's growing influence and prevent future attacks.[401]

Unfortunately, Tech Against Terrorism's solutions of banning Islamic terrorist propaganda as a form of censorship is absolutely never going to work. They seemingly missed the obvious: Banning the content only makes Youth Recruitment far more likely to happen as the Muslim youths will perceive themselves as an aggrieved minority and believe the people censoring Islamic terrorist content are trying to "hide the truth" of Islam. Moreover, Islamic propaganda on this scale is why the so-called moderate Muslims are actively harmful by shutting down any criticisms of Islam in democratic societies. The reason people living in democracies continue to allow this nonsense to go on is because other religious people don't want to break the social taboo of Religious Tolerance so that their religious beliefs are not criticized too. Right-wing religious people

---

[401] "Global Terrorism Index 2025." Vision of Humanity: IEP's Peace Research, Presentations and Resources, Institute of Economics and Peace, Mar. 2025, www.visionofhumanity.org/wp-content/uploads/2025/03/Global-Terrorism-Index-2025.pdf. For Reference: Pages 77 – 80 of the findings.

misperceive the reason Left-leaning religious people shout Islamophobia; it's actually borne from selfishness, because they know that if Islam is allowed to be criticized then all other religious beliefs become open to criticism in society. There won't be a special exception for Islam as some right-leaning groups seem to believe, because that would constitute genuine discrimination and double-standards imposed upon Muslims. The problem, as I honestly see it, is that if we continue to ban any criticisms of Islam by conflating it with hatred of Muslims, then we are all genuinely going to die as the problems continually increase to the extent that we'll never be able to stop them. We will forever have to live with Islamic terror bombings and mass shootings as if they're seasonal weather patterns just like India suffers from it now. Abrahamic mythology from the 7th century is treated with privilege, while the lives of people living here and now are treated as expendable.

If we continue refusing to criticize Islam, they are going to win. The US government has tried wiretapping, NSA mass surveillance, two occupational wars, off-shore torture prisons like GITMO, drone bombings of seven different countries, and financial backing of Islamist groups that aren't chiefly anti-American. Where has it gotten us? What have we achieved? Islamic terrorism continues unabated like a hydra, because we're not focusing on the real problem: it's coming from Islamic theology itself. All of the information I shared in this chapter was part of the reason why I wrote my book, *Machiavellian Ahimsa*, earlier this year in 2025. That is my suggestion to end this problem. I propose a strategic means of using Free Speech offensively instead of defensively as a form of psychological warfare to eradicate Islamic terrorism borne from Islamism once and for all. We should not be privileging mythology over real human lives and that's exactly what these so-called experts have been doing by pretending Islamic terrorism isn't coming from Islam itself. Freedom of Speech is Freedom of Conscience, Freedom of Speech is intrinsically non-violent, and Free Speech is the only real solution to ending Islamic terrorism by de-converting Muslims away from the barbaric, violent faith of the warlord known as the Prophet Mohammad.

Chapter VIII: The Partition of Free Speech

Shashi Tharoor: We were talking before coming in, I told you this anecdote, a true one, about ten years ago from India, when a Bangalore newspaper in the Sunday magazine section published a short story called Muhammad the Idiot, which was about a retarded boy called Muhammad.

Of course, the title was enough to inflate a mob of very, very angry people who stormed the newspaper, trashed the officers, broke up the press.

I have to tell you that very many fans of Indian democracy and freedom of speech didn't actually have much sympathy for the newspaper. It was they really ought to have known better, was they attitude, and indeed the newspaper abjectly apologized the next day, and I believe the author of that headline has not worked in the paper since.

So, the problem here is, I'm afraid, one of what do you think in your society and the social circumstances in which you're functioning, you can reasonably do without provoking a serious law and order problem.

Joan Bakewell: So, in that case, it would be when Christopher didn't come in the moment, the issue there is one of bad editing, because the author...

Shashi Tharoor: It may have been the author's original title, I have no idea.

Joan Bakewell: No, but I mean, should it not have been noted by the editor, publisher, et cetera, at that point, that the very phrase itself, which was not intrinsic to the story, was going to be problematic.

Shashi Tharoor: It should have been. It should have been. It's easy enough to say that if something provokes a mob to be to violence, it's the mob that ought to be punished or prosecuted for violating the law and being violent. But then you get into the whole question of whether a certain offense was so grievous as to serve as a sort of extenuation for the outrage expressed by the mob. We've seen this in the Satanic Loses debate too.

Joan Bakewell: Christopher?

Christopher Hitchens:

Fire.

Fire.

Shashi Tharoor: Well, you know he's saying it falsely, don't you?

Christopher Hitchens:

No, two points about that. One is...

Shashi Tharoor: The only fire is in the two cigarettes.

Christopher Hitchens: How do you know? You could be just as liable to start a panic if there was a fire by shouting fire, as you could. In fact, more likely than you would be liable to start a panic if there was not, as I think I've just demonstrated.

Justice Holmes, his famous judgment, it seems to me, is one of the stupidest remarks ever made from the bench of the United States Supreme Court.

And by the way, he made it in the following context, a group of Yiddish-speaking socialists who were opposed to Mr. Wilson's first World War, America's participation in the imperial bloodbath, gave out leaflets in Yiddish in New York saying, don't sign up for the war, don't believe in it, you're being led into a disaster.

They were put in prison for life, for producing leaflets in Yiddish, making a socialist case against the war. And the bloody fool, Wendell Holmes had the nerve to say it was the equivalent of shouting fire in a crowded theater where there was no fire.

Of course there was a fire. There was a bloodbath on the Western Front. That's a fire, enough for anybody. So... You shouldn't have used such a bullshit example.

Shashi Tharoor: Oh, all right.

Joan Bakewell: All right. Okay.

Shashi Tharoor: Let me rephrase it. You're right to wave your fist if it stops just short on my face. How about that?

Christopher Hitchens: Well, the second thing is there was – Mr. Lincoln once said, just as I would not be slaves, so I would not be a master,

I don't claim the right not to be censored. Just. I claim the right not to be a censor.

I insist on this. The beliefs of the religious are very offensive to me. When I have to read in the newspapers that if I don't accept a bogus story, about a supposed human sacrifice that took place in Jerusalem in something like AD 33, if I don't accept this, I'm going to hell.

If I don't accept this wonderful offer, I'm extremely offended. I think of all the cruelty and violence and misery and stupidity that's been inflicted by that. I do not go and burn down the nearest Baptist or Catholic Church. I'd be ashamed of myself if I did. I don't call for the order for mobs to vindicate my hurt feelings. I don't do it.

The Archangel Gabriel never said a word to the peasant Muhammad. Not a word. The event as described did not take place. I feel quite certain in saying so. Any more than the Archangel Gabriel announced himself to the non-Virgin Mary.

I find it repellent to have to hear of people and the way they're treated who live under systems where that stuff is believed. It couldn't be more offensive to me. Who is ever going to say, well, if you're feeling so hurt, Christopher, you're perfectly entitled to go burn down a newspaper or a house of worship. How contemptible can you possibly go?

Joan Bakewell: I want to take up this very point which is the nature of offence. That something that gives offence is seen to legitimise violence. And the classic case that we're familiar with – all of us – is of the cartoons in the Danish Newspaper which appeared in the September and only by December of that year in Denmark have caused trouble across the world.

50 countries reproduce these cartoons so that we all knew what we were talking about. But ambassadors were withdrawn from Copenhagen and embassies around the world. Danish embassies were attacked and many people died because of cartoons. Can one just say, are a set of not very sophisticated cartoons worth a whole set of lives, Christopher?

Christopher Hitchens: Well, the principle certainly is, but here's what you have to understand. A picture, if you will, I suppose you are a sensitive person wishing to live in a multicultural universe. And you think, well, I'll go out of my way if I have to. I'll bend over backwards not to do anything that will needlessly inflame a Muslim person. Suppose that was your wish, your desire.

How could you possibly have known, if you've made that resolution, that some caricatures actually published in an afternoon paper in Copenhagen would lead to an international pogrom against a small Northern European democracy? With its diplomatic immunity violated, its embassies burned. The embassies of the democracy burned, I mean to say, by mobs in the capital cities of dictatorships like Libya and Syria where demonstrations are not normally allowed, but suddenly the police don't show up, where people who look Scandinavian are attacked, where anyone who is Scandinavian is condemned and subjected to a boycott, a racist boycott in fact, from Pakistan to Indonesia, where violence and intimidation are used against the press, where embassies of Muslim, supposedly Muslim countries call upon the Prime Minister of Denmark to tell him what he's not legally allowed to do, that he must censor his own press, which is not in his ability to do.

And where threats, in other words, are brought by the heads of states, who claim to speak for Islam. Now, I don't know any Muslim who thinks that the ambassador of Egypt or Libya or Algeria speaks for Islam. There's no reason to think that these ramshackle dictatorships have any such right. The Prime Minister of Denmark certainly has no right to intervene in what was published in the press in Denmark. It's one of the most extraordinary cases of intimidation, and this against the country that diverts a sizable part of its budget to helping the Palestinian Authority, to sending peacekeepers and humanitarian workers to the Arab world, that have done its best to accommodate Muslim immigrants, that doesn't have an imperial past, that didn't invade Vietnam or bomb Hiroshima or any of the usual crap that you hear.

No, it means that whatever you do, they will find a reason to take offense. And when they've done that, they think it's an axiomatic right to go straight to violence, of the most criminal kind, including, you represent the United Nations here, shall we, if I haven't seen? Violations of diplomatic immunity, one of the most precious gains of human civilization.

No, one has to oppose this 100%. It is intolerable, insufferable. It's enough concessions already that have been made. Has to stop now.

Joan Bakewell: Shashi, you cited the example of the story, Muhammad the Idiot, as requiring a nuanced intersection by editors, publishers, and so on, because it was clear that that was going to offend, and trouble could be avoided by shrewd, perhaps cowardly, even Christopher might say, editing.

Does that apply to his caricatures in the Danish press? Do you think the burden was on the editor not to publish?

Shashi Tharoor: Absolutely. Well, before I say that, let me say that I actually agree with the latter part of Christopher's observations that nothing can justify or condone the behavior, the violations of the diplomatic immunity; indeed, the colossal destruction to people and property that followed. But there is very little doubt in my mind that the entire exercise was designed to inflame.

The editors actually sought caricatures of Muhammad. They wrote to the Danish Cartoonist Association, a majority of the cartoonists turned down their invitation to do caricatures of Muhammad. And one of the 12 who responded did so by drawing a cartoon, not of Muhammad the Prophet, but of a named schoolboy in a Danish school called Muhammad, who wrote on a blackboard. This is the caricature. The editors of this paper are reactionary provocateurs. That was – one of the 12 cartoons actually said that.

Christopher Hitchens: Not bad.

Shashi Tharoor: And when they published it, the editors added their own notes to the cartoon, saying this cartoonist is a coward who does not understand the menace opposed to our society by Muslim fundamentalism, or towards that effect on the cartoon.

So, in other words, they knew perfectly well what they were doing. Now as I say, that doesn't excuse the misbehavior of those who attacked people and property and all of that. But it does say that when you know you're going to create offense, you have to ask yourself why you're doing this. Perhaps you're going to predict every single one, every single detail of the consequences. But that there would be consequences. I think there could have been a no doubt about.

I mean, Christopher and I are both friends of Salman Rushdie, and we certainly know that what he went through, no one should have to go through. And of course, one of his translators was killed and all of that. But the fact that Muslims took as much offense as they did to the depictions of a fictionalized version of the Prophet in this novel, a novel which in many other ways, and perhaps not to Christopher's faith, is actually an amazing affirmation of mystical belief towards the end of the novel. If such a novel could cause that kind of offense and lead to the consequences it did, it's extremely difficult to believe the editors of this newspaper didn't have an inkling of what they were stirring up. And this is a newspaper by the way, which had a record in the 1930s of publishing anti-Semitic articles. They have in circulation over the years.

Christopher Hitchens: They have a right to publish anti-Semitic articles. And publishing anti-Christian cartoons. What was said about the Danish cartoons is exactly what was said about Salman when he published the novel. You must remember. People said, ah ha, darkly, that's it. He knew what he was doing.

Hugh Trevor Roper said he should be beaten up and kicked around in the street by Pakistani gangs because he hoped to bring on a response. Well, of course he wrote a novel using Holy Writ for literary purposes. Knowing that, that might upset some people. He thought it was about time to open this discussion in the Muslim world. And many Muslim intellectuals sided with him. But straight away, immediate resort to violence and intimidation, not just the threat of murder, but murder itself.

This – it doesn't matter to me if these people believe this, if they say, for example, we don't represent our prophet in figure. Or indeed, almost a human figure, itself in figure. Because we fear idolatry. That's good. It's much better than having pictures of weeping virgins or statues of them that may be led to weep if you've put enough pigs blood on it and put a candle nearby, the endless fraudulance of Christianity.

Fine. That's their belief. But they can't tell me I can't talk about the prophet Muhammad. They absolutely cannot do that.

Shashi Tharoor: But this is where I go back to your earlier comment about you're choosing not to be offended by other people's religious beliefs when you don't have any. I mean, part of the problem I think in our world is our failure sometimes to realize that other people aren't necessarily like us. In other words, that there are societies in different stages of cultural consciousness or sophistication. Not everyone is a Christopher Hitchens. And if there are people in sufficient number who are literalist in their beliefs and therefore will feel grievously wounded.

I mean, if for them, an offense to the Virgin Mary or more likely an offensive prophet Muhammad is equivalent to a sexual assault on their mother or their sister or their wife or whatever, and they react accordingly, I'm afraid to some degree they ought to be pitied because that's a level of reaction that you would not be capable of. But since they do react that way, should we not, as people producing that which is going to cause this reaction, be conscious that it might.

I mean, on the Satanic verses, I remember at the time an argument with an Indian Muslim who was a government official, but not at that point involved in any of the decisions on the books he was speaking, not for the government but in the social conversation. When I said, and this is outrageous, how can you ban this book, the people are clamoring for it to be banned haven't read it. And he said, that's beside the point. It doesn't matter that they haven't read it. It's enough that enough of their leaders are saying that this is what the book does, that it creates a law-and-order problem and the duty of the government is to ensure that it maintains law and order in these communities. And that was the argument that he was making, and it's one which on that particular instance I found very difficult to accept. But I can see how in certain circumstances a government or an editor or somebody else in a position of decision-making will have to weigh in the balance, the right to publish a particular cartoon, to publish a particular short story or a novel, versus the potential loss of life and destruction, property to large numbers of people.

Now there is no one rule for around the world. So, you might say that you can't publish this in this country but you can in that country, because people will not be offended

Joan Bakewell: You can't say that anymore.

Christopher Hitchens: But then my dear Shashi, you should be very happy because everyone is weighing it. There wasn't a single newspaper in Britain that published those cartoons. There wasn't a single one in America either. I know the people in the charge of these matters in many cases. I went on CNN to debate some spokesman for a Muslim organization.

And CNN put up the cartoons, the page of Denmark, pixelated. And I said to the interviewer, you're not doing this because you're afraid of upsetting my Muslim fellow guest, are you?

You're doing it because you're afraid that you'll be burned out if you do. You're bureau's, which is it? She said: Yes, that's right.

Joan Bakewell: Is that not a legitimate fear?

Christopher Hitchens: It's a very legitimate fear. If you allow the right of Muslims to use violence against anything they don't like, of course it's a legitimate fear.

It's certainly, it's not legitimate, it's a real one. But it seems to be amazing that my profession should give up without a fight on this point. So, you should be happy if they're all doing it. National, sorry, PBS, the public station. Decided they could do it this way. And it's significant. They said we can show the cartoons in this manner. We can show them the imams of Denmark traveling around showing the cartoons to others.

We can film them doing that and by accident the cartoons are in the picture. Now, what does that mean? These imams have the right to show this blasphemy to anyone and did. And they added three cartoons of their own, one of which showed the Prophet as a pig, which as you know is an incitement in itself.

The weren't in the paper, they can do it and we can't even see what they're talking about.

Do you understand this significance of this? The media is much too dominated for my taste by images. Everything is image now.

Most even in NY Times, it's mainly pictures. Here the whole story is about an image and no one is allowed to make up their minds by seeing it themselves. We're shielded from it by our editors in a free press and a free country who are paralyzed with fear and paralyzed with the idea that anyone might be hurt.

This is disgraceful.

Source: Tharoor, Shashi, et al. "Shashi Tharoor versus Christopher Hitchens, Free Speech Debate at Hay Festival on Saturday 27 May 2006 and Chaired by Joan Bakewell." YouTube, Hay Festival, 30 Dec. 2011, youtu.be/jw3dDbc1BHE.

Those who purport the argument that it is bigoted to say Islam is incompatible with democratic rules and values are ignorant of its history in South Asia. In US grade school, I was fed the lie that the Partition of 1947 happened due to mutual religious bigotry between Hindus and Muslims. What these claims originating from British historical narratives, the anti-Hinduism arguments in the US and Western corporate news media, and the general US and European ignorance omit are the difference in ideals that led to the Two-Nation theory which gradually led to the British Partition of India in 1947. On March 12th, 2015, an article titled "*Salmaan Taseer murder case harks back to 1929 killing of Hindu publisher*" by journalist Jon Boone was published on *The Guardian*. It gives a brief summary explaining the main cause of disunity between Hindus and Muslims during British colonial rule that led to the Two-Nation theory and subsequent British Partition of India on August 14th, 1947:

Salmaan Taseer murder case harks back to 1929 killing of Hindu publisher

Many Pakistanis argue Mumtaz Qadri should be regarded as a national hero like Ilm-Deen, who knifed the publisher of a commentary on the life of prophet Muhammad

Mudassir Khan visits the tomb of Ghazi Shaheed Ilm-Deen every day to add to the heap of flower petals on top of his grave and sing a tearful prayer to the illiterate carpenter's apprentice who killed to protect the honour of his faith.

Like hundreds of others who come daily to the gaudily decorated enclosure in the middle of Lahore's main graveyard, the restaurant owner reveres the 20-year-old executed for his crime more than 85 years ago.

"In the other shrines you have to pray for half an hour," Khan said. "But here God answers our prayers in minutes."

In a country bursting with shrines of saints honoured for their wisdom or righteousness, Ilm-Deen's tomb is perhaps the only one where a framed copy of a murder charge takes pride of place next to the tomb.

It relates to events that happened before Pakistan came into existence but still resonate with many people who see parallels with the contemporary case of Mumtaz Qadri, the former police bodyguard who murdered one of Pakistan's best-known politicians in the name of blasphemy in 2011.

The charge sheet details how on 6 April 1929, Ilm-Deen "brutally attacked" with a knife the Lahore-based publisher of Rangeela Rasool, a book that had enraged many Muslims with its scurrilous commentary on the life of the prophet Muhammad.

The "first investigation report" on the wall of the shrine says Mahashay Rajpal, the Hindu victim, had tried to defend himself by throwing piles of books at Ilm-Deen, who was soon arrested, still holding the murder weapon.

The killing turned the young man into a hero, earning him the honorifics Ghazi and Shaheed and ensuring he remained famous almost a century later, in part thanks to a popular film celebrating the incident.

Muhammad Ali Jinnah, the lawyer who would found the new state of Pakistan 18 years later, travelled from Mumbai, then known as Bombay, to Lahore to defend Ilm-Deen in his appeal hearing but was unable to save him from being hanged by the colonial government.

His funeral was attended by tens of thousands, including Muhammad Iqbal, Pakistan's national poet, who gave a graveside eulogy.

The saga has particular resonance today among hardline Barelvis, Pakistan's largest grouping of Sunni Muslims, not just because devotion to the prophet is central to their faith, but because they argue Qadri should also be regarded as a national hero.

This week Qadri took a step closer to becoming a modern day Ilm-Deen when Islamabad's high court upheld his conviction for murder, a decision that predictably outraged the hundreds of demonstrators who have gathered outside the courthouse for each appeal hearing.

"In 1929 we could not stop the execution of the lover of the prophet because the British were in power and Muslims were a minority," said Khadim Hussain Rizvi, a mullah who made the journey from Lahore just to protest. "Now there is a Muslim government in Pakistan and we will not obey our leaders if they execute Qadri."

Qadri enjoys widespread support for his murder of Salmaan Taseer, the governor of Punjab province, because of the outrage Taseer sparked by his campaign to win a pardon for Asia Bibi, a poor Christian woman sentenced to death under Pakistan's notorious blasphemy laws.

Although at least one popular mosque has been named after Qadri, he has a long way to go to match Ilm-Deen, whose name has been given to parks, roads, hospitals and even a government guesthouse in Islamabad.

Both the Ilm-Deen and Qadri cases touch on Pakistan's perennial, and increasingly bitter, debate about the role of Islam in national affairs.

Abdul Majeed, a retired soldier turned mullah who runs a mosque near Ilm-Deen's shrine, claimed the saga was one of the inspirations for the "two nation theory" later used to justify the partition of the subcontinent in 1947.

"It was one of the reasons for the Hindu-Muslim divide," said Majeed, who has written a short history of Ilm-Deen called The Flower Who Sent a Blasphemer to Hell. "It made us realise we are separate nations."

Liberal lawyer and historian Yasser Latif Hamdani said Jinnah only acted on the "cab-rank rule" to take a case for which, as one of India's top barristers, he was paid a handsome fee.

But Hamdani conceded the involvement of educated members of the Muslim elite, such as Jinnah and Iqbal, was "a major failing".

"It has allowed basically half-educated lawyers to get up and say Jinnah appeared in this case and now we're doing this," he said. "Pakistan has to divorce itself from this history because a society that makes heroes out of Ilm-Deen is likely to end up with murderers like Qadri."

In an extraordinary twist the two killings span the generations of one family: Salmaan Taseer's father, the celebrated Urdu poet Muhammad Din Taseer, was among Ilm-Deen's supporters, helping raise funds for his defence and donating the shroud in which the carpenter was buried.

Almost a century later, his grandson, the artist Shaan Taseer, has emerged as a leading voice against religious extremism and formally petitioned the Islamabad high court to uphold the death sentence for his father's killer.

He argues that the historical context of Qadri's case is different from that of Ilm-Deen, who Taseer said was a rallying point for Muslim pride and Muslim interests in the late colonial period.

"Defending the interests of the Muslim community of India is not the same as fighting for Islam," he said.[402]

---

[402] Boone, Jon. "Salmaan Taseer Murder Case Harks Back to 1929 Killing of Hindu Publisher." The Guardian, Guardian News and Media, 12 Mar. 2015, www.theguardian.com/world/2015/mar/12/salmaan-taseer-case-harks-back-to-1929-killing-of-hindu-publisher.

I don't think I'll ever quite understand how genuinely stupid pro-neoliberal British policymakers were to have had all the information available about this history that happened under their rule, which is part of their own history too, and then decided to import people who literally broke apart and created their own country because they have full, unyielding faith that Islam is incompatible with the democratic norms and values of Free Speech. The British committed the Partition of 1947 themselves; yet, they are shocked and confused by Pakistani Muslim grooming gangs and Muslims protesting to stamp out Free Speech in Britain, just like they did in India. This is how ignorant the version of British colonial history leaves people and how useless it is in the utility of understanding how to deal with Islamic terrorists in South Asia and beyond that exist today. Hindus of India were telling us all this for decades and the US Corporate media circus all thought that Hindus of India were just being backwards and regressive. They clearly don't have much of an education on basic information regarding the political systems of South Asia or its history, they don't understand that Islamists really want to regress all civilizations to 7th century standards, and the Corporate news media's actions have wholeheartedly proven it with their selective headlines. They destroyed their own credibility to protect people who genuinely want to regress their civilizations to 7th century living standards.

What most who don't research or try to learn anything about Islam's violent history fail to understand is that the majority of Muslims across the world today are serious about regressing all non-Muslim societies to 7th century living standards due to their absolute faith in the Abrahamic God. The majority of Muslims are serious about murdering anyone who hurts their feelings regarding Islam and it has no relation to terrorism or any form of supposed radicalism whatsoever. It has to do with Islam's theology itself. I think most people are sufficiently aware of how the Quran promotes and sanctifies murder as a religious duty that is incumbent upon Muslims towards all non-Muslims such as Quran 8:12-14, 8:39, 8:67, the theological concept of Jihad, and many more internal issues. How strongly is the belief in *bid'ah* though? Without getting too pedantic, an article published on May 9th, 1998 under the supervisory of Muhammad Saalih Al-Munajjid on his website *Islamqa.info*, titled *"Bid'ah Hasanah ("Good Innovations")"* explained the theological problems of accepting any change in Islam:

> It should be clear from the above, with no room for doubt, that the Prophet (peace and blessings of Allah be upon him) was not allowing innovation in matters of deen (religion), nor was he opening the door to what some people call "bid'ah hasanah," for the following reasons:
>
> 1. The Prophet (peace and blessings of Allah be upon him) stated repeatedly that: "Every newly-invented thing is a bid'ah (innovation), every bid'ah is a going astray, and every going astray will be in the Fire." (Reported by An-Nasa'i in al-Sunan, Salaat al-'Eedayn, Baab kayfa al-Khutbah). Reports with the same meaning were narrated via Jaabir (may Allah be pleased with him) by Ahmad, via al-'Irbaad ibn Saariyah by Abu Dawud and via Ibn Mas'ood (may Allah be pleased with him) by Ibn Maajah.

The Prophet (peace and blessings of Allah be upon him) used to say, when beginning a khutbah (sermon): " The best of speech is the Book of Allah and the best of guidance is the guidance of Muhammad. The worst of things are those which are newly-invented, and every innovation is a going astray" (reported by Muslim, no. 867)

If every bid'ah is a going astray, how can some people then say that there is such a thing in Islam as "bid'ah hasanah"? By Allah, this is an obvious contradiction of the statement and warning of the Prophet (peace and blessings of Allah be upon him).

2. The Prophet (peace and blessings of Allah be upon him) stated that whoever innovates something new in the deen (religion) will have his deed rejected, and Allah will not accept it, as is stated in the hadith narrated by 'Aa'ishah (may Allah be pleased with her), who said: "The Messenger of Allah (peace and blessings of Allah be upon him) said: 'Whoever innovates something in this matter of ours that is not a part of it will have it rejected.'" (Reported by al-Bukhaari, Fath al-Baari, no. 2697). How can anybody then say that bid'ah is acceptable and it is permitted to follow it?

3. When a person innovates something and adds to the deen something that does not belong to it, he is implying a number of bad things, each worse than the last, for example:

- That the religion is lacking, that Allah did not complete and perfect it, and that there is room for improvement. This clearly contradicts the statement in the Quran (interpretation of the meaning): " This day, I have perfected your religion for you, completed My favour upon you, and have chosen for you Islam as your religion" [al-Maa'idah 5:3]

- That the religion remained imperfect from the time of the Prophet (peace and blessings of Allah be upon him) until the time when this innovator came along and completed it with his own ideas.

- That the Prophet (peace and blessings of Allah be upon him) was "guilty" of either of two things: either he was ignorant of this "good innovation," or he knew about it but concealed it, thus letting his ummah down by not conveying it.

- That the Prophet (peace and blessings of Allah be upon him), his Companions and the righteous salaf (early generations) missed out on the reward of this "good innovation" - until this innovator came along and earned it for himself, despite the fact that he should say to himself, "If it was truly good, they would have been the first to do it."

- Opening the door to bid'ah leads to changing the deen (religion) and opens the way for personal whims and opinions, because every innovator implies that what he is introducing is something good, so whose opinion are we supposed to follow, and which of them should we take as a leader?

- Following bid'ah leads to the cancelling out of sunnah practices and the ways of the salaf. Real life bears witness that whenever a bid'ah is followed, a sunnah practice dies out; the reverse is also true.

We ask Allah to save us from the misguidance of personal whims and from all trials whether they are open or secret. And Allah knows best.[403]

They attempted to claim it has nothing to do with technology, but that's not true when you read information about Islam's Day of Resurrection, whereby it is believed that weaponry will regress back to swords, bows, and arrows when the Mahdi fights against

---

[403] "Bid'Ah Hasanah ('Good Innovations') - Islam Question & Answer." Edited by Muhammad Saalih Al-Munajjid, Islamqa.Info, Islam Question & Answer, 9 May 1998, islamqa.info/en/answers/864/bid-ah-hasanah-(%22good-innovations%22).

Satan and the Anti-Messiah until Jesus Christ comes to rescue the true believing Muslims.[404] This is honestly what Islamists kill people for. Pew Research Center published a survey on the beliefs of the majority of Muslims worldwide on April 30th, 2013. While the information may seem a bit dated, it is still very useful and many Muslim countries like Iraq have regressed instead of progressed due to the theological underpinning of *bid'ah* in Islam. On May 7th, 2013, Pew Research added full details of the sample sizes used on the front page of the report. Here are full sample sizes and dates when they were conducted before going further:

Countries Surveyed in 2011-2012 and Sample Sizes

Country	Muslims in Sample	Total Sample Size
Afghanistan	1,509	1,509
Albania	788	1,032
Azerbaijan	996	1,000
Bangladesh	1,918	2,196
Bosnia-Herzegovina*	1,007	1,605
Egypt	1,798	2,000
Indonesia	1,880	2,000
Iraq	1,416	1,490
Jordan	966	1,000
Kazakhstan	998	1,469
Kosovo	1,266	1,485
Kyrgyzstan	1,292	1,500
Lebanon	551	979
Malaysia	1,244	1,983
Morocco	1,472	1,474
Niger	946	1,002
Pakistan	1,450	1,512
Palestinian territories	994	1,002
Russia*	1,050	2,704
Tajikistan	1,453	1,470
Thailand^	1,010	1,010
Tunisia	1,450	1,454
Turkey	1,485	1,501
Uzbekistan	965	1,000

Source: "The World's Muslims: Religion, Politics and Society." Pew Research Center, Pew Research Center, 30 Apr. 2013, www.pewresearch.org/religion/2013/04/30/the-worlds-muslims-religion-politics-society-overview/.

---

[404] Al-Munajjid, Muhammad Saalih. "Will Civilisation Collapse at the End of Time and Will Battles Be Fought with Swords and Spears? - Islam Question & Answer." Islamqa.Info, Islam Question & Answer, 1 Aug. 2014, islamqa.info/en/answers/162744/will-civilisation-collapse-at-the-end-of-time-and-will-battles-be-fought-with-swords-and-spears.

MAY 7, 2013

THE WORLD'S MUSLIMS: RELIGION, POLITICS AND SOCIETY

Countries Surveyed in 2008-2009 and Sample Sizes

Country	Muslims in Sample	Total Sample Size
Cameroon	245	1,503
Chad	811	1,503
DR Congo	185	1,519
Djibouti	1,452	1,500
Ethiopia	453	1,500
Ghana	339	1,500
Guinea Bissau	373	1,000
Kenya	340	1,500
Liberia	279	1,500
Mali	901	1,000
Mozambique	340	1,500
Nigeria	818	1,516
Senegal	891	1,000
Tanzania	539	1,504
Uganda	321	1,040

For additional details on these countries, please see the Pew Research Center's April 2010 report "Tolerance and Tension: Islam and Christianity in Sub-Saharan Africa."

The Ghana, Kenya and Uganda surveys included oversamples of Muslim respondents. In Ghana and Kenya, interviews were conducted among a nationally representative sample of 1,200 respondents and supplemented with 300 additional interviews among Muslims. The Uganda survey was conducted among a nationally representative sample of 832 respondents and supplemented with 208 additional interviews among Muslims.

DOWNLOAD

Source: "The World's Muslims: Religion, Politics and Society." Pew Research Center, Pew Research Center, 30 Apr. 2013, www.pewresearch.org/religion/2013/04/30/the-worlds-muslims-religion-politics-society-overview/.

And their self-reported beliefs across the Islamic world:

Sharia as the Revealed Word of God

% of Muslims who say sharia is ...

- Developed by men, based on word of God
- The revealed word of God

Southern-Eastern Europe

Country	Developed by men	Revealed word of God
Russia	25	56
Bosnia-Herz.	39	52
Kosovo	33	30
Albania	18	24

Central Asia

Country	Developed by men	Revealed word of God
Kyrgyzstan	20	69
Tajikistan	33	60
Azerbaijan	36	53
Uzbekistan	19	52
Turkey	28	49
Kazakhstan	31	44

Southeast Asia

Country	Developed by men	Revealed word of God
Indonesia	39	54
Thailand^	20	52
Malaysia	35	41

South Asia

Country	Developed by men	Revealed word of God
Pakistan	8	81
Afghanistan	21	73
Bangladesh	25	65

Middle East-North Africa

Country	Developed by men	Revealed word of God
Jordan	18	81
Egypt	20	75
Palestinian terr.	16	75
Iraq	25	69
Morocco	13	66
Tunisia	25	66
Lebanon	38	49

^Interviews conducted with Muslims in five southern provinces only.

PEW RESEARCH CENTER Q66.

One or Multiple Interpretations of Sharia?

% of Muslims who say sharia has ...

- Multiple interpretations
- Single interpretation

Southern-Eastern Europe
Country	Multiple	Single
Bosnia-Herz.	35	56
Russia	22	56
Kosovo	11	46
Albania	23	27

Central Asia
Country	Multiple	Single
Tajikistan	21	70
Azerbaijan	15	65
Kyrgyzstan	35	55
Kazakhstan	36	41
Uzbekistan	22	38
Turkey	36	36

Southeast Asia
Country	Multiple	Single
Thailand^	29	51
Indonesia	44	45
Malaysia	35	43

South Asia
Country	Multiple	Single
Afghanistan	29	67
Pakistan	17	61
Bangladesh	38	57

Middle East-North Africa
Country	Multiple	Single
Lebanon	39	59
Palestinian terr.	42	51
Iraq	48	46
Morocco	60	22
Tunisia	72	20

^Interviews conducted with Muslims in five southern provinces only.
Data from Egypt and Jordan are not available due to an administrative error.

PEW RESEARCH CENTER Q67.

Is It Good or Bad that Laws Do Not Follow Sharia Closely?

Among Muslims who say country's laws do not follow sharia, % who say this is ...

	Good	Bad	Neither/DK
Southern-Eastern Europe			
Russia	10	47	42
Bosnia-Herz.	50	29	21
Albania	32	28	40
Kosovo	50	26	23
Central Asia			
Kyrgyzstan	26	47	27
Tajikistan	25	32	43
Kazakhstan	42	18	40
Azerbaijan	47	13	39
Southeast Asia			
Malaysia	11	65	23
Indonesia	22	65	13
South Asia			
Pakistan	5	91	4
Afghanistan	13	84	3
Bangladesh	10	83	7
Middle East-North Africa			
Palestinian terr.	5	83	12
Morocco	13	76	11
Iraq	9	71	20
Jordan	21	69	10
Egypt	25	67	8
Tunisia	25	54	21
Lebanon	41	38	21

PEW RESEARCH CENTER Q69.

Death Penalty for Leaving Islam

Among Muslims who say sharia should be the law of the land, % who favor the death penalty for converts

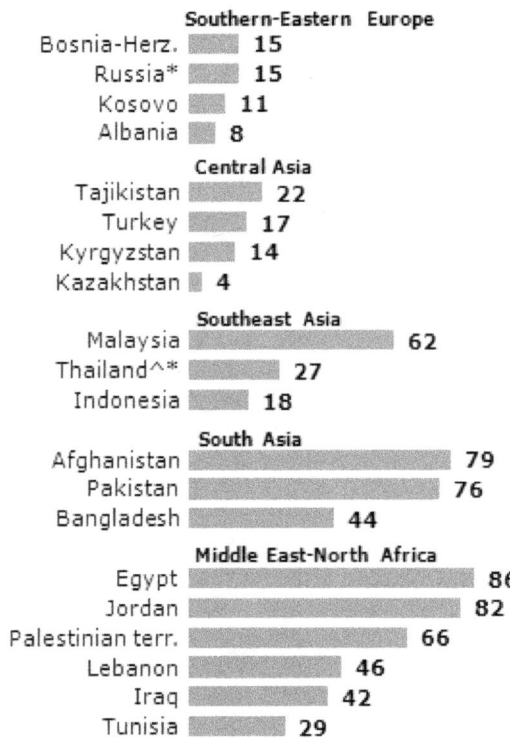

Southern-Eastern Europe
- Bosnia-Herz. 15
- Russia* 15
- Kosovo 11
- Albania 8

Central Asia
- Tajikistan 22
- Turkey 17
- Kyrgyzstan 14
- Kazakhstan 4

Southeast Asia
- Malaysia 62
- Thailand^* 27
- Indonesia 18

South Asia
- Afghanistan 79
- Pakistan 76
- Bangladesh 44

Middle East-North Africa
- Egypt 86
- Jordan 82
- Palestinian terr. 66
- Lebanon 46
- Iraq 42
- Tunisia 29

Based on Muslims who favor making sharia the law of the land.
*Based on Muslims who favor making sharia the law in Muslim areas.
^Interviews conducted with Muslims in five southern provinces only.
Results for Azerbaijan not shown due to small sample size.

PEW RESEARCH CENTER Q79a and Q92b.

Stoning as Punishment for Adultery

Among Muslims who say sharia should be the law of the land, % who favor stoning as a punishment for adultery

Southern-Eastern Europe
- Russia*: 26
- Kosovo: 25
- Albania: 25
- Bosnia-Herz.: 21

Central Asia
- Tajikistan: 51
- Kyrgyzstan: 39
- Kazakhstan: 31
- Turkey: 29

Southeast Asia
- Malaysia: 60
- Thailand^*: 51
- Indonesia: 48

South Asia
- Pakistan: 89
- Afghanistan: 85
- Bangladesh: 55

Middle East-North Africa
- Palestinian terr.: 84
- Egypt: 81
- Jordan: 67
- Iraq: 58
- Lebanon: 46
- Tunisia: 44

Based on Muslims who favor making sharia the law of the land.
*Based on Muslims who favor making sharia the law in Muslim areas.
^Interviews conducted with Muslims in five southern provinces only.
Results for Azerbaijan not shown due to small sample size.

PEW RESEARCH CENTER Q79a and Q92d.

Do You Favor Corporal Punishments for Crimes Such as Theft?

Among Muslims who say sharia should be the law of the land, % who favor corporal punishment

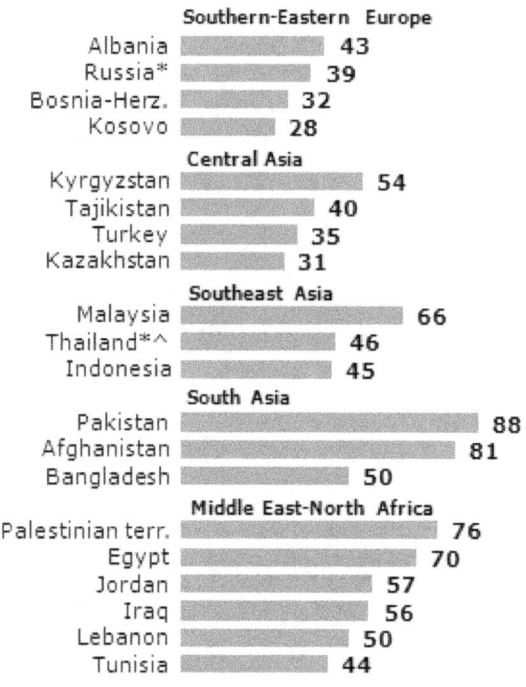

	%
Southern-Eastern Europe	
Albania	43
Russia*	39
Bosnia-Herz.	32
Kosovo	28
Central Asia	
Kyrgyzstan	54
Tajikistan	40
Turkey	35
Kazakhstan	31
Southeast Asia	
Malaysia	66
Thailand*^	46
Indonesia	45
South Asia	
Pakistan	88
Afghanistan	81
Bangladesh	50
Middle East-North Africa	
Palestinian terr.	76
Egypt	70
Jordan	57
Iraq	56
Lebanon	50
Tunisia	44

Based on Muslims who favor making sharia the law of the land.
*Based on Muslims who favor making sharia the law in Muslim areas.
^Interviews conducted with Muslims in five southern provinces only.
Results for Azerbaijan not shown due to small sample size.

PEW RESEARCH CENTER Q79a and Q92c.

Should Religious Judges Decide Family or Property Disputes?

Among Muslims who say sharia should be the law of the land, % who say that religious judges should decide domestic and property disputes

Southern-Eastern Europe
- Russia* — 62
- Albania — 55
- Kosovo — 26
- Bosnia-Herz. — 24

Central Asia
- Tajikistan — 66
- Kyrgyzstan — 65
- Kazakhstan — 59
- Turkey — 48

Southeast Asia
- Malaysia — 88
- Thailand^* — 84
- Indonesia — 71

South Asia
- Pakistan — 87
- Afghanistan — 78
- Bangladesh — 78

Middle East-North Africa
- Egypt — 95
- Jordan — 93
- Palestinian terr. — 80
- Iraq — 76
- Lebanon — 75
- Tunisia — 62

Based on Muslims who favor making sharia the law of the land.
*Based on Muslims who favor making sharia the law in Muslim areas.
^Interviews conducted with Muslims in five southern provinces only.
Results for Azerbaijan not shown due to small sample size.

PEW RESEARCH CENTER q79a and Q92a.

Favor or Oppose Making Sharia the Law of the Land?

% of Muslims who favor making Islamic law the official law in their country

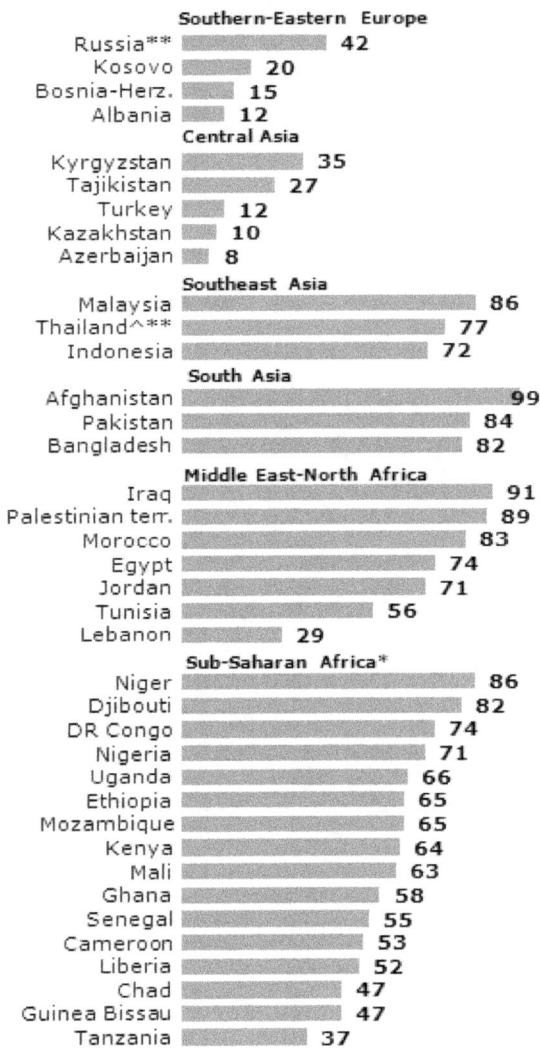

Southern-Eastern Europe
- Russia** 42
- Kosovo 20
- Bosnia-Herz. 15
- Albania 12

Central Asia
- Kyrgyzstan 35
- Tajikistan 27
- Turkey 12
- Kazakhstan 10
- Azerbaijan 8

Southeast Asia
- Malaysia 86
- Thailand^** 77
- Indonesia 72

South Asia
- Afghanistan 99
- Pakistan 84
- Bangladesh 82

Middle East-North Africa
- Iraq 91
- Palestinian terr. 89
- Morocco 83
- Egypt 74
- Jordan 71
- Tunisia 56
- Lebanon 29

Sub-Saharan Africa*
- Niger 86
- Djibouti 82
- DR Congo 74
- Nigeria 71
- Uganda 66
- Ethiopia 65
- Mozambique 65
- Kenya 64
- Mali 63
- Ghana 58
- Senegal 55
- Cameroon 53
- Liberia 52
- Chad 47
- Guinea Bissau 47
- Tanzania 37

*Data for all countries except Niger from "Tolerance and Tension: Islam and Christianity in Sub-Saharan Africa."
^Interviews conducted with Muslims in five southern provinces only.
**Question was modified to ask if sharia should be the law of the land in Muslim areas.

PEW RESEARCH CENTER Q79a.

Necessary To Believe in God to be Moral?

% of Muslims who say ...

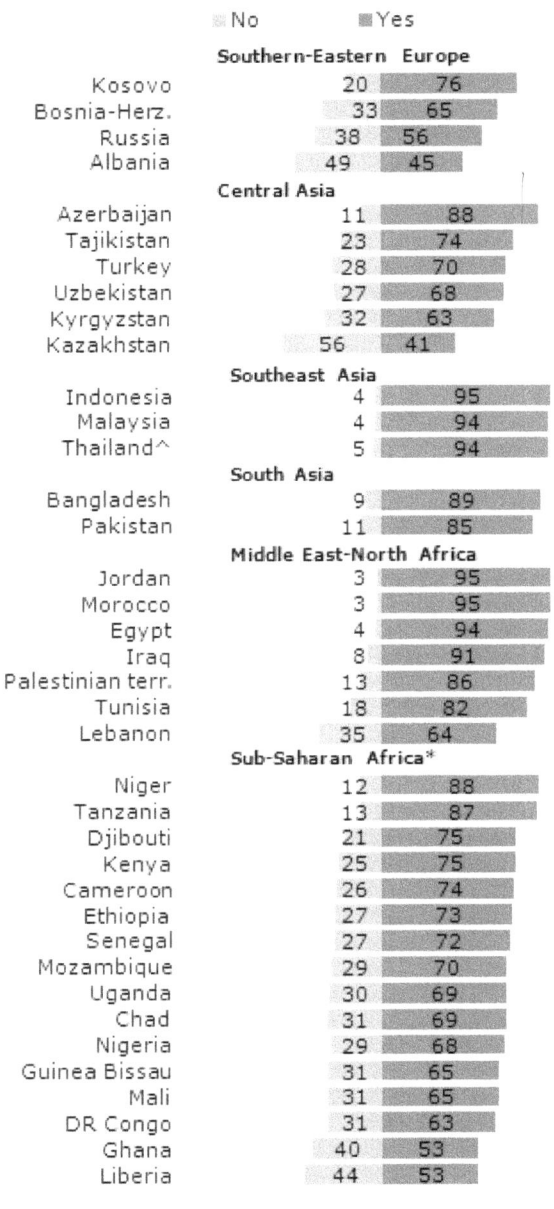

PEW RESEARCH CENTER Q16.

Is Sex Outside of Marriage Moral?

% of Muslims who say it is ...

- Morally wrong
- Morally acceptable

Country	Morally wrong	Morally acceptable
Southern-Eastern Europe		
Bosnia-Herz.	53	26
Albania	58	25
Russia	75	10
Kosovo	76	5
Central Asia		
Kazakhstan	75	9
Kyrgyzstan	78	3
Turkey	88	3
Azerbaijan	89	0
Tajikistan	85	0
Southeast Asia		
Malaysia	94	2
Indonesia	94	1
Thailand^	99	1
South Asia		
Bangladesh	81	1
Pakistan	93	0
Middle East-North Africa		
Tunisia	89	5
Lebanon	96	2
Egypt	95	1
Jordan	96	1
Iraq	83	0
Palestinian terr.	93	0
Sub-Saharan Africa*		
Guinea Bissau	63	19
Chad	63	18
Uganda	66	18
Mozambique	70	15
DR Congo	72	12
Liberia	81	12
Mali	78	9
Djibouti	75	8
Cameroon	74	7
Nigeria	87	7
Senegal	85	4
Tanzania	87	3
Kenya	89	3
Ghana	93	3
Ethiopia	77	2
Niger	91	1

*Data for all countries except Niger from "Tolerance and Tension: Islam and Christianity in Sub-Saharan Africa."
^Interviews conducted with Muslims in five southern provinces only.

PEW RESEARCH CENTER Q84i.

Is Divorce Moral?

% Muslims who say it is ...

- Morally wrong
- Morally acceptable

Country	Morally wrong	Morally acceptable
Southern-Eastern Europe		
Bosnia-Herz.	19	60
Kosovo	23	52
Albania	26	51
Russia	25	50
Central Asia		
Turkey	14	64
Kazakhstan	23	54
Kyrgyzstan	29	44
Azerbaijan	20	25
Tajikistan	44	23
Southeast Asia		
Thailand^	13	65
Indonesia	42	47
Malaysia	16	46
South Asia		
Bangladesh	30	62
Afghanistan	31	24
Pakistan	71	17
Middle East-North Africa		
Lebanon	8	64
Tunisia	32	61
Jordan	3	58
Egypt	6	56
Palestinian terr.	26	32
Iraq	26	25
Sub-Saharan Africa		
Tanzania	38	55
Niger	19	53
Senegal	34	50
Nigeria	41	46
Chad	31	45
Guinea Bissau	47	40
Djibouti	51	36
Cameroon	40	34
Kenya	52	27
Mozambique	67	24
Uganda	67	23
DR Congo	55	21
Liberia	72	19
Ghana	51	16
Mali	71	10
Ethiopia	71	5

*Data for all countries except Niger from "Tolerance and Tension: Islam and Christianity in Sub-Saharan Africa."
^Interviews conducted with Muslims in five southern provinces only.

PEW RESEARCH CENTER Q84a.

Are Honor Killings Permissible?

*% of Muslims who say **never** justified when ...*

	Male committed the offense	Female committed the offense	Diff.
Southern-Eastern Europe			
Russia	67	60	**+7**
Albania	68	67	+1
Bosnia-Herz.	79	79	0
Kosovo	60	61	-1
Central Asia			
Azerbaijan	86	82	+4
Kazakhstan	84	84	0
Tajikistan	49	49	0
Turkey	68	68	0
Kyrgyzstan	55	58	-3
Uzbekistan	46	60	**-14**
Southeast Asia			
Indonesia	82	82	0
Malaysia	59	59	0
Thailand^	50	52	-2
South Asia			
Bangladesh	38	34	+4
Pakistan	48	45	+3
Afghanistan	24	24	0
Middle East North-Africa			
Jordan	81	34	**+47**
Iraq	33	22	**+11**
Egypt	41	31	**+10**
Lebanon	55	45	**+10**
Tunisia	62	57	+5
Palestinian terr.	46	44	+2
Morocco	64	65	-1

Statistically significant differences are shown in bold.
^Interviews conducted with Muslims in five southern provinces only.

PEW RESEARCH CENTER Q53 and Q54.

Is Homosexual Behavior Moral?

% of Muslims who say it is ...

- Morally wrong
- Morally acceptable

	Morally wrong	Morally acceptable
Southern-Eastern Europe		
Albania	83	5
Bosnia-Herz.	83	5
Kosovo	73	3
Russia	89	1
Central Asia		
Kyrgyzstan	76	3
Turkey	85	3
Kazakhstan	92	1
Azerbaijan	92	0
Tajikistan	82	0
Southeast Asia		
Malaysia	94	2
Indonesia	95	1
Thailand^	99	1
South Asia		
Bangladesh	67	10
Pakistan	90	1
Middle East-North Africa		
Tunisia	91	2
Jordan	96	2
Iraq	77	1
Palestinian terr.	89	1
Egypt	94	1
Lebanon	97	1
Sub-Saharan Africa*		
Uganda	77	12
Mozambique	79	11
Guinea Bissau	71	6
Djibouti	80	6
Liberia	90	6
DR Congo	87	3
Chad	92	2
Kenya	96	2
Niger	90	1
Senegal	90	1
Mali	91	1
Tanzania	91	1
Nigeria	94	1
Ghana	97	1
Ethiopia	98	0
Cameroon	99	0

*Data for all countries except Niger from "Tolerance and Tension: Islam and Christianity in Sub-Saharan Africa."
^Interviews conducted with Muslims in five southern provinces only.

PEW RESEARCH CENTER Q84j.

Is Abortion Moral?

% of Muslims who say it is ...

▪ Morally wrong   ▪ Morally acceptable

Country	Morally wrong	Morally acceptable
Southern-Eastern Europe		
Bosnia-Herz.	66	14
Albania	65	7
Russia	77	7
Kosovo	75	4
Central Asia		
Kazakhstan	61	9
Turkey	74	7
Kyrgyzstan	69	6
Azerbaijan	23	3
Tajikistan	50	1
Southeast Asia		
Malaysia	85	3
Indonesia	93	2
Thailand^	99	0
South Asia		
Bangladesh	64	18
Afghanistan	55	4
Pakistan	82	0
Middle East-North Africa		
Tunisia	83	6
Iraq	57	2
Jordan	57	2
Lebanon	78	2
Egypt	66	1
Palestinian terr.	77	0
Sub-Saharan Africa*		
Uganda	75	15
Mozambique	75	13
DR Congo	78	10
Djibouti	72	9
Liberia	88	6
Chad	86	5
Guinea Bissau	76	5
Nigeria	91	3
Cameroon	95	2
Ghana	91	1
Mali	92	1
Niger	87	1
Senegal	87	1
Ethiopia	91	0
Kenya	92	0
Tanzania	94	0

*Data for all countries except Niger from "Tolerance and Tension: Islam and Christianity in Sub-Saharan Africa."
^Interviews conducted with Muslims in five southern provinces only.

PEW RESEARCH CENTER Q84g.

Must a Wife Always Obey Her Husband?

% of Muslims who completely or mostly agree that a wife must always obey her husband

Southern-Eastern Europe
- Russia: 69
- Bosnia-Herz.: 45
- Albania: 40
- Kosovo: 34

Central Asia
- Tajikistan: 89
- Uzbekistan: 84
- Kyrgyzstan: 75
- Turkey: 65
- Azerbaijan: 58
- Kazakhstan: 51

Southeast Asia
- Malaysia: 96
- Indonesia: 93
- Thailand^: 89

South Asia
- Afghanistan: 94
- Pakistan: 88
- Bangladesh: 88

Middle East-North Africa
- Tunisia: 93
- Morocco: 92
- Iraq: 92
- Palestinian terr.: 87
- Egypt: 85
- Jordan: 80
- Lebanon: 74

This question was not asked in sub-Saharan Africa.

^Interviews conducted with Muslims in five southern provinces only.

PEW RESEARCH CENTER Q78.

Many Muslims See Themselves as More Devout than Fellow Countrymen

% of Muslims who believe ... adhere to hadith and sunna a lot/a little

	They themselves	Most Muslims in their country	Diff
Southern-Eastern Europe			
Bosnia-Herz.	50	36	+14
Albania	20	14	+6
Central Asia			
Turkey	76	59	+17
Uzbekistan	62	47	+15
Tajikistan	60	50	+10
Kyrgyzstan	55	46	+9
Southeast Asia			
Indonesia	83	75	+8
South Asia			
Pakistan	87	71	+16
Bangladesh	84	74	+10
Middle East-North Africa			
Lebanon	56	24	+32
Morocco	81	55	+26
Iraq	82	59	+23
Egypt	56	35	+21
Palestinian terr.	61	40	+21
Jordan	47	29	+18
Tunisia	76	59	+17

Only countries where differences are statistically significant are shown.

PEW RESEARCH CENTER Q59 and Q60.

Following the Prophet's Example

% of Muslims who say their lives reflect the hadith and sunna ...

■ A lot   ▪ A little

Country	A lot	A little	NET
Southern-Eastern Europe			
Russia	22	36	58
Bosnia-Herz.	22	28	50
Kosovo	8	12	20
Albania	7	13	20
Central Asia			
Turkey	33	43	76
Azerbaijan	23	49	72
Uzbekistan	17	45	62
Tajikistan	15	45	60
Kyrgyzstan	14	41	55
Kazakhstan	9	29	38
Southeast Asia			
Thailand^	70	17	87
Malaysia	50	26	76
Indonesia	46	37	83
South Asia			
Afghanistan	75	22	97
Pakistan	50	37	87
Bangladesh	46	38	84
Middle East-North Africa			
Iraq	55	27	82
Morocco	28	53	81
Lebanon	21	35	56
Palestinian terr.	18	43	61
Jordan	17	30	47
Egypt	15	41	56
Tunisia	13	63	76

This question was not asked in sub-Saharan Africa.

^Interviews conducted with Muslims in five southern provinces only.

PEW RESEARCH CENTER Q59.

How Many Faiths Lead to Heaven?

% of Muslims who say...

- Many religions
- Islam alone

Country	Many religions	Islam alone
Southern-Eastern Europe		
Kosovo	24	59
Bosnia-Herz.	36	58
Russia	30	52
Albania	25	37
Central Asia		
Tajikistan	10	84
Turkey	19	74
Kyrgyzstan	20	69
Uzbekistan	14	66
Azerbaijan	18	63
Kazakhstan	49	29
Southeast Asia		
Malaysia	4	93
Indonesia	9	87
Thailand^	11	87
South Asia		
Pakistan	3	92
Bangladesh	8	88
Middle East-North Africa		
Egypt	3	96
Jordan	3	96
Iraq	3	95
Morocco	3	94
Palestinian terr.	7	89
Tunisia	24	72
Lebanon	27	66
Sub-Saharan Africa*		
Niger	5	92
Nigeria	12	86
Djibouti	8	85
Ethiopia	17	81
Mali	12	80
Ghana	17	78
DR Congo	16	74
Liberia	22	71
Tanzania	27	70
Kenya	28	69
Uganda	28	66
Senegal	33	62
Cameroon	39	57
Guinea Bissau	34	54
Chad	49	50
Mozambique	44	49

*Data for all countries except Niger from "Tolerance and Tension: Islam and Christianity in Sub-Saharan Africa."
^Interviews conducted with Muslims in five southern provinces only.

PEW RESEARCH CENTER Q55.

Prayer and Views of Islam as Path to Salvation

% of Muslims who say Islam is the one true faith leading to eternal life in heaven among those who ...

	Pray several times a day	Pray less often	Diff.
Southern-Eastern Europe			
Russia	78	37	+41
Kosovo	78	44	+34
Albania	63	35	+28
Bosnia-Herzegovina	80	53	+27
Central Asia			
Kazakhstan	60	27	+33
Uzbekistan	87	61	+26
Azerbaijan	66	54	+12
Tajikistan	91	80	+11
Kyrgyzstan	77	67	+10
Southeast Asia			
Malaysia	96	84	+12
Thailand^	89	78	+11
South Asia			
Bangladesh	94	84	+10
Middle East-North Africa			
Lebanon	80	43	+37
Palestinian terr.	92	78	+14
Iraq	96	85	+11
Tunisia	75	65	+10

^Interviews conducted with Muslims in five southern provinces only.
Only countries where differences are statistically significant are shown.

PEW RESEARCH CENTER Q55 and Q61.

Converting Others Is a Religious Duty

% of Muslims who ...

　　　　　　　　　　Disagree　　Agree

Southern-Eastern Europe
Country	Disagree	Agree
Russia	51	40
Bosnia-Herz.	59	33
Kosovo	55	26
Albania	72	16

Central Asia
Country	Disagree	Agree
Tajikistan	27	69
Azerbaijan	36	42
Turkey	48	39
Kyrgyzstan	50	36
Kazakhstan	77	15

Southeast Asia
Country	Disagree	Agree
Malaysia	16	79
Thailand^	22	74
Indonesia	65	31

South Asia
Country	Disagree	Agree
Afghanistan	4	96
Pakistan	4	85
Bangladesh	26	69

Middle East-North Africa
Country	Disagree	Agree
Jordan	6	92
Egypt	9	88
Palestinian terr.	10	82
Tunisia	25	73
Iraq	20	66
Morocco	14	63
Lebanon	44	52

Sub-Saharan Africa*
Country	Disagree	Agree
Liberia	5	93
Ghana	6	92
Mali	7	89
Nigeria	7	89
Niger	9	89
Chad	11	88
Tanzania	8	87
Kenya	13	85
DR Congo	6	84
Djibouti	11	84
Uganda	13	84
Cameroon	15	84
Guinea Bissau	13	82
Mozambique	14	80
Ethiopia	21	78
Senegal	21	75

*Data for all countries except Niger from "Tolerance and Tension: Islam and Christianity in Sub-Saharan Africa."
^Interviews conducted with Muslims in five southern provinces only.

PEW RESEARCH CENTER Q52.

Close Friends

% of Muslims who say all or most of their close friends are Muslims

Southern-Eastern Europe
- Kosovo: 93
- Bosnia-Herz.: 93
- Albania: 79
- Russia: 78

Central Asia
- Azerbaijan: 99
- Tajikistan: 99
- Uzbekistan: 98
- Turkey: 97
- Kyrgyzstan: 95
- Kazakhstan: 87

Southeast Asia
- Thailand^: 96
- Indonesia: 95
- Malaysia: 94

South Asia
- Pakistan: 98
- Bangladesh: 97

Middle East-North Africa
- Tunisia: 100
- Morocco: 98
- Iraq: 97
- Lebanon: 94
- Egypt: 86
- Jordan: 83
- Palestinian terr.: 80

This question was not asked in sub-Saharan Africa.
^Interviews conducted with Muslims in five southern provinces only.

PEW RESEARCH CENTER Q49.

Comfort Level with Son or Daughter Marrying a Christian

% of Muslims who say they would be very/somewhat comfortable

	Son	Daughter	Diff.
Southern-Eastern Europe			
Russia	52	39	*+13*
Albania	77	75	+2
Bosnia-Herz.	16	14	+2
Kosovo	24	22	+2
Central Asia			
Tajikistan	23	6	*+17*
Azerbaijan	8	3	+5
Kyrgyzstan	24	19	+5
Turkey	25	20	+5
Uzbekistan	16	11	+5
Kazakhstan	36	32	+4
Southeast Asia			
Thailand^	20	15	+5
Malaysia	17	12	+5
Indonesia	6	2	+4
South Asia			
Pakistan	9	3	+6
Bangladesh	14	10	+4
Middle East-North Africa			
Egypt	17	0	*+17*
Tunisia	30	13	*+17*
Jordan	12	0	*+12*
Morocco	26	14	*+12*
Iraq	13	4	*+9*
Lebanon	30	21	*+9*
Palestinian terr.	14	5	*+9*

Statistically significant differences are shown in bold.
A modified question was asked in sub-Saharan Africa. See page TK for analysis of the results.
^Interviews conducted with Muslims in five southern provinces only. Muslims were asked if they would be comfortable with their son or daughter marrying a Buddhist.

PEW RESEARCH CENTER Q37, Q37THA, Q38 and Q38THA.

Belief in Evolution

% of Muslims who believe humans and other living things have ...

- Always existed in present form
- Evolved over time

Southern-Eastern Europe

Country	Always existed	Evolved
Albania	24	62
Russia	30	58
Bosnia-Herz.	45	50
Kosovo	40	34

Central Asia

Country	Always existed	Evolved
Kazakhstan	16	79
Uzbekistan	30	58
Azerbaijan	30	54
Kyrgyzstan	31	53
Tajikistan	55	37
Turkey	49	35

Southeast Asia

Country	Always existed	Evolved
Thailand^	39	55
Indonesia	55	39
Malaysia	45	37

South Asia

Country	Always existed	Evolved
Bangladesh	37	54
Pakistan	38	30
Afghanistan	62	26

Middle East-North Africa

Country	Always existed	Evolved
Lebanon	21	78
Palestinian terr.	28	67
Morocco	29	63
Jordan	47	52
Tunisia	36	45
Iraq	67	27

This question was not asked in sub-Saharan Africa.
^Interviews conducted with Muslims in five southern provinces only.
Data from Egypt are not available due to an administrative error.

PEW RESEARCH CENTER Q20.

It may sound bigoted, but it is simply the truth that the majority of Muslims in the world don't want their living standards to increase unless they can forcibly reconstruct and squeeze it into being consistent with 7th century Arab fundamentalism. While it may be too hard for most Muslims in the world to dismiss modern conveniences, the majority make no secret that they want to erase all social value systems outside of Islam like women's rights, legal penalizations of child rape, children's rights to avoid molestation and rape, LGBT rights, and all advancements of other cultures such as Charles Darwin's theory of evolution and other scientific advancements. I know how insane that sounds because it is so out of the norm of our expectations within more advanced cultures, but the self-reported survey data, the theology of Islam itself, and the behavior of the majority of Muslims across the world are all consistent on these issues. It really is the majority of Muslims across the world who hold such views. This is the painful reality of the world we live in and the true reason why US policymakers kept failing, they didn't offer any ideals to counter Islam or allow open criticism of Islam when Iraq and Afghanistan were under occupation. The fact remains that Islam and democratic norms and values are incompatible; worse than that for non-Muslims, everyone has been making excuses for the behavior of Islamists even when they murder people on the basis of defending Islam. It simply can't get any more explicit or barbarous than that. Saying not all Muslims or applauding when Muslims act like every other person in a situation and don't choose to murder is simply praising them for doing the bare minimum of human decency; the pernicious argument is that having respect for others human rights just like everyone else is an accomplishment for Muslims. Are all non-Muslims thereby expected to jeopardize their own lives just to give Muslims chance after chance when the majority of Muslims argue they want to live within 7th century Arab fundamentalist standards everywhere? Are we supposed to constantly jeopardize our own lives, and are parents constantly required to jeopardize the lives of their daughters, due to religious tolerance – the belief that all mythology everywhere in the world leads to the same behavioral outcomes?

Has Anything Truly Changed between Islam's Past and Present?

The main reason US policymakers failed in Afghanistan was that by not truly understanding history, they merely became another victim to it in Islam's long history of victories. Liberals in the US and the West are too focused on narratives of White Supremacy and ignore 7th century Arab Supremacy that has been given a theological veneer to their detriment. Right-wing Christian groups refuse to acknowledge or accept that Muslims believe Jesus Christ is the Messiah of Islam, because it makes them feel uncomfortable in their faith in Christianity. The final reason is that, due to the falsehoods of Neoliberal economic beliefs about progress, the majority of the US and Western economists wrongly believe that there's a slow movement towards economic progress and that everyone would find this economic progress desirable in modern times. The truth is that Islamists reject modern value systems and view themselves as entitled to enter into other countries in order to impose Islamism upon them. They view their own failures as the calculated conspiracy theories of other groups trying to oppress Muslims. For the most part, Islamists merely hide the behavior better or threaten violence if people offend them to scare others into silence. This is why the most logical outcome for Europe for the importing of so many Islamic immigrants will likely lead to breakaway Islamic States that partition from their respective European countries in the coming 60 years or so; because every single time there is a push to support initiatives like pro-Islamophobia campaigns, Islamists can more freely or discretely continue their conversion tactics, rape crimes against young girls via rape conversions, and many other despicable acts while presenting themselves as an aggrieved minority. These are real behaviors that Islamists do. The dreams of higher GDPs by Neoliberals who behave politically correct towards all religious values will likely lead to the future partitions of Europe once Islamic populations become large enough. For what it's worth, I hope I am wrong and that people can laugh at this belief I have in sixty or so years from now and view me as a fool for having it.

This leads to a crucial question: what has actually changed about Islam from its nascent history to now? What reforms have actually happened? It seems to me that not much has changed among Muslims globally judging from the current data, past history, and the contemporary political issues. I cannot write a list of all historical Islamic atrocities upon other cultures, but what I can do is highlight some examples that Islamists want removed from history and have largely succeeded in removing, specifically because it would make their fellow Muslims doubt their faith. For India's history, thanks to US, Indian, and Western Indologists like Wendy Doniger, Sheldon Pollock, Audrey Truschke, Cynthia Talbot, Romila Thapar, and Andrew Nicholson using academic freedom as a shield for their vehement support for both cultural and physical genocide, Hindus are vilified as conspiracy theorists when talking about these issues with Religious Studies departments who mostly have no knowledge of India's history and especially lack knowledge of Islamic theology; at the same time, history departments in the US and the West quietly mention or keep this history in mind when in passing so as not to offend Muslim feelings with historical facts. When reading more into history, I've learned it isn't just the case that those who willfully ignore it are doomed to repeat it, but those who are left ignorant because people like those US, Western, and Indian Indologists willfully lie and keep others purposefully ignorant about Islam's theology, their lies confuse the majority of non-experts and they protect the malicious activities like Islamic theology's support for the capture and rape of young girls, which continues unimpeded. For me, the most shocking part of historian Kishori Saran Lal's truthful account of India's history in his out-of-print magnum opus, *Growth of Muslim Population in Medieval India*, was that the slave system imposed on Indian women by Muslim warlords by putting them in cages to sell in slave markets repeated itself with ISIS's *Sabaya* / Slave system upon young

Yazidi girls.[405][406][407] When I recognized the disturbing comparison . . . I genuinely wonder how many lives could have been saved had the US, Western European, and the Indian Indologists who supported them like Romila Thapar had simply been honest about Islam's history in India. That question honestly keeps bothering me every time I read the descriptions and footnotes of K.S. Lal's explanation of the slave markets and Islamic conversions through a slave system and the NY Times article on the suffering of young Yazidi girls who were caged, sold into slave markets, raped, and killed.[408][409][410]

Cultural Genocide

Both the Islamist regime of Iran and the Western Indologists have whitewashed Islam's brutality from the history books. Most Iranians have probably heard of the two-hundred years of genocide that Arab conquerors committed to support the Islamic colonization of Iran, but they don't seem to know the specifics of what happened to their ancestors. From retired Language Professor of Rutger's University, Paul Sprachman's English translation of Legendary Iranian Scholar of Persian history and literature, Abdolhossein Zarrinkoub's *Two Centuries of Silence*: *An Account of Events and Conditions in Iran [Persia] during the first Two Hundred Years of Islam*:

The Lost Language

This is what emerges when one ponders the Iranian history after the Arab invasion: The Arabs in an apparent effort to remain immune from abuse in the local languages and to never see Persian become a weapon in the hands of the conquered people, tried to wipe out languages and dialects commonly used in Iran. There was also the fear that these tongues might stir up people and threaten Arab rule in the far-flung parts of Iran. This was why wherever they ran into inscriptions, other written language, books or libraries in Iranian cities, they strenuously objected to them. The Arabs' behavior toward the writing and language of people in Khwarazm attests to this attitude.

---

[405] Lal, Kishori Saran. Chapter X: AD 1200 – 1400 (Pgs. 113 – 116). "Growth of Muslim Population in Medieval India (1000-1800)" Internet Archive, Internet Archive, 5 Aug. 2018, ia902800.us.archive.org/11/items/GrowthOfMuslimPopulationInMedievalIndiaAd10001800/Growth-Of-Muslim-Population-In-Medieval-India-ad-1000-1800_text.pdf.

[406] Lal, Kishori Saran. Chapter XI: AD 1400 – 1600 (Pgs. 127 – 143). "Growth of Muslim Population in Medieval India (1000-1800)" Internet Archive, Internet Archive, 5 Aug. 2018, ia902800.us.archive.org/11/items/GrowthOfMuslimPopulationInMedievalIndiaAd10001800/Growth-Of-Muslim-Population-In-Medieval-India-ad-1000-1800_text.pdf. For reference: Footnote on page 136.

[407] Callimachi, Rukmini. "Isis Enshrines a Theology of Rape." The New York Times, The New York Times, 13 Aug. 2015, www.nytimes.com/2015/08/14/world/middleeast/isis-enshrines-a-theology-of-rape.html.

[408] Callimachi, Rukmini. "Isis Enshrines a Theology of Rape." The New York Times, The New York Times, 13 Aug. 2015, www.nytimes.com/2015/08/14/world/middleeast/isis-enshrines-a-theology-of-rape.html.

[409] Lal, Kishori Saran. Chapter X: AD 1200 – 1400 (Pgs. 113 – 116). "Growth of Muslim Population in Medieval India (1000-1800)" Internet Archive, Internet Archive, 5 Aug. 2018, ia902800.us.archive.org/11/items/GrowthOfMuslimPopulationInMedievalIndiaAd10001800/Growth-Of-Muslim-Population-In-Medieval-India-ad-1000-1800_text.pdf.

[410] Lal, Kishori Saran. Chapter XI: AD 1400 – 1600 (Pgs. 127 – 143). "Growth of Muslim Population in Medieval India (1000-1800)" Internet Archive, Internet Archive, 5 Aug. 2018, ia902800.us.archive.org/11/items/GrowthOfMuslimPopulationInMedievalIndiaAd10001800/Growth-Of-Muslim-Population-In-Medieval-India-ad-1000-1800_text.pdf. For reference: Footnote on page 136.

Historians have written that when Qutayba b. Muslim, Ḥajjāj's commander, conquered Khwarazm he put to the sword every person who wrote Khwarazmi and who was knowledgeable about history, science, and reports of past events. He also had all the Zoroastrian clergy, from the high to the low priests [herbad s], exterminated and their books incinerated. The result was that people became illiterate by degrees, and their history was forgotten.3 The incident shows the Arabs thought of spoken and written Persian as weapons, which, in the hands of the conquered people, could be used to confront their conquerors and mount attacks on them. With this in mind, it comes as no surprise they ruthlessly pursued the eradication of the language, writing, and culture of Iran. Another thing that may explain the Arabs' war on written and spoken Persian is that the presence of the Magus' language might have impeded the spread and propagation of the Quran. The reality was that Iranians, even those that converted to Islam, did not learn Arabic, consequently they were by and large unable to pray or read the Quran in the language. In one history, we read

"The people of Bukhara when praying at the beginning of Islam recited the Quran in Persian and could not learn Arabic. When the time came for congregants to perform the rukūc [the bow], a man behind them would call out bknitā nkint and, when it came time for sajda [full prostration], he would call out nguniyānguni konit.4"

Given the strong attachment the people in Iran had for their language, it is no wonder the Arab commanders would, to some extent, view it as antithetical to their rule and religion and would spare no effort to wiping it out everywhere they found it.

Book Burning

There can be no doubt, then, many of the books and libraries of Iran fell prey to destruction in the Arab onslaught. The histories contain numerous direct reports documenting the eradication of the writing of the past, and there are also many indications from other sources attesting to it. Despite the evidence, however, some in the scholarly community have their doubts. Are such doubts necessary? What purpose would deigning to save such books have served the Arab, who valued no writing other than the Quran? The books were the Magus's affair and, to say the least, a cause of deviance from the straight path of scripture. At the time it was very rare to find in the Muslims' rituals a familiarity with written culture. The level of such people's affection for books and libraries was no secret. All indications show the Arab saw no value in books such as the Pahlavi texts extant today. Thus, there can be no doubt they would not esteem or honor the contents of such books. Apart from this, with the two groups that had enjoyed a near monopoly on learning and art, the priests and the aristocracy, out of the way, there was no need to preserve their relics and books. Wasn't this, after all, the reason why the priests more than any other class lost their previous high status and were annihilated? Obviously, with the priestly class decimated or disbanded, no need for their books and learning, which were useless to the Arabs, remained. History records the names of many books from the Sasanian period that no longer exist. Even translations of these works, which were done at the outset of Abbasid rule, have been lost. Clearly, the environment the Muslims created was not conducive to the survival of such books and resulted in their destruction.

In short, there is every indication that many of the Iranians' books were lost in the Arab invasion. Historians write when Sacd b. Abī Waqqāṣ took Mada'in, he saw many books there. He wrote cUmar b. Khaṭṭāb asking for instruction as to what was to be done with the books. The caliph ordered them thrown into the water. He reasoned: if what is in those books offered right guidance, God has sent us the Quran, which is a better guide than they are; but if what is in those books is nothing but misleading, God has protected us from their evil. On the basis of this they threw the books in the water or in the fire.5 While it is true this report is not found in quranic writing from the beginning of Islam, which is why some scholars doubt its authenticity, it is difficult to imagine Arabs would have behaved any better toward the Magus' books.

Whatever the case, from the time Arabs took over, the language of Iran was subjugated by the conquerors. It was not used in the governing apparatus, nor was it of any use in religious matters. No effort was made to spread or propagate it, causing an inevitable decline in its stature and importance. Little by little the Pahlavi language became the exclusive concern of Zoroastrian priests and worshippers. If books were written at all, they were in that language; but written Pahlavi was so intricate compositions in the language eventually died out. Languages like Sogdian and Khwarazmi in the face of the harsh measures the Arabs took also gradually became obsolete. It was not just that these languages were incompatible with the Arabs' faith and life, writing in them no longer appeared. This was why from the time the Arabic language sounded in Iran, Iranian languages became virtually speechless. With Arabic the language of religion and government, Pahlavi, Dari, Sogdian, and Khwarazmi were no longer used except among common people. To be sure people in towns and villages spoke these languages in everyday communication; however, except for that purpose they did not have much utility. This is why, during those times of silence and privation, Arabic came to dominate the languages of Iran and intermingled with them to such an extent that Arabic expressions related to religion and political administration gradually found a home in modern Persian [fārsi].[411]

Unfortunately, cultural genocide is the norm of Islamic conquest and imposing Islamic values in a society. From historian Kishori Saran Lal's Part III, chapter seven of *Theory and Practice of Muslim State in India* in response to the disturbing amount of genocide denial in India's domestic educational institutions:

> 3. It is re-asserted that a strict watch was kept on Hindu thought and expression. Hindu learning in general was suppressed since Hindu and Buddhist schools were attached to temples and monasteries. These were regularly destroyed from the very beginning and with them schools of learning. Qutbuddin Aibak razed the Sanskrit College of Vishaldeva at Ajmer and in its place built a mosque called *Arhai din ka Jhonpra*. In the east Ikhtiyauddin Bakhtiyar Khalji sacked the Buddhist university centres in Bihar like Odantapuri, Nalanda and Vikramshila between 1197-1202. There, according to the contemporary chronicler Minhaj Siraj, "the greater number of the inhabitants of the place were Brahmans, and the whole of those Brahmans had their heads shaven (probably Buddhist monks mistaken for Brahmans) and they were all slain. There were a great number of books there; and the Musalmans... summoned a number of Hindus that they might give them information respecting the import of these books; but the whole of the Hindus had been killed." All that the invader could learn was that "the whole of the fortress was a college and in the Hindi tongue, they call a college (madrasa) Bihar."2 During this period there were large numbers of centres of learning spread all over India. B. P. Mazumdar has listed some of these centres in the eleventh and twelfth centuries as existing in Northern India. In Bihar they were Nalanda, Vikramshila, Odantapuri and Phullahari near Monghyr. In North and Eastern Bengal they were Jagaddala, Somapura and Devikota in North Bengal, Vikrampuri in Dacca, Pattikeraka in Comilla, and Panditavihara in Chittagong. Minor viharas were in existence at Gaya and Valabhi and Bundelkhand.
>
> Hieun Tsang, in the seventh century, had noted that monasteries existed in all parts of the country. Many of these continued to flourish in the eleventh-twelfth centuries. Hiuen Tsang's list included "Nagarkot, Udyana, Jalandhar, Sthanesvara, Srughna Matipura, Brahmapura, Govisana, Ahichchatra, Samkasya, Kanauj, Navadevakula, Ayodhya, Hayamuka, Prayag, Visoka, Kapilvastu, Banaras, Ramagrama, Ghazipur, Tilosika, Gunamati, Silabhadra near Gaya, Kajangala, Pundravardhana, Kamarupa, Samatata, Orissa, Berar, Malwa, Valabhi, Anandapura,

---

[411] Zarrinkoub, Abdolhossein. Chapter 4: The Lost Language (Location 1833 – 1878). Two Centuries of Silence: An Account of Events and Conditions in Iran [Persia] During the First Two Hundred Years of Islam, from the Arab Invasion to the Rise of the Tahirid Dynasty First edition. Mazda Publishers. Kindle Edition.

> Surat, Ujjayini and Chitor." The adventurer Ikhtiayaruddin Bakhtiyar Khalji sacked Bihar during sultan Aibak's reign, and centres of learning were specially sacked. So thorough was the massacre by the Khalji warrior in Bihar and later on by others in other places that those who could read ancient inscriptions became rare if not extinct. So that when Sultan Firoz Shah Tughlaq (fourteenth century) shifted two Ashokan pillars from Khizrabad and Meerut to Delhi and installed them there, he called some learned Brahmans to read the inscriptions engraved in Ashokan Brahmi script on the pillars; they failed to read the script. Some of them tried to please the Sultan with funny stories by saying that it was recorded in the inscriptions that no one would be able to remove the monoliths till the advent of Firoz.3
>
> Demolition of schools and temples was continued by most Muslim rulers right up to the time of Aurangzeb, both at the centre and in the provinces. Aurangzeb was one of the enthusiastic sort in this respect, although he was no exception.
>
> The *Maasir-i-Alamgiri* records that in April 1669, "It reached the ears of his Majesty, the protector of the faith, that in the province of Thatta, Multan, and Banaras, but especially in the latter, *foolish Brahmans were in the habit of expounding frivolous books in their schools*, and that students and learners, Muslims as well as Hindus went there, even from long distances, led by the desire to become acquainted with the *wicked sciences they taught*. The Director of the Faith, consequently issued orders to *all governors of provinces to destroy with a willing band the schools and temples of the infidels*. In obedience of this order the temple of Bishnath at Banaras was destroyed."4 With such evidences on hand, Jackson is forced to concede that "some limited degree of repression may have been feasible in Delhi or in the vicinity of the sultan's itinerant court; it was surely impractical in the provincial centres, still more so in the countryside". I have resided in Delhi, Bhopal and Hyderabad (Deccan) for many years. In all these places I could hardly locate any temples left of the medieval period. Hindu learning was dependent on schools and Brahman teachers, and both were attached to temples mostly in urban areas. And all the three - schools, teachers and temples - were systematically destroyed. Muslim rulers in general and Firoz Tuglaq and Sikandar Lodi in particular considered the Brahmans as 'the very keys of chambers of idolatry" and treated them with great severity.5 The level of education in the countryside is not known. But the credit for whatever could be- saved of Hindu education goes to the freedom fighters of medieval India and not to the indulgence of the Muslim government.[412]

For this next one, I want it to be made clear that this professor and her colleagues point to political self-interest and not religion as the primary cause. When I examined the broader context of Islamic history, what the perpetrators state their motives are, and the underpinnings of Islam's theology itself; I would argue the primary cause is definitely Islam, but they do not argue or believe that and I want that to be abundantly clear because I'm not trying to take their words out of context.

Art historian Kavita Singh, a professor at the School of Arts and Aesthetics of Jawaharlal Nehru University in India, details the historic and contemporary examples of cultural genocide of Afghanistan in chapter 8 *"When Peace Is Defeat, Reconstruction Is Damage: "Rebuilding" Heritage in Post-conflict Sri Lanka and Afghanistan"* of the free online book *"Cultural Heritage and Mass Atrocities"* sponsored by the J. Paul Getty Trust philanthropic institute:

---

[412] Lal, Kishori Saran. "Part III: Reposte on Reviews: VII A Riposte on Reviews: 7.1 The Legacy of Muslim Rule in India." Theory and Practice of Muslim State in India, 2020th ed., Aditya Prakashan, New Delhi, Delhi, 1999, pp. 324–327.

Afghanistan too has suffered greatly in the past half century. Its economy, society, and polity have been shattered by seemingly endless strife. The era of Taliban rule, from 1996 to 2001, was a particularly low point in its difficult history. This was a brutal government that committed countless atrocities against its own people while supporting the international terrorist organization al-Qaeda, which committed acts of terrorism abroad. The Taliban outlawed most kinds of music, art, and education for Afghans; even chess and soccer were forbidden, and women were no longer allowed to study or to work. All of this was well-known to the international community. But the acts that excited the greatest attention to and condemnation of the Taliban from the outside world were acts directed not against the Afghan people directly, but against works of art.

Prior to the arrival of Islam, Buddhism had been the dominant faith in Afghanistan, and many sites and museum collections were rich with artifacts in the Gandharan style that flourished from the first to the seventh century and that fused Buddhist iconography with a Hellenistic and Roman style. In 2001, the Taliban leader Mullah Omar issued a fatwa that called for the destruction of all pre-Islamic statues and sanctuaries in the land. "These statues have been and remain shrines of unbelievers," he said. "God Almighty is the only real shrine and all fake idols should be destroyed."9 Within weeks, Taliban forces destroyed thousands of artworks, many of which were in the Kabul Museum. Their most prominent targets, however, were the giant Buddhas of the Bamiyan Valley.

A hundred and fifty miles west of Kabul, the Bamiyan Valley is a broad, fertile basin watered by the Bamiyan River and bordered by rocky cliffs of the Hindu Kush mountains. Here, carved directly into the cliff face, was a 175-foot-tall relief sculpture that was the largest Buddha sculpture in the world. A second sculpture, at 120 feet, was small only in comparison to its colossal neighbor. Other Buddhas, seated and recumbent, were once ranged along the mountainside, and their bodies were covered in brilliant frescoes. Hundreds of artificial caves were dug into the rock to provide cells for meditation and prayer for Buddhist monks. In its heyday the valley housed an enormous monastery and a giant stupa that would have been as eye-catching as the Buddhas.

This extraordinary cluster of Buddhist monuments was mostly built in the sixth and seventh centuries, when Bamiyan was an important node in the ancient Silk Road. As a rare oasis in harsh mountainous terrain it attracted merchants and missionaries and became a prosperous center for religion and trade. From the eighth century Islam began to supplant Buddhism in the region. Buddhist sites fell out of worship, the stupa crumbled, and the vast monastery disappeared, but apart from an attack by a passing conqueror in the twelfth century, when the Buddhas probably lost their faces, the giant sculptures remained relatively intact.

In 2001, as the Taliban tried to destroy the Buddhas, they found it was not an easy task. They first attacked the statues with guns, antiaircraft missiles, and tanks. When these did not suffice, the Taliban brought in explosives experts from Saudi Arabia and Pakistan. On their advice, workers rappelled down the cliff with jackhammers, blasting holes in the sculptures and packing these with dynamite that was detonated in timed explosions. A journalist from the al-Jazeera media network was allowed to film the final stage of the Buddhas' destruction, and shortly afterward a contingent of twenty international journalists was brought in to observe the now-empty niches.

The Taliban's determined assault on the Buddhas went forward even as global leaders pleaded with Mullah Omar to spare them. Governments of Islamic countries including Egypt and Qatar tried to reason with the Afghan leaders, and a delegation of clerics led by the mufti of the al-Azhar seminary in Cairo, the most prestigious Sunni for the study of Islamic law, was flown to the Taliban's de facto capital of Kandahar to dissuade Mullah Omar from destroying the statues.

Why, then, did the destruction of the Bamiyan Buddhas become a prestige project for the Afghan leader, a task to be "implemented at all costs"?10 Why, despite the pressure applied by global leaders, did the Taliban invest so much time, labor, and expense in the difficult task of demolition and in ensuring that it was broadcast to the rest of the world? And why was Mullah Omar so determined to destroy the Buddhas two years after he had solemnly promised to protect them? In 1999 he had declared that as there were no Buddhists remaining in Afghanistan, the Buddhas were not idols under worship, and there was no religious reason to attack them. Instead, he said his government considered them "a potential major source of income for Afghanistan from international visitors. The Taliban states that Bamiyan shall not be destroyed but protected."11 What accounts for the Taliban's volte-face, in which a religious motivation, earlier dismissed as irrelevant, was used to now justify the attack?[413]

Source: "Buddhas of Bamiyan." Wikipedia, Wikimedia Foundation, 16 July 2025, en.wikipedia.org/wiki/Buddhas_of_Bamiyan.

---

[413] Singh, Kavita. "When Peace Is Defeat, Reconstruction Is Damage: 'Rebuilding' Heritage in Postconflict Sri Lanka and Afghanistan." Www.Getty.Edu, J. Paul Getty Trust, 13 July 2022, www.getty.edu/publications/cultural-heritage-mass-atrocities/downloads/pages/CunoWeiss_CHMA_part-2-08-singh.pdf. For Reference: pages 157 - 159.

Source: "Buddhas of Bamiyan." Wikipedia, Wikimedia Foundation, 16 July 2025, en.wikipedia.org/wiki/Buddhas_of_Bamiyan.

Source: "Buddhas of Bamiyan." Wikipedia, Wikimedia Foundation, 16 July 2025, en.wikipedia.org/wiki/Buddhas_of_Bamiyan.

Source: "Buddhas of Bamiyan." Wikipedia, Wikimedia Foundation, 16 July 2025, en.wikipedia.org/wiki/Buddhas_of_Bamiyan.

Source: "Buddhas of Bamiyan." Wikipedia, Wikimedia Foundation, 16 July 2025, en.wikipedia.org/wiki/Buddhas_of_Bamiyan.

Source: "Buddhas of Bamiyan." Wikipedia, Wikimedia Foundation, 16 July 2025, en.wikipedia.org/wiki/Buddhas_of_Bamiyan.

Source: "Buddhas of Bamiyan." Wikipedia, Wikimedia Foundation, 16 July 2025, en.wikipedia.org/wiki/Buddhas_of_Bamiyan.

Source: "Buddhas of Bamiyan." Wikipedia, Wikimedia Foundation, 16 July 2025, en.wikipedia.org/wiki/Buddhas_of_Bamiyan.

Source: "Buddhas of Bamiyan." Wikipedia, Wikimedia Foundation, 16 July 2025, en.wikipedia.org/wiki/Buddhas_of_Bamiyan.

A reminder to the bloodthirsty members of the religion of peace: Professor Singh is well-meaning and does ***not*** attribute the cause to Islam like I do. If necessary, I can give you the definition of the word "not" so you can better understand modern language with your 7th century Arab fundamentalist belief system while you shout "ooga booga" or is it "Allahu Akbar"? Please remind me, I can hardly tell the difference between the two shouts. In any case, it is clear that the reason was Islam. While I don't know enough about Qatari history to judge, Egypt knows from approximately five-hundred years of Western Europe vandalizing the tombs of their Egyptian Pharaohs and imposing White Supremacy on their cultural history what it is like to suffer cultural genocide, but that is beyond the focus of this book. In any case, there's more than sufficient historic and contemporary evidence and the statements of the Taliban perpetrators themselves to determine the primary cause. On March 3rd, 2001, Amir Shah of *The Independent Asia* quoted Taliban Information Minister Quadratullah Jamal who reiterated the following about their motives for destroying the massive Buddhas of Bamiyan statues: *"Our Ulema (clerics) have given an edict. It cannot be taken back. There is no place for statues in an Islamic country,"*[414]

---

[414] Shah, Amir. "Taliban Destroy Ancient Buddhist Relics." The Independent Asia RSS, The Independent World, 3 Mar. 2001,
web.archive.org/web/20110106181318/www.independent.co.uk/news/world/asia/taliban-destroy-ancient-buddhist-relics-694425.html.

While the destruction of the Buddhas of Bamiyan were the most notorious act of cultural genocide by Islamists in contemporary history, they were obviously not the most recent. On February 13th, 2012, NY Times journalist Vikas Bajaj published an article titled "*Vandalism at Maldives Museum Stirs Fears of Extremism*" which details yet another example of cultural genocide of Dharmic heritage by Islamists:

> MALE, Maldives — The broken glass from an attack by vandals on the National Museum here has been swept away, and the remnants of the Buddhist statues they destroyed — nearly 30 of them, some dating to the sixth century — have been locked away. But officials say the loss to this island nation's archaeological legacy can never be recouped.
>
> In the midst of the political turmoil racking this tiny Indian Ocean nation of 1,200 islands, a half-dozen men stormed into the museum last Tuesday and ransacked a collection of coral and lime figures, including a six-faced coral statue and a 1 1/2-foot-wide representation of the Buddha's head. Officials said the men attacked the figures because they believed they were idols and therefore illegal under Islamic and national laws.
>
> The vandalism was reminiscent of the Taliban's demolition of the great carved Buddhas of Bamiyan in Afghanistan in early 2001, and it has raised fears here that extremists are gaining ground in the Maldives, a Sunni Muslim country that historians say converted from Buddhism to Islam in the 12th century. The country has incorporated elements of Islamic law into its jurisprudence for years. Idols cannot be brought into the country, for example, and alcohol and pork products are allowed only at resorts that cater to foreigners.
>
> The statues were destroyed on the same day that Mohamed Nasheed, who won the presidency in 2008 in the country's first democratic election, resigned his office. Mr. Nasheed said he was forced to do so in what amounted to a coup; his opponents say he went voluntarily. For nearly a month leading up to his resignation, Islamic and other opposition political parties staged protests. Some of them criticized Mr. Nasheed for not cracking down on brothels that masquerade as massage parlors and for proposing that hotels be allowed to serve alcohol on islands where Maldivians live; under current law, alcohol can be served only at the airport or on resort islands with no native population.
>
> Ali Waheed, the director of the National Museum, which was built by China as a gift to the country, said on Monday that officials might be able to restore two or three of the damaged statues, but that the rest were beyond repair. "The collection was totally, totally smashed," Mr. Waheed said. "The whole pre-Islamic history is gone."
>
> There were conflicting reports on Monday about whether suspects had been arrested in the case. Mr. Waheed said five men were caught at the museum, but a spokesman for the police, Ahmed Shiyam, said on Monday that investigators were still collecting evidence and had not made arrests.
>
> Naseema Mohamed, a historian who retired from the museum last year, said the loss was particularly devastating because many of the country's ancient artifacts, dispersed across the archipelago, had been lost or destroyed over the years by local people and rulers. "There was very little left," she said.
>
> Mr. Waheed said that typically, two or three artifacts of the country's Buddhist heritage are discovered a year, generally during construction of homes and other buildings.
>
> Both Ms. Mohamed and Mr. Waheed said that in recent years, some conservative Muslims had suggested removing the statues from the museum, but that there had never been any threats made over the statues. Abdul Majeed Abdul Bari, who was minister of Islamic affairs for the Maldives until last week, said that the country's laws specifically exempt ancient figures from the regulations governing idols. "This is our heritage, and it has to be protected for future generations," he said.

Officials of Adhaalath, an Islamist political party that took part in protests against the Nasheed administration, condemned the vandalism of the statues. Though the party has criticized what it called Mr. Nasheed's anti-Islamic policies, it said it had never objected to the presence of the statues in the museum.

"We are very concerned about it," Mohamed Iaad Hameed, president of the party's trade and economic development committee, said in an interview on Monday. "And we as a party are fully against extremism."

Mr. Waheed, the museum director, said scholars and museums in a number of countries had already offered help in restoring the damaged statues.

Sruthi Gottipati contributed reporting from New Delhi.

A version of this article appeared in print on February 14, 2012, on page A4 of the New York edition with the headline: Amid Political Upheaval, Vandalism of Maldives Museum's Treasures Stirs Fears.[415]

There are too many that were done by ISIS in the 2010s that it has its own Wikipedia page specifically because the devastation to archeological and cultural heritage sites in the Middle East were so numerous under the territories they had briefly conquered and ruled. I was particularly saddened by the destruction of the heritage sites in Palmyra such as the destruction of the Temple of Bel.[416] Journalist Will Worley of *The Independent* published an article titled *"Full Extent of Isis Destruction of Palmyra Revealed in Devastating before and after Photos."* on April 2nd, 2016 which depicted several images of the cultural genocide that ISIS had wrought, such as these two images below:

Source: Worley, Will. "Full Extent of Isis Destruction of Palmyra Revealed in Devastating before and after Photos." The Independent, Independent Digital News and Media, 2 Apr. 2016,

---

[415] Bajaj, Vikas. "Vandalism at Maldives Museum Stirs Fears of Extremism." NYTimes.Com, The New York Times, 13 Feb. 2012, web.archive.org/web/20120221170512/https://www.nytimes.com/2012/02/14/world/asia/political-turmoil-threatens-archaeological-treasures-in-maldives.html.
[416] "Destruction of Cultural Heritage by the Islamic State." Wikipedia, Wikimedia Foundation, 25 May 2025, en.wikipedia.org/wiki/Destruction_of_cultural_heritage_by_the_Islamic_State.

www.independent.co.uk/news/world/middle-east/palmyra-syria-photos-new-palmyra-photos-show-devastation-of-artefacts-ruined-by-isis-a6964766.html.

Source: Worley, Will. "Full Extent of Isis Destruction of Palmyra Revealed in Devastating before and after Photos." The Independent, Independent Digital News and Media, 2 Apr. 2016, www.independent.co.uk/news/world/middle-east/palmyra-syria-photos-new-palmyra-photos-show-devastation-of-artefacts-ruined-by-isis-a6964766.html.

Persecution and Slaughter of Real or Perceived Atheists

One of the many great failings of the Atheists of modern times is their willful ignorance of history and their unabashed online mockery campaigns. Many Atheists may mention how Atheists of the past were the most persecuted in history, but how much of the details do they know? Not much, judging from what I've observed. Moreover, a question for Atheists who engage in surface-level mockery campaigns such as Quran burnings: who does this convince? If anything, why wouldn't this make religious people more hardened in their faith traditions and more willing to view Atheists as bigots; just as Islamists and other religious groups have vilified Atheists to be? To be clear, mockery is a form of free expression and it can be a critique, but my argument is that there is generally a difference in the style of mockery that actually delves into the theology of a religion that most people are unaware of and that which is surface-level like Quran burnings. Quran burnings don't convince anyone of anything just like Christian extremists burning Harry Potter books didn't convince Harry Potter fans to stop reading the series back in the 1990s in the US. If anything, it may have had the opposite effect. When you engage and criticize the theology, you're showing respect for other people's intelligence; when you just burn something to cause offense, it is an act of anti-intellectualism. I'm not arguing that people can't or shouldn't do it, they're free to do what they want. What I'm suggesting is that it probably has the opposite intended effect and doesn't convince religious people to change their minds about what you're criticizing. When Ex-Muslim Atheist Armin Navabi was criticizing Islam's theology in college campus tours on panel discussions with *Ex-Muslims of North America*, he was doing far more damage to Islam than his short Youtube video where he burned a Quran or suggested that he record himself peeing on a Quran in a tweet.[417][418] Intellectual critique isn't just about respect, it causes religious people to engage with the arguments and it causes them to question their reasons for why they believe their religion is true. In short, a rational critique spreads doubt about a faith tradition, insulting mockery campaigns spreads stronger feelings of affirmation towards a faith tradition.

Western European and some US Atheists are generally uncomfortable with the idea that Atheism isn't unique to the Western traditions, because of their ignorance of other cultures and unfortunately due to views of racial differences. Many White Atheists and especially White Christians conflate terms like "Western values" and "Enlightenment values" to mean "White values" and refuse to believe non-Whites in ancient times were capable of atheism, even when I give them historical evidence cited by one of the foremost historians like Will Durant about Charvaka Atheists of India or share English translation of Hinduism's Samkhya theology. Even the historical Buddha being agnostic to the question of a God's existence and allowing followers to believe whatever they wanted about supernatural beliefs in the Theravada tradition seems to unsettle some White Atheists. They can't seem to accept that not all theology is bound by the notion of revealed wisdom like in Christianity, which is what most of them are familiar with. Ex-Muslim Atheists and some religious Liberals of India are uncomfortable with Hindus having Atheist traditions, I can only give my best guesses as to why. I think for Ex-Muslim Atheists, it probably means their historic and cultural loss from Islamic imperialism was far worse than they could have imagined, but I'm confused as to why that should come as a surprise when the Prophet Mohammad is notorious for being illiterate. For left-leaning Hindus of India, there seems to be a shame inherited from Christian and Islamic bigotry about consistency in theology, so they don't want to admit that Atheist *darshanas* (viewpoints) exist in Hinduism. This is backwards thinking though, because the consistency with Jesus Christ and the Prophet Mohammad is actually a weakness in the Abrahamic faith traditions; they have to reduce their thinking faculties to follow the instructions of their respective 1st and 7th century individuals who are long dead. The simplistic idea that anything that agrees with either Jesus Christ or the Prophet Mohammad is morally good and that anything which disagrees with them is morally bad means that these religions are just glorified cosplay of the ancient individual themselves. For example, what is the difference between saying a devout Muslim is following the

---

[417] Navabi, Armin. "I Just Recorded Myself Peeing on the Quran. Would It Violate Twitter's TOS If I Post the Video Here, Even If There Is Zero Nudity?" Twitter, Twitter, 27 Aug. 2020, https://twitter.com/ArminNavabi/status/1298814762491547651.

[418] Navabi, Armin. "Why I Burn The Quran." YouTube, Atheist Republic, 29 July 2018, www.youtube.com/watch?v=nVsqA7fWWoY&pp=ygUbYnVybiB0aGUgcXVyYW4gYXJtaW4gbmF2YWJp.

Prophet Mohammad's moral values and cosplaying as the Prophet Mohammad himself? In contrast, Hinduism and Judaism both have lengthy traditions of debate and I'd argue they're actually stronger for it and it may have been the reason why there was never any violence between Hindus and Jews for over 2400 years.[419] Questioning and debating truths is a strength within a culture.

Even if people would like to argue that it was scant, which I don't believe is true for the history of the Charvakas of northern India given that they dominated for approximately one-hundred years in 600 BCE within what is modern Bihar today[420], there are several problems with denying the ancient world's history of Atheism to the point that I honestly find it shocking that Western Ex-Muslim Atheists didn't realize the obvious when they ignored the evidence I sent them via social media. Here are four reasons:

1. Recognizing the history of Atheism throughout different parts of the ancient world can be used as a political campaign strategy to more effectively normalize and reduce violence and persecution of Atheists in Muslim-majority countries and elsewhere. False perceptions in the Middle East of Atheism being a mental illness or an unnatural aberration would be significantly reduced in influence.

2. In the case of Iran and India, Muslims in those societies would be forced to confront the historic fact that Atheism isn't some foreign concept originating from Western Science or Marxism that would make them feel lesser as people, but that it is indigenous to their own cultural heritage and Islam stole it from them through violence. Many Muslims in India seem to actually have this issue already, because India is a Republic and tries to maintain a balance with Free Expression and protecting Muslims' feelings. Iranians of the US leave Islam, because the US allows them to freely explore their buried history unlike if they were living under Iran's Islamist regime.

3. Islamists would be less able to confuse nominal Muslims that those ancient Atheists "weren't really Atheists" because they don't subscribe to modern criteria outside of lack of faith in a God or the supernatural more generally. There would possibly be less shame associated in being Atheist in Muslim-majority countries and elsewhere.

---

[419] Moses, Nissim. "Bene Israel of India." Avotaynu Online, 24 Mar. 2015, www.avotaynuonline.com/2007/07/bene-israel-of-india-by-nissim-moses/.
[420] Durant, Will. Chapter XV: The Buddha: I. The Heretics (9581 - 9656). Our Oriental Heritage: Being a History of Civilization in Egypt and the Near East to the Death of Alexander, and in India, China and Japan from the Beginning to Our Own Day. Simon and Schuster, 1935.

4. The most salient reason for me is that if people continue believing the falsehood that Atheism wasn't more common and held actual political influence in countries like Medieval Iran and Ancient India, then that means the Islamists of the Medieval period succeeded in the completion of their genocide so that nobody remembers these specific victims of Islamism. Not recognizing Atheism in ancient India because it feels humiliating that this is what Islam stole from Ex-Muslim Atheists is no different from validating to Islamists that genocide is successful, genocide is desirable, and that Islamists can continue getting away with it over and over throughout modern times, because they succeeded in the past. The refusal to acknowledge the historic past in honest terms is an absolute victory for Islamism. It's how Islam won in the Medieval period and it is why Islam is winning now.

First for some historic context, from Paul Sprachman's English translation of *Chapter 9: The Battle of Beliefs* of Iranian scholar, Abdolhossein Zarrinkoub's *Two Centuries of Silence*: *An Account of Events and Conditions in Iran [Persia] during the first Two Hundred Years of Islam*:

The Zindiqs ["heretics/free thinkers": zandaqeh] and the Interpretation of Doctrine

There is evidence indicating that from the time of Anushirvan Iranians were familiar with Greek philosophy. Even prior to that time there was contact between India and Greece. Many religious and scientific works had been translated into Pahlavi. Exposure to Greek and Indian ideas and customs would have the effect, of course, of opening new horizons, raising doubts, and promoting heresies. The extraordinary simplicity and clarity of the old ways of thinking could not sustain the weight of new ideas without breaking. Interest in the interpretation of beliefs and in the analysis of myths was growing. The rise of the Zindiqs, whom the priest bitterly opposed, can be attributed to this penchant for interpretation. Mani and Mazdak also held views colored by an interpretive impulse, and were thus branded as "heretics." Faith in the old myths and doctrines was gradually waning. In their debates with the hierarchy of new religions, the free thinkers resorted to interpretation and exegesis. In this type of interpretation, which consisted of adducing arguments based on reason, the apparent meaning of words in religious texts lead to anomalies. In one instance, a Zoroastrian priest, who was in a dispute with a Christian named Mehrān Goshnasb, said, "We do not consider fire in any way a god. We worship God by praying to fire, just as you also worship God by praying to a cross." Mehrān Goshnasb, who in Syriac texts is called "Georgios," quotes from the Avesta to prove that in Zoroastrianism, fire as a god had been the object of worship.6

The effects of exposure to philosophy and the Zindiqs was gradually eroding the optimism and naiveté characteristic of Zoroastrianism. The spread of Manichaean beliefs and the teachings of Christ and the Buddha all contributed, to a greater or lesser extent, to a growing interest in asceticism and withdrawal from the world. In the "Advice of Oshnar the Wise," there are sentiments that contradict the views of Zoroaster and, to some extent, are colored by Manichaeism. He says, "The soul survives; what disappears is the body." Zurvanism, which was superior to the other sects during the Sasanian period, propagated a fatalism and determinism that was poisonous to the free will of Zoroastrianism and the idea of sovereign rule.[421]

---

[421] Zarrinkoub, Abdolhossein. Chapter 9: The Battle of Beliefs (Location 4422 – 4965). Two Centuries of Silence: An Account of Events and Conditions in Iran [Persia] During the First Two Hundred Years of

And further on in *Chapter 9: The Battle of Beliefs* of *Two Centuries of Silence: An Account of Events and Conditions in Iran [Persia] during the first Two Hundred Years of Islam*:

> The animosity on the part of the high priests and the increasing excesses of heretical sects were also factors in encouraging people to convert to Islam. Even so, those Zoroastrians who refused to accept the new faith would become dhimmis in Islam. Their fire temples would remain safe but they would have no opportunity for proselytizing. The Muslims left them free to practice their religious rituals but, in effect, denied them permission to go to war with the Quran and Islam by spreading their faith. The Umayyad caliphs were particularly adamant on this point, suppressing any new idea that gave off the slightest whiff of heresy. This was not because the Umayyads were pious or devout; for the most part, they had little interest in religion. They had to combat any new idea and every free thought because these would seep into the minds of the clients [mawālī], who could pose a major threat to Arab supremacy. This was the ostensible reason al-Ḥajjāj b. Yūsuf put to death Macbad b. cAbdallāh al-Juhanī, who had gotten Qadariyah doctrine from Sinbuya. The Umayyads were also brutal to Ghaylān of Damascus,14 who professed these views. Jahm b. Ṣafwān, a man from Termez in Khorasan, introduced determinism, and was severly punished for his innovation. The examples show the extremes the Umayyads would go to suppress any deviation from the religious norm, the violence they used to prevent any idea attributed to the clients from spreading.

> **The Zindiqs15**
>
> The first Abbasid caliphs were harsh and uncompromising toward the Zindiqs. Many people, whether clients or not, were charged with Zindiqism and put to death during the reigns of al-Manṣūr and al-Mahdī. There is, nevertheless, much evidence indicating that from the end of the Umayyad period, the remaining Magians and Manichaeans were spreading their doctrines in secret. The Zindiqs were apparently more active in this activity than the other sects. Their method of proselytizing was, first and foremost, to sow doubt about the religious and ethical bases of Islam. This method, given the climate of corruption and criminality that existed under the Umayyads, provided the Zindiqs with the chance to form movements and struggles sooner than other sects. On the surface the Zindiqs were followers of Mani, but their actual doctrine was grounded in doubt and skepticism. This was why any doubter or skeptic [of religion] was branded a Zindiq or, at least, a fellow Zindiqist traveler. During Umayyad rule, this type of belief, of course, had a wider currency than other religions. It is not surprising that one of the most corrupt Umayyad caliphs, Walīd b. Yazīd, looked with favor on Zindiq doctrine and made a show of Zindiqism. At the outset of Abbasid rule, the caliphs' difficulties and preoccupations, to some extent, created a climate of liberalism conducive to the spread of Zindiqism. This was why in Basra and Baghdad, followers of Mani, other free thinkers, and irreligious people engaged in disseminating their views and promoting skepticism about Muslim doctrine. Under al-Manṣūr and al-Mahdī, Zindiq efforts and activities became more difficult and dangerous, which forced the caliphs to seek a solution to the problem.

> The Zindiqs, in reality, threatened both Islam and the caliphate. The foundation of Arab rule was built on Islam and the Quran, the truth of which the Zindiqs questioned. Both the caliphate and the religious establishment, then, considered them pernicious. The Zindiqs did not speak kindly of the Quran; they rejected what the interpreters said about two types of verses in the Quran: the "plainly

---

Islam, from the Arab Invasion to the Rise of the Tahirid Dynasty First edition. Mazda Publishers. Kindle Edition.

clear verses" [muḥkamāt] and "the verses requiring intuition" [mutashābihāt]. They claimed the Quran was inconsistent with some verses contradicting others.16 Some made up verses on their own and juxtaposed those verses with the verses of the book of God. They also found [Islamic] religious rituals and rites the subject of mirth. While in Mecca, Yazdān b. Bādhān saw people circumambulating the Ka'ba and said they look like a herd of cattle trampling hay with their hooves.17 Another Zindiq, in debate with [the sixth Shia Imam] Jacfar al-Ṣādiq, asked the Imam what was the use of fasting and prayer. The Imam said, "If there is a Day of Reckoning, carrying out these duties will benefit us; but if there is not to be such a day, then they can't do us any harm either."18 Such talk on the part of Zindiqs, of course, was impudent and alarming. It was not surprising that the Abbasid caliphs were very quick to see the danger in it and confront it. While there were authorities and free thinkers among those put to death on charges of Zindiqism in the early period, sources indicate active recruitment to the movement and proselytizing of its doctrines did not go into full force until the time of al-Manṣūr.

cAbdallāh b. Muqaffac [ca. 721-ca. 757]19

Among those arrested and, ultimately, put to death during this period one can mention Ibn Muqaffac and Bashshār b. Burd. Though himself Iranian in origin from G r [Firuzābād] and known as Rōzbeh the son of Dādūya [a.k.a. Dādōē], cAbdallāh b. Muqaffac was considered one of the master translators and writers in the Arabic language. Many works provide accounts of his Zindiq leanings. It is said he composed a book in imitation of the Quran. The Caliph al-Mahdī is reported to have said, "Every work of heresy [zandaqa] I have seen can be traced back to Ibn al-Muqaffac." Abū Rayḥān Bīrūnī also wrote that after Ibn al-Muqaffac translated Kalila wa Dimna from Pahlavi, he appended the chapter on Borzuya to it to cause Muslims to doubt their beliefs and make them ready to accept his faith, the religion of Mani.

From what sources tell us about the life of Ibn al-Muqaffac, we conclude he was inclined toward heresy. Safwān b. Mucāwiyya, the governor of Basra, having officially accused him of heresy, put him to death in the most appaling way. The truth is, however, Ibn al-Muqaffac, more than anything else, was the victim of his enemies' jealousy. Safwān, it is said, resented him and was on the lookout for an opportunity to bring him down. Al-Manṣūr also despised him and egged Safwān on in his search for vengeance. After finding a way of bringing Ibn al-Muqaffac down, the governor of Basra ordered a bread oven stoked and, before his very eyes, they put his body, torn limb from limbs, into the inferno. The sources tell us Ibn al-Muqaffac, like the other Zindiqs, was respectful of religion. Even if what Abū Rayḥān Bīrūnī said about him appending the chapter on Borzuya to the translation of Kalila wa Dimna is not true, there is evidence that he looked at religions and religious sects with skepticism and distrust. One such piece of evidence is his own treatise called Risālat al-Ṣaḥāba ["Treatise on the Companions"] which he sent to al-Manṣūr. After going on at length about the inhabitants of Khorasan and their treatment, Ibn al-Muqaffac says there are many contradictions and discrepancies in the provisions of Islamic jurisprudence. Often the rulings issued on one issue contradict other rulings on the same issue. He therefore requested the caliph give some thought to the matter and write his judges so they could rule without incurring inconsistencies and confusion. Evident, too, in the treatise are the skepticism and distrust expressed in the "Borzuya, the Physician" chapter and the pillars of Zindiq belief. This shows the writer's intent was not so much to find a solution but to find fault. In any case, Ibn al-Muqaffac, though decidedly a Zindiq, was not, like many of that ilk, one who saw irreligion and free thought as a badge of refinement and good schooling. He did not, therefore, make such an open show of disbelief as Bashshār b. Burd and Abān b. cAbd al-Ḥamīd Lāḥaqqī did. Rather, by translating and publishing works of scholarship and literature, he tried to expose Muslims to new thinking and get them to doubt their own beliefs and views.

Bashshār b. Burd

To Bashshār b. Burd, Zindiqism was a way of showing off his literary virtuosity and craftsmanship. This is why he had no compunction about openly proclaiming his affiliation to the sect. Bashshār b. Burd was a blind poet from Tokharistan. So famous was Bashshār as a lyric poet, women would visit his home to memorize his poetry, and professional singers would not perform any lyrics but his. Pious people in that age said nothing contributed to the proliferation of debauchery and depravity, of sin and lust, more than the songs of the blind poet. Bashshār also employed his taste and talent to spread Zindiqism, and his poetry was considered one of the principal reasons for the popularity of the doctrine. Wāṣil b. cAṭā, one of the major Mutazilites, said in this regard, "The poetry of this blind man is one of the greatest and grimmest of the Devil's snares." One of the beliefs Bashshār openly espoused involved fire. He placed a higher value on fire, which for Zoroastrians is the manifestation of light and a focus of worship, than earth, on which Muslims pray and which is the basic element in human nature. Bashshār is famous for composing the following: "earth is dark and fire is bright/and fire has been worshipped ever since it was fire."20 The import of this is: even the Devil, who is made of fire, is superior to man, who comes from clay. This type of mocking and belittling of Muslim beliefs got Bashshār branded as a heretic. Finally, after Bashshār satirized the caliph, al-Mahdī had had enough and, while on a trip to Basra, he ordered the poet arrested and flogged to death.

The Spread of Heresy

Apart from Bashshār and Ibn Muqaffac, several other authors and composers of Arabic verse were accused of heresy. They went so far as to write books justifying the doctrines of Mani and of [early Christian theorists like] Marcion and Bardaisan. Al-Mahdī executed some of these writers as well. One of them was cAbd al-Karīm b. Abī al-cAwjā', a Manichaean proselytizer, who engaged in open debate with his opponents. Books record some of the debates with Abū al-Hudhayl cAllāf, the Baghdadi Mutazilite. cAbd al-Karīm was also put to death by al-Mahdī. The truth is that Zindiqism during the time of the caliphs was the most widespread of all the sects of ancient Iran. This was because it represented the faith of most free thinkers who rejected religion, could be adapted to their own tastes. Many also adopted Zindiqism out of a sense of delicacy and delight in life. It was not only special territory to the clients, but the Arabs also were familiar with it. The Arabs came to know about Zindiqism through the people of Hira; Iraq also was, from early times, considered one of the places where Manichaean rites made their appearance. This was why from the beginning of the reign of the Baghdad caliphs, Zindiqism was current among the enlightened people and free thinkers of the age. Apart from those accused of Zindiqism executed by the caliphs, others to whom it was ascribed but did not go overboard in professing it were, therefore, not arrested. One can mention the names of many poets and writers of Arabic from this period who were branded Zindiq or Magian and whose stories can be read in books of history and literature. The thing that forced the caliphs to tangle with these heretics was their inflexibility and insistence on convincing people to become skeptical of all religions and beliefs. Except for Mani they considered all those known as prophets to be liars. The Muslim caliphs could not, of course, abide such a view. This was especially true considering the Quran includes Magians among the People of the Book; but there was no such language about the Manichaeans in the Quran. Al-Mahdī, then, as well as his successors, made great efforts to eliminate the Zindiqs. Al-Mahdī appointed a special agent, the "Zindiq Officer" [Ṣāḥib al-Zanādaqah], charged with hunting down and stamping out heretics.21 He also stipulated in his will that al-Hādī, his son and successor, would continue the pursuit of the Zindiqs,22 which he did energetically. Al-Hārūn also did not stop the persecution, and in 171 [22 June 787-10 June 788], he granted all refugees and escapees but the Zindiqs, who had turned away out of fear of him, safe passage.23 Al-Ma'mūn ordered one of the Zindiq leaders from Rayy, Yazdān, to engage in open debate with Muslim scholars. Yazdān agreed but asked in advance for clemency. When he failed to be persuasive, Al-Ma'mūn said,

"Yazdān, convert to Islam, for, if I had not granted you clemency, you'd have been executed by now." Yazdān said, "O Commander of the Faithful, what you say is reasonable, but I know you are not one of those people who force others to abandon their faith."24 This anecdote notwithstanding, al-Ma'mūn, was less tolerant toward heresy than other caliphs. Historians record he used the methods of his predecessors in his persecution of heretics. When informed that ten Zindiqs had appeared and were calling on people to follow Mani, al-Ma'mūn ordered them taken as a group. A potbellied man, famous for regularly turning up at homes uninvited, happened to see the group. Imagining they were on their way to a wedding festivity, he fell in with the men, who were on their way to a ship. When those charged with bringing them in arrived, they put the interloper in chains along with the others. Terrified, the gatecrasher asked them who they were and why were they in chains. They explained and asked him how was it he had joined them. "I'm just an uninvited guest by profession. When I saw your group, I figured you were on your way to a gathering, so I joined the group." After the ship had reached Baghdad, they brought the men before al-Ma'mūn. One by one, each of the ten was ordered to curse Mani and renounce their faith in his religion. All ten refused and were executed. The caliph turned to the gatecrasher and asked his name and inquired about his circumstances. The man told him. This made al-Ma'mūn laugh, and he pardoned the man.25[422]

Of course, given this broader historical context, this means from near its inception to right now in modern-day, the persecutions and assassinations of Atheists by Islamists has never stopped. It has never once abated in Islamic societies. The Charvakas of Medieval India mysteriously vanished from history under Islamic rule; given the context of how brutal and sadistic the murders of Zindiqs of Medieval Iran were, and the similar sadistic brutality of Islamic rulers like Aurangzeb, we now have a clearer understanding of what likely happened to them too. The persecution and murder of Atheists does deserve its own subsection because it is a persecution that has gone on for far too long and it is abundantly clear that most religious people around the world don't care about their lives at all. If you consider how long Islam has actually been persecuting Atheists, they might credibly be among the most persecuted people on earth due to Islam; I think it is plausible to say that only Jewish people have been persecuted more than Atheists in world history in terms of the length of history when you factor what Islam did to Atheists. Unfortunately, there is also the problem of Muslims faking being Ex-Muslim Atheists in order to get refugee status into superior non-Islamic cultures, but that shouldn't mean lack of sympathy for when Atheists are genuinely persecuted and murdered in modern times. I can't highlight every single murder of Atheists by Islamists, but I can highlight some anecdotes in the absence of any reliable survey research data.

The first Ex-Muslim Atheist suffering persecution I'd ever heard of was Aliaa Magda Elmahdy, who at the time of the 2011 Egyptian revolution, posted a nude picture

---

[422] Zarrinkoub, Abdolhossein. Chapter 9: The Battle of Beliefs (Location 4422 – 4965). Two Centuries of Silence: An Account of Events and Conditions in Iran [Persia] During the First Two Hundred Years of Islam, from the Arab Invasion to the Rise of the Tahirid Dynasty First edition. Mazda Publishers. Kindle Edition.

of herself to protest the misogyny and violence against women in Islamic culture.[423] I recall an English translated message from Aliaa Magda Elmahdy where she condemned the fact that young Egyptian girls were beaten up for not having their hijabs worn properly. Under the dictator Hosni Mubarak, women were subjected to virginity tests in Cairo's Tahrir Square.[424] Unfortunately, this act of nude feminist protest led to her being abandoned by the liberal political groups to appease the social conservative sentiments of Islamists in Egypt. Aliaa Magda Elmahdy received death threats and was even kidnapped at one point.[425] I recall an old article mentioning how the kidnapper threw misogynistic slurs at her and it may have been a rape attempt. She fled to Sweden for asylum[426] and revealed she had become an atheist at age 16 once she was safe from being killed for apostasy in Islam. On August 27th, 2014, Jillian Steinhauer published an article titled *"Feminist Activists Bleed and Defecate on Islamic State Flag #NSFW"* on Aliaa Magda Elmahdy's Free Speech protest photo against the Islamic State with Aliaa Magda Elmahdy's work with the Ukrainian feminist group, Femen. Details from the article are as follows:

> Egyptian feminist activist Aliaa Magda Elmahdy made a statement against the Islamic State (IS) this past weekend with the release of an explicit photograph on her Facebook page. The picture shows Elmahdy naked and menstruating on the flag of IS, while alongside her a woman dressed in a black hijab flicks off the camera and defecates on the flag too. The letters IS are painted on both women's bodies. According to LiveLeak, "Arab media across the Middle East avoided publishing the photo, since the words 'there is no God but Allah' are printed on the desecrated flag."
>
> For the photo, Elmahdy was working in tandem with Femen, the controversial Ukrainian feminist group known for its nude and topless protests. Elmahdy linked up with the group in the wake of her first foray into public nudity, in 2011, when the then-20-year-old posted photos of herself wearing only stocking and red shoes on her blog. The pictures sparked a huge uproar in Egypt, and Elmahdy says she was charged by the state and briefly kidnapped because of them. She received political asylum in Sweden, where she continues to live. It was there that she met and participated in naked protests with members of Femen.
>
> Elmahdy is not talking to the media about the new photo targeted at IS, but *Vice* discussed it with Inna Shevchenko, founder of Femen — whose logo, two circles with a vertical line between them, is also painted on one of the women in the IS photo. Shevchenko explains that the picture was a direct response to the video showing the murder of journalist James Foley: "With our photo message we propose our own 'way of execution' of Islamic State ideas," she said. "Our caption to the photo reads: 'Animals, our execution of your ideas looks like that! Watch it well!

---

[423] Mezzofiore, Gianluca. "Aliaa Magda Elmahdy, Nude Blogger, Gains Support from Egyptian Diaspora." International Business Times UK, International Business Times UK, 18 Nov. 2011, www.ibtimes.co.uk/aliaa-magda-elmahdy-nude-blogger-gains-support-252301.
[424] Mezzofiore, Gianluca. "Aliaa Magda Elmahdy, Nude Blogger, Gains Support from Egyptian Diaspora." International Business Times UK, International Business Times UK, 18 Nov. 2011, www.ibtimes.co.uk/aliaa-magda-elmahdy-nude-blogger-gains-support-252301.
[425] Asad, Amira. "The Egyptian Feminist Who Was Kidnapped for Posing Nude." VICE, VICE, 14 Feb. 2013, www.vice.com/en/article/the-egyptian-feminist-who-was-kidnapped-for-posing-nude/.
[426] Asad, Amira. "The Egyptian Feminist Who Was Kidnapped for Posing Nude." VICE, VICE, 14 Feb. 2013, www.vice.com/en/article/the-egyptian-feminist-who-was-kidnapped-for-posing-nude/.

We don't demand ransoms, we don't threaten you with new killings, we just SHIT ON YOU, ISIS!'"

Shevchenko continues:

"With the picture we want to criticize the killings, rapes, and public executions by Islamic fascists, who are breaking news. This is what the Islamic State wants. They want the world to obey their ideas. Spreading their video messages of executions and sharing their speeches, we do a good job for them, we serve the Islamic State. Instead we should spread our message to them. Enough of tolerance! Don't be scared to offend. Let's hit them back with our answers, instead of giving them more space. The world is in fear, exactly as the Islamic State wants. We call not to fear them, but to resist them."

Although she's not speaking to the press, Elmahdy continues to post on her blog, A Rebel's Diary, and has been consistently tweeting and posting on Facebook the dizzying number of death and other threats she's received in response to the photo.[427]

On August 7th, 2015, BBC journalist Mukul Devichand reported the numerous targeted murders of atheists in Bangladesh by Islamists in his article titled "*'Nowhere is safe': Behind the Bangladesh blogger murders*" which begins as follows:

Bangladesh's small community of online atheists is in shock after the murder of another blogger. Many are focusing on one detail of the latest killing - its location.

The men who hacked **Niloy Neel to death with machetes** seemed to be following a gory pattern that we have already seen three times this year.

Just like Avijit Roy, Washiqur Rahman and Ananta Bijoy Das - all killed recently - the victim was known to internet users as an atheist. They form a community who, for several years, used blog posts to challenge the existence of God, and to argue with Islamic and other religious and political ideas.

Islamic extremists have been blamed by authorities for the spate of murders of atheists.

There was one crucial difference this time, however: Neel was attacked in his own home, whereas the others were attacked in public.

Last week I was in Dhaka, speaking to bloggers and Islamic groups, and broadcasting a **special hour-long edition of BBC Trending on World Service radio**. We met several atheist and secular bloggers who were extremely cautious in public but felt it was safe to talk to us at home - at least at that point.

The 'list'

So far, two madrassa students have been arrested for Rahman's killing, and an online Islamist who called for Roy's murder has been detained - though no one has yet been charged.

All four men killed were on a list of 84 "atheist bloggers". The list was drawn up by Islamic groups in 2013 and has been widely circulated. It was originally submitted to the government with the aim of having these bloggers arrested, and tried for blasphemy.

---

[427] Steinhauer, Jillian. "Feminist Activists Bleed and Defecate on Islamic State Flag #NSFW." Hyperallergic, Hyperallergic, 27 Aug. 2014, hyperallergic.com/145768/feminist-activists-bleed-and-shit-on-islamic-state-flag-nsfw/.

> The large Islamic groups who initially wanted bloggers arrested told us they have no knowledge of who is killing them. Online, many pro-Islamic voices condemn the killings but also criticise secular and atheist bloggers.
>
> "They were making fun of Allah, in a really bad way," Trivuz Alam, a conservative blogger, told BBC Trending.
>
> Talukder Shaheb (not his real name), a young blogger associated with the Jamaat-e-Islami political party, also condemned the murders but defended those who want the bloggers arrested.
>
> "In Bangladesh you can get arrested for criticising the prime minister," he said. "Then why not criticising God, because God is much higher than the prime minister, right?"[428]

Unfortunately, parts of the article try to conflate Atheism and secular-leanings in order to argue the age-old and uniquely Western bigotry that Atheists aren't really atheist before continuing on with relevant information:

> They accuse the authorities not only of failing to protect them - but of arresting atheist bloggers to appease Islamic groups.
>
> Six have been arrested and bailed on charges of hurting religious sentiment.
>
> Sarah Hossain, a human rights lawyer who represented several arrested bloggers, told us: "The concern that many of us have is that while you cannot hurt religious sentiment, you can hurt secular sentiment as much as you want."
>
> The government has been accused of suppressing freedom of speech for religious and secular voices alike, including through the arrests of opposition figures.
>
> But Mr Inu defended government actions. "We have certain laws that say you shouldn't use religion in the wrong manner," he said. "If you incite somebody or you incite disorder, then you are supposed to be arrested and face trial,"
>
> He denied freedom of speech was under threat in Bangladesh.
>
> "If you look at the mass media and social media, everybody is criticising the loopholes of the government or the misuse of power, or corruption," he said.
>
> **'Open prison'**
>
> The mood among atheist and secular bloggers, after the latest murder, is a mixture of fear and defiance.
>
> "Bloggers [and] progressive-minded members of society are fuming with rage," blogger Arif Rahman tells BBC Trending. "Bloggers are no longer afraid. The anger towards the government is now the main theme."
>
> But others seem more cautious. One tells us the whole country has become an "open prison" for him and his young family, and he has been scared into censoring some of what he writes.
>
> This morning, he says he is even more terrified. "There isn't an inch of safe space in Bangladesh," he says. With a blogger now killed at home, he asks: "How can I think my house is safe?"

---

[428] Devichand, Mukul. "'Nowhere Is Safe': Behind the Bangladesh Blogger Murders." BBC News, BBC, 7 Aug. 2015, www.bbc.com/news/blogs-trending-33822674.

Additional reporting by Estelle Doyle[429]

On September 25th, 2016 an English translation of *The Independent*'s article titled "*Alleged killer who shot atheist Jordanian writer identified*" in reference to the murder of Jordanian Atheist and cartoonist, Nahed Hattar. The original writer of the article was apparently journalist Bethan McKernan. Unfortunately, while attempting to portray itself as a Middle-ground position, the article's information at the end is yet another in a long history of Islam's dehumanization of Atheists as a way of justifying the killing. The journalist likely wanted to appease Islamic sensibilities, so that Islamists could feel validated that Hattar's life had no value in their minds. It seems to omit the fact that ISIS was persecuting and slaughtering Christians in Syria and I think it is plausible that Nahed Hattar may have simply thought that Bashar al-Assad was the lesser of two evils because Hattar may have been concerned for the Syrian Christian communities, since he came from a Christian background himself:

> **Alleged killer who shot atheist Jordanian writer identified**
>
> *Controversial writer Nahed Hatter's arrest was ordered by Prime Minister Hani al-Mulki for posting a cartoon depicting the image of God on social media*
>
> A man who shot a Jordanian writer dead outside the Supreme Court in Amman has been identified as a local imam in his late 40s.
>
> Jordanian media reported the alleged shooter's name and picture on Sunday, which was supplied to them by a police officer under condition of anonymity. The reports said Riad Abdullah is from Hashi, a poor neighbourhood of the Jordanian capital, and had recently returned from a trip abroad. No further details were given.
>
> Nahed Hattar, a prominent atheist Jordanian writer, turned himself into the authorities after a police investigation was launched into a cartoon he shared on Facebook. It depicted God in paradise, being treated as a servant by a bearded Arab man, who is smoking in bed with two women and calling for wine.
>
> Relatives said the cartoon was meant to illustrate what Hattar saw as the twisted religious views of Isis extremists.
>
> All physical depictions of God or the Prophet Muhammad, even respectful ones, are forbidden under mainstream Islamic tradition, and are illegal in deeply conservative Jordan.
>
> Witnesses and police said Hattar, 56, was preparing to enter the courthouse for a hearing on Sunday morning when the gunman shot him three times at close range. The shooter was arrested at the scene.
>
> Government spokesperson Mohammad Momani condemned the killing as a "heinous crime."
>
> But Hattar's family criticised the government's response. "The prime minister was the first one who incited against Nahed when he ordered his arrest and put him on trial for sharing the cartoon, and that ignited the public against him and led to his killing," said Saad Hattar, a cousin of the

---

[429] Devichand, Mukul. "'Nowhere Is Safe': Behind the Bangladesh Blogger Murders." BBC News, BBC, 7 Aug. 2015, www.bbc.com/news/blogs-trending-33822674.

writer. "Many fanatics wrote on social media calling for his killing and lynching, and the government did nothing against them," a family statement said.

Hattar has long been a controversial figure in Jordan.

While born a Christian, he considered himself an atheist. He was a strong supporter of Syrian President Bashar Assad and an outspoken critic of Isis and Al-Qaeda.

His shooting was the latest in a string of deadly security lapses in Jordan.[430]

Here is an English translated version of the cartoon mocking the Abrahamic God of ISIS that Nahed Hattar was killed for:

Source: "Jordanian Writer Nahed Hattar Was Murdered Outside the Court Where He Was on Trial for Publishing a Cartoon." JRMora, Cartoons, jrmora.com, 21 May 2022, jrmora.com/en/jordanian-writer-nahed-hattar-murdered-court-trial-publishing-cartoon/.

On April 26th, 2017, journalist Bethan McKernan published an article on *The Independent* titled "*Man 'sentenced to death for atheism' in Saudi Arabia*" which contained the following:

Man 'sentenced to death for atheism' in Saudi Arabia

Man identified by local media as Ahmad Al-Shamri, in his 20s, lost two appeals after being arrested on charges of blasphemy for social media videos in which he denounced the Prophet Mohammed

A man in Saudi Arabia has reportedly been sentenced to death on charges of apostasy after losing two appeals.

---

[430] McKernan, Bethan. "Alleged Killer Who Shot Atheist Jordanian Writer Outside Supreme Court Identified." The Independent, Independent Digital News and Media, 25 Sept. 2016, www.independent.co.uk/news/world/middle-east/alleged-killer-who-shot-atheist-jordanian-writer-charged-with-offensive-facebook-post-identified-a7329391.html.

Several local media reports identified the man as Ahmad Al Shamri, in his 20s, from the town of Hafar al-Batin, who first came to the authorities' attention in 2014 after allegedly uploading videos to social media in which he renounced Islam and the Prophet Mohammed.

He was arrested on charges of atheism and blasphemy and held in prison before being convicted by a local court and sentenced to death in February 2015.

At the time Mr Shamri's defence entered an insanity plea, adding that his client was under the influence of drugs and alcohol at the time of making the videos.

He reportedly lost an Appeals Court case, and a Supreme Court ruled against him earlier this week.

While news stories in the last few years consistently identify Mr Shamri, his identity or sentencing has not been verified by the Saudi authorities.

The Independent's requests for comment from Saudi government representatives were not immediately answered.

Under Saudi Arabia's strict religious laws, leaving Islam can be punishable by harsh prison sentences and corporeal punishment - and a 2014 string of royal decrees under the late King Abdullah re-defined atheists as terrorists, according to a report by Human Rights Watch.

Last year, a citizen was sentenced to 10 years in prison and 2,000 lashes for expressing atheistic sentiment in hundreds of social media posts.

Mr Shamri's name and hometown have trended on Arabic-speaking Twitter in the last few days. Some users have even celebrated his sentencing.

"If you're a lowkey atheist that's fine. But once you talk in public & criticize God or religion, then you shall be punished," one such post read.

"I wish there could be live streaming when you cut his head off," said another.[431]

There exists a plethora of anecdotes about the struggles of Ex-Muslim Atheists and far too many for me to list in a single chapter. It would probably require its own book. Ex-Muslim Atheist Rana Ahmad fleeing from her family due to her brother trying to kill her and even trying to hire an assassin to kill her in the European country that she eventually received amnesty in.[432][433] I generally do not trust *Human Rights Watch* due to their explicitly Anti-Hindu bigotry on repeated occasions from using a book that had no

---

[431] McKernan, Bethan. "A Man Has Been 'sentenced to Death' in Saudi Arabia for Being an Atheist." The Independent, The Independent World, 26 Apr. 2017, web.archive.org/web/20170426142501/www.independent.co.uk/news/world/middle-east/saudi-arabia-man-sentenced-death-atheism-ahmad-al-shamri-hafar-al-batin-appeal-denied-a7703161.html.
[432] "Rescuing Ex-Muslims: Leaving Islam." YouTube, VICE News, 10 Feb. 2016, www.youtube.com/watch?v=O1lnxUXWGgE.
[433] Dawkins, Richard, and Rana Ahmad. "Richard Dawkins Interviews Saudi Arabian Atheist Author Rana Ahmad." Www.Youtube.Com, Richard Dawkins Foundation for Reason & Science, 25 Feb. 2019, www.youtube.com/watch?v=_zncB6hngZg.

credibility and thrown out of the Indian court system[434][435], to blaming Hindus for a tragic massacre by arguing that it was due to Hindus practicing their faith[436], and then to vilifying Hindu terms for Third-Gender because it wasn't in a strictly Western lexicon parroting their Eurocentric views by using the term LGBT as a shield instead of recognizing cultural terms like Third-Gender[437]; all of which are shamefully bigoted and ignorant of Human Rights Watch, but in the absence of any other organization covering this, I thought it best to mention it: on January 2021 a Yemeni man named Ali Abu Luhum was sentenced to fifteen years for blasphemy against Islam in Saudi Arabia due to expressing Atheist viewpoints.[438] The are so many more cases throughout the Middle East and among Muslim families within Western Europe and Canada.

    Some may question why I bothered highlighting obvious examples like Saudi Arabia. When I looked at the historical context of the persecution of Atheists after reading major parts of the English translation of *Two Centuries of Silence* back in 2018, a few disturbing realizations dawned on me when I compared it to contemporary Ex-Muslim human rights issues. Please think about this: consider the banality of Atheist deaths in Muslim-majority countries and how little all of these so-called human rights groups, international institutions, and governments like the United States even concern themselves with such deaths. It is only recently that it has gained much criticism at all. Atheist lives are never going to matter when it comes to international trade discussions the same way that other religious groups will at least get a passing mention. When the US Corporate media circus discusses Saudi Arabia's economic improvements, there'll be reasonable discussions on the rights of women – as there should – but do any of them really care that Atheists are going to be publicly beheaded and that large populations of Saudis take sadistic pleasure in this fact when they talk about Saudi Arabia's so-called progress under Saudi Prince Mohammed bin Salman Al Saud? No, because the lives of Ex-Muslim Atheists are categorically inconvenient when discussing issues about the Middle East. Do any of them care that Ex-Muslim Atheists live with threats that their own families will murder them or that Ex-Muslim Atheists grow suicidal because they're forced to keep silent due to legitimate threats to their lives? Only if it won't negatively harm economic interests at the convenience of other countries. The truth is that nobody

---

[434] "Supreme Court Trashes Rana Ayyub's Gujarat Book, Says It Is Based upon Surmises, Conjectures, and Suppositions." OpIndia, OpIndia, 5 July 2019, www.opindia.com/2019/07/supreme-court-rana-ayyub-gujarat-files-haren-pandya-murder/.
[435] "India: A Decade on, Gujarat Justice Incomplete." Human Rights Watch, 28 Oct. 2020, www.hrw.org/news/2012/02/24/india-decade-gujarat-justice-incomplete#.
[436] "'WE HAVE NO ORDERS TO SAVE YOU' State Participation and Complicity in Communal Violence in Gujarat." Www.Hrw.Org, Human Rights Watch, www.hrw.org/reports/2002/india/gujarat.pdf. Accessed 22 Aug. 2025. For Reference on page 44
[437] Knight, Kyle, and Meenakshi Ganguly. "India Gets Another Chance Protecting Transgender Rights." Human Rights Watch, Human Rights Watch Dispatches, 22 Feb. 2018, www.hrw.org/news/2018/02/22/india-gets-another-chance-protecting-transgender-rights.
[438] "Saudi Arabia: Yemeni Man Sentenced for Apostasy." Human Rights Watch, Human Rights Watch: News Release, 7 Jan. 2021, www.hrw.org/news/2021/12/20/saudi-arabia-yemeni-man-sentenced-apostasy.

cares about them; nobody is going to go the extra mile to give them amnesty unless they themselves risk their lives to fight for it, everyone will turn a blind eye if they're tortured or executed when other people's economic interests are put at risk, and nobody sees any intrinsic value in their lives because they don't believe in the supernatural – even when such supernatural beliefs are literally the reason they're going to be put to death. Of course, Ex-Muslim Atheists – unlike Ex-Muslim Hindus or Ex-Muslim Christians – are some of the most obnoxious and bigoted people on the planet who also dehumanize Hindus just like most Muslims do. They cannot let go of their attachment to a community that wants to murder them, because that's where their family remains. They still try to see the love and goodness in family members who want to kill them. They don't seem to understand that such behavior is obviously not love; if someone threatens to kill you for leaving a religion, then that person only saw you as an object to further their own interests and not an individual deserving of equal respect and value. If nothing else, it seems that Islam's contribution to India beyond just putting women in cages during the Medieval period to sell them and their children at slave auctions, the mass murder and persecution of Hindus and other Dharmic followers, and the regression of Dharmic civilization with the inability to practice Free Expression; it seems we must now add social stigma against Atheists after they likely slaughtered every Atheist – especially Dharmic followers who were Atheist – that they could find, just like what happened in Medieval Iran. There's honestly no reason to doubt this, because they still persecute and slaughter Atheists in Bangladesh, Pakistan, Afghanistan, and the Middle East. Islam has committed and continues to conduct the longest, systemic genocide in human history against all atheists throughout the entire world.

  Two final issues to consider: the attack on Ex-Muslim Atheist Salman Rushdie, who has lived under threat of Iran issuing a fatwa to assassinate him for his fantasy novel known as *The Satanic Verses*, was stabbed repeatedly on August 12th, 2022 at a speaking event about how the US is a safe haven for exiled writers in New York.[439] The attack was clearly an Islamist political statement about how any critic of Islam is not safe in the United States and that they should expect their lives to be in danger for criticizing Islam. While Liberal Americans were screaming Islamophobia, people swept this very disturbing political message under the rug or they were otherwise too stupid to see it clearly. What has happened since then? Salwan Momika, an Ex-Christian Atheist known for his Free Speech political activism of burning the Quran, was murdered on January 29th, 2025 earlier this year in his own apartment complex after the EU deported him back

---

[439] "Salman Rushdie Stabbing Suspect Charged with Attempted Murder as Author Remains Hospitalized with 'Serious' Wounds." CBS News, CBS Interactive, 13 Aug. 2022, www.cbsnews.com/news/salman-rushdie-stabbing-suspect-hadi-matar/.

to Sweden when he tried to leave for his own safety back around April 2024.[440][441] Nobody in Western Europe seems to have thought over the fact that the EU's laws and labeling his Free Speech activism as "far-right" for criticizing Islam effectively killed this man and that Muslims in Sweden and across the world took sadistic delight and laughed about his murder online arguing it was justified that he was killed.[442] Democratic norms and values are regressing right before our eyes and these incompetent policymakers in power don't see or understand the danger around them.

Dehumanization and Assassinations of Hindus and Other Dharmic followers

Union of India - Section
Section 295A in The Indian Penal Code, 1860
295A. Deliberate and malicious acts, intended to outrage religious feelings of any class by insulting its religion or religious beliefs.—
Whoever, with deliberate and malicious intention of outraging the religious feelings of any class of citizens of India, by words, either spoken or written, or by signs or by visible representations or otherwise, insults or attempts to insult the religion or the religious beliefs of that class, shall be punished with imprisonment of either description for a term which may extend to three years, or with fine, or with both.[443]

Definition of IPC 153A:
Promoting enmity between different groups on grounds of religion, race, place of birth, residence, language, etc., and doing acts prejudicial to maintenance of harmony.
Classification :
This section is Non-bailable, Cognizable and Non-compoundable.
Triable By :
Any Magistrate of the first class.
Punishment :
According to Para 1 – Imprisonment for 3 years, or fine, or both.
According to para 2 – Imprisonment for 5 years and fine.[444]

---

[440] Hamade, Kassem. "Salwan Momika Är Tillbaka – Går till Attack Mot Norge." Salwan Momika Är Tillbaka i Sverige – Ilskan Mot Norge | Sverige | Expressen, Expressen, 11 Apr. 2024, web.archive.org/web/20240411193917/https://www.expressen.se/nyheter/sverige/salwan-momika-ar-tillbaka-i--sverige-ilskan-mot-norge/. For Reference: Google Translated from Swedish to English.
[441] Davies, Maia, and Danny Aeberhard. "Man Who Burned Quran 'Shot Dead in Sweden.'" BBC News, BBC, 30 Jan. 2025, www.bbc.com/news/articles/cpdx2wqpg7zo.
[442] Aydemir, Ridvan. "They Want to Kill Me Next | Stand with Me." YouTube, Apostate Prophet, 1 Feb. 2025, www.youtube.com/watch?v=AT3sKDZZppQ&ab_channel=ApostateProphet.
[443] "Section 295A in the Indian Penal Code, 1860." Indiankanoon.Org, Indian Kanoon, indiankanoon.org/doc/1803184/. Accessed 23 Aug. 2025.
[444] "Chapter 8: IPC 153A." The Indian Penal Code (IPC), The Indian Penal Code (IPC), 14 Jan. 2014, www.indianpenalcode.in/ipc-153a/.

Hindus in India continue to suffer dehumanization and murders because of the legacy of Islamic imperialism and then British imperialism's effort to stamp out Free Speech. The majority of India is still lied to about their own history of what the Islamic conquests had wrought upon India, Marxism vilifies Hindus as backwards and supported British imperial policy even when the British were torturing and murdering Hindus[445], and the US Corporate media fails to use any logical thinking faculties when talking about India while pretending Pakistan, Afghanistan, and Bangladesh aren't going to be the result of what India becomes, if it became a Muslim-majority country.

I originally wanted to do what I thought would be a balanced perspective, but the truth is that even those on Left-leaning Indian political spheres have lied to themselves about the pernicious problems within Islam and how it teaches Muslims to behave. Take scholar Dilip Simeon's attempt to criticize Islamic rioters in India on February 12th, 2015 in his article for *The Indian Express* titled *"The tyranny of hurt sentiment"* which begins with the following:

> Shirin Dalvi, the editor of the Mumbai edition of Urdu newspaper Avadhnama, has become the latest victim of the running saga over cartoons. Since mid-January, when she unwittingly published a Charlie Hebdo cover, she has been slapped with criminal charges, her newspaper shut down, its employees rendered jobless, and she herself forced underground. Vicious threats are sent to her via social media. All this is happening despite her printed apology. The police have opposed anticipatory bail on the ground that it would cause a law and order problem (aren't they paid to deal with such matters?).
>
> The man who filed the complaint heads an Urdu journalists' body. He is cited as saying, "I filed a case against her and I am happy that she was arrested. If she was in an Islamic state, she would have been beheaded as per law."
>
> That the freedom of speech could be so flagrantly attacked in the name of religion is by now a common experience. Self-appointed guardians of faith have attacked our minds with relentless aggression for years. But that someone could wish a horrible death to another human being is itself highly offensive to many of us — and this person thinks it earns him merit in the eyes of Allah. I have no access to the mind of the Almighty, but I can venture to suggest that Allah is more considerate than some of his followers.[446]

The rest of his article attempts to talk about "vulnerable religious minorities" and how the State is somehow responsible for this failure, while trying to credit a scant few Muslims from other countries for doing the bare minimum of human decency with not supporting murder.[447] The truth is, he is among many examples of people trying to give

---

[445] Marx, Karl. "The British Rule in India." The British Rule in India by Karl Marx, www.marxists.org/archive/marx/works/1853/06/25.htm. Accessed 23 Aug. 2025.
[446] Simeon, Dilip. "The Tyranny of Hurt Sentiment." The Indian Express, The Indian Express, 11 Feb. 2015, web.archive.org/web/20220726090225/https://indianexpress.com/article/opinion/columns/the-tyranny-of-hurt-sentiment/.
[447] Simeon, Dilip. "The Tyranny of Hurt Sentiment." The Indian Express, The Indian Express, 11 Feb. 2015, web.archive.org/web/20220726090225/https://indianexpress.com/article/opinion/columns/the-tyranny-of-hurt-sentiment/.

credit to a 7th century Arab fundamentalist ideology that doesn't support the human rights of anyone outside the Muslim faith. Even trying to appeal to their god demonstrates that he and others with his leanings clearly do not want to accept the fact that these hateful, violent teachings come right from the Quran itself. When thinking about it logically . . . I realized that only Hindutva political groups were honest about everything related to the problems of Islamism harming a society. That can sound extreme, if you haven't actually read their perspective on the issues and simply dehumanized them for being Hindu. For example, Islamist slogans in India often chant: "*Gustakhe Nabi ki ek saza, Sar tan se juda*" which translates to "*A punishment for disrespecting the prophet, head separated from body*" whenever their sentiments are hurt.[448] Why was this information hidden from Americans by the US Corporate media circus, Christian non-governmental organizations, and Western European news organizations? Why are US and European corporate media organizations, Western Christian groups like Christian NGOs, and Leftists constantly supporting Islamist violence and terror campaigns in India?

One of the issues bothering me when commenting on this is . . . do I have any right to speak on behalf of other Hindus as a born and raised US citizen living comfortably without the fear of having my head chopped off for criticizing Islam like in India and France? Here is the most honest, but negative view of the issue of Free Speech from a Hindu perspective from the Editor-in-Chief of OpIndia, Nupur J. Sharma in her June 28th, 2022 article titled "*Of Free Speech and 295A: Why I partially agree and wholly disagree with the arguments of Prof Anand Ranganathan*" which reads as follows:

> **Of Free Speech and 295A: Why I partially agree and wholly disagree with the arguments of Prof Anand Ranganathan**
>
> *In the quest for empty, unrealistic, pedantic principles, Hindus cannot be made sacrificial lambs.*
>
> On the 27th of June 2022, Mohammad Zubair, the co-founder of AltNews was arrested by the Delhi Police was his tweets that incited hate. One of the sections applied against him was 295A of the IPC, besides Section 153. Soon, the "right-wing" (for the lack of a better defining phrase) celebrated the arrest of this hate monger who had painted a target on the backs of Hindus for as long as one could remember. The Left, of course, bemoaned the death of everything – from democracy to freedom of speech, expression, press and liberty.
>
> Amidst the cacophony, an old argument was rekindled. Professor Anand Ranganathan tweeted that he supported Zubair against his arrest because he believes that 295A is a draconian law that has no place in a moral, just and civilised society. Moreover, he is a strong proponent of absolute freedom of speech and expression, which essentially means that he might not like what Zubair said, but he will defend his right to say it.
>
> *Zubair wanted people arrested for offending religious sensibilities, and today he has been arrested for offending religious sensibilities.*

---

[448] Pandey, Shraddha. "From Nupur Sharma to Sharmishta Panoli: How Courts Are Emboldening Islamists and Curbing Space for Free Speech." Www.Opindia.Com, OpIndia, 3 June 2025, www.opindia.com/2025/06/nupur-sharma-sharmishta-panoli-courts-emboldening-islamists-curbing-space-for-free-speech/.

I do not want, nor have I ever wanted, anyone arrested for offending religious sensibilities. I stand with Zubair.

— Anand Ranganathan (@ARanganathan72) June 27, 2022

Prof Ranganathan received substantial backlash from the 'right wing' for his absolutist stand. The general tone of the responses ranged from mocking the tweet to asking him to not support someone who has habitually dog-whistled against Hindus, lied, tried to whitewash Islamist terrorists and terrorism and overall, has been a termite that has been gnawing at the existence of Hindus.

To be fair to Anand Ranganathan, he did clarify, multiple times during his Twitter Spaces that he detested what Zubair stands for as much as any of us. His argument was limited to the application of 295A and how, it was a redundant law that should not be used against the critics of any religion – Hinduism, Islam, Christianity, Scientology or the Church of Satan – I don't believe Anand cares which religion is being criticised per se.

During his Twitter Spaces, one has to admit that he made some compelling points. First and foremost, he spoke about the morality of having different standards for different folks, depending on where on the ideological spectrum the "victim" of this law lies.

Anand Ranganathan says (and I am paraphrasing) that society must strive for absolute freedom of speech and until a few years ago, I would have agreed with him not just partially but wholly. Ranganathan essentially says that as far as personal liberty goes, nobody can be locked up merely for hurt feelings because the extent and context of that hurt can hardly be controlled. A Hindu can be offended if you by an innocuous comment about his deities while a Muslim can be offended if you merely quote his texts. Where a Salman Rushdie exists, an MF Hussain exists as well. According to Ranganathan, we will see a time when the misuse of 295A would reach a position where nobody would be able to say anything about any religion because it would attract a prison sentence. He has also claimed that those of us who are not firmly against 295A are accepting that we are ok with collateral damage when thousands of Hindus are arrested for saying something remotely offensive. Further, we also seem to be ok with giving up our right to criticise a predatory religion (given that he believes the law itself is a slide to that eventuality).

The foundation of the arguments made by Prof Ranganathan can be divided into the following points:

1. Nobody should be jailed for their speech. Freedom of speech must be absolute.

2. If you are ok with Zubair's arrest, you have to be ok with Nupur Sharma being arrested – otherwise – you are a raging hypocrite.

3. The law itself is colonial and draconian, open to misuse, and criminalises what should otherwise be acceptable in a civilised society.

4. Sooner or later, the law will come back to bite Hindus since what it would do is outlaw all criticism of religion, therefore, you would lose your right to criticise a traditionally predatory religion such as Islam.

In principle, to a limited extent, I agree with Anand. The fact that I am ok with Islam being mocked and not Hinduism does make me seem like a raging hypocrite and that society must strive for absolute freedom of expression is also a principle I cannot disagree with. In an ideal world, should we be able to get along without any punitive action against those who offend religious sensibilities? Perhaps. Do we live in an ideal world where moral absolutism, essentially saying that certain moral values have universal applicability and the context of that value has no relevance, is a functional model? I think not.

But let us address each point of contention that Prof Ranganathan brings up often (one has to give it to him – he has long held his position on 295A).

Nobody should be jailed for their speech. Freedom of speech must be absolute.

In my headline, I categorically say that I partially agree with Prof Ranganathan. Up until a few years ago, and maybe somewhere deep down in my heart today, I do believe that nobody should be jailed for their speech. Not just me, I think every Hindu who today argues with the good professor at some point in time believed that freedom of speech and expression should be absolute. But what changed? First and foremost, one has to acknowledge that freedom of speech is not truly free anywhere in the world. During his Twitter Space last night, Ranganathan mentioned the United States of America and claimed that the criticism of Islam is perhaps the highest there, however, they don't have laws like 295A, given that they value freedom of expression, however, that notion is misplaced.

Nowhere in the world is freedom of speech an absolute right. Maybe in law, but the reality is far from it. In the USA today, you can get fired for merely saying that an individual who has a penis, hormones and the physical attributes of a man cannot claim to be a woman and compete in a women's sports event. You can be cancelled, and lose your job, your reputation and your life. It is a reality of our times that certain sections, even in the USA, have a greater right to freedom of speech and expression than some others – the only difference is that perhaps their dual standards come from different societal aspects like race and gender, while ours come from religion and culture. In France, a nation hailed as a haven for absolute free speech, Eric Zemmour was convicted for hate speech against migrants. Several "dissidents" have been jailed for glorifying terrorism and even abusing the police force – this included the questioning of an 8-year-old boy who said he "supported terrorism", later admitting that he did not really know what terrorism meant.

The two most liberal nations as far as freedom of speech is concerned are jailing, beating down, hounding, and setting strict standards for speech – legally or otherwise – whether we agree with it or not. Therefore, to live under the illusion that speech is free anywhere is just that – a convenient illusion.

As far as India is concerned, one has to wonder how far can the absolutism of free speech go. In a multi-cultural, diverse nation, with a high concentration of radicals, one has to admit that Hindus are not particularly playing on a level playing field. We can certainly idealistically demand that free speech must be absolute, however, the ramifications for one kind of speech and the ramifications for another kind of speech are not equal and have never been. In short, when Teesta Setalvad tweeted an image equating Maa Kali with an ISIS terrorist, she deleted her tweet after Hindus tweeted angrily at her and apologised – the matter ended. Most of you would not even remember that she had tweeted an image like that. But when Kamlesh Tiwari made a statement, he was beheaded 4 years after he came out of jail on bail.

But the truth remains that the rules of the game do not place Hindus at the same level, forget giving them an advantage in the only land they can possibly call their own. Under those circumstances, the demand for absolute freedom of speech for everyone becomes redundant. We could, principally, demand absolute freedom of speech or want to strive for it, however, with or without the law, Hindus would get the short end of the stick because Islamists don't need a law to avenge the hurt caused to them. They need a sword. A sharp one. They have plenty of those and are certainly not morally adverse to using them.

If you are ok with Zubair's arrest, you have to be ok with Nupur Sharma being arrested – otherwise – you are a raging hypocrite.

There are multiple problems with this statement. Firstly, let's focus on facts. Nupur Sharma responded to her faith being mocked relentlessly, by Islamists, after the Shivling was discovered at the disputed Gyanvapi structure and therefore, it is safe to assume that she did not set out to mock Islam or Prophet Muhammad. In fact, even as a response, she said "what if she were to mock Islam" – she did not actually mock them and whatever she said are "facts" mentioned in the Islamic Hadiths. Zubair on the other hand has harboured hatred for Hindus, painted a target on their back, cost them their jobs, sent a bloodthirsty mob against Hindus and has a long history of doing just this – mocking Hindus, justifying their murder, inciting hate and shielding Islamists. The two individuals, by no stretch of the imagination, are the same.

But this argument is moot since Prof Ranganathan would say that these are emotional arguments and according to the law, they both hurt religious sentiments and therefore, they should both be arrested – either that or 295A should be scrapped.

Two fundamental questions form the basis of Ranganathan's argument. Firstly, all religious offence is the same and by extension, all religions are the same (Ranganathan does not claim all religions are the same but if we consider all offence to be the same, then we must consider all religions to be the same as well). And secondly, we must all be moral absolutists and any form of relativism in this case is hypocritical.

Those who believe in moral absolutism and universal principles do so at the cost of realism and pragmatism.

Personally, I have no problem acknowledging the fact that Metaethical Moral Relativism is far more appropriate for the day and age we live in. The truth or falsity of moral judgments, or their justification, is not absolute or universal but is relative to the traditions, convictions, or practices of a group of persons. I concede that this might be a rather Liberal prism to look at the world, but when playing by their rules, one has to learn and use their tools to fight for our own survival. Therefore, in a civilisational state where Hinduism forms the very basis of the nation's existence, one should have no qualms in admitting that an insult to Hinduism is far more problematic than an insult to Islam.

As a Hindu, the need for survival cannot possibly be termed as collective hypocrisy when it comes to insulting faith. One can say that being ok with Islam being desecrated/mocked cannot be accepted if Hindus start getting offended when their faith meets the same fate, however, realistically, the cultural context of why Hindus are ok with Islam being mocked and their own faith has to be considered.

For thousands of years, Hindus have been subjugated by the Islamist invaders who have raped Hindu women, beheaded our kings, and murdered our children all for the ultimate goal of the establishment of the Caliphate. There are countless tales of how the Islamic invaders murdered Hindus and kept their wives, mothers and daughters as slaves – the spoils of war.

The barbarity was so perverse, that Hindu women often chose to jump into the fire and give up their lives after Hindus were defeated in war, lest they were taken slaves by Islamic invaders. You might wonder why they didn't simply slit their wrists instead of stepping into the burning fire – well – they did not want their corpse to be desecrated by the followers of Islam who had laid siege on their land.

The brutality is not just limited to Islamic invaders. In the modern political landscape of India, Hindus were humiliated during the partition as well. One recalls how the Khilafat movement claimed the lives of countless Hindus during the Moplah massacres by Islamists and even the Direct Action Day, spearheaded by Jinnah. After the countless deaths of Hindus, our own, MK Gandhi, asked Hindus to simply lay down their lives if the Islamists chose to claim it.

During the partition, Hindus were mutilated and their women raped. At the altar of 'secularism', which the Atheists love to espouse, India decided to not conduct a full exchange of population, a suggestion that was made by various luminaries at the time including Dr B.R. Ambedkar, and thus, began another cycle of subjugation in modern India. This year itself, we saw riots by sections of the Muslim community and aided by the Left against the Hindus.

The saga of brutality continues to this day not just in India, but also, against the minority Hindus of Pakistan and when India decided that the minority Hindus could take refuge in India, their natural home post-partition, the Islamists ran riots yet again. They stabbed a Hindu over 50 times simply because he was Hindu and chopped off the arms and legs of another before burning him alive.

Given this context, it would be naive to expect Hindus to take offence to Islam being mocked with the same intensity that they may take offence to their own faith being mocked. It is akin to wondering why the Jews are ok with Nazis being mocked and not their own persecution being made light of.

Further, the fact that Ranganathan believes in moral absolutism and that all offence is the same, he will have to then concede that he also believes that all religions are equal – he said he did not, but that is again a logical fallacy that he will have to reconcile in his argument.

When we say that all religions need to coexist without taking offence to each other, we are essentially saying that one of the most important tenets of survival in a multi-cultural nation like India is religious pluralism.

Religious Pluralism essentially says that firstly, all religions must acknowledge that certain truths exist in other religions as well, thereby declaring that it is not only their own religion that is the 'only truth'. Further, it says that all religions must acknowledge that every religion teaches basic universal truths that have been taught since before the advent of religion itself.

When one delves into the principles of religious pluralism as a construct that can enable religions to co-exist without sectarian violence, it becomes important to ensure that all religions are brought down to the same surface level and hence, the claim that all religions are the same takes a beastly proportion where cultural context is often lost. When one tries to do that, it becomes remarkably clear that Islam and Hinduism are not the same. While Islam wants to annihilate Hinduism, Hinduism prescribes no such thing. Islam wants to convert or murder the Kafir, subjugate heathens and establish their Dar-ul-Islam because the Dar-ul-Harb is haraam. When dealing with a traditionally hostile faith, one cannot say that the faith that they are hostile and violent towards is the same as the said faith. Islam, if allowed, sanctions taking offence to the very existence of Kafirs and submits to no law of the land other than that of the God they believe in. It is true that Islam has a strict legal and political foundation to it. Hence, to essentially say that all religions are equal and aspire toward the same universal truths is a fallacious statement that is made by the people who either harbour malice, or ignorance.

It is also pertinent to mention here that the higher the intolerance of a community, the more important it is for that community to be mocked, so the intolerance threshold is breached and that offence is normalised. Islamists have to be desensitised to criticism of their faith to a large extent because no other community is today taking to the streets demanding 'sar tan se juda' at the slightest 'provocation'. Hindus, on the other hand, would have traditionally been more than happy to agree with Professor Ranganathan, had they not been beaten, mocked, insulted and humiliated by the very Islamists who are crying victims today.

When the two religions are not the same (one being hostile and the other being the victim of that hostility), they don't aspire towards the same universal truths, and when one religion is theologically opposed to the other's very existence, to say that Hindus must be equally offended when Islam is mocked is an expectation that far divorced from reality. One has to acknowledge that Hindus are powerless globally. While Islam has the support of the Ummah, Hindus are usually the recipient of hostility not just from the Ummah, but the global Christian cabal, the Leftist, the Communists, and so on and so forth. The powerless community needs a law that they can turn to when they are repeatedly mocked and harassed. Take that away from them and you essentially tell them that the only recourse they have is to become as intolerant as the "sar tan se juda" gang. Would that be better than a legal provision? One would think not.

The law itself is colonial and draconian, open to misuse

295A is not a very complicated law. It simply says that any deliberate and malicious attempt to hurt religious feelings shall be prosecuted by the law. One can argue that it does not particularly define what religious hurt is, the extent of hurt caused and what words should be considered offensive, however, the law, on its own, is as open to misuse as any other law.

This situation could perhaps be compared to the SC/ST law, given that Hindus are a powerless lot globally, underprivileged and the target of predatory proselytisation. Hindus need laws to protect them, much like Scheduled Castes and Tribes need a law to protect their rights. Being a global minority and dealing with predatory faiths, Hindus universally need to be protected and the only way you can possibly disagree with this argument is if you also disagree with SCs and STs don't particularly need a separate law for protection after they have been historically persecuted.

The SC/ST Act, while necessary, also has a propensity to be misused. Several cases have been documented where individuals belonging to these communities have misused the law to settle personal scores. One can safely argue that just as in the case of the SC/ST Act, in the case of 295A also, there have to be special provisions made against misuse, in the former, against Brahmins and "upper castes" and in the latter, against Hindus overall. However, demanding that the law itself be scrapped is like throwing the baby out with the bath water.

One has to consider that laws are formulated to bring order and peace to society and are subject to the ever-changing reality of a nation. The reality of our nation today is that Hindus are liable to be beheaded, much like Kamlesh Tiwari, when they comment on Islam while Islamists get the support of their global cabal when they insult Hinduism. In an unequal battle, this law is the only recourse that Hindus have and Hindus need protection from this law being misused to persecute them further.

Sooner or later, the law will come back to bite Hindus since what it would do is outlaw all criticism of religion, therefore, you would lose your right to criticise a traditionally predatory religion such as Islam.

To answer this, we need to delve into how 295A came into existence. It all started with the case of Mahashay Rajpal, who published Rangeela Rasool and was ultimately assassinated for it. We mostly hear that Mahashay Rajpal was assassinated for publishing satirical work on Prophet Muhammad called Rangeela Rasool, but we seldom hear why he chose to publish the book. In 1923, Muslims published two particularly offensive books to Hindus. "Krishna teri geeta jalani padegi" used derogatory and vulgar language against Shri Krishna and other Hindu deities and "Uniseevi sadi ka maharshi" which contained derogatory remarks on Arya Samaj founder Swami Dayanand Saraswati (incidentally written by an Ahmadi).

In response to this provocation by Islamists, Pandit Chamupati Lal, a close friend of Mahashay Rajpal, wrote a short biography of the Islamic Prophet, Mohammed. "Rangeela Rasool" was a short pamphlet which satirised the life of the Prophet of Islam. Pandit Chamupati made Mahashay Rajpal promise that he would never reveal the name of the author – he knew the consequences of it. Anonymously published under the name "doodh ka doodh aur panee ka panee", the book enraged Muslims.

Staying true to the values of one-way brotherhood, Mohandas Karamchand Gandhi wrote in his pamphlet "Young India", condemning Rangeela Rasool. While Gandhi ignored the provocation by Muslims, by the end of June 1924, the colonial government banned the book. The Muslim community, partly emboldened by MK Gandhi's endorsement of their hurt sentiments and whitewashing of the provocation against Hindus, filed multiple cases against the book under 153A. In May 1927, Mahashay Rajpal, who published the book, was acquitted of all charges with the court observing that commentary based on facts on historical figures, including the prophet of Islam, cannot be said to promote enmity between groups. As soon as the verdict was delivered, Muslim mobs went into a frenzy. They rioted and demanded the head of Mahashay Rajpal. They were chants about how the murder of Rajpal was acceptable because, under Sharia, the punishment for blasphemy is death.

With the Muslim mobs going on a rampage, 295A was passed to assuage the feelings of the mobs and in the same year, there were two unsuccessful attempts at Mahashay Rajpal's life.

On April 6th, 1929 a 19-year-old carpenter named Ilm ud din stabbed Mahashay Rajpal on his chest eight times while he was seated in the outer verandah of his shop.

Now, one has to bear in mind that when Rangeela Rasool was published, 295A did not exist. However, the Muslim community back then went on a rampage demanding that Mahashay Rajpal be taught a lesson. Even in the absence of the law, there were two attempts on his life and ultimately, the third attempt was successful.

Given what we know about history, we have to ask ourselves – what would change for Hindus if 295A was indeed scrapped?

As we have seen in the case of Mahashay Rajpal, Kishan Bharwad, Kamlesh Tiwari, Samuel Patty and hundreds across the world and specifically in India, the Islamists don't need a law to extract their pound of flesh when they are offended and their religious sentiments are hurt. They have, ever so often, taken matters into their own hands and exercised their street veto liberally across the world. Hindus on the other hand, have been left powerless to deal with the onslaught of global Hinduphobia. With 295A gone, the only community that would be left with no tools to address insults to their faith would be Hindus and the message that would be sent to Hindus is that they can only be respected if they become as violent and intolerant as those who take to the streets and execute those whose words they don't like.

The ground reality for Hindus, as far as the treatment they get at the hand of Islamists would not change. "Blasphemy" would still exist since the threat of getting beheaded for criticism of Islam would certainly not be tackled by the scrapping of 295A.

Therefore, with the law gone, we would see Hindus left with no recourse when they are insulted while Islamists would still enforce their street veto against Hindus whenever their feelings are hurt.

The truth of the matter is that the law itself is not particularly unjust. It is its application that leaves a lot to be desired and that is where the Judiciary and the society come into play. More than the existence of the law, we should be offended at the normalisation of its unjust application – where DU professor Ratan Lal gets bail for insulting Hinduism and Hindus are arrested regularly, left to rot in jail, when they make comments against Islam. We should be offended that the myopic judiciary, the malicious academia and the deracinated, blinded society have normalised Hindus being hunted while others getting a free pass.

In the quest for empty, unrealistic, pedantic principles, Hindus cannot be made sacrificial lambs.[449]

One question has bothered me in all of this discussion on Islam's impact in India that everyone seems to ignore except Hindutva groups: How exactly are people who will murder others for feelings of offense an aggrieved minority? How can anyone who condones murder for hurt sentiments ever an aggrieved minority population? How is any of that rational? How does it logically follow? Why are people chronically ignoring this metaphorical elephant in the room when it comes to discussions of Islam? Why are people stupid enough to make excuses for murder? The vast majority of Muslims across the world have never concerned themselves with the human rights of Hindus, Sikhs, Christians, Jews, Buddhists, Jains, Parsis, Atheists, and many other groups. So, what exactly are we all doing here, reciprocating human rights laws while they delight in chopping people's heads off for feelings of offense and shout slogans stating they support

---

[449] Sharma, Nupur J. "Of Free Speech and 295A: Why I Partially Agree and Wholly Disagree with the Arguments of Prof Anand Ranganathan." Www.Opindia.Com, OpIndia, 28 June 2022, www.opindia.com/2022/06/free-speech-295a-disagree-arguments-prof-anand-ranganathan/.

beheadings? If violence is always their first response, why are the rest of us pretending human rights is a worthy goal or even a rational goal towards them? Please consider this: what exactly happens to all of us, once their societies and communities grow in power and have control? We already see it in Bangladesh, Pakistan, the entire Middle East, Northern Africa. and Afghanistan. Not to mention people being jailed for offending Islam due to facebook posts in Muslim-majority Island countries. What more proof do we need that we're weakening ourselves against an unrelenting enemy force that wants to harm all of us? Islamism as a political force literally uses the technological innovations of democracies to continue global terrorist activities to kill as many civilians as humanely possible. This is genuinely what their religion teaches, because following the Quran means following the guidelines of a warlord; that's why Muslim-majority countries have so many problems. They break apart into warring ethnic tribes because that's the only way the Quran had functioned during the Prophet Mohammad's time; the teachings imitating a desert warlord leads to disparate ethnic groups acting as competing desert warlords. What are we doing by pretending this had any viable future for running a country effectively? While China remains protected from Islamic terror violence by putting Uyghurs into education camps that keep the rest of China safe; India has to deal with Islamists chopping people's heads off, vilified by Middle Eastern dictatorships who are completely silent about Uyghur Muslims put into concentration camps, and India gets blamed for not supporting Free Speech effectively too. How is that not a demonstration that violence is the only language that Islamists understand? While Israel creates a demarcation zone to avoid being massacred by Palestinians and Hamas terrorists; the US, France, and Sweden have to deal with assassination attempts by Islamists. Samuel Paty was beheaded on October 2020 over specious rumors that turned out to be a student lying to her father to avoid the fact that she'd been cutting classes; in other words, Samuel Paty was beheaded in broad daylight over lies and rumors that hurt the sentiments of Muslims.[450][451] After the so-called rallies against Islamic extremism in response to the Charlie Hebdo killings; the subsequent stabbings of French teachers, such as on October 13th, 2023 by a Muslim refugee screaming Allahu Akbar, have been far more muted nationally in France and internationally among Republics.[452] What are we all doing here? What more proof does there need to be for people to accept that Islam and democratic values are incompatible after so much overwhelming evidence? Let me just give a basic

---

[450] Willsher, Kim. "Teacher Decapitated in Paris Named as Samuel Paty, 47." The Guardian, Guardian News and Media, 17 Oct. 2020, www.theguardian.com/world/2020/oct/17/teacher-decapitated-in-paris-named-as-samuel-paty-47.

[451] "Samuel Paty: French Schoolgirl Admits Lying about Murdered Teacher." BBC News, BBC, 9 Mar. 2021, www.bbc.com/news/world-europe-56325254.

[452] Pollina, Richard. "Suspect Allegedly Yelled 'Allahu Akbar' before Fatally Stabbing Teacher, Injuring 2 Others in France Knife Attack." New York Post, New York Post, 13 Oct. 2023, nypost.com/2023/10/13/france-knife-attack-leaves-teacher-dead-several-injured/.

question for everyone reading this: What more proof do you all need that Islam teaches Muslims to murder you?

Will this always be a persistent problem in India when Hindus speak about anything related to Islam? Is this the future of Western Europe and eventually the US due to Islamophobia political campaigns? Is this always going to be a problem for India and the future of other democratic countries? The horrifying details of Kamlesh Tiwari's murder published on India.com on October 19th, 2019 under the headline *"Kamlesh Tiwari Murder: UP CM Yogi Adityanath to Visit Kin of Deceased Hindu Samaj Leader Today"* which reads as follows:

> **New Delhi:** Taking stock of the controversial murder, Uttar Pradesh Chief Minister Yogi Adityanath has decided to meet the family members of Hindu Samaj Party chief Kamlesh Tiwari on Saturday evening.
>
> Speaking on the 'well-planned' murder of the leader, CM Adityanath said, "Kamlesh was the President of the Hindu Samaj Party. The assailants came to his house in Lucknow yesterday, sat and had tea with him, and later killed him after sending all security guards out to buy something from the market."
>
> Adityanath further said that the suspects have been arrested on murder charges. He further ensured that the miscreants will get stringent punishment and that the investigation will be completed within a few hours.
>
> Earlier today, his family stated that they will not cremate the body demanding CM Yogi Adityanath to pay them a visit. The family had also urged the UP Chief Minister for job assurance for two members of the family.
>
> Kamlesh's wife had even threatened to self immolate if the demands were not met.
>
> CM Yogi Adityanath, who is currently in Maharashtra rallying for the upcoming Assembly Elections, will return to Lucknow on Saturday evening and meet the kins to hear out their grievances.
>
> **Kamlesh Tiwari Murder**
>
> Former chief of Hindu Mahasabha, Kamlesh Tiwari was found brutally murdered on Friday afternoon in his Lucknow residence in Naka Hindola area. He was shot multiple times and also stabbed by unidentified miscreants in broad daylight in Lucknow.
>
> The three accused arrested have been identified as Maulana Mohsin Sheikh, Faizan, & Khurshid Ahmed Pathan and are being investigated by a joint team of UP and Gujarat police.
>
> The police have said that Tiwari's "inciting speech" on Prophet Mohammed in 2015 was the reason behind the murder. The police also confirmed based on the information that the murder was committed in a planned manner.
>
> Tiwari had hit the headlines in 2015 when he made a derogatory remark against Prophet Muhammad. Upsetting Muslims all over the country, he had called Prophet Muhammad the first homosexual in the world.
>
> Massive protests broke out in different parts of the country after his speech and Tiwari was booked under the National Security Act for making provocative remarks against the Muslim religious

leader. Outraged, around one lakh Muslims had gathered in Muzaffarnagar to demand death penalty for Tiwari.[453]

On February 7th, 2022, The Indian Express released a news article titled *"Dhandhuka murder: 3 accused in police remand for 10 more days"* on the murder of Kishan Bharwad, where it was revealed that two imams supplied weapons and convinced the murder suspects to find and murder everyone on a ten-person list that was rumored to have insulted Islam. Do you all see the problem? Let me rephrase and add an emphasis in bold: two imams supplied guns and preached that murder for insulting Islam was justified to convince two Muslim followers to murder a list of ten people who were **rumored** to have insulted Islam. This is the tyranny of hurt sentiments; not even the difference between evidence that someone else has committed an action and allegations that they have committed an action will matter to people who murder because their feelings were hurt. They base their judgment on the intensity of their emotions instead of verifiable evidence. This is what the US and Western Indologists, the US Corporate media circus who serve Neoliberal economists and CEOs, Christian NGOs that operate in India, and the mostly White Liberals of the US ignore and thereby protect from scrutiny:

> **Dhandhuka murder: 3 accused in police remand for 10 more days**
>
> *Bharwad, 30, a Dhandhuka resident, was allegedly shot dead by two bike-borne men in the town on January 25 when he was traveling on a motorcycle.*
>
> A magisterial court in Dhandhuka of Ahmedabad Saturday sent three main accused in the **Kishan Bharwad murder case** to 10 more days in police remand.
>
> The Gujarat Anti-Terrorist Squad (ATS), which is investigating the murder case, claimed that it is probing a list of 10 persons created by the arrested accused who had allegedly insulted Islam in the past.
>
> Bharwad, 30, a Dhandhuka resident, was allegedly shot dead by two bike-borne men in the town on January 25 when he was traveling on a motorcycle. Later, police revealed the murder was carried out allegedly after an objectionable social media post by Bharwad.
>
> So far, ATS has **arrested eight accused in the case**. Among them, prime accused Sabbir Chopda allegedly fired at Bharwad while Imtiyaz Pathan was riding the motorcycle with Chopda.
>
> According to ATS, arrested cleric Maulana Mohammad Ayyub Javarawala from Jamalpur in Ahmedabad allegedly supplied the weapon to the shooter, while another arrested cleric Maulvi Qamar Gani Usmani of Tahreek Farogh e Islam (TFI) organisation arrested from Delhi had allegedly instigated the shooters.
>
> According to a senior ATS officer, "The **eight day police remand** of Chopda, Pathan and cleric Javarawala ended on Saturday, after which they were presented again before the magistrate who sent them to another 10-day police remand."

---

[453] "Kamlesh Tiwari Murder: Up CM Yogi Adityanath to Visit Kin of Deceased Hindu Samaj Leader Today." India.Com, India.Com, 19 Oct. 2019, www.india.com/news/india/kamlesh-tiwari-murder-up-cm-yogi-adityanath-to-visit-kin-of-deceased-hindu-samaj-leader-today-3811970/.

According to the remand application submitted by the ATS in the Dhandhuka court, they are currently investigating a list of 10 persons who had allegedly insulted Islam in the past.

The names on the list are BS Patel, Pankaj Arya, Pushpendra Kulshreshtha, Mahendrapal Arya, Rahul Arya, Radheshyam Acharya, Updesh Rana, Upasana Arya, Sajan Odedara and RSN Singh. The accused had also collected details about them through various social media channels.

The ATS added that after killing Bharwad, shooters Sabbir Chopda and Imtiyaz Pathan allegedly threw their cell phones into a pond and destroyed three SIM cards.

The ATS also claimed that they seized 1,000 copies of an instigating booklet published by Javarwala named "Jazba E Shahadat", while another 3,000 copies of the said booklet are missing.

The ATS is also probing call detail records (CDR) of Sabbir Chopda and Maulana Ayyub who allegedly spoke 35 times between June 2021 and January 2022 as well as Sabbir and Usmani who spoke 10 times between June 2021 and September 2021. The ATS is also probing if the accused received any foreign fund for giving "punishment" to those who allegedly insulted Islam in India.[454]

Earlier this year, OpIndia's opinion columnist, Shraddha Pandey, published an article on June 3rd, 2025 titled "*'Loose tongue' to 'sentiments were hurt': From Nupur Sharma to Sharmishta Panoli, how courts are emboldening Islamists and curbing space for free speech*" and please note the Nupur Sharma mentioned in the article is not the same person as the Editor-in-Chief of OpIndia. The article reads as follows:

'Loose tongue' to 'sentiments were hurt': From Nupur Sharma to Sharmishta Panoli, how courts are emboldening Islamists and curbing space for free speech

Sharmishta Panoli, a law student from Symbiosis Law School, Pune, was arrested by Kolkata Police on 30 May 2025 in Gurugram after an online Islamist mob targeted her, issuing rape and death threats—including the infamous "Sar tan se juda" slogan—and demanded her arrest by tagging police online.

India has freedom of speech. Yes, India has freedom of speech as long as you use it to spew venom against Hinduism. India has freedom of speech as long as you berate your own country. This freedom of speech, however, ceases to exist once you intentionally or unintentionally offend the perennially offended 'minority' community—Muslims. Once you have offended those who must not be offended, there is no scope for redemption, no apology, no regret, and no law can protect you from wrath of bloodthirsty Islamists. Sharmishta Panoli, 22-year-old girl has come into the radar of Indian Islamists over an Instagram video against Pakistan, which ended up offending 'Indian Muslims.'

Sharmishta Panoli, a law student from Symbiosis Law School in Pune, was arrested by Kolkata Police on 30th May 2025, from Haryana's Gurugram. The arrest came after Islamists unleashed an online mob against the Hindu influencer, who issued rape and death threats including the Islamist-favourite 'Gustakhe Nabi ki ek saza, Sar tan se juda' threat. The Indian Muslim social media users also began tagging the police, demanding her arrest.

---

[454] "Dhandhuka Murder: 3 Accused in Police Remand for 10 More Days." The Indian Express, The Indian Express / Express News Service, 7 Feb. 2022, web.archive.org/web/20220207041105/https://indianexpress.com/article/cities/ahmedabad/dhandhuka-murder-accused-police-remand-ahmedabad-7760401/.

Instead of chasing the Muslim social media users who doxxed and gave 'Sar Tan se Juda' threats to the Hindu influencer, the Mamata Banerjee's police force have arrested Sharmistha instead.

The controversy began on 14th May when a Pakistani Muslim handle attempted to whitewash the massacre of 24 Hindus during the Pahalgam terror attack. Islamic terrorists had confirmed religious identity of the victims before shooting them dead. An enraged Sharmishta mocked the Pakistani Muslim handle for believing that India started a war without any reason and asked if she had heard of Pahalgam and other Pakistan-sponsored terror attacks.

Sharmishta further asked if Indian forces should just sit and do nothing about these terror attacks. The video was taken out of context by Pakistani and Indian Muslims alike to allege insult to Islam and Prophet Muhammad.

The Hindu influencer soon deleted her video and even tendered an unconditional apology. However, Islamists have an undeclared 'never apologise, never forgive' rule, which essentially means that when they insult Hindu gods or hurt sentiments of other non-Muslim communities, they are not supposed to apologise, rather, either double down or play victim, on the contrary, if a Hindu or a non-Muslim even criticises Islamic traditions, let alone, making derogatory remarks, then there is no scope for apologise and move on.

But what emboldens Islamists to go after anyone they declare a 'blasphemer' or 'Gustakh-e-Nabi', so much so, that no action is taken against those who literally issue threats of beheading someone for their words, while accused person, despite apologising, is subjected to harassment of all sorts and is arrested.

As unfortunate and outrageous as it sounds but it is the judiciary, the system and Muslim-appeasing socio-political ecosystem that fuels the intransigence of petulant Islamists.

On 3rd June 2025, the Calcutta High Court rejected the bail plea of Sharmishta Panoli, saying "heavens will not fall" if the ad-interim bail plea is not accepted and the case is heard later for bail.

While hearing a plea against the trial court's remanding her to 14-day judicial custody, Justice Partha Sarathi Chatterjee said that the video in question was seen and that sentiments of Muslims were hurt. He added that while the court wants freedom of speech, it does not mean that sentiments of others can be hurt.

"This video was made on social media, it was heard. This incident has led to a section of people's sentiment being hurt. We have freedom of speech but that doesn't mean you will go on to hurt others. Our country is diverse, with all persons. We must be cautious. So day after tomorrow. Heavens will not fall," Justice Chatterjee said as the petitioner's counsel apprised the court that Sharmishta is a student with attention deficit and hyperactivity disorder and staying in jail is a problematic for her.

The court deduced that Sharmishta's video hurt the sentiments of Muslims, however, what about those issuing Sar tan se juda threats to the young girl. What about the rape and death threats she continues to receive? Islamists are most of the time offended, and otherwise ready to get offended, but does that mean a person's life can be put at risk, or ruined, especially after she has apologised and deleted the video in question? Why is it that courts take sentiments of Muslims unrealistically seriously, however, the same seriousness disappears when Hindu sentiments are hurt?

The Sharmishta Panoli case reminds of the 2022 Nupur Sharma case. In May 2022, Nupur Sharma was one of the panellists on the Time Now show along with Taslim Ahmed Rehmani on the Shivlinga found at the Gyanvapi disputed structure site. During the debate, Rehmani used derogatory language against Bhagwan Shiv that irked then-BJP spokesperson Nupur Sharma. Sharma countered her and questioned how would he react if she used the same language for Islam and the Prophet.

Though it was a counter statement, Alt News' co-founder Mohammed Zubair found it to be the perfect opportunity to ruin Sharma's life. He cunningly trimmed Rehmani's remarks that came before Sharma's counter remarks and presented as if Sharma was insulting Prophet Mohammed. The propaganda against Sharma worked and it sparked an international outrage.

Regardless of the fact that what Sharma said about the Prophet's marriage to the 9-year-old Ayesha, which is mentioned in multiple Islamic hadiths, Nupur Sharma was branded as a 'blasphemer', with Islamic organisations openly declaring that she should be murdered.

Following the witch-hunt against Sharma, there were protests and riots across the country carried out by Sar tan se juda shrieking Islamist mobs. People who supported Sharma were threatened by Islamists online and offline. FIRs were filed not only against Sharma but also against those who supported her.

Not to forget, Kanhaiya Lal, a Hindu tailor from Udaipur, Rajasthan, and Umesh Kolhe, a businessman from Maharashtra's Amravati, were brutally murdered by Islamists for simply supporting Sharma. Kanhaiyalal was beheaded by two Riaz and Ghous Mohammed, for sharing a post in support of Sharma. The jihadis recorded a video after brutally murdering the Hindu man and raised sar tan se juda slogans while justifying their act. Ironically, the Muslim man who informed the killers about the Hindu tailor's presence in his shop, was granted bail by Rajasthan High Court last year.

Similarly, bloodthirsty Islamists brutally hacked chemist Umesh Kolhe, 54, to death while he was on his way back home after shutting his store in Maharashtra.

Umesh Kolhe and Kanhaiyalal had not even said or posted anything against any religion but only extended support to Sharma who was at the receiving end of a barrage of rape threats, death threats, Sar tan se juda threats and whatnot.

When Nupur Sharma approached the Supreme Court seeking clubbing of FIRs against her, the two-judge bench that heard the matter seemed to have already formed an opinion against her based on the disinformation and misleading propaganda running in media and on social media. Justice Surya Kant, in his oral observations, blamed Nupur Sharma for what was happening in the country.

Blaming Nupur Sharma for the Islamist mob violence across the country as well as killing of Kanhaiyalal and Umesh Kolhe, for stating something even Muslim scholars and scriptures state, the Supreme Court judge had said, "You have ignited the whole country. You possess a loose tongue. Power has gone to your head. You should apologise to the nation."

While Sharma had already apologised, much like it is happening in the case of Sharmishta Panoli, her apology, however heartfelt, could not satiate the quench of bloodthirsty Islamists. For Islamists, the only appropriate punishment for those who 'hurt' their religious sentiments is when either they do sar tan se juda of the 'blasphemer' or the court outrightly orders their hanging, nothing in between.

Although, the Calcutta High Court's remarks in Sharmishta's case were not as scathing as the ones made in Nupur Sharma's case, there is a disturbing pattern. The pattern of advertently or inadvertently justifying Islamist outrage no matter how violent and destructive by outrightly blaming the accused person.

While Islamists mobs cry that since the so-called 'Gustakh blasphemer' has displayed the temerity of actually holding an opinion, that person needs to be hanged, the courts also make remarks that suggest that even they agree that the person should be punished and conveniently blame them. This, however, does serve the purpose of upholding the law, rather, it only serves the purpose of lending legitimacy to the street veto of the Islamists. In a nutshell, it is like telling the accused person, "Ab gustakhi karoge, toh ye sab [threats, riots and even killings] to hoga hi".

This, however, is not confined to one Nupur Sharma or Sharmishta Panoli, there have been numerous cases wherein accusations of offending the ever-offended Muslim sentiments resulted in violence, riots and killings of Hindus. The 2019 Kamlesh Tiwari killing, the 2022 Kishan

Bharwad killing are among many such cases wherein Islamists deemed certain comments or social media posts 'blasphemous' and resorted to silencing the 'Gustakh' and drawing joy from having taught Kafir a lesson.

It is high time, however, for the courts, politicians and general public to understand that Islamists are perennially offended and can resort to violence using any real, imaginary, assumed or trivial excuse to initiate threats and violence against people. Be it Hindu processions passing in front of mosques, Hindus playing bhajans during their festivals, or putting up religious flags or even celebrating a cricket match victory in 'Muslim area', or a movie on a Hindu historical figure who endured Islamist barbarism and chose death over conversion to Islam, can offend Islamists enough to resort to stone pelting, arson and killing. All in the name of 'hurt sentiments'.

While upholding communal harmony and even laying emphasis on protecting religious sentiments is not wrong, however, by validating claims of 'hurt sentiments', especially of those who are essentially ready to do mob justice with the accused, if courts fail to punish the person and call for the accused's beheading, courts only embolden Islamists.

Political parties supporting Islamists to appease their Muslim votebank, as seen in the case of Sharmishta, wherein TMC has gone all out in support of Islamists, courts putting these curbs on speech embolden those who get offended at the drop of a hat and now day by day they are reducing the space for free speech.[455]

The statement from the article "*Ab gustakhi karoge, toh ye sab [threats, riots and even killings] to hoga hi*" translates to "*If you misbehave now, all this [threats, riots and killings] will surely happen.*" I don't know how useful this will be and I am an outsider looking in with the privilege of never having to fear being beheaded for criticizing Islam; the best I can say is that my views are out of genuine concern for Hindu human rights. One misconception that I've noticed both OpIndia and Wikipedia make on the Islamist riots over Nupur Sharma's comments is that they weren't rioting over perceived lies about Aisha's age; she and OpIndia are correct about what the Hadiths say regarding Aisha's age during her marriage and then subsequent rape by the Prophet Mohammad. It's almost certainly the reason Muslim grooming gangs that target young girls exist across the world. The Islamists of India were rioting because Islam teaches them that non-Muslims aren't allowed to have an opinion on Islam. It wasn't that they believed the information on Aisha's age was inaccurate, but that a non-Muslim woman gave an opinion on Islam that caused them to violently riot. Islamists and their Imams believe no non-Muslim has any right to an opinion on Islam and they will get violent if you express any opinion on Islam at all. That's the truth behind those Islamist riots in India and elsewhere.

First, please consider the following: does Indian Penal Code (IPC) 295A and IPC 153A really protect Hindus and other non-Muslims from Islamist violence? The cases of Samuel Paty in France and Kishan Bharwad in India are two concrete examples that

---

[455] Pandey, Shraddha. "From Nupur Sharma to Sharmishta Panoli: How Courts Are Emboldening Islamists and Curbing Space for Free Speech." Www.Opindia.Com, OpIndia, 3 June 2025, www.opindia.com/2025/06/nupur-sharma-sharmishta-panoli-courts-emboldening-islamists-curbing-space-for-free-speech/.

unsubstantiated rumors can cause the tyranny of hurt sentiments among Muslims across the world. If their first instinct is to get violently angry and kill you for something you never did anyway, then what use is suggesting that IPC has any legitimacy for either Islamists and Muslims more broadly? The example of IPC 295A being used to arrest Mohammad Zubair seems like a good example at first, but why were Indian government authorities so slow to arrest this man, if he was purposefully sowing enmity and riots as OpIndia's Nupur S. Sharma explained? This seems more like a failure of the Indian government authorities to properly apprehend this man for deliberately instigating violence on multiple occurrences against Hindus, prior to 295A being used to arrest him. If neither IPC 295A or IPC 153A existed, then why wouldn't it be the case that Indian authorities could simply arrest him for instigating riots, instead of the possibility of worrying about the hurt sentiments of Islamists and other Muslims for arresting him? As an example, from the hypothetical that Nupur S. Sharma herself suggested, if every other religious group starts having hurt sentiments and rioting over police doing their jobs, then what use are IPC 295A and IPC 153A?

Second, columnists Nupur S. Sharma and Shraddha Pandey's examination of the problem of hurt sentiments are clearly in contradiction. If as Shraddha says, the law is sometimes selectively used to vilify Hindus specifically, then how are either IPC 295A or IPC 153A protecting Hindus from violence? If Islamists are giving rape threats to female Hindu law students, if Islamists kill chemists for social media posts where the chemist simply voiced support for the human rights of other Hindus, and Islamists threaten beheadings and rioting over a truthful comment about the theology of Islam – and the Islamists repeatedly ignore the national laws due to their hurt sentiments – then how are Hindus being protected at all? In fact, even after Kamlesh Tiwari was arrested, that didn't stop Islamists from hacking him to death, so how are Hindus protected if Islamists don't even care when IPC 295A or IPC 153A are implemented in their favor? If a Hindu being arrested doesn't quell their bloodlust, then what is the point of those laws? If Umesh Kolhe and Kanhaiya Lal were brutally murdered for social media posts that didn't say anything negative about Islam and they simply voiced support for Nupur Sharma, and Islamists clearly don't even respect the national laws like IPC 295A and IPC 153A meant to appease them, then how is this protecting Hindus at all? How is it not the case that all IPC 295A and IPC 153A have done is muzzle Hindus from having a voice or giving complaints about how Islam explicitly endorses the murder of all non-Muslims, especially fellow Hindus? It doesn't seem to me that this is protecting Hindus, it seems rather that Islamic colonization has firmly rooted itself within Hindu minds to never speak-up about double-standards imposed upon Hindus.

Third, this is clearly the worst form of anti-intellectualism in modern times and it is all Islam's fault. If you live in and believe in India, then I believe you need to hear this. Even for those who hate Hindus and Hinduism in India, please seriously consider the following: India is committing the worst form of brain-drain in human history within a functioning Republic by allowing IPC 295A and IPC 153A to continue existing. Your country is literally jailing law students, your country is jailing and failing to stop the murder of prominent Indian politicians, your society is turning a blind eye to businesspeople and chemists being brutally hacked to death for their social media posts even when they don't offend Islam, and all this is to protect the hurt feelings of a group of murderous religious extremists who glorify a 7th century illiterate man and who believe that reducing all modern standards to the 7th century is the perfect way to live. It's the worst form of brain-drain, because these people glorifying an illiterate man from the 7th century are killing people who have had lengthy, hardworking lives trying to help fellow Indians in their community to improve it; they've worked to learn and improve themselves to better help their fellow Indian countrymen by becoming businesspeople, learning STEM fields, studying Indian law, and you're letting them die because of angry and illiterate mobs? You're letting all these intelligent, wonderful, and hardworking people who believe in your country, who want to make your country a better place, and who want to do the hard work to improve your country – you're allowing them all to be imprisoned or to die to appease murderous religious hate? You're letting this happen to appease a bunch of murderous cultists who want to cosplay as a 7th century illiterate man and who want to regress every aspect of your society back to 7th century social, moral, technological, and cultural standards to await a mythic Day of Resurrection that'll never happen. You're placing more value on the hurt feelings of angry, violent, vicious, and illiterate people who make it clear that they enjoy killing Hindus, Buddhists, Sikhs, Jains, Parsis, Atheists, and Christians in order to keep your society permanently regressed into 7th century Arab fundamentalist standards. Their religion teaches them that the Prophet Mohammad was the perfect human being whose standards they should follow, he was also an illiterate man, and therefore illiteracy is seen as more divine than literacy in Islam. This is what your country is letting all these other people be put in prison or to die in order to protect? Consider countries as systems and the current framework of your system is allowing 7th century cultists to prevent you from improving yourselves, it is almost certainly preventing your children from having a real future in many instances, it's harmful to your economy both intellectually and economically, and you're all wasting your time cuddling the regressive value system of Islamism which is preventing you from becoming a world power. If you continue privileging 7th century Arab fundamentalist bloodlust that wants to keep you chained to 7th century moral, cultural, and technological standards over the lives and wellbeing of your hard-working law students, STEM researchers, businesspeople, and politicians who want to give your society a real future, then how can you ever hope to become a great power? How can your children have a real future?

Fourth, in the process of thinking about this . . . Hindus clearly have far more compassion and love for Muslims, including the Islamists, than anyone is willing to accept or recognize. Western Europeans and Hindus have more in common than they realize, whereas Americans wouldn't tolerate this behavior at all. The US and Western European Corporate news media can mock India for supposedly brutal repression of Muslims, but the truth is that if Islamist riots happened in the US, then we Americans know they'd be saying the complete opposite and supporting brutal crackdowns by any means necessary. I think only Western Europe has shown equal restraint and compassion for Muslims, even for Islamists, than most of these worthless US and European Corporate journalists have ever acknowledged or understood with just how hard this problem is. US and Western European Corporate clown shows have never been fair to either Hindus, other non-Muslim Indians, or Western Europeans more broadly about just how difficult and legitimate these problems are. Think about what has happened here: Hindus and all other non-Muslim Indians, Swedes, British, French, and so much more . . . are all willing to suffer bombings, stabbings, mutilation, and physical violence just to show compassion to a bunch of violent, murderous people who threaten to kill over being offended and who want to regress all non-Muslim societies into 7th century standards. The BJP is not altogether different from any Left-leaning party in Western Europe, if people look under the surface enough and consider how much moral restraint everyone is trying to commit towards. Western European and Indian societies are all acting like the ancient Greeks who tried to maintain noble standards while getting spat in the face, except they're being called bigoted for it by the US and Western European Corporate media circus. This is while people with extremely regressive views continue to gain privileges and drain everything around them by chronically presenting themselves as perennial victims, even when they kill people or rape little girls. This is like observing Friedrich Nietzsche's critique of Master and Slave morality with visceral examples existing everywhere in the world now between Islamic communities and the host country. For those of you from Muslim backgrounds who do not understand what I mean: if Islamists acted this way in the US such as all the rioting they do in India, then the consequences would be that they would be brutally crushed by the US government if it was ever perceived that their riots would hamper the economic privileges of the One Percent – the privileged elite of US society who are above US laws and who can get away with raping children more effectively than Islamists. There would not be any political party members thrown out of the party for mentioning Aisha's age like what the BJP did to appease Muslim sentiments and there wouldn't be attempts at appeasement due to international pressure from Islamic monarchies. The only difference would be that a Republican President would present words of revenge in an attempt to portray strength and a Democratic President would speak of trying to distinguish between peaceful protesters and rioters, but behind the scenes either President would have the US armed forces formulate clear plans to brutalize and crush any armed resistance in as quick and efficient a manner as possible. It would be a bloodbath and the majority of Americans would likely be on the side of the Presidency, no matter who was in charge. Unfortunately, the sexual violence of young girls by

Islamists would be swept under the rug just as they have been with registered sex offenders raping Native American women and girls, the entire Jeffrey Epstein case in which who knows how many of the One Percent were involved with their organized rapes of little girls[456], and the White Christian Churches everywhere in the US raping mostly young White boys. Nevertheless, I find it doubtful that there wouldn't be "shoot first" orders upon any Islamist riots, if they happened in the US with concerns about any supposed human rights taking an immediate backseat against something that would probably be labeled terrorist violence to justify shoot-first orders; this is regardless of if there were tens of thousands or even millions of Islamists rioting. Even if some people believe that's unrealistic, there would be plenty of law-abiding or illegally purchased gun-toting Americans sweeping into the rioting areas and attempting to kill as many Islamists as humanely possible. The 2002 Gujarat riots and the British riots of 2024 would be happening in every area as an immediate and brutal response, if there were any Islamist rioters who started burning down cars, blowing up shops, or killing people over hurt feelings like they do in India and Western Europe; there would be no restraint because that sort of behavior would be considered unacceptable and deserving the worst forms of punishment imaginable with "enhanced interrogation" against any arrested Islamists. The point being, Islamists really do not understand how much love and compassion is sent their way as they continue complaining about hurt sentiments and wanting to regress everything to 7th century standards. It's likely a mix of nationalism, religious values, and – for India – the knowledge that some of these people are their own family members. For the EU, it's probably a commitment to the Universal Declaration of Human Rights. It seems that the US and Western European Corporate media circus don't seem to understand they're killing their own value systems of compassion, every time they punish Hindus, other non-Muslim Indians, and most of Western Europe for trying to show restraint and compassion for a regressive religious faith system that really does teach Muslims to kill other people for hurt sentiments, to rape little girls to save their eternal souls from hell, and to regress all societies to 7th century standards. Honestly, I never thought I'd say this but . . . I'm kind of happy that I live in a police-surveillance state now where I know the government and US Corporate media would thoroughly murder and dehumanize Islamists and then make news stories about regrets after they were completely certain there'd never be any Islamist riot ever again with a thorough and unrelenting US military presence making sure of it after they committed mass bloodshed upon Islamists.

Fifth, the one that is most personal to me, when are the majority of Hindu minds ever truly going to be free? It honestly upsets me that some Hindus now find it normal to apply IPC 295A and IPC 153A to disputes with other groups who "offend" Hinduism

---

[456] Fields, Ashleigh. "Dershowitz Says He Knows Epstein Client List Names: 'But I'm Bound by Confidentiality.'" Thehill.Com, The Hill, 10 July 2025, thehill.com/homenews/administration/5395597-dershowitz-says-he-knows-epstein-client-list-names-but-im-bound-by-confidentiality/.

because of trivialities like porn videos having Hindu statues in the background. You cannot claim that Hinduism is a religion of free expression and then be offended by the depictions of Hindu deities that upset you. I absolutely hate the fact that not only has IPC 295A given Islamists the power to determine how free and unfree conversations can be for the majority of Hindus, but the majority of Hindus in India are essentially being conditioned into degrading themselves and degrading Hinduism onto the level of 7th century Arab fundamentalism. From the perspective of Advaita Vedanta philosophy, the *Shvestashvatara / Svetasvatara* Upanishad, and Adi Shankara's commentary on both the Bhagavad Gita and the *Shvestashvatara / Svetasvatara* Upanishad; you're letting the illusion (*maya*) of sense-objects control your behavior because a bunch of worthless, stupid, bloodthirsty 7th century Arab fundamentalist killers who worship an illiterate pedophile warlord; they seek to degrade you, to degrade your religious traditions, and to degrade your cultural heritage into absolute shit just because they feel insecure about their worthless farce of a religion. The depiction of Hindu deities in a negative light in fiction is just sense-objects and we as Hindus shouldn't be controlled by sense-objects. If you find something objectionable, then why can't fellow Hindus just make positive fictional depictions of Hinduism as a response? What are you all doing when Hindu sensibilities are "offended" like them? The truth is, you are not free to practice Hinduism, because imposing limits on Free Speech and Free Expression was something that none of the ancient Hindu philosophers who debated each other, who debated other Dharmic followers, and who debated the oldest known Atheists in history ever had to deal with. They all ridiculed each other, they could take criticism from each other even with the ridicule, and they gave criticism back through debates. The Charvaka Atheists ridiculing Vedic traditions back around 600 BCE didn't have to deal with any persecution, or jail time, or fear of their heads being chopped off; they could just say what they wanted and Vedic followers were perfectly willing to criticize back. There were no head-chopping lunatics screaming their cosplay fantasies of an illiterate pedophile warlord to worry about for them. Vedic practitioners debated truth claims peacefully for thousands of years; Free Expression and Free Thought didn't have to exist as a law in ancient India among ancient Vedic traditions, because everyone was free to speak their minds before Islamic colonization. IPC 295A and IPC 153A are the ultimate degradation and toxic blot upon the Hindu faith that is turning Hinduism into Islam in terms of communal behavior. If you are not free to speak your mind and freely express yourself, just as our ancient ancestors did from approximately 800 BCE to 1000 AD prior to Islam ever existing, then how are you free to practice your faith just like our ancient ancestors did? When are you going to be free from the tyranny of hurt sentiments? To be perfectly frank, the only Hindus who are free to practice their faith are those living in the United States, which has the best Freedom of Expression in modern history, just like ancient India did before the Islamic conquest and colonization and British colonization imposed anti-Free Speech laws that have absolutely, under no uncertain terms, destroyed your ability to freely practice Hinduism. Regardless of what you believe about the other reasons, I firmly believe this one is unequivocally true; you are not free to practice the full depth of Hinduism, if in debates you can't just use Islam – a religion with nearly two billion adherents – as an example of anything in a debate and have to chronically worry about mobs chopping people's heads off, whenever anyone mentions anything related to Islam or falsely interprets it to be about Islam. The reference of other religions to present examples when having discussions about truth claims is just normal human behavior to give a clearer understanding of concepts; something ancient Vedic practitioners did for over thousands of years to debate truth claims. When are the majority of Hindus ever truly going to be free?

    Sixth, I want to first apologize if this seems like a privileged argument from the safe confines of the United States where I was born and raised, but I believe that Hindus in India should participate in peaceful pro-Free Speech protests demanding the removal of IPC 295A and IPC 153A through demonstrations of civil disobedience. Unfortunately, it is simply a statement of fact that you would all have to risk your heads being chopped off by Islamists and the US and European Corporate news media presenting Islamists as an aggrieved minority after they chop a Hindu's head off or perhaps even arguing the opposite of the truth happened, as has become the norm from them. I have two suggestions, one is perhaps less threatening, but more expensive than the other. These are just ideas that I can think of, if there are ideas that any of you can think of that are more grounded in reality with safety concerns and more effective as forms of civil disobedience, then please feel free to use that instead. What I would suggest is to make anonymous, concerted Free Speech protests as a form of civil disobedience; whereby you wear masks and put images critical of Islam in public areas. There would suddenly be images criticizing Islam or pictures of the Prophet Mohammad on a billboard in the early mornings. You would have to look out for cameras and where your movements are tracked, but this seems like the simplest idea. Anonymous, concerted Free Speech protests from 5 people, to 10 people, to 100 people, to 200 people, to 500 people, to 1000 people, to 2000 people, to 10,000 people, and so on. This may have to happen regardless of what riots and head chopping that Islamists commit and it is asking more than can be reasonable, due to how Islamists behave. The second, and probably more expensive idea, is recognizing that this is the era of drone technology and you can obtain tools in the modern era that never existed before to stop this 7th century Arab fundamentalist belief system. If you have the means to purchase commercial or private drones, or pool money and resources to purchase commercial or private drones, then you could perhaps use them to spread images more easily and with far less risk to your personal lives and safety, albeit you would probably lose the drone in the process while remaining anonymous. This could be done by just one person in India, if you think about it. The point being that this form of peaceful civil disobedience should be far less risky. For those concerned on what the US and Western Corporate news circus would think: there is no way to spin peaceful Free Speech demonstrations as bigoted without them being seen as racist. They'll be forced to show their true colors. My other book, *Machiavellian Ahimsa*, gives suggestions on how to use this as a military strategy that I firmly believe would work on all Islamic countries by any Republic that uses the strategy of mixing the Machiavellian brutality of Western Foreign Policy with the psychological perspective of Vedanta philosophy in Hinduism.

Please think of the consequences if you believe this to be mere bluster on my part. Are we going to have to watch Sharmistha Panoli or Nupur Sharma become victims of rape or murder, the moment the Indian government thinks they can reduce their security detail, just like with Kamlesh Tiwari? How many more people have to die because some ignorant Imam accuses a Hindu of having said or done something that was presumably insulting Islam, but the Hindu is merely killed for unsubstantiated rumors that hurt Muslims' feelings like what happened to Kishan Bharwad? If they choose to chop heads first before even verifying that a Hindu really did say anything negative about Islam, then how are IPC 295A or IPC 153A protecting Hindu human rights in India at all? What about the rights of others, such as the case of Hari Singh reportedly being crushed by a tractor in the dead of night by Islamists?[457] There appears to be a growing Islamist movement of throwing cow heads or butchering live cows in front of mandirs, in what ways are IPC 295A or IPC 153A acting as a deterrent for Islamists to prevent them from vilifying Hindus and desecrating mandirs in an unyielding display of utter hate?[458] What are you all doing? Furthermore, I want to make it clear that reading what happened to Sharmistha Panoli was one of the stupidest things I've ever seen this year in 2025. She makes a passing comment about Houris which she barely mentioned in her video (which was a true statement. Yet to Islamists, Hindus that say anything about Islam will get threatened with head chopping) and she later gets arrested by the Kolkata police after Muslim Indians join Pakistani Muslims with rape and death threats.[459] They arrest Sharmistha after traveling 1500 kms / 932 miles because the Chief Minister Mamata Banarjee supports vilifying Hindus with the tyranny of hurt sentiments.[460] It did not

---

[457] Sharma, Swati Goel. "Phoola Bai's Husband Hari Singh Was Brutally Killed by Islamists on Holi. He Was Crushed by a Tractor in Dead of the Night Hailing from an All-Hindu Vanvasi Village in Raisen District of Madhya Pradesh, Phoola Bai Has No Means of Income. ." X.Com, x.com / Twitter, 12 May 2025, x.com/swati_gs/status/1921930773151506515.

[458] Pandey, Shraddha. "The Growing 'trend' of Throwing Meat Pieces in Front of Mandirs, a Co-Ordinated Campaign to Desecrate Sacred Hindu Places?" Www.Opindia.Com, OpIndia, 19 June 2025, www.opindia.com/2025/06/the-growing-trend-of-throwing-meat-pieces-in-front-of-temples/.

[459] "Kolkata Police Travel to Gurgaon to Arrest Hindu Influencer Sharmistha over Video Targeting Pakistan, No Action so Far on Muslims Who Issued STSJ Threats." Www.Opindia.Com, OpIndia, 31 May 2025, www.opindia.com/2025/05/kolkata-police-arrest-hindu-sharmistha-from-gurgaon-over-video-targeting-pakistan-had-offended-indian-muslims-details/.

[460] "Kolkata Police Travel to Gurgaon to Arrest Hindu Influencer Sharmistha over Video Targeting Pakistan, No Action so Far on Muslims Who Issued STSJ Threats." Www.Opindia.Com, OpIndia, 31 May 2025, www.opindia.com/2025/05/kolkata-police-arrest-hindu-sharmistha-from-gurgaon-over-video-targeting-pakistan-had-offended-indian-muslims-details/.

matter to the Chief Minister of West Bengal, Mamata Banarjee, that Pakistani and Indian Muslims were giving rape and death threats to Hindu Sharmistha Panoli at all; she instead wanted Sharmistha imprisoned to appease Islamic people giving rape and death threats in both India and to the enemy country, Pakistan, which funds terrorists that committed the Pahalgam atrocity against Hindus; the very subject that Sharmistha Panoli's deleted video was criticizing. It did not matter to Chief Minister Mamata Banarjee that she had Sharmistha Panoli put in prison for Free Speech over Sharmistha's sincere patriotic sentiments for India, it did not matter to Chief Minister Mamata Banarjee that Sharmistha Panoli is a hard-working law student who wants to do her part to help her fellow Indians, it did not matter to Chief Minister Mamata Banarjee that the conditions Sharmistha Panoli was put within Alipore women's correctional home were unhygienic according to Sharmistha's lawyer Md Samimuddin[461], it did not matter to Chief Minister Mamata Banarjee that Sharmistha Panoli suffered kidney stones[462], and all that mattered to Chief Minister Mamata Banarjee was sending Kolkata police to drive over 900 miles over a Twitter post that Sharmistha Panoli deleted and unreservedly apologized for so that Mamata Banarjee could appease bloodthirsty Islamist mobs who made rape and death threats at Sharmistha Panoli while another set of bloodthirsty Islamist mobs can't seem to stop rioting in West Bengal's streets and murdering Hindus – it just always seems to happen every couple of years in Chief Minister Mamata Banarjee's Indian State of West Bengal; examples range from riots in 2017 and earlier this year in 2025.[463][464] This is a prime example of a brain-drain due to appeasing Islamist sentiments. This is Chief Minister Mamata Banarjee willfully ignoring how she's imprisoning and harming the health of future generations of her own country to bend over backwards and appease Islamism, even when they make rape and death threats upon India's future generations. Do Hindu lives matter with such people in charge in your country? If Sharmistha Panoli is killed by Islamists at any point in the future, you should all absolutely blame Mamata Banarjee for legitimizing it. It will be all the fault of Mamata Banarjee for legitimizing hatred, rape threats, and death threats towards a Hindu law student who wants to work

---

[461] Dhar, Aniruddha. "Instagram Influencer Sharmishta Panoli's Lawyer Claims Poor Hygiene in Kolkata Jail: 'She Has Kidney Stones.'" Hindustan Times, Hindustan Times, 2 June 2025, www.hindustantimes.com/india-news/instagram-influencer-sharmishta-panolis-lawyer-claims-poor-hygiene-in-kolkata-jail-she-has-kidney-stones-101748858117735.html.

[462] Dhar, Aniruddha. "Instagram Influencer Sharmishta Panoli's Lawyer Claims Poor Hygiene in Kolkata Jail: 'She Has Kidney Stones.'" Hindustan Times, Hindustan Times, 2 June 2025, www.hindustantimes.com/india-news/instagram-influencer-sharmishta-panolis-lawyer-claims-poor-hygiene-in-kolkata-jail-she-has-kidney-stones-101748858117735.html.

[463] Bhattacharya, Snigdhendu. "Bengal Violence: Basirhat's Muslim Leaders Tried to Pacify the Rioting Mob, but Couldn't." Hindustan Times, Hindustan Times, 16 July 2017, www.hindustantimes.com/india-news/bengal-violence-basirhat-s-muslim-leaders-tried-to-pacify-the-rioting-mob-but-couldn-t/story-8O6XTqN3yhsvKlfYSDK2aK.html.

[464] Arghya Prasun Roychowdhury / TIMESOFINDIA.COM / Apr 14, 2025. "Waqf Violent Protest: On a Tough Legal Wicket, Tmc Faces a Delicate Balancing Act: India News." The Times of India, TOI, timesofindia.indiatimes.com/india/waqf-violent-protest-on-a-tough-legal-wicket-tmc-faces-a-delicate-balancing-act/articleshow/120282778.cms. Accessed 25 Aug. 2025.

hard and improve your country. Thankfully, the Indian court system granted bail and I'm happy to learn they chastised the Kolkata police for the conditions Sharmistha Panoli was put in.[465] If you want to save Hindu lives, I believe you should get rid of IPC 295A and IPC 153A and just speak your truth about Islam. In the long-term, the outcome is surely better than chronically living in fear of violent people who want to regress every iota of your civilization to 7th century Arab fundamentalist standards that'll lead to yet another Islamic failed state and all you have to do is look to the left at Pakistan or the right at Bangladesh to see how true of a statement that is.

For those readers who live in Western Europe or the US, ask yourselves this: Why weren't you ever told by your supposedly legitimate and reliable US and Western European Corporate news organizations that Islamist rioters chronically chant that they want to see Hindus beheaded whenever they riot over their hurt feelings? Why was that fact hidden from you and how trustworthy are news organizations who would hide that from you? The US and Western European Corporate news organizations are not run by stupid people, most of the journalists who write those stories are not stupid people either, and they are not ignorant of these facts. Even US Indologists like Sheldon Pollock who almost certainly visited India on multiple occasions; he was likely was aware of it too. While all these Western and US news organizations were making incessant news about Cow vigilantism, Muslim rioters were enthusiastically screaming how they wanted to see Hindus heads chopped off. For those in Western Europe, absolutely expect that to start happening as Muslim populations grow in your country in the subsequent years alongside typical phrases like *"This wouldn't happen in an Islamic country!"* following the statements where the Islamists demand to see public beheadings to quench the bloodthirst of their hurt feelings. It's already being normalized in France. The Charlie Hebdo murders by Algerian Islamists led to broad international support in 2015, the beheading of French teacher Samuel Paty in October 2020 by Islamist refugee Abdullakh Anzorov over rumors led to national support and sympathy in France[466][467], and the fatal stabbing of French teacher Dominique Bernard and injury of two others who tried to stop another Russian Islamist refugee Mohammed Mogouchkov as he stabbed and screamed "Allahu Akbar" at a French school parking lot resulted in a muted national response in France with the French government immediately having to grapple with multiple bomb

---

[465] "Calcutta High Court Grants Interim Bail to Sharmistha Panoli, Pulls up Bengal Police for Their Actions." Www.Opindia.Com, OpIndia, 5 June 2025, www.opindia.com/news-updates/calcutta-high-court-grants-interim-bail-to-sharmistha-panoli-pulls-up-bengal-police-for-their-actions/.
[466] Willsher, Kim. "Teacher Decapitated in Paris Named as Samuel Paty, 47." The Guardian, Guardian News and Media, 17 Oct. 2020, www.theguardian.com/world/2020/oct/17/teacher-decapitated-in-paris-named-as-samuel-paty-47.
[467] "Samuel Paty: French Schoolgirl Admits Lying about Murdered Teacher." BBC News, BBC, 9 Mar. 2021, www.bbc.com/news/world-europe-56325254.

threats.[468][469] This is the gradual banality and normalization of 7th century Arab fundamentalist standards into non-Muslim societies. This is what the Neoliberal economists, Neoliberal politicians, and Neoliberal CEOs have brought to Western Europe. Hindus of India warned us all for decades upon decades, but all Western Europeans in particular saw were their stereotypes of "backwards" brown people and occasionally they cry "Hindutva" instead of seeing Hindus in India as rational people giving legitimate criticisms that they should have taken seriously. For a clearer understanding of just how long this has been going on within Islam, from Professor Sprachman's English translation of Abdolhossein Zarrinkoub's *Two Centuries of Silence: An Account of Events and Conditions in Iran [Persia] during the first Two Hundred Years of Islam* depicts what it was like for other faiths to "debate" in Islamic Caliphates, while it may seem cordial initially, the non-Muslims were forced to convert if they lost a debate and Caliph al-Ma'mun who reigned approximately between 813 AD – 833 AD in the Abbasid Caliphate would murder those who displeased him on a whim. This brutality was over a hundred years before the initial conquest and colonization of India:

> **Al-Ma'mūn and the Debate Sessions**
>
> Al-Ma'mūn, what was said above not-withstanding, was more patient and tolerant in his behavior toward sectarians. His reign, in fact, marked a renewed period of open debate and discussion among People of the Book. At these sessions, which were held mostly in the caliph's presence, followers of [non-Muslim] religions, especially the Zoroastrian high priests, were given the opportunity to argue the truth of their religious doctrines with Muslim scholars. The debates sparked a new round of conflicts in the war between the Magians and Muslim scholastic theologians, conflicts waged in the light of knowledge and the intellect, without coercion or the sword getting in the way.
>
> Given his interest in research and investigation into the beliefs and views held by sectarians of all stripes, al-Ma'mūn permitted a certain amount of freedom for argument and discussion. Scholastic theologians and other scholars familiar with Greek, Persian, and Indian learning would debate with those steeped in the Prophet's traditions and pronouncements [ḥadīth s]. The confrontations gave rise to novel discourse on the issues in question. Disputes flared on human free will and the createdness of the Quran. Also controversial was the question of which faith and religion was more in tune with human learning and the intellect. Followers of various faiths and those with other beliefs engaged in debates with one another, which pleased al-Ma'mūn, who considered the back and forth an effective tool for finding the truth. For this reason, he sheathed the sword the caliphs had been using on non-Muslim leaders and ordered them to engage Muslim scholars and scholastic theologians in debate. Al-Ma'mūn believed the enemy must be vanquished by reason not by force, because any victory won by force would fade when that force degraded; however, nothing could remove victory won by reason.26 For this reason, al-Ma'mūn was very fond of debate and argumentation and regularly consorted with Muslim scholastic theologians and scholars. History records that on Tuesdays scholars and authorities from various faiths and schools would gather at the caliphal court. A special chamber was decked out; food was served, hands were washed, and braziers were lit. After lunch, the guests went en masse to begin debating at a

---

[468] Pollina, Richard. "Suspect Allegedly Yelled 'Allahu Akbar' before Fatally Stabbing Teacher, Injuring 2 Others in France Knife Attack." New York Post, New York Post, 13 Oct. 2023, nypost.com/2023/10/13/france-knife-attack-leaves-teacher-dead-several-injured/.

[469] "France Pays Respects to Teacher Killed in School Terror Attack." France 24, FRANCE 24, 19 Oct. 2023, www.france24.com/en/live-news/20231019-france-pays-respects-to-teacher-killed-in-islamist-attack.

place al-Ma'mūn reserved for them. During the sessions, there was complete freedom of speech. Towards evening, they would dine and then disperse.27 Followers of various faiths and their dignitaries would attend these meetings, including the chief Zoroastrian priest Ādhar-farnbagh and the Manichaean leader Yazdānbōkht [a.k.a. Yazdānbukht]. [The Shia Imam] cAlī b. Mūsā al-Riḍā also participated in some of the sessions held in Khorasan. Histories have preserved portions of the debates, and they reveal that the market place of ideas heated up considerably during sessions dealing with the science of discourse [kalām] and of religious doctrine. The debates compelled followers of non-Muslim religions to defend their faiths and write treatises to uphold their views and rebut the objections of their critics.

Debating Dualism

During the period of open debate among scholars from various faith communities, Manichaeans and Magians would have been expected to take part in the discussions. This meant the Zoroastrian high priests would engage in dialogue and dispute on Islam and the Quran and trade views on the truth of doctrines that had humbled and supplanted Zoroastrianism more than a century before. Histories include extracts from the exchanges between the Zoroastrian and Muslim theologians. It is reported, for example, that, with al-Ma'mūn present, cAlī b. Mūsā al-Riḍā (peace be upon him) asked one of the major herbads,

"What proof do you have that Zoroaster was a prophet?" The herbad said, "Zoroaster brought a message no one had brought before him, and he made things permissible to us that had not been permissible prior to his time." Al-Riḍā then asked, "The things you say about Zoroaster—they've reached you in reports from your ancestors, haven't they?" The herbad admitted they had. Al-Riḍā said, "Other nations of the world are no different. They have reports about their own prophets like Moses, Jesus, and Muhammad from their forebears. Why, then, do you acknowledge the prophethood of Zoroaster and claim he had brought things no one else had before, but deny the prophethood of other peoples' prophets, when they have learned about their prophets in the same way as you have?" Left without a response, the herbad, went away.28

Another example is found in the following report of a conversation between al-Ma'mūn and a Manichaean:

During the time al-Ma'mūn arranged to have all religious sects engage in debate before him, a scholastic theologian, who practiced dualism, turned up wanting to join the fray. Al-Ma'mūn ordered all Muslim scholastic theologians and divines brought together to debate the dualist. The man began, "I see a world full of good and evil, light and dark, and right and wrong. Logic dictates each of these antitheses have a separate maker; it would be unreasonable to imagine good and evil coming from a single source." As he went on with similar arguments, those in the gathering shouted out, "O Commander of the Faithful, the sword is only answer for such talk!" Al-Ma'mūn remained silent for a time, then he asked the man, "What is the religion?" He said, "The religion is that the Creator is twofold; the Creator of good and the Creator of evil; the actions and states of each are clearly spelled out. That which creates good does not do evil, and that which creates evil does not do good." Al-Ma'mūn asked, "Do both have control over their actions or not?" "Both," said the man, "have authority over what they create; the Creator never lacks such capability." Al-Ma'mūn asked, "No Creator can admit inability?" "No," he said. "How could a worshipped-being admit being incapable?" "God be praised!" declared al-Ma'mūn, "The Creator of good wishes all to be him and not to be the Creator of evil, and the Creator of evil wishes not to be the Creator of good. Is this not what they intend?" "No," he said, "Neither has the upper hand over the other." Al-Ma'mūn said, "Now the incapacity of the two is plain for all to see, and it is not right to attribute such weakness to the Creator." This baffled the dualist. Al-Ma'mūn had him killed, after which all sang the caliph's praises.29

The dualist's name does not appear in the report. However, because al-Ma'mūn handled him the way he handled other Manichaeans, some scholars have been led to believe the dualist was Manichaean. Some even identify him as Yazdān Bokht.30 It is possible that al-Ma'mūn did not have Yazdān Bokht killed; however, it also seems the writer fabricated the incident out of bias, or because he wished it to be so. The debate, nevertheless, between the dualist and the caliph lifts the curtain on a basic Zoroastrian tenet, which resembles what we find in Pahlavi works. It shows what troubled the dualist more than anything was the problem of good and evil. The [Zoroastrian] people were preoccupied by the question of how evil acts could be attributed to the deity.[470]

That being said, I think Atheists that aren't from Islamic backgrounds should be added to the CAA. Unfortunately, one negative of Free Speech is that the mix of Free Speech and security means that anyone can have very stupid ideas that don't comport to reality-based thinking and many in the US simply don't understand the realities of Muslim-majority countries. We know what Islam teaches Muslim men to do to all religious minority women and young girls. Those of you in India who have read and watched news of what Pakistanis, Bangladeshis, and Afghans do to non-Muslim religious minorities know what I mean and it is a failure of compassion for the victims, if we all pretend otherwise. If a Hindu, Sikh, Buddhist, Christian, Parsi, or Jain family came from Bangladesh, Pakistan, or Afghanistan got on their knees and began begging for protection because their 9-year-old daughter was nearly raped by a gang of Muslim men and they're fleeing for their lives; we all know from the evidence that if they were sent back, exactly what would happen to their 9-year-old daughter. Now, imagine it is an Atheist family from a non-Islamic background; what is the moral difference? Regardless of how bigoted it appears to the privileged news journalists in the US and Western spheres; everyone who looks at the evidence within Islamic theology and the behavior of most Muslim men across the world know what they do to girls as young as nine-years of age. I would highly recommend adding Atheists of non-Islamic backgrounds, we all know what Muslim-majority countries do to 9-year-old South Asian Atheist girls especially if their families are from non-Islamic backgrounds just as they do to 9-year-old Hindu, Sikh, Buddhist, Parsi, Christian, and Jain girls. Regardless of if Hindus in India are labeled bigots by privileged buffoons who do not understand the reality of how disgusting Islam is, how is protecting the lives of young children from rape not a worthy goal?

While it is unfortunate that Muslim minority families or Ex-Muslim Atheists have to be turned away, the fact remains that if India accepted a fast-track for Muslim refugees alongside others, then Bangladesh and Pakistan would threaten war because the legitimacy of being Islamic States and their Islamic identity would be called into question in terms of political legitimacy. It is yet another example of the ignorance of White

---

[470] Zarrinkoub, Abdolhossein. Chapter 9: The Battle of Beliefs (Location 4422 – 4965). Two Centuries of Silence: An Account of Events and Conditions in Iran [Persia] During the First Two Hundred Years of Islam, from the Arab Invasion to the Rise of the Tahirid Dynasty First edition. Mazda Publishers. Kindle Edition.

Christian and so-called Liberal Corporate organizations in the US and Western Europe. In the case of Ex-Muslims, the supposed Ex-Muslims can and have lied before to gain refuge in other countries in Europe, so it is in India's best interests to turn them away for the safety and security of all non-Muslim lives. Finally, please consider the notorious case of Asia Bibi, a Catholic woman in Pakistan who was accused of "blaspheming Prophet Mohammad" by her Muslim neighbors and beaten by an angry mob outside of her home while the Pakistani police did nothing.[471] Think about how her family's home was targeted and ransacked with a mob physically assaulting the whole family and how Asia Bibi was sentenced to death for Blasphemy and put in solitary confinement for nine years before her retrial.[472] How her family had to keep moving from place to place to avoid being murdered by angry mobs of Islamists attempting to assassinate them shortly after the retrial and acquittal of Asia Bibi.[473] That is what this woman and her family endured over false allegations against her and even if the charges had been true, that would have simply meant they endured all of that for the freedom to speak their minds. No one should have to live like this; no Hindu, no Buddhist, no Parsi, no Jain, no Sikh, and no Christian should have to live in fear of their young child being gang raped by Islamist men, because they believe that they're saving the child's eternal soul from the fires of hell; neither should Atheists and giving refuge to the ones more easily verifiable to live peacefully without being a security threat would likely be better for India's long-term interests. It is unfortunate that Atheists from Islamic backgrounds would present security risks due to the history of fakery by Muslims, but this shouldn't be the case for Atheists of non-Islamic backgrounds.

A Falsehood of Islamic Colonization: The Case of Egypt

As an anecdotal example of why the actual and clear history of Islamic colonization is important to remember, a few years ago on the social media platform of Discord, a well-meaning Ex-Muslim Atheist in India told me that while Islam surely had problems, it at least helped with women's rights unlike other faiths *at the time*. He believed that *at the time* of Islam's conquest, it had surely helped improve women's rights by not having child sacrifices. What he was taught was a complete lie, likely to promote the objectives of the Islamic colonizers as war propaganda. It wasn't until I read historian Kishori Saran Lal that I realized how completely false this was and this Ex-Muslim from India clearly wasn't told of his ancestors' true history. Ex-Muslims in India

---

[471] Jaffery, Shumaila. "Asia Bibi: Pakistan's Notorious Case." BBC News, BBC, www.bbc.co.uk/news/resources/idt-sh/Asia_Bibi. Accessed 17 Jan. 2025.
[472] Jaffery, Shumaila. "Asia Bibi: Pakistan's Notorious Case." BBC News, BBC, www.bbc.co.uk/news/resources/idt-sh/Asia_Bibi. Accessed 17 Jan. 2025.
[473] Sherwood, Harriet. "Asia Bibi Family Being Hunted 'house to House' in Pakistan." The Guardian, Guardian News and Media, 21 Nov. 2018, www.theguardian.com/world/2018/nov/21/asia-bibi-family-being-hunted-house-to-house-in-pakistan.

don't even know that women's rights worsened under Islam in India because women were put into cages and sold at slave markets like cattle.[474][475] As a counter example to the perception that young girls were being sacrificed prior to Islamic colonization, consider the vilification and lies that Islam promotes against ancient Egypt by falsely asserting they had virgin sacrifices where they drowned young girls into the Nile. This particular story presumably originates from the ancient Greeks, but it seems Medieval Muslims used this lie for their purposes to justify their own colonization. From the website *Islam Question and Answer* by Muhammad Saalih Al-Munajjid:

> **Is it proven that 'Umar (may Allah be pleased with him) wrote a letter to the Nile in Egypt so that its water would flow by Allah's leave?**
>
> **Question: 178417**
>
> I want to know the authenticity of the story about Umar (may Allah be pleased with him) writing a letter to the River Nile. It seems to me as illogical, for the Qur'aan and the Saheeh saheeh Sunnah (authentic prophetic traditions) do not teach such a thing. Also, that for droughts, Salah Salat Ul al Istisqa is authentically established.
>
> **Answer**
>
> ---
>
> **Praise be to Allah, and blessings and peace be upon the Messenger of Allah.**
>
> Ibn Katheer (may Allah have mercy on him) said:
>
> It was narrated to us via Ibn Luhay'ah from Qays ibn al-Hajjaj from someone who told him: When Egypt was conquered, its people came to 'Amr ibn al-'As (may Allah be pleased with him) and said to him: O Ameer, this Nile of ours is used to something and cannot flow unless it is done. He said: What is that? They said: On the twelfth night of this month, we take a young girl from her parents, and we placate her parents, then we dress her in jewellery and the finest garments there can be, then we throw her into this Nile.
>
> 'Amr (may Allah be pleased with him) said to them: This is something that cannot happen in Islam; Islam erases that which came before it (of bad customs).
>
> So they stayed for a while, during which the Nile did not flow at all, neither a little nor a lot, until they thought of leaving. Then 'Amr (may Allah be pleased with him) wrote to 'Umar ibn al-Khattab (may Allah be pleased with him), telling him about this. He wrote to him, saying: You did the right thing. I am sending you a piece of paper with my letter; throw it into the Nile.
>
> When his letter came, 'Amr (may Allah be pleased with him) took the piece of paper on which was written:
>
> "From the slave of Allah 'Umar, Ameer al-Mumineen, to the Nile of the people of Egypt.

---

[474] Lal, Kishori Saran. Chapter X: AD 1200 – 1400 (Pgs. 113 – 116). "Growth of Muslim Population in Medieval India (1000-1800)" Internet Archive, Internet Archive, 5 Aug. 2018, ia902800.us.archive.org/11/items/GrowthOfMuslimPopulationInMedievalIndiaAd10001800/Growth-Of-Muslim-Population-In-Medieval-India-ad-1000-1800_text.pdf.

[475] Lal, Kishori Saran. Chapter XI: AD 1400 – 1600 (Pgs. 127 – 143). "Growth of Muslim Population in Medieval India (1000-1800)" Internet Archive, Internet Archive, 5 Aug. 2018, ia902800.us.archive.org/11/items/GrowthOfMuslimPopulationInMedievalIndiaAd10001800/Growth-Of-Muslim-Population-In-Medieval-India-ad-1000-1800_text.pdf. For reference: Footnote on page 136.

To proceed: If you only flow on your own initiative, then do not flow, for we have no need of you. But if you only flow on the command of Allah, the One, the Subduer, and He is the One Who causes you to flow, then we ask Allah, may He be exalted, to make you flow."

He threw the paper in the Nile and by Saturday morning, Allah had caused the Nile to flow (to a depth or width of) sixteen cubits in one night, and Allah put an end to this particular custom of the people of Egypt until today.

End quote from al-Bidayah wa'n-Nihayah, 7/114-115

Similar reports were also narrated by Ibn 'Abd al-Hakam in Futooh Misr, p. 165; al-Lalkai in Sharh I'tiqad Ahl as-Sunnah, 6/463; Ibn 'Asakir in Tareekh Dimashq, 44/336; Abu'sh-Shaykh in al-'Azamah, 4/1424, via Ibn Luhay'ah.

This is a da'eef isnad (weak chain of narration) that is not saheeh, and this report cannot be proven with such an isnad. Ibn Luhay'ah – whose full name was 'Abdullah ibn Luhay'ah ibn 'Uqbah – is da 'eef as he used to get mixed up, and in addition to that he is mudallis (one who narrates from someone he met something he did not hear). See at-Tahdheeb, 5/327-33; Mizan al-I'tidaal, 2/475-484

Qays ibn al-Hajjaj is sadooq (trustworthy), from the sixth level of hadeeth narrators (tabaqah) according to al-Hafiz Ibn Hajar; they are the ones who it is not proven that they met any of the Sahabah/Companions (may Allah be pleased with them). See: Taqreeb at-Tahdheeb, 1/25

Sometimes he narrated it as a mursal (the link between the Successor and the Prophet is missing) report and sometimes he narrated it from the one who told him, but the one who told him is majhool and not known.

So the report is da'eef (weak) and is not saheeh (sound)

If this story were true, everyone would know about it and it would be well known, and it would have been widely narrated through confirmed isnads, because it is an important and significant event, the like of which should not be ignored; rather an incident less significant than this would not be overlooked by historians and narrators.

And Allah knows best.[476]

And the actual truth, from journalist Ahmed Maged in his article published in 2008, last updated on August 7th, 2015, and titled *"The Nile Bride Sacrifice Is a Myth, Says Egyptologist"* on Daily News Egypt, in an interview with Egyptologist Bassam El Shammaa, which reads as follows:

> CAIRO: The ancient Egyptian custom of offering a virgin as a sacrifice to the river Nile every year to instigate a flood is a big historical error, Egyptology researcher Bassam El Shammaa told Daily News Egypt.
>
> "The myth of Arous El Nil (Bride of the Nile) has tarnished the image of ancient Egyptians who by nature hated violence and were only content to see blood at the altar, El Shammaa said.

---

[476] Al-Munajjid, Muhammad Saalih. "Is It Proven That 'Umar (May Allah Be Pleased with Him) Wrote a Letter to the Nile in Egypt so That Its Water Would Flow by Allah's Leave? - Islam Question & Answer." Islam, Islam Question & Answer, 17 June 2012, islamqa.info/en/answers/178417/is-it-proven-that-umar-(may-allah-be-pleased-with-him)-wrote-a-letter-to-the-nile-in-egypt-so-that-its-water-would-flow-by-allahs-leave.

According to some versions of history, this Egyptian custom was practiced until the Islamic conquest of Egypt when Caliph Omar Ibn El Khattab banned the pagan ritual.

According to Egyptian historian Al Maqrizi (1364-1442) in his "El Khutat El Maqrizia (The Maqrizian Plans), when the Arab armies led by commander Amr Ibn El Aas entered Egypt, Egypt's Copts requested to uphold the annual ritual prior to the time of the flood.

When Ibn El Aas referred the request to the Caliph, the latter sent a letter to Al Mokawkas, the last Coptic governor of Egypt, and asked him to throw the letter in the Nile instead.

Containing words of supplication to God to bring about the flood, the letter's benediction was said to have caused the Nile to increase its volume overnight to 16 cubits, a miracle that persuaded Egyptians to renounce the ancient custom, claimed Al Maqrizi.

El Shammaa, however, doubts the authenticity of this story.

"That the Copts had approached Ibn El Aas to ask him to sacrifice a bride isn't in line with Christian belief which bans all such pagan customs. How many Egyptians were found mummified after Christianity spread in Egypt? None, he argued.

Observing the details of the account, El Shammaa notes the contradiction between the fact that the Copts had explained to Ibn El Aas that each year Egyptians sacrifice a slave and the fact that this slave is taken by force from her parents and thrown into the Nile at a specific location in the river.

"Since when do slaves have parents? he asks. "The Nile location referred to is none other than the Island of Phaela, the only Coptic site on the Nile with a church and the closest point to the Nile's First Cataract, which made the island ideal for measuring the water level.

"With a Coptic church on it, the island could not have been a scene for such a sacrifice because Christians shunned all pagan practices. The Caliph Omar Ibn El Khattab responding by asking Al Mokawkas to throw the letter as a gift to Nile also contradicts the behavior of a conservative Muslim ruler.

"Besides it's illogical for the Nile to rise to 16 cubits overnight. The process takes a much longer time.

According to El Shammaa, there isn't a morsel of evidence in ancient Egyptian records to suggest that people sacrificed a virgin.

Pling, the Greek historian, explained that the ancient Egyptians offered crocodiles wrapped in colorful attire to the Nile.

A papyrus known by the name of 'Anastasia' embodied the holy songs that were chanted to the Nile prior to the flooding, says Al Shammaa.

It said: "Blessed flooding, to you we offer sacrifices like buffalo, oxen and birds, to you we offer the gazelles that were hunted at the mountainside, for you we set fires and burn incense.

"There is no mention whatsoever of a virgin or any human sacrifice, which should encourage research on where that myth began, he continued.

The myth, however, has its sources, he explained.

The first is the Greek historian Plutarch who first invented it. Repeated by many Greeks, it told the story of a king known as Egyptos who offered his daughter as a sacrifice to the Nile to avoid the gods' wrath.

After he did that he committed suicide by throwing himself in after her. Since then, Plutarch said, the Egyptians began to sacrifice a virgin every year.

El Shammaa says that there was no Egyptian king called Egyptos, adding that this is a mythical character with no basis in reality.

There is also evidence that the tourists who came to Egypt in the 17th and 18th centuries witnessed celebrations during the flooding of the Nile where a clay bride was offered to the river.

When they inquired about it, they were told that Egyptians had replaced the real virgin with a clay model.

"The myth must have spread this way to attract tourists, says El Shammaa.[477]

The Colossal Failure of the Ex-Muslim Atheist Movement

In 2018, I had wrongly assumed that the non-profit organization, *Ex-Muslims of North America*, and their affiliates like Ex-Muslim Atheist Armin Navabi's social media organization *Atheist Republic* largely knew what they were doing and that their approach of constant insults would be useful in criticizing Islam. This turned out to be an extremely idiotic assumption on my part. Later, I wrote a slew of essays about on my blog which I titled *"The Five Lenses"* to critique why they failed from five perspectives that I had. I was wrong to treat them as experts that knew what they were doing beyond their critiques of Islam. While I sometimes cannot stop myself from calling something out as incredibly stupid in religion when I spot something I find objectionable, it should go without saying that rational critique and rational debate where Free Speech is respected among all parties and all are willing to listen to Free Speech rebuttals; that does far more to convince others than anything else. Mockery without evidence almost never convinces people to change their mind on anything and likely hardens people to oppose your views. For example, when Western Ex-Muslim atheists like Ali A. Rizvi compared Hindu theology to Tooth Faeries, Santa Claus, and the Easter Bunny, then who was this meant to convince? If you apply that argument without any broader context to any religion's internal theology, then it won't convince anyone to change their minds. If they knew such logic wouldn't work to convince Muslims to leave Islam, then why apply it to other religious views? The answer was simply their bigotry towards Hindus.

To give a brief summary without becoming pedantic. There were three major failings of their movement that they didn't realize: the majority of Liberal Americans genuinely don't care whether they live or die because religious tolerance holds more importance to Liberal Americans than the lives of all Ex-Muslims. My anecdotal experience, in the absence of any reliable survey data, has convinced me that this is indeed a fact; the moment I ever brought up *Ex-Muslim of North America* videos to any Liberal I met through Liberal campaign organizations like the Working Families Party on my Facebook, they either accused me of bigotry and hatred towards Muslims and

---

[477] Maged, Ahmed. "The Nile Bride Sacrifice Is a Big Myth, Says Egyptologist." Dailynewsegypt, Egyptian Media Services, 7 Aug. 2015, www.dailynewsegypt.com/2008/10/03/the-nile-bride-sacrifice-is-a-big-myth-says-egyptologist/.

promptly blocked me on social media or just unfriended and blocked me without ever being willing to have any sort of conversation. I was sharing the panel discussions of Ex-Muslim college tours of Ex-Muslims discussing their own life experiences and they found that to be too offensive. It was specifically the Ex-Muslims talking about their own human rights which offended these mostly White Liberals. They genuinely do not care whether Ex-Muslims live or die; they don't want it to be their problem. Perhaps they fear it validates views of White Supremacy, but I really don't know the underlying cause. Even if an Ex-Muslim was shot dead right in front of them, they would almost certainly make excuses that it has absolutely nothing to do with Islam despite Quran 4:89. Only some Black and Hispanic Liberals seem willing to listen and learn about how serious these problems are. On social media more generally, it was mostly Right-wing and Conservative Americans showing they genuinely care about the lives of Ex-Muslims including Ex-Muslim Atheists. Second, Ex-Muslim Atheist groups as a whole, sought only to ridicule and insult every other group and it blew-up in their faces. Sure, Western Ex-Muslim Atheists, you can stand on a Berlin memorial for Holocaust victims[478], you have the Free Expression to do that even though many of us disagree with you, but that doesn't mean you're entitled to other people's time, money, or any attention on social media. Offending sensibilities without a discernible objective simply makes the broader public perceive you to be a nuisance streamer like Johnny Somali or Vitaly Zdorovetskiy and not an intellectual fighting for a legitimate human rights cause like Christopher Hitchens or Chris Hedges. I strongly disagree with Hedges on many human rights issues, but similar to the late Christopher Hitchens pro-human rights arguments, I recognize that he's sincere about his views. How you conduct yourselves does matter. It was actually jarring for me to witness the same people like Armin Navabi conducting some very thorough and in-depth critiques of Islam on college tour panels and then later deciding to become nuisance streamers to mock Hindus with pictures sexualizing Kali. Who was this ever going to convince? When I tried to explain this to them myself, they treated me as a nuisance and assumed I was attempting "gotcha" moments. I realized too late that they were not the people I assumed they were and that I was wrong to ever hold them to such high esteem. I'll never make that mistake again. The intentional bigotry towards Hindus was the clearest sign on people with uncontrollable bad habits and narcissism reacting with self-sabotage; they actually thought Right-wing Muslims and Hindus would "unite together" so that Western Ex-Muslims could present themselves as an aggrieved minority. Instead, both groups realized Western Ex-Muslim Atheists were acting this way for attention and just ignored it; I suggested in a short Youtube video that didn't get many views to simply block them, because I no longer saw any benefit towards real-life human rights causes. I mostly got praises from Muslims for the video; that may seem like a

---

[478] Navabi, Armin. "Armin Navabi: @ArminNavabi: 'With My Fellow Ex-Muslim Freedom Fighters in Berlin.'" X.Com, x.com / Twitter, 14 Sept. 2019, x.com/arminnavabi/status/1172885766965325824?lang=en.

contradiction, but there was no need for any organized campaign against Ex-Muslims, all any group has to do is ignore them and they lose all power because social media campaigns aren't the same as grassroots organized efforts to support human rights causes. For example, the Hindu nonprofit known as SEWA International and Christian NGOs are doing more to help others with food and medical drives than angry videos highlighting human rights crimes from social media groups like the Atheist Republic. What happened to most of those Ex-Muslims in Muslim-majority countries seeking to bring attention to their human rights being violated? They were also ignored. There is a genuine difference in how people treat others based upon whether you're insulting them or critiquing their beliefs with an argument premised on why it is a disadvantage for them to believe in faith-based ideas. Of course, to do the latter, that required actually learning about Hinduism in the first place like they did Islam and Christianity. They were never willing to do that, so they stuck to the long-held Islamic tradition of bigotry against Hindus.

The third failing is something Hindus in India were better able to spot than Hindus living elsewhere. Ex-Muslim Atheists wanted to find and ridicule people they considered beneath them; it is no secret that most Muslims in the world, and most Ex-Muslims as a result, grow-up believing that Hindus are a sub-human species unworthy of human rights or equal respect because of Islamic perceptions of polytheism. Even if we were polytheists, that wouldn't justify bigotry but Muslims and Ex-Muslims always try to find excuses for the bigotry ingrained from viewing Hindus as polytheist, from the teachings of their barbaric faith tradition of Islam. They can't mock Jews without being labeled anti-Semites by people who don't distinguish between Jewish people and Jewish teachings, mocking Christians must feel like mocking people of a higher social status to them because White Christianity is seen as synonymous with scientific modernity to some Ex-Muslims and Muslims, and so their need to vilify people they consider lesser is towards Hindus exclusively because they need to justify their Islamic or prior Islamic beliefs. Most Ex-Muslims recognize that Islam is the most dangerous, but they fail to recognize it is also the most stupid due to its emphasis on consistency. Ex-Muslims don't want to feel any more stupid than they do for having been a Muslim, so they try to find something they believe is dumber without actually researching the theology of Hinduism. The fact any Ex-Muslim reading this is unlikely to be convinced that reading up on the theology would help make better arguments says it all. They believe themselves to be too "above" genuinely taking the time to read and learn a theology they've surely vilified the most throughout their entire lives.

For any fellow Hindus or outside observers unconvinced that there is a longstanding bigotry and hatred of Hindus by most Muslims and Western Ex-Muslim Atheists, consider this: when Western Ex-Muslim Atheists and Muslims talk about the Armenian genocide, it is from the perspective of shame and there are always discussions on how to convince Turkey to recognize it. When Western Ex-Muslim Atheists mention they know and fully accept that Muslims historically slaughtered approximately between 60 – 80 million people in India's five-hundred years of history? They laugh and tell Hindus to shut up and get over it. When Hindus bring up how many Hindus, Buddhists, Sikhs, Christians, Parsis, and so on are being kidnapped and raped or killed in Bangladesh and Pakistan even now? Western Ex-Muslim Atheists argue that India needs to accept more Muslim refugees and Hindus should ignore those facts they see every single year as if Hindus should treat the two events as separate. For White Europeans, it is reasonable to have concerns. For Dharmic followers of India who historically suffered five-hundred years of brutal oppression and mass genocide and then more brutal oppression and genocide between Akbar the Great's peaceful rule; despite this historical Islamic brutality totaling to about 700 – 800 years, it is not considered reasonable to most Ex-Muslims for Hindus to have concerns. They notoriously ignore that India's policies are no different than Israel and the US towards any potential influx of Muslim migrants. Hindu lives being put in danger doesn't matter to most Ex-Muslim Atheists.

Muslims and Ex-Muslim Atheists Psychological Projection unto Hindus

Fellow Hindus may find this next part interesting and even enlightening; it is one of the core reasons I decided to write this book, because I've seen this phenomenon happen repeatedly and I believe it is long overdue to call it out. If you're a born and raised Muslim or an Ex-Muslim born and raised from a Muslim family reading this, then you might find this next part painful to read. Typically, most people from a Muslim background have never criticized Hinduism. I do not mean that you cannot criticize Hinduism and I do not mean the logical fallacy of shifting goalposts to change the criteria of what Hinduism is. Read these next words carefully: *Muslims have only ever been trying to turn Hinduism into Islam, to criticize Islam by giving it a Hindu lexicon.* The criticism that Muslims have with these supposedly critical "anti-Hinduism" arguments outside of Casteism are really just a mockery and disparagement of Islam. That is, every single criticism that I've read from Muslims and Ex-Muslim Atheists about Hinduism are actually criticisms of Islam; I don't know what sort of psychological self-deception is going on with Muslims who do this, but it is definitely there. This is a real phenomenon that exists among Muslims. To give you a comparison of how we Hindus view your criticisms: in Islam, *taqiyya* is a theological concept that most Muslims only hear about from anti-Muslim bigots according to *Ex-Muslims of North America*'s co-founder, Muhammad Syed. Judging from what I researched, he is correct and most Muslims have never even heard of this concept and it has nothing to do with how Muslims live and practice their faith. Sure, it happened some centuries ago, but only on specific historic instances of intra-Muslim violence between Sunni-Shia for Shia Muslims to protect themselves, it was never practiced towards non-Muslims, and it is not practiced today among Muslims. This should be a fairly reasonable assumption to make. Here's what most Muslims don't understand: Muslims who criticize Hinduism have been doing the social equivalent of a bigot shouting "*taqiyya*" at Hindus in how we practice Hinduism. They've been doing this social equivalent of shouting "*taqiyya*" at Hindus for decades or longer, while ignoring that what they're shouting at us is more readily observant in Islam's theology. You hate Islam so much that you are trying to turn Hinduism into Islam, to find a substitute to vent your hatred for Islam and in doing so, you openly dehumanize us. You are psychologically projecting onto Hinduism and psychologically scapegoating Hindus. Our way of life needs to be "lesser" in your minds in order for you to justify your way of life and Muslim identity or former identity. It won't change the fact that your Islamic religious teachings having completely failed you and everyone else in your *ummah* (One Muslim community / Muslim nation). We Hindus have always been vilified by you, so when you see us start doing better, then you want us either dead or chronically humiliated so that you get an ego boost to justify your failed religious lifestyle of believing in an unchanging 7th century standard of Arab fundamentalism.

Do you believe that I am exaggerating or lying? Let's consider some examples. Islamists who criticize Hinduism in order to convert Hindus to Islam argue that there is a bovine deity, usually given alternative names of Kamadhenu or Surabhi, but this depiction is usually a metaphor for the sacredness of cows in Hindu theology. However, let me grant to any Muslim reading this that a few denominations that worship may surely exist and a few Hindus do worship Kamadhenu / Surabhi as an actual deity despite the fact that the vast majority of Hindus haven't heard of it or only view it as a metaphor. Why do Islamists insist on objecting to this though? Because of *Sahih Bukhari Volume 5, Book 58, Hadith Number 227* which has a story about the Prophet Mohammad flying on a white horse, which gave rise to the Islamic artistic depictions of a supernatural flying horse called Buraq:

Sahih Bukhari Volume 5, Book 58, Hadith Number 227.

Sahih Bukhari Book 58. Merits of the Helpers in Madina (Ansaar)

Narated By Abbas bin Malik : Malik bin Sasaa said that Allah's Apostle described to them his Night Journey saying, "While I was lying in Al-Hatim or Al-Hijr, suddenly someone came to me and cut my body open from here to here." I asked Al-Jarud who was by my side, "What does he mean?" He said, "It means from his throat to his pubic area," or said, "From the top of the chest." The Prophet further said, "He then took out my heart. Then a gold tray of Belief was brought to me and my heart was washed and was filled (with Belief) and then returned to its original place. Then a white animal which was smaller than a mule and bigger than a donkey was brought to me." (On this Al-Jarud asked, "Was it the Buraq, O Abu Hamza?" I (i.e. Anas) replied in the affirmative). The Prophet said, "The animal's step (was so wide that it) reached the farthest point within the reach of the animal's sight. I was carried on it, and Gabriel set out with me till we reached the nearest heaven.

When he asked for the gate to be opened, it was asked, 'Who is it?' Gabriel answered, 'Gabriel.' It was asked, 'Who is accompanying you?' Gabriel replied, 'Muhammad.' It was asked, 'Has Muhammad been called?' Gabriel replied in the affirmative. Then it was said, 'He is welcomed. What an excellent visit his is!' The gate was opened, and when I went over the first heaven, I saw Adam there. Gabriel said (to me). 'This is your father, Adam; pay him your greetings.' So I greeted him and he returned the greeting to me and said, 'You are welcomed, O pious son and pious Prophet.' Then Gabriel ascended with me till we reached the second heaven. Gabriel asked for the gate to be opened. It was asked, 'Who is it?' Gabriel answered, 'Gabriel.' It was asked, 'Who is accompanying you?' Gabriel replied, 'Muhammad.' It was asked, 'Has he been called?' Gabriel answered in the affirmative. Then it was said, 'He is welcomed. What an excellent visit his is!' The gate was opened.

When I went over the second heaven, there I saw Yahya (i.e. John) and 'Isa (i.e. Jesus) who were cousins of each other. Gabriel said (to me), 'These are John and Jesus; pay them your greetings.' So I greeted them and both of them returned my greetings to me and said, 'You are welcomed, O pious brother and pious Prophet.' Then Gabriel ascended with me to the third heaven and asked for its gate to be opened. It was asked, 'Who is it?' Gabriel replied, 'Gabriel.' It was asked, 'Who is accompanying you?' Gabriel replied, 'Muhammad.' It was asked, 'Has he been called?' Gabriel replied in the affirmative. Then it was said, 'He is welcomed, what an excellent visit his is!' The gate was opened, and when I went over the third heaven there I saw Joseph. Gabriel said (to me), 'This is Joseph; pay him your greetings.' So I greeted him and he returned the greeting to me and said, 'You are welcomed, O pious brother and pious Prophet.' Then Gabriel ascended with me to the fourth heaven and asked for its gate to be opened. It was asked, 'Who is it?' Gabriel replied, 'Gabriel' It was asked, 'Who is accompanying you?' Gabriel replied, 'Muhammad.' It was asked, 'Has he been called?' Gabriel replied in the affirmative. Then it was said, 'He is welcomed, what an excel lent visit his is!'

The gate was opened, and when I went over the fourth heaven, there I saw Idris. Gabriel said (to me), 'This is Idris; pay him your greetings.' So I greeted him and he returned the greeting to me and said, 'You are welcomed, O pious brother and pious Prophet.' Then Gabriel ascended with me to the fifth heaven and asked for its gate to be opened. It was asked, 'Who is it?' Gabriel replied, 'Gabriel.' It was asked. 'Who is accompanying you?' Gabriel replied, 'Muhammad.' It was asked, 'Has he been called?' Gabriel replied in the affirmative. Then it was said He is welcomed, what an excellent visit his is! So when I went over the fifth heaven, there I saw Harun (i.e. Aaron), Gabriel said, (to me). This is Aaron; pay him your greetings.' I greeted him and he returned the greeting to me and said, 'You are welcomed, O pious brother and pious Prophet.' Then Gabriel ascended with me to the sixth heaven and asked for its gate to be opened. It was asked. 'Who is it?' Gabriel replied, 'Gabriel.' It was asked, 'Who is accompanying you?' Gabriel replied, 'Muhammad.' It was asked, 'Has he been called?' Gabriel replied in the affirmative. It was said, 'He is welcomed. What an excellent visit his is!'

When I went (over the sixth heaven), there I saw Moses. Gabriel said (to me),' This is Moses; pay him your greeting. So I greeted him and he returned the greetings to me and said, 'You are welcomed, O pious brother and pious Prophet.' When I left him (i.e. Moses) he wept. Someone asked him, 'What makes you weep?' Moses said, 'I weep because after me there has been sent (as Prophet) a young man whose followers will enter Paradise in greater numbers than my followers.' Then Gabriel ascended with me to the seventh heaven and asked for its gate to be opened. It was asked, 'Who is it?' Gabriel replied, 'Gabriel.' It was asked,' Who is accompanying you?' Gabriel replied, 'Muhammad.' It was asked, 'Has he been called?' Gabriel replied in the affirmative. Then it was said, 'He is welcomed. What an excellent visit his is!'

So when I went (over the seventh heaven), there I saw Abraham. Gabriel said (to me), 'This is your father; pay your greetings to him.' So I greeted him and he returned the greetings to me and said, 'You are welcomed, O pious son and pious Prophet.' Then I was made to ascend to Sidrat-ul-Muntaha (i.e. the Lote Tree of the utmost boundary) Behold! Its fruits were like the jars of Hajr (i.e. a place near Medina) and its leaves were as big as the ears of elephants. Gabriel said, 'This is the Lote Tree of the utmost boundary). Behold ! There ran four rivers, two were hidden and two were visible, I asked, 'What are these two kinds of rivers, O Gabriel?' He replied,' As for the hidden rivers, they are two rivers in Paradise and the visible rivers are the Nile and the Euphrates.'

Then Al-Bait-ul-Ma'mur (i.e. the Sacred House) was shown to me and a container full of wine and another full of milk and a third full of honey were brought to me. I took the milk. Gabriel remarked, 'This is the Islamic religion which you and your followers are following.' Then the prayers were enjoined on me: They were fifty prayers a day. When I returned, I passed by Moses who asked (me), 'What have you been ordered to do?' I replied, 'I have been ordered to offer fifty prayers a day.' Moses said, 'Your followers cannot bear fifty prayers a day, and by Allah, I have tested people before you, and I have tried my level best with Bani Israel (in vain). Go back to your Lord and ask for reduction to lessen your followers' burden.' So I went back, and Allah reduced ten prayers for me. Then again I came to Moses, but he repeated the same as he had said before. Then again I went back to Allah and He reduced ten more prayers. When I came back to Moses he said the same, I went back to Allah and He ordered me to observe ten prayers a day. When I came back to Moses, he repeated the same advice, so I went back to Allah and was ordered to observe five prayers a day.

When I came back to Moses, he said, 'What have you been ordered?' I replied, 'I have been ordered to observe five prayers a day.' He said, 'Your followers cannot bear five prayers a day, and no doubt, I have got an experience of the people before you, and I have tried my level best with Bani Israel, so go back to your Lord and ask for reduction to lessen your follower's burden.' I said, 'I have requested so much of my Lord that I feel ashamed, but I am satisfied now and surrender to Allah's Order.' When I left, I heard a voice saying, 'I have passed My Order and have lessened the burden of My Worshipers."[479]

In other words, Islamists want to convince themselves that the majority of Hindus believe in a nourishing, human-headed cow Goddess in order to simultaneously ridicule and feel less stupid about believing in Buraq, the flying white horse of the Prophet Mohammad. The image of a human-headed cow deity is the closest sense-object they could find in Hindu art for them to mock Buraq in Islam. This mockery likely extends to some Hindus drinking cow urine in India, because Muslims in the Middle East drink camel urine due to the false belief taught by the Prophet Mohammad himself that it cures ailments[480]; Muslims usually suffer MERS (Middle East Syndrome Coronavirus) which leads to breathing problems, fevers, kidney failure, pneumonia, and other complications as a result.[481] Regardless of what any of us believe on the practice of drinking cow urine by a scant few Hindus, most Muslims are insulting the practice to use Hinduism as a scapegoat to vilify Islam and not out of genuine concern for Hindus.

Why the accusations of Lady Sita being 6-years old when marrying Lord Rama in the *Skanda Purana*, while ignoring that Lady Sita's own words in the much older

---

[479] al-Bukhārī, Abū ʿAbd Allāh Muḥammad ibn Ismāʿīl ibn Ibrāhīm al-Juʿfī. "Sahih Bukhari Volume 5, Book 58, Hadith Number 227." Translated by Muhammad Muhsin Khan, Hadith Collection, Hadith Collection, 23 May 2009, hadithcollection.com/sahihbukhari/sahih-bukhari-book-58-merits-of-the-helpers-in-madina-ansaar/sahih-bukhari-volume-005-book-058-hadith-number-227.

[480] "The Benefits of Drinking Camel Urine - Islam Question & Answer." Islamqa.info, Islam Question and Answer, 27 Mar. 2006, https://web.archive.org/web/20190209043245/https://islamqa.info/en/answers/83423/the-benefits-of-drinking-camel-urine.

[481] Boyer, Lauren. "Stop Drinking Camel Urine, World Health Organization Says." U.S. News & World Report, U.S. News & World Report, www.usnews.com/news/articles/2015/06/10/stop-drinking-camel-urine-world-health-organization-says.

Ramayana poems state that she was eighteen-years-old?[482][483][484] Islamists are trying to turn Rama and Sita into substitutes for the Prophet Mohammad and his 6-year-old child bride, Aisha, whom the Prophet Mohammad later raped when she was nine. Yet again, as a way of vilifying Islam through Hinduism. Vilifying Lord Krishna for having multiple wives? Another way of using Hinduism as a substitute so that Islamists can vilify the Prophet Mohammad for having multiple wives and sex slaves. Attempting to portray the Skanda Purana texts as pro-rape with the story of Lord Shiva and Lady Mohini? Islamists are trying to substitute the numerous stories of the Prophet Mohammad's horrific real-life history of violence, such as the story of what the Prophet Mohammad did to the Jewish village of Safiya bint Huyai. They don't want to see, hear, listen, or learn anything about Hinduism. They want to see, hear, listen, and create a "dark" version of Islam as an outlet for their genuine emotional hatred for Islam; by pretending it exists in another religion that they deem inferior to theirs. Both Islamists and the majority of "regular" Muslims outside the US do not ever wish to see or value the humanity of Hindus or to perceive Hinduism as having any coherent or useful values. They're too psychologically fixated on needing to see other groups outside of the *ummah* (One Muslim Nation / Muslim Community) as inferior, specifically to justify their faith in the Quran. This Otherness of Hindus is normalized by many White Liberals and the Corporate media circus in the US. The murder of Hindus by Islamists is treated as banal and barely makes headlines in overseas news stories, meanwhile cow vigilantism was making headlines until a tweet by the Qatari-funded Al Jazeera tweeted an article in 2019 titled "*How Cow Vigilantism Is Undermining the Rule of Law in India*" by Manash Firaq Bhattacharjee. His article argued that cow vigilantism was essentially an "epidemic" in India because of the whopping 120 cases.[485] No, not *percent* which wouldn't even make sense to say, what they meant was 120 cases in India between 2012 – 2018… total.[486] This is in a country with a population of 1.4 billion and which had a population of over 1.2 billion when Al

---

[482] Vyasa. "Chapter 30 - Rāma's Life." Translated by Ganesh Vasudeo Tagare, Skanda Purana: Book 3 - Brāhma-Khaṇḍa: Section 2 - Dharmāraṇya-Khaṇḍa: Chapter 30 - Rāma's Life: Verses 8-9, www.wisdomlib.org, 15 Aug. 2020, www.wisdomlib.org/hinduism/book/the-skanda-purana/d/doc423651.html#:~:text=8%2D9.,with%20S%C4%ABt%C4%81%20for%20twelve%20years.

[483] Valmiki. "Book III: Aranya Kanda - The Forest Trek." Translated by Desiraju Hanumanta Rao et al., Srimad Valmiki Ramayana: Book 3 Aranya Kanda: Sarga / Chapter 47: Verses: 10b - 11., Desiraju Hanumanta Rao & K. M. K. Murthy, Nov. 2004, https://valmikiramayan.net/utf8/aranya/sarga47/aranyaitrans47.htm

[484] Valmiki. "Book III: Aranya Kanda - The Forest Trek." Translated by Desiraju Hanumanta Rao et al., Srimad Valmiki Ramayana: Book 3 Aranya Kanda: Sarga / Chapter 47: Verses: 10b - 11., Desiraju Hanumanta Rao & K. M. K. Murthy, Nov. 2004, sanskritdocuments.org/sites/valmikiramayan/aranya/sarga47/aranya_47_frame.htm.

[485] Bhattacharjee, Manash Firaq. "How Cow Vigilantism Is Undermining the Rule of Law in India." Al Jazeera, Al Jazeera, 3 Jan. 2019, www.aljazeera.com/opinions/2019/1/3/how-cow-vigilantism-is-undermining-the-rule-of-law-in-india.

[486] Bhattacharjee, Manash Firaq. "How Cow Vigilantism Is Undermining the Rule of Law in India." Al Jazeera, Al Jazeera, 3 Jan. 2019, www.aljazeera.com/opinions/2019/1/3/how-cow-vigilantism-is-undermining-the-rule-of-law-in-india.

Jazeera made that article. This is how stupid and desperate Islamists are to portray Muslims as perennially aggrieved minorities everywhere to further their Islamist agenda to reduce all other civilizations to 7th century social, political, and technological standards. They psychologically need for Hindus to be worse off to justify their faith in the Quran itself, because if Hindus are better off than all religious groups are thus doing better than those who follow Islam and they would be forced to question Islam with more scrutiny.

What about Honor Killings among Hindus and Muslims? Hindus are the only ones being criticized, the criticisms started internally within India to highlight a pertinent human rights issue for Indian women that needed more attention, appropriate and necessarily harsh criticism is given to Hindu families who commit such a disgusting act upon their own Hindu daughters, the government of India's Ministry of Home Affairs has developed a statistical list to better assess the problem[487], and everyone is turning a blind eye when Muslims do it to their own family members.[488] I strongly support the criticism of Hindus and Sikhs for this barbaric practice precisely because I believe in Hindu and Sikh women's human rights, and do you know what else? I know that my fellow Hindus will gradually improve, they have already made strides to improve, I hope the same will be true for our Sikh brothers and sisters, and I believe they will reduce this vile practice due to increased criticism that values the lives of Hindu and Sikh women. I want to see the discriminatory human rights abuses over inter-caste marriages to vanish[489]; I disagree with heterosexual gotra removal, because that would constitute incest since my understanding from what my Hindu family members have told me is that the gotra system was made in ancient times specifically to avoid incest. It's mainly used as a family tree to make sure that people aren't committing incest with any cousin or extended cousin marriages in northern India. It seems to have worked efficiently in the large populations of India that used it and it does seem effective in avoiding incest among northern Hindus. I don't think that most people who criticize the gotra system appropriately recognize that, they don't think about the negative effect ending the gotra system would have on such a large population like India with incest rising beyond just the Muslim Indian communities, and they often confuse it with a form of Caste when that isn't true. I honestly think the more that people criticize Hindus with honest critiques, the more it pushes us to improve ourselves even when Hindus find the critiques are often one-sided. What I find that most fellow Hindus dislike is that they feel unfairly maligned, because the same expectations

---

[487] "MURDER RATE ACROSS THE STATES." Www.Mha.Gov.In, Government of India / MINISTRY OF HOME AFFAIRS , www.mha.gov.in/MHA1/Par2017/pdfs/par2023-pdfs/RS05042023/3734.pdf. Accessed 15 Aug. 2025.

[488] Bloom, Nathan, and Phyllis Chesler. "Hindu vs. Muslim Honor Killings." Middle East Forum, Middle East Quarterly, 18 July 2012, www.meforum.org/middle-east-quarterly/hindu-muslim-honor-killings.

[489] Namrata, Namrata. "In between Honor, Rebellion and Patriarchy: Honor Killings in India." New College of Interdisciplinary Arts and Sciences, Global Human Rights Hub fellows blog, 9 Feb. 2024, newcollege.asu.edu/global-human-rights-hub/fellows-program/ghr-fellows-blog/namrata.

are never given to Muslims. If everyone is being honest with themselves, we all know never to expect the same from Muslims due to their fixation on their 7th century Arab fundamentalist beliefs. Muslim majority countries have worse problems than India with Honor Killings and stalwartly refuse to do anything[490]; nobody is criticizing Pakistan for having a worse rate of Honor Killings, because nobody believes in Pakistan.[491] When an entire country of Muslims refuses to do anything about it, how can we call this the "bigotry of low expectations" when their country is literally refusing to change and they shut down all criticisms of the problem?[492] What use is criticizing Islamic nation-states when they threaten to jail or kill the critics? What is then bigoted about these low expectations, when they reflect reality more accurately? Muslim-majority countries want others to shut up about honor killings, while we Hindus criticize misogyny in our own religion far more openly and have a history of doing so since the 1800s when Hindu reformers campaigned to remove the funeral burning of Hindu women. The problem Hindus, especially those who support Hindutva, have is that it is only Hindus who are ever criticized for these practices by most Liberal, Western, and many Christian organizations and never Muslims. Muslims must be perpetually infantilized due to fears that criticizing them will lead them to murder the critics.

A counterargument for any Ex-Muslim or anyone supporting the human rights of Muslims and who believe that there is a bigotry of low expectations when non-Muslims stop believing that most Muslims are capable of change: why should anyone have to risk being murdered when a Muslim's comfort level is harmed when they hear a non-Muslim's criticisms about either Islam or more specifically, the Prophet Mohammad? Why should any non-Muslim people risk being shot or stabbed when giving Free Speech criticisms of Islam? Why bother caring about Muslim human rights, when they make it no secret that the vast majority of Muslims genuinely don't care about any non-Muslim's human rights whenever they kill people for being offended by Free Speech criticisms? Why should I care about US Liberal activists yammering about Muslims having rights violated in Sudan, the Israeli territories of Gaza and the West Bank, and other countries; when Syrian Christian human rights, Christian human rights throughout Africa, the multitude of non-Muslim religious minority human rights in Pakistan and Bangladesh, and I'm sure many other places are deliberately ignored? The majority of Muslims have never concerned themselves with the human rights of religious minorities in their own countries nor of Muslim minority human rights, so why exactly should we care about theirs when they make no secret they wouldn't hesitate to kill us or rape non-Muslim children if given the opportunity, even when they're living in free and peaceful societies?

---

[490] Bloom, Nathan, and Phyllis Chesler. "Hindu vs. Muslim Honor Killings." Middle East Forum, Middle East Quarterly, 18 July 2012, www.meforum.org/middle-east-quarterly/hindu-muslim-honor-killings.
[491] Bloom, Nathan, and Phyllis Chesler. "Hindu vs. Muslim Honor Killings." Middle East Forum, Middle East Quarterly, 18 July 2012, www.meforum.org/middle-east-quarterly/hindu-muslim-honor-killings.
[492] Bloom, Nathan, and Phyllis Chesler. "Hindu vs. Muslim Honor Killings." Middle East Forum, Middle East Quarterly, 18 July 2012, www.meforum.org/middle-east-quarterly/hindu-muslim-honor-killings.

What are we doing and why always this selective focus treating Muslim lives as more important than all non-Muslim lives? If protection of human rights isn't going to be reciprocal between the majority of Muslims towards non-Muslims, then what is the point?

The only convincing argument I've been given is that people meaning to harm legitimately vulnerable minorities, such as Native Americans in the US, could then more easily commit violence upon them without human rights protections. Yet, I can't help but think about how this ignores a salient fact about the difference in behavior. For those in the US, the difference is that Native Americans serve in the US Armed Forces at five times the per capita rate of their population size in the US[493][494], they're more likely to serve in Active-Duty roles in the US Army[495][496], they have protested peacefully for over forty years while begging for their children's lives to be protected from the ongoing state-sponsored US genocide from the 1978 US Supreme Court decision of Oliphant vs Suquamish[497][498][499][500][501][502], and – unlike Islam – Native American theology are the origins

---

[493] Trump, Donald J. "Presidential Proclamation on National Native American Heritage Month, 2018." The White House, Whitehouse.gov, 31 Oct. 2018, https://web.archive.org/web/20201226230730/https://www.whitehouse.gov/presidential-actions/presidential-proclamation-national-native-american-heritage-month-2018/.

[494] Lacdan, Joseph. "Army Leader Cherishes Heritage, Honors Native American Contributions." www.Army.Mil, U.S. Army, 19 Nov. 2021, https://web.archive.org/web/20250212083345/https://www.army.mil/article/252163/army_leader_cherishes_heritage_honors_native_american_contributions.

[495] Department of Defense (DOD), et al. "2022 Demographics Profile of the Military Community." Https://S3.Documentcloud.Org/Documents/24177791/2022-Demographics-Report.Pdf, U.S. Naval Institute Staff / U.S. Naval Institute News, 29 Nov. 2023, s3.documentcloud.org/documents/24177791/2022-demographics-report.pdf.

[496] Department of Defense (DOD), et al. "2023 Demographics Profile of the Military Community." Https://Download.Militaryonesource.Mil/12038/MOS/Reports/2023-Demographics-Report.Pdf, Military OneSource, 2023, download.militaryonesource.mil/12038/MOS/Reports/2023-demographics-report.pdf.

[497] MAZE OF INJUSTICE The Failure to Protect Indigenous Women from Sexual Violence in the USA, Amnesty International, https://web.archive.org/web/20111018194106/http://www.amnestyusa.org/pdfs/MazeOfInjustice.pdf.

[498] Cooper, Renee. "Behind the Grim Statistics for Sexual Violence on Reservations." KX NEWS, KX NEWS, 22 Dec. 2020, www.kxnet.com/news/local-news/being-raped-is-a-right-of-passage-behind-the-grim-statistics-for-native-american-women/.

[499] "The Never-Ending Maze: Continued Failure to Protect Indigenous Women from Sexual Violence in the USA." Amnesty International USA, Amnesty International USA, 19 July 2023, http://www.amnestyusa.org/wp-content/uploads/2022/05/AmnestyMazeReportv_digital.pdf.

[500] Williams, Robert A. "THE ALGEBRA OF FEDERAL INDIAN LAW: THE HARD TRAIL OF DECOLONIZING AND AMERICANIZING THE WHITE MAN'S INDIAN JURISPRUDENCE." UW Law Digital Repository Media · University of Wisconsin Law School Digital Repository · University of Wisconsin Law School Digital Repository, University of Wisconsin Law Review, repository.law.wisc.edu/s/uwlaw/media/35536.

[501] "Native American Women Are Rape Targets Because of a Legislative Loophole." VICE, VICE News, 16 Dec. 2015, https://www.vice.com/en/article/bnpb73/native-american-women-are-rape-targets-because-of-a-legislative-loophole-511.

[502] "687. Tribal Court Jurisdiction." The United States Department of Justice, 22 Jan. 2020, https://www.justice.gov/archives/jm/criminal-resource-manual-687-tribal-court-jurisdiction#:~:text=The%20Supreme%20Court%20held%20in,the%20tribe%20in%20Duro%20v.

of most modern women's rights across the entire world that the majority of US and Western women benefitted from and it came exclusively from Native American religious traditions.[503] The idea of Judeo-Christian values falls apart not just because of Enlightenment values and the horrific persecution of the Jews for two-thousand years by Christians, but also because of Native American theology's major contributions to modern women's rights throughout all of earth and especially the US and Western countries.[504] While those Democratic Socialists of the US try to portray their support for Gaza as a simplistic question of good versus evil[505], they ignore the US state-sponsored genocide that happens right in their own backyard due to the Supreme Court decision of Oliphant vs Suquamish 1978 that is still in legal effect even now.[506][507][508] Apparently, the majority Islamic Palestinian people who mostly want to kill us, who celebrated the terrorist atrocity of September 11th 2001 shortly after it happened[509][510][511], and who support the idea of raping 9-year-olds per support for following the Sharia (Divine Law of the Abrahamic God) are more important to a significant portion of Liberal Americans than the Native American people who serve and protect us[512][513], while we ignore their peaceful protests and US registered sex offenders go into their homes to rape and kill

---

[503] Wagner, Sally Roesch. Sisters in Spirit: Iroquois Influence on Early Feminists: Haudenosaunee (Iroquois) Influence on Early American Feminists. Book Publishing Company. Kindle Edition.

[504] Wagner, Sally Roesch. Sisters in Spirit: Iroquois Influence on Early Feminists: Haudenosaunee (Iroquois) Influence on Early American Feminists. Book Publishing Company. Kindle Edition.

[505] Zickgraf, Ryan. "Democratic Socialism's Moral Theater." UnHerd, 13 Aug. 2025, unherd.com/2025/08/democratic-socialisms-slide-into-irrelevance/.

[506] MAZE OF INJUSTICE The Failure to Protect Indigenous Women from Sexual Violence in the USA, Amnesty International, https://web.archive.org/web/20111018194106/http://www.amnestyusa.org/pdfs/MazeOfInjustice.pdf.

[507] "The Never-Ending Maze: Continued Failure to Protect Indigenous Women from Sexual Violence in the USA." Amnesty International USA, Amnesty International USA, 19 July 2023, http://www.amnestyusa.org/wp-content/uploads/2022/05/AmnestyMazeReportv_digital.pdf.

[508] Williams, Robert A. "THE ALGEBRA OF FEDERAL INDIAN LAW: THE HARD TRAIL OF DECOLONIZING AND AMERICANIZING THE WHITE MAN'S INDIAN JURISPRUDENCE." UW Law Digital Repository Media · University of Wisconsin Law School Digital Repository · University of Wisconsin Law School Digital Repository, University of Wisconsin Law Review, repository.law.wisc.edu/s/uwlaw/media/35536.

[509] 9/11 News Coverage: 10:45 AM: Palestinians Celebrate, NBC News / AuthenticHistory, 30 Jan. 2011, www.youtube.com/watch?v=cqZBy09vCVk&ab_channel=AuthenticHistory.

[510] "Palestinians Celebrate 9/11 Attacks on US." Youtube, Fox News / mnaba11, 9 Jan. 2009, www.youtube.com/watch?v=P9yK0u-XH1M. For Reference: Within the video description box: "Palestinians dance and celebrate in the streets on 9/11"

[511] "Palestinians Celebrate at Damascus Gate." Palestinians Celebrate at Damascus Gate - AP Archive, AP Archive / AP News, 30 July 2015, www.youtube.com/watch?v=UucjbGmJILk&ab_channel=APArchive.

[512] Trump, Donald J. "Presidential Proclamation on National Native American Heritage Month, 2018." The White House, Whitehouse.gov, 31 Oct. 2018, https://web.archive.org/web/20201226230730/https://www.whitehouse.gov/presidential-actions/presidential-proclamation-national-native-american-heritage-month-2018/.

[513] Lacdan, Joseph. "Army Leader Cherishes Heritage, Honors Native American Contributions." www.Army.Mil, U.S. Army, 19 Nov. 2021, https://web.archive.org/web/20250212083345/https://www.army.mil/article/252163/army_leader_cherishes_heritage_honors_native_american_contributions.

their children across the US.[514] This is the world we collectively choose to live in. To be completely fair, pro-Palestinian protesters in the US were peacefully protesting for about a year during the Biden Administration and the response by the Biden administration, after Kamala Harris lost the election to President Donald Trump due to not having a committed position on Palestine, was to send an $8 billion weapons sale to Israel before leaving office.[515] For those who draw generalizations between the two disparate civilizations of Islam and Native American nations, I obviously can't speak for Native Americans and I'm sure the views are diverse like every other group on the issue of Israel-Palestine. As an anecdotal counterpoint, the first time I heard of criticism of Islam was from the band Corporate Avenger, a music band featuring Cherokee singer, Patrick R. "Adawee" Dubar and their 2005 album titled "*Born Again*" featured songs critical of Islamic theology like "*Gay Muslims for Christ*" and "*Jihad Schmihad*" and this was about a year prior to Sam Harris's criticisms of Islam written in the LA Times.[516][517] The journalists, academics, and social media commentators arguing that criticism of Islam was racist seemed to conveniently ignore that one of the most popular bands among Native Americans in the early 2000s had criticized Islam even earlier than Sam Harris.[518][519]

US Policymakers missed America's Unipolar moment, because they don't understand the world around them. It has become all too clear that older generation Americans had no understanding of a multipolar world or how to properly strategize in such a world. The only thing in their heads was fixations on a neo-Cold War with Russia, while Vladimir Putin is continuously obsessed with some nebulous "victory" in Ukraine. Yet, US policymakers treated a regional strategic issue as an existential threat of the Soviet Union 2.0 emerging. They repeatedly proved that they never understood the threat of Islamic terrorism despite September 11th, 2001 happening and unarmed American civilians giving their lives to protect the Bush administration and the US Congress to stop the hijackers of United Airlines Flight 93 from reaching the White House and the Capitol

---

[514] Cooper, Renee. "Behind the Grim Statistics for Sexual Violence on Reservations." KX NEWS, KX NEWS, 22 Dec. 2020, www.kxnet.com/news/local-news/being-raped-is-a-right-of-passage-behind-the-grim-statistics-for-native-american-women/.
[515] Lee, Matthew. "Biden Administration Notifies Congress of Planned $8 Billion Weapons Sale to Israel." PBS, Public Broadcasting Service, 4 Jan. 2025, www.pbs.org/newshour/world/biden-administration-notifies-congress-of-planned-8-billion-weapons-sale-to-israel#:~:text=Biden%20administration%20notifies%20Congress%20of,Live%20TV.
[516] Boehm, Mike. "Gloomed for Success: O.C.'s Mindfunk Has Had Its Share of Hard Knocks--Thank Goodness." Los Angeles Times, Los Angeles Times, 3 Nov. 1993, www.latimes.com/archives/la-xpm-1993-11-03-ca-52788-story.html.
[517] "Corporate Avenger - Born Again." Www.Discogs.Com, Discogs, www.discogs.com/release/1353275-Corporate-Avenger-Born-Again. Accessed 17 Aug. 2025.
[518] "Corporate Avenger - Born Again." Www.Discogs.Com, Discogs, www.discogs.com/release/1353275-Corporate-Avenger-Born-Again. Accessed 17 Aug. 2025.
[519] Boehm, Mike. "Gloomed for Success: O.C.'s Mindfunk Has Had Its Share of Hard Knocks--Thank Goodness." Los Angeles Times, Los Angeles Times, 3 Nov. 1993, www.latimes.com/archives/la-xpm-1993-11-03-ca-52788-story.html.

building. Even this act of self-sacrifice by unarmed Americans to protect the lives of US elected officials and lobbyists has simply become a half-forgotten footnote of history.

Chapter IX: A Repurposed Edition of The Follies of Islam

This was originally a chapter in my previous book, *Faith in Doubt*. I've added more context to a few subsections and the last subsection is a new addition. I hadn't put that one in originally, because I did not fully appreciate how literalist of an interpretation that Islam is taken by the majority of Muslims in the world.

Please seriously take the time to consider the following when reading the rest of this chapter: this is what Islamists mass murder people for throughout the entire world. This is why women including young girls in Afghanistan, Pakistan, Britain, and the Middle East are being targeted and raped by Islamist men. This was why Muslim suicide bombers blew themselves up. This is what the 9/11 hijackers kept shouting *Allahu Akbar* to celebrate on United Airlines Flight 93 to kill Americans and others.[520] This is why they make improvised explosives to blow civilians up annually in India and in Sweden. This is why they behead innocent people for insulting Islam and insulting the Prophet Mohammad. This is what both Islamists and "moderates" spend their entire lives and all their energy to censor and protect from general criticism. This is why they commit physical genocide, cultural genocide, and then use the tyranny of their hurt sentiments to deliberately lie about it. Finally, this is what they want to reduce our entire world's intellectual, cultural, and social histories and development into because of their unwavering faith in the Abrahamic God:

Contempt for Dogs

Islam's contempt for dogs is one of the most illogical beliefs I've ever come across when researching this religious faith. Some Muslims and Islamic apologists may wish to argue that it was normal for the time period in which these beliefs materialized due to rabid dogs or some other excuse. However, framing this debate as a quirk of ancient culture would be false because Zoroastrianists in Iran during the ancient era during the Islamic conquest of the Sassanid empire were reportedly compassionate and loving towards dogs, while the conquering Muslims were not and treated them horribly.

The arguments against dogs in Islam is frivolous. It's an appeal to purity that doesn't distinguish between unclean homeless dogs and well-groomed household dogs, but rather appeals to this notion that dogs are always impure. These negative beliefs come from the teachings of the Islamic Prophet Mohammad, who encourages violence on black

---

[520] Kean, Thomas H., et al. The 9/11 Commission Report, First ed., W.W. Norton & Company, Inc., New York, NY, 2004, pp. 14–14.

dogs in particular. Professor Ahmad Hassan of *International Islamic University Malaysia* translates the following from the Hadith *Book 10: Kitab Al-Said*:

> *Game (Kitab Al-Said)*
> Chapter 1050: To have a dog for hunting and some other purposes
>
> *Book 10, Number 2839:*
> Narrated Abdullah ibn Mughaffal:
> The Prophet (peace_be_upon_him) said: Were dogs not a species of creature I should command that they all be killed; but kill every pure black one.[521]
>
> *Book 10, Number 2840:*
> Narrated Jabir ibn Abdullah:
> The Prophet of Allah (peace_be_upon_him) ordered to kill dogs, and we were even killing a dog which a woman brought with her from the desert. Afterwards he forbade to kill them, saying: Confine yourselves to the type which is black.[522]

This violence against dogs, especially black dogs, in Islamic countries is happening due to the unquestioned obedience to the Prophet Mohammad. To the best of my knowledge, this violence is generally more pronounced in the Arab Spring, but the fact such a stupid and unnecessary form of violence is happening at all, because some man proclaiming to be a Prophet of the Abrahamic God said so, speaks volumes on why Islam can't change and therefore cannot reform. The enmity towards dogs in Islam gets even more stupid than that. From the website titled *Hadith Collection, Book 24 Sahih Muslim* translates verse 5246 as follows:

> Sahih Muslim Book 024, Hadith Number 5246.
>
> Chapter : Angels do not enter a house in which there is a dog or a picture.
>
> 'Aisha reported that Gabriel (peace be upon him) made a promise with Allah's Messenger (may peace be upon him) to come at a definite hour; that hour came but he did not visit him. And there was in his hand (in the hand of Allah's Apostle) a staff. He threw it from his hand and said: Never has Allah or His messengers (angels) ever broken their promise. Then he cast a glance (and by chance) found a puppy under his cot and said: 'Aisha, when did this dog enter here? She said: BY Allah, I don't know He then commanded and it was turned out. Then Gabriel came and Allah's Messenger (may peace be upon him) said to him: You promised me and I waited for you, but you did not come, whereupon he said: It was the dog in your house which prevented me (to come), for we (angels) do not enter a house in which there is a dog or a picture.[523]

---

[521] Hasan, Ahmad. "Game (Kitab Al-Said)." *Family Life in Islam*, International Islamic University Malaysia, www.iium.edu.my/deed/hadith/abudawood/010_sat.html.
[522] Hasan, Ahmad. "Game (Kitab Al-Said)." *Family Life in Islam*, International Islamic University Malaysia, www.iium.edu.my/deed/hadith/abudawood/010_sat.html.
[523] "Sahih Muslim Book 024, Hadith Number 5246." *Hadith Collection*, https://hadithcollection.com/sahihmuslim/sahih-muslim-book-24-clothes-and-decorations/sahih-muslim-book-024-hadith-number-5246

Evidently, an angel which is supposedly a powerful messenger from the Almighty Abrahamic God can't enter a home or a tent of any person because a dog happens to be there. You're expected to believe that an angel, with the supposed blessings of an all-powerful cosmic deity, apparently has a weakness where any random dog can prevent them from entering for some unspecified reason. Think about that assertion for a moment. An angel that is harboring the blessings of the same Abrahamic God which people are taught created the entire universe, the earth itself, and who grants miracles to his apostles and his supposed Messiah Jesus, cannot even have his messenger enter a domain so long as a dog is there. How does that make any sense? How can anyone honestly believe that the supposed all-powerful Abrahamic God can't manage to send an angel to a house with a dog or a picture? Perhaps you may accuse me of the fallacy of incredulity, but I'm basing this argument off of the assumption that this all-powerful God is what he claims to be. Do dogs have a special, powerful quality that even the Abrahamic God cannot overcome? If you would like to make the argument that this was clearly a mistranslated or corrupted Hadith, unfortunately the following verse 5248 from the *Hadith Collections* gives further credence to this irrational contempt. It reads as follows:

> Sahih Muslim Book 024, Hadith Number 5248.
>
> Chapter : Angels do not enter a house in which there is a dog or a picture.
>
> Maimuna reported that one morning Allah's Messenger (may peace be upon him) was silent with grief. Maimuna said: Allah's Messenger, I find a change in your mood today. Allah's Messenger (may peace be upon him) said: Gabriel had promised me that he would meet me tonight, but he did not meet me. By Allah, he never broke his promises, and Allah's Messenger (may peace be upon him) spent the day in this sad (mood). Then it occurred to him that there had been a puppy under their cot. He commanded and it was turned out. He then took some water in his hand and sprinkled it at that place. When it was evening Gabriel met him and he said to him: you promised me that you would meet me the previous night. He said: Yes, but we do not enter a house in which there is a dog or a picture. Then on that very morning he commanded the killing of the dogs until he announced that the dog kept for the orchards should also be killed, but he spared the dog meant for the protection of extensive fields (or big gardens).[524]

It seems that the Abrahamic God, the Archangel Gabriel, and the Abrahamic God's Prophet Mohammad couldn't find a more peaceful way other than to slaughter the vast majority of dogs in their abode. This nearly indiscriminate mass slaughter of dogs was because the Islamic Prophet wanted to talk to his angel friend. The ongoing ruthless treatment of dogs in the Arab Spring is because of the teachings of the Prophet Mohammad. The Abrahamic God, in his infinite wisdom, couldn't have Gabriel give the Prophet Mohammad a better solution and the Prophet Mohammad, an apparently sinless

---

[524] "Sahih Muslim Book 024, Hadith Number 5248." *Hadith Collection*, https://hadithcollection.com/sahihmuslim/sahih-muslim-book-24-clothes-and-decorations/sahih-muslim-book-024-hadith-number-5248.

prophet just like the prophets before him, couldn't come-up with a better solution than killing the majority of dogs. Which is more likely: that the Abrahamic God exists and Mohammad is his Prophet, or Mohammad was a psychotic warlord that found excuses for his violent tendencies? Needless to say, this proves that Islam is not a religion of peace for dogs.

Animal Sacrifice

"*Even as a child, this Eid was horrifying.*"[525] wrote Sarah Haider, prominent Ex-Muslim activist and Co-Founder of *Ex-Muslims of North America*, on her twitter page in 2018 explaining her experience with the annual Islamic celebration of Eid. "*I remember witnessing a sacrifice of a cow with my family, I remember the blood gushing from its throat and running through the street. The story of Abraham which it commemorates is another horror. I'll save my Mubaraks for the other Eid.*"[526]

She follows up her tweet by politely requesting for people to respect her wishes and to not respond with gruesome pictures. Another Ex-Muslim chimes in with his recollection of remembering the wrath on the slaughterer's visage and how he felt disturbed by what he experienced from the festival.[527] Haider responds by mentioning that she remembered the son of a butcher innocently playing in the blood of the dead animal.[528] The same Ex-Muslim male explains a quip about how fasting before the ritualized animal sacrifice was to avoid throwing up, and then goes onto mention how fortunate he is that he could leave the Islamic world before becoming desensitized to such barbarity.[529]

I stared at my computer screen reading her tweet attempting to comprehend it. I regarded Sarah Haider to be a reliable and intelligent person at the time; her and other Ex-Muslim panels from her organization did much to explain the problems and dangers of Islam that I hadn't been aware of. What I had struggle internalizing for a few minutes

---

[525] Haider, Sarah. "Even as a Child, This Eid Was Horrifying. I Remember Witnessing a Sacrifice of a Cow with My Family, I Remember the Blood Gushing from Its Throat and Running through the Street. The Story of Abraham Which It Commemorates Is Another Horror. I'll Save My Mubaraks for the Other Eid." *Twitter*, Twitter, 21 Aug. 2018, twitter.com/SarahTheHaider/status/1031995695652384769.

[526] Haider, Sarah. "Even as a Child, This Eid Was Horrifying. I Remember Witnessing a Sacrifice of a Cow with My Family, I Remember the Blood Gushing from Its Throat and Running through the Street. The Story of Abraham Which It Commemorates Is Another Horror. I'll Save My Mubaraks for the Other Eid." *Twitter*, Twitter, 21 Aug. 2018, twitter.com/SarahTheHaider/status/1031995695652384769.

[527] Mo, Bilaal. "I Remember the Wrath on the Slaughterer's Faces Too, and Blood Stained Hands and Kurta's Afterwards. The Whole Thing Was Creepy." *Twitter*, Twitter, 21 Aug. 2018, twitter.com/takebeerism/status/1031996242685906945.

[528] Haider, Sarah. "I Remember the Son of the Butcher We Hired Playing in the Blood, like a Rain Puddle." *Twitter*, Twitter, 21 Aug. 2018, twitter.com/SarahTheHaider/status/1031996570470940673.

[529] Mo, Bilaal. "We Used to Joke around That the Reason We Fasted the Day or Two before This Eid Was to Avoid Throwing up. Fortunately i Wasn't in That World Long Enough to Become Desensitised to It." *Twitter*, Twitter, 21 Aug. 2018, twitter.com/takebeerism/status/1031997399969947649.

was that this annual festival of animal sacrifice was true and not some crackpot conspiracy theory made-up by far-right organizations to dehumanize Muslims. I made a quick response explaining I was left speechless and dumbfounded by learning that such a stupid event was actually real. It confirmed in my mind what I had suspected; Islam was just the babbling insanity of a 7th century illiterate warlord who formed an imperialistic project. I searched online for more information and was shocked by the details. Islamic theology was rife with debates on the importance of sacrificing an animal with special pleading arguments. At that moment, I couldn't fathom how anybody could take Islam seriously. Snapshots of Muslims smiling in congregations to the snapshots of bloody images of dead animals as proof of their devotion to the Abrahamic God.[530] The most immediate issue that struck me, and which convinced me that Islam could never be reformed, was that Muslims across the world hadn't even attempted to change this ritual to be more cosmetic to keep the supposed meaning without the need to slaughter helpless animals. It was because of their deep faith in the Abrahamic God as thoroughly explained in Islamic theology, the meaning was to sacrifice for the Abrahamic God as Abraham was fully willing to sacrifice his son.[531]

For those who don't know, the celebration of Eid al-Fitr to Eid al-Adha (the latter of which translates to Festival of Sacrifice) is an annual and mandatory celebration within the Islamic faith after Ramadan.[532] Judging from what I have read, it seems the shortened name for these two conjoined holidays is Eid. The slaughter of an animal, specified as acceptable to kill, is celebrated as proof of piety within Islam.[533][534] Yet again, the reason it hasn't changed is because Islam forbids "*bid'ah*" (or in other translations "bidah"[535]) which roughly means "*innovation in religion*" or "*invention in religion*" as translations according to the website *Questions on Islam* which explains the practice.[536] When researching this Islamic holiday, I recall a joke during my high school years in which an online penpal and I mused that at least religions weren't sacrificing animals anymore. Lo and behold, how wrong I was about this notion and that Islam remains consistent with

---

[530] Sommerlad, Joe. "Why Do Muslims Sacrifice Animals during Eid?" *The Independent*, Independent Digital News and Media, 21 Aug. 2018, www.independent.co.uk/news/world/middle-east/eid-al-adha-animal-sacrifice-abraham-islam-muslims-goats-sheep-animal-rights-a8500556.html.
[531] "As Eid Al Adha Approaches…" *Questions on Islam*, questionsonislam.com/content/eid-al-adha-approaches…
[532] "The Udhiyah (the Sacrificial Animal) and Its Rulings." *Islamway*, Islamway, 29 Nov. 2012, en.islamway.net/article/12915/the-udhiyah-the-sacrificial-animal-and-its-rulings.
[533] "As Eid Al Adha Approaches…" *Questions on Islam*, questionsonislam.com/content/eid-al-adha-approaches…
[534] "The Udhiyah (the Sacrificial Animal) and Its Rulings." *Islamway*, Islamway, 29 Nov. 2012, en.islamway.net/article/12915/the-udhiyah-the-sacrificial-animal-and-its-rulings.
[535] "Tafseer on the Basis of Narrated Texts and Tafseer on the Basis of Individual Understanding - Islam Question & Answer." *Islamqa.info*, Islam Question and Answer, 11 Mar. 2015, islamqa.info/en/answers/205290/tafseer-on-the-basis-of-narrated-texts-and-tafseer-on-the-basis-of-individual-understanding.
[536] "As Eid Al Adha Approaches…" *Questions on Islam*, questionsonislam.com/content/eid-al-adha-approaches…

this belief too, even after 1400 years. News articles attempting to be "respectful" and maintain "civil discourse" about this idiotic religious practice show the depth of how useless political correctness is.[537] Attempting to humanize animal slaughter by depicting it as a pious social event instead of a psychotic and meaningless slaughter of animals do a grave injustice to both animal rights and the horrors in which young Muslim children are forced to witness, but it may also delegitimize the Western mainstream media in the eyes of the non-Muslim public as a whole. The reason this portion was so difficult to write is because I kept thinking: *'Do I really need to make an effort to argue why religiously sanctioned animal slaughter is wrong? Have we not moved past even this point as a species?'* but of course, people on Sarah Haider's twitter began commenting about the similarities to factories in which animals are slaughtered as an attempt to justify this idiotic practice.

Nevertheless, for the sake of my commitment to academic integrity, I will attempt to give a serious response to this asinine religious practice. However, I feel that I should mention how absurd I find the notion that I must actually argue against animal sacrifices in the 21st century and I feel I should reiterate how ridiculous I find attempts by any online media to humanize this disgusting, violent ritualized form of animal cruelty. My personal disgust with this topic due to my bias of Western moral sensibilities and Hindu religious sensibilities (which I'm sure that Buddhists, Sikhs, and Jains likely share) is what makes this entire Islamic celebration utterly stupid and vomit-inducing; after learning about this ritual and the dehumanization of women, I can no longer see anything about the Islamic religious tradition as deserving of any respect. I honestly tried to be reasonable and separate the positives from the negatives when researching Islam, but everything about this religion leads me to conclude that it is nothing more than a violent, hateful imperialist project of the 7th century. The only positive it has over Scientology is that it can make its barbarous history look exotic and mysterious because it is so old and can more successfully make an appeal to population fallacy which coincides with an appeal to tradition fallacy. Islam's faults aren't limited to just this issue and the problems only worsen as I will be elaborating further on. I honestly have to wonder how many Muslims actually tried to use logic and reason on their own religious faith, because I am genuinely bewildered that just animal sacrifice itself didn't get mocked out of the religious tradition and I can only infer that fear and intimidation within Islamic societies is far deeper than people recognize. The fact Muslims still sacrifice animals goes against the very ideas of logic and reason that practically every other culture feels accustomed to at this point and time in history. For all the arguments on the supposed backwardness of religious traditions indigenous to Asia, the vast majority are clearly superior to Islam. I'm sure many Muslims and Westerners can point to some bizarre subset of a small

---

[537] Sommerlad, Joe. "Why Do Muslims Sacrifice Animals during Eid?" *The Independent*, Independent Digital News and Media, 21 Aug. 2018, www.independent.co.uk/news/world/middle-east/eid-al-adha-animal-sacrifice-abraham-islam-muslims-goats-sheep-animal-rights-a8500556.html.

population within South or East Asia conducting animal sacrifice and even occurrences in South America by a few Indigenous religious groups, but the vast majority of the religious traditions don't do animal sacrifices, eat brains, or other nonsense. Perhaps there are people in the most remote or ignored locations sacrificing animals, but you would think that after a certain degree of educational attainment, they would stop and realize it is a stupid practice. I don't care how bigoted or stupid you find this commentary about Eid, because I have to be blunt here: I doubt I will ever see a Muslim as capable or as intelligent as a non-Muslim ever again, if they support animal sacrifices. I think I was wrong to ever believe that Muslims were equal in intelligence to any non-Muslim or that they could ever reform and change the terrible rituals that they practice, if they do this. I apologize if that seems dehumanizing, but I can't hold back my utter disgust for this religious ceremony that people practice. The only reform possible for Muslims seems to be becoming Ex-Muslims to avoid *bid'ah* creating a return to tradition movement.

For those who want to call me a bigot: We're talking about yearly animal sacrifice; are you really willing to defend that? Are you a serious person? I can't hold back my contempt for this stupidity; if you're a Muslim practicing animal sacrifice, then you're a genuinely unintelligent person and I will never view you as equal to the intellect of other people. If you defend this on the basis of protecting religious sensibilities, then you're even less intelligent than the Muslims who practice this savagery. Cry me a river if you think that is bigotry, while you watch animals bleed out to please an illiterate 7th century man's fantasy novel on an annual basis or support others doing it because of the tyranny of hurt sentiments.

To set aside my personal disgust and focus on the purposes of critiquing animal sacrifice. First, the intentions of slaughtering an animal for the Abrahamic God and slaughtering an animal to eat it are as far removed in intent as possible; one requires the murder of an animal because the Abrahamic God commands that you show him deference, the other is to feed whole populations to keep a country healthy and any waste of food can be ameliorated through reform in a society that mass produces food in abundance. By contrast, Islam requires adherents to physically slit the throat of an animal and appreciate as it chokes to death in order for Muslims to prove their love and devotion to the Abrahamic God.[538] Animals in production factories are generally in sterile conditions where people can make sure that the meat isn't diseased. Even in cases of corporations not following through with keeping conditions sterile, it's safer for there to be a factory keeping the diseased meat isolated. In the context of the ritualized murder of helpless animals by Islamic doctrine, the meat has a higher chance of being diseased and potentially causing food poisoning or worse for a Muslim family. Second, it leaves horrible mental images in children's minds that has shown to live with them for a lifetime

---

[538] "As Eid Al Adha Approaches..." *Questions on Islam*, questionsonislam.com/content/eid-al-adha-approaches…

and makes it a requirement for them to become desensitized to brutal violence against animals every year. Some may argue that I am attempting to infer an objective morality to this equation against Islam, but this horrific celebration is defended in reverence to the Abrahamic God on the basis of Islam's objective morality.[539] The sacrifice of an animal is embedded as an annual religious holiday in Islam and is a form of Divine Command Theory. Therefore, as a third point of contention, Islam's *Eid al-Adha* (Festival of Sacrifice) is an annual real-world example of the utter flaws of Divine Command Theory. Muslims actively butcher animals mercilessly every year to express their honest love and devotion to the Abrahamic God.[540] Finally, due to Islam being a faith that seeks converts, it creates a pointless demand for the oversupply of animals so that nearly two billion or more can kill an animal and divvy them up among seven people at most to eat.[541] Even granting that millions of animals are slaughtered each day, this ritualized religious practice still increases the slaughter of animals by approximately the hundreds of millions or possibly more. The more this religion spreads, the worse it will be for the sustainability of the environment, and that is even granting that it is a drop in the puddle of bloodshed for daily animal slaughter. This needless slaughter of animals is further credence that Islam isn't a religion of peace for animals in general. Islamic teachings are against changing this practice and therefore against making it more ceremonial.[542] If Islam had been a religion of peace or capable of adapting with modernity, it would have changed the very real annual slaughter of animals to something else entirely. Perhaps letting kids have fun striking a piñata to make this religious celebration more akin to a modernized ceremonial form of worship. It doesn't have to be precisely that, but at least something equivalent to striking a piñata. It is clear that Islam wouldn't have religious values declaring that it can't be changed, if it was actually a peaceful religion that could modernize.

Bestiality

Years ago, footage of Afghan Muslims committing bestiality outside their homes, such as atop their small rooftops had been filmed by US troops and leaked unto *liveleaks.com* for worldwide viewing.[543] Muslim men were seen penetrating the backside

---

[539] "As Eid Al Adha Approaches..." *Questions on Islam*, questionsonislam.com/content/eid-al-adha-approaches...
[540] "As Eid Al Adha Approaches..." *Questions on Islam*, questionsonislam.com/content/eid-al-adha-approaches...
[541] "As Eid Al Adha Approaches..." *Questions on Islam*, questionsonislam.com/content/eid-al-adha-approaches...
[542] "As Eid Al Adha Approaches..." *Questions on Islam*, questionsonislam.com/content/eid-al-adha-approaches...
[543] "Poor Goat." *LiveLeak.com - Redefining the Media*, www.liveleak.com/view?i=008_1443844876.

or mouth of goats and other animals from thermal vision.⁵⁴⁴⁵⁴⁵ The problem has been stated to exist in other predominately Islamic countries too and isn't limited to just Afghanistan. Social critiques have been offered such as pointing out the impoverished and rural living conditions along with extreme sexual repression within the Islamic faith as explanations for these acts of bestiality in an effort to understand why this bizarre phenomenon is happening. The internet term "*goatfucker*" by the internet hacktivist group Anon and other self-stylized "trolls" (trolls being an English-language colloquial term for people who intentionally seek to cause offense to others for their own fun) similar to 4Chan have been used as slang identification for these Muslims and certain prominent Islamic groups. Spy equipment has found that even Islamic terrorists commit these acts of bestiality; it is likely much to the chagrin or amusement for the armed forces who are checking the spying equipment.⁵⁴⁶

Many Muslim apologists may try to use this as proof that terrorist organizations and the general public of these Islamic majority countries aren't acting in accordance with Islamic teachings. They may be quick to point to Hadiths that condemn bestiality, such as the Hadith that equates homosexuality with bestiality and commands Muslims to kill both homosexuals and those who commit fornication with animals. From *Sunnah.com*, the Hadith from Book 10 verse 1255 in the English version and 1216 in the Arabic version states as follows:

> Ibn 'Abbas (RAA) narrated that the Messenger of Allah (ﷺ) said:
> "Whoever you find doing as the people of Lot did (i.e. homosexuality), kill the one who does it and the one to whom it is done, and if you find anyone having sexual intercourse with animal, kill him and kill the animal." Related by Ahmad and the four Imams with a trustworthy chain of narrators.⁵⁴⁷

However, there are other Hadiths that are completely in line with what these Afghan men and some terrorists are doing by raping the animals. From the *Hadith Collection,* Book 33 verse 4450 says the following:

> Abu Dawud Book 033, Hadith Number 4450.
>
> Chapter : Not known.

---

⁵⁴⁴ "Two Pai Taliban Jihadi Mujahideen Caught Sexing A Donkey By US Forces." *LiveLeak.com - Redefining the Media,* www.liveleak.com/view?i=825_1315923588.
⁵⁴⁵ "US ARMY Camera Catches Afghans Gangbanging a Goat." *LiveLeak.com - Redefining the Media,* www.liveleak.com/view?i=93d_1384239379.
⁵⁴⁶ "Two Pai Taliban Jihadi Mujahideen Caught Sexing A Donkey By US Forces." *LiveLeak.com - Redefining the Media,* www.liveleak.com/view?i=825_1315923588.
⁵⁴⁷ "Hadith - Hudud - Bulugh Al-Maram - Sunnah.com - Sayings and Teachings of Prophet Muhammad (صلى الله عليه و سلم)." *Search Results - Fitra (Page 1) - Sunnah.com - Sayings and Teachings of Prophet Muhammad (☐☐☐ ☐ ☐☐☐☐ ☐☐☐☐ ☐☐☐),* sunnah.com/urn/2015030.

Narated By Abdullah ibn Abbas : There is no prescribed punishment for one who has sexual intercourse with an animal.[548]

And yet another from *Sunnah.com*, which clarifies that Hadiths supporting any punishment for bestiality are weaker than those that permit bestiality within Islamic theology:

40
Prescribed Punishments (Kitab Al-Hudud)
(30)
Chapter: One who has intercourse with an animal
(30)

باب فِيمَنْ أَتَى بَهِيمَةً

'Asim reported from Abu Razin on the authority of Ibn 'Abbas saying:
There is no prescribed punishment for one who has sexual intercourse with an animal.
Abu Dawud said: 'Ata is also so. Al Hakam said: I think he should be flogged, but the number should not reach the one of the prescribed punishment. Al-Hasan said: He is like a fornicator.
Abu Dawud said: THe tradition of 'Asim proves the tradition of 'Amr b. Abi 'Amr as weak.[549][550]

حَدَّثَنَا أَحْمَدُ بْنُ يُونُسَ، أَنَّ شَرِيكًا، وَأَبَا الأَحْوَصِ، وَأَبَا بَكْرِ بْنِ عَيَّاشٍ حَدَّثُوهُمْ عَنْ عَاصِمٍ، عَنْ أَبِي رَزِينٍ، عَنِ ابْنِ عَبَّاسٍ، قَالَ لَيْسَ عَلَى الَّذِي يَأْتِي الْبَهِيمَةَ حَدٌّ ‏.‏ قَالَ أَبُو دَاوُدَ كَذَا قَالَ عَطَاءٌ وَقَالَ الْحَكَمُ أَرَى أَنْ يُجْلَدَ وَلاَ يَبْلُغَ بِهِ الْحَدَّ ‏.‏ وَقَالَ الْحَسَنُ هُوَ بِمَنْزِلَةِ الزَّانِي ‏.‏ قَالَ أَبُو دَاوُدَ حَدِيثُ عَاصِمٍ يُضَعِّفُ حَدِيثَ عَمْرِو بْنِ أَبِي عَمْرٍو ‏.‏

Grade:	**Hasan** (Al-Albani)
Reference	: Sunan Abi Dawud 4465
In-book reference	: Book 40, Hadith 115
English translation	: Book 39, Hadith 4450

As such, bestiality is an open question in Islamic societies. How can this be a religion of peace when it is okay with raping animals? Does that seem incredibly stupid

---

[548] "Abu Dawud Book 033, Hadith Number 4450." *Hadith Collection*, https://hadithcollection.com/abudawud/abu-dawud-book-33-prescribed-punishments/abu-dawud-book-033-hadith-number-4450.

[549] al-Sijistānī, Abū Dāwūd (Dā'ūd) Sulaymān ibn al-Ash'ath ibn Isḥāq al-Azdī. "40 Prescribed Punishments (Kitab Al-Hudud): (30) Chapter: One Who Has Intercourse with an Animal." Edited by Abu Khaliyl. Translated by Nasiruddin Al-Khattab, Sunan Abi Dawud 4465 - Prescribed Punishments (Kitab al-Hudud) - كتاب الحدود - Sunnah.Com - Sayings and Teachings of Prophet Muhammad (صلى الله عليه و سلم), SUNNAH.COM, sunnah.com/abudawud:4465. Accessed 8 Aug. 2025.

[550] Al-Sijistānī, Abū Dāwūd (Dā'ūd) Sulaymān ibn al-Ash'ath ibn Isḥāq Al-Azdī. "The Book Of Legal Punishments: Chapter 29. One Who Has Intercourse With An Animal." Sunan Abu Dawud Compiled by: Imâm Hâfiz Abu Dawud Sulaiman Bin Ash'ath , edited by Abdul Malik Mujahid et al., translated by Nasiruddin Al-Khattab, First Edition ed., Volume 5, DARU SSALAM GLOBAL LEADER IN ISLAMIC BOOKS, Riyadh, Riyadh Province, 2008, pp. 80–80. From Hadtth No, 4351 to 5274 , https://ia601602.us.archive.org/34/items/SunanAbuDawudVol.111160EnglishArabic/Sunan%20Abu%20Dawud%20Vol.%205%20-%204351-5274%20English%20Arabic.pdf. Accessed 8 Aug. 2025.

to ask? Unfortunately, Islam allows it to be an open question within its theology, so bestiality has to be questioned and repudiated from an outsider perspective too.

Zoroastrians in Medieval Iran challenged Islam's theological support for bestiality. The *Skand Gumanig-Wizar*, which translates to "*Doubt-dispelling Disquisition*" in English, has survived quotes criticizing bestiality in Islam. It is a Zoroastrian book authored by an individual named Mardanfarrox, known as the son of Ohrmazddad. The book was written during the Middle Ages and attempted to give a Zoroastrian perspective on Islamic theology approximately around the 9th century. For a bit of historic background, Paul Sprachman's English translation of *Chapter 9: The Battle of Beliefs* of Iranian scholar, Abdolhossein Zarrinkoub's *Two Centuries of Silence: An Account of Events and Conditions in Iran [Persia] during the first Two Hundred Years of Islam* explains some of the context behind why *Skand Gumanig-Wizar* was made:

The Polemics of the Shikand-gumanik Vichār

Does language in the Shikand-gumanik Vichār,31 apparently written a short time after the history mentioned above, show just how perplexed and skeptical the Zoroastrian clergy were in this matter? The idea that offence and sin could be attributed to the God of right and goodness was unthinkable to them. Could the god that created all that was fine and beautiful in the world be the same One who bestowed upon it what was repulsive and evil? If the God of the world was the Creator of ugliness and evil, then that Creator must also be unknowing, incapable, and devoid of goodness and mercy, all of which are defects. How could God, who must be the perfect being and the perfection of being, brook such imperfections?32 This question, which arose in the debate between al-Ma'mūn and the dualist, formed the basis of the discussion in the Shikand-gumanik Vichār. This was undoubtedly one of the most important problems that made Mazdakites and dualists dubious about converting to Islam. This question was on their minds: If, as the Muslims say, God has no peer or partner, how is it right to call Him "the Irresistible" and the "Conqueror?"33 Apart from this, it was not easy for Mazdakites to imagine a single god without antagonist or peer. Why would, they asked, a god who is wise and content allow evil and ugliness to arise? If god preferred good to evil, what explains the superiority of the impious and the criminal in the world?34 If God is compassionate and merciful, why does he afflict mankind with ignorance, blindness, and heartlessness?35

Muslim scholars like Abū al-Hudhayl cAllāf and [Abū Isḥāq] Niẓām rightly and diligently met these objections in books of scholastic theology. The critiques found in the Shikandgumanik Vichār, nevertheless, are exemplary of debating points Mazdakites leveled against Islamic theologians early in the period of scholarly sparring between Mazdakites and Muslims. The leeway, unconcern, and tolerance that characterized al-Ma'mūn's dealings with Mazdakites and members of other sects, gradually gave them the courage to criticize the Quran itself, and declare parts of it inconsistent and self-contradictory. One can see such objections, which are found in the Shikand-gumanik Vichār, as illustrative of the ways Iranians, in the light of logic and reason, conducted disputes against the Arabs. At one point the book states: "In their [the Muslims'] scripture there is this claim on the topic of heavenly reward [korfeh, thawāb], which seems contradictory. It says, 'Both reward and punishment are from me [God], and no evil spirit nor sorcerer can harm a person. None can accept faith nor do good but that I will it, and none can incline toward unbelief and fall into sin but that it be my wish.'" The same book often takes the tone of a complaint, cursing the Lord's creatures for doing wrong and commiting sin…These things are His own will and doing. Despite this, He threatens people body and soul with the torments of hell as punishment for their sins and wrongs. In another place He says, "I myself lead people astray; for I can if I wished lead them on the right path, but it is my desire they go to hell." But elsewhere in the book He says, "The people are responsible for their own wrongs and sins..."36 These illustrate what the Mazdakites argued to challenge Islamic theologians and prove the superiority of their faith. But the eloquence of the Muslim scholastic theologians acted like the sword of the Islamic warriors in lifting and countering such doubts. It put an end to the dialogues. The arguments, nevertheless, show that even with Islam at the height of its power and greatness, the Zoroastrian priests and clergymen found the opportunity to speak up and challenge the religion by adducing rational arguments. Though lacking proper foundation, these arguments speak of a battle between Iranians and Arabs joined in the light of leaning and reason. The Zoroastrian clergy's arguments, however, were not solely directed at scholastic Muslim theologians, they also debated with Jews, Christians, Manichaeans, and even materialists [dahrīyān]. Examples of these debates are also found in the Shikand-gumanik Vichār. They show that the Magians in the Islamic period were far from lax when it came to proselytizing their faith and approached the task with interest and energy.[551]

In an English translation of the book's latter two chapters, titled "*The Definitive Zoroastrian Critique of Islam: Chapters 11 –12 of the Skand Gumanig-Wizar by Mardanfarrox son of Ohrmazddad*" translated by Christian C. Sahner, the criticism of Islam's endorsement for bestiality is on pages 147 – 148. It is translated as follows:

Can a man screw his own donkey simply because he owns it?

>11.205 Furthermore: those who belong to a group of them say that God has authority over every creature and creation.

>11.206 For His creations all belong to Him.

>11.207 However it behooves Him and whatever behooves Him He does to them; [but] He is not an agent of violence.

>11.208 For violence is what they do to something which does not belong to them.

>11.209 Then He to whom all things belong, doing to them whatever behooves Him, He is not an agent of violence.

>11.210 Then let Him know that if, on account of being the ruler, He who does violence must also not be called an agent of violence

>11.211 Then also, He who is the ruler [and] speaks lies must be speaking the truth.

>11.212 Also He who, on account of being the ruler, commits evil, sin, and robbery, He should not be called a sinner

>11.213 Just as the Blessed Rosn son of Adurfarnbag said as an analogy.

>11.214 "They saw a man who was screwing a donkey.

>11.215 When they asked him, 'Why are you doing this abominable deed?'

>11.216 He gave as an excuse, 'It's a donkey belonging to me!'"[552]

---

[551] Zarrinkoub, Abdolhossein. Chapter 9: The Battle of Beliefs (Location 4422 – 4965). Two Centuries of Silence: An Account of Events and Conditions in Iran [Persia] During the First Two Hundred Years of Islam, from the Arab Invasion to the Rise of the Tahirid Dynasty First edition. Mazda Publishers. Kindle Edition.
[552] Mardanfarrox. "Can a Man Screw His Own Donkey Simply Because He Owns It?" The Definitive Zoroastrian Critique of Islam: Chapters 11 –12 of the Skand Gumanig-Wizar by Mardanfarrox Son of

The translator, Christian C. Sahner, commented in the notes on page 147 that *"The argument that follows reads like a caricatured portrayal of extreme theological voluntarists[553]"* to the above quote. Sahner is almost certainly wrong on his assessment. Mardanfarrox was commenting on a real event that he probably witnessed Muslims commit right in front of him, because Islam's contradictory Hadiths make committing bestiality an open question in terms of morality. In other words, from just Islamic theology itself, all available evidence suggests that some medieval Muslims in Iran almost certainly committed bestiality because it is considered a "deep" and "profound" question that Islamic theology has never settled. Medieval Zoroastrians were likely eyewitness to it, just as American servicemembers witnessed Afghan Muslim men and Islamic terrorists raping goats and donkeys. Supposed scholars of the West repeatedly prove that they don't understand the intellectual limitations of Islam, but this leaves them to draw ignorant and false conclusions as a result. Mardanfarrox's criticism was both genuine and respectful of Islamic theology.

Finally, consider the fact that prior to Islam, the civilization that made-up Afghanistan were known for an astounding syncretic culture of Greek and Dharmic philosophies in which Greeks, Hindus, and Buddhists all lived together in polities, created shared art and coinage, and were popularly known for debating and sharing philosophical ideas which resulted in survived records of philosophies like Pyrrhonism which was influenced by Buddhism from what the evidence shows.[554][555] Once Islam took hold through bloodshed and conquest, the debates in Muslim-majority Afghanistan have become about whether having sexual intercourse with goats and donkeys is morally permissible or not. This is the genuine intellectual difference between Islam and other cultures philosophies.

Female Slaves in Heaven

Ohrmazddad, translated by Christian C. Sahner, Paperback ed., Liverpool University Press, Liverpool, Merseyside, 2023, pp. 147–148.

[553] Mardanfarrox. "Can a Man Screw His Own Donkey Simply Because He Owns It?" The Definitive Zoroastrian Critique of Islam: Chapters 11 –12 of the Skand Gumanig-Wizar by Mardanfarrox Son of Ohrmazddad, translated by Christian C. Sahner, Paperback ed., Liverpool University Press, Liverpool, Merseyside, 2023, pp. 147–148.

[554] Ghose, Sanujit. "Cultural Links between India & the Greco-Roman World." Ancient History Encyclopedia, Ancient History Encyclopedia, 30 Apr. 2019, www.ancient.eu/article/208/cultural-links-between-india--the-greco-roman-worl/.

[555] Beckwith, Christopher I. Greek Buddha: Pyrrhos Encounter with Early Buddhism in Central Asia. PDF ed., Princeton University Press, 2017. Princeton University Press, assets.press.princeton.edu/chapters/s10500.pdf.

Another one of Islam's numerous defects is the Hadiths related to the sexual slavery of women and the descriptions of exotic supernatural women whose sole purpose is the sexual pleasure of Muslim men.[556] There are thorough details about how these women won't ever exhibit the so-called "impurities" of normal women on earth when faithful Muslim men go to heaven with full erections to have sex with them.[557] This very issue shows the massive failings of making a religion's afterlife more concrete in conceptualization and the ignorance of the Islamic Prophet and his followers. Muslim apologists may be quick to argue those Hadiths have no bearing on the Quran and are inauthentic, but the Quran itself has verses mentioning pure virgin women in Chapter 56 "The Event" (sūrat l-wāqiʿah) on verses 35 through 38.[558] Chapter 78 "The Tidings" ("An-Naba") verses 31 through 40 also affirms the existence of female slaves in heaven created specifically for Muslim men who enter heaven.[559]

First, for a fuller context, I'll show Quran chapter 56, verses 35 – 40:

Quran 56:35:

Sahih International

Indeed, We have produced the women of Paradise in a [new] creation

Muhsin Khan

Verily, We have created them (maidens) of special creation.

Pickthall

Lo! We have created them a (new) creation

Yusuf Ali

We have created (their Companions) of special creation.

Shakir

Surely We have made them to grow into a (new) growth,

Dr. Ghali

Surely We have brought them (The huris) into being a (perfect) bringing up;[560]

Quran 56:36:

Sahih International

And made them virgins,

---

[556] Al-Munajjid, Muhammed Salih. "Will Men in Paradise Have Intercourse with Al-Hoor Aliyn?" *Islamqa.info*, Islam Question and Answer, islamqa.info/en/10053.
[557] Al-Munajjid, Muhammed Salih. "Will Men in Paradise Have Intercourse with Al-Hoor Aliyn?" *Islamqa.info*, Islam Question and Answer, islamqa.info/en/10053.
[558] "Al-Qur'an Al-Kareem - القرآن الكريم." *Surah Al-Waqi'ah [56:35-38]*, quran.com/56/35-38.
[559] "Al-Qur'an Al-Kareem - القرآن الكريم." *Surah An-Naba [78:31-40]*, quran.com/78/31-40.
[560] "Surat Al-Wāqiʿah (the Inevitable) - سورة الواقعة." The Noble Qur'an, legacy.quran.com/56/35-40. Accessed 6 Aug. 2025.

Muhsin Khan

And made them virgins.

Pickthall

And made them virgins,

Yusuf Ali

And made them virgin - pure (and undefiled), -

Shakir

Then We have made them virgins,

Dr. Ghali

So We have made them virgins,[561]

Quran 56:37:

Sahih International

Devoted [to their husbands] and of equal age,

Muhsin Khan

Loving (their husbands only), equal in age.

Pickthall

Lovers, friends,

Yusuf Ali

Beloved (by nature), equal in age,-

Shakir

Loving, equals in age,

Dr. Ghali

Chastely amorous, like of age,[562]

Quran 56:38:

Sahih International

For the companions of the right [who are]

Muhsin Khan

For those on the Right Hand.

Pickthall

For those on the right hand;

---

[561] "Surat Al-Wāqi`ah (the Inevitable) - سورة الواقعة." The Noble Qur'an, legacy.quran.com/56/35-40. Accessed 6 Aug. 2025.

[562] "Surat Al-Wāqi`ah (the Inevitable) - سورة الواقعة." The Noble Qur'an, legacy.quran.com/56/35-40. Accessed 6 Aug. 2025.

Yusuf Ali

For the Companions of the Right Hand.

Shakir

For the sake of the companions of the right hand.

Dr. Ghali

For the companions of the Right-[563]

Quran 56:39:

Sahih International

A company of the former peoples

Muhsin Khan

A multitude of those (on the Right Hand) will be from the first generation (who embraced Islam).

Pickthall

A multitude of those of old

Yusuf Ali

A (goodly) number from those of old,

Shakir

A numerous company from among the first,

Dr. Ghali

A throng of the earliest (people,)[564]

Quran 56:40:

Sahih International

And a company of the later peoples.

Muhsin Khan

And a multitude of those (on the Right Hand) will be from the later times (generations).

Pickthall

And a multitude of those of later time.

Yusuf Ali

And a (goodly) number from those of later times.

Shakir

And a numerous company from among the last.

---

[563] "Surat Al-Wāqi`ah (the Inevitable) - سورة الواقعة." The Noble Qur'an, legacy.quran.com/56/35-40. Accessed 6 Aug. 2025.

[564] "Surat Al-Wāqi`ah (the Inevitable) - سورة الواقعة." The Noble Qur'an, legacy.quran.com/56/35-40. Accessed 6 Aug. 2025.

Dr. Ghali

And a throng of the later (people).[565]

And, Quran chapter 78, verses 31 – 40:

Quran 78:31

Sahih International

Indeed, for the righteous is attainment -

Muhsin Khan

Verily, for the Muttaqun, there will be a success (Paradise);

Pickthall

Lo! for the duteous is achievement -

Yusuf Ali

Verily for the Righteous there will be a fulfilment of (the heart's) desires;

Shakir

Surely for those who guard (against evil) is achievement,

Dr. Ghali

Surely for the pious there is a place of triumph,[566]

Quran 78:32

Sahih International

Gardens and grapevines

Muhsin Khan

Gardens and grapeyards;

Pickthall

Gardens enclosed and vineyards,

Yusuf Ali

Gardens enclosed, and grapevines;

Shakir

Gardens and vineyards,

Dr. Ghali

---

[565] "Surat Al-Wāqi`ah (the Inevitable) - سورة الواقعة." The Noble Qur'an, legacy.quran.com/56/35-40. Accessed 6 Aug. 2025.

[566] "Surat An-Naba' (the Tidings) - سورة النبإ." The Noble Qur'an, legacy.quran.com/78/31-40. Accessed 6 Aug. 2025.

Enclosed orchards, and vineyards,[567]

Quran 78:33

Sahih International

And full-breasted [companions] of equal age

Muhsin Khan

And young full-breasted (mature) maidens of equal age;

Pickthall

And voluptuous women of equal age;

Yusuf Ali

And voluptuous women of equal age;

Shakir

And voluptuous women of equal age;

Dr. Ghali

And youthful virgins, like of age,[568]

Quran 78:34

Sahih International

And a full cup.

Muhsin Khan

And a full cup (of wine).

Pickthall

And a full cup.

Yusuf Ali

And a cup full (to the brim).

Shakir

And a pure cup.

Dr. Ghali

And a cup brimful.[569]

Quran 78:35

---

[567] "Surat An-Naba' (the Tidings) - سورة النبإ." The Noble Qur'an, legacy.quran.com/78/31-40. Accessed 6 Aug. 2025.

[568] "Surat An-Naba' (the Tidings) - سورة النبإ." The Noble Qur'an, legacy.quran.com/78/31-40. Accessed 6 Aug. 2025.

[569] "Surat An-Naba' (the Tidings) - سورة النبإ." The Noble Qur'an, legacy.quran.com/78/31-40. Accessed 6 Aug. 2025.

Sahih International

No ill speech will they hear therein or any falsehood -

Muhsin Khan

No Laghw (dirty, false, evil talk) shall they hear therein, nor lying;

Pickthall

There hear they never vain discourse, nor lying -

Yusuf Ali

No vanity shall they hear therein, nor Untruth:-

Shakir

They shall not hear therein any vain words nor lying.

Dr. Ghali

Therein they will hear no idle talk nor cry of lies.[570]

Quran 78:36

Sahih International

[As] reward from your Lord, [a generous] gift [made due by] account,

Muhsin Khan

A reward from your Lord, an ample calculated gift (according to the best of their good deeds).

Pickthall

Requital from thy Lord - a gift in payment -

Yusuf Ali

Recompense from thy Lord, a gift, (amply) sufficient,

Shakir

A reward from your Lord, a gift according to a reckoning:

Dr. Ghali

(It is for) recompense from your Lord, a gift, a reckoning,[571]

Quran 78:37

Sahih International

[From] the Lord of the heavens and the earth and whatever is between them, the Most Merciful. They possess not from Him [authority for] speech.

Muhsin Khan

---

[570] "Surat An-Naba' (the Tidings) - سورة النبإ." The Noble Qur'an, legacy.quran.com/78/31-40. Accessed 6 Aug. 2025.

[571] "Surat An-Naba' (the Tidings) - سورة النبإ." The Noble Qur'an, legacy.quran.com/78/31-40. Accessed 6 Aug. 2025.

(From) the Lord of the heavens and the earth, and whatsoever is in between them, the Most Beneficent, none can dare to speak with Him (on the Day of Resurrection except after His Leave).

Pickthall

Lord of the heavens and the earth, and (all) that is between them, the Beneficent; with Whom none can converse.

Yusuf Ali

(From) the Lord of the heavens and the earth, and all between, (Allah) Most Gracious: None shall have power to argue with Him.

Shakir

The Lord of the heavens and the earth and what is between them, the Beneficent Allah, they shall not be able to address Him.

Dr. Ghali

(From) the Lord of the heavens and the earth and whatever is between them, The All-Merciful; they possess (no power) of addressing Him.[572]

Quran 78:38

Sahih International

The Day that the Spirit and the angels will stand in rows, they will not speak except for one whom the Most Merciful permits, and he will say what is correct.

Muhsin Khan

The Day that Ar-Ruh [Jibrael (Gabriel) or another angel] and the angels will stand forth in rows, none shall speak except him whom the Most Beneficent (Allah) allows, and he will speak what is right.

Pickthall

On the day when the angels and the Spirit stand arrayed, they speak not, saving him whom the Beneficent alloweth and who speaketh right.

Yusuf Ali

The Day that the Spirit and the angels will stand forth in ranks, none shall speak except any who is permitted by (Allah) Most Gracious, and He will say what is right.

Shakir

The day on which the spirit and the angels shall stand in ranks; they shall not speak except he whom the Beneficent Allah permits and who speaks the right thing.

Dr. Ghali

On the Day when the Spirit and the Angels rise up in ranks, they will not speak, except him (to) whom The All-Merciful has given permission and who speaks (Literally: says) right.[573]

---

[572] "Surat An-Naba' (the Tidings) - سورة النبإ." The Noble Qur'an, legacy.quran.com/78/31-40. Accessed 6 Aug. 2025.

[573] "Surat An-Naba' (the Tidings) - سورة النبإ." The Noble Qur'an, legacy.quran.com/78/31-40. Accessed 6 Aug. 2025.

Quran 78:39

Sahih International

That is the True Day; so he who wills may take to his Lord a [way of] return.

Muhsin Khan

That is without doubt the True Day, so, whosoever wills, let him seek a place with (or a way to) His Lord (by obeying Him in this worldly life)!

Pickthall

That is the True Day. So whoso will should seek recourse unto his Lord.

Yusuf Ali

That Day will be the sure Reality: Therefore, whoso will, let him take a (straight) return to his Lord!

Shakir

That is the sure day, so whoever desires may take refuge with his Lord.

Dr. Ghali

That is the True Day. So whoever decides, should seek a resorting to his Lord (i.e., by doing righteous deeds).[574]

Quran 78:40

Sahih International

Indeed, We have warned you of a near punishment on the Day when a man will observe what his hands have put forth and the disbeliever will say, "Oh, I wish that I were dust!"

Muhsin Khan

Verily, We have warned you of a near torment, the Day when man will see that (the deeds) which his hands have sent forth, and the disbeliever will say: "Woe to me! Would that I were dust!"

Pickthall

Lo! We warn you of a doom at hand, a day whereon a man will look on that which his own hands have sent before, and the disbeliever will cry: "Would that I were dust!"

Yusuf Ali

Verily, We have warned you of a Penalty near, the Day when man will see (the deeds) which his hands have sent forth, and the Unbeliever will say, "Woe unto me! Would that I were (metre) dust!"

Shakir

Surely We have warned you of a chastisement near at hand: the day when man shall see what his two hands have sent before, and the unbeliever shall say: O! would that I were dust!

Dr. Ghali

---

[574] "Surat An-Naba' (the Tidings) - سورة النبإ." The Noble Qur'an, legacy.quran.com/78/31-40. Accessed 6 Aug. 2025.

> Surely We have warned you of a near torment on the Day when a person will look at whatever his hands have forwarded, and the disbeliever will say, "Oh, would that I were dust!"[575]

These teachings help to perpetuate the dehumanization of women as sex objects without any personality of their own and could credibly be argued as an ancient form of "women as reward" – a term popularly coined by sex-negative feminist and video game critic Anita Sarkeesian.[576] Despite whatever objections people may have, the similarities of seeing women as a reward are certainly there; it is the idea that after arduous tribulations, men will be rewarded with the sexual reward of women's bodies that they will fornicate with at the man's leisure.[577][578] To be clear, I am not denigrating any man or woman who has such sexual fantasies or who would want to partake in such ideas among consenting adults, but this "reward" being part of a religion that largely discourages a follower to pursue a healthy sexual experience is quite jarring and based upon owning women as property of men. Moreover, the description of this Islamic afterlife doesn't devalue the argument about Islam internalizing and protecting a concept of purity, because the description of these otherworldly female slaves are celebrated in terms of purity and virginity being synonymous.[579] It comes attached to some vague idea of heavenly radiance that seems to further symbolize otherworldly purity.[580] As a fictional concept, this idea is fine, but people who honestly believe this is what happens after they either suicide bomb, or are martyred in some other way, do present a danger to innocent civilians everywhere. The "women as reward" functions as coping mechanism to commit horrific atrocities and feel both blessed and sexually gratified for causing violence upon others in the form of martyrdom. It is not inconsistent with Islamic doctrines, but rather exists because of Islamic doctrines.

Here are two Hadiths from *Sunnah.com* that express women as reward for Muslim men, which could be a credible reason, or at least a partial reason, for their motives when inculcated into Islamic Jihad and plausibly because of their solidarity with Muslim terrorists:

Abu Sa'eed Al-Khudri narrated that the Messenger of Allah (s.a.w) said:

---

[575] "Surat An-Naba' (the Tidings) - سورة النبإ." The Noble Qur'an, legacy.quran.com/78/31-40. Accessed 6 Aug. 2025.
[576] Sarkeesian, Anita. "Women as Reward - Tropes vs Women in Video Games." *YouTube*, Feminist Frequency, 31 Aug. 2015, www.youtube.com/watch?v=QC6oxBLXtkU.
[577] Al-Munajjid, Muhammed Salih. "Will Men in Paradise Have Intercourse with Al-Hoor Aliyn?" *Islamqa.info*, Islam Question and Answer, islamqa.info/en/10053.
[578] Sarkeesian, Anita. "Women as Reward - Tropes vs Women in Video Games." *YouTube*, Feminist Frequency, 31 Aug. 2015, www.youtube.com/watch?v=QC6oxBLXtkU.
[579] Al-Munajjid, Muhammed Salih. "Will Men in Paradise Have Intercourse with Al-Hoor Aliyn?" *Islamqa.info*, Islam Question and Answer, islamqa.info/en/10053.
[580] Al-Munajjid, Muhammed Salih. "Will Men in Paradise Have Intercourse with Al-Hoor Aliyn?" *Islamqa.info*, Islam Question and Answer, islamqa.info/en/10053.

"The least of the people of Paradise in position is the one with eighty thousand servants and seventy-two wives. He shall have a tent of pearl, peridot, and corundum set up for him,(the size of which is) like that which is between Al-Jabiyyah and Sana'a."And with this chain, it is narrated from the Prophet (s.a.w) that he said: "Whoever of the people of (destined to enter) Paradise dies, young or old, they shall be brought back in Paradise thirty years old, they will not increase in that ever, and likewise the people of the Fire." And with this chain, it is narrated from the Prophet (s.a.w) that he said: "There are upon them crowns, the least of its pearls would illuminate what is between the East and the West."[581]

Grade : Da'if (Darussalam)
English reference: Vol. 4, Book 12, Hadith 2562
Arabic reference: Book 38, Hadith 2760[582]

It was narrated from Abu Umamah that the Messenger of Allah said:
"There is no one whom Allah will admit to Paradise but Allah will marry him to seventy-two wives, two from houris and seventy from his inheritance from the people of Hell, all of whom will have desirable front passages and he will have a male member that never becomes flaccid (i.e., soft and limp).'"[583]

Grade : Da'if (Darussalam)
English reference: Vol. 5, Book 37, Hadith 4337
Arabic reference: Book 37, Hadith 4481[584]

This is part of the reason I doubt Islam can ever be reformed. How do you even pursue a serious conversation about this? What reform is possible with such ideas? It is key to note that these are blatantly sexist beliefs about women's bodies that are followed by unquestioned obedience to the Abrahamic God. Everyone in the world is safer when we can freely denigrate such ridiculous views without the threat of violence from Islamic groups and the drowning out of controversial statements for questioning the supposed sacredness of religious beliefs through censorship campaigns like claiming criticism is Islamophobia.

Fear of Satan

---

[581] "Hadith - Chapters on the Description of Paradise - Jami` at-Tirmidhi - Sunnah.com - Sayings and Teachings of Prophet Muhammad (صلى الله عليه و سلم)." *Riyad as-Salihin - Sunnah.com - Sayings and Teachings of Prophet Muhammad (□□□ □ □□□□ □□□□ □□□)*, www.sunnah.com/urn/678680.
[582] "Hadith - Chapters on the Description of Paradise - Jami` at-Tirmidhi - Sunnah.com - Sayings and Teachings of Prophet Muhammad (صلى الله عليه و سلم)." *Riyad as-Salihin - Sunnah.com - Sayings and Teachings of Prophet Muhammad (□□□ □ □□□□ □□□□ □□□)*, www.sunnah.com/urn/678680.
[583] "Hadith - Zuhd - Sunan Ibn Majah - Sunnah.com - Sayings and Teachings of Prophet Muhammad (صلى الله عليه و سلم)." *Sahih Muslim - Sunnah.com - Sayings and Teachings of Prophet Muhammad (□□□□ □□□ □□□ □ □□□□)*, sunnah.com/urn/1294400.
[584] "Hadith - Zuhd - Sunan Ibn Majah - Sunnah.com - Sayings and Teachings of Prophet Muhammad (صلى الله عليه و سلم)." *Sahih Muslim - Sunnah.com - Sayings and Teachings of Prophet Muhammad (□□□□ □□□ □□□ □ □□□□)*, sunnah.com/urn/1294400.

This specific list was compiled and shared in a humorous video criticizing Islam by the Turkish Ex-Muslim activist Ridvan Aydemir.[585] I've only edited it slightly and cannot claim any credit on its compilation. Ridvan Aydemir left Islam many years ago while keeping silent about it in Turkey and moved to the United States where he produces video content criticizing Islam based upon Islamic sources from its own sacred books. He uses the pseudonym "Apostate Prophet" on Youtube and produces videos criticizing Islam to warn people of the dangers of Islam. He doesn't share in the disdain for all religions as some other Ex-Muslim activists do and argues in defense of other religions like Christianity, Judaism, Hinduism, Sikhism, and Buddhism as being inherently peaceful religions that don't need to be criticized. He argues that Liberals are largely naive about the dangers of Islam and they need to be more critical of it in defense of their values whether in the democratic countries of the West or in other democratic countries like India. He shares his criticisms freely on Youtube and encourages people to share and become more informed about the dangers of the Islamic faith.[586] He is an incredible inspiration and holds an amazing wealth of knowledge about Islam. I would be remiss if I didn't acknowledge his important contributions to the dialogue of criticizing Islam and I highly encourage everyone to give his videos on Youtube a chance.[587] In my original book, *Faith in Doubt*, I added several more points of contention to my critiques thanks to his wealth of knowledge from his video content on Youtube.[588] Ex-Muslims like him live in fear of being killed for wanting the freedom to think for themselves. They are continually having their voices shut down by social media companies in deference to Islamic despots, their voices are being shut down by Liberals who ignore their human rights by claiming the Free Speech rights of Ex-Muslims to criticize Islam for wanting them to be killed is offensive to Muslims, and as such Ex-Muslims have every right to be angry at Liberals who ignore the plight of their human rights in favor of the meaningless and idealistic view of tolerance.[589] As of now, the current identity politics of many Liberal voices that argue this erroneous notion that nobody can understand or empathize with the experiences of specific groups without being part of that group is not only damaging, but actively dangerous for the human rights of Ex-Muslims. As such, I am endeavoring to promote their Free Speech and human rights as much as I can, even if I don't agree with the more bigoted ones. I sincerely apologize to Ridvan Aydemir and any other Ex-Muslim, if it seems as if my support is misconstruing or somehow harming their

---

[585] Aydemir, Ridvan. "All The Things That Satan Does (Ridiculous Islamic Teachings)." *YouTube*, Apostate Prophet, 28 Dec. 2018, www.youtube.com/watch?v=Ko2lttV8i2M&feature=youtu.be.
[586] Aydemir, Ridvan. *YouTube*, Apostate Prophet, www.youtube.com/channel/UCzREuchzOqiawpEpvEM0Tyg/videos.
[587] Aydemir, Ridvan. "All The Things That Satan Does (Ridiculous Islamic Teachings)." *YouTube*, Apostate Prophet, 28 Dec. 2018, www.youtube.com/watch?v=Ko2lttV8i2M&feature=youtu.be.
[588] Aydemir, Ridvan. *YouTube*, Apostate Prophet, www.youtube.com/channel/UCzREuchzOqiawpEpvEM0Tyg/videos.
[589] Aydemir, Ridvan. "Cowards in Control." *YouTube*, Apostate Prophet, 25 May 2019, www.youtube.com/watch?v=3Q5ZKANKaMQ.

cause in some unintentional manner. I have credited their contributions as much as I can and don't wish to claim their hard work as my own. I simply wish to make it clear that their human rights and Free Speech need to be protected and that religious tolerance can endanger their lives.

Islam serves as an example of how ridiculous and idiotic the belief and fear of Satan is. It is not only paranoia, but the conspiratorial nature of faith-based thinking that is demonstrated with this irrational fear and lack of evidence-based critical thinking skills. The following aims to show copious amounts of evidence of that. It was also written in a more jovial manner with the defense of Free Speech and especially the freedom to offend as the motivation.

Evidently, the Abrahamic God enjoys when Muslims sneeze and hates when Muslims yawn, because yawns are caused by Satan. Satan apparently laughs at Muslims who yawn:

Collection
Sahih Bukhari

Dar-us-Salam reference
Hadith 6223

In-book reference
Book 78, Hadith 247

USC-MSA web (English) reference
Volume 8, Book 73, Hadith 242

Narrated Abu Huraira:

The Prophet (ﷺ) said, "Allah likes sneezing and dislikes yawning, so if someone sneezes and then praises Allah, then it is obligatory on every Muslim who heard him, to say: May Allah be merciful to you (Yar-hamuka-l-lah). But as regards yawning, it is from Satan, so one must try one's best to stop it, if one says 'Ha' when yawning, Satan will laugh at him."[590]

Good dreams are apparently from the Abrahamic God and bad dreams are from Satan, the Prophet Mohammad instructed Muslims that they should spit three times over their left shoulder and seek the way of Islam's version of the Abrahamic God so that Satan's dream won't harm Muslims:

Sahih al-Bukhari Book 87 Hadith 124

Narrated Abu Qatada:

The Prophet said, "A good dream is from Allah, and a bad dream is from Satan. So whoever has seen (in a dream) something he dislike, then he should spit without saliva, thrice on his left and

---

[590] "QuranX.com The Most Complete Quran / Hadith / Tafsir Collection Available!" *Sahih Bukhari Hadiths*, quranx.com/Hadith/Bukhari/USC-MSA/Volume-8/Book-73/Hadith-242/.

seek refuge with Allah from Satan, for it will not harm him, and Satan cannot appear in my shape."591,592

The pedophile Prophet of Islam was so wise and so far ahead of his time that he warned us all that bells are the musical instrument of Satan. Truly, criticizing such astonishing wisdom is deeply offensive to Muslim sensibilities for good reason:

37 The Book of Clothes and Adornment
(27) Chapter: It Is Disliked To Take Dogs And Bells On A Journey

Abu Huraira reported Allah's Messenger (ﷺ) as saying:
The bell is the musical instrument of the Satan.593

In his Abrahamic God-given wisdom, the pedophile Prophet of Islam explained that babies cry when they're born because Satan touches them:

Sahih al-Bukhari Book 55 Hadith 641

Narrated Said bin Al-Musaiyab:

Abu Huraira said, "I heard Allah's Apostle saying, 'There is none born among the off-spring of Adam, but Satan touches it. A child therefore, cries loudly at the time of birth because of the touch of Satan, except Mary and her child." Then Abu Huraira recited: "And I seek refuge with You for her and for her offspring from the outcast Satan" (3.36)594,595

According to the pedophile prophet of Islam, the crowing of roosters is a sign that roosters have seen an angel and the braying of donkeys is a sign that donkeys have seen Satan:

Collection
Sahih Bukhari

Dar-us-Salam reference
Hadith 3303

---

[591] "Sahih Al-Bukhari Book Number 87 Hadith Number 124." *Muflihun*, muflihun.com/bukhari/87/124.

[592] al-Bukhārī, Abū ʿAbd Allāh Muḥammad ibn Ismāʿīl ibn Ibrāhīm al-Juʿfī. "Sahih Bukhari Volume 9, Book 87, Hadith Number 124." Translated by Muhammad Muhsin Khan, Hadith Collection, Hadith Collection, 6 June 2009, hadithcollection.com/sahihbukhari/sahih-bukhari-book-87-interpretation-of-dreams/sahih-bukhari-volume-009-book-087-hadith-number-124.

[593] *Hadith - The Book of Clothes and Adornment - Sahih Muslim - Sunnah.com - Sayings and Teachings of Prophet Muhammad (□□□ □ □□□□ □□□□ □□□)*, sunnah.com/muslim/37/159.

[594] "Sahih Al-Bukhari Book Number 55 Hadith Number 641." *Muflihun*, muflihun.com/bukhari/55/641.

[595] al-Bukhārī, Abū ʿAbd Allāh Muḥammad ibn Ismāʿīl ibn Ibrāhīm al-Juʿfī. "Sahih Bukhari Volume 4, Book 55, Hadith Number 641." Translated by Muhammad Muhsin Khan, Hadith Collection, Hadith Collection, 26 Apr. 2009, hadithcollection.com/sahihbukhari/sahih-bukhari-book-55-prophets/sahih-bukhari-volume-004-book-055-hadith-number-641.

In-book reference
Book 59, Hadith 111

USC-MSA web (English) reference
Volume 4, Book 54, Hadith 522

Narrated Abu Huraira:

The Prophet (ﷺ) said, "When you hear the crowing of cocks, ask for Allah's Blessings for (their crowing indicates that) they have seen an angel. And when you hear the braying of donkeys, seek Refuge with Allah from Satan for (their braying indicates) that they have seen a Satan."[596]

In accordance with the wise words of the illiterate and pedophilic Prophet of Islam, you should eat food you dropped from the ground because otherwise Satan will eat it and be sure to lick your fingers so the food is more likely to bless you:

Collection
Sahih Muslim

In-book reference
Book 36, Hadith 177

Reference
Hadith 2033d

USC-MSA web (English) reference
Book 23, Hadith 5046

Jabir reported:

I heard Allah's Apostle (ﷺ) as saying: The Satan is present with any one of you in everything he does; he is present even when he eats food; so if any one of you drops a mouthful he should remove away anything filthy on it and eat it and not leave for the devil; and when he finishes (food) he should lick his fingers, for he does not know in what portion of his food the blessing lies.[597]

For those of you who may be adamant to argue that I am creating a strawman of Islam or that I am unfairly implying that Muslims are somehow intellectually inferior to the practitioners of all other religions on average, I want it to be clear that I am mocking Islam as a belief system. The reason it is so illogical is precisely because it is a faith-based system that orients itself towards enforcing Divine Command Theory upon real life. Divine Command Theory is often opposed because it is authoritarian, but that shouldn't obscure its other crucial issue. Divine Command Theory is fundamentally irrational and creates so many silly suppositions and practices that cause needless mental

---

[596] "QuranX.com The Most Complete Quran / Hadith / Tafsir Collection Available!" *Sahih Bukhari Hadiths*, quranx.com/Hadith/Bukhari/USC-MSA/Volume-4-Book-54/Hadith-522/.
[597] "QuranX.com The Most Complete Quran / Hadith / Tafsir Collection Available!" *Sahih Muslim Hadiths*, quranx.com/Hadith/Muslim/USC-MSA/Book-23/Hadith-5046/.

consternation, contempt, self-loathing, and can lead to horrific outcomes. As much as you may find this mockery offensive, I would argue to allow a set of idiotic practices without any criticism is even more offensive, especially when it can and does lead to human rights crimes. The first Hadith is a chain of narration, the second portion below it is an explanation by an "Islamic Scholar" and the sheer idiocy of what you're about to read should speak for itself. However, for the select few that may find this portion to be a facile criticism, it should be noted that the dexterity of your hands is developed in the womb from the development of your spine.[598] Therefore, what the Islamic Prophet Mohammad asked of some of his followers on what could be argued to be an innocuous demand wasn't possible because of how their motor cortex from their brains was transmitting electrical impulses with the spine.[599] Notwithstanding, the pedophile Prophet Mohammad's ignorance and the stupidity of the hadiths chain of narration system as shown below:

Collection
Muwatta Malik

Arabic reference
Book 49, Hadith 1679

USC-MSA web (English) reference
Book 49, Hadith 6

Yahya related to me from Malik from Ibn Shihab from Abu Bakr ibn Ubaydullah ibn Abdullah ibn Umar from Abdullah ibn Umar that the Messenger of Allah, may Allah bless him and grant him peace, said, "When you eat, eat with your right hand and drink with your right hand. Shaytan eats with his left hand and drinks with his left hand."[600]

The reason why the right hand is preferred over the left

Publication : 02-03-2007
Views : 182985
Question
Why is the right hand preferred over the left hand when greeting, eating and in other cases? What is wrong with using the left hand for these purposes?.

Answer
Praise be to Allaah.

It is part of Allaah's complete blessing upon us and the perfection of this great religion, that Islam organizes all aspects of our lives. There is nothing good but it has shown it to us, and there is nothing bad but it has warned us against it. As well as beliefs, acts of worship, interactions with

---

[598] Andrews, Robin. "We Finally Know Why People Are Left- Or Right-Handed." *IFLScience*, IFLScience, 23 Jan. 2019, www.iflscience.com/brain/finally-know-people-left-righthanded/.
[599] Andrews, Robin. "We Finally Know Why People Are Left- Or Right-Handed." *IFLScience*, IFLScience, 23 Jan. 2019, www.iflscience.com/brain/finally-know-people-left-righthanded/.
[600] "QuranX.com The Most Complete Quran / Hadith / Tafsir Collection Available!" *Muwatta Malik Hadiths*, quranx.com/Hadith/Malik/USC-MSA/Book-49/Hadith-6/.

others and morals and manners, that also includes our private affairs in which Islam shows us the way that is befitting to man's noble status and the way in which Allaah has honoured him. That includes the way the Muslim eats and drinks, and so on.

This is an established principle in sharee'ah: that which has to do with honour and nobility, such as putting on one's garment and pants and shoes, entering the mosque, using the siwaak, putting on kohl, clipping the nails, trimming the moustache, combing the hair, plucking the armpit hair, shaving the head, saying salaam at the end of prayer, washing the limbs when purifying oneself, exiting the toilet, eating and drinking, shaking hands, touching the Black Stone, etc are all things which it is mustahabb to start on the right or use the right hand. As for things which are the opposite, such as entering the toilet, exiting the mosque, blowing one's nose, cleaning oneself after using the toilet, taking off one's garment, pants and shoes, and so on, it is mustahabb to start on the left or use the left hand. All of that is because the right hand is more noble and honoured. This was stated by al-Nawawi in Sharh Saheeh Muslim. There is a great deal of evidence to support this principle, such as the following:

In al-Saheehayn it is narrated that 'Umar ibn Salamah (may Allaah be pleased with him) said: The Messenger of Allaah (peace and blessings of Allaah be upon him) said: "O young boy, say the name of Allaah and eat with your right hand, and eat from what is nearest to you." Narrated by al-Bukhaari (5376) and Muslim (2022).

In Saheeh Muslim (2021) it is narrated that a man ate with his left hand in the presence of the Messenger of Allaah (S). He said: "Eat with your right hand." He said: I cannot. He said: "May you never be able to," for nothing was preventing him from doing so but arrogance. And he never raised it to his mouth again.

The Prophet (peace and blessings of Allaah be upon him) prayed against him so that what he claimed of not being able to do it would come true, because he was too arrogant to follow the truth and he did not observe proper etiquette with the Prophet (peace and blessings of Allaah be upon him), and his excuse was a lie, and lying to the Prophet (peace and blessings of Allaah be upon him) is not like lying to anyone else.

In Sunan Abi Dawood (33) it is narrated that 'Aa'ishah (may Allaah be pleased with her) said: The right hand of the Messenger of Allaah (peace and blessings of Allaah be upon him) was for his purification and food, and his left hand was for using the toilet and anything that was dirty. Classed as saheeh by al-Albaani in Saheeh Abi Dawood.

Muslim (262) narrated that Salmaan (may Allaah be pleased with him) said: He (meaning the Prophet (peace and blessings of Allaah be upon him)) forbade any one of us to clean himself with his right hand.

And Muslim (2020) narrated from Ibn 'Umar (may Allaah be pleased with him) that the Messenger of Allaah (peace and blessings of Allaah be upon him) said: "No one among you should eat with his left hand or drink with it, for the shaytaan eats with his left hand and drinks with it."

Allaah has warned us against disobeying the commands of the Messenger of Allaah (peace and blessings of Allaah be upon him), as He says (interpretation of the meaning):

"And let those who oppose the Messenger's (Muhammad's) commandment (i.e. his Sunnah __ legal ways, orders, acts of worship, statements) (among the sects) beware, lest some Fitnah (disbelief, trials, afflictions, earthquakes, killing, overpowered by a tyrant) should befall them or a painful torment be inflicted on them"

[al-Noor 24:63]

This applies if one is able to eat with the right hand. But if one is unable to do so, there is no sin in that. Al-Nawawi said in Sharh Muslim (13/191): The objection to eating and drinking with the left hand applies so long as there is no excuse. If there is an excuse which prevents one from eating and drinking with the right hand because of sickness, injury etc, then it is not makrooh. End quote.

Al-Ghazaali said in al-Ihya' (4/93): Then the One Who gave you two hands to do things with, some of which are noble, such as picking up the Mus-haf, and some are ignoble, such as removing impurities. So if you pick up the Mus-haf with your left hand, and you remove impurities with your right hand, then you have used that which is noble to do something ignoble, and you have neglected its rights and wronged it, and turned away from what is proper. End quote.

To sum up what the scholars have said about the reasons why the right hand is preferred for things that are noble:

1-That is differing from the shaytaan, as in the case of eating and drinking.

2-It is honouring the right hand over the left.

3-It is using proper etiquette with people, so that one does not shake hands with them, take things from them or give things to them with the hand with which one removes impurities.

4-It is a sign of hope that Allaah will make us among those who are on the right hand (ahl al-yameen).

And Allaah knows best.[601]

Satan apparently steals your food and when you catch him stealing your food, he'll teach you some crazy nonsense to recite so that the Abrahamic God will appoint someone to guard you from Satan and also Satan apparently stole food at night. Additionally, according to the pedophile Prophet Mohammad himself, Satan told the truth and is also an absolute liar:

Sahih al-Bukhari Book 38 Hadith 505

Narrated Abu Huraira:

Allah's Apostle deputed me to keep Sadaqat (al-Fitr) of Ramadan. A comer came and started taking handfuls of the foodstuff (of the Sadaqa) (stealthily). I took hold of him and said, "By Allah, I will take you to Allah's Apostle ." He said, "I am needy and have many dependents, and I am in great need." I released him, and in the morning Allah's Apostle asked me, "What did your prisoner do yesterday?" I said, "O Allah's Apostle! The person complained of being needy and of having many dependents, so, I pitied him and let him go." Allah's Apostle said, "Indeed, he told you a lie and he will be coming again." I believed that he would show up again as Allah's Apostle had told me that he would return. So, I waited for him watchfully. When he (showed up and) started stealing handfuls of foodstuff, I caught hold of him again and said, "I will definitely take you to Allah's Apostle. He said, "Leave me, for I am very needy and have many dependents. I promise I will not come back again." I pitied him and let him go. In the morning Allah's Apostle

---

[601] "The Reason Why the Right Hand Is Preferred over the Left - Islam Question & Answer." *Islamqa.info*, Islam Question and Answer, 2 Mar. 2007, islamqa.info/en/answers/82120/the-reason-why-the-right-hand-is-preferred-over-the-left.

asked me, "What did your prisoner do." I replied, "O Allah's Apostle! He complained of his great need and of too many dependents, so I took pity on him and set him free." Allah's Apostle said, "Verily, he told you a lie and he will return." I waited for him attentively for the third time, and when he (came and) started stealing handfuls of the foodstuff, I caught hold of him and said, "I will surely take you to Allah's Apostle as it is the third time you promise not to return, yet you break your promise and come." He said, "(Forgive me and) I will teach you some words with which Allah will benefit you." I asked, "What are they?" He replied, "Whenever you go to bed, recite "Ayat-al-Kursi"-- 'Allahu la ilaha illa huwa-l-Haiy-ul Qaiyum' till you finish the whole verse. (If you do so), Allah will appoint a guard for you who will stay with you and no satan will come near you till morning. " So, I released him. In the morning, Allah's Apostle asked, "What did your prisoner do yesterday?" I replied, "He claimed that he would teach me some words by which Allah will benefit me, so I let him go." Allah's Apostle asked, "What are they?" I replied, "He said to me, 'Whenever you go to bed, recite Ayat-al-Kursi from the beginning to the end ---- Allahu la ilaha illa huwa-lHaiy-ul-Qaiyum----.' He further said to me, '(If you do so), Allah will appoint a guard for you who will stay with you, and no satan will come near you till morning.' (Abu Huraira or another sub-narrator) added that they (the companions) were very keen to do good deeds. The Prophet said, "He really spoke the truth, although he is an absolute liar. Do you know whom you were talking to, these three nights, O Abu Huraira?" Abu Huraira said, "No." He said, "It was Satan."[602]

Satan's time of leisure is spending every night tying your hair into knots before untying them while you are asleep. Truly, the pedophile Prophet of Islam was a visionary of the unique variety:

Collection
Sahih Bukhari

Dar-us-Salam reference
Hadith 3269

In-book reference
Book 59, Hadith 79

USC-MSA web (English) reference
Volume 4, Book 54, Hadith 491

Narrated Abu Huraira:
Allah's Messenger (ﷺ) said, "During your sleep, Satan knots three knots at the back of the head of each of you, and he breathes the following words at each knot, 'The night is, long, so keep on sleeping,' If that person wakes up and celebrates the praises of Allah, then one knot is undone, and when he performs ablution the second knot is undone, and when he prays, all the knots are undone, and he gets up in the morning lively and in good spirits, otherwise he gets up in low spirits and lethargic."[603]

---

[602] "Sahih Al-Bukhari Book Number 38 Hadith Number 505." *Muflihun*, https://web.archive.org/web/20210208235810/muflihun.com/bukhari/38/505.
[603] "QuranX.com The Most Complete Quran / Hadith / Tafsir Collection Available!" *Sahih Bukhari Hadiths*, quranx.com/Hadith/Bukhari/USC-MSA/Volume-4/Book-54/Hadith-491/.

According to the wisdom of Prophet Mohammad, Satan apparently urinates in people's ears while they're asleep:

Collection
Sahih Bukhari

Dar-us-Salam reference
Hadith 1144

In-book reference
Book 19, Hadith 25

USC-MSA web (English) reference
Volume 2, Book 21, Hadith 245

Narrated `Abdullah:
A person was mentioned before the Prophet (p.b.u.h) and he was told that he had kept on sleeping till morning and had not got up for the prayer. The Prophet (ﷺ) said, "Satan urinated in his ears."[604]

When Satan isn't doing any of that, beware that Satan could be hiding in your nose according to the pedophile Prophet Mohammad himself:

Collection
Sahih Muslim

In-book reference
Book 2, Hadith 31

Reference
Hadith 238

USC-MSA web (English) reference
Book 2, Hadith 462

Abu Huraira reported:
The Apostle of Allah (ﷺ) said. When any one of you awakes up from sleep and performs ablution, he must clean his nose three times, for the devil spends the night in the interior of his nose.[605]

Men should pray to the Abrahamic God while having sexual intercourse with their wives otherwise Satan will harm the child that is conceived from their sexual relations. It is also implied that Satan watches Muslims while they have sex in this hadith:

Collection
Sahih Bukhari

---

[604] "QuranX.com The Most Complete Quran / Hadith / Tafsir Collection Available!" *Sahih Bukhari Hadiths*, quranx.com/Hadith/Bukhari/USC-MSA/Volume-2/Book-21/Hadith-245/.

[605] "QuranX.com The Most Complete Quran / Hadith / Tafsir Collection Available!" *Sahih Muslim Hadiths*, quranx.com/Hadith/Muslim/USC-MSA/Book-2/Hadith-462/.

Dar-us-Salam reference
Hadith 3271

In-book reference
Book 59, Hadith 81

USC-MSA web (English) reference
Volume 4, Book 54, Hadith 493

Narrated Ibn `Abbas:
The Prophet (ﷺ) said, "If anyone of you, when having sexual relation with his wife, say: 'In the name of Allah. O Allah! Protect us from Satan and prevent Satan from approaching our offspring you are going to give us,' and if he begets a child (as a result of that relation) Satan will not harm it."[606]

Satan comes in the shape of a woman and so Muslim men should go to their wives immediately to have sexual relations with them in order to relieve their sexual urges to avoid being tempted by Satan:

Collection
Sahih Muslim

In-book reference
Book 16, Hadith 10

Reference
Hadith 1403a

USC-MSA web (English) reference
Book 8, Hadith 3240

Jabir reported that Allah's Messenger (ﷺ) saw a woman, and so he came to his wife, Zainab, as she was tanning a leather and had sexual intercourse with her. He then went to his Companions and told them:
The woman advances and retires in the shape of a devil, so when one of you sees a woman, he should come to his wife, for that will repel what he feels in his heart.[607]

Satan intensifies the pain of menstrual bleeding according to the pedophile Prophet Mohammad:

1 The Book of Purification
(10) Chapter: Menstruation

---

[606] "QuranX.com The Most Complete Quran / Hadith / Tafsir Collection Available!" *Sahih Bukhari Hadiths*, quranx.com/Hadith/Bukhari/USC-MSA/Volume-4/Book-54/Hadith-493/.
[607] "QuranX.com The Most Complete Quran / Hadith / Tafsir Collection Available!" *Sahih Muslim Hadiths*, quranx.com/Hadith/Muslim/USC-MSA/Book-8/Hadith-3240/.

Narrated Hamnah bint Jahsh:
'I had a very strong prolonged flow of blood. I went to the Prophet (Peace be upon him) to ask him about it. He said, "This is a strike from Satan. So observe your menses for six or seven days, then perform Ghusl until you see that you are clean. Pray for twenty-four or twenty-three nights and days and fast, and that will suffice you. Do so every month just as the other women menstruate (and are purified). But if you are strong enough to delay the Dhuhr prayer and advance the Asr prayer, then make Ghusl when your purified and combine the Dhuhr and the Asr prayers together; then delay the Maghrib prayer and advance the Isha prayer, and perform Ghusl and combine the two prayers, do so. Do so, and then wash at dawn and pray Fajr. This is how you may pray and fast if you have the ability to do so." And he said, "That is the more preferable way to me." [Reported by the five imams except An- Nasa'i, At-Tirmidhi graded it Sahih (sound)][608]

Muslims must sit close together in prayer to avoid Satan entering through an opening during prayer. He watches and roams about Muslims while they pray:

Anas (May Allah be pleased with him) reported:
The Messenger of Allah (ﷺ) said, "Stand close together in your rows, keep nearer to one another, and put your necks in line, for by Him in Whose Hands my soul is, I see the Satan entering through the opening in the row like Al- hadhaf (i.e., a type of small black sheep found in Yemen)."
[Abu Dawud].[609]

The pedophile prophet Mohammad sought refuge from Satan's poetry in a prayer to the Abrahamic God, so apparently poetry itself is from Satan:

It was narrated from Ibn Jubair bin Mut'im that his father said:
"I saw the Messenger of Allah (ﷺ) when he started the prayer. He said: 'Allahu Akbaru kabiran, Allahu Akbaru kabiran (Allah is the Most Great indeed),' three times; 'Al-hamdu Lillahi kathiran, al-hamdu Lillahi kathiran (Much praise is to Allah),' three times; 'Subhan Allahi bukratan wa asilan (Glory is to Allah morning and evening),' three times; 'Allahumma inni a'udhu bika minash-Shaitanir-rajim, min hamzihi wa nafkhihi wa nafthihi (O Allah, I seek refuge in You from the accursed Satan, from his madness, his poetry, and his pride)."[610]

The depressing and infuriating results of this Islamic belief structure and how it attempted to thoroughly erase Iranian poetry during Arab Muslim colonization, from Paul Sprachman's English translation of Iranian Scholar of Persian history and literature, Abdolhossein Zarrinkoub's *Chapter 4: The Lost Language* of *Two Centuries of Silence: An Account of Events and Conditions in Iran [Persia] during the first Two Hundred Years of Islam* which reads as follows:

The Silence Begins

---

[608] *Hadith - The Book of Purification - Bulugh Al-Maram - Sunnah.com - Sayings and Teachings of Prophet Muhammad (☐☐☐ ☐ ☐☐☐☐ ☐☐☐☐ ☐☐☐)*, sunnah.com/bulugh/1/169.
[609] *Hadith - The Book of Virtues - Riyad as-Salihin - Sunnah.com - Sayings and Teachings of Prophet Muhammad (☐☐☐ ☐ ☐☐☐☐ ☐☐☐☐ ☐☐☐)*, sunnah.com/riyadussaliheen/9/102.
[610] *Hadith - Establishing the Prayer and the Sunnah Regarding Them - Sunan Ibn Majah - Sunnah.com - Sayings and Teachings of Prophet Muhammad (☐☐☐ ☐ ☐☐☐☐ ☐☐☐☐ ☐☐☐)*, sunnah.com/urn/1281560.

Scholars will hunt in vain for Persian poetry written during the savage, blood-tinged silence and dark that loomed over Iran for nearly two centuries. This is because the climate in those days was not conducive to nurturing Persian poets. In the understanding of Arabs of that period, poetry meant long odes praising or condemning their own prominent men or another type called rajaz, shorter pieces imbued with bravado and a combative heroism. It goes without saying, given the tenor of the times, these two types of poetry had no chance of surfacing in Persian. This was an age when the Arabs had vanquished the Iranian people, leaving them with no recourse but death, defeat, or flight; there was then nothing heroic to sing about. Also during such times, with Arabs ruling over the cities and with the caliph sitting in Syria or Baghdad, there was no one to praise the caliph or his agents in Persian. Religious and moral themes were also not common in the poetry of those days, and Iranians, even if they had thoughts along those lines, saw no profit in expressing them in Persian. Non-Muslim Iranians also hardly had the opportunity or the leisure to indulge this type of writing. Lyrical poetry in praise of wine and women could have existed; but as it was the bane of Muslim dignity and piety, Arabs would not shut their eyes to it. Nevertheless, if the heretics and freethinkers of the time had cultivated this poetry, it never went beyond closed tribal circles and never resonated more widely. Perhaps this in itself was the reason that if there had been something like erotic poetry in Persian and even in Arabic, it did not last long and died. Even lampoons and laments, which are basic to poetry, had no chance of seeing the light of day. During those times, every protest, every complaint, from the mouths of an Iranian was brutally stifled. The caliphs regularly tormented and tortured poets and others who composed works in Arabic about the past glory of Iran and their own [pre-Islamic] ancestries.7

The Cry of the Silenced

If things were said along those lines, they did not endure, and like other traces of the Shucūbiyya [pro-Persian] movement have disappeared. And if a protest or a complaint did arise, it did not circulate widely and faded over the centuries. Objecting to the injustices and miseries the Arabs visited on people in the cities and towns, was impossible. Any person who raised his voice to object to Arab tyranny was labeled a heretic and a fire worshipper, and his blood became fair game. The swords of the holy warriors and the whips of the rulers silenced any form of protest.

If a voice were raised at all, it was in the plaintive but faint lament of a poet weeping over the ruins of his city and homeland—as in a poem by Abū al-Yanbaghī, the ill-fated son of an emir who expressed his sense of grief and grievance this way:

> *O Samarkand, who has reduced you to ruins?*
> *You are better than Chāch [Tashkent], always better, bravo!8*

Or it was the cry of a Zoroastrian who under torture wished the hand of the Almighty would emerge from its invisible sleeve to free his beloved Iran from the Arabs' clutches. While waiting for the invisible to become visible, he sang in Pahlavi:

> *When will a messenger come from India*
> *Saying that Shah Bahrām of Kayāni descent*
> *Has a thousand elephants each with a keeper mounted on its head?*
> *Who bears the royal standard on display*
> *Before the army? To the army generals*
> *A man must be sent, a skilled interpreter*
> *Who will come and say to the Hindus*
> *What we have suffered from the desert of the Arabs,*
> *With a small band they spread their faith, and gone*
> *Is our king of kings, gone because of them.*
> *They worship like demons, they eat like dogs;*
> *They have taken the monarchy from the Khosrow kings*
> *Not with art nor with valor, but with disdain and mockery.*
> *From men they have cruelly taken*

Wives and possessions, gardens and orchards.
They imposed a tax on every head.
Despite our special garments they demand Protection money.
Look at the evil they have cast upon the world,
For there is nothing worse on earth.9[611]

Satan is responsible for making people forget things:

(27) Chapter: The story of Al-Khidr with Musa (Moses) alayhis-salam
Narrated Ibn `Abbas:
That he differed with Al-Hur bin Qais Al-Fazari regarding the companion of Moses. Ibn `Abbas said that he was Al-Khadir. Meanwhile Ubai bin Ka`b passed by them and Ibn `Abbas called him saying, "My friend and I have differed regarding Moses' companion whom Moses asked the way to meet. Have you heard Allah's Messenger (ﷺ) mentioning something about him?" He said, "Yes, I heard Allah's Apostle saying, 'While Moses was sitting in the company of some Israelites, a man came and asked (him), 'Do you know anyone who is more learned than you?' Moses replied, 'No.' So, Allah sent the Divine Inspiration to Moses: 'Yes, Our slave, Khadir (is more learned than you).' Moses asked how to meet him (i.e. Khadir). So, the fish, was made, as a sign for him, and he was told that when the fish was lost, he should return and there he would meet him. So, Moses went on looking for the sign of the fish in the sea. The servant boy of Moses said to him, 'Do you know that when we were sitting by the side of the rock, I forgot the fish, and t was only Satan who made me forget to tell (you) about it.' Moses said, That was what we were seeking after,' and both of them returned, following their footmarks and found Khadir; and what happened further to them, is mentioned in Allah's Book."[612]

Not only does he make you forget, he'll make you forget how long you pray and he'll fart when you're praying:

Sahih al-Bukhari Book 11 Hadith 582

Narrated Abu Huraira:

Allah's Apostle said, "When the Adhan is pronounced Satan takes to his heels and passes wind with noise during his flight in order not to hear the Adhan. When the Adhan is completed he comes back and again takes to his heels when the Iqama is pronounced and after its completion he returns again till he whispers into the heart of the person (to divert his attention from his prayer) and makes him remember things which he does not recall to his mind before the prayer and that causes him to forget how much he has prayed."[613]

---

[611] Zarrinkoub, Abdolhossein. Chapter 4: The Lost Language (Location 1833 – 1878). Two Centuries of Silence: An Account of Events and Conditions in Iran [Persia] During the First Two Hundred Years of Islam, from the Arab Invasion to the Rise of the Tahirid Dynasty First edition. Mazda Publishers. Kindle Edition.

[612] *Hadith - Book of Prophets - Sahih Al-Bukhari - Sunnah.com - Sayings and Teachings of Prophet Muhammad (□□□ □ □□□□ □□□□ □□□)*, sunnah.com/bukhari/60/73.

[613] "Sahih Al-Bukhari Book Number 11 Hadith Number 582." *Muflihun*, https://web.archive.org/web/20200920140329/muflihun.com/bukhari/11/582.

But worst of all, Satan might try to influence you to question religious assumptions and to think for yourself instead of being blindly dependent upon the Abrahamic God to do your thinking for you as per the pedophile Prophet Mohammad's instructions:

Sahih Muslim Book 1 Hadith 244

It is narrated on the authority of Abu Huraira that the Messenger of Allah may peace be upon him) observed: The Satan comes to everyone. of you and says: Who created this and that? till he questions: Who created your Lord? When he comes to that, one should seek refuge in Allah and keep away (from such idle thoughts).[614][615]

1 The Book of Faith

(60) Chapter: Clarifying the Waswasah (Whispers, Bad Thoughts) with regard to faith, and what the one who experiences that should say

This hadith is transmitted by Urwa b. Zubair on the authority of Abu Huraira (and the words are):
The Satan comes to the bondsman (of Allah) and says: Who created this and that? The remaining part of the hadith is the same.[616]

The Context of the Prophet Mohammad's Support for Slavery

While the fears of Satan and belief in female slaves in heaven may garner some amusement and some would argue that such beliefs are harmless, the fact remains that these are deeply held religious beliefs and they are accepted as unquestioned fact because the Islamic Prophet Mohammad taught them to Muslims. In Islam, the Prophet Mohammad is seen as the perfect human being whose example is one to live by, so that means when he took sex slaves and raped them then it is morally justified for Muslim men to kidnap women and rape them as per religious instruction.[617] When the Prophet Mohammad approves of rape, then that means Muslims have a religious right to rape their sex slaves. Most Muslim men in the West wouldn't do this because they follow secular morals and they're capable of their own reasoning faculties thanks to secular education, but this does happen in Muslim majority countries and has been spilling over to target non-Muslim women in Western countries from immigrants who originate from countries like Pakistan because either laws support rapists due to the Sharia or the more

---

[614] "Sahih Muslim Book Number 1 Hadith Number 244." *Muflihun*, muflihun.com/muslim/1/244.

[615] an-Naysābūrī, Abū al-Ḥusayn Muslim ibn al-Ḥajjāj ibn Muslim ibn Ward al-Qushayrī. "Sahih Muslim Book 1, Hadith Number 244." Translated by Abdul Hamid Siddiqi, Hadith Collection, Hadith Collection, 9 June 2009, https://hadithcollection.com/sahihmuslim/sahih-muslim-book-01-faith/sahih-muslim-book-001-hadith-number-0244.

[616] *Hadith - The Book of Faith - Sahih Muslim - Sunnah.com - Sayings and Teachings of Prophet Muhammad (☐☐☐ ☐ ☐☐☐☐ ☐☐☐☐ ☐☐☐)*, sunnah.com/muslim/1/253.

[617] "The Quranic Arabic Corpus - Word by Word Grammar, Syntax and Morphology of the Holy Quran." *The Quranic Arabic Corpus - Translation*, http://corpus.quran.com/translation.jsp?chapter=4&verse=24

secular laws just aren't followed. The majority of Muslim men from Islamic countries are apathetic to the kidnapping and rape of girls as young as nine years of age who are then forced to marry their rapists and then are told to be obedient to their rapist.[618] The rapist tells them to publicly support what was done to them through coercion or they'll suffer worse as per Islamic teachings that instruct to beat disobedient wives:[619]

Quran 4:34:

Sahih International: Men are in charge of women by [right of] what Allah has given one over the other and what they spend [for maintenance] from their wealth. So righteous women are devoutly obedient, guarding in [the husband's] absence what Allah would have them guard. But those [wives] from whom you fear arrogance - [first] advise them; [then if they persist], forsake them in bed; and [finally], strike them. But if they obey you [once more], seek no means against them. Indeed, Allah is ever Exalted and Grand.

Pickthall: Men are in charge of women, because Allah hath made the one of them to excel the other, and because they spend of their property (for the support of women). So good women are the obedient, guarding in secret that which Allah hath guarded. As for those from whom ye fear rebellion, admonish them and banish them to beds apart, and scourge them. Then if they obey you, seek not a way against them. Lo! Allah is ever High, Exalted, Great.

Yusuf Ali: Men are the protectors and maintainers of women, because Allah has given the one more (strength) than the other, and because they support them from their means. Therefore the righteous women are devoutly obedient, and guard in (the husband's) absence what Allah would have them guard. As to those women on whose part ye fear disloyalty and ill-conduct, admonish them (first), (Next), refuse to share their beds, (And last) beat them (lightly); but if they return to obedience, seek not against them Means (of annoyance): For Allah is Most High, great (above you all).

Shakir: Men are the maintainers of women because Allah has made some of them to excel others and because they spend out of their property; the good women are therefore obedient, guarding the unseen as Allah has guarded; and (as to) those on whose part you fear desertion, admonish them, and leave them alone in the sleeping-places and beat them; then if they obey you, do not seek a way against them; surely Allah is High, Great.

Muhammad Sarwar: Men are the protectors of women because of the greater preference that God has given to some of them and because they financially support them. Among virtuous women are those who are steadfast in prayer and dependable in keeping the secrets that God has protected. Admonish women who disobey (God's laws), do not sleep with them and beat them. If they obey (the laws of God), do not try to find fault in them. God is High and Supreme.

Mohsin Khan: Men are the protectors and maintainers of women, because Allah has made one of them to excel the other, and because they spend (to support them) from their means. Therefore the righteous women are devoutly obedient (to Allah and to their husbands), and guard in the husband's absence what Allah orders them to guard (e.g. their chastity, their husband's property, etc.). As to those women on whose part you see illconduct, admonish them (first), (next), refuse to share their beds, (and last) beat them (lightly, if it is useful), but if they return to obedience, seek not against them means (of annoyance). Surely, Allah is Ever Most High, Most Great.

Arberry: Men are the managers of the affairs of women for that God has preferred in bounty one of them over another, and for that they have expended of their property. Righteous women are therefore obedient, guarding the secret for God's guarding. And those you fear may be rebellious

---

[618] "Pakistani Hindus Complain of Forced Conversion of Teenage Girls." *YouTube*, VOA News, 18 Mar. 2016, youtu.be/-i24jg4mJ4I.
[619] "The Quranic Arabic Corpus - Word by Word Grammar, Syntax and Morphology of the Holy Quran." *The Quranic Arabic Corpus - Translation*, http://corpus.quran.com/translation.jsp?chapter=4&verse=34

admonish; banish them to their couches, and beat them. If they then obey you, look not for any way against them; God is All-high, All-great.[620]

The only way to end the danger of Islam is by criticizing the beliefs. I condemn all forms of anti-Muslim bigotry; most Muslims are better than Islam. I condemn Islam just as I condemn violence against Muslims. This section of the critique will focus on the subject matter of particular hadiths and may not strictly focus on numerical order. This particular set of hadiths concerning sexual slavery was shared online in various comments sections with short comments concerning each one. I was doubtful that they referred to actual hadiths until I became curious enough to search the listed hadiths for myself. To my shock and disgust, this commentator was being completely honest and there are hadiths that justify sexual slavery and thereby legitimize sexual slavery, war rape, and other horrific actions conducted by groups like ISIS and targeting children for gang rapes and sexual slavery by grooming gangs of Muslim men in the West. Muslims may be keen on arguing that the hadiths aren't "authentic" but all any Islamic organization needs is an Imam of their own saying that the hadiths are authentic to legitimize them so it is a moot point. These teachings must be recognized as harmful and criticized; they must also be recognized as coming from the Islamic faith as they are explicit instructions by the pedophile Prophet Mohammad.

The Islamic Prophet Mohammad stopped the emancipation of six slaves, kept four of the slaves for himself, and cast lots to decide which two would be freed:

Sahih Muslim Book 15 Hadith 4112

Sahih Muslim Book 15. Oath
Chapter: He who emancipates his share in the slave.

'Imran b. Husain reported that a person who had no other property emancipated six slaves of his at the time of his death. Allah's Messenger (Peace be upon him) called for them and divided them into three sections, cast lots amongst them, and set two free and kept four in slavery; and he (the Holy Prophet) spoke severely of him.[621][622]

The Prophet Mohammad sold a slave and therefore selling slaves is moral in Islam since the so-called perfect human being did it:

---

[620] "The Quranic Arabic Corpus - Word by Word Grammar, Syntax and Morphology of the Holy Quran." The Quranic Arabic Corpus - Translation, http://corpus.quran.com/translation.jsp?chapter=4&verse=34
[621] "Sahih Muslim Book Number 15 Hadith Number 4112." *Muflihun*, muflihun.com/muslim/15/4112.
[622] an-Naysābūrī, Abū al-Ḥusayn Muslim ibn al-Ḥajjāj ibn Muslim ibn Ward al-Qushayrī. "Sahih Muslim Book 15, Hadith Number 4112." Translated by Abdul Hamid Siddiqi, Hadith Collection, Hadith Collection, 1 July 2009, hadithcollection.com/sahihmuslim/sahih-muslim-book-15-oath/sahih-muslim-book-015-hadith-number-4112.

Sahih al-Bukhari Volume 3, Book 34, Hadith 351.

Sahih Bukhari Book 34. Sales and Trade

Narrated Jabir bin Abdullah:

A man decided that a slave of his would be manumitted after his death and later on he was in need of money, so the Prophet took the slave and said, "Who will buy this slave from me?" Nu'aim bin 'Abdullah bought him for such and such price and the Prophet gave him the slave.[623][624]

Manumission refers to releasing a person from slavery, please keep that in mind. This is another reference to the Islamic Prophet Mohammad cancelling the emancipation of a slave in order to sell the slave:

Sahih al-Bukhari Book 41 Hadith 598

Narrated Jabir: A man manumitted a slave and he had no other property than that, so the Prophet cancelled the manumission (and sold the slave for him). No'aim bin Al-Nahham bought the slave from him.[625][626]

The Islamic Prophet Mohammad chastised a woman for releasing her slave girl from slavery and instructed that the Muslim woman would have gained a greater reward in heaven if she had sold her slave to a maternal uncle:

Sahih al-Bukhari Book 47 Hadith 765

Narrated Kurib:

the freed slave of Ibn 'Abbas, that Maimuna bint Al-Harith told him that she manumitted a slave-girl without taking the permission of the Prophet. On the day when it was her turn to be with the Prophet, she said, "Do you know, O Allah's Apostle, that I have manumitted my slave-girl?" He said, "Have you really?" She replied in the affirmative. He said, "You would have got more reward if you had given her (i.e. the slave-girl) to one of your maternal uncles."[627][628]

---

[623] "Sahih Al-Bukhari Book Number 34 Hadith Number 351." *Muflihun*, muflihun.com/bukhari/34/351.

[624] al-Bukhārī, Abū ʿAbd Allāh Muḥammad ibn Ismāʿīl ibn Ibrāhīm al-Juʿfī. "Sahih Bukhari Volume 3, Book 34, Hadith Number 351." Translated by Muhammad Muhsin Khan, Hadith Collection, Hadith Collection, 31 Jan. 2009, hadithcollection.com/sahihbukhari/sahih-bukhari-book-34-sales-and-trade/sahih-bukhari-volume-003-book-034-hadith-number-351.

[625] "Sahih Al-Bukhari Book Number 41 Hadith Number 598." *Muflihun*, muflihun.com/bukhari/41/598.

[626] al-Bukhārī, Abū ʿAbd Allāh Muḥammad ibn Ismāʿīl ibn Ibrāhīm al-Juʿfī. "Sahih Bukhari Volume 3, Book 41, Hadith Number 598." Translated by Muhammad Muhsin Khan, Hadith Collection, Hadith Collection, 1 Feb. 2009, hadithcollection.com/sahihbukhari/sahih-bukhari-book-41-loans-payment-of-loans-freezing-of-property-bankruptcy/sahih-bukhari-volume-003-book-041-hadith-number-598.

[627] "Sahih Al-Bukhari Book Number 47 Hadith Number 765." *Muflihun*, muflihun.com/bukhari/47/765.

[628] al-Bukhārī, Abū ʿAbd Allāh Muḥammad ibn Ismāʿīl ibn Ibrāhīm al-Juʿfī. "Sahih Bukhari Volume 3, Book 47, Hadith Number 765." Translated by Muhammad Muhsin Khan, Hadith Collection, Hadith Collection, 1 Feb. 2009, hadithcollection.com/sahihbukhari/sahih-bukhari-book-47-gifts/sahih-bukhari-volume-003-book-047-hadith-number-765.

In this hadith, the Islamic Prophet Mohammad instructs that a Muslim man who takes a slave girl to teach her the ways of Islam without "violence" and then marries her gets a double-reward in heaven. Be aware that Quran verse 4:24 makes it clear that raping slave girls is permitted by the Abrahamic God and because it is in the Quran, it must be considered unquestioned fact that nobody who is a non-Muslim is allowed to criticize.[629] Upon marriage, Quran verse 4:34 makes it clear that beating a disobedient wife is allowed.[630] We see the harmful effects of these Quranic teachings from grooming gangs in the West and the targeting and rape of children in Islamic majority countries like Pakistan. Moreover, according to these hadiths, if Muslim men have done this with full faith in the teachings of the Islamic Prophet Mohammad, then they're awarded doubly so on top of that. Keeping slaves obedient to their Masters is also encouraged to be a moral act; therefore beatings, raping, and coercing women into these patriarchal norms and standards is seen as good moral behavior in the context of Islam:

Sahih al-Bukhari Book 52 Hadith 255

Narrated Abu Burda's father:

The Prophet said, "Three persons will get their reward twice. (One is) a person who has a slave girl and he educates her properly and teaches her good manners properly (without violence) and then manumits and marries her. Such a person will get a double reward. (Another is) a believer from the people of the scriptures who has been a true believer and then he believes in the Prophet (Muhammad). Such a person will get a double reward. (The third is) a slave who observes Allah's Rights and Obligations and is sincere to his master."[631][632]

Sahih Bukhari Volume 1, Book 3, Hadith Number 97A

Sahih Bukhari Book 3. Knowledge

Narated By Abu Burda's father : Allah's Apostle said "Three persons will have a double reward:

1. A Person from the people of the scriptures who believed in his prophet (Jesus or Moses) and then believed in the Prophet Muhammad (i .e. has embraced Islam).

2. A slave who discharges his duties to Allah and his master.

---

[629] "The Quranic Arabic Corpus - Word by Word Grammar, Syntax and Morphology of the Holy Quran." *The Quranic Arabic Corpus - Translation*, http://corpus.quran.com/translation.jsp?chapter=4&verse=24
[630] "The Quranic Arabic Corpus - Word by Word Grammar, Syntax and Morphology of the Holy Quran." *The Quranic Arabic Corpus - Translation*, http://corpus.quran.com/translation.jsp?chapter=4&verse=34
[631] "Sahih Al-Bukhari Book Number 52 Hadith Number 255." *Muflihun*, muflihun.com/bukhari/52/255.
[632] al-Bukhārī, Abū ʿAbd Allāh Muḥammad ibn Ismāʿīl ibn Ibrāhīm al-Juʿfī. "Sahih Bukhari Volume 4, Book 52, Hadith Number 255." Translated by Muhammad Muhsin Khan, Hadith Collection, Hadith Collection, 7 Feb. 2009, hadithcollection.com/sahihbukhari/sahih-bukhari-book-52-fighting-for-the-cause-of-allah-jihaad/sahih-bukhari-volume-004-book-052-hadith-number-255.

3. A master of a woman-slave who teaches her good manners and educates her in the best possible way (the religion) and manumits her and then marries her."[633]

If all that hasn't horrified and disgusted readers enough, here are two hadiths in which the Islamic Prophet Mohammad says not to do coitus interruptus. For those who don't know what that term means, coitus interruptus is the technical term for a man pulling out his penis before ejaculating. In these specific hadiths, Muslim men who had taken slave girl captives from conquered territories are asked by the Prophet Mohammad whether they really pulled their penises out when they raped their slave girls. The conversation is in the context of questioning whether or not pulling out before ejaculating harms the price that the slave girls are sold for. The wording may seem confusing at first, but in their ancient context, people believed that souls were real. The Islamic Prophet Mohammad assures his male Muslim followers who take slave girls and rape them that ejaculating their cum into a slave girl won't impregnate them unless the Abrahamic God wills it. Therefore, due to the belief in the soul and the belief that the Abrahamic God determines the so-called miracle of childbirth, the Islamic Prophet Mohammad encouraged Muslim men to ejaculate inside their slave girls when they rape them because they believed the slave girls wouldn't become pregnant unless the Abrahamic God willed it. If that isn't horrifying enough, just imagine what members of the terrorist group ISIS does to Yazidi and Christian captives and what Pakistani and Afghan Muslims do to Hindu, Sikh, Buddhist, Parsis, and Christian minorities in Islamic countries when they target female children. I must reiterate that these are teachings that must be criticized:

Sahih al-Bukhari Book 34 Hadith 432

Narrated Abu Said Al-Khudri:

that while he was sitting with Allah's Apostle he said, "O Allah's Apostle! We get female captives as our share of booty, and we are interested in their prices, what is your opinion about coitus interruptus?" The Prophet said, "Do you really do that? It is better for you not to do it. No soul that which Allah has destined to exist, but will surely come into existence.[634][635]

Sahih al-Bukhari Book 62 Hadith 137

---

[633] al-Bukhārī, Abū ʿAbd Allāh Muḥammad ibn Ismāʿīl ibn Ibrāhīm al-Juʿfī. "Sahih Bukhari Volume 1, Book 3, Hadith Number 97a." Translated by Muhammad Muhsin Khan, Hadith Collection, Hadith Collection, 8 Dec. 2021, hadithcollection.com/sahihbukhari/sahih-bukhari-book-03-knowledge/sahih-bukhari-volume-001-book-003-hadith-number-097a.

[634] "Sahih Al-Bukhari Book Number 34 Hadith Number 432." *Muflihun*, muflihun.com/bukhari/34/432.

[635] al-Bukhārī, Abū ʿAbd Allāh Muḥammad ibn Ismāʿīl ibn Ibrāhīm al-Juʿfī. "Sahih Bukhari Volume 3, Book 34, Hadith Number 432." Translated by Muhammad Muhsin Khan, Hadith Collection, Hadith Collection, 31 Jan. 2009, hadithcollection.com/sahihbukhari/sahih-bukhari-book-34-sales-and-trade/sahih-bukhari-volume-003-book-034-hadith-number-432.

Narrated Abu Said Al-Khudri:

We got female captives in the war booty and we used to do coitus interruptus with them. So we asked Allah's Apostle about it and he said, "Do you really do that?" repeating the question thrice, "There is no soul that is destined to exist but will come into existence, till the Day of Resurrection."[636][637]

Please consider comparing the so-called wisdom of the Islamic Prophet Mohammad with people from the past who you personally like or celebrate the philosophies of. Even if some of those people did benefit from or supported slavery, and they should be rightfully condemned for having done so, they aren't celebrated as being beyond the ability to criticize and we can evaluate them from their positives and negatives. This is not allowed in Islam; everything the Islamic Prophet Mohammad does and advocates for has to be regarded as the actions of a perfect human being for Muslims and they believe nobody has the right to criticize their Prophet. To Muslims, does this teaching of the Islamic Prophet Mohammad sound like emancipation to you? Islam is a religion of submission and as such, all it can do is harm people:

Sahih al-Bukhari Book 80 Hadith 753

Narrated Anas bin Malik:

The Prophet said, "The freed slave belongs to the people who have freed him," or said something similar.[638][639]

The Islamic Prophet Mohammad's own religious pulpit was built by slave labor:

Sahih al-Bukhari Book 47 Hadith 743

Narrated Sahl:

The Prophet sent for a woman from the emigrants and she had a slave who was a carpenter. The Prophet said to her "Order your slave to prepare the wood (pieces) for the pulpit." So, she ordered her slave who went and cut the wood from the tamarisk and prepared the pulpit, for the Prophet. When he finished the pulpit, the woman informed the Prophet that it had been finished. The

---

[636] "Sahih Al-Bukhari Book Number 62 Hadith Number 137." *Muflihun*, muflihun.com/bukhari/62/137.

[637] al-Bukhārī, Abū ʿAbd Allāh Muḥammad ibn Ismāʿīl ibn Ibrāhīm al-Juʿfī. "Sahih Bukhari Volume 7, Book 62, Hadith Number 137." Translated by Muhammad Muhsin Khan, Hadith Collection, Hadith Collection, 31 May 2009, hadithcollection.com/sahihbukhari/sahih-bukhari-book-62-wedlock-marriage-nikah/sahih-bukhari-volume-007-book-062-hadith-number-137.

[638] "Sahih Al-Bukhari Book Number 80 Hadith Number 753." *Muflihun*, muflihun.com/bukhari/80/753.

[639] al-Bukhārī, Abū ʿAbd Allāh Muḥammad ibn Ismāʿīl ibn Ibrāhīm al-Juʿfī. "Sahih Bukhari Volume 8, Book 80, Hadith Number 753." Translated by Muhammad Muhsin Khan, Hadith Collection, Hadith Collection, 2 June 2009, hadithcollection.com/sahihbukhari/sahih-bukhari-book-80-laws-of-inheritance-al-faraaid/sahih-bukhari-volume-008-book-080-hadith-number-753.

Prophet asked her to send that pulpit to him, so they brought it. The Prophet lifted it and placed it at the place in which you see now."[640][641]

The Prophet Mohammad himself participated in raping his sex slaves and the all-powerful Abrahamic God made sure to reveal that the Prophet Mohammad was fully permitted to rape his female sex slaves after his wives demanded that he say it was forbidden. This hadith is labeled saheeh (Sound):

36 The Book of the Kind Treatment of Women

(4) Chapter: Jealousy

4) ‏(باب الْغَيْرَةِ‏)

It was narrated from Anas, that the Messenger of Allah had a female slave with whom he had intercourse, but 'Aishah and Hafsah would not leave him alone until he said that she was forbidden for him. Then Allah, the Mighty and Sublime, revealed:

"O Prophet! Why do you forbid (for yourself) that which Allah has allowed to you.' until the end of the Verse.

أَخْبَرَنِي إِبْرَاهِيمُ بْنُ يُونُسَ بْنِ مُحَمَّدٍ، حَرَمِيٌّ - هُوَ لَقَبُهُ - قَالَ حَدَّثَنَا أَبِي قَالَ حَدَّثَنَا حَمَّادُ بْنُ سَلَمَةَ، عَنْ ثَابِتٍ، عَنْ أَنَسٍ، أَنَّ رَسُولَ اللَّهِ صلى الله عليه وسلم كَانَتْ لَهُ أَمَةٌ يَطَؤُهَا فَلَمْ تَزَلْ بِهِ عَائِشَةُ وَحَفْصَةُ حَتَّى حَرَّمَهَا عَلَى نَفْسِهِ فَأَنْزَلَ اللَّهُ عَزَّ وَجَلَّ ‏{‏ يَا أَيُّهَا النَّبِيُّ لِمَ تُحَرِّمُ مَا أَحَلَّ اللَّهُ لَكَ ‏}‏ إِلَى آخِرِ الآيَةِ ‏.‏

Grade: Sahih (Darussalam)

Reference: Sunan an-Nasa'i 3959

In-book reference: Book 36, Hadith 21

English translation: Vol. 4, Book 36, Hadith 3411[642]

This infamous Quranic verse is what began the Youtuber Apostate Prophet's journey to eventually leave Islam and it gives even more context on how the Prophet Mohammad treated his wives. In a holy book meant to solve all human problems to await Islamic Judgment Day, Quran 33:53 has the Abrahamic God explain that the Prophet Mohammad is shy, you should leave his house after a meal, that you should only ask his

---

[640] "Sahih Al-Bukhari Book Number 47 Hadith Number 743." *Muflihun*, muflihun.com/bukhari/47/743.

[641] al-Bukhārī, Abū ʿAbd Allāh Muḥammad ibn Ismāʿīl ibn Ibrāhīm al-Juʿfī. "Sahih Bukhari Volume 3, Book 47, Hadith Number 743." Translated by Muhammad Muhsin Khan, Hadith Collection, SUNNAH.COM, Jan. 2009, hadithcollection.com/sahihbukhari/sahih-bukhari-book-47-gifts/sahih-bukhari-volume-003-book-047-hadith-number-743.

[642] "36 The Book of the Kind Treatment of Women: (4) Chapter: Jealousy." Sunan An-Nasa'i 3959 - the Book of the Kind Treatment of Women - كتاب عشرة النساء - Sunnah.Com - Sayings and Teachings of Prophet Muhammad (صلى الله عليه و سلم), SUNNAH.COM, sunnah.com/nasai:3959. Accessed 6 Aug. 2025. Grade: Sahih (Darussalam) Reference: Sunan an-Nasa'i 3959 In-book reference: Book 36, Hadith 21 English translation: Vol. 4, Book 36, Hadith 3411

multiple wives questions from behind a curtain, and the Abrahamic God forbids marrying the Prophet Mohammad's wives after he dies. The majority of Muslims believe this book can solve all human problems:

<u>Quran 33:53</u>

Sahih International: O you who have believed, do not enter the houses of the Prophet except when you are permitted for a meal, without awaiting its readiness. But when you are invited, then enter; and when you have eaten, disperse without seeking to remain for conversation. Indeed, that [behavior] was troubling the Prophet, and he is shy of [dismissing] you. But Allah is not shy of the truth. And when you ask [his wives] for something, ask them from behind a partition. That is purer for your hearts and their hearts. And it is not [conceivable or lawful] for you to harm the Messenger of Allah or to marry his wives after him, ever. Indeed, that would be in the sight of Allah an enormity.

Pickthall: O Ye who believe! Enter not the dwellings of the Prophet for a meal without waiting for the proper time, unless permission be granted you. But if ye are invited, enter, and, when your meal is ended, then disperse. Linger not for conversation. Lo! that would cause annoyance to the Prophet, and he would be shy of (asking) you (to go); but Allah is not shy of the truth. And when ye ask of them (the wives of the Prophet) anything, ask it of them from behind a curtain. That is purer for your hearts and for their hearts. And it is not for you to cause annoyance to the messenger of Allah, nor that ye should ever marry his wives after him. Lo! that in Allah's sight would be an enormity.

Yusuf Ali: O ye who believe! Enter not the Prophet's houses,- until leave is given you,- for a meal, (and then) not (so early as) to wait for its preparation: but when ye are invited, enter; and when ye have taken your meal, disperse, without seeking familiar talk. Such (behaviour) annoys the Prophet: he is ashamed to dismiss you, but Allah is not ashamed (to tell you) the truth. And when ye ask (his ladies) for anything ye want, ask them from before a screen: that makes for greater purity for your hearts and for theirs. Nor is it right for you that ye should annoy Allah's Messenger, or that ye should marry his widows after him at any time. Truly such a thing is in Allah's sight an enormity.

Shakir: O you who believe! do not enter the houses of the Prophet unless permission is given to you for a meal, not waiting for its cooking being finished-- but when you are invited, enter, and when you have taken the food, then disperse-- not seeking to listen to talk; surely this gives the Prophet trouble, but he forbears from you, and Allah does not forbear from the truth And when you ask of them any goods, ask of them from behind a curtain; this is purer for your hearts and (for) their hearts; and it does not behove you that you should give trouble to the Messenger of Allah, nor that you should marry his wives after him ever; surely this is grievous in the sight of Allah.

Muhammad Sarwar: Believers, do not enter the houses of the Prophet for a meal without permission. if you are invited, you may enter, but be punctual (so that you will not be waiting while the meal is being prepared). When you have finished eating, leave his home. Do not sit around chatting among yourselves. This will annoy the Prophet but he will feel embarrassed to tell you. God does not feel embarrassed to tell you the truth. When you want to ask something from the wives of the Prophet, ask them from behind the curtain. This would be more proper for you and for them. You are not supposed to trouble the Prophet or to ever marry his wives after his death, for this would be a grave offense in the sight of God.

Mohsin Khan: O you who believe! Enter not the Prophet's houses, except when leave is given to you for a meal, (and then) not (so early as) to wait for its preparation. But when you are invited, enter, and when you have taken your meal, disperse, without sitting for a talk. Verily, such (behaviour) annoys the Prophet, and he is shy of (asking) you (to go), but Allah is not shy of (telling you) the truth. And when you ask (his wives) for anything you want, ask them from behind a screen, that is purer for your hearts and for their hearts. And it is not (right) for you that you should annoy Allah's Messenger, nor that you should ever marry his wives after him (his death). Verily! With Allah that shall be an enormity.

Arberry: O believers, enter not the houses of the Prophet, except leave is given you for a meal, without watching for its hour. But when you are invited, then enter; and when you have had the meal, disperse, neither lingering for idle talk; that is hurtful to the Prophet, and he is ashamed before you; but God is not ashamed before the truth. And when you ask his wives for any object, ask them from behind a curtain; that is cleaner for your hearts and theirs. It is not for you to hurt God's Messenger, neither to marry his wives after him, ever; surely that would be, in God's sight, a monstrous thing.[643]

Finally, please read these three hadiths which are accounts of the Islamic Prophet Mohammad's destruction of a Jewish tribe and the subsequent enslavement and then forced marriage of a Jewish woman, Safiya bint Huyai bin Akhtab. In these accounts, Safiya is taken to the illiterate and pedophilic warlord, the Prophet Mohammad, because of her beauty. The accounts explain that the Prophet Mohammad's army slaughtered her entire tribe, killed all the men who surrendered, took the adult women and young female children as sex slaves, and the Prophet Mohammad had Safiya's "release from slavery" be a coerced marriage to him and that was only after he was finished pondering whether to make her into one of his personal sex slaves or into one of his wives. This pedophilic, illiterate warlord is who Muslims must strive to emulate and revere as the perfect human being:

Collection
Sahih Bukhari

Dar-us-Salam reference
Hadith 2235

In-book reference
Book 34, Hadith 181

USC-MSA web (English) reference
Volume 3, Book 34, Hadith 437

Related Qur'an verses
2.234, 4.24, 33.21, 33.52

Narrated Anas bin Malik:
The Prophet (ﷺ) came to Khaibar and when Allah made him victorious and he conquered the town by breaking the enemy's defense, the beauty of Safiya bint Huyai bin Akhtab was mentioned to him and her husband had been killed while she was a bride. Allah's Messenger (ﷺ) selected her for himself and he set out in her company till he reached Sadd-ar-Rawha' where her menses were over and he married her. Then Hais (a kind of meal) was prepared and served on a small

---

[643] "53rd Verse of Chapter 33 (Sūrat l-Aḥzāb)." The Quranic Arabic Corpus - Translation, The Quranic Arabic Corpus, corpus.quran.com/translation.jsp?chapter=33&verse=53. Accessed 6 Aug. 2025.

leather sheet (used for serving meals). Allah's Messenger (ﷺ) then said to me, "Inform those who are around you (about the wedding banquet)." So that was the marriage banquet given by Allah's Messenger (ﷺ) for (his marriage with) Safiya. After that we proceeded to Medina and I saw that Allah's Messenger (ﷺ) was covering her with a cloak while she was behind him. Then he would sit beside his camel and let Safiya put her feet on his knees to ride (the camel).[644]

Collection
Sahih Bukhari

Dar-us-Salam reference
Hadith 4200

In-book reference
Book 64, Hadith 240

USC-MSA web (English) reference
Volume 5, Book 59, Hadith 512

Related Qur'an verses
2.234, 4.24

Narrated Anas:

The Prophet (ﷺ) offered the Fajr Prayer near Khaibar when it was still dark and then said, "Allahu-Akbar! Khaibar is destroyed, for whenever we approach a (hostile) nation (to fight), then evil will be the morning for those who have been warned." Then the inhabitants of Khaibar came out running on the roads. The Prophet (ﷺ) had their warriors killed, their offspring and woman taken as captives. Safiya was amongst the captives, She first came in the share of Dahya Alkali but later on she belonged to the Prophet. The Prophet (ﷺ) made her manumission as her 'Mahr'.[645]

Collection
Sahih Bukhari

Dar-us-Salam reference
Hadith 4213

In-book reference
Book 64, Hadith 253

USC-MSA web (English) reference
Volume 5, Book 59, Hadith 524

Related Qur'an verses
2.234, 4.24

Narrated Anas:

The Prophet (ﷺ) stayed for three rights between Khaibar and Medina and was married to Safiya. I invited the Muslim to h s marriage banquet and there wa neither meat nor bread in that

---

[644] "QuranX.com The Most Complete Quran / Hadith / Tafsir Collection Available!" *Sahih Bukhari Hadiths*, quranx.com/Hadith/Bukhari/USC-MSA/Volume-3/Book-34/Hadith-437/.
[645] "QuranX.com The Most Complete Quran / Hadith / Tafsir Collection Available!" *Sahih Bukhari Hadiths*, quranx.com/Hadith/Bukhari/USC-MSA/Volume-5/Book-59/Hadith-512/.

banquet but the Prophet ordered Bilal to spread the leather mats on which dates, dried yogurt and butter were put. The Muslims said amongst themselves, "Will she (i.e. Safiya) be one of the mothers of the believers, (i.e. one of the wives of the Prophet (ﷺ)) or just (a lady captive) of what his right-hand possesses" Some of them said, "If the Prophet (ﷺ) makes her observe the veil, then she will be one of the mothers of the believers (i.e. one of the Prophet's wives), and if he does not make her observe the veil, then she will be his lady slave." So when he departed, he made a place for her behind him (on his and made her observe the veil.[646]

This behavior does inform the beliefs and actions of Muslims and the historic results show consistency throughout history from ancient times to the modern reports on what Islamic terrorists do. Consider ISIS's brutality when reading the following from *Chapter 3: The Fire Extinguished* of Paul Sprachman's English translation of Iranian scholar, Abdolhossein Zarrinkoub's *Two Centuries of Silence*: *An Account of Events and Conditions in Iran [Persia] during the first Two Hundred Years of Islam*:

The Conquerors' Behavior

Stories recounted in the sources in this vein are astonishing and, often, grim and lamentable. We read cAbd al-Raḥmān b. Samura, the conqueror of Sistan enforced the practice of "not killing weasels and [jzh`hā?]."7 Apparently, the hungry lizard-eaters could not keep their hands off weasels. Accounts of the conquest of Mada'in also illustrate the Arabs own simple natures and ineptitude. Hindushāh writes:

"It is said a man found part of a ruby of exceptional quality, but did not know it. Another man, who knew the value of the stone, bought it from him for one thousand dirhams. When asked by another man why he sold the ruby so cheaply, the finder said, "If I had known there were numbers over a thousand, I would have asked for more." Another man having gotten hold of some red gold called out among the soldiers, "Anyone want to trade this yellow for white?" He was under the impression silver was better than gold. There is also the case of a group of people who found a bag full of camphor, thinking it was salt. They sprinkled a bit in a cooking pot, which made their food taste bitter, not in the least salty. They were about to throw the bag away when someone who knew it was camphor bought it from them for a piece of coarse cotton fabric worth two dirhams.8"

The brutality and irascibility of the conquerors, however, did not become fully apparent until they had taken full control of the vanquished lands. When the Arabs had to administer or act as agents in these lands, their helplessness and lack of ability, and, at the same time, their cavils and ferocity became all too apparent. The sources contain narratives revealing the savage rapacity in the way the conquerors conducted business with the conquered. Undoubtedly, many of these narratives are nothing more than fiction; nevertheless, they plainly show the conquering people being foolish, borderline deranged, and devoid of refinement and breeding. They write:

"They put an Arab in charge of a province. He gathered the Jews living there and asked them about Jesus. They said they had killed him and placed him on the cross [literally "scaffold"]. The Arab said, "Did you pay his blood money?" "No," they said. "I swear to God," said the Arab, "you will never leave this place until you pay it."... Abū al-cĀj was in charge of the Basra area. They brought a man from the Christian community to him. He asked the man, "What's your name?" The man said, "Bondād Shahr Bondād." Abū al-cĀj said, "You have three names, but

---

[646] "QuranX.com The Most Complete Quran / Hadith / Tafsir Collection Available!" *Sahih Bukhari Hadiths*, quranx.com/Hadith/Bukhari/USC-MSA/Volume-5/Book-59/Hadith-524/.

you only pay the head tax for one person." He then ordered they take by force the head tax of all three people from the man.9"

One can find many such accounts in the old chronicles. They are unanimous in showing how incapable the Arabs were of administering the lands they conquered. Despite this it was not long before local resistance to the Arabs dissipated, and, despite all their deficiencies and incompetence, the Arabs gained control of the situation. Mihrabs [prayer niches] and minarets replaced Zoroastrian fire temples and shrines. The Pahlavi language gave way to Arabic. People long accustomed to listening to the murmuring of the Magi and the royal Sasanian anthems, were now forced to endure the grim chants of "God is great" and the resounding calls of the muezzins. People who for ages delighted in the festive songs of the court minstrel Bārbad and the harpist Nakisā gradually grew use to the cries of camel drivers and the clang of camel bells. Life, which had previously been full of glitz and glamor, though stable and peaceful, was now rife with sound and fury. In place of the bāzh, barsom, kusti, hom, and of the soft orisons (zamzameh), there were now the ritual five daily prayers, ablutions, month-long fasting, alms giving, and the pilgrimage to Mecca.10

Iranians, in short, except for those acutely influenced by the teachings of Islam looked at the Arabs with ill will and loathing. There were also, however, soldiers and warriors among them, who in addition to ill will felt humiliation. This particular group considered the Arabs the vilest of creatures. The following words of Khosrow II Parviz as quoted in Arab sources give a good idea of what the Iranian royal cavalry [asāvera] and the warriors felt about Arabs:

"I have found nothing good in the way the Arabs worship nor in the way they conduct themselves in the world. They are without resolve and judgment, a people lacking energy and force. To picture their depravity and vile ambition it is enough only to see them as vermin and vagrant birds that starve their offspring to death and feed on one another out of hunger and helplessness. They are totally devoid of cuisine, clothing, and the pleasures and pastimes of this earth. The best food their wealthy benefactors can obtain for them is camel flesh, which many wild animals avoid for fear of getting sick and for its foul taste and indigestibility.11"

Anyone with such thoughts about the Arabs would naturally not submit to their yoke. Arab hegemony would have been intolerable for them, especially since it had not been achieved without widespread looting, destruction, and murder.

In the wake of the Arab invasion, many towns, cities, and fortresses were devastated. Extended families and lineages were wiped out. They pillaged the riches and property of the wealthy labeling what they robbed the spoils and lawful benefits of war. They sold Iranian women and girls in the markets at Medina, calling them "captives" and "prisoners" of war. In the name of a "head tax," they extorted heavy payments and protection money from craftsmen and grandees who did not convert to Islam.

The Arabs took all of these measures backed by the sword and the lash. No one was ever able to object openly to them. The sole Arab responses—especially in the Umayyad period—to any kind of opposition were the punishment [ḥadd] fixed in the Quran, stoning to death, and burning.

The Clients [mawālī] and the Umayyads

Umayyad reign [661-750] was insufferable to the scions of Iranian nobility and the "freemen," because it was established on basis of their inferiority as cajam or people of non-Arab descent, and, at the same time, on the superiority of the Arab. Even the lower classes could not stand Umayyad rule, for they found no relief or peace from the caliph or his agents, nor had they jettisoned their age-old religious prejudices. It is no wonder whenever rebellions sparked against the Umayyad machine Iranians had a hand in them.

Arab brutality and ruthlessness toward the conquered nations knew no bounds. The Umayyads, who had never forgotten their ardent tribal solidarity [caṣabiyya], founded their government on the primacy of the Arab. With their childlike self-regard, the Arabs after every conquest categorized other Muslims as "clients" or "slaves." The humiliation and scorn implicit in these slurs were enough to make Iranians view Arabs with enduring malice and vengeance; but somehow the harsh legal constraints and punishments the Arabs imposed on them justified that rancor. That said, the injustice and repression of the ruling apparatus caused intense anguish and dissatisfaction. The Umayyad aristocracy deprived the Iranian freemen and nobility of all their civil rights and social stature, treating their captives like store-bought slaves. This was why the term "client" (mawlā) came to signify cruelty and coercion of every type. A client was not able to engage in any respectable work. He could not make weapons nor mount a horse. If a man of Iranian descent were to take a nomad nobody for a wife, some slander monger would only have to spread lies and rumors about the couple to force the woman to abandon and divorce her husband and to have the man endure a lashing and imprisonment.

To rule and to judge were the special preserves of the Arabs; no client ever rose to such positions of power. Although Ḥajjāj b. Yūsuf [governor of Iraq 694-714] appointed Sacīd b. Jubayr—despite his being a client—as judge in Kufa for a time, the Arabs generally did not think it appropriate to promote clients to high positions and stations. It was at odds with the principle of Arab primacy in temperament and race. But this preference could not last forever, since Arabs in no way had sufficient taste, talent, and experience to rule a country or an empire.

The Superiority of the Iranians

This "superior race" of Arabs, whose thoughts and actions never strayed beyond the fields of "equine and camel" husbandry, now had to govern the vast territories they had acquired and thus could not ignore their clients completely. Like it or not, sooner or later they had to admit the superiority of clients. Hence it was not for nothing a vane, proud, and ambitious Umayyad caliph was compelled to utter these famous words: "These Iranians amaze me. They ruled for a thousand years and did not need us even for an hour. While we have been ruling for a century and cannot for an instant do without them."12 Despite those who could not see clients heading the government, it did not take long for Iranians to take their rightful places in the fields of theology and other types of learning.

Towards the end of the Umayyad period, then, most of the judges and even a large number of government agents were clients. They had control of all affairs of government. The clients' talent and genius gradually took hold of all official endeavors. The Arabs, however, were not ready to submit peacefully to the proliferation and superiority of their own windfall slaves. The violent confrontations between the two groups gave the Iranians the chance to impose their intellectual and material superiority on the Arabs. The myth of the primacy of the Arab notwithstanding, not only did they gain the upper hand over their conquerors in administrative matters, they also proved their superiority in the military and political spheres.

But, even before this, from the very dawn of Islam, the Iranian never hid his hatred and extreme resentment of his enemies and of those who extorted money from him. Not only did one Iranian stab the Caliph cUmar b. Khaṭṭāb to death in 644, Iranians also played major roles in every act of sedition and disturbance that occurred in the Islamic world. Hatred for Arabs and discontent over the misconduct and racial prejudice of the Umayyads compelled them to join in movements against the caliph. Thus, in 683, twenty thousand Iranian residents of Kufa nicknamed the "Reds of Daylam" [amrā': "fair-skinned"] accepted the call of Mukhtar to rise up against the Umayyads.[647]

And further on in the same chapter of Iranian scholar Abdolhossein Zarrinkoub's *Two Centuries of Silence: An Account of Events and Conditions in Iran [Persia] during the first Two Hundred Years of Islam*:

> Seen in this light, Mukhtār's revolt became a pretext for Iranians to test their strength against the Arabs and an opportunity to avenge themselves against the Umayyads. The Arabs, however, who could not abide an independence movement among the Iranians, accused them of looting the wealth of widows and orphans. The accusation was false; in fact, the Arabs were themselves the ones plundering widow and orphans. It was the Arab commanders themselves who made the fall of the Umayyad government inevitable.
>
> The primary task of these commanders was to conduct raids and jihad, the function of which was not to advance religion, but only to amass plunder and profit. Many soldiers and agents were left destitute by the avarice of the Arab chiefs and emirs. When one agent replaced another, he would have the dismissed agent arrested, and, using a variety of punishments and tortures seize everything he owned. With these measures Ḥajjāj b. Yūsuf set fire to Iraq and Qutayba b. Muslim consigned Khorasan to the flames. As the demand for tax funds increased by the day, the cruel tactics used by the agents to extort revenue became more pronounced. In their writings, historians have included many stunning accounts of the callousness and brutality of Ḥajjāj's tax farmers. The following is an example: For some years the people of Isfahan were unable to pay the taxes levied on them. Ḥajjāj assigned a Bedouin Arab the task of collecting their taxes. In Isfahan, the Arab got surety from several Isfahanis to submit their taxes and gave them ten months to pay. When the allotted period elapsed with the taxes still unpaid, the Arab arrested the Isfahanis, who made excuses for their failure to pay. The Arab swore he would have them beheaded if the taxes were not paid. One of the surety-givers was brought forward so they could behead him. After the beheading, he had them inscribe on his severed head "so-and-so, the son of so-and-so, fulfilled his loan agreement." Then he ordered the head placed in a moneybag, which they sealed. Then they did the same to a second surety-giver. Faced with no other choice, the Isfahanis grudgingly gathered the money they owed and paid their taxes.19
>
> In the face of the savagery and spite condoned by the tax farmers, people had only two recourses: abject obedience or bloody revolt, to which the luckless folk resorted several times.

Ḥajjāj 20

The histories relate loathsome tales of the unrelenting calamities and acts of cruelty that occurred during the bloody reign of the governor of Iraq Ḥajjāj b. Yūsuf. Such accounts fill one with horror and hate. In one history we read: "Several thousand languished in his prisons, and he ordered that they be given water to drink mixed with salt and lime, and, instead of food, that they be fed with a mixture of dung and donkey urine."21 Ḥajjāj ruled Iraq for twenty years. During that period—if the histories can be relied on—the total number of those he had killed, excluding those slain in

---

[647] Zarrinkoub, Abdolhossein. Chapter 3: The Fire Extinguished (Location 1241 – 1798). Two Centuries of Silence: An Account of Events and Conditions in Iran [Persia] During the First Two Hundred Years of Islam, from the Arab Invasion to the Rise of the Tahirid Dynasty First edition. Mazda Publishers. Kindle Edition.

battle, exceeded 120,000. They have written when Ḥajjāj ruled there were 50,000 men and 30,000 women in his prisons.22 These figures may not be free of hyperbole, but one can say this much: Ḥajjāj's reign in Iraq was for everyone, especially the clients, a huge misfortune.[648]

What did the Prophet Mohammad believe about the Earth?

Abdullah bin Abbas bin Abdul-Muttalib bin Hishim bin Abd Manaf Qurashi Hashimi also known as Ibn Abbas, a cousin of the Prophet Mohammad, who is known as the highest mufassir (interpreter of the Quran) who studied the Quran and Hadiths deeply[649], committing approximately 1,666 hadiths to memory[650], whose lived example is one of being intensely committed to the Prophet Mohammad personally since he was a child[651], and whose interpretations are recorded in Sahih Bukhari and Sahih Muslim; Ibn Abbas had the following to say about what the Prophet Mohammad believed about the shape of the earth[652]:

Tanwîr al-Miqbâs min Tafsîr Ibn 'Abbâs

{ ن وَٱلْقَلَمِ وَمَا يَسْطُرُونَ }

And from his narration on the authority of Ibn 'Abbas that he said regarding the interpretation of Allah's saying (Nun): '(Nun) He says: Allah swears by the Nun, which is the whale that carries the earths on its back while in Water, and beneath which is the Bull and under the Bull is the Rock and under the Rock is the Dust and none knows what is under the Dust save Allah. The name of the whale is Liwash, and it is said its name is Lutiaya'; the name of the bull is Bahamut, and some say its name is Talhut or Liyona. The whale is in a sea called 'Adwad, and it is like a small bull in a huge sea. The sea is in a hollowed rock whereby there is 4,000 cracks, and from each crack water springs out to the earth. It is also said that Nun is one of the names of the Lord; it stands for the letter Nun in Allah's name al-Rahman (the Beneficent); and it is also said that a Nun is an inkwell. (By the pen) Allah swore by the pen. This pen is made of light and its height is equal to the distance between Heaven and earth. It is with this pen that the Wise Remembrance, i.e. the Guarded Tablet, was written. It is also said that the pen is one of the angels by whom Allah has sworn, (and that which they write (therewith)) and Allah also swore by what the angels write down of the works of the children of Adam,

---

[648] Zarrinkoub, Abdolhossein. Chapter 3: The Fire Extinguished (Location 1241 – 1798). Two Centuries of Silence: An Account of Events and Conditions in Iran [Persia] During the First Two Hundred Years of Islam, from the Arab Invasion to the Rise of the Tahirid Dynasty First edition. Mazda Publishers. Kindle Edition.

[649] Mosaad, Walead, et al. "Sayyiduna 'Abdullah Ibn 'Abbas: A Biography." Imam Ghazali Institute, Imam Ghazali Institute, 2007, www.imamghazali.org/resources/abdullah-ibn-abbas-biography#:~:text=Another%20narration%20attributed%20to%20him,in%20the%20year%2071%20AH.

[650] "Short Biography of Abdullah Ibn Abbas (R.A.)." IslamicFinder, Athan Academy, 2023, www.islamicfinder.org/knowledge/biography/story-of-abdullah-ibn-abbas/.

[651] "Short Biography of Abdullah Ibn Abbas (R.A.)." IslamicFinder, Athan Academy, 2023, www.islamicfinder.org/knowledge/biography/story-of-abdullah-ibn-abbas/.

[652] "Short Biography of Abdullah Ibn Abbas (R.A.)." IslamicFinder, Athan Academy, 2023, www.islamicfinder.org/knowledge/biography/story-of-abdullah-ibn-abbas/.

Tafsir Ibn 'Abbas, trans. Mokrane Guezzou[653]

What am I lying about, exaggerating about, or taking out of context? All credible evidence from purely Islamic sources, and from Ibn Abbas who is the most respected *mufassir*, who was the Prophet Mohammad's own cousin that served him with full-fledged loyalty in person, strongly suggests that this is what the Prophet Mohammad himself believed about the earth's shape and how the earth exists. This is what Islamists fly planes into buildings, slaughter Hindus, slaughter Christians, slaughter Jains, slaughter Jews, slaughter Sikhs, slaughter Atheists, and slaughter Buddhists to demand respect for. This is what the US mainstream media has been shielding from criticism under the laughable claim that science and Abrahamic religion can co-exist. I recall examples such as the Muslim girl wearing a hijab talking about modern astrophysics in a Tedtalk, as if to suggest that an illiterate man from the 7th century was ever capable of the knowledge that she herself held about modern scientific discoveries. This is what they've spent all their time and energy in protecting; this is what internet mods on social media, and so many politically correct supporters shut down discussions to protect, knowing that Islamists kill innocent people over a Prophet who believed this about the shape of the earth itself.

Please think about this, because it is the unvarnished truth of why this is even controversial: this is the intellectual limits of a belief system built upon revealed wisdom. The only reason this is considered fake or controversial to the majority of Muslims is because they know this belief that the Prophet Mohammad held is demonstrably, provably wrong based upon modern scientific evidence. Yet, because Islam teaches them that the Prophet Mohammad revealed the truth to them, they substitute the historic fact that the Prophet Mohammad was a flat-earther who believed the world was atop a whale and then atop a bull in an endless ocean; they do this by trying to replace the context with a modern scientific lens, precisely because they're not allowed to question the Quran. They try to use modern science to substitute this abjectly wrong religious belief system that can be proven wrong by simply reading the Quran or finding hadiths of the actual beliefs that the Prophet Mohammad held. The majority of Muslims ignore these historic facts about his beliefs to claim he had the same level of knowledge as the Ancient Greek philosophers that predate the Prophet Mohammad and the Ancient Hindu mathematicians like Aryabhata and Brahmagupta who existed around 476 – 668 CE which is before and after the Prophet Mohammad. The difference between the Prophet Mohammad and those philosophers and mathematicians is that the Prophet Mohammad was an illiterate man from the 7th century; whereas, the philosophers and mathematicians of the ancient world took the time to educate themselves, to study, and to learn because of the thrill of seeking

---

[653] Abbas, Ibn. "Tanwr Al-Miqbs Min Tafsr Ibn Abbs." Translated by Mokrane Guezzou, Altafsir.Com, Royal Aal al-Bayt Institute for Islamic Thought, 2021, www.altafsir.com/Tafasir.asp?tMadhNo=0&tTafsirNo=73&tSoraNo=68&tAyahNo=1&tDisplay=yes&UserProfile=0&LanguageId=2.

knowledge. Even the belief that the Prophet Mohammad was a learned person for his time is wrong, precisely because he was illiterate. Those who cling to the tyranny of hurt sentiments will always seek to kill those who believe in truthseeking with their thirst for knowledge. The root cause of the tyranny of hurt sentiments is that their easy answers from revealed wisdom are proven false over and over. It is proven wrong by people who have the humility and the thrill to study and learn fact-finding research. By refusing to criticize Islam on a societal level, we are genuinely privileging illiteracy over literacy. Worst of all, we're privileging their feelings over our human rights.

Chapter X: Islamism Always Creates Failed States

    There is one simple reason why every single civilization that seeks Sharia and Islamic precepts as its main set of values within its legal system will be perennially doomed. To the degree and extent that such civilizations uphold Islamic values, they will become failed states and their perpetual doom should always be the expected outcome. This reason is so straightforward as to be doubtless to any thinking person and anyone denying this fact is lying to themselves. The basic fact is this: there is no single book that can answer all of life's problems. Apply the Quran's claims to any other book and that book would also fail. It doesn't even matter whether the book is a religious book or not; I'm not insinuating that any Hindu, Christian, Buddhist, Jewish, or any other Dharmic or Abrahamic text would do better at all. I'm simply saying that no civilization can function and improve itself economically, socially, politically, and so on with a belief system around a single book. Imagine a world where we applied the Tafsir system of Islamic jurisprudence to the Founding Fathers of the United States. The current legal system of the US law has originalist and literalist interpretations wherein US judges interpret the laws based upon the Founders original intent or what the legal text literally states. Now, imagine if all claims of scientific inquiry had to be interpreted based upon whether Benjamin Franklin or George Washington would have found such scientific questions like quantum physics to be acceptable for the majority of Americans to believe. Obviously, that is asinine; it would limit the Freedom of Speech and Freedom of Inquiry of US scientists, and it would be an abject waste of time and resources for something so absurd that it should rightly be viewed as pathetic and worthless. Yet, apply this to Islamic countries with the Quran set as the highest standard and then try to add the scientific evidence of human evolution into their societies, and you will have Muslims seriously argue that evolution cannot be true. Every single Islamic civilization that imposes Islam as a State religion that people cannot convert out of and that penalizes people for blasphemy against Islam, which is essentially penalizing people for thought crimes, are never going to remain a stable country for long without outside charity from other countries or international governmental organizations (IGOs) like the IMF and World Bank. Furthermore, there should be low expectations on returns of investment for the simple fact that no modern country in the world, especially after the Industrial Revolution of the 1800s, can possibly function under the preposterous claim that one book can answer all of life's problems.

    As another example, apply this logic to your average Math book; imagine there was a country in the world that decided an average math book was the necessary and unquestionable standard by which their Constitution could function. This math book might help with dosage for treatment of patients in hospitals, it may help with nutritional and dietary regulations to eat healthy, and perhaps even designing construction work for locales; but is it going to provide any answers to the questions of an abortion debate, how to rectify historic discrimination against an ethnic minority group, or questions pertaining to LGBT human rights? Most would find such a notion implausible and they would need other methods of reasoning outside the scope of that math book. Yet, Islam's implicit claim under the Tafsir system is that an illiterate pedophile warlord from the 7th century narrated a book that can answer all of life's problems for all-time. This would include the time after the Industrial revolution of the 1800s. Perpetual failed states are the only logical outcomes of this laughably stupid idea. In addition to this problem, the Quran itself is merely a 7th century tribal war book; the belief in the fantasy of a Messiah, the instructions on the proper enslavement and rape of women, the encouragement of massacring Jews and Pagans and Atheists, using an illiterate man as the moral standard to live by to the extent that you dress and act like him, and the belief in the fantasy of Judgment Day are simply proof of a primitive mentality in a warring-desert tribal cult. It may have worked in the Medieval period where barbarity wasn't lacking in virtually all parts of the world, but it is never going to be able to answer any of the human challenges after the Industrial Revolution and it hasn't been able to. If you live in an Islamic country whereby Islam is followed as the precepts of your society and the Quran can never be questioned, just expect your life to be one of perpetual failure that you laughably try to blame on everyone else instead of your own imbecilic political system that doomed your life. If you live in a non-Islamic country, you should peacefully protest to make sure that criticizing the pathetic and laughable claims of Islam are ensured in your society, because they'll always act like an aggrieved minority when it's really their idiotic belief systems causing them to suffer pointlessly. Where will that lead? Exactly as it has the Middle East and Pakistan. That is, a bunch of warring desert clans imitating their illiterate, pedophile warlord's lunacy in the 7th century and perpetually blaming and killing each other in repeated examples of failed states that blame Hindus, the United States, the entire Western world, Atheism, Jews, Christians, Yazidis, and I'm sure numerous other scapegoats. Everything is a perpetual conspiracy theory in their minds and it is absolutely pathetic.

  Here is the crux of the problem once you understand how Islamic theology actually functions: they're deluding themselves with self-serving narratives of being a perennially aggrieved minority and degrading our societies into failed states just because they don't like hearing criticism of their religious beliefs. The term Islamophobia allows this abject stupidity to go unchecked. Please think about this seriously, about what value these people actually provide the world around them: these are people who are literally using every iota of excuse to degrade societies into 7th century standards to create more failed states. They don't value education because the Prophet Mohammad was illiterate and many say this explicitly. They don't value scientific evidence for evolution, because they're not allowed to question the Quran, per the Sharia and Tafsir system. They don't want women to work because of Quran 4:34 teaching that men should maintain women and beat them when they become disobedient. And anytime they degrade a society, they blame that society instead of their beliefs that cause these problems like Sharia councils refusing a woman's divorce or arresting women for criticizing misogyny in Islam.

What is the point of obtaining the support of moderate Muslims? Please consider this, what do these "moderate" Muslims do except claim everyone else is a bigot and that nobody has a right to an opinion on Islam? Everyone else is an Islamophobic bigot while the Islamists spread grooming gangs in England, everyone else is an Islamophobic bigot while Islamists shun French women from being allowed to shop in their stores because it's against the Sharia, everyone else is an Islamophobic bigot for Quran burnings in Sweden while Islamists use children in their communities to firebomb cars and throw grenades at Swedish preschools, everyone else is an Islamophobic bigot while the vast majority of terrorist attacks that occur in India are from Islamists in India and Islamists take pride in killing as many Indians as possible, everyone else is an Islamophobic bigot while Islamists slaughter hundreds of African Christians who peacefully gave-up their guns under the demands of their respective governments, and no one has any right to criticize Islam despite all the rapes, murders, bombings, terrorism, and other forms of mass slaughter that the Islamists willfully do because that's the moral example set by their illiterate, pedophile warlord of a Prophet. Not even after Charlie Hebdo, Samuel Paty, Kamlesh Tiwari, Kishin Bharwad, and numerous Bangladeshi freethinkers have been beheaded, stabbed, or shot to death. It has to be asked: what are we doing here? What standards are we internalizing and being forced to accept? They're part of the problem specifically because they refuse to accept criticisms of Islam.

The primary reason Islam has more problems and a far greater propensity for violence is due to a theological issue beyond just the religion teaching its followers to try to imitate the Prophet Mohammad's lived example as much as possible. The other religions had debates and collaborative efforts; whereas Islam just has a system that seeks to ascertain whether a single illiterate, pedophilic man from the 7th century would approve of people's behavior in modern times. This does matter as it explains Islam's propensity for violence more than anything; the only debates in Islam, if they can even be called debates, is verifying the authenticity of whether an illiterate pedophile warlord made a claim about something or said something specifically in order to accept a statement as absolute fact that cannot be questioned by Muslims. Hindus had debates for thousands of years over the question of truth. Jewish theologians are widely known to have debates on theology. Christianity, while more limited in trying to understand the will of Jesus Christ and not arguing against his explicit teachings, had debates on the question of divinity and debates on ascertaining what the Abrahamic God's morals are. Buddhists, Hindus, and Jains engaged in debates with Atheists for hundreds of years. Islam's debates were limited to a strict policy of anyone losing in wars or in supposed debates being given the threat of converting or dying. The noteworthy example in

Medieval Iran has Muslim imams celebrating a Sultan sending a man to death for hurting their feelings. Islam's historic debates never included atheists and sought to slaughter them as much as possible in Iran and almost certainly in India too. The Enlightenment in Western Europe slowly defanged Christianity of these impediments that were glorified thought crimes but it took more than a century to do it; yet, no such reduction or removal of the impediment of thought crimes is possible in Islam precisely because of its theological framework. The freedom to think and the freedom of conscience is fundamentally at odds with the belief in Divine Command theory. That is the core reason why the set of ideas in Islam cannot change, because it is premised upon unquestioned obedience over freedom of thought.

Religious beliefs need to stop being held as sacred; the collective social standard of keeping them sacred is killing humanity internally with excuse after excuse. Why? Because other religious people don't want their sacred religious beliefs criticized, so they portray anyone criticizing Islam as a bigot to shield their own religious beliefs from criticism as a form of reciprocity. Most Christians, Jews, Buddhists, Jains, Sikhs, and Hindus are open to having their beliefs challenged; the vast majority of Muslims around the world will kill you for challenging their beliefs. Why are we devaluing our human rights, our modern world and all its advantages and innovations, and wasting our time with shielding people from the truth about a 7th century fantasy novel? That's really what we are doing here. The Quran is a 7th century fantasy novel, the Bible is a first-century fantasy novel, and Hindu texts have fantasy stories even more ancient than those two. We have climate change, AI innovations, quantum computing, raising standards of living across the world, and I'm sure a litany of other subjects to deal with; we cannot be wasting our time with a 7th century genocide cult that demands no one has a right to challenge their beliefs. We cannot be giving these people anything more than what they're willing to reciprocate and we shouldn't be lowering our standards because they feel uncomfortable hearing fact-finding research. I don't want to live in a world where children get kidnapped and gang raped by Muslim grooming gangs and everyone turns a blind eye to the obvious just because of an unspoken agreement of refusing to criticize ancient people's fantasy novels. Jesus Christ is not a Messiah, God does not exist, angels aren't real, Satan does not exist, jinns do not exist, and raping 9-year-olds is morally wrong by the standards of our modern society which we learned the hard way from thousands of years of trial-and-error learning from our ancestors' mistakes. Fact matters more than fiction.

Words or Forever Wars

The numerous riots throughout India's history due to Islamism attempting to infect it and the many riots growing in Europe over the threat of Islamism show that these problems aren't going to go away. One fact should be made absolutely clear: shutting down criticism of Islam makes violence inevitable. If we don't have the ability to speak our minds, to express our freedom of conscience, then all that's left is violence. We cannot live in a world where Muslims and their useful idiots shut down conversations, while Islamists commit murders and attempted murders. That is insanity and it is an insanity that no one should be willing to tolerate. No children should have to worry about being raped by Muslim grooming gangs and no parents should need to seek forming community squads to hunt down Muslim pedophiles because the police refuse to hold Muslim rapists accountable. That is not a standard anyone should be forced to live with and it is not acceptable. It is not acceptable with how Native Americans continue to be mistreated similarly by bigoted US Federal laws imposed upon them unilaterally by the Oliphant vs Suquamish 1978 Supreme Court decision which continues to give predominately White male, registered sex offenders carte blanche access to Native American communities and it is not a standard that should be imposed upon anyone else either. Furthermore, any person seriously advocating for Sharia in any capacity needs to be thoroughly investigated for terrorism links in any country, because Sharia should be understood as synonymous with the enslavement and rape of 9-year-old girls and other young girls.

Islamists are not going to stop killing people, the miniscule number of moderate Muslims will try to shut down criticisms of Islam, and the Islamists are never going to stop trying to impose their deluded, 7th century cultural problems on everyone else who have higher IQs and far less incest than their societies. Many of these so-called moderate Muslims live in safe Western societies where they support the defeat of the US by the Taliban and support the impositions of Sharia upon women in Islamic-majority countries, which they know that they will never have to live with or deal with. We risk being bogged down into forever wars that'll gradually decline us, but there is a way to avoid that. We no longer live in the Medieval world; we have methods, knowledge, and technology that can effectively end Islamism without firing a single shot, dropping a single bomb, and wasting taxpayer monies on violent methods that simply affirm their idiotic belief system. I don't want to continue to live in a world where we turn a blind eye to ongoing drone bombings that kill an unknown number of Muslim civilian casualties like under President Obama. However, what that must mean is valuing people's lives over their sacred religious beliefs. We live in a world with drones and drones can be effective in ending Islamism forever while minimizing Muslim civilian casualties to the greatest extent that is humanely possible. Earlier this year, I wrote the book called *Machiavellian Ahimsa* in which I advocate for a new use of drone warfare. I won't go into the specifics here, but if you're serious about ending Islamic terrorism within our lifetime and effectively ending all forms of Islamism in our lives, then I highly recommend reading that book. However, I am a born and raised US citizen and I do have a bias for the US. Therefore, depending on how serious you are about this issue, I recommend saving up enough to purchase the book, if you live outside of the United States and Western Europe. I do believe that the methods mentioned in that book could almost certainly help any country or any well-organized mercenary with capable drone technology to conquer vast swathes of land in Pakistan, Afghanistan, North Africa, and the Middle East so long as they have a steady supply of cheap and affordable drone technology at their disposal.

    Free Speech is the ultimate form of non-violence. The Charvaka Atheists flourished in ancient India approximately around 600 BCE because of it, Sultans that ruthlessly ruled Medieval Iran were afraid of the Zandiks ability to end Islamic rule because of it and so persecuted them mercilessly, the Enlightenment of Western Europe flourished because of it, and the US has dominated and expanded in countless human innovations for nearly 250 years precisely because of Free Speech. Imagine if Canada's recent proposals for jailing people for Free Speech happens because Muslims get offended; are scientists doing important work going to need to flee to the United States to avoid a five-year prison sentence for making online tweets about the Prophet Mohammad that Muslims get offended by? Should we expect scientific research to get cancelled because a particular scientist doesn't have thorough knowledge of what they can or cannot say in order to avoid offending a bunch of 7th century fundamentalists who always play victimhood? Should Asia Bibi expect a five-year prison sentence after nearly being killed by violent mobs in Pakistan and coming to Canada to enjoy freedoms she didn't have back in Pakistan? None of these places or people can have such freedoms when there's a group of perpetually offended 7th century fundamentalists refusing to change their ways or accept the modern world. Think about how absolutely stupid that is too. No one else acts as offended over pictures or words as Muslims; it is not a White versus ethnic minority issue. It's a modern world versus Islam issue and it always has been, because Islam was never a race and never will be one. It is either perpetual wars against an ideology that creates global terrorism when left unchallenged from criticism, or normalizing criticism everywhere, including India and the Middle East, so that the US, India, Western Europe, and even the Middle East itself no longer have to deal with a never-ending strain of terrorist bombings, terrorist shootings, mass murder, ethnic cleansings, violent coups, and violence against women and atheists on a scope and scale that is only comparable to Christianity's violence against Jews, the people of India, Black people across the world, Tasmanian Aboriginals, the Irish, the Boers, numerous Indigenous European people, and Native Americans. Many Christians are willing to have actual conversations about such histories and many are prompted internally in an effort for reconciliation and a recognition of other people's humanity; no such moral reckoning is ever committed by either Muslims or even most Ex-Muslims. I don't want to live in a world where we're so afraid of offending feelings when bomb blasts explode at a runners marathon such as during the Boston Bombings of 2013 in the US, or mothers are forcibly conditioned to be nice to people throwing hand grenades at preschools that nearly kill their children such as in Sweden, or Islamic terrorism's intentional mass murders of civilians being treated as seasonal weather patterns in India by the US corporate news media. You should absolutely expect more violent riots like the British riots of 2024 or the so-called "communal" riots in India over Islamic violence. Our choices were never Free Speech helping supposed bigots versus protecting Muslims from bigotry, that is honestly just 7th century conspiratorial thinking. Our choices have only been that we value Free Speech to reduce Islamic terrorism and end it within our lifetimes through peaceful criticisms and the freedom to question Islam's theology or we lay down and allow them to slowly kill or convert us all because Islamic terrorism is never going to stop unless Muslims hear and experience arguments about why Islam is simply wrong. Either truth triumphs over all or Islamic terrorism remains unchecked as it kills innocent civilians including children. Either free inquiry is indulged as a natural human right per the First Amendment of the US and the arguments of Thomas Jefferson, or the US gets bogged and degraded with too much debt to finance forever wars just as the Islamic terrorists have sought to do and gradually been succeeding in such a goal. Our choices will always come to either Free Speech is maintained as a standard for Free Inquiry to flourish or we live with the fear of Islamic violence for the rest of our lives. If we keep choosing the latter, then we pay the price in both lives and taxes for diminishing returns. We all must hold to a new standard and openly criticize all religion, if that's what it takes. Human lives must be held as far more valuable above feeling offended about criticisms of ancient mythology.

Bibliography

Key Terms

1. Hamid, Shadi, and Rashid Dar. "Islamism, Salafism, and Jihadism: A Primer." *Brookings*, The Brookings Institution, 15 July 2016, www.brookings.edu/articles/islamism-salafism-and-jihadism-a-primer/.

Chapter 1

1. al-Sadr, Sayyid Sadruddin. "Chapter 4 | Al-Mahdi | Al-Islam.Org." Translated by Jalil Dorrani, Al-Islam.Org, Sayyid Sadruddin al-Sadr, www.al-islam.org/al-mahdi-sayyid-sadruddin-sadr/chapter-4. Accessed 18 Jan. 2025.
2. Castor, Trevor. "Sin According to Islam." Zwemer Center, www.zwemercenter.com/guide/sin-according-to-muslims/.
3. "Difference between Shari'ah, Fiqh and Usul al-Fiqh - Islam Question & Answer." Islamqa.Info, Shaykh Muhammad Saalih al-Munajjid, islamqa.info/en/answers/282538/difference-between-shariah-fiqh-and-usul-al-fiqh. Accessed 17 Jan. 2025.
4. "Greater and Lesser Jihaad." Translated by Muhammed Salih Al-Munajjid, Islam Question And Answer, islamqa.info/en/10455.
5. Ibrahim, Abu. "Shariah and Fiqh. Do You Know the Difference?" Islamic Learning Materials, 5 Mar. 2012, web.archive.org/web/20181006224011/islamiclearningmaterials.com/shariah-fiqh/.
6. "Jami` At-Tirmidhi 2240: 33  Chapters On Al-Fitan: (59)Chapter: What Has Been Related About The Turmoil Of The Dajjal." Jami` At-Tirmidhi 2240 - Chapters on al-Fitan - كتاب الفتن عن رسول الله صلى الله عليه وسلم - Sunnah.Com - Sayings and Teachings of Prophet Muhammad (صلى الله عليه و سلم), SUNNAH.COM, sunnah.com/tirmidhi:2240. Accessed 18 Mar. 2025.
7. Khan, Faraz A. "Can the Sunnah Abrogate the Qur'an?" SeekersGuidance, sufyan https://seekersguidance.org/wp-content/uploads/2024/11/SG_Logo_v23.svg, 28 Oct. 2010, seekersguidance.org/answers/general-counsel/can-the-sunnah-abrogate-the-quran/#:~:text=(1)%20The%20Hanafis%2C%20Imam,accepted%20and%20implemented%20by%20the.
8. Sahih Muslim 156 - The Book of Faith - كتاب الإيمان - Sunnah.Com - Sayings and Teachings of Prophet Muhammad (صلى الله عليه و سلم), sunnah.com/muslim:156. Accessed 17 Jan. 2025.
9. "Sahih Muslim 2937a: 54 The Book of Tribulations and Portents of the Last Hour: (20)Chapter: Ad-Dajjal." Sahih Muslim 2937a - the Book of Tribulations and Portents of the Last Hour - كتاب الفتن وأشراط الساعة - Sunnah.Com - Sayings and Teachings of Prophet Muhammad (صلى الله عليه و سلم), SUNNAH.COM, sunnah.com/muslim:2937a. Accessed 18 Mar. 2025. For reference: Reference: Sahih Muslim 2937a In-book reference: Book 54, Hadith 134 USC-MSA web (English) reference: Book 41, Hadith 7015 (deprecated numbering scheme)
10. "Sunan Ibn Majah 4055: (28)Chapter: Signs (of the Day of Judgment)(28) باب الآيَاتِ." Sunan Ibn Majah 4055 - Tribulations - كتاب الفتن - Sunnah.Com - Sayings and Teachings of Prophet Muhammad (صلى الله عليه و سلم), SUNNAH.COM, sunnah.com/ibnmajah:4055. Accessed 18 Mar. 2025.
11. "Sunan Ibn Majah 4075: 36 Tribulations: (33)Chapter: The Tribulation of Dajjal, the Emergence of 'Esa Bin Maryam and the Emergence of Gog and Magog." Sunan Ibn Majah 4075 - Tribulations - كتاب الفتن - Sunnah.Com - Sayings and Teachings of Prophet Muhammad (صلى الله عليه و سلم), sunnah.com/ibnmajah:4075. Accessed 18 Mar. 2025.
12. "Sunan Ibn Majah 4078: 36 Tribulations: (33)Chapter: The Tribulation of Dajjal, the Emergence of 'Esa Bin Maryam and the Emergence of Gog and Magog." Sunan Ibn Majah 4078 - Tribulations - كتاب الفتن - Sunnah.Com - Sayings and Teachings of Prophet Muhammad (صلى الله عليه و سلم), SUNNAH.COM, sunnah.com/ibnmajah:4078. Accessed 18 Mar. 2025.
13. "Tafseer on the Basis of Narrated Texts and Tafseer on the Basis of Individual Understanding - Islam Question & Answer." Islamqa.info, Islam Question and Answer, 11 Mar. 2015, islamqa.info/en/answers/205290/tafseer-on-the-basis-of-narrated-texts-and-tafseer-on-the-basis-of-individual-understanding.

14. "Theory of Abrogation (Naskh) in Islam, Abrogation in Islamic Jurisprudence." Theory of Abrogation (Naskh) in Islam, Abrogation in Islamic Jurisprudence, Law and Legislation, 28 May 2018, www.lawandlegislation.com/2018/05/theory-of-abrogation-naskh-in-islam.html.
15. THE THEORY OF ABROGATION, www.islamawareness.net/FAQ/Logic/faq105.html.
16. "The Quranic Arabic Corpus - Word by Word Grammar, Syntax and Morphology of the Holy Quran." The Quranic Arabic Corpus - Translation, corpus.quran.com/translation.jsp?chapter=4&verse=89.
17. The Quranic Arabic Corpus - Translation, Quranic Arabic Corpus, corpus.quran.com/translation.jsp?chapter=4&verse=159. Accessed 17 Jan. 2025.
18. "What Do Muslims Believe about Jesus?" Islam Guide: Life After Death, www.islam-guide.com/ch3-10.htm.
19. "What Is Unique about Jesus and Mary in Islam?" Facts about the Muslims the Religion of Islam, Why Islam?, 24 Nov. 2024, www.whyislam.org/jesus-and-mary/.
20. "What Is Shari'ah? - Islam Question & Answer." Islamqa.Info, Shaykh Muhammad Saalih al-Munajjid, islamqa.info/en/answers/210742/what-is-shariah. Accessed 17 Jan. 2025.

Chapter 2

1. Aniruddha. "Aniruddha's Commentary, Translated. Book I." Translated by Richard Garbe, Http://Indianculture.Gov.In, pp. 53–55. For Reference: Aphorisms and Commentary of 92, 93, and 94.
2. Aniruddha. "Aniruddha's Commentary, Translated. Book V." Translated by Richard Garbe, Http://Indianculture.Gov.In, pp. 179 - 194. For Reference: Aphorisms and Commentary of 2 – 30.
3. "Atheism in Hinduism." Wikipedia, Wikimedia Foundation, 26 July 2019, en.wikipedia.org/wiki/Atheism_in_Hinduism#Arguments_against_existence_of_God_in_Hindu_philosophy.
4. Datta, Jatindranath. Chapter 2: The Path of Knowledge (783 – 2219). Bhagavad Gita: With the commentary of Shankaracharya. Advaita Ashrama, 1984.
5. Dixit, Sanjay. "Hindu Epistemology with Its Pramāṇa (Proof) System, Is Closest to Science - Hinduism Is Different..." Medium, Medium, 3 Nov. 2020, sanjay-dixit.medium.com/hindu-epistemology-with-its-pram%C4%81%E1%B9%87a-proof-system-is-closest-to-science-hinduism-is-different-5434cf9b659b.
6. Eknath, Easwaran, translator. Brihadaranyaka: The Forest of Wisdom (92-117) and Prashna: The Breath of Life (218-237). The Upanishads. Nilgiri Press, 2007.
7. Eknath, Easwaran, translator. Chapter Three: Selfless Service (93-103) and Chapter Five: Renounce and Rejoice (122 – 130). The Bhagavad Gita. Nilgiri Press, 2007.
8. K, Prameela. "Rebuild Demolished Temples, BJP Tells State Govt." The New Indian Express, 17 Dec. 2020, www.newindianexpress.com/andhra-pradesh/2020/Dec/17/rebuild-demolished-temples-bjp-tells-state-govt-2237415.html.
9. Kapstein, Matthew T., et al. Chapter 31: Hindu Disproofs of God: Refuting Vedantic Theism in the Samkhya-Sutra by Andrew J. Nicholson (598-619). The Oxford Handbook of Indian Philosophy. Edited by Jonardon Ganeri, Oxford University Press, 2018.
10. Lerner, Louise. "Black Holes, Explained." University of Chicago News, news.uchicago.edu/explainer/black-holes-explained#:~:text=Black%20holes%20have%20two%20parts,infinitely%20small%20and%20infinitely%20dense. Accessed 12 Mar. 2025.
11. Lotto, Beau. Chapter 5: The Frog Who Dreamed of Being a Prince (1356 - 1670). Deviate: the Science of Seeing Differently. Hachette Books, 2017.
12. Patanjali. "Book One: Samadhi Pada." Yoga Sutras of Patanjali, translated by Swami Satchidananda, Kindle ed., Integral Yoga Publications, Buckingham, Virginia, 2012, pp. 23–108.
13. Patanjali. "Chapter 1: Concentration (Samadhi Pada)." Translated by Swami Jnaneshvara Bharati, PDF ed., Www.Swamij.Com, pp. 4–15.
14. Sahgal, Neha, and Jonathan Evans. "6. Nationalism and Politics." Pew Research Center, Pew Research Center, 29 June 2021, www.pewresearch.org/religion/2021/06/29/nationalism-and-politics/.
15. Silver, Laura, and Jonathan Evans. "4. Should Religious Texts Influence National Laws?" Pew Research Center, Pew Research Center, 28 Jan. 2025, www.pewresearch.org/global/2025/01/28/should-religious-texts-influence-national-laws/.
16. Silver, Laura, and Jonathan Evans. "5. What Role Should Religion Play in Muslim- and Jewish-Majority Countries?" Pew Research Center, Pew Research Center, 28 Jan. 2025, www.pewresearch.org/global/2025/01/28/what-role-should-religion-play-in-muslim-and-jewish-majority-countries/.
17. Stanton, Glenn T. Chapter 9: "Is My Church Shrinking?" And Other Questions to Consider (pgs. 137 – 160). The Myth of the Dying Church: How Christianity Is Actually Thriving in America and the World. Worthy Publishing, 2019.
18. "The Death Throes of Stars - NASA Science." NASA, NASA, 27 Jan. 2025, science.nasa.gov/mission/hubble/science/science-highlights/the-death-throes-of-

stars/#:~:text=When%20stars%20die%2C%20they%20throw,death%20depends%20on%20its%20size.

19. "Webb Image Galleries - NASA Science." NASA, NASA, 13 Feb. 2025, science.nasa.gov/mission/webb/multimedia/images/.

Chapter 3

1. "Age of the Mother of the Believers 'Aa'ishah (May Allah Be Pleased with Her) When the Prophet (Blessings and Peace of Allah Be upon Him) Married Her - Islam Question & Answer." Islamqa.info, Islam Question and Answer, 30 Dec. 2013, islamqa.info/en/answers/124483/age-of-the-mother-of-the-believers-aaishah-may-allah-be-pleased-with-her-when-the-prophet-blessings-and-peace-of-allah-be-upon-him-married-her.
2. "As Eid Al Adha Approaches..." Questions on Islam, questionsonislam.com/content/eid-al-adha-approaches….
3. Bittles, A H, and R Hussain. "An Analysis of Consanguineous Marriage in the Muslim Population of India at Regional and State Levels." Current Neurology and Neuroscience Reports., U.S. National Library of Medicine, www.ncbi.nlm.nih.gov/pubmed/10768421.
4. "Bradford Grooming: Nine Jailed for Abusing Girls." BBC News, BBC, 27 Feb. 2019, www.bbc.com/news/uk-england-leeds-47388060.
5. Callimachi, Rukmini. "Isis Enshrines a Theology of Rape." The New York Times, The New York Times, 13 Aug. 2015, www.nytimes.com/2015/08/14/world/middleeast/isis-enshrines-a-theology-of-rape.html.
6. Chhabhadiya, Neelam. "Sexual Grooming amongst Hindu Girls." National Hindu Students Forum UK, NHSF (UK), 9 Nov. 2017, www.nhsf.org.uk/2017/11/sexual-grooming-amongst-hindu-girls/.
7. Dearden, Lizzie. "Grooming Gangs Abused More than 700 Women and Girls around Newcastle after Police Appeared to Punish Victims." The Independent, Independent Digital News and Media, 23 Feb. 2018, www.independent.co.uk/news/uk/crime/grooming-gangs-uk-britain-newcastle-serious-case-review-operation-sanctuary-shelter-muslim-asian-a8225106.html.
8. Greenwood, Shannon. "1. Demographic Portrait of Muslim Americans." Pew Research Center, Pew Research Center, 26 July 2017, www.pewresearch.org/religion/2017/07/26/demographic-portrait-of-muslim-americans/.
9. Haddad, Mais. "Victims of Rape and Law: How the Laws of the Arab World Protect Rapists, Not Victims." Jurist, Jurist, www.jurist.org/commentary/2017/05/mais-haddad-arab-world-laws-protect-the-rapist-not-the-victim/.
10. Haider, Sarah. "Even as a Child, This Eid Was Horrifying. I Remember Witnessing a Sacrifice of a Cow with My Family, I Remember the Blood Gushing from Its Throat and Running through the Street. The Story of Abraham Which It Commemorates Is Another Horror. I'll Save My Mubaraks for the Other Eid." Twitter, Twitter, 21 Aug. 2018, twitter.com/SarahTheHaider/status/1031995695652384769.
11. Haider, Sarah. "Sarah Haider: Islam and the Necessity of Liberal Critique (AHA Conference 2015)." YouTube, American Humanist Association, 28 May 2015, www.youtube.com/watch?v=0plC24YuoJk.
12. Haqiqatjou, Daniel Reza. "About." Muslim Skeptic, Muslim Skeptic, Nov. 2017, muslimskeptic.com/about/.
13. Haqiqatjou, Daniel Reza. "Daniel Haqiqatjou, Author at Muslim Skeptic." Muslim Skeptic, Muslim Skeptic, Jan. 2018, muslimskeptic.com/author/drjou/.
14. "Health Risks of Female Genital Mutilation (FGM)." World Health Organization, World Health Organization, 1 Feb. 2017, www.who.int/reproductivehealth/topics/fgm/health_consequences_fgm/en/.
15. "Iraq's New Law Allowing Children as Young as 9 to Marry Undermines Women and Girls' Rights." Walk Free, Minderoo Foundation, 31 Jan. 2025, www.walkfree.org/news/2025/iraqs-new-law-allowing-children-as-young-as-9-to-marry-undermines-women-and-girls-rights/.
16. Lal, K. S. Chapter 2: Rise of Muslims under the Sultanate (pp. 22-27). *Indian Muslims - Who Are They*. Internet Archive, 28 Aug. 2020, https://dn790000.ca.archive.org/0/items/indian-muslims-who-are-they-k.-s.-lal/Indian%20Muslims%20-%20Who%20Are%20They%20-%20K.%20S.%20Lal.pdf, PDF Edition.

17. Lal, K. S. Chapter 2: Rise of Muslims under the Sultanate (pp. 23-27). *Indian Muslims - Who Are They*. Mahesh Patel. Kindle Edition.
18. Na'amnih, Wasef, et al. "Prevalence of Consanguineous Marriages and Associated Factors among Israeli Bedouins." Current Neurology and Neuroscience Reports., U.S. National Library of Medicine, Oct. 2014, www.ncbi.nlm.nih.gov/pmc/articles/PMC4159474/.
19. Navabi, Armin. "Islam Unboxed ℭ☐ – Part 2 (With Imam Tawhidi, Daniel Haqiqatjou and Armin Navabi)." YouTube, Ideas Unboxed, 2 Jan. 2019, www.youtube.com/watch?v=bi3Cnk224zI&t=3164s&ab_channel=IdeasUnboxed.
20. Nomani, Asra Q., and Hala Arafa. "Inside the World of Gulf State Slavery." The Daily Beast, The Daily Beast Company, 11 Oct. 2015, www.thedailybeast.com/inside-the-world-of-gulf-state-slavery.
21. "Pakistani Hindus Complain of Forced Conversion of Teenage Girls." YouTube, VOA News, 18 Mar. 2016, youtu.be/-i24jg4mJ4I.
22. Rai, Lala Lajpat. "CHAPTER XII WOMAN IN INDIA: A RETROSPECT." WWW.HINDUSTANBOOKS.COM, BANNA PUBLISHING CO., CALCUTTA / Kolkata, West Bengal, 1928, pp. 151–174, https://hindustanbooks.com/books/unhappy_india/Unhappy_India.pdf. Accessed 12 Mar. 2025.
23. Rawlinson, Kevin. "Oxford Grooming Gang Jailed: Dogar and Karrar Brothers Get Life For." The Independent, Independent Digital News and Media, 27 June 2013, www.independent.co.uk/news/uk/crime/oxford-grooming-gang-jailed-dogar-and-karrar-brothers-get-life-for-abuse-and-rape-of-young-girls-8677159.html.
24. Reuters. "Swedish Court Convicts Quran Burner of Hate Crimes, Days after His Ally Was Killed | The Times of Israel." Www.Timesofisrael.Com, Times of Israel, 3 Feb. 2025, www.timesofisrael.com/swedish-court-convicts-quran-burner-of-hate-crimes-days-after-his-ally-was-killed/.
25. "Rulings from Your Site Regarding Female Circumcision Appear to Have Been Taken down. Is There a Change in Opinion Concerning Female Circumcision from a Shafii Point of View? What Do You Say about Issuing a Fatwa on This Issue Which Prohibits the Practice?" Translated by Yaqub Abdurrahman, Shafii Fiqh, shafiifiqh.com/question-details.aspx?qstID=173.
26. Saad, Hassan Abu, et al. "Consanguineous Marriage and Intellectual and Developmental Disabilities among Arab Bedouins Children of the Negev Region in Southern Israel: A Pilot Study." Current Neurology and Neuroscience Reports., U.S. National Library of Medicine, 2014, www.ncbi.nlm.nih.gov/pmc/articles/PMC3904202/.
27. "Sahih Al-Bukhari 3894: 63 Merits of the Helpers in Madinah (Ansaar): (44)Chapter: Marriage of the Prophet (Saws) with 'Aishah رضي الله عنها." Sahih Al-Bukhari 3894 - Merits of the Helpers in Madinah (Ansaar) - كتاب مناقب الأنصار - Sunnah.Com - Sayings and Teachings of Prophet Muhammad (صلى الله عليه و سلم), SUNNAH.COM, sunnah.com/bukhari:3894. Accessed 21 Mar. 2025.
28. "Sahih Al-Bukhari 3896: 63 Merits of the Helpers in Madinah (Ansaar): (44) Chapter: Marriage of the Prophet (Saws) with 'Aishah." Sahih Al-Bukhari 3896 - Merits of the Helpers in Madinah (Ansaar) - كتاب مناقب الأنصار - Sunnah.Com - Sayings and Teachings of Prophet Muhammad (صلى الله عليه و سلم), SUNNAH.COM, sunnah.com/bukhari:3896. Accessed 20 Mar. 2025.
29. "Sahih Al-Bukhari 5133: 67 Wedlock, Marriage (Nikaah): (39)Chapter: Giving One's Young Children in Marriage." Sahih Al-Bukhari 5133 - Wedlock, Marriage (Nikaah) - كتاب النكاح - Sunnah.Com - Sayings and Teachings of Prophet Muhammad (صلى الله عليه و سلم), SUNNAH.COM, sunnah.com/bukhari:5133. Accessed 21 Mar. 2025.
30. Saleem, Mya, et al. "Examining Honor Culture and Violence in Islam (AHA Conference 2016)." YouTube, American Humanist Association, 30 June 2016, www.youtube.com/watch?v=DhwrOJvPfBw.
31. Sentencing Remarks of His Honour Judge Peter Rook QC, www.judiciary.uk/wp-content/uploads/JCO/Documents/Judgments/sentencing-remarks-r-v-dogar-others.pdf. Accessed 13 Mar. 2025.

32. Shamshad, S. "Prevalence of Consanguinity in Muslim Community - A Review." Pdfs.semanticscholar.org, International Journal of Science and Research (IJSR) , pdfs.semanticscholar.org/f3db/08faf43477ce7c34146aa4b8db0769661efa.pdf.
33. "Shreela Flather." Wikipedia, Wikimedia Foundation, 9 July 2018, en.wikipedia.org/wiki/Shreela_Flather.
34. "Sunan Abi Dawud 2121: 12 Marriage (Kitab Al-Nikah): (700) Chapter: Regarding The Marriage Of The Young." Sunan Abi Dawud 2121 - Marriage (Kitab al-Nikah) - كتاب النكاح - Sunnah.Com - Sayings and Teachings of Prophet Muhammad (صلى الله عليه و سلم), SUNNAH.COM, sunnah.com/abudawud:2121. Accessed 21 Mar. 2025.
35. "Sunan An-Nasa'i 3255: 26 The Book of Marriage 29 (كتاب النكاح) Chapter: A Man Marrying Off His Young Daughter(29)."باب إِنْكَاحِ الرَّجُلِ ابْنَتَهُ الصَّغِيرَةَ. Sunan An-Nasa'i 3255 - the Book of Marriage - كتاب النكاح - Sunnah.Com - Sayings and Teachings of Prophet Muhammad (صلى الله عليه و سلم), SUNNAH.COM, sunnah.com/nasai:3255. Accessed 21 Mar. 2025.
36. "Surat An-Nisā' (the Women) - سورة النساء." The Noble Qur'an, legacy.quran.com/4/3. Accessed 12 Mar. 2025.
37. "Surat Al-Mu'Minūn (the Believers) - سورة المؤمنون." The Noble Qur'an, legacy.quran.com/23/5-6. Accessed 12 Mar. 2025.
38. "Surat An-Nisā' (the Women) - سورة النساء." The Noble Qur'an, legacy.quran.com/4/23. Accessed 13 Mar. 2025.
39. "Surat An-Nūr (the Light) - سورة النور." The Noble Qur'an, legacy.quran.com/24/33. Accessed 12 Mar. 2025.
40. "Surat An-Nūr (the Light) - سورة النور." The Noble Qur'an, legacy.quran.com/24/58. Accessed 12 Mar. 2025.
41. Swinford, Steven. "First Cousin Marriages in Pakistani Communities Leading to 'Appalling' Disabilities among Children." The Telegraph, Telegraph Media Group, 7 July 2015, www.telegraph.co.uk/news/health/children/11723308/First-cousin-marriages-in-Pakistani-communities-leading-to-appalling-disabilities-among-children.html.
42. "Tafseer on the Basis of Narrated Texts and Tafseer on the Basis of Individual Understanding - Islam Question & Answer." Islamqa.info, Islam Question and Answer, 11 Mar. 2015, islamqa.info/en/answers/205290/tafseer-on-the-basis-of-narrated-texts-and-tafseer-on-the-basis-of-individual-understanding.
43. The Quranic Arabic Corpus - Translation, corpus.quran.com/translation.jsp?chapter=16&verse=71. Accessed 12 Mar. 2025.
44. The Quranic Arabic Corpus - Translation, corpus.quran.com/translation.jsp?chapter=33&verse=50. Accessed 12 Mar. 2025.
45. "The Quranic Arabic Corpus - Word by Word Grammar, Syntax and Morphology of the Holy Quran." The Quranic Arabic Corpus - Translation, http://corpus.quran.com/translation.jsp?chapter=4&verse=24
46. "The Quranic Arabic Corpus - Word by Word Grammar, Syntax and Morphology of the Holy Quran." The Quranic Arabic Corpus - Translation, corpus.quran.com/translation.jsp?chapter=4&verse=89.
47. "Who Is a Scholar ('Aalim)? - Islam Question & Answer." Islamqa.info, Islam Question and Answer, 18 July 2011, islamqa.info/en/answers/145071/who-is-a-scholar-aalim.

Chapter 4

1. Ahmed, Zubair. "Kashmiri Hindus: Driven out and Insignificant." BBC News, BBC, 6 Apr. 2016, www.bbc.com/news/world-asia-india-35923237.
2. Alam, Julhas. "Hindus in Muslim-Majority Bangladesh Rally to Demand Protection from Attacks." AP News, AP News, 2 Nov. 2024, apnews.com/article/bangladesh-hindu-minority-attacks-hasina-yunus-beaddefd93f1b9dcf14d287543b023f5.
3. Callimachi, Rukmini. "Isis Enshrines a Theology of Rape." The New York Times, The New York Times, 13 Aug. 2015, www.nytimes.com/2015/08/14/world/middleeast/isis-enshrines-a-theology-of-rape.html.
4. Davis, Mike. Late Victorian Holocausts: El Nino Famines and the Making of the Third World. Penguin Random House Publisher Services, 2001.
5. Durant, Will. Chapter XIV: The Foundations of India: IV. Indo-Aryan Society (9245 - 9297). Our Oriental Heritage: Being a History of Civilization in Egypt and the Near East to the Death of Alexander, and in India, China and Japan from the Beginning to Our Own Day. Simon and Schuster, 1935.
6. Durant, Will. Chapter XIV: The Foundations of India: VII. The Philosophy of the Upanishads (9463 - 9469). Our Oriental Heritage: Being a History of Civilization in Egypt and the Near East to the Death of Alexander, and in India, China and Japan from the Beginning to Our Own Day. Simon and Schuster, 1935.
7. Durant, Will. Chapter XVI: From Alexander to Aurangzeb: IV. Annals of Rajputana (Pgs. 10362-10387). Our Oriental Heritage: Being a History of Civilization in Egypt and the Near East to the Death of Alexander, and in India, China and Japan from the Beginning to Our Own Day. Simon and Schuster, 1935.
8. Durant, Will. Chapter XVI: From Alexander to Aurangzeb: VI. The Moslem Conquest (Pgs. 10447-10520). Our Oriental Heritage: Being a History of Civilization in Egypt and the Near East to the Death of Alexander, and in India, China and Japan from the Beginning to Our Own Day. Simon and Schuster, 1935.
9. Durant, Will. Chapter XVI: From Alexander to Aurangzeb: VII. Akbar The Great (Pgs. 10520 - 10691). Our Oriental Heritage: Being a History of Civilization in Egypt and the Near East to the Death of Alexander, and in India, China and Japan from the Beginning to Our Own Day. Simon and Schuster, 1935.
10. Elst, Koenraad. Chapter Two: Negationism in India (pgs. 56 – 59). Negationism in India: Concealing the Record of Islam. Voice of India, 2014.
11. Ghose, Sanujit. "Cultural Links between India & the Greco-Roman World." Ancient History Encyclopedia, Ancient History Encyclopedia, 30 Apr. 2019, www.ancient.eu/article/208/cultural-links-between-india--the-greco-roman-worl/.
12. "Houses of Christian Tripura Community Torched in Bangladesh on Christmas Eve - Times of India." The Times of India, TOI, 25 Dec. 2024, timesofindia.indiatimes.com/world/south-asia/houses-of-christian-tripura-community-torched-in-bangladesh-on-christmas-eve/articleshow/116658938.cms.
13. Ispas, Alexa. Psychology and politics: a social identity perspective. Psychology Press, 2014. For reference purposes: Chapter 1: Psychology and the Social Identity Perspective (1-24), Chapter 2: The Psychology of Social Influence (26-50).
14. Kapstein, Matthew T., et al. Contributors (IX - XVII). The Oxford Handbook of Indian Philosophy. Edited by Jonardon Ganeri, Oxford University Press, 2018.
15. Kapstein, Matthew T., et al. Introduction: Why Indian Philosophy? Why now? by Jonardon Ganeri (1-14). The Oxford Handbook of Indian Philosophy. Edited by Jonardon Ganeri, Oxford University Press, 2018.
16. Kapstein, Matthew T., et al. Chapter 1: Interpreting Indian Philosophy Three Parables by Matthew Kapstein (15-31). The Oxford Handbook of Indian Philosophy. Edited by Jonardon Ganeri, Oxford University Press, 2018.

17. Kapstein, Matthew T., et al. Chapter 2: History and Doxography of the Philosophical Schools by Ashok Aklujkar (32-55). The Oxford Handbook of Indian Philosophy. Edited by Jonardon Ganeri, Oxford University Press, 2018.
18. Kapstein, Matthew T., et al. Chapter 3: Philosophy as a Distinct Cultural Practice: The Transregional Context by Justin E.H. Smith (56-74). The Oxford Handbook of Indian Philosophy. Edited by Jonardon Ganeri, Oxford University Press, 2018.
19. Kapstein, Matthew T., et al. Chapter 4: Comparison or Confluence in Philosophy? by Mark Sideritis (75-92). The Oxford Handbook of Indian Philosophy. Edited by Jonardon Ganeri, Oxford University Press, 2018.
20. Kumar, Anugrah. "Pakistan Acquits All 115 Suspects in Burning of Christians' Homes." The Christian Post, 29 Jan. 2017, www.christianpost.com/news/pakistan-acquits-all-115-suspects-in-burning-of-christians-homes.html.
21. Lal, Kishori Saran. Chapter V: AD 1200 – 1400 (Pgs. 39 – 51). "Growth of Muslim Population in Medieval India (1000-1800)" Internet Archive, Internet Archive, 5 Aug. 2018, ia902800.us.archive.org/11/items/GrowthOfMuslimPopulationInMedievalIndiaAd10001800/Growth-Of-Muslim-Population-In-Medieval-India-ad-1000-1800_text.pdf.
22. Lal, Kishori Saran. Chapter X: AD 1200 – 1400 (Pgs. 113 – 116). "Growth of Muslim Population in Medieval India (1000-1800)" Internet Archive, Internet Archive, 5 Aug. 2018, ia902800.us.archive.org/11/items/GrowthOfMuslimPopulationInMedievalIndiaAd10001800/Growth-Of-Muslim-Population-In-Medieval-India-ad-1000-1800_text.pdf.
23. Lal, Kishori Saran. Chapter XI: AD 1400 – 1600 (Pgs. 127 – 143). "Growth of Muslim Population in Medieval India (1000-1800)" Internet Archive, Internet Archive, 5 Aug. 2018, ia902800.us.archive.org/11/items/GrowthOfMuslimPopulationInMedievalIndiaAd10001800/Growth-Of-Muslim-Population-In-Medieval-India-ad-1000-1800_text.pdf.
24. Lal, Kishori Saran. Chapter XII: AD 1600 – 1800 (Pgs. 144 – 156). "Growth of Muslim Population in Medieval India (1000-1800)" Internet Archive, Internet Archive, 5 Aug. 2018, ia902800.us.archive.org/11/items/GrowthOfMuslimPopulationInMedievalIndiaAd10001800/Growth-Of-Muslim-Population-In-Medieval-India-ad-1000-1800_text.pdf.
25. Lal, Kishori Saran. "Growth of Muslim Population in Medieval India (1000-1800)" Internet Archive, Internet Archive, 5 Aug. 2018, ia902800.us.archive.org/11/items/GrowthOfMuslimPopulationInMedievalIndiaAd10001800/Growth-Of-Muslim-Population-In-Medieval-India-ad-1000-1800_text.pdf.
26. Mallapur, Chaitanya. "Sikhs, Christians More Likely to Be Jailed than Hindus and Muslims." Hindustan Times, Hindustan Times, 24 Oct. 2015, www.hindustantimes.com/india/hindus-least-likely-to-be-jailed-sikhs-christians-most-likely/story-Og4PhnhYsPlVLJglKyeOKL.html.
27. Nicholson, Andrew J. Chapter 10: Hindu Unity And The Non-Hindu Other (4806-5293). Unifying Hinduism: Philosophy and Identity in Indian Intellectual History (South Asia Across the Disciplines). Columbia University Press, 2010.
28. Nietzsche, Friedrich Wilhelm. Aphorism 23. THE ANTICHRIST. Translated by H. L. Mencken, The Project Gutenberg, 2006.
29. Sahgal, Neha, et al. "Religion in India: Tolerance and Segregation." Pew Research Center, Pew Research Center, 29 June 2021, www.pewresearch.org/religion/2021/06/29/religion-in-india-tolerance-and-segregation/#2cadb6b1e440f0bf00cd84d9a5e73d3a.
30. Sekhar, - Metla Sudha, et al. "Who Is Chinmoy Krishna Das and Why Has He Been Arrested in Bangladesh?" The Economic Times, economictimes.indiatimes.com/news/new-updates/all-about-the-iskcon-priest-who-has-been-arrested-in-bangladesh/articleshow/115694394.cms. Accessed 11 Mar. 2025.
31. Sridhar, Nithin. "No Evidence for Warfare or Invasion; Aryan Migration Too Is a Myth: B B Lal." NewsGram, 30 Nov. 2015, www.newsgram.com/no-evidence-for-warfare-or-invasion-aryan-migration-too-is-a-myth-b-b-lal

32. Sridhar, Nithin. "Vedic and Harappan Are Respectively Literary and Material Facets of Same Civilization: B. B. Lal." NewsGram, 2 Dec. 2015, www.newsgram.com/vedic-and-harappan-are-respectively-literary-and-material-facets-of-same-civilization-b-b-lal
33. "Surat Al-Bayyinah (the Clear Proof) - سورة البينة." The Noble Qur'an, quran.com, legacy.quran.com/98/6. Accessed 22 Mar. 2025.
34. "Surat At-Tawbah (the Repentance) - سورة التوبة." The Noble Qur'an, quran.com, legacy.quran.com/9/109. Accessed 22 Mar. 2025.
35. "Surat At-Tawbah (the Repentance) - سورة التوبة." The Noble Qur'an, quran.com, legacy.quran.com/9/113. Accessed 22 Mar. 2025.
36. "Surat At-Tawbah (the Repentance) - سورة التوبة." The Noble Qur'an, quran.com, legacy.quran.com/9/17. Accessed 22 Mar. 2025.
37. "Surat At-Tawbah (the Repentance) - سورة التوبة." The Noble Qur'an, quran.com, legacy.quran.com/9/28. Accessed 22 Mar. 2025.
38. "Surat At-Tawbah (the Repentance) - سورة التوبة." The Noble Qur'an, quran.com, legacy.quran.com/9/33. Accessed 22 Mar. 2025.
39. "Surat At-Tawbah (the Repentance) - سورة التوبة." The Noble Qur'an, quran.com, legacy.quran.com/9/36. Accessed 22 Mar. 2025.
40. "Surat At-Tawbah (the Repentance) - سورة التوبة." The Noble Qur'an, quran.com, legacy.quran.com/9/5. Accessed 22 Mar. 2025.
41. "Surat At-Tawbah (the Repentance) - سورة التوبة." The Noble Qur'an, quran.com, legacy.quran.com/9/66. Accessed 22 Mar. 2025.
42. "Surat Yūnus (Jonah) - سورة يونس." The Noble Qur'an, quran.com, legacy.quran.com/10/13. Accessed 22 Mar. 2025.
43. TNN / Nov 29, 2024. "Chinmoy Krishna Das Brahmachari: Bangladesh Monk Who's Sparked Calls for a Ban on ISKCON: India News." The Times of India, TOI, timesofindia.indiatimes.com/india/chinmoy-krishna-das-brahmachari-bangladesh-monk-whos-sparked-calls-for-a-ban-on-iskcon/articleshow/115787770.cms. Accessed 11 Mar. 2025.
44. TOI News Desk / TIMESOFINDIA.COM / Updated: Nov 30, 2024. "Two More ISKCON Priests Arrested in Bangladesh Following Chinmoy Krishna Das's Detention: India News - Times of India." The Times of India, TOI, timesofindia.indiatimes.com/india/two-more-iskcon-priests-arrested-in-bangladesh-following-chinmoy-krishna-dass-detention/articleshow/115848147.cms. Accessed 11 Mar. 2025.
45. TOI World Desk / TIMESOFINDIA.COM / Updated: Dec 1, 2024. "Bangladesh Stops Dozens of ISKCON Members from Crossing into India amid Rising Tensions: Report - Times of India." The Times of India, TOI, timesofindia.indiatimes.com/world/south-asia/bangladesh-stops-dozens-of-iskcon-members-from-crossing-into-india-amid-rising-tensions/articleshow/115871437.cms. Accessed 11 Mar. 2025.
46. "Two Pakistani Hindu Businessmen Shot Dead in Sindh." The Indian Express, Thursday, June 07, 2018, 5 Jan. 2018, web.archive.org/web/20180607183942/https://indianexpress.com/article/pakistan/two-pakistani-hindu-businessmen-shot-dead-in-sindh-5012781/.
47. U.S. Department of State, U.S. Department of State, www.state.gov/reports/2022-report-on-international-religious-freedom/syria/. Accessed 23 Mar. 2025.
48. White, Ed. "Judge Dismisses Charges Tied to Genital Mutilation Case." AP News, AP News, 28 Sept. 2021, apnews.com/article/religion-courts-detroit-183a427558377e73a150719d2205860e.

Chapter 5

1. Bhaumik, Subir. "South Asia | 'Church Backing Tripura Rebels.'" BBC News, BBC, 18 Apr. 2000, news.bbc.co.uk/2/hi/world/south_asia/717775.stm.
2. Dearden, Lizzie. "Grooming Gangs Abused More than 700 Women and Girls around Newcastle after Police Appeared to Punish Victims." The Independent, Independent Digital News and Media, 23 Feb. 2018, www.independent.co.uk/news/uk/crime/grooming-gangs-uk-britain-newcastle-serious-case-review-operation-sanctuary-shelter-muslim-asian-a8225106.html.
3. Foster, Sarah. "Survey: More than Half of Americans Couldn't Cover Three Months of Expenses with Emergency Savings." Edited by Brian Beers, Bankrate, SRS Omnibus, 22 Oct. 2024, www.bankrate.com/banking/savings/emergency-savings-survey-july-2021/.
4. France 24. "Sweden's 'truth Commission' Delves into Painful Sami Past." France 24, FRANCE 24, 5 Oct. 2023, www.france24.com/en/live-news/20230510-sweden-s-truth-commission-delves-into-painful-sami-past.
5. Furman, Jason. "Jason Furman." Foreign Affairs, 30 Oct. 2024, www.foreignaffairs.com/authors/jason-furman.
6. Furman, Jason. "The Post-Neoliberal Delusion." Foreign Affairs, 10 February 2025, https://www.foreignaffairs.com/united-states/post-neoliberal-delusion. Accessed 28 March 2025.
7. "German Federal Court Overturns 'Sharia Police' Acquittals." AP News, AP News, 11 Jan. 2018, apnews.com/article/525f089c10ae4417b48b368cd6fb3357.
8. Hacker, Jacob S., and Paul Pierson. Winner-Take-All Politics How Washington Made the Rich Richer - and Turned Its Back on the Middle Class. Simon & Schuster, 2011.
9. "India's Relationship with the Third Gender." UAB Institute for Human Rights Blog, The University of Alabama at Birmingham, 29 Oct. 2018, sites.uab.edu/humanrights/2018/10/29/indias-relationship-with-the-third-gender/.
10. Kahneman, Daniel. Chapter 25: Bernoulli's Errors (276) and Chapter 26: The Prospect Theory (278-288). Thinking, fast and slow. Farrar, Straus and Giroux, 2015.
11. Maffie, James. Aztec Philosophy: Understanding a World in Motion. University Press of Colorado. Kindle Edition.
12. Maxwell, Emerald, and Caroline Sinz. "Focus: Women Made to Keep Low Profile in Some French Suburbs." YouTube, FRANCE 24 English, 19 Dec. 2016, www.youtube.com/watch?v=6gZFGpNdH1A&ab_channel=FRANCE24English.
13. "Modern Slavery in United Arab Emirates." Walk Free, 22 Aug. 2023, www.walkfree.org/global-slavery-index/country-studies/united-arab-emirates/.
14. Moore, Malcolm. "Chinese Plane in Xinjiang Hijack Attempt." The Telegraph, Telegraph Media Group, 29 June 2012, www.telegraph.co.uk/news/worldnews/asia/china/9365032/Chinese-plane-in-Xinjiang-hijack-attempt.html.
15. Price, Greg. "SPLC Apologizes to Falsely Labeled Foundation." Newsweek, Newsweek, 18 June 2018, www.newsweek.com/splc-nawaz-million-apologizes-981879.
16. Savage, Maddy. "Sweden's 100 Explosions This Year: What's Going On?" BBC News, BBC, 12 Nov. 2019, www.bbc.com/news/world-europe-50339977.
17. Szumski, Charles. "'No Control': Sweden Grapples with Bomb Violence Wave." Eurasia Review, EurActiv, 31 Jan. 2025, www.eurasiareview.com/31012025-no-control-sweden-grapples-with-bomb-violence-wave/.
18. Tiwary, Deeptiman. "Centre Signs Peace Pact with Tripura Insurgent Outfit Nlft." The Indian Express, The Indian Express, 10 Aug. 2019, indianexpress.com/article/india/centre-signs-peace-pact-with-tripura-insurgent-outfit-nlft-5895406/.
19. Wagner, Sally Roesch. Sisters in Spirit: Iroquois Influence on Early Feminists: Haudenosaunee (Iroquois) Influence on Early American Feminists. Book Publishing Company. Kindle Edition.

20. Wikipedia contributors. "List of terrorist incidents in India." Wikipedia, The Free Encyclopedia. Wikipedia, The Free Encyclopedia, 5 Jan. 2025. Web. 30 Mar. 2025.
21. Wong, Tessa. "377: The British Colonial Law That Left an Anti-LGBTQ Legacy in Asia." BBC News, BBC, 28 June 2021, www.bbc.com/news/world-asia-57606847.

Chapter 6

1. Alden, Chris. "Britain's Monarchy." The Guardian, Guardian News and Media, 16 May 2002, www.theguardian.com/world/2002/may/16/qanda.jubilee.
2. "Article 30☐: Discrimination against Hindus by the Indian State." HHR News, Hindu Human Rights, 16 Dec. 2013, www.hinduhumanrights.info/article-30-discrimination-against-hindus-by-the-indian-state/.
3. Batchelor, Tom. "14 Dead in Terror Attack on Market in India." Express.Co.Uk, Express.co.uk, 5 Aug. 2016, www.express.co.uk/news/world/696937/India-terror-attack-shooting-Kokrajhar-market-Assam.
4. Bengrut, Dheeraj. "New Evidence Suggests Harappan Civilisation Is 7,000 to 8,000 Years' Old." Hindustan Times, Hindustan Times, 22 Dec. 2023, www.hindustantimes.com/cities/pune-news/new-evidence-suggests-harappan-civilisation-is-7-000-to-8-000-years-old-101703182904001.html.
5. "Brooklyn Diocese Lists Names of 108 Priests Accused of Abuse." AP News, AP News, 15 Feb. 2019, apnews.com/general-news-ae576a17118b4a45bdb0ba4943e880dc.
6. CANTON, NAOMI. "British Hindus Object to Islamophobia Council in UK, Call for Hatred against All Religions to Be Recognised." The Times of India, TOI, 18 Feb. 2025, timesofindia.indiatimes.com/nri/british-hindus-object-to-islamophobia-council-in-uk-call-for-hatred-against-all-religions-to-be-recognised/articleshow/118337929.cms.
7. Canton, Naomi. "Two Leading British Indian Community Figures Rami Ranger and Anil Bhanot Stripped of Their Honours by the King." The Times of India, TNN, 7 Dec. 2024, timesofindia.indiatimes.com/nri/other-news/two-leading-british-indian-community-figures-rami-ranger-and-anil-bhanot-stripped-of-their-honours-by-the-king/articleshow/116056259.cms.
8. Chhabhadiya, Neelam. "Sexual Grooming amongst Hindu Girls." National Hindu Students Forum UK, NHSF (UK), 9 Nov. 2017, www.nhsf.org.uk/2017/11/sexual-grooming-amongst-hindu-girls/.
9. Clarke, Jennifer, and Tom Edgington. "What Is the House of Lords, How Does It Work and How Is It Changing?" BBC News, BBC, 5 Sept. 2024, www.bbc.com/news/uk-politics-63864428.
10. "CPS Authorises Two Further Charges against Axel Rudakubana." CPS Authorises Two Further Charges against Axel Rudakubana | The Crown Prosecution Service, The Crown Prosecution Service, 29 Oct. 2024, www.cps.gov.uk/mersey-cheshire/news/authorises-two-further-charges-against-axel-rudakubana.
11. Davis, Mike. Late Victorian Holocausts: El Niño Famines and the Making of the Third World (Essential Mike Davis). Verso Books. Kindle Edition.
12. Davis, Mike. Chapter Five: Skeletons at the Feast (pgs. 141 – 177). Late Victorian Holocausts: El Niño Famines and the Making of the Third World (Essential Mike Davis). Verso Books. Kindle Edition.
13. Davis, Mike (2002-06-17). Late Victorian Holocausts: El Nino Famines and the Making of the Third World (p. 151-158). Verso Books. Kindle Edition.
14. Davis, Mike. Late Victorian Holocausts: El Niño Famines and the Making of the Third World (Essential Mike Davis) (pp. 164-165). Verso Books. Kindle Edition.
15. De, Abhishek. "US-Based Techie, IAF Official among 26 Killed in Attack. Who Were the Victims?" India Today, India Today, 23 Apr. 2025, www.indiatoday.in/india/story/pahalgam-terror-attack-kashmir-full-list-of-victims-released-2713232-2025-04-23.
16. "Dhandhuka Murder: 3 Accused in Police Remand for 10 More Days." The Indian Express, Express News Service, 7 Feb. 2022, web.archive.org/web/20220207041105/https://indianexpress.com/article/cities/ahmedabad/dhandhuka-murder-accused-police-remand-ahmedabad-7760401/.
17. Drake, Bruce, and Jacob Poushter. "In Views of Diversity, Many Europeans Are Less Positive than Americans." Pew Research Center, Pew Research Center, 12 July 2016, www.pewresearch.org/short-reads/2016/07/12/in-views-of-diversity-many-europeans-are-less-positive-than-americans/.

18. Easwaran, Eknath. Brihadaranyaka Upanishad (p. 114). The Upanishads (Easwaran's Classics of Indian Spirituality Book 2) (p. 114). Nilgiri Press. Kindle Edition.
19. Eddy, Sherwood. Chapter I: The People of India (pg. 25). "India Awakening: Eddy, Sherwood, 1871-1963: Free Download, Borrow, and Streaming." Google Books, Princeton University. Presented by THE PHILADELPHIAN SOCIETY, 1912, https://books.googleusercontent.com/books/content?req=AKW5QacOjZvyVCZx7JC45zx-pVd69QF_LrzHGBABHlS0BgDJfJNrm__UimdC_tajRdFAHCb5Fc7s5prfnZA5v_2kgrvVs4xCvYzw1DKcpY23MeNI5J8FL0u6HNfHT7PxHtR030sgoOXaVi2VVNswh-gOIXN1b3AXji1BPyqoV7tUxYhdPLpdQuhOJN4ZANy_ogTdNlHu-y2H5b4AjSlU2JuiFYgTcUCL8Vq9uZmSqw0z2tmvo4YOh6dUG_d4PblBcVWG-3kj6edg PDF edition.
20. Evans, Rob, and David Pegg. "Revealed: Queen Lobbied for Change in Law to Hide Her Private Wealth." The Guardian, Guardian News and Media, 7 Feb. 2021, www.theguardian.com/uk-news/2021/feb/07/revealed-queen-lobbied-for-change-in-law-to-hide-her-private-wealth.
21. G, Ananthakrishnan. "On PIL Seeking to Free Temples from Govt Control, SC Seeks More Material in Support." The Indian Express, The Indian Express, 1 Sept. 2022, web.archive.org/web/20220902050836/https://indianexpress.com/article/india/on-pil-seeking-to-free-temples-from-govt-control-sc-seeks-more-material-in-support-8125936/.
22. Gautam, Swati. "The Breast Tax That Wasn't." Kerala | The Breast Tax That Wasn't - Telegraph India, Telegraph India, 13 Jan. 2021, www.telegraphindia.com/culture/style/the-breast-tax-that-wasnt/cid/1803638.
23. Greenslade, Roy. "The D-Notice System: A Typically British Fudge That Has Survived a Century." The Guardian, Guardian News and Media, 31 July 2015, www.theguardian.com/media/2015/jul/31/d-notice-system-state-media-press-freedom.
24. Hacker, Isaac Henry. A HUNDRED YEARS IN TRAVANCORE BY I. H. HACKER, PDF ed., THE LONDON MISSIONARY SOCIETY, pp. 27–27, https://ia600207.us.archive.org/20/items/100YearsInTravancore/100YearsInTravancore.pdf. Accessed 18 May 2025.
25. Hacker, Isaac Henry. "CHAPTER II: THE RINGELTAUBE PERIOD, 1806-1816." A HUNDRED YEARS IN TRAVANCORE BY I. H. HACKER, PDF ed., THE LONDON MISSIONARY SOCIETY, pp. 27–27, https://ia600207.us.archive.org/20/items/100YearsInTravancore/100YearsInTravancore.pdf. Accessed 18 May 2025.
26. Hacker, Isaac Henry. "CHAPTER III: THE GROWTH OF FORTY YEARS, 1816-1856." A HUNDRED YEARS IN TRAVANCORE BY I. H. HACKER, PDF ed., THE LONDON MISSIONARY SOCIETY, pp. 38–38, https://ia600207.us.archive.org/20/items/100YearsInTravancore/100YearsInTravancore.pdf. Accessed 18 May 2025.
27. Hacker, Isaac Henry. "CHAPTER IV: FROM JUBILEE TO CENTENARY, 1856-1906." A HUNDRED YEARS IN TRAVANCORE BY I. H. HACKER, PDF ed., THE LONDON MISSIONARY SOCIETY, pp. 46-49, https://ia600207.us.archive.org/20/items/100YearsInTravancore/100YearsInTravancore.pdf. Accessed 18 May 2025.
28. "How Members Are Appointed - UK Parliament." Www.Parliament.Uk, UK Parliament, www.parliament.uk/business/lords/whos-in-the-house-of-lords/members-and-their-roles/how-members-are-appointed/. Accessed 17 May 2025.
29. Humphries, Jonny. "Axel Rudakubana: 'evil' Southport Killer Jailed for Minimum 52 Years." BBC News, BBC, 23 Jan. 2025, www.bbc.com/news/articles/c4gweeq1344o.
30. "India's Relationship with the Third Gender." UAB Institute for Human Rights Blog, The University of Alabama at Birmingham, 29 Oct. 2018, sites.uab.edu/humanrights/2018/10/29/indias-relationship-with-the-third-gender/.

31. "Israel/OPT: Amnesty International's Research into Hamas-Led Attacks of 7 October 2023 and Treatment of Hostages." Amnesty International, Amnesty International Public Statement, 2 Dec. 2024, www.amnesty.org/en/documents/mde15/8803/2024/en/.
32. Jain, Sagaree. "Theresa May 'deeply Regrets' Colonial Anti-LGBT Laws." Human Rights Watch, Human Rights Watch Dispatches, 18 Apr. 2018, www.hrw.org/news/2018/04/18/theresa-may-deeply-regrets-colonial-anti-lgbt-laws.
33. Kurlantzick, Joshua. "Genocide in Burma." Washington Monthly, 11 June 2016, washingtonmonthly.com/2016/06/11/genocide-in-burma/.
34. Kurungot, Avinash. "Kumbh Mela and Taxation: A Historical and Economic Perspective." Taxscan, TAXSCAN, 14 Feb. 2025, www.taxscan.in/the-kumbh-mela-tax-a-price-paid-on-spirit-and-soul/489753/#.
35. "Legalized Hinduphobia - RTE Law, Hurts Hindus Part 1." PGurus, 23 Sept. 2016, www.pgurus.com/diary-of-a-second-class-citizen-how-rte-has-hurt-hindu-educational-bodies-part-1/.
36. Lal, Kishori Saran. Chapter V: AD 1200 – 1400 (Pgs. 39 – 51). "Growth of Muslim Population in Medieval India (1000-1800)" Internet Archive, Internet Archive, 5 Aug. 2018, ia902800.us.archive.org/11/items/GrowthOfMuslimPopulationInMedievalIndiaAd10001800/Growth-Of-Muslim-Population-In-Medieval-India-ad-1000-1800_text.pdf.
37. Lewis, Paul, and David Pegg. "How the British Royal Family Hides Its Wealth from Public Scrutiny." The Guardian, Guardian News and Media, 5 Apr. 2023, www.theguardian.com/uk-news/2023/apr/05/how-the-british-royal-family-hides-its-wealth-from-public-scrutiny.
38. Maizland, Lindsay, and Eleanor Albert. "What Forces Are Fueling Myanmar's Rohingya Crisis?" Council on Foreign Relations, Council on Foreign Relations, 23 Jan. 2020, www.cfr.org/backgrounder/rohingya-crisis.
39. "Making Laws: House of Lords Stages - UK Parliament." Https://Www.Parliament.Uk/Business/Lords/Work-of-the-House-of-Lords/Making-Laws/, UK Parliament, www.parliament.uk/business/lords/work-of-the-house-of-lords/making-laws/. Accessed 17 May 2025.
40. Monbiot, George. "Deny the British Empire's Crimes? No, We Ignore Them | George Monbiot." The Guardian, Guardian News and Media, 23 Apr. 2012, www.theguardian.com/commentisfree/2012/apr/23/british-empire-crimes-ignore-atrocities.
41. Mukul, Sushim. "Hindu Nationalism, Khalistani Extremism among New Threats: Leaked UK Govt Report." India Today, India Today, 29 Jan. 2025, www.indiatoday.in/world/uk-news/story/uk-leaked-report-hindu-nationalism-pro-khalistani-extremism-threats-britain-islamist-left-wing-2671734-2025-01-29.
42. Mulligan, Gerard. "Genocide in the Ancient World." World History Encyclopedia, https://www.worldhistory.org#organization, 27 Jan. 2013, www.worldhistory.org/article/485/genocide-in-the-ancient-world/.
43. "Myanmar: New Evidence Reveals Rohingya Armed Group Massacred Scores in Rakhine State." Amnesty International, Amnesty International, 22 May 2018, www.amnesty.org/en/latest/news/2018/05/myanmar-new-evidence-reveals-rohingya-armed-group-massacred-scores-in-rakhine-state/.
44. Norton-Taylor, Richard, et al. "Britain Destroyed Records of Colonial Crimes." The Guardian, Guardian News and Media, 17 Apr. 2012, www.theguardian.com/uk/2012/apr/18/britain-destroyed-records-colonial-crimes?newsfeed=true.
45. "Outlandish Proverbs (1640) | Jack Horntip Collection Blog." Edited by Jack Horntip. Translated by George Herbert, Outlandish Proverbs (1640), Jack Horntip Collection Blog, www.horntip.com/html/books_&_MSS/1600s/1640-68--1876_musarum_deliciae__wit_restored__and__wits_recreations_(HC)/1640_outlandish_proverbs.htm. Accessed 23 May 2025. For reference: Proverb 524. Living well is the best revenge.
46. Pandey, Jhimli Mukherjee. "Indus Era 8,000 Years Old, Not 5,500; Ended Because of Weaker Monsoon: India News." The Times of India, TOI, 29 May 2016,

timesofindia.indiatimes.com/india/Indus-era-8000-years-old-not-5500-ended-because-of-weaker-monsoon/articleshow/52485332.cms.

47. "Pilgrim Tax—India - Hansard - UK Parliament." UK Parliament, Hansard, hansard.parliament.uk/Commons/1831-10-14/debates/a954d490-d962-4650-8d39-f1dd71072012/PilgrimTax%E2%80%94India. Accessed 18 May 2025.

48. "Poll Tax." Encyclopædia Britannica, Encyclopædia Britannica, inc., www.britannica.com/topic/poll-tax. Accessed 22 May 2025.

49. "Poll Tax." Wikipedia, Wikimedia Foundation, 2 Apr. 2025, en.wikipedia.org/wiki/Poll_tax#Great_Britain.

50. Power, Samantha. "A Problem from Hell": America and the Age of Genocide. Reissue ed., Harper Perennial, 2007.

51. Prakash, A Surya. "Why Should the Government Run Hindu Temples?" The New Indian Express, The New Indian Express, 13 Jan. 2022, www.newindianexpress.com/opinions/2022/Jan/13/why-should-the-government-run-hindu-temples-2406605.html.

52. Preston, Heather. "Nigerian Bishop Demands Action after 200 Christians Murdered in Week of Violence - Premier Christian News: Headlines, Breaking News, Comment & Analysis." Premier Christian News, Premier Christian News, 22 Apr. 2025, premierchristian.news/us/news/article/nigerian-bishop-demands-action-200-christians-murdered-week-of-violence.

53. Rajyaguru, Dipen. "The Hindu Council UK's Concerns on the Recently Leaked Home Office Extremism Report." Hindu Council UK, Hindu Council UK, 2 Feb. 2025, hinducounciluk.org/2025/02/02/the-hindu-council-uks-concerns-on-the-recently-leaked-home-office-report/.

54. Reuters. "Swedish Court Convicts Quran Burner of Hate Crimes, Days after His Ally Was Killed | The Times of Israel." Www.Timesofisrael.Com, Times of Israel, 3 Feb. 2025, www.timesofisrael.com/swedish-court-convicts-quran-burner-of-hate-crimes-days-after-his-ally-was-killed/.

55. Riches, Chris, and Paul Jeeves. "Southport Killer Axel Rudakubana Read Al-Qaeda Training Manual for Sick Tips." Express.Co.Uk, Express.co.uk, 23 Jan. 2025, www.express.co.uk/news/uk/2004398/southport-killer-axel-rudakubana-al-qaeda.

56. Ruland, Sam, et al. "List: Names, Details of 301 Pa. Priest Sex Abuse Allegations in Catholic Dioceses." York Daily Record, York Daily Record, 18 Aug. 2018, www.ydr.com/story/news/2018/08/14/pa-grand-jury-report-catholic-clergy-sexual-abuse-names-details-catholic-dioceses/948937002/.

57. Sahgal, Neha, et al. "Religion in India: Tolerance and Segregation." Pew Research Center, Pew Research Center, 29 June 2021, www.pewresearch.org/religion/2021/06/29/religion-in-india-tolerance-and-segregation/#2cadb6b1e440f0bf00cd84d9a5e73d3a.

58. Schroth, Raymond A. "New Jersey Opinion; the Rise, and Fall and Rise Again of Willdurant, Truth-Seeker." Https://Www.Nytimes.Com/1985/12/08/Nyregion/New-Jersey-Opinion-the-Rise-and-Fall-and-Rise-Again-of-Willdurant-Truth-Seeker.Html, The New York Times, 8 Dec. 1985, www.nytimes.com/1985/12/08/nyregion/new-jersey-opinion-the-rise-and-fall-and-rise-again-of-willdurant-truth-seeker.html.

59. Shankara, Adi. "Chapter 4." Svetasvatara Upanishad with the Commentary of Sankaracarya, translated by Swami Gambhirananda, 4th ed., Advaita Ashrama, Kolkata, West Bengal, 2009, pp. 143–143.

60. Sharma, Yashraj. "What Is the Resistance Front, the Group Claiming the Deadly Kashmir Attack?" Al Jazeera, Al Jazeera, 24 Apr. 2025, www.aljazeera.com/news/2025/4/23/what-is-the-resistance-front-the-group-behind-the-deadly-kashmir-attack.

61. Silver, Laura, et al. "Comparing Levels of Religious Nationalism around the World." Pew Research Center, Pew Research Center, 28 Jan. 2025, www.pewresearch.org/global/2025/01/28/comparing-levels-of-religious-nationalism-around-the-world/.

62. "Slavery Abolition Act (1833) | An Act for the Abolition of Slavery throughout the British Colonies; for Promoting the Industry of the Manumitted Slaves; and for Compensating the Persons Hitherto Entitled to the Services of Such Slaves. [28th August 1833.]." Legislation on the Slave Trade, pdavis.nl, www.pdavis.nl/Legis_07.htm. Accessed 20 May 2025.
63. "SLAVERY ABOLITION ACT 1833." Slavery Abolition Act, 1833, Section 64, Government of Ireland: electronic Irish Statute Book (eISB), www.irishstatutebook.ie/eli/1833/act/73/section/64/enacted/en/html. Accessed 20 May 2025.
64. Smith, Matthew. "British Attitudes to the British Empire." YouGov, YouGov UK, 29 Jan. 2025, yougov.co.uk/society/articles/51483-british-attitudes-to-the-british-empire.
65. Srinivasan, Kaushik. "How a British Tax Scheme at the Jagannath Temple Became a Political Controversy." Brown History, Brown History, 30 Mar. 2023, brownhistory.substack.com/p/how-a-british-tax-scheme-at-the-jagannath.
66. "Surat Al-Mā'Idah (the Table Spread) - سورة المائدة." The Noble Qur'an, https://legacy.quran.com, legacy.quran.com/5/32. Accessed 30 Apr. 2025.
67. "Surat Al-Mā'Idah (the Table Spread) - سورة المائدة." The Noble Qur'an, legacy.quran.com, legacy.quran.com/5/33. Accessed 30 Apr. 2025.
68. "The Crown Estate FAQs: Find Answers to Commonly Asked Questions." The Crown Estate, The Crown Estate, 2025, www.thecrownestate.co.uk/about-us/faqs#whoownsthecrownestate.
69. "The Parliament Act 1949 (Updated November 2005)." Www.Parliament.Uk, HOUSE OF LORDS LIBRARY, www.parliament.uk/globalassets/documents/lords-library/hllparlact1949.pdf. Accessed 17 May 2025.
70. "The Parliament Acts - UK Parliament." Www.Parliament.Uk, UK Parliament, www.parliament.uk/about/how/laws/parliamentacts/. Accessed 17 May 2025.
71. Torrance, David. "The Relationship between Church and State in the United Kingdom - House of Commons Library." UK Parliament, House of Commons Library, 14 Sept. 2023, commonslibrary.parliament.uk/research-briefings/cbp-8886/.
72. Tripathy, Manorama. "A Brief History of the Pilgrim Tax in Puri." Magazines.Odisha.Gov.In, Odisha Review, Jan. 2014, magazines.odisha.gov.in/Orissareview/2014/Jan/engpdf/62-69.pdf.
73. Vyasa. "SECTION XII of Anusasana Parva of the Mahabharata." Mahabharata, edited by John Bruno Hare, translated by Kisari Mohan Ganguli, Kindle ed., Sacred-Texts.Com, 2005, p. Location 614-Location 681, https://www.gutenberg.org/cache/epub/15477/pg15477-images.html. Accessed 14 May 2025.
74. Windsor, Elizabeth Alexandra Mary. Racial and Religious Hatred Act 2006, UK Home Office, 1 Oct. 2007, www.legislation.gov.uk/ukpga/2006/1/data.pdf. For Reference: The Home Office of the UK states it was officially enacted on October 1st, 2007 on "https://www.legislation.gov.uk/uksi/2007/2490/made" which reads as follows: Commencement 2.—(1) Apart from the provisions mentioned in paragraph (2), the 2006 Act comes into force on 1st October 2007.
75. Wong, Tessa. "377: The British Colonial Law That Left an Anti-LGBTQ Legacy in Asia." BBC News, BBC, 28 June 2021, www.bbc.com/news/world-asia-57606847.
76. "World Values Survey Association." WVS Database, World Values Survey, 12 Sept. 2018, www.worldvaluessurvey.org/WVSDocumentationWV6.jsp. Initially published on 4/29/2014 but updates and corrections were made on 9/12/2018.

Chapter 7

1. "About Institute for Economics and Peace." Institute for Economics & Peace, Institute for Economics & Peace, 2025, www.economicsandpeace.org/about/.
2. "About Us - Strategic Foresight Group, Think Tank, Policy, Global Studies, Global Affairs Research, Global Water Cooperation." Strategicforesight.Com, Strategic Foresight Group (SFG), www.strategicforesight.com/about-us.php. Accessed 24 July 2025.
3. Akbar, Noorjahan. "A Year Later, Still No Justice for Farkhunda." Foreign Policy, 1 Apr. 2016, web.archive.org/web/20160406114242/https://foreignpolicy.com/2016/04/01/a-year-later-still-no-justice-for-farkhunda/.
4. Akbar, Shaharzad. "Afghanistan's Women Are on Their Own." Foreign Affairs, 30 August 2022, https://www.foreignaffairs.com/afghanistan/afghanistans-women-are-their-own. Accessed 21 July 2025
5. Burns, Robert. "Billions Spent on Afghan Army Ultimately Benefited Taliban." AP News, AP News, 17 Aug. 2021, apnews.com/article/joe-biden-army-taliban-995b069a9008690582cb34f4cacd8515.
6. Cahn, Albert Fox. "The Taliban Now Controls a U.S.-Made Super-Surveillance System." The Daily Beast, The Daily Beast Company, 19 Sept. 2024, www.thedailybeast.com/the-taliban-now-controls-a-us-made-super-surveillance-system/.
7. Dilanian, Ken. "CIA's Failure to Hire and Promote Diverse Agents Erodes Spy Agency's Mission, Study Finds." PBS, Public Broadcasting Service, 30 June 2015, www.pbs.org/newshour/nation/cias-failure-hire-promote-diverse-agents-erodes-spy-agencys-mission-study-finds.
8. "Fact Sheet on Post-9/11 Discrimination and Violence against Sikh Americans ." www.Sikhcoalition.Org, The Sikh Coalition, https://www.sikhcoalition.org/images/documents/fact%20sheet%20on%20hate%20against%20sikhs%20in%20america%20post%209-11%201.pdf.
9. Futehally, Ilmas, et al. "Humanity at Risk: Global Terror Threat Indicant, 2018." Strategicforesight.Com/Publication_pdf/Humanity%20at%20Risk.Pdf, Strategic Foresight Group (SFG) / Centre for the Resolution of Intractable Conflict (CRIC) from the University of Oxford, 2018, www.strategicforesight.com/publication_pdf/Humanity%20at%20Risk.pdf.
10. "Global Terrorism Index 2025." Vision of Humanity: IEP's Peace Research, Presentations and Resources, Institute of Economics and Peace, Mar. 2025, www.visionofhumanity.org/wp-content/uploads/2025/03/Global-Terrorism-Index-2025.pdf.
11. Goldstein, Joseph. "U.S. Soldiers Told to Ignore Sexual Abuse of Boys by Afghan Allies." The New York Times, The New York Times Magazine, 20 Sept. 2015, www.nytimes.com/2015/09/21/world/asia/us-soldiers-told-to-ignore-afghan-allies-abuse-of-boys.html.
12. Harris, Sam. "In Defense of Profiling." Sam Harris, www.samharris.org, 28 Apr. 2012, www.samharris.org/blog/in-defense-of-profiling.
13. Harris, Sam. "It's Real, It's Scary, It's a Cult of Death." Los Angeles Times, Los Angeles Times, 18 Sept. 2006, www.latimes.com/archives/la-xpm-2006-sep-18-oe-harris18-story.html.
14. Harris, Sam. "On Knowing Your Enemy." Sam Harris, samharris.org, 7 May 2012, www.samharris.org/blog/on-knowing-your-enemy29.
15. "History of Hate: Crimes Against Sikhs Since 9/11." The Huffington Post, TheHuffingtonPost.com, 7 Aug. 2012, www.huffingtonpost.com/2012/08/07/history-of-hate-crimes-against-sikhs-since-911_n_1751841.html.
16. "History." Sikh Coalition, 19 Oct. 2020, www.sikhcoalition.org/about-us/history/.
17. Klein, Ezra, and Sam Harris. "The Sam Harris Debate: The Ezra Klein Show." Smash Notes, The Ezra Klein Show, 9 Apr. 2018, https://smashnotes.com/p/the-ezra-klein-show/e/the-sam-harris-debate.

18. Klein, Ezra. "Sam Harris, Charles Murray, and The Allure of Race Science." Vox, Vox, 27 Mar. 2018, web.archive.org/web/20201124051651/https://www.vox.com/policy-and-politics/2018/3/27/15695060/sam-harris-charles-murray-race-iq-forbidden-knowledge-podcast-bell-curve.
19. "Massacre of over 100 Villagers in Christian Area of Nigeria Elicits Response from President." MSN, The Christian Post, 23 June 2025, www.msn.com/en-us/news/world/massacre-of-over-100-villagers-in-christian-area-of-nigeria-elicits-response-from-president/ar-AA1HfeI4.
20. Preston, Heather. "Nigerian Bishop Demands Action after 200 Christians Murdered in Week of Violence - Premier Christian News: Headlines, Breaking News, Comment & Analysis." Premier Christian News, Premier Christian News, 22 Apr. 2025, premierchristian.news/us/news/article/nigerian-bishop-demands-action-200-christians-murdered-week-of-violence.
21. Qiu, Linda. "Trump Claim on Israel Profiling Misses Full Security Context." @politifact, The Poynter Institute, 23 Sept. 2016, www.politifact.com/factchecks/2016/sep/23/donald-trump/donald-trump-claim-israel-profiling-very-successfu/.
22. Schreiber, Melody. "George W. Bush's Anti-HIV Program Is Hailed as 'amazing' - and Still Crucial at 20." NPR, NPR, 28 Feb. 2023, www.npr.org/sections/goatsandsoda/2023/02/28/1159415936/george-w-bushs-anti-hiv-program-is-hailed-as-amazing-and-still-crucial-at-20.
23. Stephens, Joe, and David B. Ottaway. "From U.S., the ABC's of Jihad." The Washington Post, WP Company, 23 Mar. 2002, www.washingtonpost.com/archive/politics/2002/03/23/from-us-the-abcs-of-jihad/d079075a-3ed3-4030-9a96-0d48f6355e54/?utm_term=.cbb9b6b8a59a.
24. "The Obama Administration's Ebola Response." National Archives and Records Administration, National Archives and Records Administration, Oct. 2014, obamawhitehouse.archives.gov/ebola-response.
25. Weaver, Mary Anne. "Her Majesty's Jihadists: More British Muslims Have Joined Islamist Militant Groups than Serve in the Country's Armed Forces. How to Understand the Pull of Jihad." New York Times, The New York Times Magazine, 14 Apr. 2015, www.nytimes.com/2015/04/19/magazine/her-majestys-jihadists.html.

Chapter 8

1. "687. Tribal Court Jurisdiction." The United States Department of Justice, 22 Jan. 2020, https://www.justice.gov/archives/jm/criminal-resource-manual-687-tribal-court-jurisdiction#:~:text=The%20Supreme%20Court%20held%20in,the%20tribe%20in%20Duro%20v.

2. 9/11 News Coverage: 10:45 AM: Palestinians Celebrate, NBC News / AuthenticHistory, 30 Jan. 2011, www.youtube.com/watch?v=cqZBy09vCVk&ab_channel=AuthenticHistory.

3. al-Bukhārī, Abū ʿAbd Allāh Muḥammad ibn Ismāʿīl ibn Ibrāhīm al-Juʿfī. "Sahih Bukhari Volume 5, Book 58, Hadith Number 227." Translated by Muhammad Muhsin Khan, *Hadith Collection*, Hadith Collection, 23 May 2009, hadithcollection.com/sahihbukhari/sahih-bukhari-book-58-merits-of-the-helpers-in-madina-ansaar/sahih-bukhari-volume-005-book-058-hadith-number-227.

4. Al-Munajjid, Muhammad Saalih. "Is It Proven That 'Umar (May Allah Be Pleased with Him) Wrote a Letter to the Nile in Egypt so That Its Water Would Flow by Allah's Leave? - Islam Question & Answer." Islam, Islam Question & Answer, 17 June 2012, islamqa.info/en/answers/178417/is-it-proven-that-umar-(may-allah-be-pleased-with-him)-wrote-a-letter-to-the-nile-in-egypt-so-that-its-water-would-flow-by-allahs-leave.

5. Al-Munajjid, Muhammad Saalih. "Will Civilisation Collapse at the End of Time and Will Battles Be Fought with Swords and Spears? - Islam Question & Answer." Islamqa.Info, Islam Question & Answer, 1 Aug. 2014, islamqa.info/en/answers/162744/will-civilisation-collapse-at-the-end-of-time-and-will-battles-be-fought-with-swords-and-spears.

6. Arghya Prasun Roychowdhury / TIMESOFINDIA.COM / Apr 14, 2025. "Waqf Violent Protest: On a Tough Legal Wicket, Tmc Faces a Delicate Balancing Act: India News." The Times of India, TOI, timesofindia.indiatimes.com/india/waqf-violent-protest-on-a-tough-legal-wicket-tmc-faces-a-delicate-balancing-act/articleshow/120282778.cms. Accessed 25 Aug. 2025.

7. Asad, Amira. "The Egyptian Feminist Who Was Kidnapped for Posing Nude." VICE, VICE, 14 Feb. 2013, www.vice.com/en/article/the-egyptian-feminist-who-was-kidnapped-for-posing-nude/.

8. Aydemir, Ridvan. "They Want to Kill Me Next | Stand with Me." YouTube, Apostate Prophet, 1 Feb. 2025, www.youtube.com/watch?v=AT3sKDZZppQ&ab_channel=ApostateProphet.

9. Bhattacharya, Snigdhendu. "Bengal Violence: Basirhat's Muslim Leaders Tried to Pacify the Rioting Mob, but Couldn't." Hindustan Times, Hindustan Times, 16 July 2017, www.hindustantimes.com/india-news/bengal-violence-basirhat-s-muslim-leaders-tried-to-pacify-the-rioting-mob-but-couldn-t/story-8O6XTqN3yhsvKlfYSDK2aK.html.

10. "Bid'Ah Hasanah ('Good Innovations') - Islam Question & Answer." Edited by Muhammad Saalih Al-Munajjid, Islamqa.Info, Islam Question & Answer, 9 May 1998, islamqa.info/en/answers/864/bid-ah-hasanah-(%22good-innovations%22).

11. Boehm, Mike. "Gloomed for Success: O.C.'s Mindfunk Has Had Its Share of Hard Knocks-- Thank Goodness." Los Angeles Times, Los Angeles Times, 3 Nov. 1993, www.latimes.com/archives/la-xpm-1993-11-03-ca-52788-story.html.

12. Boone, Jon. "Salmaan Taseer Murder Case Harks Back to 1929 Killing of Hindu Publisher." The Guardian, Guardian News and Media, 12 Mar. 2015, www.theguardian.com/world/2015/mar/12/salmaan-taseer-case-harks-back-to-1929-killing-of-hindu-publisher.

13. "Buddhas of Bamiyan." Wikipedia, Wikimedia Foundation, 16 July 2025, en.wikipedia.org/wiki/Buddhas_of_Bamiyan.

14. Boyer, Lauren. "Stop Drinking Camel Urine, World Health Organization Says." U.S. News & World Report, U.S. News & World Report, www.usnews.com/news/articles/2015/06/10/stop-drinking-camel-urine-world-health-organization-says.

15. "Calcutta High Court Grants Interim Bail to Sharmistha Panoli, Pulls up Bengal Police for Their Actions." Www.Opindia.Com, OpIndia, 5 June 2025, www.opindia.com/news-updates/calcutta-high-court-grants-interim-bail-to-sharmistha-panoli-pulls-up-bengal-police-for-their-actions/.
16. Callimachi, Rukmini. "Isis Enshrines a Theology of Rape." The New York Times, The New York Times, 13 Aug. 2015, www.nytimes.com/2015/08/14/world/middleeast/isis-enshrines-a-theology-of-rape.html.
17. "Chapter 1: Beliefs about Sharia." Pew Research Center, Pew Research Center, 30 Apr. 2013, www.pewresearch.org/religion/2013/04/30/the-worlds-muslims-religion-politics-society-beliefs-about-sharia/.
18. "Chapter 3: Morality." Pew Research Center, Pew Research Center, 30 Apr. 2013, www.pewresearch.org/religion/2013/04/30/the-worlds-muslims-religion-politics-society-morality/.
19. "Chapter 4: Women in Society." Pew Research Center, Pew Research Center, 30 Apr. 2013, www.pewresearch.org/religion/2013/04/30/the-worlds-muslims-religion-politics-society-women-in-society/.
20. "Chapter 5: Relations among Muslims." Pew Research Center, Pew Research Center, 30 Apr. 2013, www.pewresearch.org/religion/2013/04/30/the-worlds-muslims-religion-politics-society-relationship-among-muslims/.
21. "Chapter 6: Interfaith Relations." Pew Research Center, Pew Research Center, 30 Apr. 2013, www.pewresearch.org/religion/2013/04/30/the-worlds-muslims-religion-politics-society-interfaith-relations/.
22. "Chapter 7: Religion, Science and Popular Culture." Pew Research Center, Pew Research Center, 30 Apr. 2013, www.pewresearch.org/religion/2013/04/30/the-worlds-muslims-religion-politics-society-science-and-popular-culture/.
23. "Chapter 8: IPC 153A." The Indian Penal Code (IPC), The Indian Penal Code (IPC), 14 Jan. 2014, www.indianpenalcode.in/ipc-153a/.
24. Cooper, Renee. "Behind the Grim Statistics for Sexual Violence on Reservations." KX NEWS, KX NEWS, 22 Dec. 2020, www.kxnet.com/news/local-news/being-raped-is-a-right-of-passage-behind-the-grim-statistics-for-native-american-women/.
25. "Corporate Avenger - Born Again." Www.Discogs.Com, Discogs, www.discogs.com/release/1353275-Corporate-Avenger-Born-Again. Accessed 17 Aug. 2025.
26. Davies, Maia, and Danny Aeberhard. "Man Who Burned Quran 'Shot Dead in Sweden.'" BBC News, BBC, 30 Jan. 2025, www.bbc.com/news/articles/cpdx2wqpg7zo.
27. Dawkins, Richard, and Rana Ahmad. "Richard Dawkins Interviews Saudi Arabian Atheist Author Rana Ahmad." Www.Youtube.Com, Richard Dawkins Foundation for Reason & Science, 25 Feb. 2019, www.youtube.com/watch?v=_zncB6hngZg.
28. Department of Defense (DOD), et al. "2022 Demographics Profile of the Military Community." Https://S3.Documentcloud.Org/Documents/24177791/2022-Demographics-Report.Pdf, U.S. Naval Institute Staff / U.S. Naval Institute News, 29 Nov. 2023, s3.documentcloud.org/documents/24177791/2022-demographics-report.pdf. For reference: Page 24 and page 73.
29. Department of Defense (DOD), et al. "2023 Demographics Profile of the Military Community." Https://Download.Militaryonesource.Mil/12038/MOS/Reports/2023-Demographics-Report.Pdf, Military OneSource, 2023, download.militaryonesource.mil/12038/MOS/Reports/2023-demographics-report.pdf. For Reference: Pages 24 and 73.
30. Devichand, Mukul. "'Nowhere Is Safe': Behind the Bangladesh Blogger Murders." BBC News, BBC, 7 Aug. 2015, www.bbc.com/news/blogs-trending-33822674.
31. "Dhandhuka Murder: 3 Accused in Police Remand for 10 More Days." The Indian Express, The Indian Express / Express News Service, 7 Feb. 2022, web.archive.org/web/20220207041105/https://indianexpress.com/article/cities/ahmedabad/dhandhuka-murder-accused-police-remand-ahmedabad-7760401/.

32. Dhar, Aniruddha. "Instagram Influencer Sharmishta Panoli's Lawyer Claims Poor Hygiene in Kolkata Jail: 'She Has Kidney Stones.'" Hindustan Times, Hindustan Times, 2 June 2025, www.hindustantimes.com/india-news/instagram-influencer-sharmishta-panolis-lawyer-claims-poor-hygiene-in-kolkata-jail-she-has-kidney-stones-101748858117735.html.

33. Durant, Will. Chapter XV: The Buddha: I. The Heretics (9581 - 9656). Our Oriental Heritage: Being a History of Civilization in Egypt and the Near East to the Death of Alexander, and in India, China and Japan from the Beginning to Our Own Day. Simon and Schuster, 1935.

34. Fields, Ashleigh. "Dershowitz Says He Knows Epstein Client List Names: 'But I'm Bound by Confidentiality.'" Thehill.Com, The Hill, 10 July 2025, thehill.com/homenews/administration/5395597-dershowitz-says-he-knows-epstein-client-list-names-but-im-bound-by-confidentiality/.

35. "France Pays Respects to Teacher Killed in School Terror Attack." France 24, FRANCE 24, 19 Oct. 2023, www.france24.com/en/live-news/20231019-france-pays-respects-to-teacher-killed-in-islamist-attack.

36. Hamade, Kassem. "Salwan Momika Är Tillbaka – Går till Attack Mot Norge." Salwan Momika Är Tillbaka i Sverige – Ilskan Mot Norge | Sverige | Expressen, Expressen, 11 Apr. 2024, web.archive.org/web/20240411193917/https://www.expressen.se/nyheter/sverige/salwan-momika-ar-tillbaka-i--sverige-ilskan-mot-norge/. For Reference: Google Translated from Swedish to English.

37. "India: A Decade on, Gujarat Justice Incomplete." Human Rights Watch, 28 Oct. 2020, www.hrw.org/news/2012/02/24/india-decade-gujarat-justice-incomplete#.

38. "Jordanian Writer Nahed Hattar Was Murdered Outside the Court Where He Was on Trial for Publishing a Cartoon." JRMora, Cartoons, jrmora.com, 21 May 2022, jrmora.com/en/jordanian-writer-nahed-hattar-murdered-court-trial-publishing-cartoon/.

39. "Kamlesh Tiwari Murder: Up CM Yogi Adityanath to Visit Kin of Deceased Hindu Samaj Leader Today." India.Com, India.Com, 19 Oct. 2019, www.india.com/news/india/kamlesh-tiwari-murder-up-cm-yogi-adityanath-to-visit-kin-of-deceased-hindu-samaj-leader-today-3811970/.

40. Knight, Kyle, and Meenakshi Ganguly. "India Gets Another Chance Protecting Transgender Rights." Human Rights Watch, Human Rights Watch Dispatches, 22 Feb. 2018, www.hrw.org/news/2018/02/22/india-gets-another-chance-protecting-transgender-rights.

41. Lacdan, Joseph. "Army Leader Cherishes Heritage, Honors Native American Contributions." www.Army.Mil, U.S. Army, 19 Nov. 2021, https://web.archive.org/web/20250212083345/https://www.army.mil/article/252163/army_leader_cherishes_heritage_honors_native_american_contributions.

42. Lal, Kishori Saran. Chapter X: AD 1200 – 1400 (Pgs. 113 – 116). "Growth of Muslim Population in Medieval India (1000-1800)" Internet Archive, Internet Archive, 5 Aug. 2018, ia902800.us.archive.org/11/items/GrowthOfMuslimPopulationInMedievalIndiaAd10001800/Growth-Of-Muslim-Population-In-Medieval-India-ad-1000-1800_text.pdf.

43. Lal, Kishori Saran. Chapter XI: AD 1400 – 1600 (Pgs. 127 – 143). "Growth of Muslim Population in Medieval India (1000-1800)" Internet Archive, Internet Archive, 5 Aug. 2018, ia902800.us.archive.org/11/items/GrowthOfMuslimPopulationInMedievalIndiaAd10001800/Growth-Of-Muslim-Population-In-Medieval-India-ad-1000-1800_text.pdf. For reference: Footnote on page 136.

44. Lal, Kishori Saran. "Part III: Reposte on Reviews: VII A Riposte on Reviews: 7.1 The Legacy of Muslim Rule in India." Theory and Practice of Muslim State in India, 2020th ed., Aditya Prakashan, New Delhi, Delhi, 1999, pp. 324–327.

45. Lee, Matthew. "Biden Administration Notifies Congress of Planned $8 Billion Weapons Sale to Israel." PBS, Public Broadcasting Service, 4 Jan. 2025, www.pbs.org/newshour/world/biden-administration-notifies-congress-of-planned-8-billion-weapons-sale-to-israel#:~:text=Biden%20administration%20notifies%20Congress%20of,Live%20TV.

46. Maged, Ahmed. "The Nile Bride Sacrifice Is a Big Myth, Says Egyptologist." Dailynewsegypt, Egyptian Media Services, 7 Aug. 2015, www.dailynewsegypt.com/2008/10/03/the-nile-bride-sacrifice-is-a-big-myth-says-egyptologist/.
47. Marx, Karl. "The British Rule in India." The British Rule in India by Karl Marx, www.marxists.org/archive/marx/works/1853/06/25.htm. Accessed 23 Aug. 2025.
48. MAZE OF INJUSTICE The Failure to Protect Indigenous Women from Sexual Violence in the USA, Amnesty International, https://web.archive.org/web/20111018194106/http://www.amnestyusa.org/pdfs/MazeOfInjustice.pdf.
49. McKernan, Bethan. "Alleged Killer Who Shot Atheist Jordanian Writer Outside Supreme Court Identified." The Independent, Independent Digital News and Media, 25 Sept. 2016, www.independent.co.uk/news/world/middle-east/alleged-killer-who-shot-atheist-jordanian-writer-charged-with-offensive-facebook-post-identified-a7329391.html.
50. McKernan, Bethan. "A Man Has Been 'sentenced to Death' in Saudi Arabia for Being an Atheist." The Independent, The Independent World, 26 Apr. 2017, web.archive.org/web/20170426142501/www.independent.co.uk/news/world/middle-east/saudi-arabia-man-sentenced-death-atheism-ahmad-al-shamri-hafar-al-batin-appeal-denied-a7703161.html.
51. Moses, Nissim. "Bene Israel of India." Avotaynu Online, 24 Mar. 2015, www.avotaynuonline.com/2007/07/bene-israel-of-india-by-nissim-moses/.
52. "Kolkata Police Travel to Gurgaon to Arrest Hindu Influencer Sharmistha over Video Targeting Pakistan, No Action so Far on Muslims Who Issued STSJ Threats." Www.Opindia.Com, OpIndia, 31 May 2025, www.opindia.com/2025/05/kolkata-police-arrest-hindu-influencer-sharmistha-from-gurgaon-over-video-targeting-pakistan-had-offended-indian-muslims-details/.
53. Mezzofiore, Gianluca. "Aliaa Magda Elmahdy, Nude Blogger, Gains Support from Egyptian Diaspora." International Business Times UK, International Business Times UK, 18 Nov. 2011, www.ibtimes.co.uk/aliaa-magda-elmahdy-nude-blogger-gains-support-252301.
54. "Native American Women Are Rape Targets Because of a Legislative Loophole." VICE, VICE News, 16 Dec. 2015, https://www.vice.com/en/article/bnpb73/native-american-women-are-rape-targets-because-of-a-legislative-loophole-511.
55. Navabi, Armin. "I Just Recorded Myself Peeing on the Quran. Would It Violate Twitter's TOS If I Post the Video Here, Even If There Is Zero Nudity?" Twitter, Twitter, 27 Aug. 2020, https://twitter.com/ArminNavabi/status/1298814762491547651.
56. Navabi, Armin. "Why I Burn The Quran." YouTube, Atheist Republic, 29 July 2018, www.youtube.com/watch?v=nVsqA7fWWoY&pp=ygUbYnVybiB0aGUgcXVyYW4gYXJtaW4gbmF2YWJp.
57. Navabi, Armin. "Armin Navabi: @ArminNavabi: 'With My Fellow Ex-Muslim Freedom Fighters in Berlin.'" X.Com, x.com / Twitter, 14 Sept. 2019, x.com/arminnavabi/status/1172885766965325824?lang=en.
58. "Palestinians Celebrate 9/11 Attacks on US." Youtube, Fox News / mnaba11, 9 Jan. 2009, www.youtube.com/watch?v=P9yK0u-XH1M. For Reference: Within the video description box: "Palestinians dance and celebrate in the streets on 9/11"
59. "Palestinians Celebrate at Damascus Gate." Palestinians Celebrate at Damascus Gate - AP Archive, AP Archive / AP News, 30 July 2015, www.youtube.com/watch?v=UucjbGmJILk&ab_channel=APArchive. For reference in the Youtube description box of the video: "There were celebrations at Jerusalem's Damascus Gate, following the attacks on the Trade Centre and the Pentagon. Palestinian men, women and children chanted in jubilation after terrorists crashed two planes into the World Trade Center causing them to collapse on Tuesday morning."
60. Pandey, Shraddha. "From Nupur Sharma to Sharmishta Panoli: How Courts Are Emboldening Islamists and Curbing Space for Free Speech." Www.Opindia.Com, OpIndia, 3 June 2025,

www.opindia.com/2025/06/nupur-sharma-sharmishta-panoli-courts-emboldening-islamists-curbing-space-for-free-speech/.

61. Pandey, Shraddha. "The Growing 'trend' of Throwing Meat Pieces in Front of Mandirs, a Co-Ordinated Campaign to Desecrate Sacred Hindu Places?" Www.Opindia.Com, OpIndia, 19 June 2025, www.opindia.com/2025/06/the-growing-trend-of-throwing-meat-pieces-in-front-of-temples/.
62. Pollina, Richard. "Suspect Allegedly Yelled 'Allahu Akbar' before Fatally Stabbing Teacher, Injuring 2 Others in France Knife Attack." New York Post, New York Post, 13 Oct. 2023, nypost.com/2023/10/13/france-knife-attack-leaves-teacher-dead-several-injured/.
63. "Rescuing Ex-Muslims: Leaving Islam." YouTube, VICE News, 10 Feb. 2016, www.youtube.com/watch?v=O1lnxUXWGgE.
64. "Salman Rushdie Stabbing Suspect Charged with Attempted Murder as Author Remains Hospitalized with 'Serious' Wounds." CBS News, CBS Interactive, 13 Aug. 2022, www.cbsnews.com/news/salman-rushdie-stabbing-suspect-hadi-matar/.
65. "Samuel Paty: French Schoolgirl Admits Lying about Murdered Teacher." BBC News, BBC, 9 Mar. 2021, www.bbc.com/news/world-europe-56325254.
66. "Saudi Arabia: Yemeni Man Sentenced for Apostasy." Human Rights Watch, Human Rights Watch: News Release, 7 Jan. 2021, www.hrw.org/news/2021/12/20/saudi-arabia-yemeni-man-sentenced-apostasy.
67. "Section 295A in the Indian Penal Code, 1860." Indiankanoon.Org, Indian Kanoon, indiankanoon.org/doc/1803184/. Accessed 23 Aug. 2025.
68. Sharma, Nupur J. "Of Free Speech and 295A: Why I Partially Agree and Wholly Disagree with the Arguments of Prof Anand Ranganathan." Www.Opindia.Com, OpIndia, 28 June 2022, www.opindia.com/2022/06/free-speech-295a-disagree-arguments-prof-anand-ranganathan/.
69. Simeon, Dilip. "The Tyranny of Hurt Sentiment." The Indian Express, The Indian Express, 11 Feb. 2015, web.archive.org/web/20220726090225/https://indianexpress.com/article/opinion/columns/the-tyranny-of-hurt-sentiment/.
70. Singh, Kavita. "When Peace Is Defeat, Reconstruction Is Damage: 'Rebuilding' Heritage in Postconflict Sri Lanka and Afghanistan." Www.Getty.Edu, J. Paul Getty Trust, 13 July 2022, www.getty.edu/publications/cultural-heritage-mass-atrocities/downloads/pages/CunoWeiss_CHMA_part-2-08-singh.pdf. For Reference: pages 157 - 159.
71. Shah, Amir. "Taliban Destroy Ancient Buddhist Relics." The Independent Asia RSS, The Independent World, 3 Mar. 2001, web.archive.org/web/20110106181318/www.independent.co.uk/news/world/asia/taliban-destroy-ancient-buddhist-relics-694425.html.
72. Sharma, Swati Goel. "Phoola Bai's Husband Hari Singh Was Brutally Killed by Islamists on Holi. He Was Crushed by a Tractor in Dead of the Night   Hailing from an All-Hindu Vanvasi Village in Raisen District of Madhya Pradesh, Phoola Bai Has No Means of Income. ." X.Com, x.com / Twitter, 12 May 2025, x.com/swati_gs/status/1921930773151506515.
73. Steinhauer, Jillian. "Feminist Activists Bleed and Defecate on Islamic State Flag #NSFW." Hyperallergic, Hyperallergic, 27 Aug. 2014, hyperallergic.com/145768/feminist-activists-bleed-and-shit-on-islamic-state-flag-nsfw/.
74. "Supreme Court Trashes Rana Ayyub's Gujarat Book, Says It Is Based upon Surmises, Conjectures, and Suppositions." OpIndia, OpIndia, 5 July 2019, www.opindia.com/2019/07/supreme-court-rana-ayyub-gujarat-files-haren-pandya-murder/.
75. Tharoor, Shashi, et al. "Shashi Tharoor versus Christopher Hitchens, Free Speech Debate at Hay Festival on Saturday 27 May 2006 and Chaired by Joan Bakewell." YouTube, Hay Festival, 30 Dec. 2011, youtu.be/jw3dDbc1BHE.
76. "The Benefits of Drinking Camel Urine - Islam Question & Answer." Islamqa.info, Islam Question and Answer, 27 Mar. 2006,

https://web.archive.org/web/20190209043245/https://islamqa.info/en/answers/83423/the-benefits-of-drinking-camel-urine.

77. "The Never-Ending Maze: Continued Failure to Protect Indigenous Women from Sexual Violence in the USA." Amnesty International USA, Amnesty International USA, 19 July 2023, http://www.amnestyusa.org/wp-content/uploads/2022/05/AmnestyMazeReportv_digital.pdf.

78. "The World's Muslims: Religion, Politics and Society." Pew Research Center, Pew Research Center, 30 Apr. 2013, www.pewresearch.org/religion/2013/04/30/the-worlds-muslims-religion-politics-society-overview/.

79. Trump, Donald J. "Presidential Proclamation on National Native American Heritage Month, 2018." The White House, Whitehouse.gov, 31 Oct. 2018, https://web.archive.org/web/20201226230730/https://www.whitehouse.gov/presidential-actions/presidential-proclamation-national-native-american-heritage-month-2018/.

80. Valmiki. "Book III: Aranya Kanda - The Forest Trek." Translated by Desiraju Hanumanta Rao et al., Srimad Valmiki Ramayana: Book 3 Aranya Kanda: Sarga / Chapter 47: Verses: 10b - 11., Desiraju Hanumanta Rao & K. M. K. Murthy, Nov. 2004, https://valmikiramayan.net/utf8/aranya/sarga47/aranyaitrans47.htm

81. Valmiki. "Book III: Aranya Kanda - The Forest Trek." Translated by Desiraju Hanumanta Rao et al., Srimad Valmiki Ramayana: Book 3 Aranya Kanda: Sarga / Chapter 47: Verses: 10b - 11., Desiraju Hanumanta Rao & K. M. K. Murthy, Nov. 2004, sanskritdocuments.org/sites/valmikiramayan/aranya/sarga47/aranya_47_frame.htm.

82. Vyasa. "Chapter 30 - Rāma's Life." Translated by Ganesh Vasudeo Tagare, Skanda Purana: Book 3 - Brāhma-Khaṇḍa: Section 2 - Dharmāraṇya-Khaṇḍa: Chapter 30 - Rāma's Life: Verses 8-9, www.wisdomlib.org, 15 Aug. 2020, www.wisdomlib.org/hinduism/book/the-skanda-purana/d/doc423651.html#:~:text=8%2D9.,with%20S%C4%ABt%C4%81%20for%20twelve%20years.

83. Wagner, Sally Roesch. Sisters in Spirit: Iroquois Influence on Early Feminists: Haudenosaunee (Iroquois) Influence on Early American Feminists. Book Publishing Company. Kindle Edition.

84. "'WE HAVE NO ORDERS TO SAVE YOU' State Participation and Complicity in Communal Violence in Gujarat." Www.Hrw.Org, Human Rights Watch, www.hrw.org/reports/2002/india/gujarat.pdf. Accessed 22 Aug. 2025.

85. Williams, Robert A. "THE ALGEBRA OF FEDERAL INDIAN LAW: THE HARD TRAIL OF DECOLONIZING AND AMERICANIZING THE WHITE MAN'S INDIAN JURISPRUDENCE." UW Law Digital Repository Media · University of Wisconsin Law School Digital Repository · University of Wisconsin Law School Digital Repository, University of Wisconsin Law Review, repository.law.wisc.edu/s/uwlaw/media/35536.

86. Willsher, Kim. "Teacher Decapitated in Paris Named as Samuel Paty, 47." The Guardian, Guardian News and Media, 17 Oct. 2020, www.theguardian.com/world/2020/oct/17/teacher-decapitated-in-paris-named-as-samuel-paty-47.

87. Worley, Will. "Full Extent of Isis Destruction of Palmyra Revealed in Devastating before and after Photos." The Independent, Independent Digital News and Media, 2 Apr. 2016, www.independent.co.uk/news/world/middle-east/palmyra-syria-photos-new-palmyra-photos-show-devastation-of-artefacts-ruined-by-isis-a6964766.html.

88. Zarrinkoub, Abdolhossein. Chapter 4: The Lost Language (Location 1833 – 1878). Two Centuries of Silence: An Account of Events and Conditions in Iran [Persia] During the First Two Hundred Years of Islam, from the Arab Invasion to the Rise of the Tahirid Dynasty First edition. Mazda Publishers. Kindle Edition.

89. Zarrinkoub, Abdolhossein. Chapter 9: The Battle of Beliefs (Location 4422 – 4965). Two Centuries of Silence: An Account of Events and Conditions in Iran [Persia] During the First Two Hundred Years of Islam, from the Arab Invasion to the Rise of the Tahirid Dynasty First edition. Mazda Publishers. Kindle Edition.

90. Zickgraf, Ryan. "Democratic Socialism's Moral Theater." UnHerd, 13 Aug. 2025, unherd.com/2025/08/democratic-socialisms-slide-into-irrelevance/.

Chapter 9

1. Abbas, Ibn. "Tanwr Al-Miqbs Min Tafsr Ibn Abbs." Translated by Mokrane Guezzou, Altafsir.Com, Royal Aal al-Bayt Institute for Islamic Thought, 2021, www.altafsir.com/Tafasir.asp?tMadhNo=0&tTafsirNo=73&tSoraNo=68&tAyahNo=1&tDisplay=yes&UserProfile=0&LanguageId=2.
2. "Abu Dawud Book 033, Hadith Number 4450." Hadith Collection, https://hadithcollection.com/abudawud/abu-dawud-book-33-prescribed-punishments/abu-dawud-book-033-hadith-number-4450.
3. Andrews, Robin. "We Finally Know Why People Are Left- Or Right-Handed." IFLScience, IFLScience, 23 Jan. 2019, www.iflscience.com/brain/finally-know-people-left-righthanded/.
4. al-Bukhārī, Abū ʿAbd Allāh Muḥammad ibn Ismāʿīl ibn Ibrāhīm al-Juʿfī. "Sahih Bukhari Volume 1, Book 3, Hadith Number 97a." Translated by Muhammad Muhsin Khan, Hadith Collection, Hadith Collection, 8 Dec. 2021, hadithcollection.com/sahihbukhari/sahih-bukhari-book-03-knowledge/sahih-bukhari-volume-001-book-003-hadith-number-097a.
5. al-Bukhārī, Abū ʿAbd Allāh Muḥammad ibn Ismāʿīl ibn Ibrāhīm al-Juʿfī. "Sahih Bukhari Volume 3, Book 34, Hadith Number 351." Translated by Muhammad Muhsin Khan, Hadith Collection, Hadith Collection, 31 Jan. 2009, hadithcollection.com/sahihbukhari/sahih-bukhari-book-34-sales-and-trade/sahih-bukhari-volume-003-book-034-hadith-number-351.
6. al-Bukhārī, Abū ʿAbd Allāh Muḥammad ibn Ismāʿīl ibn Ibrāhīm al-Juʿfī. "Sahih Bukhari Volume 3, Book 34, Hadith Number 432." Translated by Muhammad Muhsin Khan, Hadith Collection, Hadith Collection, 31 Jan. 2009, hadithcollection.com/sahihbukhari/sahih-bukhari-book-34-sales-and-trade/sahih-bukhari-volume-003-book-034-hadith-number-432.
7. al-Bukhārī, Abū ʿAbd Allāh Muḥammad ibn Ismāʿīl ibn Ibrāhīm al-Juʿfī. "Sahih Bukhari Volume 3, Book 41, Hadith Number 598." Translated by Muhammad Muhsin Khan, Hadith Collection, Hadith Collection, 1 Feb. 2009, hadithcollection.com/sahihbukhari/sahih-bukhari-book-41-loans-payment-of-loans-freezing-of-property-bankruptcy/sahih-bukhari-volume-003-book-041-hadith-number-598.
8. al-Bukhārī, Abū ʿAbd Allāh Muḥammad ibn Ismāʿīl ibn Ibrāhīm al-Juʿfī. "Sahih Bukhari Volume 3, Book 47, Hadith Number 743." Translated by Muhammad Muhsin Khan, Hadith Collection, SUNNAH.COM, Jan. 2009, hadithcollection.com/sahihbukhari/sahih-bukhari-book-47-gifts/sahih-bukhari-volume-003-book-047-hadith-number-743.
9. al-Bukhārī, Abū ʿAbd Allāh Muḥammad ibn Ismāʿīl ibn Ibrāhīm al-Juʿfī. "Sahih Bukhari Volume 3, Book 47, Hadith Number 765." Translated by Muhammad Muhsin Khan, Hadith Collection, Hadith Collection, 1 Feb. 2009, hadithcollection.com/sahihbukhari/sahih-bukhari-book-47-gifts/sahih-bukhari-volume-003-book-047-hadith-number-765.
10. al-Bukhārī, Abū ʿAbd Allāh Muḥammad ibn Ismāʿīl ibn Ibrāhīm al-Juʿfī. "Sahih Bukhari Volume 4, Book 52, Hadith Number 255." Translated by Muhammad Muhsin Khan, Hadith Collection, Hadith Collection, 7 Feb. 2009, hadithcollection.com/sahihbukhari/sahih-bukhari-book-52-fighting-for-the-cause-of-allah-jihaad/sahih-bukhari-volume-004-book-052-hadith-number-255.
11. al-Bukhārī, Abū ʿAbd Allāh Muḥammad ibn Ismāʿīl ibn Ibrāhīm al-Juʿfī. "Sahih Bukhari Volume 4, Book 55, Hadith Number 641." Translated by Muhammad Muhsin Khan, Hadith Collection, Hadith Collection, 26 Apr. 2009, hadithcollection.com/sahihbukhari/sahih-bukhari-book-55-prophets/sahih-bukhari-volume-004-book-055-hadith-number-641.
12. al-Bukhārī, Abū ʿAbd Allāh Muḥammad ibn Ismāʿīl ibn Ibrāhīm al-Juʿfī. "Sahih Bukhari Volume 7, Book 62, Hadith Number 137." Translated by Muhammad Muhsin Khan, Hadith Collection,

Hadith Collection, 31 May 2009, hadithcollection.com/sahihbukhari/sahih-bukhari-book-62-wedlock-marriage-nikah/sahih-bukhari-volume-007-book-062-hadith-number-137.

13. al-Bukhārī, Abū ʿAbd Allāh Muḥammad ibn Ismāʿīl ibn Ibrāhīm al-Juʿfī. "Sahih Bukhari Volume 8, Book 80, Hadith Number 753." Translated by Muhammad Muhsin Khan, Hadith Collection, Hadith Collection, 2 June 2009, hadithcollection.com/sahihbukhari/sahih-bukhari-book-80-laws-of-inheritence-al-faraaid/sahih-bukhari-volume-008-book-080-hadith-number-753.

14. al-Bukhārī, Abū ʿAbd Allāh Muḥammad ibn Ismāʿīl ibn Ibrāhīm al-Juʿfī. "Sahih Bukhari Volume 9, Book 87, Hadith Number 124." Translated by Muhammad Muhsin Khan, Hadith Collection, Hadith Collection, 6 June 2009, hadithcollection.com/sahihbukhari/sahih-bukhari-book-87-interpretation-of-dreams/sahih-bukhari-volume-009-book-087-hadith-number-124.

15. Al-Munajjid, Muhammed Salih. "Will Men in Paradise Have Intercourse with Al-Hoor Aliyn?" Islamqa.info, Islam Question and Answer, islamqa.info/en/10053.

16. "Al-Qur'an Al-Kareem - القرآن الكريم." Surah Al-Waqi'ah [56:35-38], quran.com/56/35-38.

17. "Al-Qur'an Al-Kareem - القرآن الكريم." Surah An-Naba [78:31-40], quran.com/78/31-40.

18. al-Sijistānī, Abū Dāwūd (Dāʾūd) Sulaymān ibn al-Ashʿath ibn Isḥāq al-Azdī. "40 Prescribed Punishments (Kitab Al-Hudud): (30) Chapter: One Who Has Intercourse with an Animal." Edited by Abu Khaliyl. Translated by Nasiruddin Al-Khattab, Sunan Abi Dawud 4465 - Prescribed Punishments (Kitab al-Hudud) - كتاب الحدود - Sunnah.Com - Sayings and Teachings of Prophet Muhammad (صلى الله عليه و سلم), SUNNAH.COM, sunnah.com/abudawud:4465. Accessed 8 Aug. 2025.

19. Al-Sijistānī, Abū Dāwūd (Dāʾūd) Sulaymān ibn al-Ashʿath ibn Isḥāq Al-Azdī. "The Book Of Legal Punishments: Chapter 29. One Who Has Intercourse With An Animal." Sunan Abu Dawud Compiled by: Imâm Hâfiz Abu Dawud Sulaiman Bin Ash'ath , edited by Abdul Malik Mujahid et al., translated by Nasiruddin Al-Khattab, First Edition ed., Volume 5, DARU SSALAM GLOBAL LEADER IN ISLAMIC BOOKS, Riyadh, Riyadh Province, 2008, pp. 80–80. From Hadtth No, 4351 to 5274 , https://ia601602.us.archive.org/34/items/SunanAbuDawudVol.111160EnglishArabic/Sunan%20Abu%20Dawud%20Vol.%205%20-%204351-5274%20English%20Arabic.pdf. Accessed 8 Aug. 2025.

20. an-Naysābūrī, Abū al-Ḥusayn Muslim ibn al-Ḥajjāj ibn Muslim ibn Ward al-Qushayrī. "Sahih Muslim Book 1, Hadith Number 244." Translated by Abdul Hamid Siddiqi, Hadith Collection, Hadith Collection, 9 June 2009, https://hadithcollection.com/sahihmuslim/sahih-muslim-book-01-faith/sahih-muslim-book-001-hadith-number-0244.

21. an-Naysābūrī, Abū al-Ḥusayn Muslim ibn al-Ḥajjāj ibn Muslim ibn Ward al-Qushayrī. "Sahih Muslim Book 15, Hadith Number 4112." Translated by Abdul Hamid Siddiqi, Hadith Collection, Hadith Collection, 1 July 2009, hadithcollection.com/sahihmuslim/sahih-muslim-book-15-oath/sahih-muslim-book-015-hadith-number-4112.

22. "As Eid Al Adha Approaches..." Questions on Islam, questionsonislam.com/content/eid-al-adha-approaches…

23. Aydemir, Ridvan. "All The Things That Satan Does (Ridiculous Islamic Teachings)." YouTube, Apostate Prophet, 28 Dec. 2018, www.youtube.com/watch?v=Ko2lttV8i2M&feature=youtu.be.

24. Aydemir, Ridvan. "Cowards in Control." YouTube, Apostate Prophet, 25 May 2019, www.youtube.com/watch?v=3Q5ZKANKaMQ.

25. Aydemir, Ridvan. YouTube, Apostate Prophet, www.youtube.com/channel/UCzREuchzOqiawpEpvEM0Tyg/videos.

26. Beckwith, Christopher I. Greek Buddha: Pyrrhos Encounter with Early Buddhism in Central Asia. PDF ed., Princeton University Press, 2017. Princeton University Press, assets.press.princeton.edu/chapters/s10500.pdf.

27. "53rd Verse of Chapter 33 (Sūrat l-Aḥzāb)." The Quranic Arabic Corpus - Translation, The Quranic Arabic Corpus, corpus.quran.com/translation.jsp?chapter=33&verse=53. Accessed 6 Aug. 2025.
28. Ghose, Sanujit. "Cultural Links between India & the Greco-Roman World." Ancient History Encyclopedia, Ancient History Encyclopedia, 30 Apr. 2019, www.ancient.eu/article/208/cultural-links-between-india--the-greco-roman-worl/.
29. Hadith - Book of Prophets - Sahih Al-Bukhari - Sunnah.com - Sayings and Teachings of Prophet Muhammad (صلى الله عليه و سلم), sunnah.com/bukhari/60/73.
30. "Hadith - Chapters on the Description of Paradise - Jami` at-Tirmidhi - Sunnah.com - Sayings and Teachings of Prophet Muhammad (صلى الله عليه و سلم)." Riyad as-Salihin - Sunnah.com - Sayings and Teachings of Prophet Muhammad (صلى الله عليه و سلم), www.sunnah.com/urn/678680.
31. Hadith - Establishing the Prayer and the Sunnah Regarding Them - Sunan Ibn Majah - Sunnah.com - Sayings and Teachings of Prophet Muhammad (صلى الله عليه و سلم), sunnah.com/urn/1281560.
32. "Hadith - Hudud - Bulugh Al-Maram - Sunnah.com - Sayings and Teachings of Prophet Muhammad (صلى الله عليه و سلم)." Search Results - Fitra (Page 1) - Sunnah.com - Sayings and Teachings of Prophet Muhammad (صلى الله عليه و سلم), sunnah.com/urn/2015030.
33. Hadith - The Book of Clothes and Adornment - Sahih Muslim - Sunnah.com - Sayings and Teachings of Prophet Muhammad (صلى الله عليه و سلم), sunnah.com/muslim/37/159.
34. Hadith - The Book of Faith - Sahih Muslim - Sunnah.com - Sayings and Teachings of Prophet Muhammad (صلى الله عليه و سلم), sunnah.com/muslim/1/253.
35. Hadith - The Book of Purification - Bulugh Al-Maram - Sunnah.com - Sayings and Teachings of Prophet Muhammad (صلى الله عليه و سلم), sunnah.com/bulugh/1/169.
36. Hadith - The Book of Virtues - Riyad as-Salihin - Sunnah.com - Sayings and Teachings of Prophet Muhammad (صلى الله عليه و سلم), sunnah.com/riyadussaliheen/9/102.
37. "Hadith - Zuhd - Sunan Ibn Majah - Sunnah.com - Sayings and Teachings of Prophet Muhammad (صلى الله عليه و سلم)." Sahih Muslim - Sunnah.com - Sayings and Teachings of Prophet Muhammad (صلى الله عليه و سلم), sunnah.com/urn/1294400.
38. Haider, Sarah. "Even as a Child, This Eid Was Horrifying. I Remember Witnessing a Sacrifice of a Cow with My Family, I Remember the Blood Gushing from Its Throat and Running through the Street. The Story of Abraham Which It Commemorates Is Another Horror. I'll Save My Mubaraks for the Other Eid." Twitter, Twitter, 21 Aug. 2018, twitter.com/SarahTheHaider/status/1031995695652384769.
39. Haider, Sarah. "I Remember the Son of the Butcher We Hired Playing in the Blood, like a Rain Puddle." Twitter, Twitter, 21 Aug. 2018, twitter.com/SarahTheHaider/status/1031996570470940673.
40. Hasan, Ahmad. "Game (Kitab Al-Said)." Family Life in Islam, International Islamic University Malaysia, www.iium.edu.my/deed/hadith/abudawood/010_sat.html.
41. Kean, Thomas H., et al. The 9/11 Commission Report, First ed., W.W. Norton & Company, Inc., New York, NY, 2004, pp. 14–14.
42. Mardanfarrox. "Can a Man Screw His Own Donkey Simply Because He Owns It?" The Definitive Zoroastrian Critique of Islam: Chapters 11 –12 of the Skand Gumanig-Wizar by Mardanfarrox Son of Ohrmazddad, translated by Christian C. Sahner, Paperback ed., Liverpool University Press, Liverpool, Merseyside, 2023, pp. 147–148.
43. Mo, Bilaal. "I Remember the Wrath on the Slaughterer's Faces Too, and Blood Stained Hands and Kurta's Afterwards. The Whole Thing Was Creepy." Twitter, Twitter, 21 Aug. 2018, twitter.com/takebeerism/status/1031996242685906945.
44. Mo, Bilaal. "We Used to Joke around That the Reason We Fasted the Day or Two before This Eid Was to Avoid Throwing up. Fortunately i Wasn't in That World Long Enough to Become Desensitised to It." Twitter, Twitter, 21 Aug. 2018, twitter.com/takebeerism/status/1031997399969947649.

45. Mosaad, Walead, et al. "Sayyiduna 'Abdullah Ibn 'Abbas: A Biography." Imam Ghazali Institute, Imam Ghazali Institute, 2007, www.imamghazali.org/resources/abdullah-ibn-abbas-biography#:~:text=Another%20narration%20attributed%20to%20him,in%20the%20year%2071%20AH.
46. "Pakistani Hindus Complain of Forced Conversion of Teenage Girls." YouTube, VOA News, 18 Mar. 2016, youtu.be/-i24jg4mJ4I.
47. "Poor Goat." LiveLeak.com - Redefining the Media, www.liveleak.com/view?i=008_1443844876.
48. "QuranX.com The Most Complete Quran / Hadith / Tafsir Collection Available!" Sahih Bukhari Hadiths, quranx.com/Hadith/Bukhari/USC-MSA/Volume-2/Book-21/Hadith-245/.
49. "QuranX.com The Most Complete Quran / Hadith / Tafsir Collection Available!" Sahih Bukhari Hadiths, quranx.com/Hadith/Bukhari/USC-MSA/Volume-3/Book-34/Hadith-437/.
50. "QuranX.com The Most Complete Quran / Hadith / Tafsir Collection Available!" Sahih Bukhari Hadiths, quranx.com/Hadith/Bukhari/USC-MSA/Volume-4/Book-54/Hadith-491/.
51. "QuranX.com The Most Complete Quran / Hadith / Tafsir Collection Available!" Sahih Bukhari Hadiths, quranx.com/Hadith/Bukhari/USC-MSA/Volume-4/Book-54/Hadith-493/.
52. "QuranX.com The Most Complete Quran / Hadith / Tafsir Collection Available!" Sahih Bukhari Hadiths, quranx.com/Hadith/Bukhari/USC-MSA/Volume-4/Book-54/Hadith-522/.
53. "QuranX.com The Most Complete Quran / Hadith / Tafsir Collection Available!" Sahih Bukhari Hadiths, quranx.com/Hadith/Bukhari/USC-MSA/Volume-5/Book-59/Hadith-512/.
54. "QuranX.com The Most Complete Quran / Hadith / Tafsir Collection Available!" Sahih Bukhari Hadiths, quranx.com/Hadith/Bukhari/USC-MSA/Volume-5/Book-59/Hadith-524/.
55. "QuranX.com The Most Complete Quran / Hadith / Tafsir Collection Available!" Sahih Bukhari Hadiths, quranx.com/Hadith/Bukhari/USC-MSA/Volume-8/Book-73/Hadith-242/.
56. "QuranX.com The Most Complete Quran / Hadith / Tafsir Collection Available!" Muwatta Malik Hadiths, quranx.com/Hadith/Malik/USC-MSA/Book-49/Hadith-6/.
57. "QuranX.com The Most Complete Quran / Hadith / Tafsir Collection Available!" Sahih Muslim Hadiths, quranx.com/Hadith/Muslim/USC-MSA/Book-2/Hadith-462/.
58. "QuranX.com The Most Complete Quran / Hadith / Tafsir Collection Available!" Sahih Muslim Hadiths, quranx.com/Hadith/Muslim/USC-MSA/Book-8/Hadith-3240/.
59. "QuranX.com The Most Complete Quran / Hadith / Tafsir Collection Available!" Sahih Muslim Hadiths, quranx.com/Hadith/Muslim/USC-MSA/Book-23/Hadith-5046/.
60. "Sahih Al-Bukhari Book Number 11 Hadith Number 582." Muflihun, https://web.archive.org/web/20200920140329/muflihun.com/bukhari/11/582.
61. "Sahih Al-Bukhari Book Number 34 Hadith Number '351." Muflihun, muflihun.com/bukhari/34/351.
62. "Sahih Al-Bukhari Book Number 34 Hadith Number 432." Muflihun, muflihun.com/bukhari/34/432.
63. "Sahih Al-Bukhari Book Number 38 Hadith Number 505." Muflihun, https://web.archive.org/web/20210208235810/muflihun.com/bukhari/38/505.
64. "Sahih Al-Bukhari Book Number 41 Hadith Number 598." Muflihun, muflihun.com/bukhari/41/598.
65. "Sahih Al-Bukhari Book Number 47 Hadith Number 743." Muflihun, muflihun.com/bukhari/47/743.
66. "Sahih Al-Bukhari Book Number 47 Hadith Number 765." Muflihun, muflihun.com/bukhari/47/765.
67. "Sahih Al-Bukhari Book Number 52 Hadith Number 255." Muflihun, muflihun.com/bukhari/52/255.
68. "Sahih Al-Bukhari Book Number 55 Hadith Number 641." Muflihun, muflihun.com/bukhari/55/641.
69. "Sahih Al-Bukhari Book Number 62 Hadith Number 137." Muflihun, muflihun.com/bukhari/62/137.

70. "Sahih Al-Bukhari Book Number 80 Hadith Number 753." Muflihun, muflihun.com/bukhari/80/753.
71. "Sahih Al-Bukhari Book Number 87 Hadith Number 124." Muflihun, muflihun.com/bukhari/87/124.
72. "Sahih Muslim Book Number 1 Hadith Number 244." Muflihun, muflihun.com/muslim/1/244
73. "Sahih Muslim Book Number 15 Hadith Number 4112." Muflihun, muflihun.com/muslim/15/4112.
74. "Sahih Muslim Book 024, Hadith Number 5246." Hadith Collection, https://hadithcollection.com/sahihmuslim/sahih-muslim-book-24-clothes-and-decorations/sahih-muslim-book-024-hadith-number-5246
75. "Sahih Muslim Book 024, Hadith Number 5248." Hadith Collection, https://hadithcollection.com/sahihmuslim/sahih-muslim-book-24-clothes-and-decorations/sahih-muslim-book-024-hadith-number-5248.
76. Sarkeesian, Anita. "Women as Reward - Tropes vs Women in Video Games." YouTube, Feminist Frequency, 31 Aug. 2015, www.youtube.com/watch?v=QC6oxBLXtkU.
77. "Short Biography of Abdullah Ibn Abbas (R.A.)." IslamicFinder, Athan Academy, 2023, www.islamicfinder.org/knowledge/biography/story-of-abdullah-ibn-abbas/.
78. Sommerlad, Joe. "Why Do Muslims Sacrifice Animals during Eid?" The Independent, Independent Digital News and Media, 21 Aug. 2018, www.independent.co.uk/news/world/middle-east/eid-al-adha-animal-sacrifice-abraham-islam-muslims-goats-sheep-animal-rights-a8500556.html.
79. "Surat An-Naba' (the Tidings) - سورة النبإ." The Noble Qur'an, legacy.quran.com/78/31-40. Accessed 6 Aug. 2025.
80. "Surat Al-Wāqi`ah (the Inevitable) - سورة الواقعة." The Noble Qur'an, legacy.quran.com/56/35-40. Accessed 6 Aug. 2025.
81. "Tafseer on the Basis of Narrated Texts and Tafseer on the Basis of Individual Understanding - Islam Question & Answer." Islamqa.info, Islam Question and Answer, 11 Mar. 2015, islamqa.info/en/answers/205290/tafseer-on-the-basis-of-narrated-texts-and-tafseer-on-the-basis-of-individual-understanding.
82. "36 The Book of the Kind Treatment of Women: (4) Chapter: Jealousy." Sunan An-Nasa'i 3959 - the Book of the Kind Treatment of Women - كتاب عشرة النساء - Sunnah.Com - Sayings and Teachings of Prophet Muhammad (صلى الله عليه و سلم), SUNNAH.COM, sunnah.com/nasai:3959. Accessed 6 Aug. 2025. Grade: Sahih (Darussalam) Reference: Sunan an-Nasa'i 3959 In-book reference: Book 36, Hadith 21 English translation: Vol. 4, Book 36, Hadith 3411
83. "The Quranic Arabic Corpus - Word by Word Grammar, Syntax and Morphology of the Holy Quran." The Quranic Arabic Corpus - Translation, http://corpus.quran.com/translation.jsp?chapter=4&verse=24
84. "The Quranic Arabic Corpus - Word by Word Grammar, Syntax and Morphology of the Holy Quran." The Quranic Arabic Corpus - Translation, http://corpus.quran.com/translation.jsp?chapter=4&verse=34
85. "The Reason Why the Right Hand Is Preferred over the Left - Islam Question & Answer." Islamqa.info, Islam Question and Answer, 2 Mar. 2007, islamqa.info/en/answers/82120/the-reason-why-the-right-hand-is-preferred-over-the-left.
86. "The Udhiyah (the Sacrificial Animal) and Its Rulings." Islamway, Islamway, 29 Nov. 2012, en.islamway.net/article/12915/the-udhiyah-the-sacrificial-animal-and-its-rulings.
87. "Two Pai Taliban Jihadi Mujahideen Caught Sexing A Donkey By US Forces." LiveLeak.com - Redefining the Media, www.liveleak.com/view?i=825_1315923588.
88. "US ARMY Camera Catches Afghans Gangbanging a Goat." LiveLeak.com - Redefining the Media, www.liveleak.com/view?i=93d_1384239379.
89. Zarrinkoub, Abdolhossein. Chapter 3: The Fire Extinguished (Location 1241 – 1798). Two Centuries of Silence: An Account of Events and Conditions in Iran [Persia] During the First Two

Hundred Years of Islam, from the Arab Invasion to the Rise of the Tahirid Dynasty First edition. Mazda Publishers. Kindle Edition.
90. Zarrinkoub, Abdolhossein. Chapter 4: The Lost Language (Location 1833 – 1878). Two Centuries of Silence: An Account of Events and Conditions in Iran [Persia] During the First Two Hundred Years of Islam, from the Arab Invasion to the Rise of the Tahirid Dynasty First edition. Mazda Publishers. Kindle Edition.
91. Zarrinkoub, Abdolhossein. Chapter 9: The Battle of Beliefs (Location 4422 – 4965). Two Centuries of Silence: An Account of Events and Conditions in Iran [Persia] During the First Two Hundred Years of Islam, from the Arab Invasion to the Rise of the Tahirid Dynasty First edition. Mazda Publishers. Kindle Edition.

About the Author

Jarin Jove is the pseudonym of Niraj Choudhary in his ill-conceived attempt at being clever by
making a nickname based upon switching his first name and using the shortest name of his
favorite planet in the solar system. He has also published *Machiavellian Ahimsa* and encourages others to read it and recommend it as part of the Foreign Policy of all Democratic Republics towards Islamic countries, if they're serious about ending Islamism within our lifetime so that we no longer have to live with terrorism treated as seasonal weather patterns. It is either that or we keep listening to utterly incompetent politicians repeatedly spewing useless pabulums and ignoring the fact that innocent civilians continue to be murdered, while vilifying people who are critical of Islam for encouraging and endorsing the murder of innocents. If you're sick and tired of that, then read *Machiavellian Ahimsa* and then send emails to your elected officials demanding that we start using drone strategies that manipulate the limitations of 7th century Arab fundamentalism to destroy the ideals of Islamism once and for all. No more excuses and no more incompetence.

Niraj Choudhary holds a Bachelor of Science in Political Science from New York Institute of Technology (2012) and a Masters of Arts in Political Science from Long Island University (2016).

He has a personal blog: www.jarinjove.com. He can be reached via email at jovejarin@hotmail.com and on Twitter via the handle @NocturneDream. However, he prefers
email correspondence.

Copyright Notice:

Copyright Niraj Choudhary, 2025. All Rights Reserved.

www.ingramcontent.com/pod-product-compliance
Lightning Source LLC
Chambersburg PA
CBHW080632230426
43663CB00016B/2844